THE PUBLIC PAPERS AND ADDRESSES

OF FRANKLIN D. ROOSEVELT

THE PUBLIC PAPERS AND ADDRESSES OF

FRANKLIN D. ROOSEVELT

WITH A SPECIAL INTRODUCTION
AND EXPLANATORY NOTES BY
PRESIDENT ROOSEVELT

Volume One

THE GENESIS OF THE NEW DEAL
1928-1932

RANDOM HOUSE · NEW YORK · 1938

The material in these volumes has been

compiled and collated by

SAMUEL I. ROSENMAN

Counsel to the Governor during the ad-

ministration of Franklin D. Roosevelt

as Governor of the State of New York

1929-1932

THESE VOLUMES ARE DEDICATED

TO THE PEOPLE OF THE UNITED STATES

WITH WHOM I SHARE BELIEF

IN THE PRINCIPLES AND PROCESSES

OF DEMOCRACY

General Introduction

I N THIS generation the people of the United States have been facing two major problems, the solution of which seems more and more vital to the continued functioning of what we call the requirements of modern civilization.

The first of these, the maintenance of that ideal of government known as the democratic process, is not new, for it goes back in our own history for nearly two centuries. During our existence as a Nation, the United States has found it necessary from time to time to carry on extended political movements for the retention of democratic processes.

We must not assume that our democracy in 1789 corresponded to the interpretation of the term in 1933. At the time of the first inauguration of George Washington, voting was, in general, restricted to the owners of a substantial amount of property. The natural result was that those chosen to fill executive and legislative positions came, virtually by common consent, from the best-educated classes. We must remember that much the greater part of the whole population of the original States was made up of men who had received either no education at all or only what we today would term a smattering of the rudiments of education. Therefore, in the early days the control of government rested in the hands of a definite minority of the male population.

As time went on, the proportion of voters to the whole population increased gradually. In our own generation universal suffrage is in effect except in a very few parts of the United States. During this gradual extension of the franchise, the actual control of government, nevertheless, passed from time to time from the hands of the voters themselves to various groups of citizens — groups which were not classes, as classes are known in Europe, but rather aggregations of power concentrated in a very small percentage of the population. In the earliest days such concentration of authority was actively sponsored by men in public life, many of whom had even been ardent supporters of the American Revolution. In later days important financial and banking interests became so powerful, not only in the economic, but also the political system, that the Jacksonian period came as a logical protest.

Still later, the clash of the plantation system, the immigration to the Middle West and the development of early industries resulted in a new emphasis on special managerial interests, using slavery and States' rights as a cloak, to halt the march of democracy and make a civil war inevitable.

This was followed by another era of unrestrained expansion, wild-cat speculation, and dishonest government, which in spite of the struggle to end the spoils system, to curb the railroads, and to maintain sound currency, lasted nevertheless into the early years of the present century.

That there has been a vast improvement in the processes of government in our own lifetime can be readily proved. History, I think, will give great credit to Theodore Roosevelt and to Woodrow Wilson for the part they played in arousing public opinion to the necessity not only of conducting honest government but, at the same time, transferring its policies and objectives from the control of minority groups often selfish, to the great mass of the citizens themselves in accordance with our more modern concept of the democratic process.

In spite of the apparently soulless decade which followed the World War, I have always felt that the surge of the previous twenty years caused by these two great personalities was by no means dead. The idealism of a score of years could not so readily be snuffed out. It is true that during the twenties of this century, control of government was allowed to slip back, in large degree, to the hands of small groups representing big finance and large industry; that most of our citizens were so busy with their occupations and with speculation, that problems of national economics and social betterment were neglected by all but a few; and that politically there was no substantial leadership to counteract a growing popular trend toward thinking in terms of the Mississippi Bubble rather than in terms of permanent security.

That decade, therefore, can be said to represent a dormant

period for democratic processes — a period, nevertheless, which was probably necessary for the revitalizing of any great movement to restore and maintain democracy. The fulfillment of the idea of the very word "democracy" presupposes a national interest on the part of a large percentage of citizens. But, unfortunately, a catastrophe seems to have been necessary to focus public attention once more on ideals in government and on its proper relationship to citizens.

The year 1929 was an ideal time for the beginning of another national movement for the restoration of democratic control — a movement old in our American history so far as its objectives are concerned, but new in its application to the greatly changed circumstances and tempo of modern life.

The second great problem which faced this generation did not have its roots so deeply embedded in our past as the case of democracy in government. Social justice is essentially a conception of this century. It was not visualized by the men who founded the Nation, and it entered little into the daily life or thought of those who expanded the original thirteen States to the empire stretching all the way to the Pacific.

It is true that prior to 1900 there were sporadic demands here and there to improve by State or local machinery the lot of factory workers and miners, the care of public health and the conditions of prisons. It is true that efforts to organize small groups of workers appeared here and there during the latter part of that period. And it is true that increasing study was being given to social and economic national problems in certain select circles.

The new surge of public conscience toward social justice appeared earlier, and progressed more rapidly in Europe than here. Several Nations had actually adopted old-age pensions and other security methods before the World War commenced. That war, by its overthrow of many monarchical Governments, stimulated the demand for further reforms — a demand which made itself felt sometimes by violence, sometimes by the setting up of wholly new and strange methods of government, and sometimes by misapplication of democratic forms to people not ready for them.

We in the United States had been ready before the World War to press for many social reforms. The War interrupted that march of progress as soon as the advance was begun. When peace came, enthusiasm for any basic social betterment was swallowed up in the very understandable demand for "a return to normalcy" — the normalcy of 1910.

Let me say with complete frankness that during the twenties, I in common with most liberals did not at the start visualize the effects of the period, or the drastic changes which were even then necessary for a lasting economy. We knew that many changes in monopolistic practices and in the concentration of the control of wealth in the hands of a few — changes fought for by Theodore Roosevelt and Woodrow Wilson — were long overdue. But we did not understand the real depths of the problem.

Almost all economists were then preaching the theory that the greater the production of goods, the greater the wealth and well-being of the Nation. That delightfully simple theory of 1928 ignored the fact that in 1928 when production was increasing unemployment was also increasing.

It required the depression itself and my experience as Governor during that period to bring home to me the more fundamental, underlying troubles which were facing all civilization. It is true that in the campaign of 1928 I had grasped the fact that the progressive decline in agriculture was a thing of danger; and that, in advocating the election of Alfred E. Smith, I had pointed to his public record on behalf of the groups who received for their labor only an inadequate and unjust share of the national income.

The 1929-1933 period was well fitted to serve as an education in social and economic needs for those who were willing to search out all the underlying causes and not merely symptoms on the surface.

During that period there were two clearly defined and opposing classes of thought. Those in charge of the national Government believed that individual and collective private action could restore the prosperity of 1928 and that the restoration of such prosperity was the sole objective. This group wholly ignored both problems of modern civilization of which I have spoken — the ideal of the democratic processes and the necessity for social justice.

The other group, to which I very definitely belonged, believed that a material recovery could not be established by the same forces which had created the depression and, furthermore, that if those forces were entrusted with the task of recovery, they would wholly ignore the needs of reform. To us, strong vital government action was therefore a prerequisite in any program for material recovery.

During my four years in Albany this prerequisite became more and more apparent because of the complete failure of the private groups actually in control of the Federal Government either to solve the economic situation or to care for the growing number of human beings who were definitely in need of assistance. The remedies proposed by these private groups were inadequate. They sought to do a patchwork job on unsound foundations. Most important of all, they clung obstinately to their opposition to all social reform.

In these volumes those who seek inconsistencies will find them. There were inconsistencies of methods, inconsistencies caused by ceaseless efforts to find ways to solve problems for the future as well as for the present. There were inconsistencies born of insufficient knowledge. There were inconsistencies springing from the need of experimentation. But through them all, I trust that there also will be found a consistency and continuity of broad purpose.

Consistently I have sought to maintain a comprehensive and efficient functioning of the representative form of democratic government in its modern sense. Consistently I have sought through that form of government to help our people to gain a larger social justice.

Washington, D. C.
January 24, 1938

XIII

The work of compilation and arrangement of the material for these volumes has involved not merely many hours of work but also a complete and clear understanding both of national problems and of details of government. I know of no one better equipped for this task by training and experience than my old friend, Samuel I. Rosenman, who served as counsel to the Governor during my term as Governor of the State of New York. It is for that reason that I asked him to undertake this task, and I am grateful for all that he has done.

At the same time I extend his thanks and mine to the members of the Cabinet and heads of other agencies and others who have assisted in the gathering of this material in the various departments of the Government and in the Executive Offices in the White House. As these volumes will be principally useful in the future to Government officials and students of history, the contribution of those who have assisted is of great value to permanent accuracy in assaying the period in which we live.

F. D. R.

Foreword

VOLUME ONE of this series is a compilation of selected public papers and addresses of Franklin D. Roosevelt as a candidate for the office of Governor of the State of New York, as Governor of the State, as candidate for the Presidency of the United States, and as President-elect. They cover the period from October 8, 1928, to March 3, 1933.

The papers selected for the period of the Governorship have been arranged by general subject matter, except the inaugural addresses, the annual messages to the Legislature, and the campaign speeches, each of which refers to several subjects. Obviously only a limited selection of the Governor's public papers for the four years of his Administration in New York and of his speeches during the three political campaigns of 1928, 1930 and 1932 could be crowded into the limits of one volume. Those were chosen which most clearly show his general policies and objectives in so far as they forecast what was to come later in the Presidency. Even these had to be limited by considerations of space. Many omitted papers have been referred to, however, and can be found in full in the appropriate annual volumes of *The Public Papers of Governor Franklin D. Roosevelt*. Documents of purely local or State interest, dealing with matters unrelated to his later programs as President, have not been included.

Volumes Two, Three, Four and Five of this series consist of the public papers and addresses of Franklin D. Roosevelt as President. Each volume covers one of the four calendar years of the first Administration from March 4, 1933, to January 19, 1937. However, Volume Two covers the year 1933, from Inauguration Day only; and Volume Five, in addition to the year 1936, covers part of January, 1937, i.e., to the date of the second Inauguration.

It is expected that a volume similar in content and format to these four volumes will be issued after each year of his second Administration.

The papers included in Volumes Two, Three, Four and Five consist of messages to the Congress, public addresses of the President, some of the press conferences, a number of the Executive Orders and Proclamations, a selection of the published letters of the President and the more important White House statements.

Practically all of the Presidential messages to the Congress have been included; the only exceptions are the formal messages merely transmitting to the Congress reports submitted to the President from time to time by various agencies of the Government. There have been excluded the numerous veto messages on private and local bills of the Congress which do not have national importance or significance.

With respect to public addresses, it has been necessary to curtail the number to be printed, in order to meet requirements of space. Practically all of the formal, prepared addresses have been included. Numerous extemporaneous and informal speeches, which have little national importance or which express the same general thoughts as other speeches, have been omitted. This is particularly true of extemporaneous speeches delivered from the rear platform of the President's train during campaigns or during the trips made by him to different parts of the United States. Only a part of the total number of these extemporaneous speeches has been printed, although reference has been made by place and date to most of those which have been omitted.

A novel feature in compilations of Presidential public papers is the inclusion in these volumes of several of the press conferences of the President and excerpts from others. Since his inauguration, press conferences have been conducted by President Roosevelt very informally, with unlimited freedom on the part of reporters to ask questions. These conferences have all been taken down verbatim by a stenographer. A few of the more important of them have been selected for this publication, not only to show the type of relationship maintained between the President and the press, but also to indicate trends of Administration policy in connection with certain public affairs. Although there were 337 press conferences during the first four years of

President Roosevelt's term of office, only 48 have been included in whole or in part in these volumes. They would themselves occupy several additional volumes if all were printed in full. The conferences, so far as they have been included, are accurate stenographic records of what transpired, with minor editing.

Only a few of the Executive Orders issued by the President during these four years have been printed. A complete list, however, of all of the Executive Orders is printed at the end of Volume Four. The vast majority of them relate to purely routine administrative matters, such as approval of codes submitted under the National Industrial Recovery Act, exemptions of various individuals from retirement age provisions, etc. Full text of Executive Orders may be obtained by application to the Division of Federal Register, National Archives, Washington, D. C. The Executive Orders have been printed without the formal beginnings and conclusions.

Similarly, only important Presidential Proclamations have been included. A complete list of these during the first four years is also printed at the end of Volume Four. The routine Proclamations have been omitted. The complete form of a Proclamation is printed on page 17 of Volume Two. Full texts of all Proclamations for the President's first term are printed in Part II of Volumes 48 and 49 of the United States Statutes at Large.

No private letters of the President have been included. On the whole, only published letters which have some national significance have been printed. During the course of each year, the President is requested to, and does, send many letters of greeting to various national organizations and associations assembled throughout the United States, either at a convention or in some public gathering. A limited number of specimen letters of this kind have been included in these volumes.

Important White House statements and an occasional Treasury or State Department release have been printed, although technically they are not utterances of the President himself. They do serve, however, to explain Administration policy toward items of legislation and other public affairs. In general, only the speeches and acts of the President himself have been included, except in cases of joint statements by the President and some-representative of a foreign Nation, or in a few exchanges of letters in which the entire correspondence has been printed.

The appointments by the President to various public offices have not been included; nor have his memoranda accompanying acts of Executive clemency.

The various documents included in these volumes have been selected with the object of presenting the more significant written and oral utterances of the Chief Executive during this period — one of the most important in American history.

The papers and addresses during the Presidency have been printed in chronological order, rather than by topical arrangement. The separate subjects discussed may be found by reference to the index for each volume.

For continuous reading on any one important subject — such as agriculture, monetary system, National Recovery Administration, foreign affairs, or others — reference should be made to the table of subjects, appearing on page xxi of this volume, which covers the documents in all five volumes.

The important papers in these volumes are covered by comments and notes written by President Roosevelt. This feature is unique in editions of Presidential papers. The object of the President in preparing and publishing these notes is to present the facts and circumstances surrounding the issuance of the various documents, the reasons and the policy underlying them, the legislative and administrative action taken pursuant to them, or the results accomplished by them. The notes were prepared chiefly during the summer and fall of 1937, and the accomplishments are in most instances detailed down to that period only. It is expected that as the succeeding volumes appear, the results accomplished will also be carried forward chronologically.

It has been the desire to present within the limits of these volumes a chronological story, by Presidential utterances and by Presidential notes, of the more important events during these critical four years — years which will have as great effect upon the future history of America as any similar period of time. It is hoped that these books in the years to come will be a source of historical data about this significant period in history. If some of the notes seem to deal with subjects well known to readers of today, it should be remembered that they are written not only for the present, but for those who in the future may seek to interpret the policies of President Roosevelt from his public utterances and acts, and from his comments with respect to them.

SAMUEL I. ROSENMAN

Topical Table

NOTE: The documents in these volumes, except in Volume I, are arranged chronologically. In order to enable the reader to follow any particular subject through this extensive material, the following Topical Table has been prepared, showing the various Item numbers dealing with the respective subject. Where a note is appended to an Item number, the note is included in the reference to the Item and should be read with the Item.

Some subjects fall within more than one of the general classifications enumerated below. For example, the subjects of proper use of land and of resettlement belong to the general topic of Agriculture and also to the topic of National Planning. They have accordingly been listed in both classifications. This practice has also been followed in other instances where documents might be placed in more than one category.

By using this table a general view may be had of the treatment during these years of any of the topics listed. The table also shows the continuity along many lines between the documents of the Governorship and the documents of the Presidency.

For more detailed itemization of any particular subjects, the reader is referred to the index at the end of each volume.

AGRICULTURE

(Including A.A.A., Cotton Crop Adjustment, Crop Adjustment, Crop Insurance, Crop Production Loans, Crop Surpluses, Ever-Normal Granary, Farm Credit Administration, Farm Mortgages, Farm Tenancy, Federal Surplus Relief Corp., Land Use, Resettlement, Seed Loans, Soil Conservation, Subsistence Homesteads, Sugar, Wild Life)

VOLUME I Items 1, 3, 13, 14 (page 81), 15 (page 92), 17 (page 105), Chapter III, 131 (page 655), 135, 140, 145, 146 (page 829), 148 (page 853).

VOLUME II Items 18, 20, 22, 22A, 23, 29, 54, 73, 83, 84, 92, 100, 106, 125, 130, 140, 151, 177, 179

VOLUME III Items 6, 21, 27, 29, 62, 64, 76, 80, 116, 124, 124A

VOLUME IV Items 18, 33, 50, 51, 59, 84, 113, 120, 135, 151, 152, 177, 181, 182, 183

VOLUME V Items 4, 6, 11, 19, 25, 28, 32, 39, 56, 131, 133, 141, 151, 155, 156, 158, 182, 218
(See also Drought, Flood and Other Natural Disasters; National Planning)

XXII

Topical Table

FOREIGN AFFAIRS

(Including Arms and Munitions, Buenos Aires Conference, Foreign Trade, Good-Neighbor Policy, Inter-American Affairs, Inter-American Highway, Montevideo Conference, Neutrality, Peace, Reciprocal Tariffs, Russia, War Debts, World Economic Conference at London)

GENERAL OBJECTIVES AND ACCOMPLISHMENTS OF THE NEW DEAL

(See also specific subjects for specific accomplishments and objectives in those fields)

HOURS AND WAGES

HOUSING AND HOME OWNERS

(Including Federal Housing Administration, Home Mortgage Foreclosures, Home Owners Loan Corporation)

INSULAR POSSESSIONS

(Including Philippine Islands, Puerto Rico, Virgin Islands)

LABOR AND LABOR RELATIONS

(Including Collective Bargaining, General Labor Legislation, Labor Disputes, Strikes)

MONETARY SYSTEM

(Including Currency, Devaluation, Foreign Exchange, Gold, Silver, Stabilization)

NATIONAL PLANNING

(Including Grazing Land, Great Plains, Land Use, National and State Parks, National Resources Board, Natural Resources, Population Distribution, Reforestation, Regional Planning, Resettlement, State Planning, Subsistence Homesteads, T.V.A.)

NATIONAL RECOVERY ADMINISTRATION

(Including N.I.R.A.)

(See also Business, Hours and Wages, Labor Relations)

OIL AND COAL

RELIEF

(Including C.W.A., Federal Emergency Relief Administration, Federal Surplus

Topical Table

(For the reader's guidance in using the foregoing Topical Table, the subjects listed below are to be found in the topics which are set down opposite each subject.)

XXVIII

Topical Table

Contents

Contents

Contents

CHAPTER IV. PUBLIC WATER POWER DEVELOPMENT AND CHEAPER ELECTRICITY IN THE HOME AND ON THE FARM. (*NOTE*)   159

Contents

Contents

Contents

Contents

Contents

Contents

Contents

Contents

CHAPTER XXIV. THE FIRST CAMPAIGN FOR THE PRESIDENCY, 1932. (*NOTE*)   621

PART I *Before the Nomination at Chicago, July 1, 1932*

PART II *After the Nomination at Chicago, July 1, 1932*

PART ONE

PART TWO

Contents

Contents

The Genesis of the New Deal

Introduction

THE TITLE of this volume, *The Genesis of the New Deal,* is intended to indicate that many of the objectives and policies of my Administration as President had their origin during my term as Governor of New York. The maintenance of the processes of democracy and the promotion of the ideal of social justice which are referred to in the General Introduction to these volumes are, in the main, the ends which I sought as Governor with the same consistency as I did during my term as President.

It must be borne in mind, of course, that the field of activity of State Government is very limited as compared with that of the Federal Government. In relief to agriculture, in protection of labor, in regulation of utilities, in attainment of economic security, in protection of investors and bank depositors — in all these and in all our other efforts to bring about a broader social justice — the extent of the action which can be taken by any State is, of course, circumscribed by the physical boundaries of the State and by the action or lack of action by sister States.

There are certain other restraining features which must be taken into consideration by the Legislature and Governor of a State in formulating a program of social legislation. Restrictions cannot be placed upon business and industry and finance in any single State which will place them at an undue disadvantage with competing business and industry and finance in neighboring States. Of course, caution with respect to this feature can at times be carried to unnecessary extremes. In fact, opponents of reform have rushed forward on nearly every occasion to urge that the slightest departure from *laissez-faire* would cause business and industry to leave their State and go elsewhere.

I have always had considerable doubt that any large number of reputable business men actually have moved their plants out of the State of New York because of the advanced social legislation of that State. But there have been some who have sought to exploit the cheaper labor of other regions and obtain an advantage over their New York competitors in terms of human misery. It is also true that some products made in some other States, under sweat-shop conditions, have come into competition with products made under more enlightened conditions in New York State. This situation has often been exaggerated and has been frequently urged as an argument for blocking action to remove even the most glaring social inequalities. The effects of this type of competition, however, must always be considered in adopting any plan for social reform which is restricted to any individual State.

Good results from social legislation in any one State cannot be obtained to the same degree when confined to that State as when it is made nationwide. For example, I am convinced that the Federal legislation which I have been recommending for more than a year, to fix a minimum wage and a maximum number of hours with some degree of uniformity throughout the Nation, will help business, industry and agriculture as much as it will help underpaid workers. It will furnish to many millions of people greater purchasing power with which more products of our factories and our farms may be bought. It will serve directly to stimulate greater production and sales in our factories and on our farms. But if a similar statute were passed for any single State, the increased purchasing power might or might not benefit the business and industry of that particular State to the same degree, for it might well be spent on the products of other States and produce its effects outside the State.

The same result follows in many other fields of reform. Where artificial State lines limit the effects of policies which should apply to entire correlated geographical areas or to the whole of one industry, the results can never be the same within the particular State as when action is taken along national lines.

It is interesting to note, as I have myself frequently seen, that opponents of reform and social betterment often object with one breath to State legislation on the ground that it drives industry to other States, and, with the next breath, decry efforts to obtain

Federal legislation on the ground that it is interference with purely local matters. Of course, the truth is that these individuals wish no such legislation, either by the State Legislatures or by the Congress.

Another major restriction on the benefits of social legislation by State action is the inability to give adequate consideration to interdependence between different economic groups, between different industries, between finance and agriculture, between labor and industry. From the time of my acceptance speech in Chicago, and even before, I have consistently and continuously stressed the importance to our national well-being of this interdependence. When one is at the head of the Government in a single State, it is obviously impossible to correlate policies of that State with the remaining forty-seven States in order to meet the necessities of interdependence in our modern economic life.

Furthermore, there are matters which are exclusively of Federal jurisdiction — such as the monetary system, tariffs, foreign trade, interstate commerce — which always have an immediate effect on attempts to meet social and economic problems by State action. These matters cannot constitutionally be handled even partially by any State Government to assist in effectuating a program of reform.

It is with these various limitations and restrictions that the title of this first volume of papers and addresses, *The Genesis of the New Deal,* should be taken. I do not mean to imply by that title that my Administration as Governor of New York was in any sense a counterpart of what came later. The objectives were the same. But for all the reasons I have mentioned, and for many others, it was impossible to use all the various methods to attain those objectives that were available during my term as President. In so far as it was possible to adapt statewide measures to the attainment of a broader social justice, it was done.

With these differences between action along State lines and action by the national Government, I trust that this volume of *Public Papers and Addresses* for the years of my Governorship may be recognized as the beginnings of the general aims and purposes of the New Deal. I trust that there will be found between this first volume and the remaining volumes a bond of consistency and continuity of objectives, and that occasional variations of method and detail coming from lack of Government precedent, from insufficient available information and from need for experimentation will not obscure the close similarity of broad purposes toward which we were striving.

I had thought of these things for many years and had talked of them too. The Governorship was the first opportunity which I had to do something about them in a practical though limited way. In the pages of this volume is the story of what was done during my Administration as Governor with respect to old-age security, development of electricity from water power, adequate regulation of public utility operating and holding companies, unemployment relief by direct aid and through public works, unemployment insurance, wages and hours of labor, assistance to agriculture, land planning and land use, improvement in the administration of justice, reforestation, aid to the blind, to crippled children, to dependent mothers, and many other steps in progressive government. The growth from this type of State action to the broader front of national action which came with the New Deal was a natural one.

The growth and expansion were promised in the Democratic National Platform of 1932. They were promised during the campaign of 1932. They were approved by the election of 1932. They were started on March 4, 1933.

It has been noticed by hostile political writers that in some instances recommendations made by me as Governor apparently do not fully square with my later recommendations to the Congress. True enough. But what they fail to call attention to is that while I was Governor, demanding action along State lines, the national Administration in many instances was consistently blocking efforts by the States to curb unsocial activities by progressive State legislation.

It is an interesting fact that during the past generation certain large corporate interests, especially in the utility field, have sometimes adopted the practice of "playing both ends against the middle." When an Administration favorable to special privilege is in power in Washington these corporations beg for Federal control in order to circumvent those State Governments and public service commissions which are trying to enforce the original conception of a public utility in the public good. When, however, we have a Federal Administration devoted to protection of the consuming public, these same corporations call loudly for State control only. During my term as Governor, for example, some of these companies relied on the sympathy of the national Administration to block every possible effort of mine to obtain adequate control and supervision in the State of New York. When I became President they transferred their efforts and their affections by an appeal to the old slogan of "States' Rights."

In saying this I am not referring to the Courts but rather to broad Government policies. In Albany I was forced to work for State action because of the attitude of Washington. When I went to Washington I was able, by reversing the national policy, to give aid to States that wished to help themselves along progressive lines.

For example, during the famous New York Telephone rate case the public was outraged by its meandering progress through the Federal Courts for seven long years. I protested this procedure in my message to the Legislature on January 27, 1930 (see Item 48). After the new national Administration started in March, 1933, with a Department of Justice wholly sympathetic with its aims, it was clear to me that Federal Courts in the future would never handle similar cases with such undue and unwarranted delay.

While I was Governor also, on many occasions I spoke in favor of "Home Rule" in its application to problems of government which could be handled properly by State legislation, and decried the encroachment of the Federal Government into such fields. It

7

must be remembered that those were the days of Prohibition, when the Federal Government had stepped in to regulate from Washington the personal lives and habits of its citizens. It was that type of unwarranted extension of power into purely State matters that I was opposing. However, an analysis of the occasion and subject in those speeches in which I stressed "States' Rights" shows no inconsistency with my advocacy as President of Federal legislation covering nationally such subjects as cannot be adequately and properly dealt with by forty-eight States separately.

In New York, as later in the Nation, I was able to accomplish reform and progress only because the public was ready for them, wanted them, and was willing to help me carry out the people's will. As Governor, it was often necessary for me to appeal for public support over the heads of the Legislature and sometimes over the almost united opposition of the newspapers of the State. In several instances, what was passed by the Legislature was literally forced from the Republican leaders by demand of public opinion which never hesitated to make its views known and which found ways of making them known.

The use of the radio by me in those days not only to appeal directly to the people, but also to describe fully the facts about legislation which were not always given by many press reports, was the beginning of similar use of the radio by me as President in what have come to be known as "Fireside Chats." The radio has proved to be a direct contact with the people which was available to only two Presidents before me. It has been invaluable as a means of public approach and will, I know, continue to be so in the years to come.

I do not mean to say that I was always successful with proposed legislation. In much of what I tried to do, I failed. But the general direction was right. The impulse of those years has since been continued in the State of New York. And that is the really most important contribution which any Administration can make to history — to provide direction toward broad objectives, to see that the great mass of the people understand the objectives, to make sure that the popular will insists upon them. In that way changes of administration and shifting of leaders cannot succeed in blocking the march of progress.

Franklin D Roosevelt

Washington, D. C.
February 15, 1938

I

The First Campaign for the Governorship

INTRODUCTORY NOTE: THIS CHAPTER contains some of the speeches made by me during my first campaign for the Governorship in 1928.

I was nominated by the Democratic State Convention at Rochester on October 3, 1928. I accepted the nomination only after very urgent persuasion by Governor Alfred E. Smith, who was at that time campaigning as the Democratic candidate for the Presidency of the United States.

During the Rochester convention I was in Warm Springs, Georgia, continuing my treatment for infantile paralysis, and my doctors had strongly advised me against reentering public life at that time. It was against their advice and largely because of the thought that I could be of service in promoting the cause of liberal and progressive government in the State and, through the election of Governor Smith, in the Nation, that I finally yielded.

Before my campaign for the Governorship began I had made several speeches in behalf of the candidacy of Governor Smith for the Presidency. Included among these were speeches at Atlanta, Ga., September 26, 1928; Manchester, Ga., October 2, 1928; Columbus, Ga., October 5, 1928; Cleveland, Ohio, October 6, 1928; Boston, Mass., October 12, 1928; New York City, October 15, 1928.

As will be seen in the speeches in this chapter, besides discussing various State issues, I actively advocated the election of Governor Smith in practically every speech made.

In addition to the speeches included in this chapter I made other speeches in New York during my campaign for the Governorship in 1928, at the following places: Oswego, October 18; Elmira, October 18; Corning, October 19; Hornell, October 19; Wellsville, October 19; Olean, October 19; Salamanca, October 19; Dunkirk, October 20; Batavia, October 22; Canandaigua, October 23; Seneca Falls, October 23; Oswego, October 24; Watertown, October 24; Boonville, October 25; Rome, October 25; Herkimer, October 26; Schenectady, October 26; Albany, October 27; New York City, October 31, November 2, November 3. They have not been printed here because of lack of space.

My opponent in this campaign was Hon. Albert Ottinger. The vote was Roosevelt 2,130,193, Ottinger 2,104,629.

1 ❡ The Candidate Accepts the Nomination for the Governorship. October 16, 1928

(Alfred E. Smith — Progressive government — Water power — Administration of justice — Farm relief — Improvement in local government.)

I ACCEPT the nomination for Governor because I am a disciple in a great cause. I have been enlisted as a private in the ranks for many years and I cannot fail to heed a call to more active service in a time when so much is at stake.

This cause needs little explaining to the citizens of the State of New York. We have a right to hold our heads high, for we have made a proud record in improving the science and practice of State Government. Where we have led, our sister States now follow. Indeed, the man to whose leadership this progress has been due has been selected by our party to bring to Washington the same constructive genius which he has shown in Albany. I am confident that the people of the United States will ratify this choice.

Study of the trend of public will in New York during the past few years makes this fact clear — our State is committed to the principle of progressive government. Under magnificent leadership we have first aroused public interest, and have then obtained public approval for a program of governmental improvement which has few parallels in any similar period of time.

It is a program which has caught public imagination, partly because of its own inherent soundness and humanity, but equally because of the clear and honorable personality of its principal exponent, the present four-times Governor of our State.

Let it be remembered, however, that the ground won was fought for, inch by inch. An overwhelming majority of voters in our past elections have made it clear that this opposition has not had their consent or approval. We must lay the blame and the responsibility on that group of Republican leaders who have either lacked vision or have sought partisan advantage by injecting politics into public problems which should have received a disinterested cooperation from all leaders regardless of party. I

13

hope that if this little group of leaders is still to remain in power in their own party, the voice of the electorate this fall will make it clear even to them that leaders must move forward and not in circles.

For much remains to be accomplished — not for this party or for that party, but for the good of the whole State. Petty partisan opposition such as these leaders have shown slows up the wheels of progress. But, with them or without them, we propose to go through to the goal.

We rejoice in the fact that the reorganization and consolidation of the administrative machinery at Albany is a thing done; but we must pay close attention to its actual operation and be prepared to improve it further in the interest of good business and clearly defined responsibility. I want to live to see the day when the business men of the Nation as well as political leaders will look to Albany as a model for business efficiency, which, in line with the most advanced modern thought, takes into consideration the human element as well as mere dollars and cents.

In the field of public works we are in the process of catching up with the fulfillment of needs that go back fifty years. We can be very certain that every dollar expended is justified by considerations of humanity and of common sense.

In social legislation, in education, in health, in better housing, in the care of the aged, we have gone far, but we must go farther.

We are, therefore, face to face with the first great issue of the State campaign: Shall the State of New York carry through, consolidate and make permanent the great reforms which will for all time attach to the name of Alfred E. Smith? My answer is "Yes."

Finally, there is the even broader question of the years to come. This State is headed in the right direction. But beyond the need of preserving what we have gained is the equal need of improving our governing methods each year as rapidly as civilization itself expands and improves. Progress means change. A perfect system of 1918 may be outworn ten years later. The strides of science and invention, the shifting of economic balance, the growing feeling of responsibility toward those who need the protection of the State, call for ceaseless improvement to keep up to date those personal relationships of the individual to other individuals and to the whole body politic which we call Government.

Four examples occur to me. First of all, these ten years have brought about a great change of economic conditions in regard to the use of power. The people own vast water-power resources and by the far-seeing insistence of our Governor were saved at the eleventh hour from the loss of control of a large portion of those resources. The time has come for the definite establishment of the principle as a part of our fundamental law that the physical possession and development of State-owned water-power sites shall not pass from the hands of the people of the State.

I would also speak very briefly of a subject that goes deep to the roots of effective government: the system by which justice is administered. I am confident that the procedure of both civil and criminal law has failed to keep pace with the advancement of business methods and with the needs of a practical age; that this procedure is too costly, too slow, too complex; and that the present methods are at least in part responsible for disregard of law and for many miscarriages of justice. It is a problem of the greatest magnitude, but that is no reason for failing to start to solve it, no matter how long its completion may take. It should be studied not only by the judiciary and the bar, but we should also bring to the solution of this problem the intelligence of the ablest citizens in other fields of endeavor.

We must realize also that the ten years since the War have brought extraordinary difficulties to the millions who live on the farms. While there have been prosperity and growth in the cities, their measure has not extended to the rural communities. This is in part a national problem, but it calls also for immediate and disinterested study in our own State. In the final analysis, the progress of our civilization will be retarded if any large body of citizens falls behind; and I am confident that those who live in the cities of this State will be glad to cooperate in initiating measures for the improvement of existing conditions in the agricultural sections.

Last of all, the splendid reorganization of our State Government calls for extension of it to the lower units of county and town government. Nobody with knowledge and honesty pretends that the present system is either economical or productive of the best results. I hope that this coming year the State will give this subject the attention it deserves.

The other great issue in this campaign is therefore this: Do we as citizens want to undertake new improvements in our governing methods to keep pace with changing times?

I stand for an affirmative answer. I am confident that the people of the State of New York are not content with preserving civilization, but that they have the will to improve it. They are in this fight to win, and I fight with them, not against them.

2 ❨ Extemporaneous Campaign Address (Excerpts), Binghamton, N. Y. October 17, 1928

(Alfred E. Smith — Reorganization of Government — Religious bigotry in the national campaign.)

Governor Walker, and my friends of Binghamton:

I was very much moved tonight, and so were my associates on the Democratic State ticket, at the perfectly splendid reception that you good people have given us, and I hope that you will tell your neighbors and friends how very deeply we appreciate it. . . .

This was to have been my first speech of the active campaign. That was the intention on the part of everybody, until I left Jersey City this morning, when the whole thing was knocked into a cocked hat — first at Middletown, and then at Port Jervis, and then at Callicoon, and then at Hancock, and then Neponsit, and then at Susquehanna. So this is the seventh speech of the campaign. . . .

I wonder if we people in the State of New York have any conception of what a perfectly splendid thing it has been for our State to have Governor Alfred E. Smith nominated for the Presidency. Everywhere that I go, whether it be in the South or in the Middle West or New England, people come up to ask me questions about the reorganization of the Government of the State of New York, about our humane legislation, about our public works, about all the great things of which we are so proud. The State of New York today stands right up on a little pedestal among all the States. They are all looking at us and they all think that we are fine. And one reason why this Governor of ours is going to carry a great many more than a majority of the forty-eight States in the Union is because people in the other States know that he put our State up on that pedestal.

I cannot take up all the subjects tonight, but I do want to talk particularly about the practical reorganization of State Government, of which we are all so proud, and which is bearing fruit in the Legislatures and the administrations of other States of the Union. The record that Governor Smith has made in four years in that regard, should properly be compared to what has been going on in the Federal Government during the same time.

I am not so certain whether I told the story of the four bears when I was last in Binghamton in the campaign of 1920. I probably did, because in that national campaign both parties were talking about the need of reorganizing our Federal Government. Down in Washington, back there in 1919 and 1920, the situation was just as bad as it was in the State of New York three years ago. They had, I think, 170 or 180 different departments and commissions and bureaus and boards and institutes and all the other things. In the last year of the Wilson Administration, the Wilson Cabinet made a very careful study, looking to a consolidation and reorganization of all of this governmental machinery.

I spent many weeks during that campaign going up and down the United States, clear out to the Coast, down South, up in New England; and almost everywhere I went I used to tell the story about the four bears. There are four different kinds of bears in the United States, and, of course, all these bears come under the jurisdiction of one Government department or another. I think it is the brown bear that comes under the jurisdiction of the Department of the Interior, and I think the black bear comes under the Department of Agriculture; and the Alaska bear comes under the Department of Commerce; and jurisdiction over the grizzly bear is held by the Department of War. That has been going on from time immemorial in Washington. Each bear — the care of the bear and everything else about the bear — falls under a different department, depending on the genus of the bear. And I am told confidentially that sometimes there is a most awful mixup, because sometimes a black bear falls in love with a brown bear, and then nobody knows under what department the puppies belong.

Well, it is not a very funny story, but it was used quite effectively in the campaign of 1920, and during that campaign Senator Harding, the Republican candidate for the Presidency, used my story about the bears. He used the story, and he claimed that if he got into power he would accomplish great things in reorganizing the departments of the Government.

Thereafter, he got into power, and we poor Democrats were thrown out into the cold. He put in a Cabinet of the best minds. Perhaps it is best that I do not recall all the names of that Cabinet. Well, one of them was the present Republican candidate for the Presidency, the Secretary of Commerce. I believe that it is perfectly true that President Harding gave to Mr. Hoover the task of drawing up a plan for the consolidation of the 160 or 170 departments, bureaus and commissions of the Federal Government. Mr. Hoover drew up a plan, and the chief feature of the plan was the consolidation of nearly all of the Federal Government machinery into Mr. Hoover's own Department of Commerce.

The other members of the Cabinet did not seem to like it, and after a number of lengthy discussions the plan disappeared into a pigeon-hole in someone's desk. It stayed there until 1924, and then President Coolidge, running for election, took out the plan, dusted it off, held it up to the audience of the United States, and said "Now, if we are returned to power we will put through this great plan of reorganization and consolidation."

The people then elected him, whereupon he and Secretary Hoover forgot all about it. The plan again went into a pigeon-hole, and there it stayed until last June, four years more. And then, to my joy, because it had gone clean out of my head, when Secretary Hoover made his speech of acceptance in August, he trotted out my story about the four bears.

So, my friends, for the third time they are asking you to believe in their promise. There is the same old collection of departments and boards and commissions today that existed on October 17, 1920; only, a few extra ones have been added for good measure. Now Mr. Hoover, hoping to succeed Mr. Coolidge and Mr. Harding, has trotted out the same old promise. Two men have disregarded the promise. Is the third man likely to carry it out, the third who has served as a part of the official family of the other two? . . .

There is a particular reason why I wish this campaign could go on for another three months instead of another three weeks. I refer to the reason that you all know. I refer to a reason that is particularly well known around Binghamton. But it is not half so bad here as it is in other States. I have just come from the South; and I have seen circulars down there in the Southern States that any man or woman in this audience would be ashamed to have in his home. I have seen circulars that were so unfit for publication that the people who wrote and printed and paid for them ought not to be put in jail, but ought to be put on the first boat and sent away from the United States.

Down in the South and out in the West, I have had people come up to me and talk to me about the Eighteenth Amendment to the Constitution, complaining about us in New York, because, they said, we do not care anything about the Eighteenth Amendment to the Constitution. Then those same people, in the same breath, would say that they would not vote for Alfred E. Smith; and they had never read and did not care to talk about the First Amendment to the Constitution of the United States, the one guaranteeing religious liberty throughout the Nation. And the curious part of it is this: I have noticed in a fairly extensive trip

19

around the country that this un-Americanism, this assault on one of the most fundamental principles on which our country was founded, is most widespread in those sections where there is least education.

You go to any State, and you will find that the religious bigotry in this campaign is more glaring in the out-of-the-way farms and hills and valleys and small towns, where there is no contact with the outside world. You do not find it in cities to anything like the same extent.

Just after I got down to Georgia, an old friend of mine in a small country town, a farmer, came in to see me, and said, "Mr. Roosevelt, I am worried. A lot of my neighbors, all Democrats — we are all Democrats down here — say that they cannot vote for Governor Smith, and I don't know what the reason is. But there must be some good answer. Will you tell me so that I can go back and talk to them? They tell me, these neighbors of mine, and they show me printed handbills saying that if Governor Smith becomes President of the United States, the Methodist and Baptist marriages over here among our neighbors will all be void and that their children will be illegitimate." Yes, you may laugh; but they were not laughing. They thought it was true; and they were honest, law-abiding citizens. They did not have the education, the contact, to know better. Oh, I could go on and tell you a thousand stories along that same line.

It was upstate in New York, over near my section of the Hudson River, that a young Irishman was running for office, a boy who had been born up there in Dutchess County and who was running for office of, I think, Town Assessor. He was going around before election seeing his neighbors, and one evening he was passing a farm, and he went to call on the farmer with a good deal of trepidation to ask the farmer to support him. The farmer said to the young Irishman, "Yes, I will be glad to support you in this election. I have known you, you are a fine young fellow, you are a good influence in the community." This young man said to the farmer, "I greatly appreciate your support. But I know you won't mind my telling you that I am a little surprised, because I had understood that you were opposed to Catholics." The farmer, stepping forward, and putting his hand on the young man's shoulder, said, "My boy, you have got it all wrong. I am not opposed to Irish Catholics. What I am opposed to is those Roman Catholics." (*Laughter.*)

I believe that the day will come in this country when education — and, incidentally, we have never had a Governor in the State of New York who has done more for the cause of education than Alfred E. Smith — when education in our own State and in every other State, in the cities and the hamlets and the farms, in the back alleys and up on the mountains, will be so widespread, so clean, so American, that this vile thing that is hanging over our heads in this Presidential election will not be able to survive.

It may be years to come, but I believe that this year we in the State of New York have got beyond those days of prejudice and bigotry. I believe that in our State we have come to visualize the right, because I like to think our education is high enough to make that possible.

And so you see that I have treated this delicate subject from the point of view of one who cares for the future of the country, from the point of view of one who wants to eradicate ignorance, because ignorance is at the bottom of it all, and let that man whom that cap fits put it on. . . .

3 ❨ Extemporaneous Campaign Address (Excerpts), Jamestown, N. Y. October 19, 1928

(Alfred E. Smith — State program for agriculture — Republican neglect of farmers — Land use.)

Mr. Chairman, my friends of Chautauqua County:

Tonight, partly because of the fact that I have been coming through agricultural counties and partly because I know that for many years Chautauqua County has been one of the greatest agricultural counties in the State of New York, I want to talk to you about a subject that is of vital importance to you who live in the cities, no matter whether they are cities of the size of Jamestown or of Buffalo or of the greatest city of all, with its seven million people. It is a subject that perhaps does not seem very close to us in the cities, but actually it is affecting our daily lives and our pocketbooks, and even more than that, it is going to affect the future of our children.

It is a mighty broad subject, and let me sum it up in one or two sentences by way of an explanation. In the early days of this Republic, at the time of the Revolution, 95 percent of the population of the thirteen States lived on farms; only 5 percent, in the cities. Gradually that farm ratio has decreased, very slowly during our first one hundred years; more rapidly during the next twenty-five; and during the past twenty-five years a situation has been brought about that is serious to our future.

We think of the agricultural population of this country as the backbone of the Nation, do we not? We were taught that in our school books, and yet today fewer than forty million people out of our one hundred and ten or one hundred and fifteen million live on the farms; and every single day that passes, more and more of them are moving into the cities.

I do not quite like the idea that some scientists and professors have, that we are approaching with rapid strides the synthetic age, when all of our food will be produced synthetically instead of being grown in the ground; that when we get up in the morning we shall go to a bottle and take out a pill, labeled "Two poached eggs" (*Laughter*), and go to another bottle and take out another pill labeled "Corn flakes and cream," and still another pill labeled "One cup of coffee."

Of course, that may be in store for future generations of Americans, but I hope it will not happen in your day or mine. Now we are confronted with this present situation, the increasing drift of the rural population into the cities. There are two causes for it, both essentially economic. The first is the attraction of the city. It is mighty slow in these modern times to live on a farm. But we are rapidly overcoming that through the advent of the automobile and of good roads, and I do not have to tell you people in this State what has happened to the roads of the State under the administration of Alfred E. Smith.

But there is another reason beyond the question of where the young people can have the best time. There is the practical question of how you can best make both ends meet; how you can best feed yourself and your family and put a little money into the savings bank. Every day that goes by — between sunrise this morning and sunrise tomorrow morning — one thousand farm families will have left their farms in the United States. That sounds almost incredible, does it not? Not farm population, but farm families. Nearly a thousand abandoned farms every single day in the year!

In one part of the country alone, out there in the corn belt, four hundred and forty-four farms are being abandoned from day to day. They are not being abandoned for anything but the good economic reason that the farm families cannot make both ends meet by staying there. . . .

Back in 1920, after the close of the World War, there began the present decline of agriculture. I do not think there is anybody in this audience who will go so far as to say that there has not been a drastic decline in agricultural conditions. I have heard a great deal today about the grape industry in this country, for instance.

Back there in 1920 both the Republicans and Democrats in their platform planks promised some kind of relief to the farmer. They were pretty vague. I do not think either party knew exactly what ought to be done. But the Republicans came into power, with their Republican President and a Republican Congress, and it was assumed that they would try to carry out their pledges.

During the first four years, although the agricultural situation was daily growing worse, nothing was accomplished. Various bills were introduced in Congress, but they did not even pass.

In 1924 there came another Presidential campaign. In that campaign both parties again promised some kind of relief. The promises still were fairly vague, although by that time expert agricultural opinion in this country was headed toward a pretty definite program.

Again in that year the Republican Party won. They elected a Republican President. They elected a Republican Congress. And during these past four years down in Washington, the whole Nation has been interested in the struggle to obtain farm relief.

Now, whether it was the fault of the Republican Party, either of their President or of their national Legislature, that nothing was done is quite immaterial. The Congress passed the first agricultural relief plan over a year ago, and it was vetoed by the Republican President. This past spring they passed another somewhat similar plan, passed it both in the Senate and in the House, and that was also vetoed by the Republican President. The result is that they now come into this third campaign this year pledging once again that they will give some relief to the farmer.

If you will read the Republican platform and in connection with it the speeches on farm relief made by President Coolidge, you will find that the Republican attitude at present on farm relief is covered by a general pledge of help in the first place, and secondly by the suggestion that they will work it out in some way through the expansion of the cooperative movement among the farmers, and that they will endeavor in some way to finance the general farm situation.

The whole plan is very vague; and when you come down to what the agricultural interests in the wheat and cotton and corn belt States are chiefly interested in, namely, the question of dealing with surplus crops, both the Republican platform and the Republican candidate have been singularly reticent. Nobody knows today what the exact attitude of Mr. Hoover is in that regard.

On the other side, the Democrats, both in their platform and through their candidate, have recognized that the crux of the matter, the meat of the cocoanut, is dealing with this problem of the surplus crops. Governor Smith in his campaign speeches has pledged definitely that if he is elected on November sixth, he will immediately call together the best farm experts that he can find to devise a definite way and means for taking care of this exportable surplus.

The Democratic Party has not any record of performance on farm relief for the past eight years, for the very simple fact that nationally we have not been in power. On the other side, the Republican Party has a record of eight years of broken promises and failure to accomplish anything. This year the Republican Party is again vague, and I think that every person in the land feels that too. The Democratic Party, on the other hand, is pretty specific as to what they intend to do about farm relief.

Why have I talked all about this national situation when I am running on a State ticket? For two reasons: In the first place, I am just as much interested in the election of the national Democratic ticket as I am in that of the State Democratic ticket. And in the second place, agriculture in any one State, while it may be a State problem, ties in necessarily in a thousand different ways with agriculture in the other States, in other words, with the whole national problem. . . .

Governor Smith well said in his Rochester speech the other day, "I have been reading the agricultural plank of the Republican State platform, and there comes to me, again and again, this thought — Oh, how the Republican Party loves the farmer in October." And if you will read that Republican platform, you will agree with me and with him that you can reduce the twenty-seven long lines that it contains to this simple sentence: "We Republicans love our farmers." . . .

Now, on the other side what do the Democrats in their State platform say of this problem of farm relief. The Democratic platform is far more specific, because it first gives specific examples of definite helpfulness to the farmer and his problems under the Administration of Governor Smith, and then goes on to pledge certain new efforts to give further help. That is the important part of it. These pledges are: first, to name a commission of experts to study the problems of distribution and to make definite constructive recommendations; second, to give scientific study and investigation to the whole farm assessment and tax situation in order to obtain a fair adjustment of the farmer's taxes. . . .

I was born and raised on an up-State farm. I am living there

25

today. Therefore I am not boasting, when I state in very simple words that all my life I have had a deep and vital interest in farm problems of all kinds; and I might add that I know by personal experience how difficult it is at the end of each year to make both ends meet on a farm, let alone to make any profit on it. I do know the incontrovertible fact that in every county in this State more and more farms are being abandoned. Today, in coming into Chautauqua County, I noted the unanswerable fact that in vineyard after vineyard thousands and thousands of tons of grapes have been allowed to rot on the vines. As I came along the road today I saw in Steuben and Cattaraugus Counties — leading potato-growing counties of the State — potatoes advertised for sale on the road at sixty-five cents per bushel. Two potato growers — Democratic Committeemen they happened to be — told me that the best they could get for mighty good potatoes alongside car was only thirty-five cents a bushel. Does anyone think that these potato growers are getting rich? At these prices these potato growers will find it difficult to pay for their fertilizer bills. In this County of Chautauqua alone I understand that 389 farms, totaling over 31,000 acres, are now being advertised for sale for unpaid taxes for the tax year 1927. This is an area greater than that of any single town in Chautauqua County, except the township of Chautauqua itself.

It seems to me that is pretty significant, and I could go on and give you similar statistics for farms abandoned and for tax sales in every single one of the rural counties of New York State. And yet they say there isn't any farm problem, and they go on and say that it is silly for any Democrat to charge that we have not the most superabundant prosperity all over our land.

I cannot help wondering a little how long Republican farmers in up-State counties are going to continue to hope for relief from their Republican leaders and legislators. These leaders and legislators have been going on year after year, talking platitudes, and watching the farm population of their home counties decrease and their agricultural lands revert to uncultivated wastes.

It is a simple matter of record that the Republican Party in

Albany and in Washington has been devoting most of its energies to building up an industrial development in the country. They have failed utterly to give anything to the plight of the rural population but fine words. . . .

And now I am going to make a somewhat unusual statement in a campaign for the Governorship. Most people who are candidates get up and say, "I subscribe to everything that is said in the State platform." Well, I think I can take about everything there is in our State platform. Part of it I might have expressed differently if I had been in Rochester instead of in Georgia at the time. But I am perfectly willing to go along and say, "I will stand on our Democratic State platform." But — and this is the unusual part — I go even further than the Democratic State platform, and I offer an ultimate objective for the State to aim at, even though it may take a long time to attain the whole of that objective.

I am satisfied with those two planks in our present platform; I am satisfied that those two pledges are excellent, the pledge for a careful study, and the pledge for investigation of that farm tax situation. Beyond those two pledges, let us ask ourselves just what we are aiming at. What is the goal? Put into plain language, it is just this: I want to see the farmer and his family receive at the end of each year as much for their labor as if they had been working not on a farm, but as skilled workers under the best conditions in any one of our great industries.

I want our agricultural population, in other words, to be put on the same level of earning capacity as their fellow Americans who live in the cities. Toward that end the Democratic platform urges that immediate study be made of the farm problem of distribution of farm products, to the end that the unnecessarily high differential between what the farmer receives and what the consumer pays may be materially lowered, giving a better price to the farmer for his products, and a lower cost to the consumer for what he buys.

Right there is just one place where the city dweller comes in. You know that the cost of living to you in the cities has gone up, gone up a lot, hasn't it — the cost of food, the cost of feeding the

27

children, the cost of feeding everybody in the household. You do not stop to think of some of the reasons why it has gone up; and you do not stop to think, while you are paying such and such a figure for such and such a farm product, how much the poor devil and his family back there on the farm who grew that product for you got for it. You do not bother to consider that the price they got for it was anywhere from, say, 20 to 40 percent of what you are paying for it, that somewhere out of that dollar you are paying for it, somebody along the road got from sixty to eighty cents and the farmer only got the balance — and those are pretty conservative figures. I suppose a complex situation such as we have in our modern life will bring that thing about. But it has been going on for a number of years now, and it is time that we found out two things: How, out of that dollar, the farmer can get more, and how, out of that dollar, you will have to pay a bit less.

And then there is that other pledge — a pledge to carry out a scientific investigation of the whole farm tax situation. If you are in business, your taxes fluctuate very largely on the success or the failure of your business; in poor years you pay less taxes, and in good years you pay more taxes; but the poor fellow out on the land — well, he never pays less, and in almost every case that I have ever known in the State of New York he pays just a little bit more, year in and year out, whether he makes more or less. Yes, I go one step further than my platform, for I am convinced that there are many other factors which a careful study will show have a direct bearing on the continued abandonment of farms and the decrease of our rural population. I propose, therefore, that the study of the problem of distribution and the study of the farm tax situation shall be broadened to cover these other factors so that we may have broad recommendations covering the entire economic farm situation.

It is obvious that the future of the State depends on the proper use of every acre within the borders of the State. It may be that adequate investigation will show that many of the farms abandoned within the period of depression since 1920 should not be restored to agriculture, but should be especially used for the growing of a future timber supply for the people of this State. At the same time we do not want the present alarming rate of farm abandonment to continue; and we must, therefore, make special efforts to make it possible for those who are now engaged in agriculture on suitable agricultural land, to continue to farm under more profitable conditions. I want this whole situation, this whole problem, studied by the representatives of some of those great bodies who know something about it, not just by Senators and Assemblymen. I want it studied by representatives of the State College of Agriculture, of the State Grange, the Farm Bureau, the Home Bureau, the Dairymen's League, and other farm cooperatives. I want it studied without regard to partisan politics, and it is my hope and belief that the recommendations resulting from this study will be acted on by the legislative branch of our Government without the interference of partisan politics. And I am very certain, too, that the people of our great cities will understand the vital need of this program, for it is obvious that their own prosperity is in large part dependent on the rural population as well. . . .

My own fight in this campaign, and the Democratic Party's fight, is not with the Republican rank and file. Our fight is with the leadership of that Republican Party, a leadership which has been so barren of imagination, so stupid year in and year out that it has contributed year in and year out to Democratic success.

I do not want, if I am elected, to have a row with the Republican Legislature. I hope that they will in most instances go along as well with my program as they have been forced to do with Governor Smith's program.

And I can tell you quite frankly that I shall have a program. You have heard part of it tonight. In the course of the next ten days the people of this State are going to hear some more programs from me. I believe in programs, because I believe in moving ahead. I am not one of those who are very keen about those periods of standing still that a Nation or a State sometimes has to have. It is just possible that after the War in 1920 it may have been in some respects a good thing for the United States to have

29

had a period of—what shall we call it, politely?—beauty sleep under President Harding and President Coolidge. (*Laughter*) It may have been a good thing for us to quiet our nerves after the struggle of the Great War. Some of the farmers of this country do not think that that beauty sleep did them much good, and some of us are beginning to realize that we have fallen pretty far behind during that beauty sleep. But be that as it may, the time has come for us to wake up; and I believe that it is better for us when we wake up, instead of stretching and yawning comfortably and putting our head back to doze upon the Hoover pillow, that it is better for us to get up and take a cold Al Smith shower and feel fit for another four years. (*Laughter*) . . .

4 ⟪ Campaign Address (Excerpts), Buffalo, N. Y. October 20, 1928

(Alfred E. Smith—Labor legislation—Republican opposition to labor legislation—Religious bigotry in national campaign.)

I AM VERY grateful to the City of Buffalo for this very splendid meeting. This great gathering tonight has come here not merely to pay tribute to the Democracy of the State of New York; it understands that we have with us, perhaps not in body but at least in spirit, the great leader of the Democracy of the Nation, our next President, Alfred E. Smith.

I had planned to talk about a lot of things, national issues and various others tonight, but when I read that in Buffalo my old and good friend Mr. Ottinger had had the nerve to talk about what the Republican Party has done for labor, I decided that that was my chance.

And so tonight I am going to tell you all about it, tell you the facts, go back in my own mind and in your mind into the history of this State. Somewhere in a pigeon-hole in a desk of the Republican leaders of New York State is a large envelope, soiled, worn, bearing a date that goes back twenty-five or thirty years. Printed in large letters on this old envelope are the words, "Promises to labor." Inside the envelope are a series of sheets dated two years apart and representing the best thought of the best minds of the Republican leaders over a succession of years. Each sheet of promises is practically the duplicate of every other sheet in the envelope. But nowhere in that envelope is a single page bearing the title "Promises kept."

I ought to know something about it, from personal experience, because I had the good fortune to be a member of the State Senate in that famous year of 1911, when the Democratic Party, aided by an almost solid delegation in the Senate and Assembly from the City of Buffalo, came into control of the State Government for the first time in a generation and started on its way a program — not of promises, but of accomplishments.

Now, the set-up in 1911 was exactly the same as it is in 1928. The Democratic Administration, the Democratic leaders in the Legislature began at that time a series of practical measures in the interest of the men and women of this State who work with their hands. That session of the Legislature was the godfather of the Workmen's Compensation Law, of the first law limiting the hours for women in industry, of the factory investigating committee, and of a series of important measures strengthening the provisions of existing labor laws and building up the effective strength of the Labor Department.

It is worth while to go as far back as 1911, because we get at that time a definite picture of the attitude of the leaders of the two parties, an attitude that has continued down to the present day. I remember well that the attitude of the Democratic Party at that time was severely criticized by the reactionary element in this State. We were called socialistic and radical, and if the term "Bolshevist" or "Red" had then been in existence, it would undoubtedly have been applied to Assemblyman Alfred E. Smith and Senator Robert F. Wagner, and many others, including myself, because of our ardent support of the whole program.

Arrayed against us on the other side was the silent, powerful pressure of the old school of thought, which held the theory that when an employer hired a working man or a working woman, he became the master of the fate of his employee; that when a worker entered the factory door it was nobody's business as to how he worked, how long he worked, or how much he was paid.

It is very difficult, seventeen years later, for this generation to understand the attitude of the old conservative element toward employment, back in 1911. But it is a fact that this attitude was subscribed to, sometimes silently, sometimes openly, but always definitely, by the Republican leaders of this State at that time. During the years 1911 to 1915, the splendid record of definite accomplishment made by the Democratic Party of this State was fought and blocked and criticized at every turn by the Republican legislative leaders, and I am simply telling you bald facts. The best example of the difference in attitude between the two parties is the fact that during the four years of Governor Whitman constructive labor legislation in the State of New York came to an end. The progress was not resumed until Governor Smith went back to Albany as the Chief Executive in 1919.

Now, in the present year of 1928 it would have been perfectly possible, away back last spring, to forecast with absolute certainty the exact words which the Republican leaders and the Republican candidates would say during this autumn campaign.

First of all, they trot out the old worn envelope, dust it off, and copy into their platform the same old words that have been used every two years for a generation back. Let me read you the labor plank of the Republican platform. It is grand.

"The Republican Party in this State has done more for labor than any other party. The Labor Law and the Workmen's Compensation Law are conceded by labor to be the best in all the States. Almost every line has been written in these laws by or with the approval of our party."

Now, how dare they say that? How do grown up and ostensibly sane political leaders perjure themselves that way, for a statement of that kind is so openly and flagrantly dishonorable that it comes pretty close to the borderline of perjury? These same leaders know perfectly well that the Republican Party has constantly fought against almost every progressive measure in the interest of labor, that the State of New York has added to its statute books during the past seventeen years. Is it not dishonorable to talk about the writing of laws by or with the approval of the Republican leaders, when every man or woman who reads the newspapers knows that our present laws were either written by a Democratic Legislature or were forced through a Republican Legislature because the Democratic Governor of this State has been able on occasion after occasion to appeal so strongly to public opinion that it became too dangerous for those Republican leaders to block the wheels of progress any longer?

The best proof is to go and get the opinion of any man or woman in this State who has been working in the interest of social betterment and the improvement of conditions of employment during all these years. You will find a definite substantiation of everything I am stating in regard to the relative attitude of the Republican and the Democratic leaders.

Let us take a practical example of the principle of limiting the hours of work for women and children in industry. Back in that session in 1911 the Democratic leaders brought forward what was then regarded as a radical, socialistic proposal to limit the hours of women and children to fifty-four hours a week, and that is only seventeen years ago. The record shows that opposition came from the Republican leaders, many of them the same individual men we have today. But after a long fight that proposal became law.

When Alfred E. Smith went back to Albany as Governor in 1919, progressive thought had advanced to the point of demanding a further limitation for women and children to a maximum of forty-eight hours a week. During six years that demand for action increased and at last, although the Democratic platform had been for it year after year, at last in 1924, four years ago, the Republican State platform for the first time came out definitely in favor of the forty-eight-hour week. It is almost needless to say that the Democratic platform had it in that year again as it had before.

It seemed, therefore, that the fight had been won. Both parties were for it. It seemed that the workers were definitely assured by both parties of the passage of the proposed law; definite assurance was given to the voters of this State by Theodore Roosevelt, Jr., who, as I remember it, was a candidate for Governor, and by the Republican leaders, that they would carry out that pledge.

Well, what happened? The Republican Legislature, wholly in their control, in the spring of 1925 failed utterly to carry out this plan in spite of the demand for it by every Democratic member, and by the Governor of the State. As a deliberate subterfuge the Republican Legislature passed the so-called Joyner Bill, which was unanimously denounced by labor and was criticized by Governor Smith as a fraud upon the people of the State — another promise gone bad.

Well, that brings us nearer home. In order to create further delay the Republican leaders in the spring of 1926 appointed a so-called Industrial Survey Commission and hoped that they would by that action take the minds of the voters off the broken promises of 1924, and in the 1926 platform they merely referred in glowing terms to what this Commission was going to do. The Democrats, on the other hand, again stood squarely by the pledge for the forty-eight-hour week.

In 1927 this Republican Commission made a report recommending a half-way measure, and the Legislature enacted not a forty-eight-hour law but a forty-nine-and-one-half-hour law. Because that was obviously the best that he could get from a reactionary and hostile Legislature, the Governor signed this law with the simple statement to the people of this State that it did not carry out the pledges hitherto made by the Republican Party. He signed it on the theory that sometimes it is better to have half a loaf than none at all.

That brings us down to date. What is the situation this year? That same old Republican Commission, the smoke-screen commission, is still in existence, and the Republican platform this year pledges — I shall read the wording — "We pledge our party to give full consideration to the recommendations of this commission."

What do we Democrats say? Compare the two. Compare the thought behind the two. We say, "We pledge ourselves to complete Governor Smith's labor and welfare program, including an eight-hour day and forty-eight-hour week for women and children in industry."

That pledge is definite, and the record of the Democratic Party is also definite. We are in the habit, as is shown by the record, of carrying out our pledges. The Republican leaders of this State have not yet formed that habit.

That is a pretty good illustration, and I have gone into it a good deal in detail; an illustration of the history of all legislation affecting the working men and the working women that has been going on for the past twenty years.

I want to go on with the consideration of what the two parties are offering to the electorate this year. Other than the quotations which I have made from the platform of the Republican Party, that party offers nothing further for social and labor legislation. The Democratic Party in its platform goes on as follows, and it is worth-while for me to give the principle points, because there are very few people, probably not more than one man or woman in a thousand, who ever bothers to read through the whole length of any party platform. I myself had to do it this year because I am a candidate. The Democratic Party goes on very simply and pledges, first, a law prohibiting the granting of temporary injunctions without notice of hearing, and trial before a jury for any alleged violation of injunctions.

Second, we pledge a consideration of the subject of old-age pensions, and I might add right here that this is a subject that may be regarded today as radical, as socialistic, or as my conservative friends would say, "Red," just exactly as workmen's compensation and factory inspection were regarded as radical twenty years ago. But I believe that the time is definitely at hand for the State of New York to give definite study to the great humanitarian question of preventing destitution among the thousands of our citizens who become too old to maintain for themselves the adequate standards of life to which as Americans they are entitled.

35

We pledge further the establishment of an advisory minimum wage board on behalf of women and children.

Fourth, we pledge the extension of the Workmen's Compensation Act to give the greatest protection to injured workers and the dependents of workers killed in industry and to extend the law to cover all occupational diseases.

We pledge, fifth, the further liberalization of the laws relating to the welfare of mothers and children.

And, finally, we pledge a declaration by law that the labor of human beings is not a commodity.

I received tonight the last bulletin of the New York State Federation of Labor. I want to read two short sentences. The State Federation of Labor says: "An analysis of the Democratic and Republican State platforms as they relate to labor shows positively that the Democratic platform is by far the most favorable to the wage earner. The Democratic platform plainly pledges to support legislation to require hearings in court before an injunction can be issued against wage earners; to provide for jury trial of persons accused of violating such injunctions, the paramount legislative reform asked for by organized labor. The Republican platform ignores organized labor's request." And then, in a very naive or a very sarcastic way, it continues and says: "The Republican platform is very indefinite on improvements in the labor laws and ignores all of organized labor's proposals stated above, which were presented to the Republican Convention by the committees representing organized labor of the State of New York."

I ask tonight the simple question of the people of this State: Are they in favor of continuation of progress in our laws relating to labor and social welfare; and, further, I ask whether on the record they think that this end can be best obtained by reliance on a Republican Governor and a Republican Legislature, or by reliance on a Democratic Governor and a Democratic Legislature? . . .

Now, one final word, the last time that I expect to speak it

36

in this campaign. Some misguided people in every section of the land have been violating by written and spoken word the Sixth Amendment to the Constitution of the United States, that great charter which forbids any religious test for the holding of public office. I hope and believe that as Election Day approaches this question will be left out of the decision of the electorate; just as I have talked up and down the land that no vote be given to Mr. Hoover because his opponent happens to be a member of another church of God, so I plead that no vote be given to me because my opponent is a member of a different church of God.

I go back in my memory ten years ago — ten years ago this autumn. I go back to the days when I saw Chateau Thierry; I go back to the days when I was following up the advance of the American Army; I go back to a day in particular when several miles behind the actual line of contact between the two armies I passed through wheat fields, wheat fields with the ripened grain uncut; wheat fields in which there were patches, little patches of color, something in the wheat, and some of those patches wore a dark gray uniform and others of those patches wore an olive drab uniform. As we went through these fields there were American boys carrying stretchers, and on those stretchers were German boys and Austrian boys and American boys being carried to the rear, and somehow in those days people were not asking to what church those German boys or those American boys belonged. Somehow we got into our heads over there and we got into our heads back here that never again would there be any question of a man's religion in the United States of America.

And I want to say to you very simply, very solemnly, that if there is any man or woman whose mind can go back ten years; if there is any man or woman who has seen the sights that I have seen, who knows what this country went through; any man or woman who knows what Germany, Poland, France, Austria, England went through — even more than we did — in those years; if any man or woman, after thinking of that, can bear in his heart any motive in this year which will lead him to cast his ballot in the interest of intolerance and of a violation of the spirit of the Constitution of the United States, then I say solemnly to that man or woman, "May God have mercy on your miserable soul."

5 ⟨ Campaign Address (Excerpts), Rochester, N. Y. October 22, 1928

(Alfred E. Smith — Human functions of Government — Education — Child Welfare — Crippled children — Aid to widowed mothers — Old-age assistance — Smith, Wagner and I as "socialists" and "radicals.")

My friends:

. . . I HAVE been trying to concentrate, so far as possible in these great night meetings, on one topic at a time, especially because nowadays one talks not just to the audience in front of him, but also to thousands of people scattered all over the State who are listening in by radio.

Tonight I want to talk facts about what I call the human function of our State Government. Today, after a long period of education, every citizen recognizes that it is the duty of the State to concern itself with the health, welfare and general education of the people of the State. We have made tremendous strides in these past ten years. Before that, the State was content to stop with the assistance of a very second-rate kind of education and did practically nothing in the other fields of welfare.

First, in the matter of our schools, I want to point out one very simple proof of what has happened since Governor Smith came into office as Chief Executive on the first of January, 1919, because while I am not a statistician, like Mr. Hoover, the use of figures once in a while is very convincing.

During the first year of Governor Smith's Administration, the State of New York spent twelve million dollars for education; during the current year of 1928, ten years later, the State of New York has spent eighty-six million dollars in the same cause. During no period in the State's history have such enormous strides been made, and I leave it to the judgment of anybody, of all the voters of this State, as to who is responsible. Was it the gentlemen who called themselves the leaders of the Republican Party? And I want to say right here, at the outset, that my fight, our fight this year, is not against the rank and file of the Republican Party, but against the leaders of that party. Were those leaders responsible for this progress in education, or was it the insistence of Governor Alfred E. Smith? As the Governor himself has said, let anyone who cares to know write to Dr. Graves, head of the Education Department, and ask him who is most responsible for the splendid progress. Incidentally, Dr. Graves is a Republican, and he is a truthful man.

The only time the Republican leaders took any initiative at all was when they thought they could embarrass the Governor a few years ago by passing a bill to increase teachers' salaries, when they knew there was no money in the treasury with which to pay the increase; and, incidentally, they absolutely declined to furnish the money by an appropriation.

While it is true that these magnificent steps for improved education have already been taken, we cannot now stand still, because in many communities of this State school facilities remain still wholly inadequate and out of date. A continuation of State aid is imperative. In many places the minimum requirements are still too low; and it is obviously the duty of the State to see to it that this minimum standard is made higher.

So, too, I am convinced that the minimum standards for the teachers of the State must also be raised. We are approaching a new era in which teaching standards will be subjected to increasing scrutiny. . . .

Now, here is a kindred subject that goes hand in hand with education. I conceive it to be of just as much importance to educate the body of the child as it is to educate the mind of the child. During the past ten years, again under the leadership of Governor Smith, the general health of the citizens of this State in the first place, and of the children in particular, has taken tremendous strides. The death rate has shown a constant decline.

Ten years ago the death rate of the babies was ninety in every thousand, whereas today it is sixty in every thousand.

Again, in this field, we have only just begun the task, for much remains to be done. I may be pardoned if I refer to my own intense interest in the care of crippled children, and, indeed, of cripples of every kind. Infantile paralysis, tuberculosis, occupational and other accidents, and various other causes give an estimate of over one hundred thousand adults and children in this State who are seriously crippled, most of them so seriously that they are unable to live normal or useful lives.

First of all, then, from the practical dollars-and-cents point of view, it is obvious that if a large proportion of these cripples can by proper treatment be restored to active and useful citizenship, the money spent on them by the State will come back many times through their increased productiveness.

We must not forget that a wheel-chair cripple is not only a dead load on the earning power of the community, but in most cases requires also the attention and care of some able-bodied person as well. Modern medical science has advanced to such a point that in the great majority of cases these cripples can be made to function. It is often a long and costly procedure, but it is worth-while for the various communities and for the State to spend this time and money, for it will be repaid a thousandfold.

Then, too, there is the great humanitarian side of the subject. I have seen thousands of examples of crippled adults and children, who by proper care have been restored to normal life among their families and friends. It is, of course, a fact that the family of the average crippled child in this State cannot afford to pay the heavy cost of obtaining proper private treatment, and we must come to a better realization that this care is as much a part of the duties of the local and State Governments as it is for those Governments to provide the funds for the development of the child's education. . . .

The work so well begun needs to be greatly expanded. There are, for instance, between twenty thousand and thirty thousand crippled children in this State, it is estimated, who have not yet been located.

There are thousands of others in this State who are not receiving adequate treatment. We need more money. We need an expansion of medical service to every out-of-the-way corner in the cities and on the farms. Money and momentum are the remaining needs. I propose to ask for the money and to accelerate the momentum.

I suppose that people readily will recognize that I myself furnish a perfectly good example of what can be done by the right kind of care. I dislike to use this personal example, but it happens to fit. Seven years ago in the epidemic in New York, I came down with infantile paralysis, a perfectly normal attack, and I was completely, for the moment, put out of any useful activities. By personal good fortune I was able to get the very best kind of care, and the result of having the right kind of care is that today I am on my feet.

And while I shall not vouch for the mental side of it, I am quite certain that from the physical point of view I am quite capable of going to Albany and staying there two years.

Unfortunately, the great majority of the people in this State, whether children or grown up, who have become incapacitated, are unable to afford the cost and the time necessary to rehabilitation. It seems to me that it is the clear duty of the State and the local governments to make up what is needed to bring about the splendid definite results that medical science can now provide. And I promise to do all in my power to make available for others that which I myself have been fortunate enough to obtain.

Then there is another side of that same broad picture. For the additional care of the little children who have been thrown on the mercy of the community by the death, the insanity, the desertion or the incapacity of their fathers, this State has now adopted the definite policy where we are no longer satisfied with the old-fashioned idea of sticking them away in the dismal recesses of an institution, there to be catalogued, classified, and merely allowed to grow up. We believe that their place is rightfully with their mothers. We believe that the money spent on institutions for those unfortunate children to go to, should instead be given to their mothers, to help bring them up at home. Money used to give these children a mother's love and a mother's rearing can never be wasted.

Now, this system of mothers' pensions has been urged by the Democratic Party for many years, and it has gradually been broadened, extended and amplified by the Democratic Administration of Governor Smith. What has been the attitude of the Republican leaders? Let us look at the record. These allowances to widows for the support of their children are made by so-called county boards of child welfare. The money comes from the county treasuries, but some of our counties have been unable to raise enough money for this purpose. Their finances in many cases could not stand the strain. Governor Smith has come forward and said: "Let the great State of New York step in and help." He has urged the Legislature time and again to appropriate money to help the counties in this humane work. Bills were introduced by Democratic Legislatures to contribute State money to these local boards, with which they could function. Those messages and those bills were ignored by the Republican leaders. They turned a deaf ear to these pleas for better childhood, for better motherhood in our State. Why? Simply because it cost money; and the other reason was that they had not thought of it first.

When we Democrats were in control of the Senate a few years ago, the Senate passed these bills: Senate Introductory Bill No. 284 of 1923; Senate Introductory Bill No. 84 of 1924. Introduced by Democrats, they were passed by Democrats. But what happened to them? When they got on the other side of the capitol to the Assembly, there was a different story. The Republican leaders were in control there. The bills were strangled to death in committee, and were not even allowed to come out for a vote. That is the record; those are the facts. On that record and on those facts, are you going to trust those Republican leaders to carry on our program of child welfare in this State? . . .

One of the unsatisfactory conditions still existing in this State is the administration of the Poor Law. I do not know how much you people come in contact with that law, how much you have ever bothered your heads to look into the administration of the Poor Law in the various counties of this State. In some counties they handle it pretty well. But I think one of the most oppressing things that I have to do on occasion in this State is to visit the County Poorhouse. Somehow it just tears my heart to see those old men and women there, more than almost anything that I know. We need a drastic revision of the poor laws, and I propose to recommend it. But beyond a mere revision of that law is the difficult problem of why it is that we have to have so many aged poor who need to be taken care of.

I have already said that in accordance with the Democratic platform I propose an immediate study of the broad subject of old-age pensions. If this State can, as I believe it will, pass a proper and adequate old-age pension law, we shall not have to revise the Poor Law of this State. We shall then be in a position, by a simple two-line act, to repeal it forever and ever.

The taking up of this subject of old-age pensions at this time is no more radical or socialistic than the initiation of the Workmen's Compensation and the Factory Inspection Laws of seventeen years ago; and I remember well, when I was in the Legislature in that year of 1911, following that fine convention in this very hall, that we people who advocated Workmen's Compensation and Factory Inspection and social legislation of that kind, were regarded by a great many of the respectable and substantial citizens of this State as radicals and socialists. As I remember, the two Senators from Rochester at that time viewed me as a "Red." If the word "Bolshevist" had been invented then, it would have been applied to people like Assemblyman Alfred E. Smith, Senator Robert F. Wagner and me. Yes, and I suppose that those of us, who, this coming winter, ask for an immediate study of the question of old-age pensions will be written down as Bolshevists.

Now, I am opposed to any form of dole. I do not believe that the State has any right merely to hand out money. But I am certain that a practical method can be worked out in the State of New York on the principle of mutual contributions. . . .

As I was coming over this afternoon from Batavia, I thought of a little verse that was taught me when I was pretty small, and I thought it was a good motto for me in this campaign, a motto that applies to what we are trying to do in this State; a motto that will apply with equal force to what our Governor is going to do in Washington after the fourth of March, next, and it is this:

"Look outward and not in; look forward and not back; look upward and not down, and lend a hand."

6 ❪ Campaign Address (Excerpts), Syracuse, N. Y. October 23, 1928

(Alfred E. Smith — Public development of the State's water-power resources.)

Mr. Chairman, my friends of Syracuse:

. . . TONIGHT I am going to talk about a very wet subject, the wet subject of water power. While it may not be quite as soul-stirring a subject as the other wet one (prohibition), in some ways it goes just as deep to the roots of our democracy.

This is a history and a sermon on the subject of water power, and I preach from the Old Testament. The text is "Thou shalt not steal."

It is the history of the development of public thought in this State over a period of twenty years, a gradual forming of public opinion made necessary by the greatest of American discoveries, electricity, and by the growth among a small group of individuals of the very human desire to add to their worldly possessions by getting something for nothing.

The story goes back twenty-one years. In 1907 the use of electricity for power purposes or for general illuminating purposes was still in its infancy, and the general public had not yet come to realize the vast expansion which has taken place since then.

44

On the other hand, the far-seeing experts and specialists in the electrical field had already begun to lay out a program, a program for the acquisition of water-power sites, realizing that the development of the turbine would soon make the production of electric power by the use of water far cheaper than by the use of coal.

It was back in 1907 that the passage by the Legislature of the State of New York of a free, gratis charter created mighty little interest. Very few people knew about it. Yet that Legislature gave away on a silver platter a charter in perpetuity, giving the right to develop the power of the Long Saulte Rapids up on the St. Lawrence River. Most of us knew nothing about it at all, and it was not until some time afterwards that the people came to realize what the Legislature had done. Probably the great majority of the members of that Legislature had considered it merely one of the usual charters for private companies, and nobody charges bad faith on the part of that Legislature.

Several years later, however, the Democratic Party came into power for the first time in both the Senate and the Assembly. By that time, in 1912 and 1913, public opinion had begun to crystallize in this State, and in the face of intense lobbying and bitter opposition, the law was passed repealing the free hand-out of the charter to the Long Saulte Development Company.

I shall always be proud of the fact that I was a member of the State Senate at that time, for I believe firmly that our action saved to the people of the State of New York its most valuable water-power asset.

Well, what happened? The power interests remained pretty quiet for a while. Nothing happened until Governor Smith became Chief Executive of the State in 1919. He immediately urged the development of the water-power resources of the State, and during two years was, as usual, as in everything else that he recommended, blocked by the Legislature of the State.

Evidently the water-power interests feared the possible future return of a Democratic Governor, because two years later, during the term of Governor Nathan L. Miller, whom some of you know, I understand, an act was passed creating a body called the Water Power Commission, that consisted of the Speaker of the Assembly, the Majority Leader of the Senate, the Conservation Commissioner, the State Engineer, and the Attorney General. The Legislature gave to this Commission the broadest sort of power to grant licenses to private persons or corporations authorizing the diversion and use for power or other purposes of any of the water resources of the State.

I suppose people who were chiefly interested thought they had all the time in the world to go ahead with their well-laid plans. But they reckoned, as they had often reckoned before, without Alfred E. Smith. Because, as we know, he came back into office on January 1, 1923, and fortunately also he has remained as our Chief Executive from that day to this.

It is only because of this fact, my friends, that we, you and I, the owners of our water power, have not lost that water power by theft. Governor Smith sought in vain to obtain a repeal of the Water Power Commission Law. The Legislative leaders blocked it, and it is interesting to note the definite appearance at this time of the Speaker of the Assembly, Mr. Machold, the open and avowed champion of the private corporations which were seeking to obtain the water-power sites from the control of the State. With the help of Mr. Machold the water-power interests made the next move and offered an amendment to the Constitution of the State, allowing the use of the waters in the forest reserves. See how clever it was! The amendment did not have to go to the Governor for signature; it went straight to the voters, and they were clever too, because they carefully camouflaged that amendment to make the voters think that it would allow the use of these waters up in the Adirondacks only for municipal canal or stream-flow purposes. But it contained a little joker, just as so many of my friend Machold's little schemes did, a little joker allowing the development of power by lessees under leases not to exceed fifty years. That, of course, would have enabled the construction of water-power plants throughout the Adirondack Park.

Governor Smith is not the kind, perhaps, that jokers get by. He dug it out, took prompt issue, labeled the amendment "the Adirondack raid" and made a personal campaign against its adoption. He made the issue so clear to the people of the State that it is worth while remembering that they sustained his position by defeating the amendment by a vote of 965,000 to 470,000, a little over two to one.

The next step in the history of the attempted theft was the announcement by Governor Smith of the adoption of a definite policy on water power, January, 1924. He brought out two points clearly. First, the people of the State are opposed to the principle of leasing the power sites which they own. Second, that leases for long-term periods, such as fifty years, are in effect perpetual grants. . . .

He proposed the development of the sites by a water-power authority, on a principle similar to that of the highly successful Port of New York Authority. . . .

Well, needless to say, the Republican Senate and Assembly, under the guidance of my friend, Speaker Machold, failed to carry out the recommendations of the Governor, or to consider what were undoubtedly the wishes of the great majority of the voters of this State. Again they tried to delay action by suggesting further investigation of a subject perfectly clear to everybody.

That same situation continued in practically the same way through 1925 and the greater part of 1926. But in the fall of 1926 — and now we are getting down to modern times, very close to the days of the attempted robbery that I am coming to in a minute — the difference in policy between the leaders of the two parties was made clear in their platforms. The Republican platform said, "We favor the prompt development of the water-power resources of the State by private capital and management, under a system of limited leases." On the other hand, the Democratic platform said, "We pledge ourselves to the enactment of laws which will guarantee the perpetual ownership and control by the people of the State of the State-owned water-power resources."

47

Which would you rather have? Which is the standard that the people of this State have so clearly adopted?

Now, it is a simple fact, which Mr. Ottinger cannot deny, that the gubernatorial campaign of 1926 was waged in large part on this issue. As all know, Governor Smith was reelected by an enormous majority, and it seemed clear that the people of the State had set the seal of their approval on his policy. As a result of the 1926 election, however, there came that episode in our State history which will be recorded in large letters for all time.

Immediately after the votes had been counted in November, the power interests of this State realized that unless prompt action were taken, their chances would be gone, for the plan of reorganization of the State Government, which had been adopted by the people the previous year, was to go into effect the following first of January. Under that plan the old Water Power Commission was to die. The power interests had less than two months to get something done, seven weeks to go. Through the subservient Republican leaders they controlled four out of five members of the Water Power Commission: the Speaker of the Assembly, the Majority Leader of the Senate, the State Engineer, and Albert Ottinger, the Attorney General of the State of New York.

In this situation the water-power interests became desperate. They induced the Water Power Commission to consent to grant them a lease on the St. Lawrence River which would have deprived the people of most of their water-power resources forever. The Governor, hearing of the plan of the Commission, promptly protested, calling the attention of the State to the fact that the Commission was about to go out of office, and that after January 1, 1927, the Governor himself was to be given the right to veto such licenses. But in spite of that this Commission had the consummate nerve to reply to the Governor that they intended to go through with the granting of the lease during the final months of their existence.

Public opinion was thoroughly aroused in every section of the State. Litigation was threatened. The situation was critical. There, on the one side, was the overwhelming and definitely proven opposition of the great majority of the citizens, demanding that this steal should not be consummated at the eleventh hour.

There, on the other side, stood the Water Power Commission, listening to the pleadings of the power magnates, asking them to act before it was too late.

I see a picture of a table: four men, among them the Attorney General of the State, the lawyer elected by the people to defend the interests of the people, the lawyer of the State whom the Governor in this crisis was so unable to trust to work for the interests of the people of the State, that he felt obliged to retain the services of Samuel Untermyer to represent the people.

There stood these four men, their pens poised in hand, ready to consummate the final steal. Telegrams poured in, protests from public meetings and editorials in the newspapers of all parties flooded Albany. And in that crisis came the decisive move, the open dare of the Governor of the State of New York, challenging the Water Power Commission to affix their names. For a few moments it looked as if the steal would be consummated. But in the nick of time the face of the Water Power Commission was saved. The power companies themselves lost their nerve. They did not dare to accept the challenge of the Governor and of the people of the State of New York. No; they decided that rather than arouse public opinion any further, they would wait until they could control, at some future date, not only the Attorney General, but also the Governor of the State. They were waiting until the election of the year 1928.

Yes, the Water Power Commission put down their pens. Attorney General Ottinger and his colleagues had also lost their nerve. It was a drama that has had a happy ending in the first act; the curtain is about to ring up on the second act. . . .

In many ways this matter of power is the outstanding controversial issue before the people of the State in this election. . . .

The record and position of Mr. Ottinger on the whole power question are too well known, too well fixed in history to do other than convince the people of this State that his election as Governor would mean the abandonment of the policy of Governor Smith, the policy that has received the support of the electorate. It means, further, the immediate handing over of our power resources to development by private corporations.

It may sound very plausible to talk about a lease for a fifty-year period. I state, and I make this statement on a fairly wide reading of history and a certain amount of common sense, that a fifty-year lease of water-power resources to a private corporation is, in effect, a grant in perpetuity. Let that sink in in this State. Does any human being suppose that when one of the great water-power companies, if it should by any mischance get the legal right to develop the Long Saulte Rapids in the St. Lawrence River, puts in its dams, its power plants, and its transmission lines, at the end of fifty years it would walk out, comfortably and quietly, and turn it over to somebody else? That is not credible. That is asking us plain people to swallow something big.

I do not want, any more than Mr. Ottinger or the power interests do, to put the State of New York into the business of distributing power to the ultimate buyer. That is a matter which can now be properly taken care of by private companies, especially because of the fact that it involves the employment of very large forces of men and women in the distribution of power to the ultimate consumer. But this function of the distribution end is a wholly separate function from that of the development of power at its sources.

Personally, I am convinced that the people of this State have made up their minds that they want their power sites developed by a Power Authority, and not by private corporations. I shall advocate legislation to carry out that policy, and I will go just one step farther. If, by some misfortune, the Legislature after the first of January should still be under the control of Mr. Machold, Chairman of the Republican State Committee, and should still decline to carry out the policy that I have suggested, I will dare them to submit the question in simple form by referendum to the people of the State of New York.

One election, just one day, two weeks from today by the way, just one day in November stands between the rights of the people of the State on one side, and the loss of their priceless heritage on the other. The rights of the people are assailed in this election. Those who would steal our heritage are within one day of success. I have been placed by my party on duty as policeman to guard that heritage. I ask your support in that difficult and great task, and I ask you to join with me in saying, as our old sailors did back there in the days against the pirates of the Barbary Coast, "Millions for defense, and not one cent for tribute."

7 ❨ Campaign Address (Excerpts), Utica, N. Y. October 25, 1928

(Prohibition and State Enforcement.)

Senator Brown, my friends of Utica:

. . . WHILE I am on the question of State's prisons, I want to make a point that the whole prison question presents a grave problem for today and possibly for the future, because of the undoubted increase in crime during the past few years. I am personally much interested in the crime question, by virtue of the fact that for several years I have been a member of the National Crime Commission, and I am familiar with the reports on this subject from every State in the Union. Any person who is familiar with this situation, not just here in New York, but in the West, the Far West, the South and in New England, must recognize two unfortunate facts that have arisen during these past few years.

First, the age of criminals and of delinquents has shown a tremendous drop from previous years. Where ten years ago the average age of people convicted of crime was a little over 21, it is today nearer 18.

Second, as shown by every record everywhere in the United States, the use of bootleg liquor bears an increasing responsibility for the commission of crime. Whether we live in the country or in the city, whether we live in this State or in another State, we know from personal observation of the effect of the present situation on the younger generation. . . .

In every State in this country there are from two to five times more arrests of minors for drunkenness and disorderly conduct than before the misnamed Prohibition Law was put upon the Federal statute books. During the past four years I have spent much time in the State of Georgia, a State which had its own dry law years and years before the Volstead Law went into effect, and I can bear witness here in the State of New York, as I have borne witness publicly in the State of Georgia, that there is more consumption of distilled liquor per capita in Georgia, whether it be in the great cities like Atlanta, or in the rural sections of the State, than there is here in our State of New York. That I believe to be the fact, and I believe that the same fact applies to a great many other States that are today casting aspersions on our record in the State of New York.

Now, it is a fact that any legislative change in the present Federal Law is, of course, a matter for the Federal Congress. Many States in the Union have State statutes similar to and based upon the Federal Volstead Law. I know from personal observation in many of these States that the enforcement of Prohibition is in those States actually less effective than it is in the State of New York, where we operate under the Volstead Law alone. It must, therefore, not be forgotten that it is still the duty of every peace officer in this State to make arrests for any violation in this State of the Volstead Law, just as much as any other Federal statute, and no one need question my position in favor of law enforcement.

In view of the experience of other States, and in view of my conviction that an overwhelming respectable opinion in this State is opposed to the creation of a new set of machinery to add to the present confusion, graft and ineffectiveness of the Federal Law Enforcement system under the present Government in Washington, there is no practical advantage in enacting another

Mullen-Gage law as a part of the statutes of the State of New York.

That, my friends, is the way I feel about it. That is where I stand, and it is an interesting fact that I have not yet been able to learn what Mr. Ottinger's policy is, or indeed whether he has any policy at all. Certainly his party has no policy. Its platform does not even mention Prohibition. Aren't the people entitled to know before they vote? . . .

8 ⟨ Campaign Address (Excerpts), Troy, N. Y. October 26, 1928

(Typical day of campaigning by the "sick" candidate.)

Mr. Van Santvoord, my friends of Troy:

WELL, I am glad to get back to the Hudson River. You know, I have been a little bit amused during the last three weeks. I understand that after the Rochester Convention took the action that it did, there was a good deal of what might be called sob stuff among the Republican editorial writers in the State of New York. They said, "Isn't it too bad that that unfortunate man has had to be drafted for the Governorship? Isn't it too bad that his health won't stand it?"

We started off nearly two weeks ago from the City of New York, consisting of a caravan — a whole flock of people, candidates, the press, the stenographic force, etc. We started in in Orange County and we went on through Sullivan, Delaware, Broome, Steuben, and so forth, out through the Southern Tier, all the way to Jamestown. One day we covered 190 miles by automobile and made seven speeches. Then we worked our way up to Buffalo and back to Rochester and Syracuse; because we were getting into our stride, we took a little side trip up to Oswego and Watertown, and then we dropped back to Utica. We left Utica this morning, intending to have an easy day of it. We got to Herkimer, where we all made speeches; then we expected to come through to Schenectady, but when we got to Fonda, there were forty or fifty automobiles in line blocking the road, and we were literally kidnapped. It threw the whole schedule out. We were told that up in that neck of the woods, Gloversville, where in the past there had been occasionally two Democrats, and sometimes three, that had gone to the polls, there were two thousand people waiting for us on the street, and that all the talk of the owners of the glove factories there could not keep them off the streets. So we changed our plans a little and went up to Gloversville. There they were, all of them going to vote the Democratic ticket. When we came on down, we were kidnapped again. We got to Amsterdam. We expected to go through Amsterdam just as fast as the traffic cops would let us, but there were sixteen hundred people in the theatre in Amsterdam, waiting. They had been waiting there two hours.

And then, for good measure, we just dropped into Schenectady and spoke there earlier in the evening, and now here we are in Troy. Too bad about this unfortunate sick man, isn't it? . . .

9 ⟨ Campaign Address (Excerpts), Queens, New York City, N. Y. October 29, 1928

(State parks program — Alfred E. Smith called a "socialist" by President Hoover.)

Mr. Chairman, and friends of Queens:

. . . Tonight I want to talk to you about something that is particularly appropriate in Queens, because here you are the great artery, the great means of access to the farmers of Long Island. I had started — it was on the tip of my tongue — to say that Queens was the neck of the bottle to Long Island. But I was afraid that the Anti-Saloon League might object.

We have heard much in the past about the drift of the rural population to the cities, and it is true. There are more and more abandoned farms up-State in New York than I have even seen in my lifetime. There are more and more farms being advertised for tax sales. The farmers cannot make both ends meet, and that is one reason why, as part of my program, a new program for this State, I propose that we should take up seriously this question of retaining our rural population. In that plan I know that I have the support of the people who live in New York City, because it is to their interest as well as that of the farmers that the farms of the State should be maintained. Many reformers and social workers have been worried about the possible effect on future generations that would come from the increased crowding in our cities. Locally, out here, you are not yet crowded, and I hope that the development of this great borough will not be along the lines of crowding. But you know there is an old military axiom that says that for every new weapon of offense that is invented, very quickly there comes along the invention of a weapon of defense, and I am convinced that that is the case with the trend of the past fifteen years of the rural populations coming into the cities. There has been at the same time the invention, you might say, of our modern civilization, that is taking city people out into the country districts.

There are two modern factors that belong to this movement. One is the great growth of popular sports that we all know about, and the other is the advent of the automobile, which is making it possible for those of us who live in the cities to get out into the country, whole families at a time. . . .

Of equal importance with the highway program has been the great program of park and parkway development initiated by Governor Smith in 1923. Up to that time, as you probably know, there had been a scattered, uncoordinated series of local efforts to create park facilities in various places throughout the State, all of this without any general policy. With his almost uncanny ability to sense the needs of the average citizenship at the inception of those needs, Governor Smith, as he has shown in dozens of other cases, was the first to call the attention of the people of the State to the need for a definite State policy on parks, for a systematic development of construction and acquisition. He realized then, as all the people have since, that the people who need those parks all throughout the State are not those that have the time and money to own great estates and enjoy outdoor life whenever the spirit moves them, but rather those millions of citizens, the great rank and file of us, and particularly the children, who have no home of their own in the country and who long for a chance to obtain appreciation at first hand of the value of outdoor life.

Outside of the Adirondack and Catskill Preserves, practically all of the lands of this State were held in private ownership; and in almost every case, as you know, there were "No Trespass" signs out against the people who did not own the lands. In New York City, especially, the problem was becoming a critical one, because the increased value, and the constantly increasing value of the land within fairly easy distance of New York — the value not only of land but of the sea beaches — was making State control soon an impossibility. Action had to be taken quickly or not at all.

It was in April, 1923, that the Governor recommended this definite State Parks Program. He asked the Legislature to authorize $15,000,000 of bonds. At the same time, he recommended the creation of the State Council of Parks to tie in all of these scattered regional parks that had no head and no tail. That bond issue was approved by the people of the State in the fall of 1924, and in January, 1925, the Governor asked the Legislature to appropriate the money to permit the starting of work on the parks program.

What happened? . . .

When he asked them to appropriate the money, the Legislature saw a chance to give him political embarrassment. They had tried before to trip him up, and each time they were the ones that fell. . . .

Right about that time, not so long ago that most of you do not remember it, occurred the famous effort on the part of a number of gentlemen living on Long Island to stop the machinery before it got into working order. Those gentlemen made such a stir in and out of court, that the people in the Legislature were influenced by it and thought that here was the chance to put a spike in the Governor's guns.

Now, to understand that battle it is necessary to call attention to the fact that Long Island, as you know, forms the natural playground for six million men, women and children who live in New York City. The north and south shores of Long Island are readily accessible, and these shores have been held in private ownership practically all the way to Montauk Point. In order to obtain access to the whole of Long Island, the Long Island Park Commission mapped out two great Parkways, one on the North Shore, and one on the South; and the Commission planned the use of beaches and bays and the providing of recreational parks at suitable intervals.

What happened? The fight by that small group of Long Island residents was sufficiently effective so that the Governor's program and his request for an appropriation failed, first at the regular session, and then at the special session of the Legislature called in the summer. This opposition was definitely in the face and against the wishes of the expressed opinion of the people as given at the polls. Of course you know, as I know, that it is characteristic of the Governor, when he gets opposition of this kind it just makes him fight the harder.

The story of that long legal battle over the taking over of Deer Range Park at Central Islip is a matter fresh in our memories. Who was it headed by, that fight? It was headed by a gentleman named W. Kingsland Macy, now the Republican County Chairman of Suffolk County. He and his associates tried every known form of legal procedure to stop the State from getting Deer Range Park. Every form of social and political pressure was brought to bear on the Governor; and to bring the story down to date, it was not until the Court of Appeals of this State affirmed the appropriation of that land, that the fight seemed won. Even then Mr. Macy and his friends appealed to the Circuit Court of the United States, and were there again turned down.

The successful outcome of the struggle of 1925 and 1926 over the Taylor Estate, an old unoccupied, overgrown acreage at Central Islip, finally seemed to convince the Legislature of the definite will of the people that the parks program should be carried out, because in the 1926 session, and in 1927 and 1928, the Legislature made large appropriations out of current revenue and out of permanent improvement bond money, for the purpose of park development and acquisition.

The resulting situation is this: we have in this State eleven park regions, into which are divided all of the counties of the State. Each of these park commissions, or authorities in charge of these regions, is carrying out a well-considered, definitely co-ordinated plan of parks and parkway developments. All of us who live in the City of New York know about the splendid play-ground up at Palisades Interstate Park. We know the splendid park development system in Westchester. We must not forget, too, that the area of this State is large, and that facilities are also being provided at other strategic points.

For instance, the Taconic Commission, of which I happened to have been the Chairman myself, so that I am speaking about it somewhat from personal knowledge, is developing the great tri-State park up the Harlem Valley, where Massachusetts, Connecticut and New York come together. That will be a splendid camping ground within fairly reasonable distance of the City of New York, only a few hours' run. It was opened last summer and already thousands of people from the City of New York are beginning to use that park. . . .

(Here followed a description in some detail of the park regions and a statement of their development.)

As a result of these activities the State now has — it is rather difficult to sense this, for you think in terms of lots in Queens — two million, two hundred and eighteen thousand acres of park lands devoted to the use of the people. That huge acreage is divided into seventy parks and reservations. The regions provide compact geographical units, and some idea of their value to the people of the State can be gleaned from the fact — this is just one example — that last year the Bear Mountain Park, from January 1st to November 1st, was visited by 4,875,000 people. That is just one park in the State. As many as 35,000 automobiles have used the Bronx River Parkway in one day, and ten thousand bathers have used one little two-by-four park down at Valley Stream, Long Island, almost every Saturday and Sunday this past summer. . . .

Last Monday night, just a week ago, in New York, somebody got into a panic. Brother Hoover got up in Madison Square Garden, looking for an issue, to stop the swell of the tide for Smith, and he said, "He is a socialist." By that token Smith will be elected.

He knows just what to do when he is called a socialist. He has a good answer, and it is a true answer. If his program for the public park system of the State is socialistic, then we are all socialists; and if his program for the reduction of hours of women and children is socialistic, we are all socialists. If his program for public improvements for the hospitals of the State and the prisons of the State is socialistic, we are all socialists. And if his programs for bettering public health in this State and for aid to the educational program of this State are socialistic, we are socialists.

Yes, anybody in public life who goes ahead and advocates improvements is called a "radical." The Democratic Party in this State has gone on and advocated improvements; it has put them through; and it has been called "radical" and everything else. The Democratic Party in this State will keep on winning as long as it goes ahead with a program of progress. . . .

10 ❡ Extemporaneous Campaign Address (Excerpts), New York City, N. Y. October 30, 1928

(Labor legislation — Collective bargaining during the navy days of F. D. R. — Fluctuations in employment.)

Mr. Chairman, My friends: . . .

. . . I REMEMBER particularly one of the first things I got into awful hot water about up in my country district — and mind you, I come from an unfortunate district up there on the Hudson River where organized labor had mighty hard sledding, and still has, in the city of Poughkeepsie. It is one of the spots that we can make some headway with, I hope, in the days to come.

And one of the first measures that we started in 1911 was the fifty-four-hour law for women and children in industry. In those days a fifty-four-hour law was considered the most radical thing that had ever been talked about. It shows the progress that our civilization is making. That was only fifteen years ago. And you have heard the history from then on down. It all goes to point out one perfectly definite fact in my mind, and that is that in this State the Democratic Party has had a kind of human vision that the other side has lacked.

Those three years were very interesting years and I learned a lot. I think that it was those three years spent up there in Albany that made it possible for me to go down to Washington in 1913 with some understanding at least of the problems of the Federal end of things.

I remember when I got down there. I had not been there more than about a week when a delegation from the Brooklyn Navy Yard came down and said, "Mr. Roosevelt" — they had not started to call me Frank; they did in about another week — "there is one thing that we want you to do. You know, you, as Assistant Secretary of the Navy, have charge of all labor matters." I said, "That is fine; I did not know it." "Will you do something to change the present method of working out the wage scale paid in the Navy Yard?" I said, "Fine. How is it done?" "Well," they said, "do it yourself." I said, "Why, hasn't it been done by the Assistant Secretary in the past?" "No, it has been done by the officers." And then they went on to tell me how unjustly the wage scales in all of the Navy Yards on both coasts and on the Gulf of Mexico had been arranged each year by a special board of naval officers.

After I had been there I think three days longer, I got Joe Daniels to sign an order making it the duty of the Assistant Secretary to fix the wage scale each year. I am very proud of one simple fact, and that is that during the seven and one-half years in Washington, we did not have one single major dispute, no strike, walk-out, or serious trouble in all of the Navy Yards all over the United States.

We established, in other words, a perfectly practical example of the practice of collective bargaining; and it worked, as it always will work, if both sides come to the table in the right spirit. They came in the right spirit and we were not only able to settle wage matters, but we were able to do something else that no Republican Administration — national Administration — in the past has ever thought of doing.

As you know, during the previous years, before 1913, in every Navy Yard in the United States there were tremendous fluctuations in employment. The naval officers were thinking only about the needs of the military side of things. The entire Atlantic Fleet would be brought to the Navy Yards for overhauling. We would take on ten or fifteen thousand additional men during a period of a month or six weeks. Then the Fleet came out again, and ten or fifteen thousand men would be laid off.

The result was great hardship. The Republicans also in previous years had taken the point of view that the Government did not need to manufacture anything in the Navy Yard, on the theory that with their fancy system of keeping accounts private materials could be bought a great deal more cheaply than they could be manufactured by the Government itself.

Well, we started investigating; and on the investigating committee we put mechanics from the yards themselves, as people who knew the most about it. The results were: first, the establishment of a system of costs that proved that over a great many years of work in the Navy Yards the Government made material more cheaply than we could buy it; and, second, an arrangement so that the schedule in employment could be maintained on a fairly even basis throughout each year.

That was maintained during seven and a half years, and the result was that employment in the Government service became a true opportunity for permanent service. . . .

11 ❲ Campaign Address (Excerpts), Bronx, N. Y. October 30, 1928

(Administration of justice — Prison reform — Modernization of criminal law procedure.)

Mr. Chairman, my friends of the Bronx:

TONIGHT I have chosen a somewhat serious subject, but a subject that comes home into the life of every man and woman in this audience.

In my speech of acceptance I spoke of four examples of improving our Government methods with the succeeding years, and I have talked about three of them already. Tonight I want to talk about the last of these. It relates to a subject that goes deep to the roots of effective government, the system by which justice is administered.

Now, justice comes pretty close home into our lives; although, as somebody said to me the other day, probably only one man or woman out of a thousand is engaged or involved in court procedure, either criminal or civil, in any way. Yet I am perfectly certain that nine hundred and ninety-nine individuals out of a thousand are interested in better justice in this State.

We ought to be very proud of this State. We ought to have pride in the contribution that we have made in the past to the system of jurisprudence. It was the New York Code of 1848 that was not only the first of the great codes of civil procedure, but became the model for other States, and it was our criminal code of 1881 that lighted the way for the rest of the Nation. In the organization of our judiciary, especially the high character of our Court of Appeals in Albany, New York has established a happy preeminence, and we have had great help from commissions and bar associations and business organizations in the improving of the administration of justice.

But I think that you will agree with me, on thinking over this very vital matter, that these constructive efforts of recent years have not been able to keep pace with the fundamental changes in our social conditions. Population has increased in a manner that previous generations could not have foreseen. The very existence of Bronx County today is the finest living example of how a great community is born in these United States. Population has increased, and the rise of great cities has been out of proportion even to this great increase, and business has been done on broader lines. All of these increased complexities of our social relations have added to the difficulties of assuring fundamental justice to the individual man and woman, the human being, and this plea of mine is merely an expansion, another step in that great program for human rights which Alfred E. Smith has so long championed.

We know conditions and we know responsible and thoughtful judges have reported that, in spite of efforts, the burden of litigation grows more rapidly than the facilities of the courts; that justice is often slow and expensive; that the jury system in certain types of cases is unsatisfactory; that perjury is all too common. Great strides have been taken in the penal phases of the criminal law in the past two years. But the unsatisfactory condition still prevails.

In other words, the whole problem of crime must remain under scrutiny until it is put on a better basis. I believe that the time has come to use intelligent effort not merely to provide adequate punishment in these days, but more modern, more American methods to eliminate the cause of crime.

Now, what is our complaint, your complaint and mine, the average citizen? Is it not along these lines, that justice is too slow, that it is too expensive, that it allows and encourages too much litigation? I need not expand on the subject of the slowness of justice. You people know here how long, very often, it takes to get into court, and then to get through court. Our record in the matter, in comparison with other Nations, is not as good as it should be. Improvements due to the cooperation of bench and bar have helped our court calendars, and I approve of all of these measures, but in the final analysis there may result from them too much congestion in the lower courts, as we know in the City of New York. . . .

Both of these premises, the slowness and the costliness of getting justice, bring up the need of studying, in addition, the possibility of reducing the volume of litigation. You know, we Americans just love to go to court. It is one of our favorite occupations. Some people would rather be in court than eat. They would rather find a new cause of action than eat their breakfast. And yet it is not a good thing for us. It is not a good thing for the communities. And I believe the time has come in the advance of our civilization when we can make one of the points in our education of the children, in our working out of the procedure of the law, that it should be a matter of pride for us Americans to avoid litigation where we can properly do so. . . .

We need a fact-finding commission to determine by scientific analysis of the thousands of cases what cases cause the delay and the expense; what kinds of cases take up the time of the courts; what courts are most crowded; and, finally, what cases ought never to have come to court at all.

I recognize that great study has been given to this problem by various committees, voluntary organizations, and by the courts themselves, but the point I would make is that the State needs a coordination of this mass of figures, and the recommendations of an official body representing the State itself. This State Commission should, of course, have on its membership judges and lawyers, but in addition, and I say this as a member of the bar of this city, we should call on the intelligence of laymen and lay women who are not members of the legal profession, so that we can have a cross-section of public opinion representing all classes of endeavor. So much has already been done in the study of judicial procedure, of arbitration, of penology, that a State Commission appointed this coming winter should be able to make a comprehensive report within the year.

When that is done, the State needs action. We have been flooded with recommendations for years, but there has been no central body capable of bringing in a report in such form that any action could be taken thereon. . . .

My friends, experience with our Republican leader friends in the Legislature makes it perfectly evident that the people of this State can expect very little from that Legislature if they are left to work out the problem themselves. I will, if elected, take immediate steps to secure the cooperation of the bench, of the bar, and bar associations, and of commercial and industrial and labor organizations, and of such other public and semi-public agencies which have a broad interest in this problem.

Here are a few suggestions that will only take me a minute to run over:

First, the question of the reduction of the number of jury trials;

Second, the elimination of perjury;

Third, stricter examination into the ethics of certain members of the bar;

Fourth, the elimination of ambulance chasing;

Fifth, the elimination of dilatory motions;

Sixth, the devising of new methods to handle many thousands of cases, particularly certain kinds of court cases, by administrative tribunals rather than by courts of law.

In many ways that last suggestion goes back to the ancient patriarchal system of the Bible, where, instead of going before a judge duly decked out, you go out and settle your troubles before a friend, without formality, without the red tape of all of the present judicial procedure.

On the criminal side of this question, here are some steps which we must study in these next few years:

First, consideration of Governor Smith's sentencing plan, a great step in the right direction, and far in advance of anything we have done yet;

Secondly, the complete overhauling of the prison labor system;

Third, the classification of prisoners in State prisons;

Fourth, reform of the system by which short term prisoners are kept in County jails;

Fifth, establishment of statewide detective service to assist District Attorneys in the running down of crime and the preparation of important cases;

Sixth, the establishment of a system of minor criminal courts to take over the criminal jurisdiction of Justices of the Peace;

Seventh, the extension of a State Criminal Identification and Statistic Service;

Eighth, further revision of the Penal Code in order to bring the substantive criminal law in harmony with new conditions;

Ninth, better provision for the education of local police officers. That does not apply in the City of New York.

Tenth, revision of the firearms law.

Eleventh, provisions for insanity proceedings in criminal cases to reduce the so-called expert testimony evil. And,

Twelfth and last, a better parole law, with adequate parole service.

We are hearing much today, with some justification, of many complaints about our legal system. We hear talk of one law for the rich and another law for the poor. Taking it by and large, I am very certain that the people of this State want a reform of their judicial procedure, and I am equally certain that the bench and the bar will cooperate with the other citizens of the State in helping to expedite this reform.

Again, I want to repeat that what we need is action, and I propose to do all in my power to see that it is brought about. . . .

12 ⟨ Campaign Address (Excerpts), Yonkers, N. Y. November 1, 1928

("Is Hoover Human?" — Rugged individualism — Democracy vs. intellectual aristocracy in Government.)

Mr. Chairman, and my old friends:

YES, I want to say something about the theory of Government. You know, campaign speeches are very different nowadays from what they were when I was young. I go back far enough to remember the Fourth of July orator. There are few of them left, thank God.

But I believe that people are interested in the philosophy of politics, in the theory of our Government. More and more the old-fashioned "pull the eagle's tail to make him scream," or "twist the lion's tail to get a howl out of the mob," has gone by. That day is gone, and we have come down with our better education all over this country to a willingness to talk about the philosophy of politics, and about the theory of Government, provided it can be made at all interesting. . . .

What leads me to think about this is the fact that this morning I happened to pick up the November number of one of the leading magazines and there on page one was an article with the following caption: "Is Hoover Human?" That title implies something. It implies the suggestion in the minds of a great many citizens that Mr. Hoover is not human. And I went on and I read it, and through seven long pages the author of that article labored, and labored heavily, to prove that the Republican candidate has the human qualities which the title of his own article puts in question.

Well, I wonder if any man or woman in the United States, writers for magazines, editors, or just plain citizens like you and me, has ever, in their wildest moments, put this question, "Is Al Smith Human?" That is the best example that I know, of the difference between the two men. In the one case the question cannot be asked. It would be ridiculous on the face of it. In the other, it is a question, not merely on the front page of that magazine, but in the minds of hundreds of thousands of men and women throughout the United States.

I want to go on. In this article there was a quotation, a quotation from a book written by the late Secretary of Commerce, Honorable Herbert Hoover, and, mind you, it is very short. It is worth taking home with you and thinking about. Here is what Mr. Hoover writes, with his own pen, out of his own head, in his own book, a book called *American Individualism*, and he says:

"Acts and deeds leading to progress are born of the individual mind, not out of the mind of the crowd. The crowd only feels, it has no mind of its own which can plan. The crowd is credulous, it destroys, it hates and it dreams, but it never builds. It is one of the most profound of exact psychological truths that man in the mass does not think, but only feels."

I know the gentleman well, and have for many years; and that, in my judgment, is the best insight that you can possibly find into the personality of Herbert Hoover, into his approach to every public and private question. It is characteristic of the man. That question gives the reason why the author of the article asked, "Is Hoover Human?" And it affirms the judgment of tens of thousands of Americans who during the past four months have been viewing him as a possible occupant of the Presidency.

Now, Mr. Hoover's theory that the crowd, that is to say, 95 percent of all the voters who call themselves average citizens, that the crowd is credulous, that it destroys, that it hates, that it dreams, but that it never builds, that it does not think, but only feels — that is in line with the training, the record and the methods of accomplishment of the Republican candidate for the Presidency.

It is another way of saying, and I say this as an analyst and not as a candidate, that there exists at the top of our social system in this country a very limited group of highly able, highly educated people, through whom all progress in this land must originate. Furthermore, that this small group, after doing all the thinking

68

and all the originating, is fully responsible for all progress in civilization and Government.

What is on the other side? It seems to me that the whole life of the man whom we still refer to as "Our Al Smith" is a refutation of this innate theory of his opponent. Governor Smith has given undoubted proof of the definite fact that the mass of humanity does think, that it can make up its own mind on the pros and cons of all public questions; that it often originates, and that there is a very definite relationship between what Mr. Hoover calls the crowd and the continuation of modern progress.

As a matter of fact, here in this State of ours we are well aware of those deeper impulses that have led in large part to the great humanitarian achievements and accomplishments in this State during these past few years. I want to cite some very simple examples of the origin of the progress.

Take, for instance, the thing that you people in Westchester know all about, the magnificent park-development program. If you look back in your own minds ten or fifteen years, you will remember that there was back from at the time of the War, just before the War and during the War, a very definite urge that started at the bottom among the mass of average citizens, an urge that expressed a need, a need of finding open spaces for those of us that have to live in the crowded confines of the cities of the State. There is no question that that first expression of this need came from the bottom, and as we remember, it produced some small results in various parts of the State through the undertaking of small parks by local communities, by the gifts of public-spirited citizens. But all of this was just the beginning. As the population grew, especially during these very years—and there came a definite impetus to this demand for somewhere to go into the country, somewhere to go that was not all plastered over with "No Trespass" signs—the spirit was communicated from the bottom up to the next step. Who? The elected officials representing the mass of the population.

One by one, these elected officials began to respond to the urge from the electorate, and that, after all, is the whole basis of our system of representative government in the United States.

Now, that urge from the bottom, it may have been a dream, as Mr. Hoover would call it; it may have come from people who do not think, as Mr. Hoover says. But the fact remains that it worked on up, first through the elected officials, until it became what we call a body of public opinion, and then it was communicated to a man at the top who knew public opinion when he saw it, a man who, by the grace of God, was the Governor of this State. . . .

And so on that question of parks Governor Smith was the first man to recognize that growth, that swelling of public opinion from the bottom, and he put the definite demand down on paper and presented it to the voters of the State. Well, you know the history of the development of that great park program. You remember how it was blocked for several years by another form of that stupid leadership. You in Westchester particularly remember the famous special session of the Legislature in 1925, which was called with the understanding that the Senator from this district was going to approve of the park program, and that after he got to Albany he turned around and there was no approval.

You remember, too, at the same time, the opposition in Long Island to the acquisition of the Southern Parkway along that great Southern Shore of the Island. If you make an analysis, you will find that it was the element in Long Island, consisting of less than 5 percent of the electorate, who thought they knew better as to what was good for Mr. Hoover's crowd than the other 95 percent of the inhabitants who made up that crowd.

It worked, after a while, public opinion, coming up from the bottom and not from the top; with leadership at the top, yes, the finest leadership that we have ever had in this State; and finally that public opinion, helped along by the leadership of our Governor, has put the park program on a firm foundation. . . .

Take some other examples. Take other examples that refute wholly that Hoover theory of the God-inspired individual at the top who is supposed to do all the thinking and the building for everybody else. The whole subject of Prohibition is in point, because it has amply proved that a statute is incapable of good enforcement unless the majority of the people themselves wish to abide by the statute and wish to aid in its enforcement.

And yet, Mr. Hoover's attitude on that subject, and I suppose the attitude of those ideal individuals of his who would do all our thinking for us, is that the present conditions in the United States—all over the United States—constitute merely a "noble experiment." Governor Smith, on the other hand, recognizes the diametrically opposite point of view; he recognizes that the great majority of the average voters do think, and by that process of thought are convinced of the outrageous conditions that have resulted from the Volstead Law and its present method of administration; furthermore, that a change in these conditions is demanded from the bottom upward. Governor Smith and I are at one in recognizing this demand from what Mr. Hoover calls the crowd. We recognize it as the thought on the part of that crowd, the thought that demands constructive action. Constructive action means change from the present conditions, and we favor change.

Take another example, water power. It is quite safe to say, I think, you know what the issue here is this year. You know that the Democratic Party is standing by exactly the same platform pledges, exactly the same general policy. The State of New York owns today two million undeveloped horsepower, and we believe that those two million horsepower sites ought to be developed by the people of the State of New York who own those sites.

But when you come right down to it, taking that same Hoover theory of the crowd, and of the little tin gods on wheels up at the top who have got some kind of heavenly right to rule, it is quite safe to say that if that Hoover type of mind had been given full authority in this Nation during the past generation, not one single lake or river or stream or waterfall capable of developing electrical energy would today remain in the possession of the people of the United States, or of any individual State. There is such a thing as too much engineering.

Take as another example the great humanitarian reforms that have been accomplished as a result of the efforts on the part of organized labor. Does Mr. Hoover imagine for a minute that the individual mind of those lucky few who are at the top of the ladder would have favored enactment of our laws limiting the hours of work of women and children in industry? Or our laws for factory inspection, or our law calling for one day of rest in seven, or any of that great program of welfare that has been put through under the guidance of Alfred E. Smith? . . .

In the final analysis the great issue in both the national and State campaigns revolves around that fundamental belief of my friend Mr. Hoover in the incapacity of the mass of average citizens either to think or to build. In the national election the great Governor of the State of New York is the most splendid living example of the opposite fact.

And in this State election, too, the same point is raised, for the Republican leadership of this State is based on that same belief that Mr. Hoover holds. I deny, and the Democratic Party denies, that the average man and woman in this State, who make up its electorate, are incapable of thought or of constructive ability. I know that the electorate does think, that it does originate, and that it does build, and it is on that fundamental belief that I base my campaign for the Governorship. It is the same belief which has brought to us the great program of the past few years; the same belief that must carry us forward during the coming years to an even greater progress. . . .

II

Governor Roosevelt's Two Inaugural Addresses and Four Annual Messages to the Legislature of New York

THIS CHAPTER contains the two Inaugural Addresses and the four Annual Messages to the Legislature made by me during my four years as Governor.

As will be seen, they each cover several subjects; and specific reference will be made to them in the chapters dealing with the respective subjects covered.

The material in the annual messages which relates exclusively to particular State matters, and which has no relevancy to the Federal policies or objectives of my Administration as President, has been omitted. The full text of these messages can, however, be found in the *Public Papers of Governor Franklin D. Roosevelt* for the years in question.

13 ❧ The First Inaugural Address as Governor. January 1, 1929

(Alfred E. Smith — Aims of progressive government — Water power — Administration of justice — Farm relief.)

Governor and Mrs. Smith, Mr. Secretary of State, my friends:

THIS day is notable not so much for the inauguration of a new Governor as that it marks the close of the term of a Governor who has been our Chief Executive for eight years.

I am certain that no Governor in the long history of the State has accomplished more than he in definite improvement of the structure of our State Government, in the wise, efficient and honorable administration of its affairs, and finally in his possession of that vibrant understanding heart attuned to the needs and hopes of the men, the women and the children who form the sovereignty known as "the People of the State of New York."

To Alfred E. Smith, a public servant of true greatness, I extend on behalf of our citizens our affectionate greetings, our wishes for his good health and happiness and our prayer that God will watch over him and his in the years to come.

It is a proud thing to be a citizen of the State of New York, not because of our great population and our natural resources, nor on account of our industries, our trade, or our agricultural development, but because the citizens of this State more than any other State in the Union, have grown to realize the interdependence on each other which modern civilization has created.

Under the leadership of the great Governor whose place you have selected me to fill has come a willingness on our part to give as well as to receive, to aid, through the agency of the State, the well-being of the men and women who, by their toil, have made our material prosperity possible.

I object to having this spirit of personal civil responsibility to the State and to the individual which has placed New York in the lead as a progressive commonwealth, described as "humanitarian." It is far more than that. It is the recognition that our civilization cannot endure unless we, as individuals, realize our personal responsibility to and dependence on the rest of the world. For it is literally true that the "self-supporting" man or woman has become as extinct as the man of the stone age. Without the help of thousands of others, any one of us would die, naked and starved. Consider the bread upon our table, the clothes upon our backs, the luxuries that make life pleasant; how many men worked in sunlit fields, in dark mines, in the fierce heat of molten metal, and among the looms and wheels of countless factories, in order to create them for our use and enjoyment.

I am proud that we of this State have grown to realize this dependence, and, what is more important, have also come to know that we, as individuals, in our turn must give our time and our intelligence to help those who have helped us. To secure more of life's pleasures for the farmer; to guard the toilers in the factories and to insure them a fair wage and protection from the dangers of their trades; to compensate them by adequate insurance for injuries received while working for us; to open the doors of knowledge to their children more widely; to aid those who are crippled and ill; to pursue with strict justice, all evil persons who prey upon their fellow men; and at the same time, by intelligent and helpful sympathy, to lead wrongdoers into right paths — all of these great aims of life are more fully realized here than in any other State in the Union. We have but started on the road, and we have far to go; but during the last six years in particular, the people of this State have shown their impatience of those who seek to make such things a football of politics or by blind, unintelligent obstruction, attempt to bar the road to Progress.

Most gratifying of all, perhaps, is the practical way in which we have set about to take the first step toward this higher civilization, for, first of all, has been the need to set our machinery of government in order. If we are to reach these aims efficiently without needless waste of time or money we must continue the efforts to simplify and modernize. You cannot build a modern dynamo with the ancient forge and bellows of the medieval blacksmith.

The modernization of our administrative procedure, not alone that of the State, but also of those other vital units of counties, of cities, of towns and of villages, must be accomplished; and while in the unit of the State we have almost reached our goal, I want to emphasize that in other units we have a long road to travel.

Each one of us must realize the necessity of our personal interest, not only toward our fellow citizens, but in the Government itself. You must watch, as a public duty, what is done and what is not done at Albany. You must understand the issues that arise in the Legislature, and the recommendations made by your Governor, and judge for yourselves if they are right or wrong. If you find them right it is your duty as citizens on next election day to repudiate those who oppose, and to support by your vote those who strive for their accomplishment.

I want to call particularly on the public press of this State in whose high standards I have the greatest confidence, to devote more space to the explanation and consideration of such legislation as may come up this year, for no matter how willing the individual citizen may be to support wise and progressive measures, it is only through the press, and I mean not only our great dailies but their smaller sisters in the rural districts, that our electorate can learn and understand what is going on.

There are many puzzling problems to be solved. I shall here mention but three. In the brief time that I have been speaking to you, there has run to waste on their paths toward the sea, enough power from our rivers to have turned the wheels of a thousand factories, to have lit a million farmers' homes — power which nature has supplied us through the gift of God. It is intolerable that the utilization of this stupendous heritage should be longer delayed by petty squabbles and partisan dispute. Time will not solve the problem; it will be more difficult as time goes on to reach a fair conclusion. It must be solved now.

I should like to state clearly the outstanding features of the problem itself. First, it is agreed, I think, that the water power of the State should belong to all the people. There was, perhaps, some excuse for careless legislative gift of power sites in the days when it was of no seemingly great importance. There can be no such excuse now. The title to this power must vest forever in the people of this State. No commission, no, not the Legislature itself has any right to give, for any consideration whatever, a single potential kilowatt in virtual perpetuity to any person or corporation whatsoever. The Legislature in this matter is but the trustee of the people, and it is its solemn duty to administer such heritage so as most greatly to benefit the whole people. On this point there can be no dispute.

It is also the duty of our legislative bodies to see that this power, which belongs to all the people, is transformed into usable electrical energy and distributed to them at the lowest possible cost. It is our power; and no inordinate profits must be allowed to those who act as the people's agents in bringing this power to their homes and workshops. If we keep these two fundamental facts before us, half of the problem disappears.

There remains the technical question as to which of several methods will bring this power to our doors with the least expense. Let me here make clear the three divisions of this technical side of the question.

First, the construction of the dams, the erection of power houses and the installation of the turbines necessary to convert the force of the falling water into electricity.

Second, the construction of many thousands of miles of transmission lines to bring the current so produced to the smaller distributing centers throughout the State; and

Third, the final distribution of this power into thousands of homes and factories.

How much of this shall be undertaken by the State, how much of this carried out by properly regulated private enterprises, how much of this by some combination of the two, is the practical question that we have before us. And in the consideration of the question I want to warn the people of this State against too hasty assumption that mere regulation by public service commissions is, in itself, a sure guarantee of protection of the interest of the consumer.

The questionable taking of jurisdiction by Federal courts, the gradual erection of a body of court made law, the astuteness of our legal brethren, the possible temporary capitulation of our public servants and even of a dormant public opinion itself, may, in the future, as in the past, nullify the rights of the public.

I, as your Governor, will insist, and I trust with the support of the whole people, that there be no alienation of our possession of and title to our power sites, and that whatever method of distribution be adopted, there be no possible legal thwarting of the protection of the people themselves from excessive profits on the part of anybody.

On another matter I tread perhaps a new path. The phrase, "rich man's justice," has become too common nowadays. So complicated has our whole legal machinery become through our attempt to mend antiquated substructures by constant patching of the legal procedure and the courts that justice is our most expensive commodity. That rich criminals too often escape punishment is a general belief of our people. The difficulty with which our citizens maintain their civil rights before the courts has not been made a matter of such public notice but is equally serious. It is my hope that within the next two years we shall have begun to simplify and to cheapen justice for the people.

Lastly, I want to refer to the difficult situation to which in recent years a large part of the rural population of our State has come. With few exceptions it has not shared in the prosperity of the urban centers.

It is not enough to dismiss this problem with the generality that it is the result of changing economic conditions. It is time to take practical steps to relieve our farm population of unequal tax burdens, to install economies in the methods of local government, to devise sounder marketing to stabilize what has been too much a speculative industry, and finally to encourage the use of each acre of our State for the purpose to which it is by nature most suited. I am certain that the cities will cooperate to this end, and that, more and more, we as citizens shall become State-minded.

May I, as your newly elected Governor, appeal for your help, for your advice, and, when you feel it is needed, for your criticism? No man may be a successful Governor without the full assistance of the people of his own commonwealth.

Were I as wise as Solomon, all that I might propose or decide would be mere wasted effort, unless I have your constant support. On many of the great State questions that confront us, the platforms and the public pledges of candidates of both parties are substantially agreed. We have passed through a struggle against old-time political ideas, against antiquated conservatism, against ignorance of modern conditions, marked by serious disagreements between the Legislative and the Executive branches of the Government. As I read the declarations of both parties in asking the support of the people at the polls, I can see little reason for further controversies of this kind.

There is a period in our history known in all our school books as the "Era of Good Feeling." It is my hope that we stand on the threshold of another such era in this State. For my part, I pledge that the business of the State will not be allowed to become involved in partisan politics and that I shall not attempt to claim unfair advantage for my party or for myself, for the accomplishing of those things on which we are all agreed.

You have honored me greatly by selecting me as your Chief Executive. It is my hope that I shall not fail you in this critical period of our history. I wish that you may have a continuance of good government and the happiest of New Years.

14 (The Annual Message to the Legislature (Excerpts). January 2, 1929

To the Legislature:

I COME before the Legislature, not only in accordance with the Constitution to communicate the condition of the State, but also to express the hope and belief that neither you nor I are entering upon our offices with partisan purpose. From the day of our election we become individually and jointly the representatives of all the people of the State.

We are charged with the duty of carrying on the existing functions of the Government, of initiating changes in present laws, made necessary by changing times, and of undertaking also new projects which an advancing civilization makes desirable.

The past six years have been an unparalleled era in our State. We have pointed the way of progress to our sister States and we must not allow this progress to flag during the coming year.

Most of our problems are not political: they can be solved by the same kind of cooperation on your part which I as the Executive of the State hereby offer to you. A few are matters of an honest difference of opinion; most of these also can, I hope, find practical solution by frank discussion and honest effort to obtain results. . . .

(Here followed a statement on State finances.)

AGRICULTURE

I want the agricultural problems studied without regard to partisan politics and it is my hope that through appointing an agricultural commission composed of members of the Legislature, master farmers, representatives of the College of Agriculture, the Grange, the Farm Bureau, the Home Bureau, the Dairymen's League and other farm cooperatives, the Legislature from their recommendations will be able to act favorably and constructively on this most important subject.

It may be that adequate investigation will show that many of the farms abandoned within the period of agricultural depression since 1920 should not be restored to agriculture but should be devoted to growing a future timber supply for the people of the State. Also we do not want the present alarming rate of farm abandonment to continue: we must therefore make special efforts to make it possible for those who are now engaged in agriculture on suitable agricultural land, to continue under more favorable and more profitable conditions.

I hope that this agricultural commission will make a special

81

study and investigation of the whole farm assessment and tax situation in order to obtain a fairer adjustment of the farmers' taxes. The ultimate goal is that the farmer and his family shall be put on the same level of earning capacity as his fellow American who lives in the city.

The problem of distribution of farm products should also be studied to the end that the unnecessarily high differential between what the farmer receives and what the consumer pays may be materially lowered, giving a better price to the farmer for his products and a lower cost to the consumer for what he buys.

WATER POWER

On the subject of the development of water power sites, owned in part or in whole by the people of the State, I am convinced of two facts: First, that there is a definite demand for the undertaking of their development — not several years hence but this year; second, that the title and constant control of the power generated at the sources shall remain definitely in the people and shall not be alienated by long term leases. This is one of those questions on which I hope we can reach an agreement.

The development of our statewide park and parkway system has, I think, ceased to be a matter of political controversy and will, I am confident, go forward with your assistance. . . .

(Here followed statements on grade crossings, public works, canals, aviation, and four-year term for Governor.)

COUNTY AND TOWN GOVERNMENTS

I can see no object in being anything but frank with you in regard to the business efficiency of our system of town and county governments. In recent years our system of State Government has been brought to a high level of efficiency. Why should any of us pretend any longer that our county and town governments do not require the same kind of overhauling which we have given to the affairs of the State? Even the school children know that we maintain many useless offices in our towns, that many functions now exercised by town officials should be assumed by county management, that there is an almost complete lack of budgeting, that there is an equal lack of proper auditing, and, in the final analysis, that the average taxpayer does not know why or where his tax money is being spent. It would be a fine thing if you and I, laying politics and partisanship aside, could take definite steps at this session of the Legislature toward this reform, which everybody knows is so vitally necessary. I am confident that the public will support an honest effort on our part, for I am not enough of a cynic to believe that the public is indifferent to wasteful or outworn governing methods.

LABOR

When I consider the extraordinary progress which has been made in labor and social legislation, I am reminded of the fact that eighteen years ago, when I was a member of the Legislature, any person advocating a large part of the laws which have been enacted in the succeeding years would have been called a dangerous radical. That is the universal history of social progress. While much has been accomplished so far, we cannot stand still, and I recommend to you the following program which I believe to be in accordance with the needs of the day:

1. A real eight-hour day and forty-eight-hour week for women and children in industry.
2. The establishment for them of an advisory minimum or fair wage board.
3. The extension of workmen's compensation to give its benefits to all occupational diseases.
4. The prohibiting of the granting of temporary injunctions in industrial disputes without notice of hearing; and provision for trial before a jury of any alleged violations of injunctions.
5. The immediate study by a commission of experts of the subject of old-age security against want.
6. The continuation of such provisions of the emergency rent laws as are necessary.

7. Further elimination of unhealthy living conditions in the congested areas.

8. Declaration by law that the labor of a human being is not a commodity or an article of commerce.

HEALTH

While we have made and are making splendid progress in caring for the general health of our citizens, there are two specific matters in which we can lay the foundations for great public benefit.

CRIPPLES

The first of these is the care of adults and children who, through accident or disease, are so crippled in body that they are unable to lead useful and happy lives. It is estimated that at least 50,000 men, women and children in the State of New York are thus seriously handicapped, and many of them require constant attendance on the part of some able-bodied person. As a matter of good business, it would pay the State to help in restoring these cripples to useful citizenship, and the great majority of them can, with the aid of modern medical science, be so restored. Most of them are, however, not today receiving adequate care or treatment for the very good reason that such treatment costs more time and money than the average family can afford.

But there is an added reason. I conceive it to be the duty of the State to give the same care to removing the physical handicaps of its citizens as it now gives to their mental development. Universal education of the mind is, after all, a modern conception. We have reached the time now when we must recognize the same obligation of the State to restore to useful activity those children and adults who have the misfortune to be crippled. I shall submit to you a carefully worked out program to initiate this much-needed care.

SARATOGA SPRINGS

The State has during recent years acquired one of the greatest gifts of nature in the whole world — the mineral springs at Saratoga. I am not satisfied that the program for their development in the past has taken sufficient account of the great benefits to mankind that can be derived from them as medicinal and therapeutic agents. We in this country are far behind Europe in the internal and external use of natural mineral springs for health purposes. The springs at Saratoga should be developed primarily for health purposes, under far more careful medical supervision than we have hitherto attempted. The physical development of the State properties at Saratoga must proceed, and I ask you to authorize the appointment of a temporary commission of scientific and medical experts, in order that a careful plan may be worked out under their advice.

EDUCATION

The principal mandatory increase in the coming budget will be the additional sum, running probably to nine million dollars, required for the extension of the better education of our citizens. The people of the State are unanimous in support of our liberal policy.

Under the present methods of apportioning State funds to rural school districts, the poorer districts in many instances fail to receive their fair share. The method of apportionment should be simplified and made to conform more closely to the relative wealth of the districts.

JUDICIAL REFORM

While I am confident that the citizens of the State demand legislation aimed to diminish crime and approve the policy of prison reform, still there are many thinking people who believe that we have not yet gone to the root of our troubles. By a long series of piecemeal enactments, covering many years, we have built up a highly complicated system of judicial procedure, both criminal and civil, which does not conform to the ideals of modern efficiency or simplicity. A growing body of our citizens complain of the complexities, of the delays, and of the costliness of private and of public litigation. I do not for a moment believe either that the situation can be greatly improved by minor amendments to the existing system, nor do I believe that a drastic reform can be accomplished in one or two years. It is time, however, that a deeper study of the whole subject should be made by a body of citizens representing the bench, the bar and laymen. After conferring with you, I hope that I can recommend the definite initiation of this at a later time in the session. . . .

(Here followed statements on "ambulance chasing," modernization of inheritance laws, election law changes, initiative and referendum of Constitutional amendments, soldiers in veterans' hospitals, state census.)

In my inaugural address to my fellow citizens I have already pledged myself to seek no mere personal or partisan advantage in the performance of my duties as Governor. I feel sure that the legislators of both parties will join me in this pledge. He best serves his party who best serves his State.

Let us all at this session rid ourselves forever of that blighting dread of following in the rear guard of another's triumphal procession along the road to better government which has too often in the past prevented any progress whatsoever. It is of small moment who first points out that road. The important thing is, having once seen the proper course, that we should turn toward it, fight for its adoption and march shoulder to shoulder with the others toward the goal.

In conclusion may I urge you all, individually, to come to me with problems, with suggestions, with honest differences of opinion as often and as freely as I hope you will let me come to you. The verdict on our relations that I most desire from you is that I have at least been fair and reasonable and friendly. Let a common desire to serve our State unite us in a common friendship.

15 ❧ The Annual Message to the Legislature (Excerpts). January 1, 1930

To the Legislature:

WE ARE entering a new year with a clean slate, and I offer to you, a new Legislature, my own hearty cooperation in carrying on our mutual tasks. You will find me ready at all times to talk over the problems of the State with you individually or collectively; as I said last year, most of our work is not partisan in its nature and should be considered and debated solely from the viewpoint of the State's welfare.

A crying need for wise and immediate legislative action on these important matters has been made manifest by events of the past year:

1. Through indifference and lack of knowledge of actual conditions on the part of our citizens, through false economy by previous legislatures and through our failure to apply to the whole problem of the convicted criminal the results of enlightened and modern research, we have allowed our prisons to become breeding places of new crimes.

2. The meshes of our banking laws have been woven so loosely as to permit the escape of those meanest of all criminals who squander the funds of hundreds of small depositors in reckless speculation for private gain. The entire Banking Law is in need of revision and the Banking Department needs immediately far more adequate inspection facilities.

3. Our antiquated Public Service Commission Law has proved itself unable to cope with the enormous growth and huge consolidations of public utility corporations and it has become evident that new methods of regulation, supervision and administration must be devised.

4. Selfish and indifferent people should no longer be favored by exemption from the burden we now impose on the generous and charitable in providing for the care of those un-

able to support themselves in their old age. This is a common duty of all citizens and should be borne, under a wise and systematic plan, by all taxpayers alike.

During the past year commissions or conferences of able and qualified public-minded citizens and legislators have studied what should be done on these matters. The determinations which result from their labors are too important to be condensed in the restricted limits of this message. At a very early date I shall call their conclusions, together with specific recommendations, to your attention by separate special messages.

JUDICIAL REFORM

Many, probably a great majority, of our citizens continue to be dissatisfied with the existing administration of justice. They object to the costliness, the delays and the complexities of civil actions and to the inequalities and slowness of criminal procedure. They ask that we go to the roots of the disease and cease our sporadic efforts merely to prune off occasional dead branches. Because the great majority of parties to court actions are not lawyers, it seems fitting that laymen should have a large part in any comprehensive study and revision of the methods by which their actions at law should be handled. I asked the last Legislature for a mixed commission of laymen and lawyers. Instead, a bill was passed creating a body composed wholly of lawyers, most of them members of the Legislature. I vetoed that bill; and now renew my recommendation of last year.

In advance of any general reorganization of the methods of doing justice, there are, of course, certain obvious things which may be accomplished at once. I desire at this time to call your attention to two such matters. The first is a general strengthening of the statutes regarding perjury. The second is the proposal to permit the prosecution in criminal cases to impeach its own witnesses when it finds itself the victim of deliberately perjured testimony. I am aware that this recommendation is not approved by all members of the bar, but I think it nevertheless deserves serious consideration at the hands of the Legislature.

MODERNIZING LOCAL GOVERNMENT

The taxpayers of the State are coming to realize that if the taxes on their farms and houses are being carelessly or extravagantly expended it is the direct fault, not of the State but of their local government agencies. National, State and city governmental machinery has been generally improved in efficiency and economy of operation but town and county government has not been modernized and therefore presents extraordinary instances of waste and inefficiency.

Several other States have already begun to modernize local government, using as a basis the principle of home rule, and making the establishment of new forms to meet new needs permissive rather than mandatory. It is my thought that the same principle could well be adopted by New York. Several years ago a legislative committee reported in favor of many drastic changes. No action followed. The necessity is today even greater.

It is time to consider and act on these particularly important questions:

1. A limitation of the debt-incurring powers of counties and of towns, to prevent unpleasant and unsound conditions such as have already arisen in a number of cases.
2. A rearrangement of the number and duties of town officers.
3. Possible new forms of county government.
4. The right to consolidate various town and county operations to avoid duplication.
5. The right of two or more counties to unite in the exercise of certain functions without loss of county individuality.

All of these changes in the Constitution or in statute can well be placed upon a permissive basis.

I am a firm believer in home rule and recognize the right of the citizens of a county to determine their own form of local government. However, under our present laws no county can modernize its machinery, although it may greatly desire so to do, without the aid of the State Legislature in removing the existing legal barriers thrown across the road to economic reform. . . .

(Here followed statements on a State crime investigating bureau, State Police, and parks.)

SARATOGA SPRINGS

At my suggestion a commission was appointed last spring to consider the development and best use of the Saratoga Springs for health purposes. An excellent and comprehensive report will shortly be presented. It appears clear that an immediate start in this humanitarian work can be made. I emphasize that definite control of the waters by the best attainable scientific and medical experts is the only way to bring about the best therapeutic results. We can provide health facilities for our own citizens and at the same time set up a model which will be of enormous future value to the proper development of other mineral springs in different sections of the United States.

LABOR

Labor legislation must keep step with changing developments in industrial life and with forward steps in social welfare.

I recommend to you the following program:

1. The inclusion within the coverage of the Workmen's Compensation Law of all diseases arising from occupational tasks — in other words, making last year's law a real law.
2. A genuine eight-hour day and forty-eight-hour week for women in industry, not the present counterfeit which masquerades under this title.
3. The establishment for women and children of an advisory minimum or fair wage board.
4. A raising of the limit for compensation to twenty-five dollars per week so as to include all types of disabilities. The present distinction between partial and total disabilities is arbitrary and without reason.

5. Regulation by the State of fee-charging employment agencies.
6. Declaration in the form of a statute, that the labor of human beings is not a commodity or an article of commerce.
7. Prohibition against the granting of temporary injunctions, without notice of hearing, in industrial disputes, with provision for trial before a jury of any violation of injunctions when granted.
8. Last year I signed the new multiple dwelling bill because it offered a definite step in advance. It still has certain defects which should be remedied. We should look to improved legislation over a period of years in order to abolish dark rooms and provide a fair minimum of sanitary provisions in all tenement houses.

ELECTRICITY

Last year after much study I made to the Legislature a definite proposal for the long delayed development of the State-owned water power of the St. Lawrence River. This was deliberately pigeonholed.

I now renew my recommendation of last year. It was based on a simple declaration of principle — that the ownership, development and operation of the St. Lawrence power resources remain forever in the actual possession of the people of the State or of an agency created by them, and that the electricity so generated be sold to distributors by contract upon a basis to insure a fair and reasonable rate to the consumer, especially the household user.

At the same time I thought it advisable that the State agency should at least provide the financing of, and retain the fee to, any system of State-wide transmission of electricity made necessary by the new power development. As a mere matter of saving in interest rates alone this would reduce the cost of electricity many millions of dollars each year, for the consumer of course pays the interest and dividend charges on the project.

Let us stop once and for all the silly talk that the electricity available by developing the St. Lawrence is not needed or not usable in a practical way. We know that private companies are only too eager to proceed if the State were to abandon its rights.

Let us establish the policy, and ask the proposed trustees to submit to the next Legislature a practical plan based on that policy. If they find a plan and it commends itself to the Legislature, let them proceed full steam ahead.

It is becoming more and more clear that the families of this State, whether they live in the cities, in the villages or on the farms, have been paying too much for their electricity, and are therefore not in a position to use to a proper degree the many labor-saving devices of modern invention. Furthermore, rates between different localities show much too great variance, and rural installations are in many cases prohibitive.

Whether mere regulation of electric utilities in the future can be made more successful than it has proved in the past remains a serious question. In the meantime the development of the great State-owned natural resources offers a definite method of relief. . . .

(Here followed statements on grade crossings and a proposed State business bureau.)

AGRICULTURE

The year 1929 was marked by the most important practical assistance to the agriculture of this State in this generation. Over a month before I actually assumed the duties of Governor, a committee of agricultural leaders met at my request to report on what steps should be taken. These gentlemen were, in January, formed into the Agricultural Advisory Commission and immediately they made important recommendations which I transmitted to the Legislature. I am happy to say that all of the principal objectives were translated into law. The chief aim of this legislation has been to relieve the rural counties of the State from a highly unequal tax burden.

Besides these tax savings, the previous Legislature, on my recommendation, appropriated over three million dollars under a new law for the assistance of small schools throughout the State.

The Governor's Agricultural Advisory Commission continues to meet and will make further recommendations. For instance, I hope that this Legislature will again pass a measure to relieve the counties of their share of building bridges on State highways; such a measure was passed last year but an accompanying appropriation to carry it into effect was unfortunately overlooked.

We need further rural tax reduction through elimination of superfluous local officials, through closer State supervision of town and county expenditures and through better business methods in local government administration. We need to encourage the farmers of the State to establish real business selling organizations — in other words, greater cooperation among the farm people for the promotion of their own interests. We need to increase the electrification of the farms by standardization of installation charges and reduction of rural electricity rates. We need to emphasize the responsibility of school trustees and school boards in handling the State aid. We need further development of the reforestation of lands not primarily suited to agriculture. Finally, we need a broad survey of all of the phases of agricultural production in this State, from a completion of the study of soils to the marketing of the products. To devote to agriculture the same interest and intelligence that is now being given to industry will mean new recruits for farming, better living conditions, and the breaking down of artificial and unnecessary barriers between the rural and the urban communities of the State. . . .

(Here followed statements on highways, four-year term for Governor, State census, election law changes, and State finances.)

* * *

In concluding my message last year I said that it is of small importance who first points out the road to progress, and expressed the hope that all measures affecting the welfare of the State would be discussed frankly and fully between us, with no consideration on either side of partisan advantage. Possibly that idea was too novel to be carried out as fully as I suggested. There was, however, one conspicuous example of the advantage of this method when it was honestly tried out, which I hope will serve as an incentive to other experiments along this line during this session. I refer to the recommendations transmitted by me to you from the Agricultural Advisory Commission.

Although these suggestions came primarily from a commission appointed by your Governor, they were considered and adopted in great part by a practically unanimous vote of the Legislature, and while the actual bills which passed were those introduced by members of the majority, I can assure you that your Governor signed them cheerfully and promptly, as the record shows. That is the way I hope all proposed legislation will be considered this year. In particular do I hope that these four subjects be treated in this spirit of friendly cooperation: the reform of the administration of justice; the permissive reorganization of town and county government; legislation relating to social welfare including the prison and hospital program, and the providing of cheaper electricity in our homes.

I express the same wish with which I concluded my message last January — that a common desire to serve our State unite us in a common friendship.

16 ❨ The Second Inaugural Address as Governor. January 1, 1931

(Improvement of local government — Interest in government.)

To ALL of you who are here today and to all the people of the State of New York I extend New Year's Greetings. May 1931 be a year of happiness, a year of greater well-being, a year in which all of us may dedicate ourselves more unselfishly and more truly to the good of our commonwealth and of our fellow men.

Twenty years ago today I first entered into public service, and on this anniversary it is not unnatural that I should think of the progress of government during that period. On January 1, 1911, the people of New York were experiencing for the first time in many decades a sustained public interest in their State Government, an interest first stimulated by the fine insistence of Governor Hughes and later translated into action at several legislative sessions. At that time were laid the foundations for the continuing general attention of our citizens toward State Government which has followed through all these years.

With this awakening of interest followed logically the studies of the structure and functioning of the State Government itself which culminated in the Constitutional Convention of 1915, and eventually resulted in the reorganization of the departments and the creation of the present businesslike budget system under the leadership of Governor Smith.

As a summing up of this quarter century I think that we can well say that we have made great strides in modernizing the Government of the State and in vastly increasing both its honesty and its efficiency; in bringing this Government into a sound and responsible relationship to the social needs and the welfare of the citizens themselves; and at the same time in avoiding the pitfalls of paternalism.

This noteworthy and continuing improvement in the theory and practice of State Government has come in part from progressive leadership, but most of all from a genuine public interest backed up by the willingness of thousands of citizens to give practical and unselfish service. Therefore while properly we recognize the many tasks, the many new problems which lie ahead, still I think we can take genuine pride and satisfaction in the structure and functioning of that instrumentality of our sovereignty known as the Government of the State of New York.

But this gratifying modernization and perfecting of our State Government serve at the same time to accentuate by contrast our lack of progress in improving local government. Not long ago I received a letter from an eminent editor, telling me tearfully that all local government had broken down, and begging me as Governor — note the unconscious willingness to accept a Tsar or absolute dictator in the Governor's chair in Albany — to usurp and assume the functions of the officials duly elected by the communities themselves. He ended with the suggestion that if I did not do so, the alternative would be to call out the militia and establish martial law.

I cite this as an illustration of the present dangerous tendency to forget a fundamental of American democracy which rests on the right of a locality to manage its local affairs — the tendency to encourage concentration of power at the top of a governmental structure alien to our system and more closely akin to a dictatorship or the central committee of a communistic regime.

Now my friend was right about one thing. Local government as a whole is open to severe criticism, and this applies to the cities, to the towns, to the counties, and to the multiplicity of other local agencies. During this century the problem of local government has been complicated by three new factors — the unparalleled growth of city populations, the birth of a new type of community known as the suburban area, and, piled on top of these, a wholly new series of human physical needs such as highways, pavements, water, sewers, lighting, bridges, tunnels, schools, which affect every inhabited area of the State. We have shifted and shuffled our population by the millions, we have made more physical changes in twenty-five years than in the previous two hundred and fifty, and we have expected the old machinery of local government without any redesigning to carry the new load. The only real wonder is that the inefficiency is not worse, and that public honesty is probably on a higher general plane among the rank and file than it was a generation ago.

But why are our local governments archaic in design, unsuited for the purpose for which they are established, unsatisfactory in their functioning, and profligate in the spending of the taxpayers' contributions? The answer is not hard to find. It is because the individual citizen is indifferent to his local government problems. The stress of business competition in this hectic twentieth century of ours, the even more feverish pursuit of pleasure to compensate for our strenuous business days — these so occupy the time and thought of our average taxpayer as to leave no inclination either to study or assist in the conduct of the community in which he lives. We do not trust our personal business affairs to strangers; we do not take our pleasures vicariously; but when it comes to running our local communities we gladly let John Doe do it. We do not even take the trouble to inquire what manner of person John Doe may be when he is nominated by a political party for a responsible local office. We do not know enough about the machinery of our local government to find out after he is elected whether he has been an efficient official or not. We know neither what his job is nor how he has performed it. We grumble at the taxes, but have not the slightest idea what could be done to lower them, because we do not know for what they are spent. We are occasionally aroused into driving out the grafter and the crook but we allow complacently a hundred times the amount of their peculations to be frittered away for needless and costly duplication of governmental functions under a system designed originally for the simple needs of our Colonial forefathers. We are far more familiar with the structure of our national Government at Washington and of our State Government at Albany than we are with the Government of our own town, village, city, or county. Our criticism is seldom valuable because we have no clear idea of what is wrong and not the faintest real conception of any practical remedy.

It would be appalling to compute the millions of dollars which our local taxpayers needlessly pay as the price of their indifference. Our State Government has been reformed because of the ability of great leaders to awaken public interest in the affairs of State. Our local communities, alas, only in rare instances, have aroused themselves to an interest in local government extending down to the average citizen.

Too often reform associations, preachers, editors, committees of eminent citizens have, with the best intentions, come forward for a few months only to right an emergency evil, or else they have represented one angle only in a many-sided problem, or else they have had an ulterior motive of mere partisanship. It is impossible to get better government locally if only 5 percent of the electorate participate in civic affairs two months of the year while the other 95 percent remain uninterested all twelve months of the year.

Let us get this picture clearly before us. We have three main divisions of Government: First, the Federal, operating, at least in theory, in the national field and in accordance with strictly limited powers of control ceded to it by the sovereign States; second, the State, moving only in the statewide field and careful not to confuse State with local functions; third, the several divisions of local government, authorized to be sure by the State, but based on the centuries-old conception of the town meeting.

When States become indifferent to their duties, the natural tendency is for the national Government to grasp for more power. In like manner if community government becomes slipshod and lax, the way of opportunism is to carry the problem to Albany and get the local legislators to introduce a bill.

Some of us for many years have striven against the multiplicity of local laws passed each year by complacent Legislatures. During the past two years I have the record of having vetoed more bills of this character than any previous Governor. Back of the immediate reason in the individual case has been the fundamental thought that the elimination of piecemeal legislation might to some degree make people think along broader lines and come back another year with a well-thought-out comprehensive plan to cover the subject as a whole. This is, of course, in direct line with what is commonly called the home rule principle. The principle is right. We have started to apply it. But at the same time its success must depend on local interest on the part of the 95 percent of the citizens as well as of the 5 percent if we are not to slip back into the system of a generation ago when even the number of dog catchers in a community was made the subject of State legislation.

How often do people stop to realize the relative influence which the three great branches of Government play in their daily lives? What daily contact has the average man or woman with the activities, the machinery or the administration of the Government in Washington? What personal touch has the average man or woman with the Government in Albany except when traveling over a State highway or visiting a State park? If you own a piece of real estate, whether it be a business property or a home or a farm, do you ever stop to realize that when you pay the taxes on it not one cent goes to Albany or to Washington?

Much has been said of the mounting burden of taxation; yet lack of thought leads most of us to forget that by far the greater part of the increase has been caused during this generation by mounting local expenditures. And this is further emphasized by the fact that over half of all the tax money collected by the State of New York is spent not by the State, but is returned by the State to the counties and communities for local expenditure.

It is my ardent hope that in the twenty years to come the people of New York will be able to accomplish as much for the cause of improved local government along American lines as we have accomplished for our State Government in the past twenty years. This can come only through leadership and through a greater dedication on the part of the individual, giving more generously of his time and thought and personal service.

First, we need to plan, to go to the root of the problem in order that specific remedies may be offered. When this is done I am very certain that the Legislature and the administration of this State will lend their aid and sympathy to the granting of the necessary authority.

I have spent two happy years in Albany and today I look forward to 1931 and 1932 as giving me, because of the experience which I have had, a greater opportunity for usefulness to the people of the State. The older I grow the more insistent I am that the average of the citizenship of the State will respond to the presentation of problems of government if the fundamentals of the issues are presented to them clearly and honorably. I am convinced, too, that the electorate has a sense of proportion and, given the facts, will of its own accord recognize them in the order of their importance.

That is why on this New Year's Day I have taken occasion to speak somewhat at length on government. One part at least of

99

our Government we can be proud of—the State is functioning well. Another part, the one which enters more closely than any other into our daily affairs, needs our attention, our interest and our earnest efforts to improve.

The vitality of our American institutions has been amply proven in the past. We have met difficulties before this and have solved them in accordance with the basic theories of a representative Democracy. Let us not at this time pursue the easy road of centralization of authority lest some day we discover too late that our liberties have disappeared. Let us pause in our pursuit of materialism and pleasure, and devote greater efforts to retain these liberties within the communities in which we dwell.

That is the New Year's message from the Governor of your State who pledges himself anew to devote the best that is in him to the whole-hearted service of the men and women and children of the State of New York.

17 ❨ The Annual Message to the Legislature (Excerpts). January 7, 1931

To the Legislature:

I REPORT to you, a new Legislature, in accordance with the Constitution. I cannot truthfully inform you that all is well with the condition of the citizens of the State for, during the past year, in common with the rest of the Nation, many of them and many of our industries have experienced a decline in prosperity which often has brought about suffering and hardship. It is greatly to be hoped that those are right who call this a period of readjustment and that the near future will bring relief.

It is not calm waters but the stress of angry seas in time of storm that tests the soundness of the construction of any ship: the Ship of State is no exception. I conceive it to be not only the duty of a State to promote the prosperity of its citizens, but to aid them in every possible way during dark days when prosperity has been succeeded by adversity.

Therefore it gives me satisfaction to be able to report to you not only that the finances of the State are in good condition, that the orderly conduct of State activities is proceeding according to law, but also that the State has taken the lead in the solution of many pressing emergency problems arising from economic causes. We have done and are doing all within our power to relieve the emergency and to build against the future. I am confident that in this I shall have your whole-hearted cooperation.

CRIME AND ITS PUNISHMENT

As a result of the passage of much needed legislation recommended by me a year ago, the State has at last developed a definite prison policy which we are now engaged in carrying out. The adequate housing of the prisoners of the State is proceeding along sound lines and you will find the report of the Prison Investigation Commission outlines a building program which, when completed in 1935, will furnish modern housing facilities and at the same time give opportunity for the much needed classification, segregation, instruction and vocational training of the many different types of individuals who, because of infringements of law, come into the custody of the State.

Better food and clothing have been provided, the corps of prison guards has been strengthened, and a new parole system is now functioning. I ask specifically that the recommendations of the Prison Investigation Commission be carried out, including the erection of a new type of prison. I ask also revision of the existing laws relating to all sentences. This will include also revision of the laws relating to commutation and compensation and clarification and systemization of the varying degrees of executive clemency.

At the same time I ask for an extension and improvement of the probation system. Probation is not to be confused with parole. Parole gives provisional release before expiration of sentence to prisoners already in prison; probation, on the other hand, keeps the individual out of prison altogether so long as good behavior continues.

All of these steps aim at two great objectives — the prevention of a repetition of crime on the part of the individual and the building up of the individual into a useful law-abiding citizen.

I renew my recommendation of last year for a State Crime Investigating Bureau to facilitate the task of local police authorities in the apprehension of criminals. It is also important that the alarming increase in perjury be checked; justice must rest upon truth.

HOSPITALS

The overwhelming approval given by the voters of the State in the recent election to the bond issue for erection of hospitals, prisons and other buildings for the care of the wards of the State assures, with the cooperation of the Legislature, the completion of the definite building program outlined by me last year whereby by the year 1935 there will be adequate provision for all patients. It is especially gratifying to note the strides being made by medical science in mental hygiene. The percentage of cures is slowly but constantly rising, and at the same time we are making progress in the prevention of mental disorders.

HEALTH

Last spring I constituted a special committee of citizens and experts, headed by President Farrand of Cornell University, to study a new health program for the State. This is the first time a comprehensive survey has been made since the splendid program sponsored by the late Dr. Biggs. The report of this committee will be transmitted to your Honorable Bodies at an early date and will, I am certain, mark a very definite advance in the general subject of public health for adults and children.

OLD-AGE SECURITY

In 1929 I recommended to the Legislature a commission to report on Old-Age Security against Want. The report of this commission resulted in the passage of the Old-Age Security bill by the last Legislature, and actual payments under the new law went into effect on January first this year. I have many times stated that I am not satisfied with the provisions of this law. Its present form, although objectionable as providing for a gratuity, may be justified only as a means intended to replace to a large extent the existing methods of poor-house and poor-farm relief. Any great enlargement of the theory of this law would, however, smack of the practices of a dole. Our American aged do not want charity, but rather old age comforts to which they are rightfully entitled by their own thrift and foresight in the form of insurance. It is, therefore, my judgment that the next step to be taken should be based on the theory of insurance by a system of contributions commencing at an early age. In this way all men and women will, on arriving at a period when work is no longer practicable, be assured not merely of a roof overhead and enough food to keep body and soul together, but also enough income to maintain life during the balance of their days in accordance with the American standard of living.

The commission which reported last year gathered ample data along these lines on which legislation may be based. I trust that your Honorable Bodies will give this great subject immediate practical consideration.

UNEMPLOYMENT

Your Honorable Bodies are well aware of the present abnormal situation in regard to unemployment not only in this State but in the Nation. The State is doing and will do what it can in the way of immediate emergency relief. Public works are being speeded to the utmost; all available funds are being used to provide employment; wherever the State can find a place for a man to work it has provided a job. Our course has been founded on truthful and accurate statistics. Those charged with the duty of collecting these figures for the State have realized the futility and folly of attempting to gloss over or conceal the real situation. In the long run the truth hurts nobody. Because the information regarding the unemployment situation given by the State Department of Labor during the past year has been accurate, it has been possible for the administration to take far-reaching steps both to mitigate and relieve the emergency, and also to plan for the future.

Since last spring the Governor's Commission on Stabilization of Industry has accomplished much to prevent the lay-off of workers, to find new employment both through public and private employment agencies, and to coordinate and stimulate local employment efforts. It has worked in close cooperation with local relief agencies. Careful surveys of every part of the State have been made, and individual localities have been greatly aided in establishing comprehensive plans for relief. This commission has been acting under my appointment but without any appropriation. I ask that it be created an official State commission to function for the coming year, and that it be given adequate funds to carry on this emergency work.

The above relates to the immediate present. The great future problems of unemployment call for close study. I have invited the Governors of Massachusetts, Rhode Island, Connecticut, New Jersey, Pennsylvania and Ohio to meet with me in Albany on January twenty-third to discuss the problem in its broader aspects. It is my thought that the industrial States of the northeastern part of the Nation can well cooperate in seeking a joint study of facts and existing or proposed methods of relief both here and abroad so that State legislation in the future may be made more nearly uniform.

I have a definite program to submit to this conference. Thereafter I shall communicate to you such recommendations as may be adopted at the conference which in my opinion will tend to promote a farsighted policy of prevention and relief, a policy carried out as uniformly as possible by neighboring States in which somewhat similar conditions exist.

LABOR

Although this State has taken the lead in labor legislation, there are still certain requirements which are necessary in order to keep step with the newest developments in industrial life and the newest conceptions of social welfare. I recommend to you the following program:

1. The inclusion within the coverage of the Workmen's Compensation Law of all diseases arising from occupational tasks.
2. A genuine eight-hour day and forty-eight-hour week for women in industry.
3. The establishment for women and children of an advisory minimum or fair wage board.
4. Strict regulation by the State of fee-charging employment agencies.
5. The raising of the limit for compensation in all classes of disabilities to twenty-five dollars per week.
6. Declaration in the form of a statute, that the labor of human beings is not a commodity or an article of commerce.
7. Establishment in the Labor Department of a special means for the enforcement of the provisions of the Labor Law relating to the eight-hour work day, the prevailing rate of wages, and preference to citizens of New York State on public works.

Many of these recommendations have been made by my predecessor and myself for a number of years. I think the time has definitely arrived for recognition by the Legislature of these fair demands by the laboring men and women of the State. . . .

(Here followed statements on a proposed business bureau of information, expediting public works, State highways, bridges and barge canal.)

AGRICULTURE

The past two years have placed the State of New York in the lead in remedial legislation for the farmers and rural dwellers. The Governor's Agricultural Advisory Commission, which has been of such inestimable help, will continue, and will make further recommendations to bring into a more sound and equitable relationship the country and the city communities. In other words, we have progressed to the point where we can visualize and formulate a practical, definite and far-reaching land policy for the State. Long range planning for the character of the use of land itself has become almost a prerequisite to the building of arteries of transportation, the development of markets, the diversification of crops, flood control, reforestation and the many other needs that fall under the general head of agriculture, conservation and the even broader head of social economics. In a special message I shall later outline this definite land policy, the adoption of which I believe would be of permanent value to every individual and every community.

WATER POWER AND PUBLIC UTILITY REGULATION

After generations of discussion of the development of the water power resources of the State, the Legislature last year created a Commission for a comprehensive study of a method of development by a public authority. This Commission will transmit its report to your Honorable Bodies within a very short time, and I trust that action will be taken at this session providing for water power development by a public agency for the purpose of producing cheaper electricity for the people of the State.

Intimately bound up with the question of water power is that of effective public utility regulation. They both stand out as pressing problems in our industrial and our home life. Two years ago I urged upon the Legislature the need of a fundamental change in our law concerning public utility corporations. The Legislature set up a Commission to study the subject. Both the majority and minority reports of that Commission disclose the ineffectiveness of our present supervision over these corporations; though it is generally conceded that the Public Service Commission is now functioning more effectively insofar as authorized by our present statutes. Regulation of monopolies for centuries under common law principles and under the theory of the original Public Service Commission Law, was based on the underlying principle that these utility companies should furnish fair service at reasonable rates. That purpose in many cases has been thwarted. In some cases rates are too high; profits are beyond any reasonable return on investment; service is not always satisfactory. The plain truth is that effective regulation as contemplated originally has not been realized.

Unfortunately the Legislature last year rejected not only the conclusions of the minority but also the recommendations of the majority of the Commission. Nothing was done. The consumers, and especially the household consumers, continue, of course, to be the losers from this inaction.

The problem is not confined to the State alone. It is nationwide. As a result of a long course of judicial decisions and of newly invented methods of financing, the householders and business men of the Nation, in a great many cases, must now pay exorbitant rates, measured not in terms of reasonableness for legitimate investors but rather in terms of speculative profit. We can, of course, have no objection to a reasonable return for the real investor in stocks of utility companies; indeed we should actually do everything possible to safeguard such reasonable return for him. The difficulty is rather with those who seek unreasonably to inflate profits and promote speculative trading by so pyramiding capital structures in holding companies and otherwise that profits are made on stock which is not always represented by actual investment.

I remain of the opinion that the proposals of the minority of the Commission last year which were rejected by the last Legislature will go far to meet the immediate problem effectively. The housewives of many parts of the State look to us for relief from rates so high as to deprive them of the advantages of modern science to release them from household drudgery.

This ever-growing public demand for more effective regulation should be met promptly. It would be a fine thing if you and I, serving a common master — the people of the State of New York — would unite in this common purpose of bringing into the homes and stores and factories of our State, these modern utilities at a cost reasonably consistent with a fair return to the legitimate investment in these corporations. . . .

(Here followed statements on reapportionment, election law changes, four-year term for Governor, State census.)

LOCAL GOVERNMENT

In the interest of economy and efficiency I again urge upon you the necessity of a complete reorganization and modernization of local government. The machinery of village, town and county government, originally created many generations ago to meet the needs of those days, is now obsolete. I ask you to authorize a commission to be appointed by the Governor to study and report advisable fundamental changes. In the meantime I recommend that a constitutional amendment be adopted permitting the Legislature to provide modern forms of government for any county, subject to referendum within that county. This, of course, does not contemplate the consolidation of counties in any sense; but rather an elimination of present overlapping functions of town and county offices so that local government may be administered more efficiently and economically.

During the past several months there has been much public discussion of the advisability of a general investigation into the conduct of the various departments of the local New York City Government and judicial officers therein. Once more it is necessary to clarify the use of well-defined governmental functions. There are three independent and separate branches of the Government.

In so far as possible interference by one of these three branches with another should be avoided. The Governor as the head of the executive branch is authorized by statute, under the so-called Moreland Act, to investigate any executive department of the State Government, thus casting upon him the burden of keeping his own executive house in order. Added to this, the Governor may on specific charges remove a few carefully limited and specifically designated municipal and county officials and no others. Finally, where evidence of crime is submitted in substantiated form to the Governor, accompanied by proof that the local machinery of prosecution has failed properly to function therein, he is empowered and it is his duty to invoke the State agency of the Attorney General's office.

In the case of the second separate branch of Government — the judiciary — a sound public policy should place the burden of supervision over the various courts and their justices upon the judicial branch itself. This principle has been recognized for many years. Under it the Appellate Divisions for many years have been charged with the duty of supervising the conduct of members of the Bar. More recently they were given authority over some inferior Civil and Criminal Courts. The wisdom of this provision is being well demonstrated by the investigation now in progress in the first department. The other Appellate Divisions are similarly under a duty to initiate proceedings whenever in their opinion they become advisable or necessary. I believe that constitutional and statutory provision should immediately be made to extend the supervisory power and functions of the several Appellate Divisions to cover other courts, such as county courts, special sessions courts, general sessions courts, city courts and other lower courts, together with the power to remove judges thereof. To the Appellate Divisions should be given the duty of seeing that the conduct of such courts and of their justices is in accordance with the laws of this State and ethical practices.

The conduct of the Supreme Court and the Appellate Divisions and of the justices thereof should likewise be subject to regulation by the judiciary itself, in this instance, I believe, by the Court of Appeals, leaving the power of removal of the judges of the higher courts in the Legislature where it now resides. In this way the primary responsibility of maintaining order in the judicial house of the Government would be placed squarely upon the shoulders of the judiciary itself.

Finally we come to the duty of the legislative branch of the Government. No one questions the right of the Legislature to investigate any matter of importance to the welfare of the State. It alone can proceed to investigate the conduct of the New York City Government generally, as I told the Legislature of 1930 in no uncertain terms. The responsibility of determining what action shall be taken by you and what justification there is therefor rests exclusively and squarely with you. It is not alone your right but your duty to conduct such an investigation if you determine that such course falls within your obligation to maintain the welfare of the State.

Two often-forgotten principles must surround the initiation and the conduct of any investigation if permanent good is to result. First, it must as a matter not only of fact but also of public opinion spring from a desire to promote the general welfare and not the political ambitions of any person or party. Second, it must be so conducted that all persons, unless or until formally charged with crime, shall be shielded from suspicion and innuendo through publicity, lest the mere fact of their appearance in the investigation destroy their reputation or impair their standing among their neighbors.

These two principles carry out the highest theory of good government as well as the American spirit of fair play. Recent flagrant violations of these principles, impairing the value of the investigations themselves, have impressed upon the public mind the need for their future observance. . . .

It seems particularly appropriate that in times of stress such as we are now witnessing, the Governor should again offer to the Legislature his willingness and desire to cooperate for the good of the State. I do so in the hope that this new Legislature will accept this in the spirit in which it is meant. Recriminations and the seeking of mere political advantage bring no rewards either to the State or to the party. It is my firm belief that we can work together for the bettering of our Government and the promotion of the happiness and well-being of the people of New York.

18 ❡ The Annual Message to the Legislature (Excerpts). January 6, 1932

Members of the Legislature:

I COME before you at a time of domestic crisis which calls for the complete laying aside of partisanship and for a unity of leadership and action as complete as if we were engaged in war. Not since the dark days of the sixties have the people of this State and of this Nation faced problems as grave, situations as difficult, suffering as severe. The economics of America, and indeed of the whole world, are out of joint; only the most skillful and concerted care will mend them. That is why I come before you as the Governor of all the citizens of the State to ask you to cooperate and counsel with me, not in your capacities as representatives of individual assembly or senatorial districts but rather as a great legislative body acting and speaking for all parts of the State, united in seeking not local advantages but rather the most courageous and hopeful solution of our common problems.

We face the necessity of employing new measures of value for the good reason that many old values have disappeared; new comparisons of property and of man's remuneration for his work, for the good reason that many of the old proportions have been proven false.

It would be useless as well as ungracious to place the blame for our present situation on individuals, or groups, or on any specific acts. What we can do is to learn from the recent years in a spirit of humility and of generosity what to avoid in the process of rebuilding our economic and social structure upon a surer foundation.

In the many groups of human beings known as Nations the structure of Government has been so inelastic that reconstruction has been possible only by revolution. We are fortunate that our fathers provided systems, both State and Federal, which permit peaceful change by intelligent and representative leadership to meet changing conditions of human society.

Let us face the facts. In the field of private endeavor we have retained in large degree, perhaps, the personal liberty of the individual; but we have lost in recent years the economic liberty of the individual. This has been swallowed up in the specialization of industry, of agriculture and of distribution, and has meant that the cog can move only if the whole machine is in perfect gear. We thus see on one hand an overproduction of food and clothing and close by many millions of men and women who lack the medium of exchange—money—with which to ward off starvation and nakedness.

We know now from bitter experience that the theory that a Nation could lift itself up by its own bootstraps was not sound; that the cheering thought that the larger the number of people engaged in manufacturing commodities the more these commodities would be used, could be carried too far; that just because a piece of paper was labeled a share of stock or a bond did not of necessity give it value; that an increasing concentration of wealth and of the power that wealth controls did not guarantee an intelligent or a fair use of that wealth or power.

We know that many of those who ran after false gods are heartily sorry for their sins of omission and commission; that many of the leaders of American thought in Government and in business appreciate the errors of their teaching. That is well; and nothing is to be gained by making them the scapegoats.

Nevertheless, more than two years have gone by and these leaders have as yet shown us few plans for the reconstruction of a better ordered civilization in which the economic freedom of the individual will be restored. Business and industry have been toiling and are toiling to salvage the old structure. They need more than just to be let alone. The public asks that they be given a new leadership which will help them and at the same time give definite recognition to a new balance based on the right of every individual to make a living out of life.

It is true that in any State of this Union of States the complete solving of those economic problems which are national in scope is an impossibility without leadership and a plan and action by our national Government. Perhaps that will come, but in the meantime we in this State have a very positive duty to do what we can to help ourselves.

For example, the larger problems of the national financial system, and therefore of banking, are to a greater degree Federal than State, yet we in New York can and ought to start to apply here the lessons learned during 1930 and 1931. Thoroughly unsound, even if wholly legal, banking practices have been growing for a generation. Many banks became mere bond-selling houses. Many bankers forgot that it was of doubtful ethics to sell their own securities to their depositors and to trust funds for which they themselves were trustees. Many billions in securities were sold to the public at prices unjustified even by the expectation that we had reached an immutable millennium, a permanent Utopia. Consolidations, mergers, holding companies, investment trusts were touted in every corner of the land, a pyramiding unequaled since the days of the Mississippi Bubble.

Today we recognize the unsoundness and the danger. The bubble has burst with all its rainbow glory. The public has burned its fingers in the flame of wild speculation and has learned now to fear the fire. While it still fears the fire is the time for us to act.

This action must come from the Legislature of the State, now as in the past. The people through their representatives have at all times found it necessary to place curbs and regulations and supervision on those who handle other people's money.

BANKING

First, we need new laws to give to the Superintendent of Banks and his department the benefit of assistance and advice in meeting a situation which is abnormal and without precedent. The inflexible provisions of our banking law do not permit adequate handling of emergencies. An advisory council could provide, under proper restrictions, flexibility with safety. With this I am confident that we can give additional protection to the deposits of millions of our people who are depending on their savings

and to the wheels of industry which require banking facilities
to meet their payrolls.

Second, unsound practices of the past must be eliminated by
law from now on. The ethics of banking need restatement; savings must be managed as savings and not confused with commercial or checking deposits.

Third, there must be revision of the laws relating to the sale
of securities to the public. It is time to differentiate between
prospects and true values, or at least to tell an unskilled public
the whole truth about the contents of what in the past has been
a package too often sold only because of the bright colors on
its wrapper.

Fourth, we must by law maintain the principle that banks are
a definite benefit to the individual community. That is why a
concentration of all banking resources and all banking control
in one spot or in a few hands is contrary to a sound public policy.
We want strong and stable banks, and at the same time each
community must be enabled to keep control of its own money
within its own borders.

MOTOR TRUCKS

I come now to another problem of the moment over which unfortunately the State can have little control. For many generations the greatest of common carriers, the railroads, have formed
the backbone of that form of wealth which seeks stable investment. Banks, insurance companies, charities, hospitals, churches,
trust funds, all, rightly or wrongly, have placed confidence in
the permanence of the underlying mortgages of the railroad.
Many people of late have seen the serious effects of a nationwide
depression on railroad traffic. The railroads are heavy sufferers,
in addition, from a new competition by great trucks and buses
on highways built by the State. In view of the fact that the taxes
paid by the railroads have helped and are helping to build these
highways and that the trucks and buses now use them almost
taxfree, a better equalization of taxes is called for in all fairness.
I shall ask in my budget message for a tax on heavy motor ve-

hicles commensurate with their use of the costly highways of the State.

Summing up, therefore, the present situation in so far as the State can give assistance to credit, to bank deposits, and to the strengthening of the general financial structure, it is incumbent on us to do everything in our power to protect the present and to rebuild for the future along far sounder lines.

UNEMPLOYMENT

The actual present conditions of life which face at least over two millions of the citizens of our State compel a reiteration of the principle to which we are committed — that the people of the State of New York cannot allow any individuals within her borders to go unfed, unclothed, or unsheltered. From that fundamental springs all of the work of relief now in progress in the State.

I report to you regretfully that the conditions of unemployment are as yet no better than those we faced during the recent special session of the Legislature. On the other hand, I report to you gladly that the measures which we adopted at that time for unemployment and distress relief are, with few exceptions, going forward in the right spirit and with measurable success. To the Temporary Emergency Relief Administration goes great credit for the businesslike and, at the same time, humane progress which under their leadership has been made in every county. To the great majority of local government units and to the hundreds of thousands of individual citizens who are giving money and services, must also go credit for coming forward unselfishly in this emergency.

It is as yet too early to determine whether further relief on the part of the State will be a necessity. We all hope that the worst is past. Much can still be done by individual citizens through community effort. Examples such as already given by the city of Rochester can well be followed by other communities.

In other words, Government and citizenry have combined to

meet the emergency. That does not mean that we can think only in terms of this winter. We must look ahead.

POPULATION DISTRIBUTION

A study of the past decade gives us at least one clue to the difficulties of today. It is a simple fact that by far the greater part of the present suffering, of the present inability on the part of hundreds of thousands to obtain any work and, therefore, to obtain food, clothing and lodging, lies in the larger communities of the State. A few of the smaller cities, because of low per capita wealth, need special assistance. But the fact remains that in the smaller cities and in the villages and the country districts, even though the shoe pinches in many households, the actual suffering and destitution are far less severe than in the big cities.

In other words, we seem to have established that the distribution of population during recent years has got out of balance, and that there is a definite overpopulation of the larger communities in the sense that there are too many people in them to maintain a decent living for all.

Great problems of distribution of the necessities of life are involved but we have sufficient studies to know that an immediate gain can occur if as many people as possible can return closer to the sources of agricultural food supply.

This is not a mere "back to the farm" movement. It is based on the fact that the pendulum has swung too far in the direction of the cities and that a readjustment must take place to restore the economic and the sociological balance.

I am a great believer in the larger aspects of regional planning and, in my judgment, the time has come for this State to adopt a far-reaching policy of land utilization and of population distribution. Let me illustrate from two extremes. At one end of the scale we are actually solving the problem of the unprofitable farming operation conducted on land unsuited to agriculture. This land, representing perhaps twenty percent of the area of the State, will be gradually returned to its most profitable use —

forestry, hunting or recreation. At the other extreme lie the industries in great metropolitan centers where land values, taxes and living costs are so high as to make the cost of production too high to compete with areas where the overhead is far lower. In between these two extremes lie tens of thousands of square miles and thousands of communities where agriculture may be made profitable enough to sustain life on a reasonable basis and where industries may with proper relationship to agriculture itself thrive more soundly than in the metropolitan areas.

From many of the larger centers of population I receive appeals from families who, springing from an agricultural background, have tried the ups and downs of city life and who are now ready to exchange its uncertainties for the comparative assurance of a livelihood given by the smaller community.

We cannot tell until we try to find out, how many urban families in this State would be glad to return to the smaller communities even with the full understanding that in so doing they would in all probability never become millionaires.

To that end I ask that you confer with me, in order that I may lay before you the studies made on this subject by an unofficial committee appointed by the Governor, and in order that we may try to work out a definite plan to restore a more normal population balance between the great cities and the rest of the State.

From a consideration of the distribution of population it is a logical step to the problem of excessive local taxation and its cause — excessive cost of local government.

LOCAL TAXES

From every corner of the State arise justified complaints of the taxes on real property, whether the property consist of stores, of city homes or of farms. We hear few complaints in regard to State taxes because the State taxes are not on real estate, but are on intangibles such as stock exchange sales, incomes, gasoline sales, etc. After three long years during which I have tried in every part of the State to make people understand that real estate taxes have absolutely nothing to do with the State Government, the public is at last coming to realize that the increase in real estate taxes is due wholly to the increase in the cost of local and not State Government.

These taxes on real estate are too high. I make that categorical assertion. By the same token I make the categorical assertion that the cost of Government is too high. The answer to the problem of excessive real estate taxation is reduction in the cost of local government. The answer does not lie in having the State Government collect general taxes and distribute these general taxes in the form of cash to the local communities for their local expenditures. That is unsound.

Local government has in most communities been guilty of great waste and duplication, of unnecessary improvements, and of thoroughly unbusinesslike practices. For three successive years I have begged the Legislature of this State to appoint a commission to study the simplification of local government, but for three successive years the Legislature has done nothing. I have given up trying to persuade the Legislature to do this. I am having a complete study made by experts in the field, on my own initiative. I expect shortly to lay before your Honorable Bodies, facts, figures, and recommendations in regard to local government, as a result of this study, which will make clear the difficulties of the past and the present and will point out remedies sufficiently definite to give to this Legislature at least a point of beginning for definite reform.

It is very satisfactory to me to know that the overwhelming majority of counties, cities, villages, improvement districts, and towns, within this State, are not only wholly solvent but are in the happy position of having mortgages on the future far below any statutory or even safe debt limit. There are, however, a few isolated instances of communities which have borrowed money beyond a reasonable limit, and I shall shortly send you a message asking for legislation to prevent a recurrence of this practice. It is safe to say that these exceptions to the general rule are so few as to be almost negligible, but I am so proud of the economic soundness of Government in this State that I seek a condition where every unit of local government will be financially above reproach. . . .

(Here followed a statement on State finances.)

STATE LAND POLICY AND REFORESTATION

Distinct progress is being made by the State in carrying out its State land survey. It has completed two years of work and has made a soil survey of the entire county of Tompkins and parts of the counties of Steuben, Orleans, Rensselaer, Broome, Monroe, Genesee, Nassau, Suffolk, Cayuga and St. Lawrence.

The Legislature during the past two years has provided the necessary funds for this work, and I shall again recommend to your Honorable Bodies a further appropriation to carry it on.

The survey has already been directed into channels which will provide the basis for future State planning dependent for complete efficacy upon accurate knowledge of land conditions. This survey is already formulating plans for future public service and public utility development and road construction for some of those regions which it has determined to be so adapted to agriculture as to justify the conclusion that they will continue to be used for farming. When the study is entirely completed, accurate data will be at hand to indicate definitely which lands of the State can profitably be continued in cultivation, which lands of the State should be devoted to reforestation, and which lands of the State should be used for industrial purposes. I look forward to the time when this information will provide the basis for planning future State and local developments dependent upon the proper and economic settling of population — for example, the location and kind of roads to be built through the rural areas of the State, the establishment of additional school facilities, the laying out and planning of electric and telephone services. This will provide the highest maximum efficiency in planning farm-to-market roads, rural electrification and telephones, and scientific allocation of school facilities, as well as a more scientifically coordinated system of assessment of rural lands.

119

As a part of this land utilization program, the people of the State have adopted the so-called reforestation amendment providing for annual appropriations of money for the purchase and reforestation of over one million acres of land better suited for forestry than for agriculture. This amendment was overwhelmingly approved by the people last fall, and provision is being made in my budget to carry out the mandate of the electorate along these lines. The reforestation program should be carried out in conjunction with the land survey, so that as little time as possible will be consumed in translating into proper State action the scientific information and data which will be furnished to us. The expenditure of money will almost immediately bring economic returns in prevention of waste.

PRISONS

The State is making good progress in carrying out the new and comprehensive prison policy. With current appropriations and those to be made by this Legislature and the next, we shall be in a position by the date set — 1935 — to eliminate the antiquated and unsanitary housing of prisoners which was such a disgrace to our modern society. The new Attica prison is already in partial use, the new medium security prison at Wallkill is under contract, and I am asking this year for the starting of two additional institutions — one to take care of mentally defective prisoners and the other to house the younger type of delinquents.

Equally important has been the progress in the classification, segregation and paroling of prisoners, but the more we give intelligent administration to this problem, the more we find a definite need for changes in the present law dealing with first offenders and the length of their sentences. I incline more and more to the enactment of an indeterminate sentence law, the foundation of which will be the individual case rather than the application of definite terms and rules laid down by the Legislature and the courts. While the establishment of the Parole Board has given a more substantial justice, we must definitely follow this up with an extension of the system of probation and with adequate provision for indeterminate sentences. The Commission to Investigate Prison Administration and Construction will shortly make definite recommendations along these lines to your Honorable Bodies.

ADMINISTRATION OF JUSTICE

At last the State seems to be making progress toward the day when we can drastically improve our present administration of justice. After a long delay, which was wholly unnecessary, the Legislature last year provided for a commission, and this commission is at work with effective diligence. It has recognized that any important improvement in the administration of justice must come not through piecemeal tinkering with rules of procedure, but through a genuinely fundamental rearrangement of the structure of the administration of justice itself. This commission plans to submit a preliminary report this year and a year hence will ask for definite remedial measures. It seeks to bring the administration of justice into harmony with modern conditions, to simplify procedure, to cut the cost to the litigant, to eliminate useless functionaries, and even unnecessary courts, to the end that justice may be easier to obtain, quicker to obtain, and cheaper to obtain. Its task covers both the criminal and the civil law, and I trust that an enlightened public opinion, not only of the Bench and Bar but especially of the great body of lay citizens, will encourage and support recommendations which, to those who are wedded to ancient precedents, may seem radical.

OLD-AGE PENSION

In January, 1929, I suggested an immediate study of the problem of the security of elderly people against want, and in 1930 a special legislative committee made a report and recommendations thereon. I had hoped that their recommendations would include a plan by which a contributory system would be set up in addition to taking care of our present old people. It was my thought that in this way the financial burden on localities and on the State would, while at first heavy, be greatly reduced over a period of years through the coming into operation of an annuity fund built up in large part by contributions made during the working years of the individual citizens. I regretted the omission of any recommendation along these lines and today we have what is in effect a straight old age pension system without contributions. Many complaints have come to me from localities regarding the operation of this system and calling attention to the increasing amounts which have to be raised through county budgets. I have requested of the department of social welfare a survey and checkup, in order to give assurance against excessive payments and especially to prevent the giving of aid to aged persons whose near relatives can and should take care of them without placing the burden on the county or on the State. It is of the utmost importance to prevent abuses of what was intended to be a great step toward the relief of those who, through no fault of their own, had come upon difficult times in their later years.

I suggest, furthermore, that your Honorable Bodies give immediate study to the establishment of a contributory system in order in future years to relieve the increasing burden upon the county and State treasuries. You already have the necessary data. By so doing we shall not in any way lessen the assistance given to the thousands of worthy cases; rather we shall encourage thrift and foresight among the younger citizens of the State. . . .

(Here followed statements on reapportionment and redistricting.)

WATER POWER

The Power Authority, created last year, has made definite progress in the performance of the duties imposed upon it by law, not only in working out the respective rights and interests of the four parties principally concerned, namely, United States, Canada, Province of Ontario, and the State of New York, but also in a further study of the economic and engineering problems and in negotiation of contracts for power distribution.

In conjunction with the mandate placed upon it by Section 5 of Chapter 772 of the Laws of 1931, directing it to provide a reasonable share of the power to be generated on the St. Lawrence for the use of municipalities and other political subdivisions of the State now or hereafter authorized by law to engage in the distribution of electricity, I desire to recommend to your Honorable Bodies the adoption of a statute similar to the one which was proposed by me last year, but which failed of adoption, authorizing municipalities of the State to form public utility districts, with the consent of their voters, for the purpose of generating, distributing and selling electricity.

LABOR

There still remain several reforms which I have urged in previous messages and which seem to me to be the very minimum which the laboring classes of our State are entitled to insist upon. These include:

1. Extension of the workmen's compensation law to cover all occupational diseases.
2. The State regulation of fee-charging employment agencies.
3. The declaration by law that the labor of human beings is not a commodity.
4. The establishment for women and children of an advisory minimum fair wage board.

I believe that if possible the laws relative to State contracts on all public work should be amended so as to insure, in so far as is possible, the actual payment of legitimately earned wages to employees where contracts are defaulted.

I believe also that the law passed in 1930 abolishing ex-parte injunctions in labor disputes should be extended to include the guaranteeing of a jury trial for persons accused of violating such injunctions. . . .

(Here followed a statement on election law changes.)

In times of stress and emergency like these we should avoid two evil extremes. At one end is the school of thought which believes that American industry and American business can pull themselves out of the slough unaided by Government. Its optimism forbids what it calls governmental interference. Its confidence in the success of individual action rejects efforts on the part of the State and Nation to lead back to better times. Too many national leaders in business, finance and politics adhered to this view — and for too long a time. Fortunately, though tardily, their views have changed. Even if such a return, without the aid of united community effort, which we call the State, were possible, it would have cost too much in human suffering and misery.

At the other extreme is the pessimism which looks upon the future with fear. It despairs not only of American business and industry but dares despair even of American Government and American character. To these timid souls the threat of a different social idea can always present itself as perpetually imminent.

Where shall we ourselves be?

We should not seek in any way to destroy or tear down, except in order to replace unsound materials with new. The American system of economics and Government is everlasting. Rather should we seek to eliminate those methods which have proved mistaken, and to apply to business and to Government, principles in which the rights of the average citizen are given a higher spiritual value. The times and the present needs call for a leadership which insists on the permanence of our fundamental institutions and at the same time demands that by governmental and community effort our business and industry be nourished and encouraged back to a basis made more sound and more firm by the lessons of the experience through which we are passing. Let us not seek merely to restore. Let us restore and at the same time remodel. To those millions who now starve we owe a duty as sacred as to those thousands who died in France — to see to it that this shall not come again. This is the duty of all of us — leaders in business, finance, agriculture, labor and government.

The mistakes of the past among men and among Nations, the effects of which now beset us, call for leadership broad enough to understand the problems not only of our Nation but of their relationship to other Nations, the problems not of New York alone but of all the other forty-seven States, the problems not of the cities alone but of the small communities and rural districts as well—a leadership practical, sound, courageous and alert. Let us, you and I, dedicate ourselves here and now to a fulfillment of this objective. Let us by our example show to the people of the State our complete confidence in the future of our commonwealth and our Nation. We know that the tragedies of the present will help in the rebuilding on a sounder basis for the days to come.

III

Agriculture, Farm Relief and Reduction of Rural Taxes

INTRODUCTORY NOTE: DURING the campaign of 1928 I had stated in general my plans for the relief of agriculture in the State of New York (see particularly Item 3). In my Acceptance Speech for the first nomination for the Governorship (see Item 1, this volume), in my first Inaugural Address (see Item 13, this volume), and in my first Annual Message to the Legislature (see Item 14, this volume) I also discussed the many aspects of this subject.

Even before I was inaugurated as Governor, I appointed an Agricultural Advisory Commission to formulate a program for the relief of farmers in the State of New York.

In most respects a farm relief program for an individual State must perforce be a limited one, for an adequate farm program must disregard State boundaries and deal in national terms. Not only is there the factor of competition from the farms of other States, but the whole agricultural problem is so tied in with the activities of every group of the Nation's population and of every section of the country, and is so closely bound up with such Federal matters as the tariff, the currency, and foreign trade, that treatment by any one State alone must necessarily be inadequate.

In New York State the major local problem of farmers and rural dwellers generally was the burden of taxation which had been placed upon them over the years. The first recommendations, therefore, of the Agricultural Advisory Commission had to do with reduction in the rural tax burden for highways, bridges and schools.

Other local agricultural matters, however, such as farm-to-market roads, farm management, soil research and soil surveys, cooperative marketing, agricultural research, testing of herds, specific crop diseases, were also the subjects of legislative and administrative attention. This appears from the documents in this chapter and also from the portions of my Annual Messages for 1930, 1931, and 1932, dealing with these subjects (see Items 15, 17, and 18 of this volume) on pages 92, 105, and 119.

The Agricultural Advisory Commission, on November 16, 1929, also took up with representatives of some of the larger power companies in the State the question of extension of electric service to the rural areas. The Commission was seeking to bring about a more uniform rate for rural service, and to devise a standardized plan, under which the farmer would not be called upon to pay for any part of the line construction. On January 30, 1930, the Agricultural Advisory Commission reported some progress in its negotiations with the utility companies for extension of rural electricity. No real accomplishments in rural electrification were made, however, until after the establishment of the Rural Electrification Administration on May 11, 1935, during my first term as President (see Item 58 of Vol. IV). On April 28, 1930, I approved a bill to provide for a Rural Electrification Division in the Public Service Commission, indicating my hope that some day the benefits of electricity would be extended to the farm areas (see page 307 of the *Public Papers of Governor Franklin D. Roosevelt, 1930*). That hope was not realized, however, until the Federal program of rural electrification was developed.

In the broader aspects of the agricultural problem the questions of soil utilization and submarginal land were also taken up in a practical way (see Chapter XVIII of this volume).

During the campaign of 1932 for the Presidency, I discussed the problems of agriculture from the national viewpoint, referring incidentally to some of the things done in New York State (see Items 131, 135, 140 and 145 of this volume).

In addition to the speeches and messages which are printed in this chapter with respect to this subject, I also delivered the following addresses and messages which could not be included here for lack of space, but which may be found in full in the volumes of my Public Papers as Governor for the years in question: Address before Legislative Committees on Taxation and on Agriculture, Albany, N. Y., January 16, 1929, *Public Papers of Governor Franklin D. Roosevelt* (1929), page 683; Address at State Press Association, Syracuse, N. Y., February 1, 1929, *Public Papers* (1929), page 685; Radio Address, Albany, N. Y., March 7, 1929, *Public Papers* (1929), page 688; Approval memoranda, April 10, 1929, *Public Papers* (1929), page 274; Statement on farm relief laws, April 10, 1929, *Public Papers* (1929), page 520; Address at State Fair, Syracuse, N. Y., August 29, 1929, *Public Papers* (1929), page 733; Address at Howe Caverns, N. Y., August 21, 1930, *Public Papers* (1930), page 750; Address at State Fair, Syracuse, N. Y., September 4, 1930, *Public Papers* (1930), page 756; Radio Address, Albany, N. Y., January 31, 1931, *Public Papers* (1931), page 701.

19 ❡ A Message to the Legislature on Rural Tax Relief (Excerpts). February 25, 1929

To the Legislature:

ON JANUARY 28, 1929, I transmitted to your Honorable Bodies the first constitutional State budget and in that document I stated that by a supplemental message I would suggest changes in taxation.

These changes are in my judgment made necessary because of certain inequalities in the tax burden under existing laws.

For some time it has been increasingly evident that the laws covering the methods of paying for county highways in the State highway system bear very unequally and unjustly on the great majority of counties. This is because, regardless of property values, and regardless of density of population, the local contribution to building cost is fixed at a flat thirty-five percent rate. The result is that whereas in some counties the tax burden for this cost of completing the State system is less than one dollar per thousand dollars of equalized valuation, in other counties it is over forty dollars per thousand dollars of such valuation. The counties principally discriminated against are those whose lack of economic prosperity forms a matter of grave concern to all citizens whether they be residents of city or of rural communities.

We have reached a point in modern civilization where we realize that a carefully planned highway system for the whole State is of direct benefit to the whole State and is no longer a matter of mere local interest. We understand the value of such a system for pleasure and recreational purposes and we have come also to know the value of concrete roads for the purpose of the direct distribution of milk, vegetables, farm products, raw materials, and manufactured articles. The large cities of the State are more and more dependent on the statewide highway system.

It is obvious that unless we impose a higher burden directly on the wealthier counties the only way to relieve the present inequality is for the State to take over a greater share of the cost of highway building and maintenance. It seems to me that it is time to recognize the principle that the burden should be based primarily on the true value of the taxable property per mile of highway.

Accordingly, the proposed legislation which accompanies the supplemental budget proposes three measures of relief, as follows:

1. Equalization of contributions to highway building by counties, by a requirement of not to exceed one-fourth of one percent per one thousand dollars of equalized value per mile of highway, nor in any event more than the existing requirement of thirty-five percent of the highway cost. This proposal is made to apply also to bridge construction. The additional cost to the State next year under this plan would be four million dollars. No county would be called on for a greater contribution than under the present law and most counties would receive a substantial reduction.

2. It is suggested that towns and incorporated villages be relieved from the present requirement of contribution for maintenance of State and county highways. This would add six hundred thousand dollars to the obligation of the State.

3. The present State and county system will not adequately be rounded out without the construction of additional lateral roads and these roads should be built under a careful plan of State supervision. It is time for the State Government to cease making any further contributions from the State treasury to counties or other local governments unless the principle is firmly established that the State shall have the right and duty to approve and give general supervision to the actual expenditure within the localities. It is in the case of highways an extension by the State of the wise provision in the Federal law which gives to the United States Government the duty to designate the highway, approve the plans and check the expenditures in all Federal aid highway

projects. The proposed system of lateral roads should be planned with the utmost care so that it will become a component part of the existing system. Additional aid by the State to help the counties to carry this proposed system forward would cost four million two hundred thousand dollars the coming year.

The above three proposals involve the expenditure of $8,800,-000 and the executive budget heretofore transmitted to you shows an estimated surplus of only $5,714,816.30. A sound business policy requires an estimated surplus of at least that amount and this is in line with the previous policy of the State.

An additional tax is, therefore, necessary if the highway tax burden is to be equalized as I have proposed.

With the advent of new forms of necessary governmental expenditure brought about by changes of modern civilization, new forms of revenue have also been devised. I believe that public opinion and political opinion is substantially agreed that a gasoline tax is the best solution of the problem. It is a tax already levied in 46 states ranging from a minimum of two cents to a maximum of five cents. It costs little to collect. Further it is a tax levied against the users of highways in proportion to benefits received; and in pursuance of a sound tax policy it should be used solely for road building and maintenance. In the last analysis the gasoline tax costs the automobile owner little. It is an investment by him in good roads. His automobile lasts longer, the cost of operation is less, the tires will travel many more miles and the repair bills on his automobile will be very considerably smaller. . . .

The justification of this tax being a charge against motorists according to benefits received, it necessarily follows that those using gasoline for industrial purposes, farm tractors and other machinery, airplanes and motor boats, etc., should be rebated in full for all taxes paid on gasoline so used. This is provided in the proposed bill.

I am recommending that the proposed gasoline tax go into

effect June 1, 1929, and I do this because the tax receipts accruing during June will not be physically received by the State treasury until July. This gives to the budget figures an apparent sum of $2,000,000 over and above the $22,000,000 estimated for the fiscal year, but I believe it is good business practice to have actual cash coming into the treasury before actual expenditures start to go out. . . .

20 ❡ A Message to the Legislature on Rural Schools and School Taxes (Excerpts).

March 4, 1929

To the Legislature:

I AM convinced, after an exhaustive study of the rural situation, that it is necessary to relieve the rural school districts by decreasing the tax burden now borne by rural taxpayers, principally farmers, through increased State aid to such rural districts. . . .

The constitutional mandate that the State shall "provide for the maintenance and support of a system of free common schools wherein all the children of this state may be educated" fixes responsibility on the State and implies that equality of educational opportunity shall be afforded the boys and girls of the State, wherever they may reside. That condition does not exist at the present time. Many school districts are too poor to maintain a school of an acceptable standard unless the tax is made prohibitive.

It has been proposed, and the bills are now pending before the Legislature, to extend the equalization quota, which under the present law stops with the five-teacher school, to the schools employing four, three and two teachers, respectively, thus giving to such additional schools all of the benefits of the equalization quota. It is estimated that this will cost the state approximately $1,000,000.

With respect to one-teacher, one-room school districts, it has been proposed that the State shall give to the one-teacher schools $1,500 each, less the amount of a tax of $4.00 per thousand of actual valuation. This would cost the State approximately $3,-250,000, which, together with the other appropriations, would deplete the balance of the budget to such an extent as to render it unsafe and inadvisable for the present year to give the full proposed State aid to such schools.

Moreover, there are hundreds of school districts now spending less than $1,200 per year in maintaining the schools. Some are spending less than $1,000. I question the advisability of suddenly saying to each such district: "Hereafter you may maintain a $1,500 school with a tax rate no higher than $4.00 per thousand, based on the full value of your taxable property."

The purpose of this plan is twofold. It is designed to equalize the school tax burden and thereby grant a large measure of tax relief to poor rural districts. It is also intended to raise the standard of education in rural schools. The standard cannot be raised overnight. To do that will require time. The mere dumping of more money into a school district will not in and of itself raise the standard of education in that district. . . .

The substantial benefits to the rural communities in case these proposals are carried out should result advantageously to the State at large and will tend very materially to equalize the school tax load, relieve the burdens now existing in the rural communities, assure to the children in such districts equality of educational opportunity and thereby carry out the evident purpose of the Constitution. . . .

21 ❡ Address at an Annual Farm Dinner (Excerpts), Syracuse, N. Y. August 28, 1929

(Future of farming in State of New York — Land use — Interdependence of farmer and city dweller.)

I WILL not recite to you the steps which, at the suggestion of the Governor's Agricultural Advisory Commission, have already been taken to relieve farmers of some of the unjust tax burdens, or other steps which might be called emergencies to equalize the burdens more satisfactorily.

The ultimate goal is, socially and economically, briefly stated. It is to arrive at the day when the average farmer in this State will be assured of as good living conditions and as much earning power in the average year as the skilled mechanic or small business man in the cities of the State.

I want tonight to discuss an economic trend which I believe to be on the way and which is sound, both from the point of view of geography and the point of view of economics.

It is perfectly true that this is one great Nation in which we live, yet we are apt to look at some of the economic features of our life too little from the regional viewpoint.

Let me cite an example of what I mean. The six million people in the City of New York are the daily users of hundreds of thousands of quarts of milk and cream. Modern medical science requires that that milk and cream be pure and free from dangerous bacteria from the moment of their production to the moment of their consumption by the man, woman or child in the city. That requires inspection by the city health authorities of the source of supply, i.e., the individual farms where the milk and cream are produced. Two years ago the Health Commissioner of New York City adopted the very wise and practical business policy of confining the area to which his inspectors could go to points within a reasonable distance of New York City, eliminating thereby costly and time-consuming visits to scattered individual farms through a dozen States of the Middle West.

Thus was created what is known as the "New York Milk-shed." It includes the whole of the State of New York and a few nearby points in New Jersey, northern Pennsylvania and Vermont. The New York City inspectors thus have only a homogeneous, easily-reached district to cover and the cost of this governmental function has been put on a practical business basis.

At the same time every effort is being made by the Dairymen's League and other cooperating agencies to bring the milk and cream production of this area up to the needs of New York City, and to keep the production up to the necessary maximum from year to year.

This is sound economics for two reasons. It means that the elimination of western milk and cream will prevent extreme fluctuations in the cost of milk and cream to the individual user in New York City; it also means that farmers engaged in the production of milk will be assured of a definite market year in and year out.

By the same token, it is good economics for the western farmer, for if the same practice is established in the cities of the Middle West, the western farmer, through proper cooperation, will build up the same kind of stabilized market in the cities of his own vicinity as exists in New York today.

In addition to all of this, the consumer, both in the West and in the East, is assured of fresher and safer milk and the railroads can make great operating savings in having definite shipping schedules instead of fluctuating hit-or-miss methods that existed in transportation up to the time this splendid step was taken.

What I am driving at is this. If the cities of New England, the city of Philadelphia, the city of Baltimore and other centers of the East could carry out the same method of the encouragement and maintenance of a local and nearby milk-shed, the dairy industry throughout the eastern states in a very few years could automatically be stabilized.

Now, if this principle can be successfully applied to milk and cream, and I am glad to say other cities and states are following our lead, why in the name of common sense can it not be applied to other agricultural products which are locally used? If we can have a successful milk-shed, why should we not have a successful vegetable-shed? I do not of course refer to the out-of-season vegetables which have necessarily a nationwide distribution. For instance, in the Spring of the year thousands of carloads of vegetables come to northern and western cities from the South several weeks before those same vegetables can ripen in the North. I refer, of course, to the seasons in which vegetables come to maturity in our own individual localities.

What, for instance, is the economic use in the spectacle in huge dump scows being towed down New York Harbor and out to sea for the purpose of throwing overboard dozens of carloads of cabbages which have come to the New York City market from the eastern and middle western States and in many cases the far western states, all arriving the same day and in such quantities that they could only be consumed, if the six million people in New York all decided to eat corned beef and cabbage three meals a day for a week. The growers of those unfortunate cabbages blame the commission merchants when they get no return and are out of pocket for the shipping charges, but the fault lies not with the commission merchants but with the lack of planning by the communities and the growers as a whole.

The manufacturer of shoes or the producer of automobiles does not send a train-load lot of shoes or automobiles to the New York market or any other large city on consignment in the fond hope that he can sell them in forty-eight hours. Why should vegetable growers and vegetable dealers and the vegetable consuming public lay down another and different rule?

The next practical step for us to take is to devise means by which, for example, the vegetable supply of the cities of New York State will be placed on a statewide basis. This can be arrived at only by cooperation between the city-dwelling public on the one side and the vegetable-growing farmers on the other.

Permit me to offer another example. The same proposition applies to fruit. Nobody would expect us in the East to limit in any way the shipping of early peaches or grapes from the further South before our own fruit is ripe. Nevertheless, when our own fruit is ripe it is an economic waste for us to be bringing in fruit, of no better grade or quality, from other sections of the country.

We all know the story of the Oregon apple. We must take off our hats to the energy and salesmanship of our friends in Oregon and Washington who have created a demand in our New York State cities for apples which have to be transported three thousand miles. The story of the success of the western apple is well known in every eastern city in spite of the knowledge that we can, if we want to, raise equally fine and perhaps better tasting apples in our own orchards.

One trouble is, of course, that too many thousands of farmers in the East continue to flood the local markets with inferior, under-sized, badly packed apples, with the result that the average retail merchant prefers to handle the product from the Pacific Coast, because the buying public wants something that looks good as well as tastes good.

If we could build up the same cooperative interest among the apple growers of the State of New York as we have succeeded in building up among the dairy farmers, we would soon be able to establish an apple-shed for the cities of our State.

In all of this work of regional planning for the production and consumption of agricultural products, we need the same coopera-tion from business men as they are now giving to city and sub-urban planning. We need their study in conjunction with farmers of the physical and material needs of marketing. We need their interest in the building up of common-sense pride in the use of our own products.

Over in New England the organization known as the New England Conference has already accomplished great things in teaching the average citizen to prefer to use the products of New England rather than to buy articles which are no better but which happen to be made in totally different sections of the country.

I am confident that the theory of regional planning for the more local use of all future situations is economically sound. It will result, in the long run, in a more stabilized price, in the pre-vention of overproduction, in the more permanent employment of labor, in the saving of transportation, duplication and waste, and in a better understanding between the city and farm popula-tions.

I look for the day when, throughout the length and breadth of the United States, zones will be established for the production and consumption of whatever the soil within that zone is best fitted to raise and whatever the local demands of consumption require. Let us not forget that the prosperity of the country, both State and national, is dependent as much on the prosperity of the agricultural population as on the prosperity of the city dweller.

If the farming population does not have sufficient producing power to buy new shoes, new clothes, new automobiles, the manufacturing centers must suffer. It is time for us, who are in business or in governmental positions, to regard this task as our own and to realize that the farm problem is not confined to wheat, corn and cotton. Much can still be done to equalize the burden of taxation, to meet the waste which undoubtedly exists in local government and to reduce other economic burdens such as the inequality of the tariff in its relation to the farmer. But in the final analysis, we need, more than anything else, a definite determination on the part of the business men, of the city dwellers and of the agricultural population to join hands in creating a permanent basis of production, transportation, sale and consumption in which the natural economic laws will take precedence.

22 ❡ Address at State College of Agriculture, Cornell University (Excerpts), Ithaca, N. Y. February 14, 1930

(Betterment of agricultural conditions — Proper land use — Rural education — Rural health.)

I THINK we are all agreed that the year 1929 will go down in history as affording the greatest amount of substantial progress for the agricultural interests of the State in modern times. Because of a more general and whole-hearted cooperation on the part of all of the interests affected and because of definite governmental aid of all kinds through the State Administration and the Legislature, marked advance has been made along economic and social lines for the bettering of agricultural conditions.

This broad attitude of intelligent interest in agriculture continues and further important steps are being taken this year to round out what we may well call a full program.

The time has come, however, to pause for a moment and ask ourselves the definite question: What is the objective of all of this interest and cooperation? Are we passing these new laws and spending all of this new money merely to correct existing conditions? In other words, is this a mere correctional policy or does it go much further? If it does go further, what is it aiming at?

To answer this question it is necessary to give a very brief survey of the fundamental reasons for the relative decline of agricultural prosperity in our State during the past decade.

The first reason is the economic one. We have come to realize that many thousands of acres in this State have been cultivated at a loss, acres which are not under modern conditions suitable for agriculture. Second, we have used many thousands of acres of soil for growing crops unsuited to the particular soil. Third, we have allowed thoroughly antiquated marketing processes to continue without intelligent change to meet the economic growth of the cities. For instance, we have built up a marvelous system of State Highways, without providing either the feeders to those roads at one end or the market facilities at the other end. Finally, we have only just begun to reorganize the tax burden so as to eliminate its inequalities.

The other reason for the past and present troubles is the social one. Modern civilization has brought wholly new methods of living. We must admit very definitely that one of the principal causes for the trek of thousands of people, especially the young people, from the farm to the city has been that the farms have been cut off from the amusements and interests which the urban communities provide. Modern inventions, such as the radio, telephone, and the automobile, are helping to correct a lop-sided situation, but we must take a more intelligent interest in the whole problem of making farm life more socially interesting as well as more financially profitable. That this can be done is evidenced by the actual cases of a growing group of individual fam-

141

ilies who are worthy to be listed as master farmers. In the same category of social needs comes the development of educational facilities in the rural communities. Much has been done, yet we still have a long way to go to make all rural education come up to the standards which have been already set.

Another definite problem of the future relates to the health of the rural communities. We are all distressed by the growing difficulty of obtaining adequate medical service and care. In many communities the actual cost of medical care is almost prohibitive and in many the medical facilities are themselves almost lacking.

In the same way we are facing the problem of the country church. The old days of the local Dominie who could live with his family on a salary of $500 a year and where the general maintenance cost perhaps another $500 a year, have gone by. We are confronted definitely in most communities with a multiplicity of church buildings, a multiplicity of different sects and the unfortunate injection of the high cost of living into our religion.

These are the outstanding economic and social causes of agricultural decline. And there is what might be called the supplementary reason that during these past years the urban and suburban communities have offered a better chance for industrial employment than ever before, and also a better chance to obtain social advantages. . . .

There is necessarily a limit to the continuance of the migration from the country to the city, and I look in fact for a swing of the pendulum in the other direction. Things all point that way. Industrially the United States has made not only the greatest strides in history in this generation, but perhaps has come to the period when industrial expansion will slow up. In other words, many economists are seriously questioning whether we have not for the time being reached the saturation point of industrial production calling for a period of digestion for a number of years to come. No matter how anxious we may be to prevent any panic of thought over the unemployment situation at this time, we must nevertheless recognize the fact that there are more people in the cities of the United States who are walking the streets looking for jobs than at any time within many years.

The effect of this condition, for it is a condition and not a theory, is that there will be less opportunity for young people to go from the farm to the city in the next few years and find work awaiting them. By the same token many people from the cities will give more serious attention than in the past to the possibility of moving to the country.

How happy is the family today located on a farm in New York State and able to say every day as they get up in the morning and as they go to bed at night, "We at least have no fear of starvation. We at least have no fear of losing our job. We may not be getting very rich, but at least we are able to go on with our lives without suffering and without drastic change."

This great objective, that I have been speaking about, aims at the great fundamental of making country life in every way as desirable as city life, an objective which will from the economic side make possible the earning of an adequate compensation and on the social side the enjoyment of all of the necessary advantages which exist today in the cities.

All sorts of factors are involved: better roads, better markets, better schools, better health facilities, better churches, lower rates for electricity, lower rates for telephones. Let us keep the objective definitely before us as we work year after year on the individual problems leading to that objective.

Perhaps great betterment can be obtained through the development of the idea of regional planning—a planning, for example, for every city in the State on the same principle which has already been applied to the milk supply for New York City. As an example of how the administration in Albany is seeking to develop better facilities throughout the whole State, I have just sent a letter to the Mayors and Health Officers of all the principal upstate cities asking them to come to Albany on March 11th, for a conference looking toward the establishment of regional milksheds for the further elimination of the bootleg milk and cream which come into our State from far distant points.

23 ❲ A Message to the Legislature Recommending Experimentation in Improvement of Dirt Roads. March 25, 1930

To the Legislature:

MANY people of the State feel that the methods of improving dirt roads have received but little study. In the case of the wider and more heavily traveled State roads much scientific progress has been made during the past twenty years, so that we are now able to build concrete roads whose life will be for a generation or more.

In the case of dirt farm roads, however, because of the enormous mileage involved, the cost of concrete, even one strip wide, laid under standard State specifications with a solid sub-base of rock is practically prohibitive for the greater part of the mileage. It is possible that experimentation with other types of construction may furnish us with data which will be very helpful in solving the serious dirt road problem. It has been suggested by the Superintendent of Public Works that the Legislature authorize the expenditure by his department of $100,000 from the funds for maintenance already allocated in order that experiments may be made.

It is further suggested that one of these experiments be made in each of the ten highway districts of the State, and each experimental strip in each district may again be subdivided into several different types of construction for purposes of comparison.

I, therefore, submit this suggestion for your consideration in the belief that we may be able greatly to profit thereby in the years to come. No additional appropriation is involved.

24 ❡ Governor's Statement Outlining Accomplishments in Fulfillment of Program for Agriculture, Farm Relief and Reduction of Rural Taxes. April 24, 1930

BEFORE I assumed the office of Governor, I organized in November, 1928, the Agricultural Advisory Commission for the specific purpose of a cooperative study of the outstanding needs of the rural population of New York State. This Commission, non-partisan in every aspect, has now completed its work so far as the two legislative sessions of the present administration are concerned, and I consider it advisable to draw the attention of the people of the State, particularly those toward whose requirements the work of the Commission was directed, to the accomplishments which have followed the Commission's work.

The first recommendations of the Commission were made available to the public on November 24, 1928, by Henry Morgenthau, Jr., the Commission's chairman. I feel that the most graphic means of presenting the results of its efforts in cooperation with the Legislature, is to state, chronologically and in sequence, the recommendations made before I assumed office, together with the final result that has followed each individual recommendation. This record stands as follows:

1. That the counties be relieved of their 35 percent contribution to the State for the construction of new highways.

RESULT: This was accomplished in 1929.

2. That the State assume the cost of removing snow from the State highways.

RESULT: In 1930 the Legislature passed a bill authorizing the State to aid the counties for snow removal from State and county highways and requiring that such snow removal be accomplished at the joint expense of the State and county. This bill is now a law by my signature.

3. That the State assume the cost of elimination of grade crossings.

RESULT: In 1929 the counties' share of the cost of eliminating grade crossings was reduced from 10 percent to one percent.

4. That a readjustment be made for the distribution of moneys for so-called dirt roads under section 101.

RESULT: In 1930 the Legislature passed the Pratt Dirt Road Bill which will give the rural counties approximately double the amount of State money which they received heretofore. This bill is now a law by my signature.

5. That a gasoline tax measure be passed.

RESULT: In 1929 a gasoline tax of two cents was put on the statute books of the State. Owners of farm tractors and stationary engines are refunded the tax paid for gasoline used. Twenty percent of the moneys received from the gasoline tax is given to the counties for construction of county highways.

6. That a study be made of the cost of local units of government.

RESULT: In spite of repeated requests and recommendations by me to the Legislature for a complete study of all phases of local government, it has refused to do anything.

7. That the State assume the minimum salary for rural school teachers.

RESULT: In 1929 a rural school bill was passed equalizing the method of raising rural school taxes. This piece of legislation has meant more in the way of tax relief to the districts that needed it most than perhaps any other single piece of legislation.

I feel that if the foregoing represented the whole work of the Commission, its members might well be proud of their achievements. It does not, however, represent the entire work of the Commission. In the Legislature just ended, an additional group of the Commission's recommendations was passed and, by my signature, these measures also have been made law. These include the following:

At the January 30, 1930, meeting of the Commission, the following recommendation was adopted:

1. That Governor Roosevelt be requested by the Commission to call as soon as possible a conference of Mayors and health officers of the cities of the State to give consideration to the establishment of such regulations governing the production and sale of milk and cream as will insure consumers the maximum health protection and will enable such cities to take advantage of nearby sources of supply.

RESULT: The conference was held and as a result I have just signed an act entitled: "An act to amend the public health law in relation to the sanitary control and inspection of milk and cream, and making an appropriation for such purposes." (This appropriation is for $90,000.)

At the January 30, 1930, meeting of my Commission, they recommended and adopted the following resolution:

a. That in view of the serious emergency confronting the peach industry by the widespread injury of oriental peach moth and of the apple industry particularly in exports, from apple maggots and spray residue, we recommend that the budget item of "Investigation of moths and insects, services and expenses, $13,000" be increased to $25,000.

RESULT: I have just signed, and it has become a law, an act entitled: "An act making an appropriation for investigation of certain moths and insects by the New York State Agricultural Experimental Station at Geneva." (This appropriation is for $37,000.)

b. That in view of the depressed condition of the potato industry in New York and of new insects and diseases which have appeared, we recommend that additional work in research be

147

carried out by the College at Ithaca and the Geneva Experimental Station, and that special work on the control of insects or diseases affecting potatoes on Long Island be done by the College of Agriculture at Ithaca.

RESULT: I have just signed an act making an appropriation for research, extension work and investigation by the New York State College of Agriculture at Cornell University, carrying a total appropriation of $43,710.

c. At the same meeting the Commission recommended and adopted a resolution which stated:

"We recognize the fact that the economic aspects of agriculture are now of predominating significance, and despite the handicaps of grossly inadequate physical facilities, the Department of Agricultural Economics at the State College of Agriculture has been and is making outstanding contributions to the present day needs of agriculture, which it cannot continue without immediately improved physical facilities."

RESULT: I have just signed an act entitled: "An act authorizing the construction of a building at Cornell University for agricultural economics, marketing and farm management, and making an appropriation therefor." (This bill carries an appropriation of $100,000.)

d. At a meeting on February 21, 1929, the Commission approved the bills now before the Legislature which would provide additional State support for the county farm and home bureaus and junior extension work in the State. These bills failed of passage in the 1929 Legislature.

RESULT: I have just signed an act by the 1930 Legislature, and it is now a law, entitled: "An act to amend the county law, in relation to the State contributions toward the support of county farm and home bureaus, and junior extension work, and making an appropriation therefor." (This bill carries an appropriation of $40,500.)

148

e. At a meeting of the Agricultural Commission at Ithaca on August 2, 1929, the Commission recommended and adopted the following resolution:

That the State take immediate steps to survey the agricultural resources of New York in order to make plans for the most profitable use of each kind of land.

RESULT: I have just signed, and it is now a law, an act entitled: "An act making an appropriation for a survey of agricultural resources of the State by the New York State College of Agriculture at Cornell University." (This bill carries an appropriation of $20,000.)

I submit to the people of the State this record of accomplishment by my Agricultural Advisory Commission with a feeling of deep personal satisfaction in their work, and I wish to extend to the individual men and women who served on the Commission my congratulations and thanks for having performed such worthy, devoted and constructive public service.

25 ❨Address at an Annual Farm Dinner (Excerpts), Syracuse, N. Y. September 3, 1930

(Farm relief program for the future.)

AT THIS dinner the men who represent every known interest in agriculture in the State of New York, I want to express my own gratitude and that of the agricultural population of the State for the splendid teamwork and cooperation which you have given during the past year and a half to the best farm relief program of any State in the Union. What is even more important is that the greater part of this is no longer a program, but has been translated into actual fact and actual law. . . .

As I see the next logical steps for us to take we must:

1. Strike out boldly to reduce the present exorbitant spread between what the farmer receives for his produce and what the

consumer pays for that same produce. Let me give some concrete examples of what this spread amounts to at the present time. These figures were taken on August 20, 1930, and are approximately correct. The wholesale price in New York City for heavy, live fowls is from 20 to 23 cents, and the retail price is from 35 to 36 cents. This represents a spread of 65 percent between the wholesale and retail prices. The wholesale price of legs of country dressed veal is 16 to 17 cents a pound; the retail price is 32 to 33 cents a pound, or a spread of 97 percent. The spread between the wholesale price of potatoes and the retail price is 47 percent. The spread between the wholesale and retail price of eggs is 41 percent. Now, it is interesting to note that in all of these cases, the spread between the wholesale price and the retail price in 1930 averages nearly double what it was in August, 1929. That is something for us to think about; it requires the best thought of all of us, city dwellers and farmers alike. But one thing is very certain, and that is that the farmers of the State of New York are neither profiteering nor getting rich on what they are receiving at this time, or for a generation past, for their produce.

Therefore, while we have done much and are doing still more through our highway systems, to bring farm produce to the urban markets, the next two definite steps are the working out of better terminal facilities in the cities and a wholly new system of city markets. These two essentials are the key of modern food distribution and it is time to put them both on an up-to-date business basis.

2. Hand in hand with city markets and terminal facilities goes one subject which relates more directly to the farmer himself, and that is the bettering of the existing grading of all kinds of farm produce. Why fool ourselves when we know definitely that in many lines of fruit and produce, other States are sending to market a more uniform and higher quality pack than we ourselves are doing?

In regard to the existing milk situation in the State, there is also need for the definite truth to be known by every family that buys milk. I take it that no dairyman and no consumer objects to activities of Government authorities which aim to locate and stop profiteering in food of any kind, but it is also axiomatic that any activities of Government officials which force farmers to sell their products below the cost of production, and especially those which lessen public confidence in milk as a food, are wrong and do irreparable damage. If it is a fact that severe drought and other adverse conditions to our dairy farmers justify a rise in the price of milk to them, in order to enable them to make both ends meet, it is wrong for public authorities to try the case in the newspapers first and investigate afterwards.

It is to the best interests of the farmer and of the consumer that the New York milk-shed be maintained and encouraged. It is wholly right, however, that every effort be made to prevent retailers of milk from using a very small and absolutely essential emergency increase in the price to the farmer as an excuse for making an additional or an unconscionable profit for themselves.

26 ❪A Message to the Legislature on Farm-to-Market Roads (Excerpts). January 20, 1932

To the Legislature:

I PROPOSE to your Honorable Bodies a concrete plan which has the twofold purpose of bringing our agricultural products more quickly and more cheaply to the centers of consumption and at the same time of lending encouragement to many who now constitute the surplus of population in the cities to return to small communities or farms under conditions more favorable than in the past.

This constitutes a step in State planning for the immediate future which can be put into operation this year without exceeding the appropriations recommended in the budget. I ask the diversion of a small part of the highway construction fund for the immediate construction of farm-to-market roads.

Let me first summarize the highway situation in our State:

The system of main roads is a source of justifiable pride to our citizens. The miles of wide, smooth highways and parkways over which motorists and trucks now roll with ease and safety provide rapid and convenient communication for long distance transportation and for recreational purposes. The construction and maintenance of these highways through the more popular and populous sections of the State is expensive. The rights of way, the permanence of the construction, and the maintenance for heavy traffic cost much; but our highways are worth what we have spent on them. We must continue to build them. State money invested in these highways is well spent and brings adequate return.

There are now approximately twelve thousand miles of these State highways. This is, however, only a small fraction of the total length of all the other roads in the State which have been opened by counties and by towns during many generations and which comprise the secondary and tertiary system of highways. There are eighty-two thousand miles of these less expensive roads, and of these, twelve thousand miles have been already improved by counties and towns. But this leaves about seventy thousand miles of so-called dirt roads which the farmers of our State must use in order to haul their supplies and get their products to market. Most of these dirt roads have served a most important function, not only to the farmer himself, but to the entire State. The facility with which the farmer transports his products from his farm either to railroad centers or to main arteries of truck transportation, is among the most important factors determining the cost of those products to the consumers in the cities and larger villages. It is obvious that vegetables, fruit or grain which can be trucked from the remote farm over dry hard roads to the market at all times of the year, can be sold more cheaply than if they have to be dragged through miles of mud or become marooned because of impassable roads.

The improvement of these roads has been primarily a function of counties and towns. Counties and towns are carrying on this work in different parts of the State with varying intensity and varying efficiency. In some of the localities good work has been done; in many others, the work has been so wastefully done that there is very little to show for the money that is being spent year in and year out.

Several years ago I requested that the Legislature allocate one hundred thousand dollars out of the highway funds, to be used by the Department of Public Works in experimental construction of rural market roads. With this money, experiments have been carried on by the department with plain gravel roads, field stone base roads, and combinations of these with various kinds of surface treatment. Careful cost accounts for each type have been kept and their respective degrees of endurance have been the subject of constant observations. As a result, the Department of Public Works now has adequate information as to the most economical basis for the construction of rural farm-to-market roads. In other words, the experiment has fully justified itself.

I believe that as the next logical step the State should proceed, at its own expense and through its own Department of Public Works, to the construction of demonstration farm-to-market roads in each county of the State. In this way, not only would many miles of improved roads be made available to the farmers of the State, but the State would furnish a practical example to follow in place of the present haphazard road-building methods in many of the rural towns and counties, as well as a powerful influence toward introducing a new spirit of emulation in good rural road building in every section. . . .

In order to conform to the new State policy of planning ahead, we must carefully guard against building any of these demonstration roads into territory which the State land utilization survey holds to be unfit for agricultural purposes. It would be folly to build one of these new roads to give an outlet to farms which will soon be abandoned for farming purposes.

Therefore, I recommend that the location of the mileage to be improved be selected upon the suggestion of, or with the approval of, the State College of Agriculture at Cornell, which, in conjunction with the land survey now being conducted by it, and with its sources of economic information, could select those stretches of roads which would best serve the purposes of demonstration and greatest usefulness.

I further recommend that the number of miles to be built in any one county be based on the ratio of the total mileage in that county to the total mileage of rural roads within the State.

I am advised that the cost of experimental roads of this type has ranged from three thousand six hundred and forty dollars per mile to eight thousand five hundred and eighty-two dollars per mile, and that a highly satisfactory type of rural road can be built not to exceed five thousand five hundred dollars per mile. This would provide a gravel or stone road in most cases with surface treatment applied after use for a year. It is my thought that the highway department of the State should be charged with the continued maintenance of these demonstration roads. At this average cost we should be able to provide the farmers of the State with an average of ten miles to the county or a total of six hundred and thirty-six miles.

This program cannot possibly be construed as signifying an intention to take over from the counties and the towns the construction of rural roads. An average of ten miles to the county is practically nothing when compared with the thirteen hundred miles' average of rural roads in each county of the State.

I therefore recommend to your Honorable Bodies that these initial steps be taken in the interest of helping the farmers of the State get their products to the markets of the State as quickly and as economically as possible, of encouraging people in the cities to return to the farms and small communities and of persuading city industries to consider locating in villages and towns.

By adopting this program your Honorable Bodies will accomplish three objectives. First, you will initiate the first practical step toward taking out of the mud the New York State farmer who lives on a dirt road. Second, you will give to local taxpayers an opportunity to compare construction and maintenance costs, and create in most communities a demand for better conducted town highway departments. Third, you will encourage the return to small communities and farms of many hundreds of families who, under present economic conditions, regret that they ever moved to the cities, and the relocating of many small industries now operating in costly city surroundings.

I regard this last as one of the most important factors in meeting the condition of unemployment in the great centers of population. No single panacea, in one year or in five years, will start all the wheels of all the factories turning again. Rather, we must seek out many basic reasons for our present situation, one of which is the present wholly unsound distribution of our population. Many steps to correct this unbalanced condition must be planned for and adopted. This step toward making the small communities and agricultural areas accessible to and from the larger centers is wise, far-sighted and wholly justified.

27 ❰ Address before the New York State Grange (Excerpts), Albany, N. Y. February 2, 1932

(Revival of world trade — Reciprocal trade agreements.)

Worthy Master and Members of the New York State Grange:

. . . I WISH to speak tonight about a more general problem, to discuss particularly means by which the products of American industry and of American farms can find a better outlet than they have now. The question of markets is today our most vital question. Without adequate markets industry is stifled and when industry is stifled the demand for farm products and the prices of farm products sink to levels that mean privation, hunger and dispossession. Without such markets an era of low prices and an army of unemployed will long be with us.

There are two outlets for our products: the first, an increase of home consumption, and the second, the sale of more of our industrial and agricultural products to other Nations throughout the world.

You, in the State of New York, whether you live on the farm

or work in the factory, are personally and deeply interested in the problem, not only of finding home markets, but of finding foreign markets. Volumes of technical phrases have been written and uttered, but it all comes down to this plain truth:

The Nations of Europe, South America and the Far East are not buying our products of factory and farm for the very good reason that they have not the means to do the buying. International cash is gold or its equivalent, and they have not got the gold.

For ten years, between 1920 and 1930, we Americans helped these other Nations to buy our goods by lending them our own money to do the buying. We have stopped doing that now for good and obvious reasons.

There was and is only one other way by which other Nations can buy our goods and that is by using the old-fashioned method of bartering or exchanging their goods for ours. Unfortunately, that is an impossibility for them because our Government, in its wisdom, put up a tariff fence so high that they could not use this old-fashioned method of exchange of goods. Furthermore, when our Smoot-Hawley Tariff Law went into effect three years ago, over the protest of thousands of our own business men and farmers, the foreign Nations, by way of retaliation, raised high tariff fences of their own.

By way of parenthesis, I might add that our own tariff fence increased the cost to the farmer of manufactured articles used by him on his farm and in his household, while at the same time it did not prevent foreign competition with him in many lines of agricultural products. It is a simple fact that the farmers of America have been buying in a protected market and selling in a market open to the competition of the whole world.

It is time for this Nation to use a little horse sense about the objective we seek and the results of our present tariff law. It is time for us to sit down with other Nations and say to them: "This tariff fence business, on our part and on yours, is preventing world trade. Let us see if we can work out reciprocal methods by which we can start the actual interchange of goods. We do not ask you to buy our goods for cash because we know you do not have the cash, but we do suggest that it would be good for us and for you if we could send to you each year a large volume of American products in exchange for your products. We recognize the fact that we can probably use many of your articles and at the same time we can start our own wheels of industry going in manufacturing the things you need and want — all with adequate safeguards for the American standards of labor."

I have good reason to believe that many Nations which, like us, are suffering from stoppage of industry, will meet us half way and put all the cards on the table for the purpose of breaking an actual deadlock which has paralyzed world trade and thrown millions here and abroad out of useful work.

Let me at the same time make it clear that a trade conference with the other Nations of the world does not and should not, by any stretch of the imagination, involve the United States in any participation in political controversies in Europe or elsewhere. Nor does it involve the renewal in any way of the problem of twelve years ago of American participation as a member of the League of Nations. . . .

28 ⟨ Governor's Statement upon Approving Bills Providing Additional Credit Facilities for Crop Production. March 17, 1932

It is a great satisfaction to me to be able to give my approval to this group of four bills whose purpose is to relieve the pressing need of farmers in this State for additional credit facilities to finance their crop production activities.

The four bills are the result of recommendations made to me by the Governor's Agricultural Advisory Commission on January twentieth of this year following a study of the acute credit situation resulting from the closing of many banks and a consequent lack of funds to meet seasonal needs. On that same date I addressed a message to the Legislature urging the early passage of legislation along the lines embodied in these bills.

Of the four bills one will permit banks to purchase stock in agricultural credit corporations to discount farmers' notes and rediscount them with the Federal Intermediate Credit Bank; the second will permit the formation of agricultural credit corporations for the same purpose under the general corporation law; the third will permit the formation of cooperative credit corporations for the same purpose, and the fourth will permit existing cooperative organizations of producers to form similar credit corporations to accomplish the same end.

I believe the enactment of this legislation will help very materially to remedy a situation that threatened to paralyze the farming industry in some sections of the State and to ruin many individual farmers.

IV

Public Water Power Development and Cheaper Electricity in the Home and on the Farm

INTRODUCTORY NOTE: The subject of water power development was discussed by me in my 1928 Acceptance Speech and in various speeches during my first campaign for the Governorship (see Items 1 and 6 of this volume). It was also discussed in detail in my first Inaugural Address, and in my first Annual Message to the Legislature (see Items 13 and 14 of this volume, on pages 77 and 82).

The speeches and messages contained in this chapter treat the question of the development of water power in greater detail.

The subject matter of this chapter must be considered contemporaneously and in conjunction with the subject matter of Chapter VII, "Regulation of Utilities." The purposes of proper public power development and proper public utility regulation are the same; namely, to restore to the people effective control by them over modern electrical services which have become essentials in modern standards of living and to make certain an ample supply of these services at a reasonable price.

During my four years as Governor, a definite pattern of policy was formulated with respect to power development and utility regulation which may be summarized as follows:

1. Development of major water power resources by agencies of government as the inalienable possession of the people.
2. Marketing of the power from such public developments, if possible, through private agencies under contracts assuring the lowest possible electric rates based on actual cost of service.
3. Cost of service to include a fair return on money actually and prudently invested in plant and working capital, the fair re-

turn to be determined in terms of actual bond interest, plus actual dividends on preferred stock, plus from 6 percent to 8 percent on the remaining equity in the property.

4. Availability of public transmission and distribution as an alternative if the companies refused to make contracts on these terms.

5. Provision for municipal operation of electrical utilities as a means of reducing rates, if authorized by a referendum vote of the citizens.

6. Strengthening of regulation by restoring the original conception of the Public Service Commission as an administrative representative of the people rather than as a judicial body holding the balance between the public and the powerful monopolistic utility corporations.

7. Determination of rate bases on the basis of actual and proper cost in order to eliminate involved valuation proceedings which had served the companies as a means of thwarting effective regulation.

8. Regulation and supervision of holding companies.

9. Extension of rural electrification to every farm, through the elimination of differentials in rates and line construction charges tending to make the service more expensive in the country than in the city, on the principle of equal pay for equal service throughout the State.

The development of this pattern will be seen from the papers in this chapter and in Chapter VII dealing with the regulation of utilities.

My attempts in 1929 to enact legislation for the public development of the water power of the State were unsuccessful (see Item 30 of this volume).

In my Annual Message of January 1, 1930 (see Item 15 of this volume on page 91), I renewed my proposal.

Finally, on January 13, 1930, the deadlock was broken, and an agreement was reached with the Republican majority in the Legislature upon a bill providing for a commission to make a survey and to bring in by January 15, 1931, the most practicable plan of development. This bill is described in my statement of January 14, 1930 (see Item 31 of this volume).

The history of the conflict between those who believed that the development of water-generated electricity should be undertaken by private capital and those who believed in public development, as well as an outline of the bill itself, were given in my speech of January 18, 1930 (see Item 32 of this volume).

The bill was finally passed, and was signed by me on March 29, 1930.

On August 13, 1930, I appointed the members of the St. Lawrence Power Development Commission — Robert M. Haig, Chairman, Julius Henry Cohen, Frederick M. Davenport, Thomas F. Conway and Samuel L. Fuller. On August 30, 1930, they met with me at the site of the St. Lawrence project, and organized for work. On December 4, 1930, the Commission conferred in Washington with President Hoover, with representatives of the State Department, and with officials of the Federal Power Commission. On December 20, the Commission conferred with the Hydro-Electric Power Commission of Ontario.

The discussion with President Hoover included the problem of cooperation between the Federal authorities and the New York agencies. At this conference the opinion was expressed by President Hoover that answers to specific questions could not be given until the problem had been developed further through negotiations between the United States and Canada.

During my campaign for reelection in 1930, I kept the St. Lawrence development continually in the foreground as a major campaign issue (see, for example, Items 87 and 90 of this volume), pointing out that the St. Lawrence Power Development Commission was about to bring in a plan, and that the crucial test would have to be met in Albany in 1931, to determine finally whether or not a plan for public development in the interest of the people, rather than private development for private interest, would prevail. I pointed out that even if a plan of public development were certain to be adopted in 1931, it would still be dangerous to leave the carrying out of the plan to the party which had always opposed public development.

The St. Lawrence Power Development Commission rendered its report on January 15, 1931, finding the project feasible from an engineering and financial point of view.

In my special message to the Legislature, dated January 19, 1931 (see Item 33, this volume), I discussed and summarized the majority and minority reports of the Commission. I pointed out the extent to which they embodied the objectives for which I had been contending, particularly that in distribution of the power, first consideration should be given to securing the lowest possible rates for small users, and that something more effective than Public Service Commission regulation must be depended upon to assure such low rates.

On March 2, 1931, a bill drafted by the majority of the Commission was introduced, the important principles of which were outlined in statements by me dated the same day and printed as Item 34 in this volume.

After the bill had been passed by the Assembly, it was announced by the Republican leader of the Senate, Senator John Knight, that the bill would be amended so as to include the names of the power authority which was proposed to be set up by the statute, instead of leaving the appointments to the Governor.

This led to the statement by me of April 2, 1931, printed as Item 35 of this volume, charging that this unacceptable amendment was deliberately proposed in order to kill the bill and postpone action for another year. The next day I announced my intention of appealing directly to the people by radio. During the next four days so many messages, telegrams and letters poured in upon the members of the Senate in support of the program of public development, that Senator Knight was forced to abandon his attempt to amend the bill, and it was passed on April 7, 1931, without amendment.

I made the scheduled radio address (see Item 36 of this volume) April 7, 1931, but used the occasion to point out the force which public opinion may exert upon legislation, as exemplified by the events of those four days.

On April 27, 1931, I signed the bill as Chapter 772 of the Laws of New York, 1931.

The bill created the Power Authority of the State of New York to improve the St. Lawrence River for commerce, navigation and hydro-electric purposes, under the definite policy declared in the law that the St. Lawrence River within the State's boundaries was a natural resource of the State, and that the bed and waters of the river and the power and power sites should always remain inalienable to the people of the State. It directed the Power Authority to develop power primarily in the interest of domestic and rural consumers, to make available such power at reasonable cost to municipalities authorized to engage in the distribution of electric current, to negotiate contracts for the transmission of power in order to obtain the lowest possible rates for domestic and rural use, and, in the event of its inability to obtain such a contract, to report that fact to the Legislature, together with plans for the transmission of the power in some other way, including the actual building of transmission lines. The proposed contract was to include terms which would enable the initial rate to consumers to be fixed in the contract and to be adjusted from time to time on the basis of true cost data.

On May 6, 1931, the five trustees were appointed as follows: Frank P. Walsh, Chairman, Delos M. Cosgrove, Morris L. Cooke, James C. Bonbright, Fred J. Freestone. Mr. Leland Olds became Executive Secretary.

The Power Authority immediately began technical studies covering in general the cost of transmitting and distributing St. Lawrence current, rural electrification with special reference to low-cost current, the coordination of St. Lawrence power with other sources of power throughout the State, and means of attracting industry to Northern New York to utilize the power at high-load factors.

Between June, 1931, and October, 1931, the Power Authority,

with such support as I could give it as Governor, made every effort to secure from the Federal Government recognition of the interests of the State of New York in the proposed treaty negotiations with Canada for the development of the St. Lawrence which were, according to reports and rumor, about to begin.

It was anticipated early in 1929 that soon after President Hoover's inauguration, negotiations between the United States and Canada for a St. Lawrence treaty would be resumed. Nothing was initiated, however, until 1930, when the two Governments exchanged brief notes. Actual negotiations were not undertaken until November, 1930.

A letter from me to President Hoover, dated June 11, 1931, suggesting the appointment of Delos M. Cosgrove, one of the members of the New York State Power Authority, as a member of the Treaty Commission, in order to represent the State of New York in the proposed treaty negotiations, received only formal acknowledgment by the President's secretary. A letter from the Power Authority to President Hoover, dated July 25, 1931, requesting a conference at which the respective rights and interests of the Federal Government and the State of New York might be considered, received a reply from the President that "an international agreement must be entered into between the United States and Canada before any steps can be taken in the matter you discuss."

This attitude toward the efforts of New York to establish a cooperative arrangement under which the State's power project would go forward harmoniously with the Federal navigation undertaking was consistently maintained by the Federal Administration until the treaty with Canada was actually signed on July 18, 1932. The Power Authority repeatedly urged that the interests of the State of New York be recognized in connection with the negotiation of the treaty, in order to avoid conflict and confusion. The Power Authority pointed out that the Canadian Government had announced its intention of consulting the interested provinces of Canada in order to reach an understanding regarding the respective rights of the Dominion and the interested provinces prior to signing the treaty. Finally, the Secretary of State arranged for a conference at the Department of State with the Power Authority, at which the Power Authority presented several views in a memorandum. The Secretary of State, on November 3, 1931, made formal reply recognizing the desirability of cooperation between the representatives of the Federal Government and of the New York Power Authority; and stating his readiness to confer with the trustees and place them in contact with the technical agents of the Federal Government. He stated, however, that whatever the rights of the State of New York may be in respect to electric power must in the end depend upon the authority and permission of the Federal Government.

On December 8, 1931, a series of conferences between representatives of the State Department and the Power Authority commenced, which extended until June, 1932, when it became apparent to the Power Authority that the Federal Administration had no intention of arriving at any definitive understanding with New York State prior to the signing of the treaty.

After many conferences with the State Department, and upon learning that a treaty between the United States and Canada was about to be signed without any arrangement between the Federal Administration and the State of New York, the trustees reported to me on July 8, 1932, on the status of the negotiations. Thereupon, the following day, July 9, 1932, I sent a telegram to President Hoover, printed in Item 38 of this volume, requesting a conference with him in order to reach an agreement with special reference to the respective shares of the cost of the entire project to be borne by the State and the Federal Government in order to make possible early submission of the treaty to the Senate.

On July 10th President Hoover replied by telegram rejecting this proposal. This telegram is also included in Item 38 of this volume.

This exchange of telegrams brought to a conclusion twelve months of effort on the part of my Administration as Governor to establish a basis of cooperation with the Federal Administration.

On July 18, 1932, a little over a week after the exchange of telegrams between President Hoover and myself, the St. Lawrence Treaty was signed.

Meanwhile the Power Authority in an interim report to me, dated December 31, 1931, pointed out the difficulty it faced in trying to negotiate the contract for the disposition of St. Lawrence power, in view of the fact that there was one huge corporation in upper New York State which occupied a monopolistic advantage in bidding for distribution of the electricity. The Power Authority therefore recommended the enactment of bills permitting municipalities, with the consent of their citizens, to engage in the distribution of electricity.

In a special message to the Legislature, dated February 15, 1932 (see Item 37 of this volume), I recommended the enactment of such legislation as a means of reducing electric rates as well as a means of providing distribution for St. Lawrence power and enabling the State more quickly to obtain all of the benefits of the development.

See also my Annual Messages to the Legislature of 1931 and 1932 (Items 17 and 18 of this volume, pages 106, 122), for further discussion of water power development and cheap electricity.

In addition to the documents printed in this chapter on the subject of development of water power, see also the following: Message to Legislature, March 26, 1929, *Public Papers* (1929), page 171; Statement on signing Development Commission Bill, March 29, 1930, *Public Papers* (1930), page 438.

During my campaign for the Presidency in 1932, and particularly in my campaign addresses at Portland, Oregon, September 21 (see Item 138 of this volume), at Los Angeles, September 24, and at Milwaukee, September 29, I referred to the significance of the St. Lawrence project and stressed particularly the importance of having these great power developments — these "yardsticks" — as a means of insuring consumers, particularly small domestic and rural consumers, against excessive rates.

For a statement of further developments in connection with the St. Lawrence Treaty, the reader is referred to Item 7 of Vol. III.

29 ❲A Letter to Senator Robert F. Wagner on Diversion of Water from the Niagara River. February 9, 1929

Dear Senator Wagner:

I HAVE delayed answering your letter of February 2nd for several days because it brings up a matter very vital to the interests of the people of the State of New York.

You ask me three specific questions in regard to the attitude of this State concerning the convention signed at Ottawa between representatives of the United States and the Government of Canada in relation to the diversion of water in the Niagara River above Niagara Falls.

This convention is intended primarily to preserve the scenic beauty of Niagara Falls by preventing rapid erosion of the center of the crest of the Falls through erection of weirs or other structures in the bed of the river above the Falls on both the New York side and the Ontario side, thus diverting sufficient water to the wings of the Falls.

This convention is the result of careful study made by the International Niagara Board. This Board worked out a plan under which an offer of the Hydro-Electric Power Commission of Ontario and the Niagara Falls Power Company, a private corporation of New York State, was recommended for acceptance. Under this offer the Ontario Commission and the New York private corporation agreed to build the necessary weirs and structures in the bed of the river and asked in return the use, for a period of seven years, during the six winter months of each year, of 10,000 cubic feet per second of water on each side of the river. It is estimated that this 10,000 cubic feet per second on the American side would enable the Niagara Falls Power Company to develop between 80,000 and 100,000 horse power.

First of all I want to call your attention to the important fact that quite aside from the merits of this proposal the State of New York was in no way invited to participate in the discussions attending this proposal; to the second important fact that the proposed weirs and structures would have to be erected on the bed of the Niagara River owned by the State of New York; and to the third important fact that use of the 10,000 cubic feet per second proposed to be withdrawn depends on the consent of the State of New York to that withdrawal and to the satisfying of the State of New York that if it is withdrawn the people of the State are to receive an adequate rental for this water.

In regard to the three categorical questions you ask me, I beg to advise you as follows:

(1) In pursuance of its long-standing policy, the State of New York requires that its consent is prerequisite before any disposition can be made of the additional 10,000 cubic feet per second of water made available for power development by the convention.

(2) In pursuance of the same policy of long standing the State of New York requires a charge for the use of such additional water, said charge or rental being determined in pursuance of the statutes of the State.

(3) In your other question you ask whether the State accepts the proposal to have the work of preserving the Falls undertaken at private expense, and at the same time making available for private utilization by the Niagara Falls Power Company of the additional water to be diverted under the convention for a temporary period.

A careful reading of the proposed convention discloses the fact that the letter of the Secretary of State transmitting the convention refers to a protocol to be agreed to between the United States and Canada. The protocol itself is appended to the convention and the protocol refers to the recommendations of the International Niagara Board. In other words, the three documents must be read together, and it becomes at once clear that the Treaty itself is essentially an agreement to carry out a specific plan heretofore adopted. If the State of New York offers no objection to the ratification of the Treaty by the Senate of the United States, the State may by inference be bound to the acceptance of the plan worked out between the International Niagara Board on the one side and the Ontario Power Commission and the Niagara Falls Power Company on the other. My easiest course, as Governor, would have been to ask you and your colleague in the United States Senate to oppose the ratification of the Treaty as strongly as possible on the ground that the Treaty ties the hands of the State of New York as to the methods by which the beautification and diversion can be arrived at, and forces the State to accept the offer of the Niagara Falls Power Company.

I think that I can speak for the whole State in telling you that we want to cooperate with the Federal Government and the Congress of the United States in every way possible to aid in the preservation of the scenic beauty of Niagara Falls and the Niagara River. That is why instead of direct opposition to the ratification of the Treaty, I have tried, in a spirit of cooperation, to enter into a plan by which the scenic beauty of the Falls can be preserved and at the same time all of the rights of the people of the State of New York in and to their property and governmental powers can be equally retained.

After a number of conferences, I am glad to say that I have been able to obtain from the Niagara Falls Power Company a written stipulation duly executed by it, which stipulation fully preserves the property rights and governmental authority of this State.

I might note the following facts in regard to the Niagara Falls Power Company:

1. It is the only private company now in a position immediately and economically to utilize the proposed experimental diversion of the additional 10,000 cubic feet per second of water.
2. The Niagara Falls Power Company has for a number of years been paying a rental to the State of New York for the water which it is now using.
3. The Niagara Falls Power Company has paid this rental to the State under protest.

The stipulation signed by the Niagara Falls Power Company states that if it is allowed to use for seven years the additional water obtained from this experimental diversion, it will

1. Withdraw all objections to the payment of the rental now being charged by the State for existing water,
2. Agree to pay such equitable rental for the additional experimental supply as may be determined by the State under the Water Power Act, and
3. Recognize the necessity of obtaining a license from the State for the use of this experimental water.

This is a complete recognition of the right and sovereignty of the State of New York to license and rent all water now being used by the company and all water to be used under the provisions of the convention and protocol.

It is, of course, clear that the proposed treaty with Canada is a temporary measure only, running for the diversion period of only seven years, and that the State of New York is in no way restricted as to its full control of this water after the seven-year period has run. The stipulation received by the State of New York clears up the matters long in dispute between it and the private company and makes it perfectly clear that the State has the full sovereignty and control over the water on the American side of the Niagara River for all time.

I am very happy that the State by this stipulation obtains all that it has in the past claimed from the Niagara Falls Power Company as its rights at this particular site and that the State can contribute in a constructive way to the beautification of the Falls which is the primary object of this convention.

It is obvious that though the factor of scenic beauty exists in this particular case it should not be considered in any way as modifying the policy of this State at other power sites in regard to the development of water power under direct State control and possession.

The State reserves every right to make a different arrangement at the termination of the seven-year period should the diversion be made permanent or be increased.

I hope that I have made my position clear in this matter.

Sincerely yours,

Hon. Robert F. Wagner,
United States Senate,
Washington, D. C.

NOTE: The proposed Convention and Protocol was subsequently rejected by the United States Senate Committee on Foreign Relations.

30 ❡ The Governor Proposes a Plan for the Development of the Water Power Resources of the St. Lawrence River. March 12, 1929

To the Legislature:

FOR a generation the need for power for industrial and domestic purposes has been steadily increasing, and during this period the ownership by the people of the State of New York of a vast potential source of energy in their portion of the waters of the St. Lawrence River has received increasing public attention.

In the past the actual necessity for the development of this potential energy has not been wholly clear but in more recent times the great preponderance of informed opinion recognizes the immediate need for action.

The State owns or controls other much smaller water-power rights but it seems to me best at this time to focus recommendations and public attention on the development of the St. Lawrence River.

In making use of this potential energy on the St. Lawrence owned by the people of the State, the objective of the problem is essentially this:

1. The physical transforming of falling water into electrical current.

2. The transmission and distribution of this current from the plant where it is developed to the industries and homes of the people of the State.

As this St. Lawrence power source is the property of the people of the State, we can, I think, all agree to the principle that the actual energy therefrom should be, for all time, under the immediate control of the people of the State and should be transmitted and distributed to the people of the State at the lowest practical cost.

Let me briefly develop these underlying principles. In the manner of the actual development of the St. Lawrence power, it is not enough that the ultimate title vest in the State. I hope there will be no difficulty in securing agreement that not only title but physical possession of the development should at all times be in direct representatives of the people.

At least of equal importance is the problem of transmission and distribution to the ultimate consumer. A mere development of power at a low production cost is insufficient unless, at the same time, we make certain that it is finally distributed to the ultimate consumer at a fair price, under which no individual or corporation, involved in the business of transmitting or distributing, will make more than a reasonable profit.

Right there we are confronted with a double difficulty.

First arises the question of who should do the transmitting and distributing of the power actually generated by representatives of the people of the State. I follow, I think, the opinion of my distinguished predecessor in saying that because of the complications involved, the actual operation of a transmission or a distribution system in this field of activity should, if possible with safety to the people, be undertaken by private enterprise, and that the State should undertake it only if private enterprise proves that it cannot, or will not, successfully carry out the task.

In regard to the second point involving the actual rates to be charged to consumers, we are confronted with what many believe to be ineffectiveness of the present rate-regulating powers of the

Public Service Commission. When this Commission was first created, about twenty-five years ago, the basic purpose was to provide fair rates based on fair return to private capital. It was recognized then that private capital entering the public utility field would be distinguished from private capital entering wholly private fields of industry, in that the profit to a public utility company would be limited, and sums earned over and above a fair return, would be passed back to the consumer in the form of lower rates.

Since that time a series of court decisions, especially in the Federal Courts, has to a large extent nullified the protection originally intended for the consumer. Originally it was intended that fair earnings should be limited to the actual cash capital invested, but today it is notorious that because of court rulings involving replacement value, "going value," so-called good-will, return on capital, and allowances for surplus, there have been made legally possible investment returns as high as fifty percent or even one hundred percent annually on the original investment.

That is why in trying to treat this whole problem of development, transmission and distribution of St. Lawrence power as a complete picture in the interests of the people of the State, I have sought a method by which we could avoid the rate-regulating power of the Public Service Commission, tied up as it is at the present time by Federal Court rulings. I have, therefore, after consultation with many experts on the subject, come to the conclusion that the representatives or trustees who develop the power can enter into contracts with transmitting and distributing companies, under which a fair price to the consumer will be guaranteed, this price to make allowances only for a fair return to the companies on the actual capital invested in the transmitting and distributing of this particular power energy. It is a method which is frankly based on the theory of contract rather than the theory of regulation.

To meet this problem the Federal Power Commission has made special rules for setting up capital investment, limited wholly to actual cash, less property deduction for obsolescence, depreciation and the like. But in the Federal Government these rules are valuable in practice only in case the Government wishes to recapture a plant built under license from the Board. There is, however, no reason why the State of New York should not apply the principle of such rules for the purpose of making contracts for the transmission and distribution of its power. Those who have thoughtfully considered the matter see but one way to protect the consumer and to prevent the exploitation of our water power again: that is, by applying the principle of making the right to have power from the power station depend absolutely on a fixed maximum return on actual investment, with books kept in accordance with rules fixed and agreed upon in advance. This is one of the methods proposed in the House of Representatives for dealing with the Boulder Dam project. It is neither Republican nor Democratic in principle. It is just a sound business method used in the public interest.

I want to reiterate that the St. Lawrence problem involves not only the actual development of the site or sites, but must be thought through to the legitimate end of guaranteeing to the consumer, after the power has been transmitted and is ready for distribution, a final price based only on a fair return on actual investment.

Now, as to machinery. I have spent many hours and many days in a study of the mechanics of the problem. I am very certain that we have today in existence sufficient data and facts to justify the elimination of any further study as to mere physical feasibility. I have gone over volumes of carefully gathered information, including a comprehensive physical survey of the suggested site or sites on the St. Lawrence River made by the Frontier Power Company. Everything points to the practicability of building a dam. Furthermore, it is my judgment that no insuperable difficulty lies in the relationship between the State of New York on the one side and the United States Government or the Canadian Government on the other side. To appoint a mere commission to make inquiries would get us nowhere, unless we create a body with authority to make, subject to the approval of the Legislature, definite agreements on the basis of a definite, carefully worked out plan.

In the same way a mere investigating body could get nowhere with conversations with the representatives of private capital in regard to transmission and distribution of power, whereas a body clothed with authority to negotiate with transmitters, distributors, and bankers, on the basis of a comprehensive and definite plan, stands an excellent chance of accomplishing results.

I propose, therefore, the creation of a body of five representative citizens, regardless of political considerations, to be known as the Trustees of the Water Power Resources on the St. Lawrence River. It is my thought that these trustees should be composed of men in whom there is great public confidence, such as former Governor Charles Evans Hughes, and former Governor Alfred E. Smith.

In its inception these trustees would constitute a planning and negotiating commission, and would be charged with the duty of reporting a definite plan and a specific contract for the approval of the Legislature, on January 15, 1930. Before such a plan could go into effect it would require legislative approval. If and when approved, by the Legislature, the trustees would automatically be charged with the duty of carrying the plan into effect.

These trustees would examine into the engineering phases of the problem and bring in figures as to the practicability and the cost, and would, of course, secure the aid of the best impartial experts available. They would confer with the various Federal authorities, with the International Joint Commission, and through proper constitutional channels with the Government of Canada and its provinces for the purpose of advising the Legislature what definite steps should be taken by treaty, Federal legislation, or otherwise, to secure complete cooperation. They would confer with representatives of existing or prospective distributors of electric power for the purpose of arranging by contract for the sale of St. Lawrence power to the ultimate consumer after allowing a fair and reasonable return on actual capital investment.

In other words, I propose that the Trustees should bring in a complete plan for the development of the State's water power resources on the St. Lawrence and that this plan should conform to a definite statement of two basic principles which I believe to be the policy desired by a great majority of our citizens.

These two basic principles are:

1. The natural water power sites on the St. Lawrence now owned by the people of the State or hereafter to be recovered, shall remain forever inalienable to the people, and any dams or plants necessary to generate power shall be built, financed, owned, operated, and occupied by the trustees, as the duly constituted instrumentality of the State.

2. Power developed therefrom shall be transmitted and distributed, if possible, through the employment of private capital so as to secure adequate distribution throughout the State. This distribution, however, shall secure the lowest rates to consumers compatible with a fair and reasonable return on actual cash investment. The rates, in other words, shall be based on actual cash outlay — that is to say, operating expenses, capital outlay representing money actually spent in plant investment, and working capital — with reasonable allowance for obsolescence and depreciation, and a return on the investment not exceeding the interest actually paid on borrowed money and dividend rates not in excess of current rates on preferred stock, and not to exceed 8 percent on all other cash capital. In other words, the power generated by the agency of the State, called the Trustees, shall be sold only on a contract basis which will take into definite consideration all the steps between the sale at the power house and the ultimate sale to the home owner or industrial establishment.

I want to see something done. I want it done in accordance with sound public policy. I want hydro-electric power developed on the St. Lawrence, but I want the consumers to get the benefit of it when it is developed. They must not be left for their sole protection to existing methods of rate-making by the Public Service Commission. Are the business men of this State willing to transmit and distribute this latent water power on a fair return on their investment? If they are satisfied, here is their opportunity. If not, then the State may have to go into the transmission business itself. It cannot on the one hand let this power go to waste, nor on the other be required to yield to anyone who would aim to exploit the State's resources for inordinate profit.

We shall soon know whether or not such a contract can be made. If the Trustees can make it and it commends itself to the people of the State, then the Legislature and I will approve it and we can go ahead. But, if no such contract can be made we shall know the reasons why and protect ourselves accordingly. I want to be in accord with sound business principles. I believe there are enough good business men in this State who see this problem as clearly as I do and will be glad to join with the State in this endeavor. I want to give to business this big opportunity to participate in a public service.

If these proposals become law we shall have the opportunity of ascertaining whether or not business and finance will accept this way of developing the State's resources for its industries, its commerce, and its homes. On the one hand is the policy of public ownership and control of our power sites, dams, and power plants, with private operation of transmission lines and distributing systems, allowing a fair return on actual cash capital investment. On the other side is one of two courses — either exploitation by private interests or else public ownership and operation not only of the site, the dam, and the power, but of the transmission lines and distribution systems as well.

Instead of asking an individual member of the Senate or the Assembly to introduce definite legislation in accordance with this message, I am appending hereto a suggested Act carrying out the principles and the plan which I am advocating. I shall, of course, be glad to confer with any of the members or committees of your Honorable Bodies in regard to what I conceive to be a matter of the utmost importance to this State. I hope you will agree with me that this problem which has been so much discussed is now ripe for some form of definite action and that it is great enough to take it wholly away from the field of partisan politics.

31 ❨ The Governor Hails the Agreement on a Bill Creating a Commission to Prepare Plan for Development of St. Lawrence Hydro-Electric Power. January 14, 1930

I HOPE and believe that yesterday will go down into the history of our State as a red letter day. The Water Power bill introduced in the Legislature, while requiring certain changes to clarify it, is of such outstanding importance that every man, woman and child in the State who uses electricity has cause to rejoice.

The bill ends a controversy over a great principle which began more than twenty years ago and has been acutely argued during each one of the past ten years.

The bill introduced last night is of far greater importance than merely the removal of this great subject from the field of temporary politics, for it represents a definite approval of what the majority of people in this State have been striving for regardless of party lines — a sincere effort on the part of the State to develop, through a State agency, the great electric power of the St. Lawrence River.

On the one side a powerful group has insisted that the State-owned water power to be developed by private corporations or leased to them for generations, relying for protection of the public consumers wholly on Public Service Commission regulation. On the other side what is, I believe, an overwhelming public sentiment has insisted that the State retain constant control of its great electric power resources, develop them, and sell the electricity by contract in such a way that the consuming public will be assured of cheap lighting and power.

The issue has been beclouded and befogged from time to time by efforts to magnify mere details and take away public interest by the cry of "politics," and the seeking of partisan advantage. In spite of this, the big principle has remained the same and a deadlock has existed between what have been clearly and definitely two schools of thought.

Now at last the deadlock is broken. Last night's bill is a definite recognition of the principle for which my school of thought has striven so long.

I had asked for practical legislation on broad lines as follows:

1. The creation of a Board of Trustees to bring in a plan. This is given by the bill with the change of the word "Trustees" to "Commissioners."

2. These Trustees (or Commissioners) to bring in a plan for development of the St. Lawrence by a State agency. This is directed by the bill.

3. The sale of electricity for consumers' use by the contract method. This is directed by the bill.

4. A report on this plan to the Legislature for approval or rejection. This is directed by the bill.

5. If accepted by the Legislature, the creation of permanent Trustees to carry out the plan. This is completely set up by the bill.

I am feeling very happy that the great principles involved are recognized by this proposed legislation and if it is passed by the Legislature I shall, of course, do everything in my power to further the practical working out of a plan based on the principles.

Let me repeat that the furtherance of the fundamental principles involved marks the greatest step forward which has been taken by any State in the Union in the solution of the much controverted power problem. It will mark a wholly new phase of the task of providing electricity to the homes of the people at low rates.

32 ❧ The Governor Discusses the History of the St. Lawrence Power Fight. Address before the State Bar Association. January 18, 1930

I WANT to outline to you tonight a subject which, on its face, is not confined to the interest of the legal profession. You, however, with the other citizens of the State, have read of the proposal made a few days ago by legislative leaders which makes possible the termination of a ten-year deadlock on the subject of the development of State-owned water power.

That the future of the great public utility known as electricity must be of some interest to the legal profession may be illustrated by an experience I had last year in seeking to find an appointee to the Public Service Commission from a certain district in this State.

In evolving a list of names of approximately fifty lawyers of real standing in their profession in this district, I came, on investigation, to the discovery that every one of these gentlemen was in some shape, manner or form the legal representative of some utility company or some utility interest. I do not mention this as being derogatory to the fitness of lawyers as a whole to represent the public interests in this particular field, but merely as an illustration of the fact that the legal profession is very much concerned with the general problems of the development of utilities.

It is interesting, also, that during the past five days I have discussed with at least one hundred people the new proposal for the development of the St. Lawrence power and only one of these individuals had even read the proposed law. All of the other ninety-nine had based their opinions either on the statements of political leaders or on the accounts which they had read in the public press.

May I, therefore, present to you as a "brief" a short account of just what has happened in the past and just what is proposed for the future.

The St. Lawrence Power Fight

More than twenty years ago, certain far-seeing gentlemen applied to the Legislature for a State franchise to develop the water power on the St. Lawrence River in what is known as the "International Section" at the Long Sault Rapids. That these gentlemen asked for a legislative charter was proof conclusive that the State has a very definite interest in the property. This charter was granted by the Legislature, but a few years later, with the growing knowledge of what the Legislature had given away without compensation to the State, another Legislature repealed the charter and every right that it conferred.

For a number of years there was no open effort on the part of private companies or of the State to develop the latent water power of the St. Lawrence. Gradually, however, an issue was joined between two schools of economic and social thought, the one holding that the development of electricity should be undertaken wholly by private capital, the other holding that this great natural resource was of such tremendous importance to the future population of the State that its constant control should never pass from the hands of the State.

The next step was the passage of a water power act by which certain State officials were given the right to lease the State power properties, and very soon an application was made by the Frontier Power Company for a lease of the St. Lawrence rights for a term of fifty years. This in itself seemed to be in the nature of a compromise offer by those who had hitherto been willing to have the State actually sell its rights. This school was willing to admit that the ultimate fee of the title should remain in the State, but at the same time insisted that the fee could be leased for long periods of time extending into the dim, distant future. As you all know, the effort to obtain this long-term lease was blocked by my predecessor not only on the technical ground that the lease actually proposed was illegal, but on the broader ground that it was contrary to a sound public policy.

For a number of years the two schools of thought remained at complete loggerheads. One, represented by the Republican Party and Republican platforms, was willing to grant leases for all of the State's rights and properties for long periods, though admitting that the nominal ownership should rest in the State. The other school of thought, represented by the Democratic Party and its platforms, asked for the actual physical development of the electrical energy on the St. Lawrence through a State agency and the retaining of the physical manufacture of electricity, and possibly its transmission, in the hands of the State agency at all times. This was the situation when I took office a year ago.

2. THE PRESENT SITUATION

The next step, and the one which has brought the question finally to a head, was the definite proposal of a law which I submitted in March to the Legislature of 1929.

The principles of this plan can best be explained by comparing its purpose with the bill introduced last Monday in the Legislature of 1930. By so doing we can arrive at a wholly fair estimate of what the new legislative offer actually is.

3. THE BILL ITSELF

1. The title of the new bill is in itself important, for it is called, "An Act to declare the policy of the State in respect to its water power resources, and to provide for the appointment by the Governor of a commission."

Please note that the title itself sets up a policy.

2. Section 1 of the bill is in very definite terms the enunciation of the policy called for by the title to the Act, and because it uses the identical language, word for word, with the language of my bill of 1929, I hope that every citizen of this State will read it. It is as follows:

"The natural water power sites in, upon or adjacent to the St. Lawrence River, owned or controlled by the people, or which may hereafter be recovered by them or come within their ownership and control, shall remain inalienable to, and ownership and control shall remain always vested in the people."

It is a simple fact that this key clause has been incorporated in identical language, without the changing of a letter or a syllable, taken directly from my bill of last year. In this fact lies the justification for the simple, unequivocal statement that this new bill of 1930 is a complete conversion to my policy on the part of the legislative leaders, and is an acceptance of the principle for which I have fought so long.

3. The new bill in Section 2 directs the Governor to appoint five commissioners to bring in a plan or plans. It calls these five gentlemen "commissioners" instead of "trustees" as I had suggested, and removes the requirement of the consent of the Senate to their appointment.

4. The third section of the new bill covers the scope of the inquiry and is in purpose and language substantially similar to the corresponding part of last year's bill. This section has the addition of a new sentence which states that in the event that the commissioners determine that the development by the State, through a State agency, is not feasible or practicable, they shall determine whether an alternative for development or distribution of power would be more beneficial, and shall report such an alternative plan. It is, of course, obvious to any reasonable person that I could have no objection to this sentence, for, as a matter of fact, there was nothing to have prevented the commissioners, suggested under my plan last year, from stating perfectly frankly that they could not bring in a feasible State agency plan, or from suggesting an alternative plan or plans.

5. The fourth section of the new bill relates to a technical superseding of prior provisions of law and is identical in language with last year's bill.

6. The fifth section of the new bill is identical with my bill of last year, except that it appropriates $200,000 instead of $100,000.

7. The next four sections of the new bill are of the utmost importance because they bear directly on the declaration of policy in the first section of the bill. These last four sections constitute a tentative setting up of an instrumentality of the State, a body

corporate and politic to be known as the "Trustees of the Water Power Resources on the St. Lawrence River."

In my bill the language set up this State agency immediately, but my bill provided, of course, that any actual work of electrical development by this State agency should be dependent upon ratification by the following Legislature of any plan proposed. In other words, I set up the agency but made it impossible for it to start any construction work until the Legislature had given its approval. The new bill merely puts this in different language, saying:

"If a development by a State Authority is recommended in a plan which is approved by the Legislature, it shall be a corporate municipal instrumentality of the State known as the Trustees of the Water Power Resources on the St. Lawrence River."

From thereon, the new bill is identical in principle and practically identical in language with the bill of last year, conferring upon the proposed Trustees of the Water Power Resources the essential duty, rights and legal authority to carry on their work of actual engineering, construction, financing and sale of power.

It is true that the new bill omits a number of sections of last year's bill which were intended to clarify and simplify the work of the proposed commissioners and make their task more simple. Most of the provisions which have been omitted relate to details, but I call your attention at this time to the omission of one declaration of purpose which I believe to be of importance and which I see no reason to leave out in any statement of policy. I refer to the following paragraph of last year's bill which has been omitted this year. It reads as follows:

"The development of the said power sites and the generation, transmission and distribution of power therefrom shall be made in such manner and on such terms as to assure fair and impartial treatment of all consumers at the lowest rates compatible with a fair and reasonable return on the actual cost thereof."

Let the people of this State read and re-read that paragraph. I hope they will. Let them ask the simple question: Does that paragraph state fairly and clearly the purpose of the development of the State's electrical resources? Why it was omitted I do not know. I am certain that the people of this State will agree with me that this paragraph should be put back into the present bill, for it carries with it a simple truth, a simple expectation, and a clear direction to the commissioners that the power must be developed primarily for the good of the consumers and at fair and impartial rates. It will be difficult for any person to defend the omission of this simple statement from any bill.

I shall be interested in knowing what valid reason can possibly be advanced for the omission of this important principle.

Such is the summary of the language and the principles of the new bill which opens a new era for the industries and the homes of the people of the State of New York. Let me briefly recapitulate:

First, the bill accepts, word for word, the same paragraph of State policy which I asked for last year.

Second, the bill creates a body of five citizens whose primary duty shall be to bring in a workable plan based on that policy.

Third, the bill sets up a permanent State agency which will begin to function in the actual work of the development of electrical power just as soon as a succeeding Legislature has approved of the plan submitted.

This does not differ in any essential of basic principle from what so many citizens of the State have demanded in the past.

The important duty of every citizen of the State — lawyers, business men, the press, the agricultural interests, and the average "man in the street" — is from now on to work whole-heartedly for the carrying out of the proposed policy and the plan which, I am confident, will result therefrom. This is not the time for us to pay heed to carping objections as to detail; to monkey wrenches which some people may try to throw into the machinery; to the magnifying of difficulties which can be surmounted if we have the will to surmount them. I am confident that the great majority of citizens of the State want to see something done and that they believe that it is practicable to work out a State agency method of development of our great natural electrical resources in such a way that the control of these resources will never pass from the ownership of the State itself.

33 ❨ The Governor Transmits the Report of the St. Lawrence Power Development Commission. January 19, 1931

To the Legislature:

IN ORDER to clarify and simplify the questions involved in the voluminous and necessarily technical reports of the St. Lawrence Power Commission, I have studied and summarized the problems and the recommendations. Here is the background:

On March 12, 1929, I sent a special message to the Legislature in which I laid down these general principles:

> "In making use of this potential energy on the St. Lawrence, owned by the people of the State, the objective of the problem is essentially this:
> 1. The physical transforming of falling water into electrical current.
> 2. The transmission and distribution of this current from the plant where it is developed to the industries and homes of the people of the State."

The first objective was seriously opposed by many people who insisted for varying motives that the physical building of a dam was fraught with danger; that the cost would be prohibitive; and that generation by steam had become as cheap as by water power.

The Commission unanimously finds:

a. The dam can be built with one hundred percent of safety, actual construction being on dry land by the method of diverting the river first on one side of an island and then on the other side.

b. The cost would be about $70,000,000 less than any previous estimate.

c. The cost of generation per horse power would be $10.00, as against a $25.00 cost for steam power.

This is an outstanding vindication for those of us who have supported the project against insidious propaganda for private development. It should foreclose for all time to come further discussion of public development of the St. Lawrence site.

Next is the question, "Who shall get the power?"

In 1929 and 1930, I consistently held that the power should be developed for the primary benefit of the consumer at the lowest possible rate compatible with a fair return on the investment; and furthermore, I have stressed the fact that the home user is the one to be given first consideration, because today the small home owners and storekeepers are carrying a relatively far greater burden than the industrial user. That is the primary objective of transmission and distribution, and both the majority and minority reports point out that the entire policy of development should be to provide the maximum benefits for domestic consumers, farmers and small users of power. This coincides with my views expressed not only in my message to the Legislature, but a great many times thereafter. I emphasized the fact that my interest in water power development was primarily to get it into the homes of the women of the State and into the small shops and stores, and that only secondarily was it to be used for the huge manufacturing industries.

The majority report says in this connection:

"All effort should be made to secure the maximum possible reduction in rates to domestic and to small commercial users. In other words, we believe that the principle of 'selling on a commercial basis' should be applied to industrial consumers of power, and that the resulting profits on this business should be applied to the reduction of rates of other consumers. . . . Not being in a position to protect themselves by an exercise of their bargaining power, they require the protection of their Government in the enjoyment of service at the lowest possible rates . . . and since the transmission and distribution costs of the industrial power supplied near

187

the site will be very small, a profit may be expected on this part of the business — a profit which should be applied to the reduction of rates to the small customers . . . it must always be borne in mind that as a practical matter, the large consumer of power is able to protect himself much more effectively than the small consumer. For example, he can usually install his own generating plant. Indeed, this possibility has actually resulted in the establishment of comparatively low rates to large industrial users. It is the small consumer who is unable to cope with the situation. It is he who stands in great need of help from the State. In the judgment of the Commissioners the accent should be put upon his needs."

Thus, the entire commission, both the majority and the minority, as well as I myself, is interested chiefly not so much in the disposition of this power to industries which might locate near the St. Lawrence River, but in its cheap sale and transmission to household consumers. Of course, by reason of the fact that the flow of the river is practically constant, the power will be generated during the entire day all the year round at a nearly constant load. Only large industrial plants can use peak power twenty-four hours a day, and it is therefore practicable and feasible to encourage certain types of industry to locate near the site of the power house for the use of this constant load.

Next comes the matter of the price which consumers away from the site itself, principally the small consumers, will have to pay for electricity.

Hitherto we have relied wholly on Public Service Commission regulation of rates. We all know the long story of how court decisions, valuation, rate bases, complicated accountings, newly invented methods of finance, and unsatisfactory leadership in the Public Service Commission itself have made impossible the fulfillment of the original purposes of regulation.

Something new had to be done. I said to the Legislature in 1929:

"That is why in trying to treat this whole problem of development, transmission and distribution of St. Lawrence power as a complete picture in the interests of the people of the State, I have sought a method by which we could avoid the rate regulating powers of the Public Service Commission, tied up as it is at the present time by Federal Court rulings. I have, therefore, after consultation with many experts on the subject, come to the conclusion that the representatives or trustees who develop the power can enter into contracts with transmitting and distribution companies, under which contracts a fair price to the consumer will be guaranteed, this price to make allowances only for a fair return to the companies on the actual capital invested in the transmitting and distributing of this particular power energy. It is a method which is frankly based on theory of contract rather than the theory of regulation."

The majority and the minority of the commission both agree with that statement made by me, — that the rates should not be subject to the control of the Public Service Commission, but should be fixed by contract based on a definite method of accounting and valuation, which would insure fair rates for all time to come.

The majority of the commission states it this way: "There can be no question but that the existence of litigation in rate cases is a waste which should be avoided by the utility companies as well as by the State. If it is found practicable through a process of negotiation to establish a system of rate control by contract which will adequately safeguard the consumer, a great step forward will have been taken."

The minority of the commission says the same thing in another way in recommendation "F": "That the trustees seek to negotiate with the utility companies a contract for the transmission and distribution of the power, which contract by its terms should bind the utility companies to transmit and distribute to consumers all of the power generated at rates or prices to consumers to be fixed in the contract, on the basis of charges, the lowest consistent with a fair return to the power authority on the investment."

The next question is, how to transmit the power, i.e., the question of the main transmission lines to carry the power to points of distribution.

I foresaw, of course, as everyone does, the possibility that existing private companies might refuse to treat with the State on fair terms for the transmission of this electricity under a contractual relationship fixing their rates and profits. It was for that reason that I viewed with such alarm the merger of the three largest holding companies of power corporations into the Niagara Hudson Power Company. The creation of this super-utility deprived the State of its right to bargain with several companies and compelled it to bargain with this company alone.

I want everybody to reread the following clear statement in my 1929 message, for it is just as true now as it was then:

"Are the business men of this State willing to transmit and distribute this latent water power on a fair return on their investment? If they are satisfied, here is their opportunity. If not, then the State itself may have to go into the transmission business. It cannot on the one hand let this power go to waste, nor on the other be required to yield to anyone who would aim to exploit the State's resources for inordinate profit.

"We shall soon know whether or not such a contract can be made. If the trustees can make it and it commends itself to the people of the State, then the Legislature and I will approve it and we can go ahead. But, if no such contract can be made, we shall know the reasons why and protect ourselves accordingly. I want to be in accord with sound business principles. I believe there are enough good business men in this State who see this problem as clearly as I do and will be glad to join with the State in this endeavor. I want to give to business this big opportunity to participate in a public service.

"If these proposals become law, we shall have the opportunity of ascertaining whether or not business and finance will accept this way of developing the State's resources for its industries, its commerce, and its homes. On the one hand is the policy of public ownership and control of our power sites, dams, and power plants, with private operation of transmission lines and distributing systems, allowing a fair return on actual cash capital investment. On the other side is one of two courses — either exploitation by private interests or else public ownership and operation not only of the site, the dam, and the power, but of the transmission lines and distribution systems as well."

What does the commission say? The chief divergence between the majority and minority reports is as follows:

Both favor a contract with a private utility company by which in effect such company can collect only for the actual cost of services rendered plus a reasonable profit. That is the objective of the proposed contract form of delivering the power.

The minority, however, recommends that if such a contract for transmission cannot be made on a fair basis with an existing utility company, the Authority should try to get some other private company, existing or to be organized, to carry the power; and that it is wholly possible to interest private investment in such a company, because the earnings would in effect be based on a firm contract with the Power Authority.

As an alternative to this, if such private transmission cannot be contracted for, the minority report recommends that the Power Authority itself build transmission lines in order to bring the cheap power into the homes and shops of small consumers. In this connection, both the majority and minority of the commission fully realize that municipalities or lighting districts could purchase this cheap power for distribution to their citizens if, because of existing poor service or exorbitant rates, it became necessary.

The majority says: "Your commission is aware that a considerable number of municipal distributing systems are already in existence in New York State, and that they are charging rates which compare very favorably with the rates charged by private companies operating under similar conditions. These municipal systems should be given full opportunity to purchase a reasonable share of the St. Lawrence River power at such prices as may be necessary to cover the cost of generation and of transmission. Moreover, any municipal or other political subdivision of the State that chooses, in the future, to engage in the distribution of electric current, should be given the opportunity to purchase St. Lawrence power on conditions at least as favorable as those which are offered to private distributing systems. In the event that all of the water power shall be sold to private transmission and distribution companies at the generating station, this sale should not be made except under a contractual agreement whereby these companies will transmit a reasonable share of the power to municipal plants at prices representing no more than a fair spread to cover the cost of transmission."

These two alternatives which the Power Authority would have

in determining the method of transmitting electricity, are of course the only bargaining club in its possession in its negotiations with the present utility monopoly. If it did not have these alternatives, the State would be at the complete mercy of the Niagara Hudson Power Company. I believe that these alternatives form the very foundation of the plan which will have its ultimate attainment only when the homes of the State get cheap electricity. I believe that these two alternatives provide the whip hand — the trump card — with which the State can treat with the power trust, and I believe that they should be emphasized to the utmost.

The majority of the commission does not lose sight of this alternative. In fact, it points out in its report, though not in so specific a manner, the efficacy of these alternatives as a bargaining weapon.

The majority report states: "Can satisfactory arrangements be made between the power authority and privately owned transmission and distribution companies. . . . We hope that it will be feasible to make an acceptable contract. A genuine effort should be made to secure such a contract before consideration is given to a plan for State transmission and distribution. . . . In the event of the inability of the trustees to make such a contract, they shall have such authority as is necessary to make other disposition of the power." Of course, the phrase "to make other disposition of the power" would necessarily include the two alternatives about which I have spoken, and it must be clear to anyone reading the report that the majority of the commission is desirous of retaining in the hands of the Power Authority these bargaining weapons with which the State should enter into negotiations with the power companies. The minority report stresses the importance of being specific and clear about the two alternatives, putting them in plain language into the law creating the Power Authority.

I desire to repeat, however, that both reports should be a source of gratification to those of us who have been interested in cheaper electricity in the homes. They show, first, that the power can be developed cheaply; second, that the rates at which it is to be sold to the ultimate consumers should be fixed by contract in the interest of the consumer; third, that if the contract is impossible to obtain, alternative methods should be pursued which would ultimately place this power in the homes of our citizens at low rates; fourth, that the authorities of the United States and Canada have so far evidenced an attitude of friendly cooperation; fifth, that the time is ripe for the creation by the Legislature of a power authority with legislative sanction to proceed to carry to completion its negotiations, as well as such further necessary studies as need be made of the building of transmission lines by the State, or the possibility of the creation of a new corporation to undertake to contract with the State, for the transmission of this cheap electricity.

I trust your Honorable Bodies will study and act on these most vital reports.

34 ❡ The Bill to Develop St. Lawrence Water Power Is Introduced. Statement by the Governor. March 4, 1931

I BELIEVE that the submission of this bill should be hailed by proponents of public, governmental water-power development as a remarkable step toward the attainment of their ultimate goal. If you had told the most ardent and enthusiastic three years ago that such a bill would be possible today, they would have laughed at you. And yet, here we are with a definite, concrete proposal, submitted after a careful survey by a commission authorized by the Legislature and equipped with expert legal and engineering assistance, which embodies every sound principle and policy which reasonable progressive opinion advocates.

The bill is in principle acceptable to me. There are a number of amendments which I should like to see made, and on which I propose to invite the legislative leaders into conference. I sincerely hope that this bill will pass, with the amendments I have in mind.

The bill conforms with the principles which I laid down in my messages of March 12, 1929 and January 19, 1931 to the Legislature on this subject, in practically all of its fundamentals:

1. It definitely establishes the policy and principle of constant, inalienable public ownership and control for all time to come.
2. It sets up a public agency, to be appointed by the Governor with the advice and consent of the Senate, to build the necessary dam and power houses by the issuance of bonds.
3. It declares that the primary purpose for the development of this electricity is the benefit of the people of the State as a whole, and particularly the domestic and rural consumers of the State so that the homes and farms of the State may receive cheap electricity; and that only the secondary purpose is the furnishing of cheaper electricity to factories and industrial establishments.
4. The people of the State can be fully and adequately protected from every angle in the sale of this power, right down to and including the time when it actually comes into their homes and farms, for the following reasons:

A. The rates to be charged for electricity shall be definitely fixed by a contract or contracts. In this way, all of the troubles which now exist in fixing rates of utilities will be avoided, in that all the judge-made law concerning good will, reproduction cost, going value, franchise value, etc., etc., will be avoided. Rates will be based only on actual costs, under accounting methods which will avoid all of the present ingenious methods of devious financing used by some of our utility companies. The Public Service Commission will not be able to grant any increase in rates under any circumstances.

B. The Power Authority is given power to enter into one or more contracts with any corporation or corporations, whether now existing or to be formed in the future, for the transmission of this electricity from the power house to the various localities in the State, and with any corporation, old or new, for its distribution into the individual homes and farms. Under the very terms of the bill, the details of these contracts are so laid out that the rates to be paid by the people, as before stated, will be fixed on an actual cost basis at the lowest possible figure. There is absolutely no limit as to which company or how many companies the Power Authority can contract with. Under the provisions of the bill, it can contract with one existing utility company or with several; if it wishes it can contract with any other kind of corporation, one or more; if it wishes it can contract with a new corporation or corporations to be organized for the purpose; and if it wishes it can be instrumental in forming a new corporation for the purpose of making a contract or contracts.

C. Any contract or contracts which it desires to enter into shall be subjected to public inspection and public hearings beforehand, after due public notice. The contract or contracts will be subject to the approval of the Governor, who will be given sufficient time and a sufficient appropriation to enable him to enter into an extended investigation of the contract and all that it means for the people of the State, and to permit him to entertain any objections made by various municipalities or groups of consumers, and so protect in every way the interests of the people.

D. In the event that the Power Authority decides that it cannot make a contract or contracts which are advantageous to the people of the State, or in the event that the Governor disapproves of the proposed contracts on the ground that they are not advantageous to the State, the Power Authority is then directed to get up a plan whereby the State can build its own transmission lines and distributing systems so as to do the whole job itself. Before, however, actually building the lines, the plan will have to be approved by the Legislature and the Governor.

E. Every municipality or municipal lighting district that has its own distribution system, or every municipality or municipal lighting district which establishes one, is to have a preference in the purchase of this electricity from the Power Authority for distribution among its citizens.

Therefore, the bill provides the two bargaining clubs which I have always insisted were necessary for the full protection of the people. The fact that these bargaining clubs clearly appear in this bill, proposed by the majority of the commission, shows plainly that the commission at all times, as I set forth in my message of January 19, 1931 to the Legislature, had in mind the necessity of these alternate methods in dealing with any existing utility company or companies which might refuse to enter into a contract which the Governor ultimately would deem advisable for the best interest of the people of the State. These alternatives are, of course, as above set forth: (1) The power to disregard any existing utility company or companies in making contracts for the transmission or distribution of the power; and (2) the definitely stated proposal for the State to enter into a plan of transmission by itself through its own transmission lines and distributing systems, built and maintained by itself.

I hope that I may be pardoned the expression of considerable pride and gratification that the Legislature and I have been able, during my short tenure in the Executive Chamber at Albany, to arrive thus far toward fulfilling what I know to be the universal desire in this State to develop the tremendous electrical energy in the St. Lawrence River by a State agency with the sole consideration in mind of providing cheap electricity to the people of the State. I hope that the principle enunciated in this bill will be the forerunner of similar legislation for the development of other water power in this State, as well as in other States. I consider it an outstanding triumph in the battle of the people for the retention for themselves of the benefits of their natural water power resources instead of turning them over to private corporations for selfish exploitation. The safeguards in this bill, whereby every proposed contract is wholly open not only to public inspection but also to approval by the Governor after careful investigation could only be circumvented in the future by a combination of complete lack of public interest plus a set of faithless public officials. There is no doubt in my mind that if contracts that are honestly in the public interest and that provide really reasonable rates for electricity cannot be made, then the Legislature and the Governor will take the next economically sound step for publicly owned transmission lines and some new form of public or quasi-public distribution.

35 ❮ Statement by the Governor on the Opposition's Attempt to Kill the St. Lawrence Power Bill. April 2, 1931

WORD has just come to me that the St. Lawrence Power Development Bill, introduced by Mr. Cornaire, and passed by the Assembly in substantially the same form as it was prepared by the St. Lawrence Commission, has been suddenly and unexpectedly amended in the Senate in a way which I cannot accept. The amendment deliberately strikes out the power of the Governor to appoint the members of the Power Authority. Instead, it substitutes therefor five individuals by name.

On Monday, March 23, in a conference with the leaders of the Legislature, I specifically and in very definite terms told the President Pro Tem of the Senate and the Speaker of the Assembly that I could not accept any amendment taking the appointive power away from the Governor and gave my reasons therefor — reasons which were apparently acceptable to the Assembly, as no change of this character was made by that body. In view of this clear understanding by the President Pro Tem of the Senate I am forced to the conclusion that this amendment is deliberately made for the purpose of making certain my veto of the bill, and thereby creating an excuse for postponing any action for another year. It is in line with the long policy of obstruction, objection and refusal even to consider any legislation which looked to conserving for the people their rights in this water power which has marked the attitude of the Republican leaders in the Legislature for many years past — a policy which public opinion forced them to abandon last year and which this year has made it impossible for them to delay in any legitimate way the final step toward the creation of the Power Authority.

I have conceded much in order to get action on power development and each concession has been followed by the raising of some new objection.

Last year, after a continued campaign of opposition and delay, the Republican leaders finally consented to my appointment of a commission of five men to study and report plans for developing power on the St. Lawrence. This bill not only provided that these five men should be appointed by the Governor, but further specifically and definitely provided that, in the event of a favorable report on a plan by this commission, the proposed Power Authority itself should "consist of five trustees . . . to be named by the Governor by and with the advice and consent of the Senate." This winter the report of the Investigating Commission itself provided that the Power Authority should consist of five trustees to be appointed by the Governor by and with the advice and consent of the Senate. The bill as introduced in the Assembly by a Republican legislator provided that the Power Authority should be appointed by the Governor in exactly the same way. And finally, the bill as passed by the Assembly, provided exactly the same thing. And now for the first time on no revealed recommendation and without any responsible authority to back it up, the Senate has arbitrarily struck this provision from the bill and has amended it by actually naming five individuals.

The action of the Senate is in direct contravention of the law of 1930, is directly opposed to the report of the commissioners and is directly opposed to the action of the Assembly which accepted the appointing power of the Governor.

Furthermore, I want to make it perfectly plain that this great project for the power development of the St. Lawrence falls very distinctly and definitely within the Executive power. A principle is involved, which I hoped was settled forever in this State by the Constitutional Convention, that Executive responsibility must be armed with Executive authority. The Governor is an important and integral part of the whole plan. No contract can be awarded without his approval; no project, no financing can even be started until the Governor has approved. In addition, the Governor must at all times be in close touch and sympathy with the trustees, not only in facilitating their work in connection with the drawing up of proposed contracts, but also in assisting them in their relations with the Federal Government, the Canadian Government and the Government of the Province of Ontario.

I am convinced that this action is dictated by forces which have prevented the development of water power on the St. Lawrence for the last generation. I am convinced that Republican leaders in and outside the Legislature have realized that this movement toward the public development of water power is from their viewpoint dangerously near to achievement. They knew that I would refuse to accept an amendment to the bill taking out the power of appointment and naming the individuals, even if it necessitated a veto. The conclusion is irresistible that this action was taken purely to hamstring, hinder and stop the power development.

I must decline to divest either the present Governor or any future Governor of his Executive authority and responsibility toward this great project. I am confident that sober second thought will persuade the Legislature to restore the bill to the original form of the law of 1930, to the original form of the report of the Commission and to the original form in which it passed the Assembly.

36 ❡ Radio Address Following Passage of the St. Lawrence Power Bill (Excerpts). April 7, 1931

I WANT to talk to you very briefly tonight about the influence of public opinion on great questions of State policy, and I shall use as an illustration an episode that has occurred in Albany during the past ten days.

Since last Thursday when I decided to make a frank appeal to the people of our State to help me save the St. Lawrence water power project, the crisis itself seems to have been averted. This afternoon I am happy to say that the State Senate has refused to pass the restrictive amendment proposed by Senator Knight, and there now seems no good reason why the Power Authority bill should not become law within a very short time. I feel very strongly that this result is due in large part to the wave of protest which swept over the State from north to south and from east to west immediately following the announcement by the Republican Senate leaders last Thursday that they had amended the power bill in a way which they knew definitely would of necessity compel its veto by the Governor. The great majority of the newspapers of the State, regardless of party, understood not only that the attempt to deprive the Governor of the power of appointing the Trustees for the St. Lawrence development was merely another of a long series of political tricks, but also that it was contrary to the law passed last year, contrary to the recommendation of the Investigating Commission and contrary to the bill as it passed the Assembly a week ago. Will you let me for a few minutes describe very briefly the existing situation in regard to the St. Lawrence Power Development? . . .

(Here followed a statement of the history of the project, which is covered in the preceding papers in this chapter.)

With the passage of this bill and its signature by me, the State of New York enters into the definite first phase for the development of the St. Lawrence through a governmental agency.

Three tasks will confront the new trustees: first, to complete and perfect the engineering plans; second, to try to make contracts for transmission and distribution with existing or new private companies; third, to negotiate with the Federal Government and with the Canadian authorities. On this latter point, I can only say that I hope that there will be no political or administrative obstruction in Washington; and the State of New

York must very properly make its plans so as to interfere in no possible way with the present or future navigation of the St. Lawrence River. The State of New York has no desire selfishly to block either our Federal Government or the Canadian Governments in any development of the St. Lawrence on which they may mutually agree. There is, therefore, no real reason for obstruction in Washington.

The bill further distinctly provides that if the power Trustees are unable to bring about a contract or contracts satisfactory to them and to the Governor, with private companies, for transmission and distribution, then the Trustees must report to the Legislature some other plan, if practicable, for either transmission or distribution, or both, which may involve the erection of transmission lines by the Authority itself. To my mind the other great keynote which is struck by the present bill is the solemn declaration of principle that the primary purpose of this St. Lawrence Development is not merely for big industrial purposes but is essentially for the providing of cheaper electricity and better facilities for distribution of electricity to the householders and small users as broadly as possible through the State.

From the very beginning I have held to a consistent course and a consistent objective. I have fought all along for development of this power by an agency of the State itself and not by any private corporation. Furthermore, I have fought from the very beginning for the use and distribution of this power for the great purposes of bringing more and cheaper electricity into the homes of the State, into the small shops and small industries, into the farms and into the flats. I am grateful for the fact that there has been such a splendid response from every corner of the State to this policy, for without that response it is clear that it would not have had a chance of going through the Legislature. The influence of a handful of political leaders is strong and so is the influence of private corporations when they see an opportunity to get something for nothing; but stronger than all of these put together is the influence of Mr. and Mrs. Average Voter. It may take a good many years to translate this influence of the people of the State into terms of law, but public opinion, when it understands a policy and supports it, is bound to win in the long run.

37 ⁅A Recommendation for Legislation Permitting Municipalities to Build Their Own Power Plants. February 15, 1932

To the Legislature:

THE intermediate report of the Power Authority points out the necessity of early adoption of legislation which will permit municipalities to buy the cheap electrical power to be developed from the St. Lawrence. In connection with this, one or more municipalities should also be enabled by law to combine into a utility district for this purpose. It is equally important that municipalities, acting either for themselves or in conjunction with other municipalities or parts thereof, should have the right, on the approval of a majority of the voters in the region affected, to manufacture, transmit and distribute electrical energy.

Last year there were introduced in the Legislature two bills to carry out this purpose. They were not passed. Nor, indeed, were they given any adequate consideration. I am causing legislation to this end again to be introduced and trust that your Honorable Bodies will adopt it so as to permit municipalities to help reduce rates for electricity for their inhabitants. A number of municipalities in the State now have this right; and it is common knowledge that the rates for electrical energy are much cheaper in those localities than elsewhere.

There can be no valid objection to this legislation, except from those utility corporations which seek to maintain as exorbitant rates as possible. If there are details of the proposed legislation which do not meet with the views of your Honorable Bodies,

I shall be glad to confer with you relative to amendments, providing only they do not change the general principle of the program. I believe that it is particularly important that this policy be written now into the statute law of our State in order more adequately and more quickly to obtain all of the benefits of the development of the St. Lawrence water power toward which the Power Authority has made marked progress.

38 ⟨ An Exchange of Telegrams between Governor Roosevelt and President Hoover on Negotiations for Canadian Treaty for Development of St. Lawrence River. July 9, 10, 1932

Hyde Park, July 9, 1932.

THE Power Authority of the State of New York has officially reported to me the status of its negotiations with the State Department in the matter of effecting an agreement between the Federal Administration and the State of New York in connection with the development of the St. Lawrence River for navigation and power.

According to this report, after many protracted conferences between the State Department and the New York State Power Authority over a period of many months, the Secretary of State has referred the issues. to you for final determination.

The question, failure to agree upon which has prevented complete accord, is the proportion of the cost to be borne by the State of New York.

I am sure that you agree with me that prompt and speedy settlement of this only question remaining unsettled is a matter of vital necessity. It is a vital necessity for the simple fact that this great project involves two objectives of equal importance and cannot in public justice accomplish one without the other.

I am deeply interested in the immediate construction of the

deep waterway as well as in the development of abundant and cheap power.

The State of New York not only owns this potential power, but seeks, through a State agency, to make it available to millions of people at reasonable cost.

That is why the determination of the share of the total cost of construction to be paid for by this State is a present factor which should not be relegated to later negotiations between us.

Four sovereignties are involved: The Dominion of Canada and the Province of Ontario, the United States and the State of New York.

In Canada, the Premier of Canada and the Premier of Ontario have directly conducted negotiations on this very subject.

In international matters affecting the joint rights and interests of the United States Government and one or more of its sovereign States, an understanding should be reached between the Federal and State Governments as a condition precedent to the conclusion of negotiations with a foreign Nation.

In view of this, therefore, it is my belief that, through a personal conference between us, this could be promptly solved.

With such an agreement between the Federal Administration and the State of New York, it would be my hope that it would be possible to submit a treaty to the Senate for immediate and, I hope, favorable action as soon as signed.

May I respectfully point out that such action would hasten greatly the initiation of this vast project — one which means cheap transportation by deep waterway for the agricultural and other products of the West; cheap electricity from the State-owned and controlled resource, to be developed for the primary interest of homes, farms and industries; and, of immediate importance, employment for thousands of workers.

If, by thus cutting red tape and eliminating formalities, we could work together to secure early and final action on this great public work, it would be greatly to the public interest. It has already been too long delayed.

I hold myself subject to your call and am ready to go to Washington on forty-eight hours' notice at your convenience.

FRANKLIN D. ROOSEVELT

The President,
The White House,
Washington, D. C.

Washington, July 10, 1932.

I am in receipt of your telegram of July 9. I am glad to assure you that the negotiations between the United States and the Dominion of Canada in respect to the Great Lakes waterway are making progress and that it will not be necessary to interrupt your cruise by a visit to Washington.

These negotiations, as you know, involving a score of intricate problems, have been under way for nearly three years and have now reached a hopeful aspect.

While under our Constitution international treaties fall within the sole jurisdiction of the Federal Government, nevertheless representatives appointed by you and leaders in other States primarily concerned have been consulted during the course of the negotiations. I am in hopes an agreement can be reached between the two Governments, but it has not yet been concluded, and I shall be glad to have you advised when this occurs.

The question of the disposal of the by-product of power which will result from the works which border the State of New York like all domestic questions of this character affecting the two countries, is reserved by the proposed treaty for purely domestic action by each country. This disposal is not the subject of international agreement.

If a treaty is concluded and is ratified by the Senate, then the domestic questions which may arise must be settled through the action of both the Senate and the House of Representatives in accordance with Federal and State law and in accord with the interests of all the States of the Union.

You will realize that neither you nor I have authority to enter upon agreements in respect to these domestic questions, but if the treaty is consummated and ratified, I shall be glad to consult with you and other Governors.

I have no doubt that we can make such recommendations to the Congress as will be helpful to them in solving the particular domestic problems relating to each State.

Having ardently advocated for over ten years the great work of completing this shipway from Duluth and Chicago to the sea, I am glad to know that it will meet with your support.

HERBERT HOOVER

Honorable Franklin D. Roosevelt,
Governor of New York, Albany, N. Y.

V

Old-Age Assistance

IN MY various campaign speeches in 1928 (see, for example, Item 5, this volume) I had discussed the question of assistance to the needy aged persons of the State. In my first Annual Message to the Legislature (Item 14, page 83, this volume) I recommended the creation of a commission to study the subject.

As a result of this and further recommendations to the Legislature (see Item 39 of this volume), a commission was set up to investigate and determine the most practical and efficient method of providing security against old-age want. The commission made its report to the Legislature of 1930, and a bill was passed which I signed on April 10, 1930. In addition to the Items in this chapter, see also in this volume Item 89, page 416; Item 17, page 102; Item 18, page 121.

39 ❧ The Governor Recommends the Creation of a Commission to Study the Problem of Old-Age Assistance. February 28, 1929

To the Legislature:

T HE majority party in your Honorable Bodies has stricken out from the appropriation bill which I submitted to you pursuant to the Constitution, an item to defray the expenses of a proposed commission to study the question of security against old-age poverty and want in this State. I cannot believe that it was your intention summarily to dismiss in this manner all consideration of the pressing needs of our numerous aged poor. For that reason, there is being introduced for your consideration a bill creating such a commission, and I urge upon you its immediate adoption.

New social conditions bring new ideas of social responsibility. The problem of how to take care of the aged poor outside of State institutions is now occupying the attention of other States of the Union as well as of foreign countries. We can no longer be satisfied with the old method of putting them away in dismal institutions with the accompanying loss of self-respect, personality, and interest in life.

This State abandoned some time ago the principle of institutional care for poor children, and adopted the method of helping them in their own homes. Similar provision should be made for old age.

Poverty in old age should not be regarded either as a disgrace or necessarily as a result of lack of thrift or energy. Usually it is a mere by-product of modern industrial life. An alarmingly increasing number of aged persons are becoming dependent on outside help for bare maintenance. While improved medical science has increased man's span of life, the rapid pace of modern industry has proportionately increased the number of years during which he is an unsought employee. While the worker of today on the average may look forward to a longer life than did his grandfather, he must necessarily count on a shorter period of industrial availability. No greater tragedy exists in modern civilization than the aged, worn-out worker who after a life of ceaseless effort and useful productivity must look forward for his declining years to a poorhouse. A modern social consciousness demands a more humane and efficient arrangement.

Some of our States and some foreign countries have dealt with the problem by adopting a straight pension system, where the Government distributes a certain periodic stipend to aged persons fulfilling the requirements as to residence, citizenship, etc. I am informed that such a system has been adopted in Montana, Kentucky, Wisconsin, Alaska and Nevada, and in Australia, Denmark, the Irish Free State, New Zealand, Norway and Uruguay. Objections have been made to this method on the ground that it savors too much of a straight governmental dole, and that it is likely to sap a man's self-reliance and discourage thrift.

On the other hand, a number of countries have adopted a system in which workers really insure themselves with the aid of the State against old-age want. They contribute certain fixed weekly amounts into a capital fund, during their more youthful years of industrial productivity. These contributions are equally matched by the Government itself; so that the worker and his Government are equally sharing the burden of insuring against the needs of old age. Provision is made under such plans, for temporary cessation of such contribution by the worker during enforced unemployment. In general this scheme of old-age insurance is followed out in England, Belgium, France, Argentina, Austria, Chile, Czechoslovakia, Germany, Greece, Iceland, Italy, Poland, Portugal, Rumania, Spain, Sweden, Switzerland and Jugoslavia.

There is no reason why our State, which is one of the foremost centers of industry in the world, should not now investigate the plans of these various jurisdictions as well as other proposed methods, and, indeed, the entire question of security against old-age want, to determine what, if anything, should be done by it to meet this rapidly growing problem within our own borders.

It must be borne in mind that although the adoption of any plan of old-age pensions or old-age insurance will be expensive, the present method by which the State's aged poor are being taken care of in institutions is also expensive. Four or five years ago, the United States Department of Labor through the Bureau of Labor Statistics made a study of the poor-farms and almshouses throughout the Nation, with a view to ascertaining the expense of maintaining them and the value of the capital invested, including the land, buildings and equipment.

In the State of New York, the investigation covered 61 institutions housing 9,203 inmates. The report shows that the capital value of these institutions was $16,321,338 or $1,773.49 per inmate, and that the annual maintenance cost was $2,753,327 or $299.19 per inmate. In other words there were then invested almost $1,800 of public moneys for each inmate of our poorhouses in this State, and almost six dollars per week was being spent by the public to maintain each person. This present high cost should be carefully considered in deciding upon the advisability of making a change in our policies of providing for the dependent aged. I look forward hopefully to the day when our poorhouses will be used, if at all, only for the helpless incurables of the State who by virtue of physical or mental handicaps are unable to provide for themselves.

Apart from the apparent justice of making some provision for our aged poor outside of institutions, a wise public policy dictates the necessity of an early formulation of a definite intelligent policy along these lines. The sooner this problem is met scientifically, the more economical will be its operation.

40 ❧ Address before the New York Women's Trade Union League on Old-Age Security (Excerpts). June 8, 1929

I FEEL that it is a great honor and a very high compliment for the New York Women's Trade Union League to celebrate its

Twenty-fifth Anniversary at the home of the Governor of their State. To have earned the confidence, to have deserved the friendship of an organization such as yours, are achievements of which I am very proud. I am prouder still that this friendship and mutual understanding between us dates back to my first entrance into public life, when, as a new Senator in the legislative halls, I found myself fighting shoulder to shoulder with your body for better working conditions, for fairer treatment of labor in this State.

I remember well our bitter struggle and eventual triumph for a shorter working day, and as I look back I think we can both feel that much real progress has been made and that even greater progress will be made in the near future.

One thing I think has been triumphantly demonstrated during the last twenty-five years, and that is that organizations of workers, wisely led, temperate in their demands and conciliatory in their attitude, make not for industrial strife, but for industrial peace. The whole tendency of our modern civilization has been toward cooperation. Employers and employees alike have learned that in union there is strength, that a coordination of individual effort means an elimination of waste, a bettering of living conditions, and is, in fact, the father of prosperity.

There were many mistakes made in the early days on both sides. There was a period when every combination of industry was designated as a trust, and the word "trust" was considered an opprobrious term. And there was a time when organized labor was too prone to strike first and negotiate afterward. That period is rapidly passing. Capital is realizing that without the friendly and intelligent cooperation of labor it cannot exist, and labor has learned that without the aid of capital it cannot earn its daily bread. Indeed, so successful has this new principle of arbitration, calm discussion, and willingness to look fairly at the arguments on the other side proved in our industrial affairs that it has led to a general demand for its adoption between Nations as the surest guarantee for the peace of the world.

There has been also a growing realization on the part of our people that the State itself is under obligations to those who labor, that the citizen who contributes by his toil to the wealth and prosperity of the commonwealth is entitled to certain benefits in return, which only the commonwealth can give. This principle, so far as it affects the healing of the sick, the amelioration of the sad lot of the insane, the care of the orphan and the education of the child, has been, I am proud to say, more clearly recognized, more firmly established in the State of New York than in any other political division of our country.

It is my feeling, and the feeling I think of a majority of our citizens, that the time has now come to take a further step, that we should forever banish the black shadow of old-age want. For those who may no longer earn their daily bread, because of some swift-falling accident or slow incurable disease, we have provided, and we are providing, hospitals, sanitaria, and institutions where, so far as is humanly possible, they may be restored to useful life or, if that is not possible, receive care and comforts. But how about those whose bodies are not stricken by sudden disaster, who work hard and faithfully through long years, until time lays its heavy hand upon them? Is there no obligation on the part of the State to look after these? It is through no fault of theirs that they cannot continue to add to our prosperity or to labor for the good of the whole State. And yet, what answer have we made, except the creation of that gloomy institution which haunts the thought of every aged worker, like some horrible nightmare, the poorhouse?

I do not believe it necessary, nor do those who have studied the matter long and thoughtfully, believe that it is an economic necessity that we herd our aged workers, dependent on their toil for their daily bread, in institutions of this character. It is not even an economic solution of the problem. It is the most wasteful and extravagant system that we could possibly devise. It belongs to that past barbaric age when we chained our insane to the walls of our madhouses.

By a proper system of old-age pensions, this dark blot on our modern civilization can be eliminated. I want New York to take the leadership in this movement as it has in other humane efforts.

The Legislature last year accepted my very strong recommendation for the appointment of a commission to study and report as to how this could best be done, and I am sure that commission will consist of citizens in thorough sympathy with the object and holding broad and comprehensive views, as well as practical experience in the handling of the financial problems involved. . . .

They will, I confidently trust, have a very definite and practical plan to present at next year's session, and I beg of the Women's Trade Union League something more than a mere lukewarm support in the effort to be made to enact their recommendations into law, if they meet with your approval. You, of all organized bodies, should feel a deep responsibility, a duty that is incumbent upon each one of you, personally, to see that this step forward is not blocked by stubborn stupidity, by incomprehensible refusal even to discuss it or to argue it fairly in our legislative halls. Make it clear that this particular thing will not be allowed to sink silently into that slimy morass called "politics" as has been the fate of so much labor legislation in the past. If by your own industry, if by your own thrift and diligence, you have provided an old-age pension of your own, do not, I beg of you, forget those less fortunate, to whom each birthday means a drawing near of a penniless old age, too horrible to contemplate calmly.

There is one other thing that I would like to urge upon you, and that is a better understanding and a closer cooperation between you who, as workers, are organized, and those who work quite as laboriously, quite as tirelessly, with hours that know no legal limitation and for wages which are often pitifully inadequate. I am speaking now of those who toil in the fields, as well as those who toil in the shops. There should be the deepest sympathy, the greatest willingness to work together, between the farmhand and the shophand. Too often have there been mutual distrust and mutual misunderstanding. They cannot live without the products of your industry, and you would starve without the products of their toil. By reason of the nature of their occupation they may not organize as you have organized. The only capital on which they can make demands is the capital which they, themselves, possess, but this is no reason why they are not as truly workers as yourselves. I hope for a better understanding of their problems on your part and for a more sympathetic interest in your problem on their part than has existed in the past. We are all citizens of the same State and the State is created to help its citizens, to make life a more pleasant thing for all of us, to provide its protection and to prevent the unscrupulous and the powerful from oppressing the weak and the helpless. I beg of you to take the lead in promoting this better understanding, this closer relationship, between our city and our rural life to the end that both city and country alike may work intelligently, harmoniously and sympathetically to solve the problems of government which still lie before us.

It is, I think, obvious to all that the problem of the needy aged cannot be solved by the mere building of vast State institutions in which to place them during their declining years. Modern thought is getting away from institutions. It is a curious fact that in all this talk about the breakdown of family life, the tendency is more and more to take care of the individual in the home. For that reason I believe that all will agree that, whatever the details of the plans which will be worked out by the new commission, it is clear that they will not advocate taking our aged poor away from their homes and placing them in hospitals and other public institutions. In the final analysis, good economics as well as a decent sense of humanity dictates that if the State is to aid them in their declining years that aid should be given to them under conditions where they may maintain their independent lives and hold up their heads as citizens of America.

41 ⟨ Governor's Statement on the Report of the Commission on Old-Age Assistance (Excerpts). February 24, 1930

WITHIN the next few weeks the people of the State are going to hear much in regard to the subject of a new law to provide against want in old age.

For many years other countries — in fact, almost all other civilized countries — have had some form of governmental system to take care of people who become dependent in their old age. Two or three States in our own country have started systems. Because I have felt for many years that New York should do something to fill this great need, I asked the Legislature in my first annual message over a year ago for the appointment of a commission to study and report. This commission, composed principally of members of the Legislature and of three appointees of the Governor, started its work last summer and has just made its report and recommendations and has caused to be introduced into the Legislature a bill by the chairman of the commission, Senator Mastick. This whole question is, of course, a large one and because of its magnitude and because of our lack of experience in this form of social legislation in this country, it is perhaps too much to expect that the Mastick Commission would have brought in a comprehensive plan.

Nevertheless, thousands of people will be disappointed in the recommendations of the commission. Frankly, I share in this disappointment and letters have begun to pour in, many of them objecting to the proposed machinery for old-age relief and many of them objecting to the fact that the commission has not gone to the real root of the needs.

The law proposed by the Mastick Commission does set up a form of machinery for old-age relief, this machinery being based primarily on an extension of the existing welfare or poor laws which are now administered primarily by local officials in the various cities and counties of the State. Right here a grave question is raised: Should the administration of a comprehensive law for the relief of the aged poor be left to the discretion of local officials or should a state wide system of administration be provided?

The difficulty with the principle of purely local administration is that we know from practical experience that it will in all probability be administered fairly, justly and economically in some counties, and extravagantly and, perhaps, unjustly in other counties.

In any event local administration undoubtedly does open the door for politics to enter into practical relief.

The amount of the relief is left wholly uncertain and may range from $5.00 to $50.00 a month—further evidence that the bill should be regarded as a wholly incomplete plan.

Finally, and of great importance, the Mastick Commission has accomplished nothing toward the setting up of a State-controlled method calculated to encourage savings on the part of individual workers.

I think I am right in saying that those who have given the deepest study to this whole subject and thoroughly understand legislation of this kind as set up in other countries, believe that a mere dole or pension for the aged poor is wrong in principle and bad in practice.

The most successful systems are based on what might be called a series of classes by which a person who has done nothing in his or her earlier life to save against old age is entitled only to old age care according to a minimum standard. Opportunity is offered, however, under these systems for wage earners to enter other classifications, contributing as the years go by toward increased incomes during their later years. In other words, a definite premium should be placed on savings, giving to the workers an incentive to save based on the prospect of not only food and shelter but on comfort and higher living standards than the bare minimum. All of this has been omitted by the Mastick Commission, yet it is a fundamental of the principle of old-age security against want unless we are to accept merely a dole system.

All in all, therefore, the Mastick report is a distinct disappointment to many people in this State. It may be argued that it is a mere stop-gap, a small beginning toward a comprehensive plan. Perhaps in this light it may be best for the State to accept the Mastick bill with the distinct understanding that it has many grave objections both in the relief to be afforded and especially in the manner in which that relief is to be administered.

In any event, I am glad to see something come out of my recommendation of a year ago and we can only hope that this will be the forerunner of a proper system of security against old-age want in the years to come.

VI

Labor Legislation

THE ATTITUDE of the Democratic Administrations in the State of New York on labor and social legislation, and the difference between it and that of the Republican leadership, were discussed in detail by me in the gubernatorial campaigns of 1928 and 1930 (see Items 4, 5, 9, 10, 12, 87 and 88 of this volume).

The papers and speeches in this chapter, as well as parts of the Annual Messages (see Item 14, page 83; Item 15, page 90; Item 17, page 104; Item 18, pages 115, 123 of this volume), deal with the general subject of this type of legislation. See also the Items in Chapter XVII of this volume, on unemployment.

It seems unnecessary to point out that my 1929-1933 principles and policies, with respect to those who are generally and popularly included within the term "labor," have been continued in large part since my inauguration as President.

42 ⦗A Recommendation for Specific Bills to Improve Social and Labor Conditions.

March 22, 1929

To the Legislature:

IN THESE closing days of the Session I desire to urge favorable action by you upon several bills now pending before your Honorable Bodies, proposed in the interests of improving social and labor conditions. This legislation has been before you for consideration for a number of years, and, while it has received at all times the support of the minority members of your houses, it has not been able to obtain the approval of the leaders of the majority party. I refer particularly to the bill providing for the establishment of a fair wage board to determine fair wages for women and minors in certain industries, Senate Print Number 883, Assembly Print Number 1542; the bill providing for the inclusion within the benefits of the workmen's compensation law all occupational diseases, Senate Print Number 4, Assembly Print Number 52; the bill providing that preliminary injunctions in industrial disputes shall be issued only after a hearing, Senate Print Number 966, Assembly Print Number 708; the bill providing that the labor of a human being shall not be deemed a commodity, Senate Print Number 66, Assembly Print Number 4; and the bill providing for a straight forty-eight-hour week for women and children in industry, Senate Print Number 57, Assembly Print Number 149.

I consider the foregoing statutory amendments which are requested by the workers of the State to be a minimum of what we should do to promote the welfare and comfort of our laboring classes. Modern social conditions have progressed to a point where such demands can no longer be regarded other than as matters of an absolute right.

43 ❦ Address before the State Federation of Labor — A Two-Year Report on Labor Legislation. Buffalo, N. Y. August 27, 1930

(Report on Labor Legislation, 1929-1930.)

I APPEAR before the State Federation of Labor not to talk politics but rather to make a report on legislation in this State during the past two years and on administrative action on labor problems.

Here is the record.

1. I have for two years asked the Legislature for an honest law guaranteeing an eight-hour day and a forty-eight-hour week for women and children in industry. A part of this was given when the Legislature this year passed a law which helps to secure a half holiday a week for women working in factories and mercantile establishments.

2. The Legislature has wholly failed to establish an advisory minimum or fair-wage board on behalf of women and children.

3. I asked for a law extending workmen's compensation to all occupational diseases. The Legislative leaders in 1929 passed a bill adding a small number of diseases to the list and in 1930 added three more diseases to the compensation list. I suppose we should be thankful for these crumbs, but it would have saved time and trouble all around to pass one complete statute to carry out my recommendations.

4. In 1929 I asked for a law prohibiting the granting of temporary injunctions without notice of hearing in industrial dispute, with provision for trial before a jury of any violation of injunctions, when granted. The Legislature did nothing. I renewed the recommendation this year, and I am glad to say that the force of public opinion and the constant hammering of President Sullivan and other officials of the Federation of Labor at last compelled the Legislative leaders to pass a bill carrying out this recommendation.

5. As usual the Legislature has failed to declare by law that the

labor of a human being is not a commodity or an article of commerce.

6. You all know the strong fight I started the day I was inaugurated to get some form of old-age security against want. We finally persuaded the Legislature to authorize the appointment of a commission to report a plan and on this commission I took the greatest of pleasure in naming our devoted friend, the late James M. Lynch of Syracuse. During his final illness I talked with him on the telephone and I think that it is right that you should know just what he told me about the Old-Age Pension plan which the majority members of the commission were about to bring in. He said:

"I don't like this plan. It has three grave defects. First, it smacks too much of being merely a dole or a handout. Second, it sets an arbitrary age of seventy before anyone can get relief, and we all know that in these strenuous times many people are too old to work when they are sixty or sixty-five. Third, the plan of almost entirely local administration raises the definite danger that the whole system may be run by politics."

Jim Lynch was one hundred percent right, but he and I had to accept the bill as the best that we could get this year. I want your backing and whether I am a public official or a private citizen, I will devote my time and energy to obtaining an honest, non-political law to provide full security for every citizen who, through no fault of his own, needs help in his later years.

Most of the civilized countries of the world have undertaken a Government-supervised program to alleviate the distress of fluctuating unemployment. You and I are very keenly aware of two very definite facts. The first is that reckless and deceptive promises that this country would never again have a widespread condition of unemployment have not only not been fulfilled but broadly speaking the unemployment situation in the United States is today more serious than at any time since 1893. Second, we are fully aware that the tendency of the present industrial system makes it increasingly difficult for any man or woman, past forty years old, to find a new job.

To meet the first fact the State of New York is now engaged in a definite effort to level, in so far as possible, the peaks and valleys of employment. Already we have obtained the cooperation of several hundred large employers of labor. I am very certain that organized labor agrees with me that it is far better for all of us to have steady employment year in and year out, rather than to have periods where there is a demand for more labor than exists, followed by periods when a large percentage of workers are either entirely out of a job or are receiving pay for only one or two days' work a week. The feasts and plenty of yesterday will never dispel the famine and need of today. This effort of the State is, I am glad to say, receiving the hearty cooperation of the more far-sighted employers, and I am confident that further study and further effort along this line will bring real results in the future.

On the second point of men and women who find it increasingly difficult to get new work, after they pass the forty-year mark, we have a definite illustration of why unemployment insurance and old age security are very similar problems and ought to be considered hand in hand with each other. I hope that the next administration and the next Legislature will take up a practical, definite study of Unemployment Insurance, avoiding, of course, any form of dole and basing their investigations on a sound insurance basis under which the employees, the employer and the State itself will all be premium payers. I have said that the feasts of yesterday do not satisfy our hunger today, but it is wholly possible to set some portion of yesterday's feast aside in cold storage, as it were, to satisfy tomorrow's hunger. It is, of course, worthy of note that one of the largest corporations within the State of New York has, recently, of its own free will set up a plan which, in effect, is unemployment insurance.

Let me clear your minds of any doubt as to my attitude toward prison labor, in view of certain grotesque misrepresentations of my position which were yesterday set forth to you. No one more clearly realizes the evil of competition of prison labor with free labor than I. The best proof of how seriously I regard this matter is that I have added to the State-created Prison Commission a

Governor's Sub-Committee to consider how we may keep our prisoners employed without competing with the labor of our free workmen. I did this because I felt that otherwise this question, which for years has troubled all penologists, might be ignored or scantily considered as it has been in the past. On this committee I have already named a man and a woman representing organized labor in the State of New York, your President, John Sullivan, and Miss Rose Schneiderman of the Women's Trade Union League, and I have asked President Green to nominate to me a representative of the American Federation of Labor as an additional member. It is almost unnecessary for me to add that I am wholly and irrevocably opposed to letting one State dump its prison-made goods on the free markets of another State. . . .

44 ❢ The Governor Approves a Bill Regulating Hours of Labor for Women and Minors.

April 20, 1931

MEMORANDUM filed with Assembly bill, Int. No. 1086, Pr. No. 2803, entitled:

"AN ACT to amend the labor law, in relation to the hours of labor of women and minors." APPROVED.

THIS bill establishes for the first time a basic schedule of hours which will give to those working under it a really enforced protective measure. The only departure from this schedule for which the bill provides is six additional hours, twice a year, for the sole purpose of taking inventory. A certain amount of flexibility is introduced into the working day and week by providing for ten additional hours during the year, which the employer may use as he needs them, in addition to the regular scheduled daily and weekly hours. But equivalent time off must be given for any time thus used so that no really additional working time is imposed by this provision.

An alternative schedule to the six-day, forty-eight-hour week is provided for which offers the advantage of a regular, steady half-holiday each week in return for a strictly limited amount of overtime. This principle of the weekly half-holiday is a recent development of the movement for the shorter work week — one which the working women themselves prize highly and for whose inclusion in the present bill they vigorously strove. It is my definite conviction that a desirable social policy, already largely a custom in industry, is thus given the sanction of law and encouraged to develop, while at the same time the underlying principle of a limitation based on the eight-hour day is preserved.

The bill contains a clause requiring that no overtime employment shall be permitted until at least four hours after a copy of the notice shall have been delivered to the Commissioner. We believe, and our legal advisers agree, that this is a great step forward in enforcement. Heretofore, the provisions of the law have been such as to make it impossible to require the records (or notices) necessary for effective enforcement. The new amendment puts the burden of delivering this notice on the employer. I believe that in this wise we shall get a check by means of which we can greatly diminish the illegal use of overtime.

The bill is an agreed measure, the fruit of long negotiations between the merchants and the women's organizations favoring hours regulation, and is believed by all of them to embody sound and fair provisions and to represent a forward step. I have been much impressed by the advantages implicit in such a negotiated measure both for the future improvement of conditions in this industry and as an example for other industries to follow.

A large number of mercantile establishments have written me asking me to approve this measure.

For all of the above reasons, I am approving the bill.

45 ❧ The Governor Endorses a Shorter Work Week as a Means of Relieving Unemployment. August 25, 1932

Dear Mr. Sullivan:

I AM glad that the State Federation is endorsing the movement for shorter hours or a shorter week as a means of relieving unemployment. I believe that at this time this is a factor in any relief program. It means the making of additional jobs by fewer hours of work per man. This can be done through agreements between industrial workers and employers to put into effect immediately either a short work day or a short work week, whichever is best adapted to the particular industry. Additional workers could thus be taken on proportionately to the shortening of the working hours. Room could be made for at least 10 or 15 percent more people in most of the plants which are at present in operation. The beneficial and wholesome effect of this method of relief would be very great. I believe it is essential that definite steps be taken at once. I am addressing this message to my friends of the New York State Federation of Labor in order that it may be communicated to all the groups and trades represented in your body. I am also making this message public with an expression of the hope that it will be read and accepted and adopted by the hundreds of employers throughout this State. A concerted effort in recognition of their mutual interests by employers and employees alike will, I am confident, bring practical and necessary results.

Mr. John Sullivan, President,
State Federation of Labor,
in Convention at Hotel Martin, Utica, N. Y.

VII

Regulation of Public Utilities

INTRODUCTORY NOTE: As I stated in my note to Chapter IV on water power development, the subject matter of this chapter is closely bound to the other. The objectives of a proper public power development policy and the objectives of an adequate regulation and supervision of public utilities are the same.

In my Inaugural Address of 1929, in discussing the development of the water power resources of the State (see Item 13 of this volume), I pointed out that regulation by public service commissions is not always a sure guarantee of protection of the interest of the consumers.

In my message of March 25, 1929, I recommended the creation by the Legislature of a public utility survey commission to study the question of public utility regulation and the reasons for its breakdown in recent years, and to make recommendations as to a proper and adequate system of regulation (see Item 46 of this volume). Pursuant to that recommendation the Legislature created such a commission and I approved the legislation on April 16, 1929 (see Item 47 of this volume).

This Commission on Revision of the Public Service Commissions Law consisted of nine members, six of whom were members of the Legislature and only three of whom were appointed by me.

On June 29, 1929, having in mind the problem of transmitting the hydro-electric power to be developed on the St. Lawrence River (see Chapter IV, this volume), and realizing that the State would have to deal with the Niagara-Hudson Power Corporation, which was about to be formed by a contemplated merger of three great power systems covering most of the State of New York, I requested the then Republican Attorney General, Hamilton Ward, to investigate the proposed merger to determine whether it was a violation of the anti-monopoly laws of New York State. The Attorney General replied on July 12, 1929, in a long discursive report which avoided stating any conclusion. I asked him again on July 26, 1929, for a definite opinion; and his reply on July 29th expressed the opinion that the proposed merger did not constitute a violation of any State law. (See *The Public Papers of Governor Franklin D. Roosevelt*, 1929, pages 560-581.)

It is interesting to note that my misgivings about this merger which would create a practical monopoly in certain parts of the State, so far as negotiations with the Power Authority were concerned with respect to transmission of St. Lawrence current, were later fully justified. As appears in the note to Chapter IV of this volume, the Power Authority subsequently reported to me its difficulties in dealing with the Niagara-Hudson Power Corporation; and as a result, on February 15, 1932, I requested the Legislature to enact legislation to permit the municipalities to build and operate their own plants for the purchase and distribution of St. Lawrence power (see Item 37, this volume).

The commission appointed in the previous year to investigate the ineffectiveness of public utility regulation made its report in February, 1930. The report was almost unanimous in acknowledging the breakdown of such regulation, and in pointing out that complicated and outworn valuation procedure was in large measure responsible for the failure.

There was, however, no unanimity in the matter of recommendations. The legislative representatives on the commission submitted a majority report, and my three appointees submitted a minority report.

The more important conclusions in the minority report were as follows:

1. The public service commissions law was designed primarily as a means of protecting the interest of the public in good service and reasonable rates.
2. Conclusive evidence showed that these objects of public service commission regulation had not been attained.
3. The commission's acceptance of a judicial rather than an administrative point of view had been an element in this failure.

4. The prime responsibility for the ineffectiveness of regulation rested squarely with the prevailing legal system of rate-making on the basis of valuation of property, subject to review both as to law and as to facts by the Federal Courts.

5. The public service commission, the evidence showed, felt obliged to sanction rates which could not possibly be justified economically. In fear of court reversal the commission had, in large part, been compelled to surrender to the utility companies the right to charge whatever rates the conditions of their business and the monopoly character of their enterprise could support.

6. The reproduction cost theory was the latest device of the companies for undermining regulation along the old over-capitalization lines. Over-valuation is the modern form of over-capitalization.

7. The electric rate situation in New York State afforded concrete evidence of the extent to which the consumer had been practically abandoned to the charges of the corporations.

8. Three holding companies, which dominated the State, had played an important part in the breakdown of effective regulation, introducing problems of over-capitalization and inter-company transactions over which the law gave the State no effective control.

9. Municipal competition, whenever attempted, revealed a measure of success in attaining what regulation had failed to provide for the consumer.

The minority report recommended:

1. Establishment of the prudent investment principle as the public policy of the State for purposes of rate control.

2. Revision of the uniform system of accounts so as to make possible the fixing of rates on the basis of actual and proper costs.

3. Publicity for all facts necessary to give the public a clear insight into the justice of rates and profits.

4. Authorization of municipalities to build their own electric plants and distribution systems, and to acquire private systems by agreement or condemnation.

5. Authorization of municipalities to join in creating power districts for joint ownership and operation of such systems.

Thirty-four bills were introduced to carry out the majority and minority reports. The four bills based on the minority report were defeated; twenty-six of the majority bills after considerable modification were passed. My action on the bills which were passed is set forth in Items 49, 51, 52, 53 and 54 of this volume.

In the memoranda on approving or vetoing these bills I also endeavored to lay down a simple program for dealing effectively with the weaknesses of present-day utility regulation which had been exposed by the commission.

Important parts of this program as indicated in these items are: (1) a change in the conception of a public service commission as a quasi-judicial body; (2) a new principle of valuation for rate-making on a prudent investment basis; (3) a new treatment of holding companies; (4) insistence upon an accurate uniform system of accounting; (5) provision for municipal ownership and operation of utilities as yardsticks for reasonable rates.

In 1931 and 1932 I continued my efforts to obtain an adequate system of regulation of public utilities in the interest of the consuming public (see Items 17 on page 106, 56 and 57 of this volume).

During the 1932 campaign for the Presidency, I discussed the problem in my speech at Portland, Oregon, September 21 (see Item 138, this volume).

In addition to the documents included in this chapter, reference is made to the following items not printed in these volumes: Communication to the Chairman of the Public Service Commission with respect to proposed increase of telephone rates. January 27, 1930. *Public Papers* (1930) page 487; Memorandum re bill in relation to jurisdiction of public service commission over small telephone companies. April 25, 1930. *Public Papers* (1930) page 298; Message re supervision over bus companies and water companies. April 10, 1931. *Public Papers* (1931) page 165.

46 ⟨A Recommendation for the Creation of a Commission to Study Public Utility Regulation. March 25, 1929

To the Legislature:

I HOPE that before your Honorable Bodies adjourn you will authorize the creation of a non-partisan commission to make a thorough study of the whole subject of the public utility field. This study should be so comprehensive as to include not merely regulation, past, present and future, by the Public Service Commission, but also other methods of supervision such as the application of the principle of contract approval by a public body as distinguished from straight rate regulation.

47 ⟨The Creation of a Commission to Study Public Utility Regulation. April 16, 1929

Memorandum filed with Senate Bill, Int. No. 986, Printed No. 1870, entitled:

"AN ACT to create a temporary commission to make a thorough survey, examination and study of the public service commission law, in relation to the operation and the effect thereof and to propose remedial or other legislation in relation thereto, and making an appropriation for the expense of such commission." APPROVED.

WHILE I was hopeful that the Legislature would create a smaller commission for the purposes of making this survey, I am approving this bill in order to have the investigation started.

I am convinced that the present public service commissions law is in need of great amendment and I hope that this survey will be instrumental in recommending legislation to provide for a more efficient and just supervision and regulation of public service corporations and allied companies. Further, the whole principle of guaranteeing to the people a fair rate for the use of services provided by private corporations ought to be restudied. The theory of twenty years ago that the return to public service corporations should not exceed a fair profit on the money actually invested is constantly and flagrantly violated. Some method must be found to return to the original principle. There is an overwhelming demand for practical, definite and immediate action.

For the above reasons, the bill is approved.

48 ❧ Recommendation for a Memorial to Congress on the Power of Federal Courts with Respect to Regulation of Public Utility Rates. January 27, 1930

To the Legislature:

THE recent decision of the Federal court in the southern district of New York, permitting the New York Telephone Company drastically to raise its telephone rates, brings to the fore in a striking way the whole question of interference by the United States courts with the regulatory powers of our Public Service Commission. Time and again we have seen utility companies rush into the Federal courts to obtain injunctions against State commissions. Although State courts are open to them, they have refused to accept State tribunals, but instead have sought the aid of Federal judges.

I consider such action to be contrary to sound theories of government and an improper encroachment upon State home rule. The control of local rates is a matter of purely State concern. The acts of State boards and commissions should be subject in the first instance to an orderly appeal by a telephone or other utility company to the United States Supreme Court after the State Court of Appeals has passed upon the question. But the system of two concurrent original jurisdictions from which the public utility may at will choose its forum is contrary to our sense of orderly administration of justice, as well as our concept of local self-rule and self-government.

The people of our State are more and more resentful of the

assumption and retention of jurisdiction by Federal judges. We have had many examples in electricity, gas, telephone and subway cases. It means that hearings and trials which rightfully should be held before our Public Service Commission or before State courts are, by a scratch of the pen, transferred to a special master appointed by the Federal court. The State regulatory body, set up by our law to inquire into matters of valuation, depreciation, operating expenses and other factors entering into rate-making, is laughed at by the utility seeking refuge with a special master, who is unequipped by experience and training, as well as by staff and assistants, to pursue that searching inquiry into the claims of the company which the consuming public is entitled to demand. The special master becomes the rate-maker; the Public Service Commission becomes a mere legal fantasy.

This power of the Federal court must be abrogated. Only the Congress can give the remedy. Legislation has been introduced in the Congress to carry out this purpose and the bill is now before the Judiciary Committee of the Senate. I recommend to your Honorable Bodies that you memorialize the Congress to pass this legislation. I believe that an enlightened public opinion earnestly asks some action by the Congress in the interest of the consumers of gas, electric light and transportation, telephone and other public utility service. Your Honorable Bodies can properly inform the Congress of the United States of the ever-growing demands of our residents for relief and for the prevention in the future of practices which are inconsistent with the American form of government.

49 ❨ The Governor Vetoes Bill for a "People's Counsel" for Public Utility Hearings.

April 22, 1930

Memorandum filed with Senate bill, Int. No. 1429, Pr. No. 1659, entitled: "AN ACT to amend the public service commissions law, in relation to creating the office of people's counsel." NOT APPROVED.

THIS bill provides that the Attorney-General shall appoint in his department an attorney, to be known as "People's Counsel," to be charged with the special duty of representing the public before the Public Service Commission at public utility hearings.

The entire purpose of this bill is based upon a fundamentally false conception of the proper function of a public service commission. Public service commissions were originally adopted, in this and other States, for the purpose of carrying out certain duties in connection with utility companies theretofore performed by the various legislatures. These duties, in essence, are to see that public utility companies furnish to the consuming public adequate service at fair and reasonable rates, and to protect legitimate investors in utility securities. The Public Service Commission has taken these legislative functions over. It is not, and never has been, merely a court. It is rather intended to represent the public interest in connection with various industries of a semi-public character subjected to its jurisdiction. The very nature of the businesses under their control renders inoperative the ordinary controlling force of competition; therefore, the State has provided this machinery to protect the public from the evils which would inevitably follow from the granting of monopolistic privileges.

Many people think that the Public Service Commission of New York State in recent years has not measured up aggressively to these standards; that this is proved by statistics showing a decrease in the number of instances in which the Commission has initiated rate cases since 1923. In a great many cases it is alleged that consumer complaints have not aggressively been followed up.

This decline in effectiveness is shown very clearly by the minority report of the Commission on Revision of the Public Service Commissions Laws at pages 68 to 74. I believe, however, that recent changes in personnel, and additional appropriations for the Commission may be expected to correct this tendency.

The testimony before the revision commission shows that whatever sentiment was developed in favor of a "People's Counsel" was due entirely to the recent letting down of commission activities in connection with these functions. The duty and function of the Public Service Commission can never remain in doubt. It can never be transferred to an individual as a counsel. . . .

Indeed, the entire testimony before the revision commission tends to emphasize the unmistakable fact that the function which this bill aims to transfer to the Attorney General's office is really the function of the Commission itself. The bill would divide this responsibility for protecting the public. It would in effect reduce the Public Service Commission to the role of a mere utility court in which the people would have to fight their unequal battle against the huge resources of public utility corporations. The functions of the "People's Counsel" provided for in this bill should be exercised by the Commission through its own counsel, assistant counsel, or any other employees whom it wishes to designate therefor.

I hope that the present Public Service Commission will more and more undertake on its own initiative to institute rate and service proceedings. It should not rely on the complainant's, but on its own efforts, to establish proper protection for the public. The idea of a "People's Counsel" as intended by this bill is antagonistic to such an attitude on the part of the Commission.

Without the help of engineers and accountants a lawyer can accomplish little because the questions involved are almost always non-legal. The bill provides that the proposed "People's Counsel" shall have the assistance and cooperation of the staff of the Public Service Commission. This is destructive of efficiency and responsibility, for no staff can work simultaneously for two masters.

The bill is disapproved.

50 ❦Radio Address on Public Utility Regulation. April 23, 1930

WHEN history is written the Legislature of 1930 will always be remembered as having taken one great step and opened the door toward another great step.

The first was the passage of the law authorizing me to appoint a commission to use every effort to bring in a plan for the development of our electrical resources on the St. Lawrence under a State agency, rather than by a private corporation. I have spoken several times before of the details of and reasons for this important State policy. I refer to it tonight only because it has a somewhat close bearing on the general subject of cheaper electric light in our homes and I hope that you will bear the fact of the St. Lawrence policy in mind when you discuss the even broader subject of the State's general policy toward what is known as public utilities.

Let us go back about fifteen months. Early in 1929, there was general agitation in many parts of the State over what was considered by many to be the failure of the Public Service Commission to function as it had been intended to function when it was first established under the administration of Governor Hughes in 1907. At that time, twenty-three years ago, Governor Hughes, fortified by his experience in the astounding revelations of the insurance investigation, obtained from the Legislature the warrant to create a Public Service Commission which was intended to supervise the activities of utility companies of various kinds. Up to 1907, the Legislature itself had from year to year sought to supervise utilities by stating maximum rates, an unsatisfactory system which resulted in log-rolling, lobbying, and actual bribery in the legislative halls. Governor Hughes and everybody else in 1907 recognized without question that there is a very great distinction between wholly private industrial companies dealing in commodities like steel or shoes or clothing or groceries or flour or automobiles or farm implements or running department stores, and on the other side, semi-public corporations dealing in services to the public such as gas, electricity, street cars and the like. In other words, services which might and probably would result in monopolies. There was no question that the State had the absolute right not merely to regulate these public utilities and to supervise their methods of carrying on business, but also to give or deny to them the right to get charters except upon terms laid down by the State. The Public Service Commission, therefore, was created in the days of Governor Hughes to act not as a court as between the public on one side and the utility companies on the other but to act definitely and directly for the public, as the representative of the public and of the Legislature, its sole function being to supervise the utilities themselves under definite rules. That is a very clear statement of the common law principle which goes back hundreds of years in the civilization from which we spring. Keep that distinction in mind when I speak of the next events.

Gradually from 1907 on there has come about a forgetfulness of the Public Service Commission's primary function. Gradually the commission had come to consider itself more and more as a court and many of the public had come to think of a utility company as very similar to any corporation engaged in private business as distinguished from public service.

As a result of the agitation early in 1929 a commission was appointed consisting of six members of the Legislature, and three people appointed by me. This commission held extensive hearings last autumn and until March 1 this year. The six legislative members brought in last month a series of over thirty bills. Let me tell you first what these bills sought to do. All but ten of them may be dismissed with the simple statement that they are of distinctly minor importance, chiefly minor changes in language and in the Public Service Commission procedure. Of the other ten bills which were of some importance, one gave authority for the first time to the Public Service Commission over holding companies; one bill proposes a new method of appeal to the Appellate Division by companies which are not satisfied with the Public

Service Commission rate-making; one bill creates a Bureau of Valuation and Research; and another seeks to set up a People's Counsel in the office of the Attorney-General. The bill to create a so-called People's Counsel, I vetoed yesterday on two very simple grounds. The first is that the Public Service Commission itself should act as the People's Counsel and should be given all the legal, engineering, and accounting assistance possible to this end; and the second, that there would be a division of responsibility if both the Attorney-General's Office and the Public Service Commission were charged with the protection of the people's rights in utility matters. All of these five bills passed both houses of the Legislature, but two others extending regulation got lost between the Senate and Assembly during the rush of the final night session and did not pass the lower house. These were the bills to provide for regulation of private water companies and of the practice of sub-metering electric light to tenants of large buildings. I wish that the public and I could some day learn the true story of where and how these bills got lost. I think it would make interesting reading.

It is greatly to be regretted that the Public Service Commission was not given authority over private water companies, because though few people realize it, a very definite drive is now being made by promoters and others to buy up private water companies and even the municipally-owned water companies in many parts of the State in order to create new holding companies and permit them through their financing arrangements to be turned into gold mines for the promoters, even though they are not always gold mines for those who buy the stock.

Now we encounter the meat in the cocoanut; and here is where my friends in the Legislature made what I honestly and sincerely believe to have been a very grave error of judgment and a very grave failure to understand the overwhelming public demand for laying down a clear and well-defined State Policy about utility companies and their rates.

I refer to two bills introduced by the Legislative members of the investigating committee, the valuation bill and the contract bill.

The first, when introduced, proposed a definite valuation by the Public Service Commission of all of the utility companies of the State over a period of years, but did not set up in any way any policy or clear-cut definition of how the valuation was to be made. The purpose of valuation is, of course, to find out how high or low the rates charged to consumers should be in order to give the utility company a fair profit. I objected to the bill from the beginning, because it failed to set up any distinct standard for the valuation. In the closing days of the session, the bill after protest by the utility companies was amended by the legislative leaders by making the so-called valuations wholly discretionary, thereby pulling out the few remaining teeth in the bill and making it, in my judgment, absolutely valueless and ineffective.

The other bill, also weakened in the closing days of the session, is equally a mere gesture by the Legislature, and I do not think it is worth the paper it is written on or the cost of having it printed. It represented originally a half-hearted attempt to provide for voluntary contracts between the Public Service Commission and the utility companies by which a company might come to some kind of agreement on valuation, this to hold good for ten years. It was perfectly clear at the hearings that the utility companies would not enter into any such contracts, unless they could get what they thought were wholly satisfactory rates and there was nothing to compel them to make the contract. It was, indeed, stated that they had no intention of making any contracts with the Public Service Commission whatsoever. This bill in the closing hours of the Legislature was practically strangled and the new bill substituted, providing that municipalities may, if they can — and let me stress the words *"if they can"* — make ten-year rate contracts with the utilities doing business within the municipality. There is nothing new in this provision. It has been tried out in the past with street railroads and has proved practically useless. This bill is also a mere gesture and means less than nothing at all.

The above is a simple statement of the way the mountain labored and brought forth a mouse, and this in spite of the fact that nearly one hundred thousand dollars has been spent trying to provide some really useful legislation.

Nevertheless I feel that the money and the time have not been wholly wasted, because more and more people are taking a greater interest in the whole subject of public utilities and the greater the discussion, the more the public will realize that the time is at hand for this State, and most of our sister States, to take definite and positive action.

The three minority members of the investigating commission, in the hearings and in their recommendations, went to what is really the root of the public utility problem. They pointed out the simple truth that the major problem of restoring proper supervision of utilities centers around the question of valuation for rate-making purposes. The question is whether the great utility companies are under present methods rendering regulation ineffective by insisting they are entitled to profits rated on inflated valuation of their properties and by starting long drawn-out controversies in the courts when they do not like the rates granted by the commission.

The minority report signed by Commissioners Walsh, Bonbright, and Adie is a model of clarity and will for many years be used as a kind of text book throughout the United States. They say that the only way to get anywhere so as to assure reasonable rates for electric light, telephone and similar service is to set up by statute a definite declaration on the part of the people of the State who grant the charters under which these companies operate, making it clear just what elements can be used to set up the rate base, these elements being composed essentially of the actual cost of the necessary properties, namely, the actual cash put into the utilities by investors. Such a rate base becomes fixed and on this rate base and no other, a reasonable rate of return should be allowed to the utility.

Take a simple example. Suppose a new electric light and power company is organized to serve a given territory and that the cost of developing the power, transmitting it, and distributing it to the homes and industries of the region is one million dollars. Under the definite plan proposed by the minority report this million dollars would be raised, let us say, by bonds which would be entitled to the actual rate of interest on the bonds, say 5 percent, in part by preferred stock which would be entitled to the actual rate of interest, say 6 percent, and in part by common stock which would be entitled to, say, 7 percent or 8 percent. This would mean that the rate would have to be high enough to pay this interest on these dividends, say an average of 6 percent or the total of sixty thousand dollars profit to the company in the first year.

The Public Service Commission would also allow an annual sum to retire the bonds, so that the net result, if the bonds ran, say for thirty years and amounted to one-half the financing, the capital of the utility company at the end of thirty years would be only one-half a million dollars because the bonds would be retired. In other words, at the end of thirty years the public in paying for this electric light and power would only have to pay enough to give about thirty-five thousand dollars of profit to the stockholders of the utility company.

Now let us see what is done by some utility companies operating under the present laws, or rather lack of laws. The same company in the same territory capitalized for one million dollars gets the same part of this capital through the issue of 5 percent bonds, through 6 percent preferred stock, and by 7 percent or 8 percent common stock, but it demands at once that it be allowed a 7 percent or 8 percent return on the whole million dollars. This means that it is getting 12 percent, 14 percent or 16 percent on the common stock, and this common stock is usually held by the insiders in the company.

Next under existing laws, the company fails to retire a portion of the bonds each year so that at the end of thirty years, the life of the bonds, they are refunded by issuing new bonds and running them another thirty years. Thus, the public has to continue to pay for all time on the original capital structure. In this example, the public would be paying at the end of thirty years from seventy to eighty instead of thirty-five thousand dollars under the bond retirement principle.

But, this is by no means all. In many cases in the United States, through the mysteries of so-called accounting, companies have been allowed to set up each year very large depreciation reserves and instead of having these depreciation reserves deducted from the original cost of the plant, the depreciation reserves have been actually added to the capital structure. Bear in mind that this depreciation reserve is paid for out of the monthly bills which are sent to you, the consumers. This method may mean very easily that at the end of thirty years a depreciation reserve may amount to one-half the original investment cost so that you are paying a profit on one and one-half million dollars instead of a million dollars.

But still this does not tell the whole story. Under the lack of a plainly-stated policy by the State Governments as to what the rate base shall be, the Supreme Court has gradually allowed large additional amounts to the rate base, based on what it would cost to reproduce the plant anew after many years have elapsed. This means that if a dam or power house actually cost only one-half million dollars when erected twenty years ago, it would now cost twice that amount to reproduce. The utility company could add one-half million dollars to this rate base, a straight out and out gift of that amount to the utility company stockholders. Suppose then, that in the case of our million dollar utility company, one-half million dollars were added by this wholly illogical depreciation reserve addition, and another one-half million dollars were added by the reproduction of plant theory, even though the old plant continued to be operated, we would have a rate-base of two million dollars instead of a rate base of one-half million dollars under the proposed investment theory.

Put it another way. On two million dollars the users of electricity in our homes would have to pay 7 percent or 8 percent or one hundred and forty thousand dollars to one hundred and sixty thousand dollars a year of profit to the company instead of thirty-five thousand dollars a year under the proposed new set-up.

It is perfectly evident that the difference between thirty-five thousand dollars and one hundred and forty thousand to one hundred and sixty thousand dollars means not only much higher electric light bills to the consumers but also profits to the original common stock investors which would be not 7 percent or 8 percent on their investments, but anywhere from 25 percent to 50 percent.

That is why I am insisting that this State should return to the original theory of granting a reasonable return and only a reasonable return to the owners of utility companies. . . .

The straight question for you and for me to ask is whether we are going to return to the three-hundred-year-old distinction between a company engaged in wholly private business and a company engaged in a monopoly of a service which must be used by all of our citizens, rich and poor alike, a monopoly which exists by the grace of you and me through the charters which we, as the people, have granted.

There are two methods of restoring reasonable rates for electricity and telephones in this State, and I say advisedly that I consider the rates charged to householders for these commodities are today too high. Unless we act definitely and promptly they are going even higher. One of these methods is to allow and restore competition either by encouraging new companies to enter the field or by setting up at least as a yardstick more municipally-operated companies, especially in the electrical field.

I think it is an established fact that those municipalities in the United States which have their own municipally-owned companies providing the light and power for their citizens give just as good service and much lower rates than in almost any of the privately-owned companies. The yardstick of municipal operation is the question of success. Almost all of the municipally-owned companies are successful today, and the yardstick which they have furnished us proves that the rates of most of the privately-owned electric companies are too high.

The other method which can well go hand in hand with the first is to give to the Public Service Commission a definite rule for valuation and to make it obligatory on the Public Service Commission to fix rates in accordance with this definitely set standard and no other. Let me say that this is not and should not be a matter of politics. If it becomes such, it will not be through my action. Nevertheless it is an issue, and I hope that the two major parties will not line up on different sides of it. It is an issue between two schools of thought, between those who would return to the fundamental that a public utility is the creature of the State, that it must give service and that it can and should earn a reasonable return on the investment which it has made and no more. The other school of thought would have us believe that a public utility company is essentially a private business operated for service perhaps, but operated in such a way that through swollen valuations past, present and future it can make the public pay rates on two- and five- and tenfold the amount of money which was actually invested.

51 ❡ The Governor Approves Two Bills on Public Utility Holding Companies. April 24, 1930

Memorandum filed with following bills:
Senate bill, Int. No. 1394, Pr. No. 2295, entitled:
  "AN ACT to amend the public service commission law, in relation to holding companies and the transactions between affiliated interests and public utility companies."
Senate bill, Int. No. 1427, Pr. No. 1657, entitled:
  "AN ACT to amend the public service commission law, in relation to the disclosure of identity of the persons owning substantial interests in the voting capital stock of corporations under the jurisdiction of the commission."
APPROVED.

IN APPROVING these feeble bills, offered by the Legislature as its only solution to the pressing problem of dealing with the great holding companies which dominate the public utilities, I wish to emphasize my belief that they are entirely inadequate. I am approving them only as temporary expedients. If the State's right to regulate these essential industries is to be preserved intact, the Legislature must face squarely the necessity of extending real control over these super-utilities.

The alleged control offered by these bills, when all the complicated provisions for its exercise are squeezed out, reaches only to certain contracts between utilities and affiliated interests. The bill in its original form provided that such contracts must be approved by the public service commission before they become effective. It is interesting to note that after the public utilities had strenuously objected to even this ineffective bill this provision as to contracts was further emasculated to provide that the contract need only be filed with the commission. It does provide that later the Public Service Commission may disprove the contract but nothing is said about the result of any such disapproval.

A real bill would have contained not only an express condition that the contracts be specifically approved, but would have given the commission plenary power to insist upon terms and conditions most favorable to consumers of public service. In any event, as a factor in the inflation of consumers' bills these contracts are far less important than the excessive capitalization of the holding companies. This is what is so largely responsible for the tremendous pressure for higher valuation of the operating properties. This, the bill does not even attempt to meet.

When the State first undertook to regulate the utilities it was dealing almost entirely with local operating properties. Today the situation has entirely changed. The State is dealing with great holding companies and many of the problems of protecting the small investor and the consumer now involve the operations of these mammoth corporations. The report of the counsel to the revision commission shows that in 1928 such holding companies controlled about 98.5 percent of all the electrical energy sold in New York State to consumers other than electrical companies. This means that consumers in New York State are buying practically all their electricity from just three companies, the Niagara Hudson Power Corporation which controls 54.6 percent, the

Consolidated Gas Company which controls 34.8 percent, and the Associated Gas and Electric Company which controls 7.6 percent.

Such figures reveal the magnitude of the problem which the bills before me entirely fail to meet. The people of New York State cannot afford to have the actual control of their public services pass to a few companies which are beyond the reach of the public service law. The present crisis in utility regulation is due to a great extent to the failure to control holding companies. Without power over these, regulatory statutes are without teeth. . . .

Regulation of the security issues of holding companies is the most important feature of control over them. This is not even touched upon in the legislation before me. Such regulation would mean protection to small investors as well as to consumers. The report of the counsel to the revision commission indicates that there can be no effective regulation of the securities of operating companies unless such control is exercised over the securities of holding companies. The report points out that such control "has been largely nullified by the ease with which operating company stocks could be placed in the ownership of holding companies and the securities of such holding companies sold to the public on a speculative basis." (Page 141.)

The speculative interests, which have been magnified in the utility industry by holding company operators, are diametrically opposed to the interests of both legitimate investors and consumers. It is bound to mean insecurity and increases in the cost of capital. It must, therefore, result in pressure for higher rates. . . .

The report of the counsel offers one suggestion which I believe should at least have been considered. It is that the provisions of the Public Service Commissions Law, now applicable to the issue of securities and acquisition of stock of operating utility companies, shall be equally applicable to the issue of securities and acquisitions of stock of every corporation which owns 50 percent or more of the voting stock of a utility corporation under the jurisdiction of the commission, and which may be found by the commission, after a hearing, to be actually dominating such operating company to such an extent as to be considered by the commission as engaged in public utility operation. The suggestion was thrown overboard.

The critical nature of the problem is recognized in the majority report of the revision commission which says:

"The domination of operating companies by holding companies may in some instances be so complete that the holding company is actually engaged in public utility operation, in which case it should be subject to regulation as a public utility corporation. . . . The interests both of consumers and investors may be abused by the adoption of unsound financial practices by holding companies. We recognize and desire to emphasize particularly these dangers." (Page 27.)

The majority, however, merely recommend that at some future time, after the completion of the Federal Trade Commission's investigation, further consideration be given to the problem.

I believe that this attitude represents a surrender to the demands of the public utility interests. I believe that the evidence before the revision commission was sufficient to warrant immediate action. I hope that in the near future a free and untrammeled Legislature will deal with the critical problem of holding company domination with more courage and concern for the interests of the consumer.

A constructive handling of the problem would certainly subject holding company financing to commission control, for it is increasingly through holding companies that the public participates in the financing of the utility industry. Protection of small investors requires such control and it appears to be the only way to prevent continued capitalization of the expectation of high rates. But I believe that the program must go even further to assert the Public Service Commission's full jurisdiction over any holding company which it determines, after hearings, is dominating operating companies so completely as to be actually engaged in public utility operation.

It is with the hope that the near future will see legislation along this line that I approve these measures which seem so hopelessly inadequate in the face of the magnitude of the problem.

The bills are approved.

52 ❧ The Governor Vetoes a Worthless Valuation Bill for Public Utilities. April 24, 1930

Memorandum filed with Senate bill, Int. No. 1433, Pr. No. 2501, entitled:

"AN ACT to amend the public service commission law, in relation to a state-wide valuation, by the public service commission, of public utility properties." NOT APPROVED.

THIS valuation bill, as it is now before me, is the fourth reprint of the bill as originally introduced. Its successive transformations have been drastic and in its final form it is an entirely different bill from that originally submitted. The introducer himself refused to vote for this bill on the ground that it was nothing like the bill for which he was responsible.

I am disapproving the bill because it tends simply to perpetuate the present valuation muddle which all agree renders effective regulation impossible. I am disapproving it because it is distinctly contrary to the proper principles of valuation and, if actually and literally carried out, it would in all probability produce higher rates than those which now burden consumers of public utility services.

The majority and minority of the revision commission agreed on the fact that revival of effective utility regulation depends upon a solution of the valuation problem. . . .

The report of the counsel to the commission asserts that rate determination has been largely a matter of guesswork, and indicates that upon proper solution of the problem of valuation depends in large measure the future of public utility regulation. It indicates also the utter hopelessness of trying to secure proper regulation if there is insistence upon guesses at valuation according to lines laid down by the courts.

The minority of the commission strikes the same note when it states that the greatest single weakness of the present system, not only in New York State but in the entire country, lies in "the hopeless difficulties inherent in the use of a physical valuation of property as the basis of rate control." The minority points out that the court decisions in determining value have made regulation under existing law completely impossible.

The plan suggested by the minority of the commission and proposed through bills introduced in the Legislature, provides the simplest approach to this major problem. It attempts to meet it by providing for a complete valuation of all utility properties in the State according to doctrines heretofore laid down by the courts only as a definite starting point. Thereafter all additions to the rate base would be on the basis of actual cost and no more. This would provide a definite and ascertainable rate base always available in the bookkeeping entries of the companies. It would guard against all future inflations.

The majority of the commission recognized the advantages of this plan in terms of simplicity and definiteness but expressed the belief that it would be declared unconstitutional. Without seeking a test on this point, the Legislature brushed this plan aside without even discussing it and took up the original print of the valuation bill which is now before me.

This bill originally provided that the Public Service Commission should make a valuation of all the utilities in the State in accordance with the court decisions. So far it followed the minority recommendations. But its fatal weakness was that it provided that this tremendously expensive process should be repeated from time to time and that regulation should never get permanently away from the unjust and impracticable present value basis.

The evidence before the commission shows that no one has a clear-cut conception of the meaning of fair value, that no one can account satisfactorily for inconsistencies in its application in recent cases, and that no definite standard exists with respect to such factors as depreciation, "going value," and the "reproduction" theory. It is inevitable that such indefiniteness in the very fundamental of rate control should produce constant controversy and litigation. The present value theory also offers a great inducement to companies to retain in service plant and equipment which have become obsolescent and inadequate. It promotes public utility speculation because of its indefiniteness. . . .

The recent New York Telephone Company case is a perfect example of the complete futility of regulation based upon so uncertain, so vague, and so flexible a standard of valuation. It has meant more than ten years of controversy. Even before the latest development it had produced about 63,000 pages of testimony and 4,300 exhibits. It has cost the company well over $5,000,000, which has, of course, been passed on to telephone users in higher rates. The attempt to guess at the fair value of the company's property in 1926 resulted in six different conclusions, ranging all the way from $367,000,000 up to $615,000,000. The telephone company itself produced two different guesses, about $100,000,-000 apart.

The bill as originally introduced would have deliberately perpetuated these absurdities. The bill in its final form offers no way of escaping them. The present breakdown of regulation cannot be corrected without laws which make possible the fixing of a definite rate base determinable by definite rules of policy and of accounting rather than by guesswork. The only solution is to get on an actual cost basis.

As I have already noted, the proposals submitted by me to the Legislature would have provided for a natural transition to such an actual cost basis. While additions to the original valuation would be on a cost basis, the initial valuation itself would be gradually worked out of the rate base through depreciation and retirement. In the end certainty and fairness would be substituted for the present absurdity. . . .

In contrast, the bill which I have before me does nothing to remove the evils of the present system. It practically gives statutory sanction to all that is unjust, unworkable and absurd in the present situation.

252

This bill is a complete acknowledgment of failure to meet the outstanding problem of regulation. It was passed during the last hours of the session in a form that was not even printed, so that few of the legislators voting on it really knew its contents. It tends to perpetuate a system of regulation which does not regulate. It is not based on any recommendation of the revision commission and can find no substantiation in the evidence submitted before the commission.

The bill is disapproved.

53 ⟨ The Governor Approves a Batch of Public Utility Regulation Bills. April 25, 1930

THE twenty bills dealing with the provision of the Public Service Commission Law, which I am approving with this memorandum, reveal clearly the failure of the Legislature to attack the main issues presented by the existing lack of effective supervision. They bulk large in point of quantity in the utility legislation passed in the session. But as I review them I wonder whether meticulous attention to the correction of typographical and verbal inaccuracies in the law did not distract the attention of those who wrote them from the crisis in the State's control of its huge utilities.

Many of these bills are too unimportant to require mention. But three groups of four bills each warrant a brief word because they reveal how bills which carry a significant title may be enacted in a form which really represents no material gain to consumers.

The first group (Senate bills, Pr. Nos. 2290, 2296, 2298 and 2328) aims to close up certain gaps in the commission's control over the acquisition of stock in the operating companies under its jurisdiction and to give legislative sanction to the commission's practice of not consenting to such acquisitions unless they are shown to be in the public interest. These bills add little to the broad authority already exercisable by the commission in this field and, in view of the recent consolidation of the utility industry under holding companies, look very much like locking the gate after the horse has been stolen.

The second group (Senate Pr. Nos. 2297, 2299, 2300 and 2301) makes certain minor changes in the commission's control over the financing operations of utilities. But two of the most important recommendations of the majority, which were embodied in the original bills, were deleted in the present bills in response to protests by the utilities.

One of these provisions, which was omitted in the final draft of these bills, would have meant a real extension in the commission's authority. It provided that a utility company must secure commission approval for all short-term loans in excess of 5 percent of the value of its outstanding securities. According to evidence gathered by the revision commission, these short term loans now afford the corporations a method of evading the commission's control over new construction financed by regular security issues. These short term loans, in the leading holding company groups, are very extensive and should be brought under more effective control.

The third group (Senate Pr. Nos. 2302, 2303, 2304 and 2307) places the burden of proof on a corporation to justify the account in which an item is entered, if questioned by the commission at a hearing. This provision was weakened by changes before it was finally passed by the Legislature and adds little to the broad authority of the commission. The majority bills do not touch the really important extension of accounting control which would make mandatory a uniform system of accounts designed to present a clear-cut cost picture for all classifications of the various services. Such an accounting system would serve as a basis for intelligent rate control. Under the present system the small consumer is paying more than his share of the profits.

In concluding this brief comment on the large assortment of unimportant bills, I wish to remark on the fact that the failure of this whole legislative program is due to the false foundation on which it rests. The majority and minority split was really fundamental.

The majority program, embodied in these bills, rests on the theory that the utility company lions can be charmed into lying down with the consumer lambs. The minority says that without State authority capable of curbing the carnivorous impulses of the lions, the lions are more likely to lie down only with the lambs inside.

In other words, the majority hopes that utility companies, which have treated regulation in the past as an unwarranted invasion of their rights, will alter this attitude and agree to accept a more elaborate and harassing invasion of those so-called rights.

The minority, on the other hand, recognizes that effective regulation has always meant coercion, an exercise of the authority of the State. Consequently, it proposed legislation which would curb the impulses to evasion and force the utility companies to live within the regulatory system.

The weight of evidence gathered by the revision commission shows the absurdity of putting any faith in the willingness of big utility corporations to give up gains. In fact, the attitude of the utility representatives at the Senate committee hearing showed beyond contradiction that they regard themselves as entirely private enterprises, that they are ready to oppose any attempt to assert the public interest.

The majority legislative program before me, in these bills, is ineffective. It is complicated. Its weakness lies in the attempt to get around the issue without meeting it squarely. The effectiveness of the minority program, on the other hand, is obvious from the utility opposition it has aroused. It can be summed up in three points:

1. Assertion of the State's determination that the return to which owners of privately owned utilities are entitled shall be the original cost of the property used and useful in the public service, as shown by their books.
2. Establishment of a uniform system of accounting which will

make available accurate unit cost analysis of all classes of service, such as any modern corporation in competitive industry would insist upon.

3. Provision for municipal ownership and operation of public services on a referendum vote of their citizens expressing their desire to undertake such enterprises. This provides the keen spur of competition so necessary to induce the privately owned utilities to accept effective regulation.

I believe that legislation along these lines would make it possible to reduce rather than increase the complexity of the regulatory machinery. I believe that it would eventually relieve the people of a considerable proportion of the burden of expense incidental to regulation and would permanently lift from the backs of consumers the burden of protracted rate controversies. I believe that it would provide the shortest possible road to reasonable rates readily ascertainable.

I am approving this large assortment of relatively unimportant utility bills in the belief that they may prove of some temporary advantage pending the adoption by a far-sighted Legislature of a truly effective program along the lines which I have indicated.

54 ❧ The Governor Vetoes Another Worthless Bill for Contracts between Municipalities and Public Utility Companies. April 25, 1930

Memorandum filed with Senate Bill, Int. No. 1599, Pr. No. 2502, entitled:

"AN ACT to amend the public service commission law, in relation to contracts between municipalities and public utility companies."

NOT APPROVED.

YESTERDAY I vetoed Senate Bill, Int. No. 1433, Pr. No. 2501, entitled, "An act to amend the public service commission law, in relation to a statewide valuation, by the public service commission, of public utility properties," on the ground that it was an ineffective and useless piece of legislation which did not improve regulation of utilities in any way. I pointed out that it would tend to perpetuate all of the features of regulation which have caused the present breakdown.

Today I am disapproving the contract bill on the same grounds. It represents a poor little last-minute effort to deal with the major problem confronting the State in this field of regulation. Nothing indicates more clearly the utter futility of the bills passed by the Legislature than this ridiculous bill, which provides merely for optional contracts between municipalities and the utility companies which serve them. Such contracts may be made, with the approval of the commission, providing that for ten years rates shall be adjusted in accordance with the excess of revenues over and above all necessary costs, including depreciation and return on the value of the property.

The bill is the third reprint of the bill as originally introduced. It is so completely different from the original draft that even the introducer of the bill refused to vote for it, stating that he could not recognize it as his own.

The original bill provided that any public utility could enter into a contract with the Public Service Commission fixing for a period of ten years the basis of rate adjustment. Such contracts were to be purely voluntary, with the utilities able to enter them or not according to the dictates of self interest. In spite of this obvious bias in their favor, the utilities opposed the bill before the committees of the Senate and Assembly, and it was thereupon amended so as practically to emasculate it.

When it was found that, even in this emasculated form, the bill could not obtain sufficient votes to pass the Legislature, it was finally exchanged for the useless piece of paper now before me. It was passed in this form without even being printed.

This bill, more than any other, shows the complete bankruptcy of the entire program of the majority of the revision commission for meeting the existing crisis in public utility regulation. In its original form it left it completely to the willingness of the utilities to enter into the contract or not as they choose. In its final form it makes no pretense at lifting the process of rate-making out of the hopeless mess of controversy and litigation into which the reproduction cost and fair value theories have plunged it. It offers the consumer of electric current and the user of telephones no protection which they do not already enjoy under the present law. . . .

It is foolish to think that any utility companies will enter into such a contract if it tends to deprive them of the benefits which they believe they derive from judicially determined reasonable returns on the so-called fair value of their properties. The evidence adduced before the revision commission must convince us of the unmistakable intent on the part of the utilities to fight on this issue to the last ditch.

The dominant leadership in the public utility field represents too much the speculative rather than the investment interest in these enterprises. Any contract which definitely curtailed speculative possibilities in the interest of the security of the non-speculative investor would not even be given consideration. . . .

Needless to say no wide-awake and honest municipal administration will enter into a contract which gives the utility the best end of it. The prospect and indeed the certainty are that there will be no contracts.

The bill in reality leaves the present condition untouched. It is not based on any recommendations from either the majority or minority members of the commission. It finds no support in the testimony before the commission. It was never considered by the legislative committees or by the members of the Legislature. It is a complete evasion of the issue. It does nothing to meet the problem.

The bill suggested by the minority would have met the situation by compelling public utility companies to accept a carefully worked out transition to the actual investment basis on which the rate base would always be definitely ascertainable by accounting methods. But the majority party refused even to pass the bills submitted by the majority of the commission. The leaders in turn refused to permit the Legislature to adjourn without passing some kind of bill. So, to break the deadlock, the bill now before me, ineffective and meaningless as it is, was passed to allow the Legislature to adjourn with the hollow claim that something had been done.

No other purpose can be served by the bill, and it is disapproved.

55 ❡ A Message Urging Regulation of Water Companies and Bus Lines. April 1, 1931

To the Legislature:

AT THIS time I desire to call your attention to two bills which have been introduced by a member of the majority in the Legislature. They seek to bring within the control of the Public Service Commission water companies and bus lines. These are the only two remaining important classes of public utilities which have not yet been placed under the supervision of the commission. I believe that the continued omission of these utilities has been highly prejudicial to the public service and that the defect in the law should be remedied at once.

I am advised that the more responsible bus companies in general are not opposed to State regulation, and are ready to accept and cooperate with legislation which places them under the same kind of public supervision which applies to their natural competitors—street railways, interurban lines, and railroads. On the other hand, many water companies have been and still are actively opposing all efforts made at State regulation. In spite of many years of effort, these companies have been successful in blocking all attempts to subject them to supervision in behalf of the public of the State. No sufficient reason can be advanced for depriving the consumers of water of the same protection as is accorded to the consumers of gas, electricity and telephone service.

In about three-quarters of the States of the Union, water companies are under the control of the public service commissions of the States, and the remaining one-quarter of the States have done very little in any direction toward public regulation of utilities. The fact is, surprising as it may be, that New York is practically the only large progressive and important State which does not publicly regulate the water companies of the State.

Irrespective of the completeness or adequacy of our present system of regulation and control of all utilities, there is no justification for continuing to permit water companies to remain without the control of our regulatory body.

I hope that your Honorable Bodies at this session will correct these unexplainable omissions in our system of public utility regulation.

56 ❨ The Governor Again Urges Passage of Adequate Legislation to Regulate Public Utility Companies. April 10, 1931

To the Legislature:

No ONE who has given the subject any thought believes that public utility companies in this State are now subject to that degree of control and supervision which was contemplated when our Public Service Commission Law was enacted in 1907. It is common knowledge, not only among utility lawyers but among the consumers of public utility services, that a long line of judicial decisions and court-made laws has to a great extent nullified the original purpose of the statute. So strong had public opinion become, indeed, that in 1929 the Legislature finally yielded to it, and appointed a commission to investigate the subject and to make recommendations for tightening the control of the Public Service Commission over the rates and services of these companies.

This legislative commission was organized, held its hearings, and made its report. Its investigation showed how completely the original theory of public utility regulation had broken down. That investigation has already cost the taxpayers of the State an appropriation of $63,500. To date no material popular benefit has come from it. Last year the majority members of the Investigating Commission and the minority members, appointed by me to the Investigating Commission, submitted legislation to carry out their own theories of what ought to be done by the State in the interest of consumers. The legislation suggested by the majority members was ineffective when introduced; but after introduction it was thoroughly emasculated at the demand of the utility companies, with the result that what was left was so utterly ineffectual and inconsequential that it would have been a fraud upon the people for me to have approved the bills, giving the impression that something had been done for them. The plain fact is that nothing was done.

I have been waiting for some signs of action by your Honorable Bodies on this problem this year. Bills have been introduced this year by the minority leaders in the Legislature (Assembly Prints 2278-2286 inclusive, Senate Prints 1733-1741 inclusive) in a constructive effort to make public regulation effective, to simplify and definitize rate making, and to establish a system whereby fair and reasonable rates might be fixed without years of investigation, hearings and law suits. . . .

I am convinced that the householders, small storekeepers, and farmers of the State are paying more for their utility services than they should under any legitimate allowance of profit for the utility companies. Large manufacturers and industrial users can, of course, protect themselves from extortionate demands. It is the smaller users of electricity — the women in the homes, the men in the small shops and stores, the farmers of the State — who have only too long been subject to rates for electricity and other services which have been all out of line with what they should normally and reasonably be expected to pay.

In the few hours that remain of the present session a great deal can be done by you for the protection of these people, who demand it.

57 ❮ The Governor Makes a Final Effort to Obtain Adequate Legislation to Regulate Public Utility Companies. March 2, 1932

To the Legislature:

I DESIRE to call your attention to the fact that the large amount of public money which was spent in 1929 and in 1930 by the legislative Commission on Revision of Public Service Commissions Law, has as yet produced no legislative action for the benefit of the people of the State. That commission was organized and created for the purpose of making recommendations to bring about a more adequate supervision and control of the large public utility corporations under jurisdiction of the Public Service Commission. The public of the State had come to realize that the degree of control and supervision which was hoped for in 1907 when the Public Service Commission Law was first enacted had become impossible of attainment because of a long line of judicial decisions and judge-made law which to a great extent has nullified the original purpose of the statute.

The report of this legislative commission amply demonstrated the great extent to which public utility regulation had disintegrated. The recommendations for legislation made by that commission have been, however, completely ignored. Even the recommendations of the majority members of the commission which were wholly inadequate, were so completely emasculated through the lobbying activities of the utility companies of the State in the legislation which was passed, that I was compelled to veto the bills so as to prevent an actual fraud being perpetrated on the public by giving to the public the impression that something substantial had been done for them. . . .

I have asked the Legislature for several years to act. Bills to accomplish something effective have been introduced by the minority leaders in the Legislature after waiting in vain this session for your Honorable Bodies to take action. If your Honorable Bodies are sincere in a desire to save money for the taxpayers of the State without at the same time throwing thousands of people out of work, this is a way to accomplish a saving that will be felt in practically every home in the State.

VIII

Toward the Reform of the Administration of Justice

IN MY SPEECH of acceptance on October 9, 1928 (see Item 1, this volume), I pointed out that the administration of justice had become too costly, too slow and too complex, and that a study of the problem should be made not only by members of the Bar, but by laymen. I repeated that suggestion during my campaign of 1928 (see Item 11, this volume), in my first Inaugural Address in 1929, and in my Annual Message of 1929 (see Items 13 and 14, page 85, of this volume). The recommendation was again made by me on March 21, 1929, in a special message to the Legislature (see Item 58, this volume).

The Legislature created a commission but provided that it should be composed exclusively of lawyers. For the reasons expressed by me in my message of April 5, 1929 (see Item 59 of this volume), I vetoed this legislation.

The following year, in my Annual Message (see Item 15, page 88, of this volume), I renewed my recommendation for a commission composed particularly of laymen. A bill carrying it out was passed and approved by me on April 23, 1930 (see Item 60 of this volume). Some of the results of this commission are set forth in my speech to the Bar Association of the City of New York on March 12, 1932 (see Item 61 of this volume). Since 1932 much has been done. See also Item 18, page 121 of this volume.

It will be noted that the problem of delayed justice in the State of New York was not caused by a scarcity of judges, whereas delays in the Federal Courts in 1937 were due in many districts and circuits, in large part, to an insufficient number of judges.

58 ⟨ The Governor Repeats His Recommendation for a Commission to Study the Administration of Justice in New York State. March 21, 1929

To the Legislature:

I HAVE already addressed your Honorable Bodies in regard to the broad necessity for the improving of our whole system of the administration of justice. Many of our citizens feel, with some right, that substantial justice is difficult to secure because of the costliness, the delays and the lack of simple business efficiency.

I recommend the authorization of the appointment of a temporary commission broad enough in scope to cover the whole field of study and more specifically:

1. To make a study of the business of the courts and how it can be simplified and expedited. This covers, among other things, the advisability of setting up new courts or re-arranging the system of old courts, especially the lower courts in large centers of population.

2. To examine into the advisability of creating a permanent commission or judicial council, or some other agency which would make a continued study of court decisions and the existing state of the law and recommend, from time to time, removal of anachronisms in the law and obsolete and burdensome requirements.

In regard to the personnel of the proposed temporary commission, I can only say that I feel very strongly that laymen should constitute a large proportion of the membership; and that its personnel should be removed wholly from the field of partisan politics.

59 ❨ The Governor Vetoes a Bill Creating a Commission, Exclusively of Lawyers, to Study the Administration of Justice. April 5, 1929

Memorandum filed with Senate Bill, Int. No. 1492, Pr. No. 1782, entitled:

"An Act to create a commission to investigate and collect facts relating to the present administration of justice in the courts of the State and report thereon, and making an appropriation therefor."

Not Approved.

In my annual message I called attention to the necessity for a scientific study to be made by representatives of the bench, the bar and laymen, of our entire system of judicial procedure, with a view to a fundamental reform thereof. On March 21, 1929, in a special message to the Legislature, I again recommended the creation of such a commission for such purposes. In that special message I strongly urged that the personnel of the commission be composed of a large percentage of laymen. The function of such a commission should be to examine not merely the superficial defects of the present administration of justice but rather the very frame-work and foundations of the system, which is universally regarded as archaic, expensive and inefficient. With that end in view, the commission should be composed of a large percentage of business men and other laymen, whose interest would be centered on this broad survey. While I favor lawyers serving on commissions, I think that this particular commission should be made up from all walks of life and, in large part, of laymen who can use their non-professional experience to good advantage.

Bills in conformity with these suggestions were introduced in the Legislature. They were completely disregarded. Instead, this present piece of legislation was rushed through, which specifically provides that every member of this commission must be a lawyer or a legislator. The personnel of such a commission in all probability would be interested only in strictly legal and technical phases of judicial administration rather than broad general questions of policy and fundamentals. No substantial benefit could possibly result from such a survey. I believe that the approval of this bill would be a wanton waste of sixty thousand dollars of public moneys appropriated by it. In its present form, this legislation would be a fraud upon the public, who demand something very different. Even the casual observer must see that this is not a sincere and honest attempt to improve the fundamentals of our judicial procedure and administration.

In the study of the broad question of bringing our system of justice to the standards of business efficiency and to the meeting of modern conditions of life, it is essential to bring to bear the experience of lay as well as technical legal experts.

The aim of the commission is to remedy conditions more important to the layman than to the lawyer. Although I am myself a lawyer, I feel that a study of this kind should have the active participation of laymen. This is not to be an investigation of the legal profession or of legal practices or of technical procedure; but rather of the underlying theories of civil and criminal judicial administration. While the bar should have a part in this study, it should not have an exclusive part.

I regret that another year must go by before we can make another attempt, and in the meantime the responsibility for delay rests squarely on a handful of gentlemen who fail to respond to the popular will.

For these reasons, I disapprove this measure.

60 ❡ The Governor Approves a Bill Creating a Commission of Laymen and Lawyers to Study the Administration of Justice. April 23, 1930

Memorandum filed with Senate Bill, Int. No. 1620, Pr. No. 1928, entitled:

"AN ACT to create a commission to investigate and collect facts relating to the present administration of justice in the State and report thereon, and making an appropriation therefor."

APPROVED.

I AM glad to approve this bill creating a commission to investigate and collect facts relating to the present administration of justice in this State.

This commission was suggested by me in my speech of acceptance made immediately after my nomination for the office of Governor in the fall of 1928. I pointed out at that time, and have pointed out many times that the proper function of such a commission was not merely the remedying of minor procedural matters, but rather a fundamental revision and speeding up of the business of our courts. It was apparent to me that such a commission should have a large proportion of laymen on it for such purposes. Last year the Legislature, disregarding my recommendation, passed a bill providing for a commission which would have been composed wholly of lawyers. I promptly vetoed it.

I am glad that this year the Legislature has seen fit to pass this bill in which laymen will undoubtedly play a most important part. I feel confident that it will go a long way toward making justice in this State cheaper and speedier.

61 ❨ "The Road to Judicial Reform"—Address before the Association of the Bar of the City of New York. March 12, 1932

WHAT IS THE PROBLEM?

I⊤ is unnecessary to take time in establishing the fact that the administration of justice is generally unpopular with the people of this country. Growing complaint with the law's injustices, delays and costs has to a great extent characterized every generation. The present one is no exception. At the present time, however, and in such a city as this, the problem rises in significance beyond the stage of mere dissatisfaction. It becomes a public problem of major importance. Speedy and efficient justice in a vast community like this is a public necessity, to be ranked with health, sanitation and police protection. I need not tell you that it has not yet been adequately provided. Moreover, in a time of economic distress such as this, the multiplication of legal actions involving debts increases. The necessity for relief is accentuated. It is impossible and unnecessary to consider here the extent to which this situation is caused by technical difficulty. It may be taken for granted that much of it is due to the fact that the rules of the legal game are such that in the absence of very strong administrative control they will be used, not for a direct search for the truth, but to permit such legal maneuvers as will further the interests of those who do not want the truth to be found. The jury trial, for example, established in order to provide the means for trustworthy decisions on matters of fact, is used all too frequently for purposes of delay. Absurd motions likewise enter the picture. In the long run the actual issue comes to be laid over with a whole network of unessential matters of strategy.

So long as years of delay are assured by the condition of the calendars of the courts, this delay itself will be used to threaten those who have rightful claims. Such delays constitute actual denials of justice. On the other hand, those defendants who have

271

legitimate defenses are threatened with long and irritating legal processes. It is a common thing among courts where reform has been attempted that the very fact that justice is made more expeditious means the quick settlement of many cases that should never have been in the courts at all. Thousands of cases find their way into the courts for the simple reason that to put them there, with the delay involved, is to set up a means to force an unjust settlement. Long delay is caused by non-meritorious cases, and non-meritorious cases are put into the courts because of long delay. The whole thing is a vicious circle.

The only way to attack the problem is by rigorous application of judicial efficiency. In the face of this congestion the remedy commonly proposed is to add new judges or new courts, but it will readily be seen that if the problem is what I have stated it to be, such a so-called remedy merely aggravates the complaint. There are, of course, legitimate demands for additional judicial man-power in sections of the State where the population has grown rapidly. But it is easy to see that to apply this remedy in all cases is to add to the ravages of the disease, to contribute to the confusion and, what is profoundly important at this time, to burden still further an already seriously embarrassed taxpayer. With taxes mounting in all of the subdivisions of Government, the time has come for a veritable searching of heart with regard to the cost of public service, and new demands should be most carefully scrutinized in the light of this problem of dollars and cents.

Moreover, the cost to the litigant is very serious. This cost applies not only to the cost imposed by the governmental authorities, but professional fees as well. An English lawyer, in a very discriminating statement concerning the administration of justice in his own country, recently said justice in no country in the world is so expensive to obtain as England, except for the United States of America. Writers and lawyers in Continental countries comment severely on this feature of Anglo-American Government. In Germany, according to this authority, Mr. Claude Mullins (*In Quest of Justice*), an ordinary civil action for fifty pounds can be brought for total fees on both sides of not more than eighteen pounds. On the other hand, in England and the United States the cost of litigation is still deeply embedded in the mysterious recesses of lawyers' accounts; but we may be certain that it is much, much higher. Justice, then, is not only delayed, but it is excessively costly.

Stripped of frills, the problem comes down to a question of administration. Some of the realism that goes into matters less clouded by theory and tradition needs to be applied to the administration of justice. There are, of course, important considerations of policy that distinguish the administration of justice from the administration of some of the more prosaic activities of life. But it is not too much to say that the fact that the law is a learned profession and that its exponents are men trained in theoretical wisdom and are quick to distinguish fine shades of meaning has permitted them to invest their business with an almost mystical attribute that forbids the laying of the hard hands of common sense on the things that they are doing. Yet, when you consider the vast portion of cases that come to our courts, the adjustment of these problems comes down pretty much to a consideration of the same items of everyday life that we have in other activities. It would seem to me that there is to be little of the sacrosanct in the problem of determining whether John Doe did actually sell a bill of defective goods to Richard Doe. The core of the matter, after all, is earthly fact, and no manner of theorizing and of invocation of precedent is going to solve the essential issue.

WHAT IS THE ROAD TO REFORM?

If the experience of England is any guide to what we may expect in the direction of reform, our progress out of the present unsatisfactory condition will be slow and, I fear, painful. In the first place, we must divest ourselves of the hope of easy reform, participated in by a few people. The day of the great law-giver is past. A modern, diversified and almost incoherent society requires that reform be the resultant of many diversified efforts. Cooperation among the innumerable interests of such a State as ours is necessary and such cooperation means vastly detailed and patient planning and labor. The history of law reform in this State has shown this. While many marked improvements have taken place in the past thirty years in connection with the administration of justice, it has been notable that altogether too many well-planned attempts at improvement have failed. If we are to succeed now it must be by widespread cooperation and unflinching labor.

One of the difficulties has been the fact that attempts to reform have concerned themselves largely with the higher courts of the State. These courts, as the result of consistent efforts on the part of reformers and largely because of the generally splendid personnel of judges who have served in them, have been a credit to New York and to the Nation. It is a matter of pride for the citizens of New York to consider how widely throughout the various States our Court of Appeals has been placed not only in the front rank, but preeminent among the courts of last resort. While these courts go far to encourage optimism, it is nevertheless true that our lower courts have been and are vastly in need of reconstructive improvement. The great delay occasioned in some of our city tribunals, the unsatisfactory nature of justice as it is administered by justices of the peace throughout the State and the unsatisfactory condition in the administration of criminal justice, all point to the necessity for serious consideration of those courts that provide the means of justice to the poor and unfortunate.

In the quest for reform there is no doubt as to the willingness of leaders of the bar to assist not only individually as lawyers, but through the various associations throughout the State. Vast energy and sums of money have been spent in order to justify the expectation of those who believe that lawyers ought to be in the forefront of reform in this field.

But in spite of this professional cooperation and assistance, I have felt from the beginning that reform cannot ultimately succeed unless it is participated in and supported by the lay public. Consequently, in the creation of a Commission on the Administration of Justice for this State, which, after repeated requests, I succeeded in bringing into existence through the Legislature, last winter, I insisted that there be lay membership. England found in the long struggle for legal reform in the Nineteenth Century that laymen were indispensable.

Kenneth Dayton, Chairman of the Committee on Law Reform of the Association of the Bar, says of the part that laymen played in law reform in England: "The lesson of the early battlers has not been lost upon the English public. Increasingly, the examination into the administration of justice and its improvement has been delegated to laymen. The first commission appointed in 1850 consisted of seven attorneys, but on petition of Parliament two business men were added to the commission. The proportion of laymen upon subsequent commissions has constantly increased. A Parliamentary committee appointed in 1909 contained but one lawyer out of ten members. The 1913 commission was made up of one judge, two lawyers and eight laymen. Of this commission it was said, 'even this meager representation of the legal profession was objected to by the commission as discrediting its report.'"

We should not forget the direct interest in the administration of justice that laymen have; in the last analysis they suffer most from the slow-moving courts. Moreover, laymen have no vested interests, except in unusual instances, in the administration of justice. They are not lawyers with the fear of antagonizing the judiciary, nor are they judges who hesitate to reconstruct the conditions under which they work. Moreover, the intelligent layman is able to cut through cobwebs that in some way frustrate the efforts of the lawyers.

It is now clear to all thoughtful observers that reform in the administration of justice means an attack much more fundamental than the mere alteration of rules of procedure. It is more a problem of government than of law. It is concerned with questions of administrative policy and with social welfare rather than mere procedure.

This involves a broad search for the experience of other States and most certainly of other countries. It means that we should, wherever possible, adopt the experience of other States. For example, there has developed throughout the country a system for the management of the calendar, which originated, as I understand, in Cleveland and details of which are familiar to many members of the bar here. Largely through the leadership of one of your own members, Mr. Harry D. Nims, the Federal courts in New York have adopted a modification of this system, and now, as I understand it, the Supreme Court of the First Department is in like manner expediting its business and at the same time saving money for litigants and taxpayers. Other useful experiments are abroad in the land which New York should not be long in examining. It is a very gratifying thing that our State Commission on the Administration of Justice is keenly aware of the necessity for a consideration of such experience, has made itself familiar with a number of these ideas and is planning a further search for the benefits of further experience in other places. To the end that reform of this type may be provided with official State leadership we have at last created a Commission on the Administration of Justice, which has set to work this past year. As is indicated in its preliminary report, it has carried on its work with a number of sound general policies.

This Commission, broadly representative in interest and viewpoint, has diligently applied itself to its task. It has selected its field of investigation with discrimination; but it has brought within its purview far more than a mere tinkering with procedure. It has initiated the study of a number of significant subjects, it has called conferences of judges, held public hearings, and in a tactful but effective manner has opened the way to a genuine appraisal and reconsideration of our judicial system.

It wisely proceeded with a decorous abstention from publicity. The trouble with some types of reform is that they celebrate before the event. They are, as Chesterton drily remarks, rejoicing in the memory of tomorrow afternoon.

The Commission has sought, through cooperation with the courts, and in many other ways, a reasonable program of improvement. It will, in the year to come, seek to move toward the achievement of this program. Its main results, it may be assumed, will be indirect, the courts themselves, through common thought on the subjects at issue, achieving the beneficial result sought for by all of us.

Because while some legislation and perhaps even a number of constitutional changes are desirable, the most important improvements can be achieved without new laws. To this end the Commission has sought and, it reports, secured the interest and cooperation of judges and lawyers throughout the State. A few weeks ago, for example, at the request of Senator Walter Westall, Chairman of the Commission, the four Presiding Justices of the Appellate Divisions of the State, and other judges, met with the Commission to consider matters of common interest. This meeting of minds, which, as I understand, will be continued, cannot help but have a beneficial effect upon the administration of justice throughout the State. Administrative readjustments of the greatest value can come by the use of customary powers or, what is more noteworthy, by the potent influence of suggestion and example.

A thoughtful judge of this city, Bernard Shientag, commenting upon the need for judicial statistics, says that "the absence of such statistics has, more than anything else, checked the progress of the law." One of the activities this Commission contemplated for the coming year is the creation throughout the State of a system by which there will be for the first time in the history of New York, adequate statewide statistics concerning all of the courts. It is planned that this work should be carried on and if and when a permanent judicial council is created, the present temporary Commission will divest itself of this function and transfer it to such a permanent body. The value of such information, systematically gathered and intelligently presented, is of extraordinary importance. It will give officials themselves a picture of the state of litigation in the courts which will permit us to know what work the courts are doing, how much of it there is, and how long it takes to dispose of cases. It will, I hope, be a permanent and accurate guide to the Legislature in the creation of new courts and new judges. It will give us the assurance that we shall not be permitted to enact legislation adding to the expense of the courts, without accurate scientific means of knowing the extent of the need and whether it is immediately necessary.

What I have said of law reform may in many respects be applied with singular appropriateness to much of public life today. The principle of fewer new laws has, it is true, been widely advocated. But it has too often been the cry of a touchy conservatism, a wish to escape the regulatory arm of the Government. The general wisdom of the demand for fewer laws is undeniable. But its necessary correlative principle is to use with intelligence and energy the powers that we have. Administration, informed, energetic, and economical, is the deep need of Government today. The public, particularly in these moments of deep stress, deserves of its servants an example of unselfish application to duty. Let us remember that every member of the bar has something of the character of a public servant and that he owes it to his profession and to the public to encourage and to give his efforts for important and even drastic improvements in the administration of justice.

IX

Modernization of Local Government

INTRODUCTORY NOTE: PEOPLE who speak of the large percentage of national income which goes to the payment of taxes very often overlook the fact that a great proportion of such taxes is paid to what is known as local government — town, village and county. For example, in most States practically all of the tax on real estate goes to local government rather than to State Government. Of course, the Federal Government does not levy any tax at all on real estate.

A great deal of the taxes paid for local government could be avoided if the inefficiencies, anachronisms and overlappings in local government were eliminated.

In the papers in this chapter, in my acceptance speech of the first nomination for the Governorship (see Item 1, this volume), in my Annual Messages to the Legislature and in my second Inaugural Address (see Item 14, page 82; Item 15, page 89; Item 16, page 95; Item 17, page 108; Item 18, page 117), and in other messages and speeches which have not been included, I pointed out the need for improvement of local government in the interest of efficiency and economy, not only in the State of New York, but throughout the United States. Repeatedly I urged the Legislature to take definite steps toward reform along these lines. The need today becomes greater each year as the functions of Government increase.

The American form of local government has come down practically unchanged from the days when rural communities were sparsely settled and when communication and transportation between communities were slow and cumbersome. The telephone, telegraph, steam engine and automobile have rendered wholly inadequate and obsolete the machinery of local government which has persisted through the years.

Of course, little can be done to remedy defects in local government by the Federal Administration in Washington, except perhaps to call attention to the need for reform (see Item 140, this volume, page 759). In my own State of New York, action has been begun for reform in local government, and it is to be hoped that the other local communities throughout the United States, for the sake of efficiency as well as for the sake of economy, will take similar steps.

62 ⟨ Address on Reorganization and Consolidation of Function of Local Government and Their Effect on Taxes. Saranac, N. Y. September 11, 1929

WHY must the American people be inconsistent? In our business life and in our social contacts we are little controlled by the methods and practices employed by our forefathers. The farmer of today does not plant, cultivate, harvest and market as did his grandfather. Methods of manufacture and of distribution and of merchandising are entirely unlike those of a century ago. We have made great changes in the budgeting and administration of the Federal and State Governments. Nevertheless, in almost every State in the Union we seem content, in the main, to accept and continue to use the local machinery of government which was first devised generations or even centuries ago.

In the State of New York, for example, I am utterly unable to understand why we remain wedded to the local system of government devised two hundred and fifty years ago by His Royal Highness, the Duke of York.

It has been well said that, while in the larger units of American Government, at Washington and at the State capitals, undoubted savings in administrative efficiency can still be made, yet the waste there is a mere drop in the bucket in comparison with the extravagance, the loss, the duplication — yes, the stupidity and, in some cases, the dishonesty — which exist in so many sections in the conduct of local government.

For Americans to be proud of their business efficiency, of their economic progress and of all the improvements which have come to them during the past generation is highly inconsistent with the attitude of the average citizen who, without objection, allows local government to continue in its time-worn groove of inefficiency.

I do not think that I am overstepping the bounds of truth, and I am fairly familiar with conditions in many States, when I assert that not one percent of the towns and counties of the United States but could save great sums for the taxpayers, if they were reorganized along modern business lines.

It should be clearly understood, of course, that while this problem is nationwide in its scope, yet its solution cannot be considered from the national standpoint but must be studied, first, from the State standpoint and, second, from the point of view of the dwellers in the counties and towns themselves. While the generalization in regard to the need of reorganization applies to all States, the details vary in each State and, indeed, even in the local units themselves.

That is why I take, merely as an example before this National Tax Conference, the situation which exists today in the State of New York. The lessons from New York may not apply in detail to the other States, but they do apply in principle.

Under the Duke of York's laws the county and the town were recognized as the two units of local government. With practically no exceptions the organization of our counties and towns remains the same today as two hundred and fifty years ago. We now have all the town offices, for example, which existed under the first State Constitution of 1777, with several more added. It is well to remember in dealing with this broad problem that the conditions of life have undergone a revolutionary change. These conditions have changed all of our relations in business, but they have not called for corresponding changes in our agencies of government. In the old days people of a community lived very much within that community with few, if any, outside contacts. Today modern transportation and modern communication have given to many things, which were originally of local concern and, therefore, functions of local government, a far broader aspect.

I recognize to the full the sentiment and home pride which cling jealously to county and town lines, especially in those parts of the country which have a long-standing historical background. As a matter of practical effort, therefore, revolutionary changes in local geographical units would seem to be out of the question for immediate relief. We do not put through great reforms all at one time. We must seek what can be practically accomplished even though the process may be piecemeal.

The two main aspects of this problem are: First, what can be accomplished toward the consolidation and reorganization of local units of government and, second, if we leave local units of government as they now exist, how we can relieve them of functions which are not purely local? . . .

In this connection, it is worth while noting that a differentiation must be made between counties which are mainly agricultural and other counties which are almost wholly suburban. For instance, in Nassau County, on Long Island, the greater part of the area of the county lies within the limit of incorporated villages. Yet in addition to the officials of these villages there exist complete sets of town officers who have jurisdiction over the fringes of land outside the incorporated villages. This brings up the serious question as to the necessity for town government in the suburban counties. Why have many complete sets of officials whose jurisdiction and duties overlap?

It is time for the recognition of the new phenomenon of the widely growing suburban areas which are constantly increasing in size, in wealth, and at the same time in the demands for all kinds of public improvements, sewers, lighting, water supply, concrete roads, special policing and the like. Why should they be governed under a system devised for a sparsely settled agricultural community?

It is this lack of study and reorganization of the suburban areas which has led to the terrible abuses of the last few years. In Monroe County in this State a suburban town has recently given the example of advertising for bids for a system of sidewalks which had been actually laid and completed two years before by a contractor who was in league with a real estate developer and the town officials. In another town in the same county various so-called improvements have, in the past few years, been put in with such a lavish hand that the per capita debt of the inhabitants of that town is over $1,000 apiece. By the same token this system has so grown without restriction or planning that, after the last session of the New York Legislature, I was compelled to veto many local bills, especially those affecting towns and villages in Westchester County, on the general ground that these bills were establishing new officials, boards and commissions, without regard to uniformity, or were enabling officials, boards and commissions to spend the taxpayers' dollars in the millions without any approval on the part of the taxpayers themselves and without recourse.

The other side of the picture relates to the relief of local units of government through functions which are no longer purely local, even though the geography of the local units may remain the same. Let me cite some examples.

During the early history of the country, roads, for instance, were used almost exclusively by the people living within a given community, and it was proper that they should be required to maintain these roads. Now, however, almost no road is a local road and this function of government, originally a purely local town function, has now become one of county and State concern.

I know of no business reason, and can think of none, why the town as a unit of administration of highway expenditure should longer exist. I shall propose to the next Legislature that the citizens of any county in this State may in their discretion substitute a county highway organization for the present large number of town highway organizations, one in each town, which now exist. If an enabling act of this kind is passed, and if the counties of this State shall avail themselves of the act, it will result in the substitution of fifty-seven county highway organizations in the place of the nine hundred and thirty-three existing town highway departments. Were this purely a business proposition, the decision would be immediately and promptly made. It would result in building more and better town highways for the same amount of money. More than that, it would result in the opening up of vast areas of the State of New York which today, because they are off a concrete State road, have shown no increase in value and have shown steadily decreasing populations.

Another example: Except for the fact that larger health districts are permissible, the town is still the unit for health administration in rural communities. With modern means of transportation no good reason exists in most cases for that form of administration. Disease germs are no respecters of political boundary lines. They will flit from one town to another without the slightest thrill when they pass over town lines. There is no doubt that administrative health units larger than the town are imperative in these modern times.

Still another example: Every two years in this State we elect in each town a collector of taxes — over 930 of them in all. In the old days when a horse and buggy furnished the most rapid means of communication, a town collector's existence was justified. The town collector today is paid by the fee system and there is a definite premium for his own pocketbook if he lets a collection of taxes slide and later gets a higher fee for the delay. It would be right, of course, in some towns to provide, as a matter of convenience, some central point and some one individual — say the town clerk — who might receive the payment of bills voluntarily brought in. But, in the main, the principal tax collecting agency might well be the office of the county treasurer.

I shall ask the next Legislature for enabling legislation which would allow the citizens of a county, if they so wished it, to place the duty of collecting taxes in the office of the county treasurer, providing at the same time for the sending out of uniform tax bills, with definite notation thereon telling each taxpayer what his money was going to be used for; how much was to go to the State; how much to the county; how much for roads; how much for schools and other purposes. It has been estimated that the consolidation of tax collecting under a county official would save the taxpayers of this State over half a million dollars a year by the elimination of unnecessary existing town officials.

Finally, it is right that we should give serious consideration to the office of Justice of the Peace. These town officials are in most cases paid by fees. Their duties are threefold, to hold and commit violators of the law, to try minor violations of the law, sitting as magistrates, and to hear and try small civil actions happening within their town. In most cases Justices of the Peace have had no legal training, and, while many of them are conscientious in the exercise of their functions, the great majority of the Justice of the Peace courts in this State give unsatisfactory and, in many cases, costly justice. Simplified and less costly justice for the average citizen is a crying need of the whole Nation. One of the first steps will be to reorganize the whole system of Justices' Courts, retaining possibly some individual in every township, who shall have the jurisdiction of a committing magistrate but placing the trial of both criminal and civil cases in the hands of qualified and trained judges. By this means we shall gain much, both for a larger measure of justice and for the saving of the taxpayer's pocketbooks. . . .

I consider this subject of local government one of the major outstanding problems confronting the people of the State of New York. I consider that it is the major outstanding problem in almost every other State. I hope that next year New York will have the courage, the common sense, and the will, through its Legislature, to start this definite reform. I want to see this State save millions in taxes for the benefit of the present generation, but even more I want to see our generation reorganize and improve an outworn system for the sake of those sons and daughters who will come after us.

63 ⟨ The Governor Persists in His Recommendation for Study and Reorganization of Local Government. April 9, 1931

To the Legislature:

LOCAL county, town, village and district government in this State during the year 1929 cost the taxpayers $192,116,594.66. This does not include the cost of city governments.

This huge total remains in spite of the fact that, as a result of the recommendations of the Agricultural Advisory Commission, which I appointed in 1928, the State has passed measures of rural tax relief which have reduced the cost of local government by $24,000,000 annually.

There is no doubt in the minds of those who have studied, even superficially, the system of local government in New York State that it is both extravagant and inefficient. It is important to bear in mind that for the last several years every penny of real estate tax which is paid in this State goes into the cost of local government; not a cent of it goes into the State treasury. Our form of local government has for the main part come down to us from a period of two hundred years ago with few, if any, fundamental changes. It is now so out of line with modern conditions that in addition to being extremely expensive, it is inconceivably inefficient. The taxpayers are not only paying an exorbitant sum for their form of government, but they are not even getting their money's worth. Millions of dollars can be saved annually by abolishing useless offices, by eliminating the pernicious fee system and by allowing local communities to create consolidations of districts and scattered functions. We can retain home rule and at the same time apply modern business methods.

For several years I have requested the Legislature merely to study this question with a view to reorganizing the whole system. There can be no justification for the steadfast refusal to investigate it. Once again I urge that your Honorable Bodies do not adjourn this year without creating a commission to study this problem, so that the taxpayers of the State, and particularly those residing in every part of the State outside of cities, may be relieved of the terrific burden of governmental expense which they now carry.

64 ❨Address at University of Virginia on the Excessive Costs and Taxes in Local Government. Charlottesville, Va. July 6, 1931

THE cost of Government in this country, particularly that of local government, is causing considerable concern. We are told that the aggregate expenditure of Federal, State and local government is approximately twelve or thirteen billion dollars yearly. Of this sum the Federal Government spends approximately one-third, State Governments about 13 percent, leaving considerably more than one-half as the cost of local government. Notwithstanding the influence of the war on Federal governmental expenditures these ratios have existed, with slight variations, since 1890. It is manifest that inasmuch as the cost of local government constitutes the major portion of our aggregate tax bill, we must, if we hope for lower taxes or less rapid increases in taxes, analyze local government and see if its workings may not be simplified and made less expensive for the taxpayers.

The form of local county and town government as we know it in most of our States dates back to the Duke of York's laws, enacted about 1670. The design was to meet conditions as they existed at the time and was continued by American States after the Revolutionary War. It is astonishing how few changes have been made in the form since the formation of our Nation. We may assume that at the time of its adoption it was suited to the conditions of that period. You will recall that no steamboats, railroads, telephones, telegraphs, motor vehicles or good roads were in existence. Means of transportation and communication were meager. The swiftest methods of travel or of communication were the saddle horse, the stage coach and the canal.

Sometimes we refer to that age as the "horse and buggy age." Perhaps it would be more accurate to describe it as the "ox-cart age." We had no urban centers—only a few overgrown villages. Our population was almost exclusively rural. In those days at least eight out of every ten workers obtained a living by tilling the soil. The people lived in small territorial groups and led local community lives. They subsisted almost entirely on the things which they produced or which were produced by others in their locality. A town form of government was the natural form. It suited the conditions of the time.

Moreover, the need for governmental service was not extensive. Trails met the need of the limited inter-community travel where expensive motor routes are now necessary. Little attention was given to public health. There might be a village pump, but otherwise each citizen took care of his own water supply, and drainage and garbage disposal were family concerns. At first police and fire protection were not considered municipal functions. Every community made provision for its own poor. An education in the three R's was deemed sufficient for the average child.

But conditions have changed. We have witnessed a most remarkable growth in population and an astonishing transformation in social and economic conditions. Factory production and a high degree of specialization even in our agriculture have kept step with improved methods of transportation and communication, with the result that community living on the old pattern has vanished. Instead of producing for our own families and neighbors to consume, we are putting our thought and labor on products that go to distant cities and States and even to foreign lands. We clothe ourselves in the fabrics of distant factories, we build our homes of materials transported perhaps thousands of miles and our food is collected from the four corners of our own continent and from all the other continents and the seas of all the world.

Our population, too, has become in part transient. We follow the call of industry, of ambition or of whim from community to community and from State to State. It is not only in the newer regions of America that the old resident may find himself in the minority. The personnel and even the character of the population in any village in one of our older States may change within a few years. Every village and every city and every community is made up of rapidly shifting groups whose members are units in a national economic and social scheme rather than fixed residents of any community. The untraveled person has become comparatively a rarity.

Things which originally were of local or community concern are now of much wider interest. This applies, as you will readily agree, to such things as roads, schools, public health, the care of the socially dependent and virtually every activity of local government. Yet we have continued to use the machine designed under radically different conditions as the major instrument through which to sell governmental service in this age of bewildering movement.

Let us inspect the machinery of local government as it exists today. In this country of ours we have, it is said, 500,000 units of government. They range from the Federal Government down to the smallest school or special district. Take my own State as an instance. We have, first, sixty-two counties and sixty cities, but this is a mere beginning. We go on from these larger wheels of the machine to find 932 towns, and according to the last count, 525 villages, 9,600 school districts and 2,365 fire, water, lighting, sewer and sidewalk districts, a grand total of 13,544 separate, independent governmental units. Carrying the analysis a step further let me cite an example: a small, densely populated suburban county adjacent to New York City where we have three towns and two cities. Again, that is only a start. To these we must add forty villages, forty-four school districts *and one hundred and fifty-six* special districts in order to understand how complicated the local governmental problem in that county really is — a total of 246 governmental units in one county.

The expenditures of local government have increased at an astonishing rate. In 1890 local government in the entire Nation cost $487,000,000. In 1927, the last year for which complete figures are available, the government of lesser units within States cost $6,454,000,000. It increased from a per capita of $7.73 in 1890 to $54.41 in 1927. Just that you may see what has happened in a small unit such as a county, let me say that in the suburban county to which I have referred, all local taxes in 1900 amounted to $337,000 and in 1929, in round figures, $22,000,000. In that space of time the valuation of taxable property increased thirty-five times, but the taxes increased sixty-five times, while population multiplied only five and one-half times. In another case, that of a rural, agricultural county, local taxes amounted to $158,000 in 1900 and to $1,150,000 in 1929. In this case taxes were multiplied seven times, tax valuations slightly more than two times, while the population of the county actually decreased 5 percent. In the suburban county per capita local taxes in 1900 were six dollars and in the rural county four dollars and thirty cents. But by 1929 per capita taxes were ninety dollars in the suburban county and fifty-two dollars in the rural community.

These figures demonstrate, first, the very rapid growth in the cost of rural government; second, that such growth was very much more rapid than the increase in either taxable wealth or population; and, third, it presents sharply the question whether we are obtaining our money's worth through this method of buying governmental service.

These conditions have presented in my State — and I think similar problems are present in every State — the question of how to finance local government. In the main, local government must depend for its revenue upon a general property tax. To a very great extent that tax has degenerated into a tax on real estate only, and as local expenditures have increased the tax on real estate has mounted. In the two counties to which I have referred the tax rates ranged in the suburban county in 1900 from fourteen to seventeen dollars per thousand and in the rural county from seven to twenty-one dollars per thousand. In 1929 the suburban county rates ranged from twenty-four to forty-six dollars, while the rates in the rural county were from twenty-five to fifty-four dollars.

The increase in taxes on farm real estate indicates in a striking way the increases in taxation that have occurred and the added burden which this places upon agriculture. Here are some illustrations from New York State.

On a selected group of good farms, taxes just doubled in the

291

period from 1914 to 1923. During the same period the general price level increased only 27 percent. In another case on three farms in an average agricultural county of the State where records are available for 100 years, the increases in taxes from 1825 to 1925 were as follows:

Farm No. 1, from $2.48 to $101.44
Farm No. 2, from $2.33 to $140.36
Farm No. 3, from $2.38 to $115.20

These are typical of increases on several other farms where records are available. This is perhaps the most graphic method of showing the increase on farm property.

On the same group of farms mentioned above, it required three bushels of wheat on the average to pay the taxes on one farm in 1825. In 1925, it required 104 bushels of wheat. In other words, the tax burden per farm on the average of six farms increased in 100 years from three bushels of wheat to 104 bushels of wheat. On these same six farms it required at the going rates for labor six days of labor to pay for the taxes per farm in 1825, and 37 days of labor per farm in 1925.

Taxes bear more heavily upon the poor farms than upon the good farms. In one township where approximately 40 percent of the farms were abandoned, the taxes averaged 3.4 percent of the real value of the farms. On six farms in that township the taxes were over 10 percent of what the farmer considered to be the market value of his farm. Many other figures could be cited from our available farm cost data to indicate similar changes that have taken place in farm taxes.

Accompanying these increases in local rates has been an increasing demand for relief of the burden on real estate. A study was made in New York of the trend in the tax burden on real property, covering a period from 1915 to 1927. That study disclosed that in the wealthy, growing counties of the State the true burden on realty increased 16½ percent in those twelve years, while in the rural, agricultural counties the increase in the burden was 43 percent. This established to our satisfaction that something must be done to equalize the burden of taxation as between different counties and communities. Various remedies were suggested, which grouped themselves as follows:

1. To abolish the direct State tax on real estate and personal property;
2. To share with localities State-collected taxes;
3. To grant State aid; and
4. To reorganize local governments, or at least transfer from local government to larger units of administration some of the functions now performed locally.

In New York we have invoked all of these methods except that of reorganizing or simplifying local government. That has been advocated by my distinguished predecessors in office and by me. As yet nothing has been accomplished in that direction. The Legislature for various reasons has almost wholly neglected or refused to act on any of the proposals either to simplify local government or to make a comprehensive study of local government, looking toward improvements. For instance, based upon the report of a commission of eminent health authorities, I urged the enactment of a law this year which would establish the county as the unit for health administration, thereby reducing from more than one thousand to about one hundred the number of health administrative units. I believed the service would be improved, the public health better protected, more efficient use of the tax dollar obtained and discrimination against the rural population as compared with the urban population eliminated. That proposal was allowed to die in the Legislature. In another case I proposed to eliminate from the fee system for handling State aid for public education an expenditure of more than $300,000 now being made under the present system in the form of a fee of 1 percent paid to town supervisors for acting as intermediaries in the transfer of funds, and again the Legislature failed to approve.

One of the remedies proposed was to abolish the direct State tax on real and personal property. That we accomplished in New York during the first year of my first term. In that respect we followed Virginia's course established by your distinguished Governor Byrd. A second remedy that we have embraced in New York is that of sharing with the localities certain taxes collected by the State. During the last completed fiscal year the State returned to the various units of local government more than eighty-five million dollars as their share of taxes collected by the State. While I am on this point, let me say that this remedy is not without its dangers. I incline strongly to the view that it should be adopted only when some form of guaranty is exacted that the funds so distributed will be efficiently and economically used. Too frequently, I fear, do the local officials view revenue obtained in this way as "easy money" and spend it accordingly. I am convinced that it is not always used to reduce the general property tax. I am opposing the further development of this program in New York unless more adequate and complete guaranties are required of the sub-divisions that the funds will be distributed so as actually to reduce the local tax burden or to provide on an efficient basis for services really needed.

Still another remedy that New York has applied to the excessive local tax load is that of granting State aid to local government for specified projects and services. This year the State is appropriating one hundred million dollars for the aid of public schools, more than three million dollars for county highways and something more than four million dollars for town highways. More than one-third of the New York State budget consists of items of this form of aid to localities.

This method of relieving the local tax burden is subject to the same dangers as that of sharing taxes with the sub-divisions of the State; it is apt to lead to extravagance and to result in the inefficient use of money. As I see the situation under the present distribution of functions, State aid is essential in New York and probably the same conditions obtain in other American States. Too frequently, however, State aid is granted and the money turned over to the localities without requiring that its expenditure shall be subject to State supervision, without exacting any guaranties that the aid so granted will be economically used or applied to reduce the local tax load. In this regard I think our New York system is lax, and I venture to believe that may be truthfully said of similar aid granted in other States.

Finally we come to the remedy of lightening the local tax burden by transferring from local government to the State Government, or at least to a larger division of government, some functions of local government, that is to say, transferring the responsibility or the obligation to pay for certain improvements or governmental services. This method of local tax relief is rather extensively used in New York. After my election in 1928, I appointed a commission known as the Agricultural Advisory Commission. The purpose put before its distinguished members was to devise methods of assisting and promoting the interests of the rural population of the State, and of agriculture as an industry in the State and to see if and to what extent justice might be done by way of equalizing taxes as between the rural and the urban communities.

The first reform the commission recommended was that the State assume the entire cost of completing and maintaining the State highway system. Under the then existing law the counties were required to contribute thirty-five percent of the cost of such highways and to pay approximately $600,000 annually for their maintenance. It worked out this way: one of the wealthiest counties could pay its share of the cost of completing the State highway system by levying one tax of thirty-seven cents per thousand dollars of taxable valuation, while in a poor rural county a tax of forty-six dollars per thousand would have to be levied.

The recommendation of the commission was adopted. Thereby the State relieved the counties of an aggregate expenditure of fifty-four million dollars for construction, and an annual charge of six hundred thousand dollars for maintenance.

The next recommendation of the commission was based on the town highway or "dirt road" situation. The State had been granting State aid to the towns, but under a plan which permitted the wealthiest town in the State to obtain out of the State treasury fifteen hundred dollars for each mile of town highway, while the most that any one of six or seven hundred poor towns succeeded in obtaining was twenty-five dollars per mile. Tax rates for the maintenance of town highways ranged from a dollar or two to as high as sixteen or eighteen dollars per thousand of taxable valuation. The high taxes were invariably found in the poor rural towns.

To remedy this condition a law was enacted which provided in substance that no town need have a tax rate higher than three dollars per thousand and that the State would give to a town as State aid the difference between the proceeds of a three-mill levy and a sum needed to create a fund equal to one hundred dollars for each mile of town highway. You will readily see that this tended greatly to relieve excessive local taxation and also to equalize the burden of supporting the town highway system.

The commission then turned to rural schools. It found that school tax rates varied from one dollar to more than twenty dollars per thousand. As in the case of highway taxes, the very high rates were found to obtain in the rural, agricultural communities. The principal of equalization was invoked here with the result that rural schools in our State can now be supported adequately with a tax rate no higher than four dollars per thousand, the State contributing the difference between the proceeds of such a tax and a sum sufficient to maintain the schools.

Attention was then given to bridges in the State highway system. The State had required the counties to pay thirty-five percent of the cost of all bridges in the State system. The commission proposed, and a law was enacted, pursuant to which the State assumed the entire cost of building bridges and of maintaining them when constructed. This automatically relieved the counties from an expenditure of $34,750,000, and to that extent eased local taxes.

In addition to these things the State relieved the counties of twenty million dollars for grade-crossing eliminations, and engaged to pay one-half of the cost for snow removal.

I have mentioned these things that you may know of the effort we have made in New York to take from the sub-divisions of the

State the burden of excessive local taxation, and I think you will agree with me that we have gone a long way.

You will readily realize, however, that in our efforts thus far we have merely shifted from local government to the State Government expenditures for these purposes. It is true that in some instances the State is certainly doing these things better and more economically than the localities would have done them, and in that way genuine economy has resulted. It is also true that through these measures we have gone far toward equalizing the tax load in New York State; but the fact remains that we are still supporting a complicated machine of local government which seems to me and to many others unreasonably expensive, wasteful and inefficient. In our effort thus far we have succeeded in reducing somewhat in the aggregate the cost of this elaborate machine. Is it not time that we should analyze this form of local government and see how far it is suited to the conditions of today? Think of it in this light if you will: No citizen of New York can live under less than four governments: Federal, State, county and city. If one lives in a town outside of a village, he is under five layers of government: Federal, State, county, town and school. If he lives in an incorporated village, another layer is added. If he lives in a town outside of the village, he may be in a fire, water, lighting, sewer and sidewalk district, in which case there are ten layers of government.

A citizen so situated has just too much governmental machinery to watch. It is too complicated for him to understand. He may not sense or realize that ten sets of officials are appropriating public funds, levying taxes and issuing bonds. His attention is not usually centered on local government, for seldom, if ever, does he know what sums are being appropriated, what taxes are being levied or what bonds issued. Means for gaining information concerning these things are altogether inadequate.

I question whether there is any real need for so many overlapping units of government. I incline strongly to the view that much can and will be accomplished by reorganizing and simplifying the machinery of local government.

297

Recently a comprehensive study of this problem was made in the State of North Carolina. The conclusion reached in the report of that survey is that a radical reorganization of local government is needed. It is intimated that county government is obsolete and that the county as a unit of administration may well be eliminated. It is conceded that it will take time to secure majority support for that proposal, and in the meantime it is urged that counties be consolidated and a greatly simplified form of county government be set up to replace present cumbersome forms and many officials. The report of a similar study in New Jersey reaches substantially the same conclusion.

I am quite convinced that the excessive cost of local government can most effectively be reduced by simplifying the local governmental organization and structure and by reallocating the responsibility for performing various services, according to a logical analysis rather than by accident or tradition. I think we need to consider each service and decide what administrative unit and what size unit can most effectively and economically perform that service. The smaller units of rural government are so unequal in wealth that some are unable to maintain satisfactory roads and schools even with excessively high tax rates, while others with very low rates are able to spend generously and even extravagantly. All overlapping of local jurisdictions should be abolished. I incline to agree with those who hold that one or at most two layers of local government subordinate to the sovereignty of the State are adequate and that we ought seriously to undertake the radical reorganization and reallocation of functions necessary to accomplish the elimination of all others.

There remains to be mentioned another remedy for the excessive cost of local government — the controlling of local expenditures by State or district authority. It is familiarly referred to as the "Indiana plan." In that State ten or more taxpayers in a tax district may appeal to the State tax commission from the local budget or from a proposed bond issue. After hearing, the State tax commission may reduce the proposed appropriation or the amount for which bonds may be issued, or eliminate the item altogether.

Much can be said in favor of this method of controlling local expenditures. It has passed beyond the experimental stage in Indiana, and the information before me indicates it is supported by public sentiment. Colorado and New Mexico have modified forms of the Indiana plan. Ohio, Oklahoma and Oregon have adopted the idea, but the control is exercised through district boards. This general method of controlling the excessive cost of local government is worthy of consideration by the authorities of every State.

If you will permit me to be conservatively prophetic, I foresee in all of the States of the Union in coming years a progressively strengthening movement for reform of the local governmental scheme. It has already, I believe, been much too long delayed and this fact has cost us many an unnecessary dollar in taxation, and on the other hand has deprived us of improvements and services in the way of better protection of our lives and property and of better facilities for orderly, happy living that we might have had with the same expenditure.

We all of us recognize, I think, that much of the increase in the aggregate of governmental expense has been inevitable and necessary. Our limited glimpse today of the functions of local government has been sufficient to show that government has been quite properly called upon to assume an increasing number of responsibilities that once belonged to the individual and the family. In the same way the larger units of government have been properly and logically forced to assume functions that once belonged to the lesser units. The demands of a different sort of civilization and a different sort of national economy have forced us to redistribute the burdens which the public service imposes.

Roads, for instance, are no longer merely local facilities. They are avenues of communication and channels of necessary commerce between all communities of a State and between a State and its neighbors, close and distant. So we have been compelled to build them on a greater scale and to find new ways of meeting and distributing the cost as far as possible upon those who are benefited.

We face the question of education and we find a mandate from the State as sovereign that the children of all shall be given opportunities to learn. In fact it is more than a State mandate, for the American system of education is in fulfillment of a national purpose intimately associated with the great experiment in democracy we are still carrying on after the lapse of three centuries since our forefathers came here to undertake it and to pass its responsibilities on to us along with the inspired ideal which created them. The State's responsibility for education cannot be escaped by passing it on in one case to a city of teeming millions and in another to a dozen farmers scattered over miles of countryside. It is not solely on an altruistic basis that we consider the educational needs of the farm boy and girl as well as those of the tenement children in the city. The character and training of our fellow foot-loose Americans of the future are a matter of concern to us and to our descendants. They will have their part in making up the civilization in which we shall live a generation hence.

We are beginning to recognize, too, that the public health is more than a local responsibility. Disease knows nothing about town lines, nor do bacilli undertake to inquire about local jurisdictions. Their carriers are on the public highways and riding in the railroad trains. If we care nothing about the fact that a farmer's children are dying of infection or malnutrition — and that can happen in the country, too — we can still give some thought to the weaklings and the sufferers whom we may have to support in some day not far off.

Crime ceased to be a local matter and the criminal adopted a statewide or national range, if not a broader citizenship, long before we thought it necessary to do anything about it. But that is a question too far-reaching to discuss here further than to say that, along with the general administration of justice and of penology and along with the care of the defective and the insane, the problem of crime has long since transcended the scope of petty jurisdictions. State sovereignty alone can cope with it, and that must be reinforced by better and more adequate and less antiquated means of cooperation between the States.

As to all these matters, I expect to see an increased measure of assumption of functions and responsibilities by the State, through one means or another. We have seen how the effort to equalize the tax burden has made the State the holder of the purse strings as to a large proportion of local expenditures. This creates a responsibility for wise expenditure that can hardly be avoided by the State, in justice to those who have been taxed on a statewide basis to replenish the State's treasury. This responsibility, it seems to me, is fairly certain to result in much closer and more authoritative supervision of all local expenditures. This will mean inevitably a closer integration of local authority with statewide authority, based on the fact that as to many functions some competent State authority with expert staffs and statewide information will possess both an advisory and a veto power over the use of funds for local expenditure.

It seems entirely logical that local authority must consolidate, eliminating many of the local government layers, in order to retain any appropriate measure of home rule over local affairs. Certainly the time has come to give serious consideration to the consolidation of a great many local jurisdictions of one kind and another.

I should like the privilege of stating as forcibly as I can one general conclusion that has long been in my mind. That is, that too many of us have been lazy-minded in this matter of government. We like to talk in large terms about the comparative advantages and defects of democracy and autocracy; we like to admire patriotically the work of our forefathers in devising our forms of government or to criticise them as too slavish imitators, but we are terrifically dilatory in following our forefathers' example by seeking to plan and devise for our own immediate needs and for the future; particularly, we hate the details of government. We talk about Russia's five-year plan and the excellence or iniquity of Mussolini's system, in preference to giving consideration to the question whether a town supervisor is good for anything or inquiring what a village health officer does to earn his pay. This may be because it is easier to form a judgment on matters that are more remote. I hate to think that it is because we prefer to have someone else form our judgments for us.

This suggests to me that those who hold public office should not be content merely to take the duties of their jobs as they find them and to carry them out according to precedent. Those who have had experience in operating the machine should be able to tell of its defects. I once heard of a public official who recommended that his job be abolished as useless. It would be a heartening and refreshing thing if there were a lot more like him.

We heard a great deal during the late war about the challenge to democracy and I think it was a good thing for our complacency to learn that democracy was being challenged. But I think, too, that democracy is being challenged today just as forcibly if not as clamorously. The challenge is heard right here among us from all who complain about the inefficiency, the stupidity and the expense of Government. It may be read in the statistics of crime and seen in the ugliness of many of our communities. It is expressed in all the newspaper accounts of official graft and blundering. It is written on our tax rolls and even in the patriotic-seeming text books that our children study in their schools. It looms large on election day when voters see before them long lists of names of men and women of whom they have never heard to be voted upon as candidates for salaried offices of whose duties and functions the voter has but the haziest impression.

The men who addressed themselves to the task of laying the framework of our national Government after freedom had been won, wrote down in enduring words that their aim was to form "a more perfect union." In writing that ideal into the preamble of the Constitution of the United States, I think they set a task for us as well as for themselves. They were forming a new Government, suited, as they believed, to the conditions of their day, but they were wise enough to look into the future and to recognize that the conditions of life and the demands upon Government were bound to change as they had been changing through ages past, and so the plan of government that they prepared was made, not rigid, but flexible — adapted to change and to progress.

We cannot call ourselves either wise or patriotic if we seek to escape the responsibility of remolding Government to make it more serviceable to all the people and more responsive to modern needs.

65 ❦ Once Again the Governor Urges a Study of Local Government to Bring About Economy and Efficiency. February 29, 1932

To the Legislature:

I INVITE your attention to a matter vital to the objects of economy and efficiency in Government. I have on other occasions pleaded with you to take some steps looking toward reform in the structure of local government in the State, but you have seen fit to delay action. I am returning to the subject now because I think the present condition of our affairs is such that any of you who think at all seriously about the burdens which Government imposes on the taxpayer and the urgent need for the maximum of service at the minimum of expenditure must realize that you owe a duty to the people of the State beyond the mere routine of legislation. I am asking you now most respectfully but insistently to lay aside partisan considerations and consider how we may find means to stop an appalling waste of public funds. I ask you to do more than merely to make a showing of economy by deferring to the future necessary expenditures. I ask you to consider a means of cutting away for all future time needless drains upon the public purse which I am advised by competent authorities run into scores of millions annually.

We have a system of local government in this State whose general form and structure can be traced back beyond the birth of our Nation back to conditions in rural England before ever a colony existed on North American soil. To assert that this structure of Government fits the conditions under which we live today is to utter the most ridiculous of absurdities. It is no more fit for its purpose than an ox-cart would be fit for the task of supplying modern transportation between New York and Chicago.

I am not alone in this belief. It is not a discovery of mine. It has been said over and over again by every authority on political science and every open-minded investigator of public affairs over a period of many years.

Nor is it a condition unique in the State of New York. Other States have been the heirs of the same traditions of customs and government and they, like us, are hampered and harassed in the conduct of their affairs of government and their affairs of ordinary business by the same or similar archaic, expensive and wasteful forms of local organization. Their people are waking to an understanding of the situation. All over the land there is a demand for change and for reform. And other States are taking action. Some have appointed commissions and experts to study their problems, but others have gone beyond that stage and are putting sweeping changes into operation.

Why should the greatest State in the Union lag behind? Are our people so rich and so well able to bear perfectly useless burdens of taxation that we should wait to be the laughing-stock of the people of every progressive commonwealth and an object of derision to every schoolboy who studies the elements of government?

Do you imagine that any set of men can go on indefinitely fooling the people of the State into the belief that they are getting their money's worth in what they spend for local government? Do you imagine that it is possible to explain satisfactorily the fact that local taxation goes on piling up no matter how much of the burden of supplying necessary services to the localities is assumed by the State and financed by other means of taxation? I do not believe it can be done much longer. The people are beginning to realize that they are burdened with a host of useless officials and an intricate mass of local machinery of Government that cannot function efficiently in this present age and cannot properly supply the services that they have a right to expect of Government. And it is through this machinery of Government that 80 percent of the taxes, exclusive of Federal taxes, raised in the State, is being expended.

Everywhere in this State in these difficult times the demand is being made for an explanation of high taxes. I have said that local officials have not been doing their full duty to the taxpayer in making savings that could have been made; and I stand by that assertion. But there is this to be said on behalf of all local officials: that while they might do better than they are doing—much better, in fact, for in many communities the conditions are scandalous—they cannot in fact do well; they cannot govern efficiently, for they have to work with a machinery of Government in which efficiency is not possible.

You do not need to take my word for this. Nor do you need to rely exclusively on your own powers of observation. There is testimony by dispassionate and able observers. Two months ago I decided to seek expert help in presenting this subject in convincing light to you and to the people of the State who have imposed responsibility upon you. I asked the Institute of Public Administration to make a cursory study of the adequacy of the forms of local government in the State and to suggest what general lines of reorganization ought to be attempted. I wish that every one of you might see and might read carefully this report. I hope that your Honorable Bodies will order it to be printed.

Obviously I cannot quote extensively from it here, but I shall cite a few significant paragraphs. . . .

The authors of this report suggested a remedy. They went so far as to outline a general scheme of reorganization. I shall not present that plan to you at this time and I do not wish to be understood as endorsing the specific proposals there suggested. It provides only a starting point for discussion. I am asking instead your cooperation in devising a plan to remedy evils that must be as apparent to you as they are to me and to the authors of this report. In concrete terms, what I am asking is that you create a commission to study this whole matter of reorganization of local government which is so manifestly necessary and urgent so that a definite, well-considered plan on which we may agree may be brought to the stage of action. The expense of such a commission would be trivial in proportion to the actual financial benefits which a sound scheme of reorganization would inevitably bring about. It is the expense of whittling a plug to drive into a hole through which our resources are leaking away.

It seems plain to me that this ought not to be merely a legislative commission. We have had legislative commissions on this subject in the past and they have spent large sums of money and have brought in nothing worth while. I suggest and ask that you create a commission of practical experts, of business men, of students of government, of men and women with real vision and with a determination to accomplish something practical and drastic—not mere tinkering. And it should go without saying that I hope you will see fit to create a commission which will act without any regard at all to partisan politics. If you recognize your duty to do this thing I think you should recognize your greater duty to do it on that basis.

Obviously any such sweeping reform implies an amendment or a series of amendments to the State Constitution. It ought to be possible to lay these amendments before the next session of the Legislature. Such a series of amendments would no doubt authorize consolidation of many existing units of Government, possibly the elimination of towns altogether or at least a consolidation of their functions, and certainly the elimination of many offices that are useless. But I am not advocating any preconceived plan. I am urging instead that you in whom rests the power to propose amendments to our form of Government take the necessary steps to procure a plan that can be put into effect.

Neither am I asking you to enforce any such fundamental change upon the people of the State. I think any amendment proposed should take into consideration the sound principle of home rule. I think the new form or alternative forms of local government to be embodied in the amendment or amendments should be made optional with counties or communities through referendum. If the plan is soundly conceived it will justify itself.

I most earnestly urge that you create such a commission before this session of the Legislature is adjourned. It will be a simple decision to make, a simple act to perform, but a pledge of a sincere desire to bring about economy and efficiency in Government.

X
Better Housing

66 ⁅ The Governor Approves a New Multiple Dwellings Law. April 18, 1929

Memorandum filed with Senate Bill, Int. No. 459, Printed No. 1876, entitled:

"AN ACT in relation to multiple dwellings, constituting chapter sixty-one-a of the consolidated laws."

APPROVED.

THIS bill is the result of long and careful study of a situation involving many conflicting interests in the greatest city in the world. It seeks to improve living conditions affecting hundreds of thousands of our citizens. It is not a perfect bill. Nevertheless, though the effort has been unsuccessfully made many times before to obtain agreement on such legislation, this bill meets with the approval of a substantial majority of civic, business, welfare and charity organizations, owners, builders, architects and tenants.

Some organizations seeking very properly improvement in the so-called old law tenements are wholly dissatisfied because of the failure of this measure to give adequate relief. So am I. That, however, is not a valid reason for disapproving the bill if it gives other needed relief; and I am convinced that it does.

In old law tenements fire retarding requirements are increased, and yard toilets are forbidden. In new law tenements various improvements are called for, such as more stairways and larger courts and yards; and the distinction between the so-called apartment hotel and the legitimate apartment house is done away with. Tall buildings and towers are not forbidden; they must hereafter be built on a larger base area, thus preventing the streets from becoming mere canyons.

On the whole, therefore, the merits of the bill outweigh the objections, and the average citizen will be benefited.

One other point remains, a legal objection involving wide diversity of opinion. Members of the bar in whose ability and sincerity I have the highest confidence have appeared before me on both sides of the question. It is unnecessary to go into the details here. I can say truthfully that the only way to determine this matter is to obtain the opinion of the courts. That would without doubt be asked in the case of any new law affecting so vitally such important property rights.

I am approving the bill in confidence that if its constitutionality is upheld it will go far to improve living conditions for large numbers of people, and that further legislation will be sought to give relief where this bill is inadequate.

67 ❨An Address on Better Housing Conditions (Excerpts). New York City. February 28, 1930

THE marvelous skyline of New York City with its human beehives reaching ever higher and higher until the very clouds hide its towers from the street below, seems always to impress the visitor as the visible symbol of wealth and power. To me, however, these vast structures have always seemed monuments of a thought finer and worthier than mere material prosperity. To me they represent the triumph of courage and vision, the two qualities which have made civilization possible and, above all else, have raised men beyond the level of the brutes. . . .

It is because I appreciate this courage, this determination, this vision which the men of New York have shown, that I make bold tonight to appeal to you to help in something which is still needed to make New York truly the city better as well as the city beautiful. You have just cause for pride in what you have achieved — the tall, slim buildings standing white and clear against the sky — but too often around their feet cluster the squalid tenements that house the very poor — buildings that should have been destroyed years ago, full of dark rooms where the sunlight never enters, stifling in the hot summer days, no fit habitation for any man, far less for the thousands of children that swarm up and down their creaking stairways.

As you have envisioned and dared to create what we have not inaptly called the "skyscraper," is it too much to ask you to cast your eyes lower and picture to your minds a city of apartment homes where light and air and sunshine are enjoyed by everyone? If you should make this a dream come true, you will have achieved that which will bring you far more than satisfied pride, an accomplishment which will bring you the most gratifying of all feelings, the consciousness that you have done much to make life a happier thing, a pleasanter thing for thousands of your fellow men. Is this not a worth-while thing that I am asking of you? This is an old problem and many worthy souls, touched with compassion for the poor, have tried to solve it, but there lie tremendous difficulties in the path.

It is easy to be philanthropic at the expense of others. But even if it were possible, it would not be fair and just to expect a few to bear the heavy financial burden which would fall upon those who convert their present properties to the far more expensive and less remunerative type of buildings.

There are those who say there is no answer, that this city and all great cities must hide in dark alleyways and dingy street buildings that disgrace our modern civilization; where disease follows poverty and crime follows both. I confess I see no clear way, but I vision just outside these walls convincing evidence of what your courage, your vision, your resourcefulness have done, and I believe you will take this up as a body, in mutual conference, and apply your most practical knowledge to this matter of the housing of our poor, that you will find the way; and I believe that if you find the way your courage and persistence will see that it is done.

We recognize, of course, that close cooperation among all of the varied interests is necessary to the solution of a big problem in a big way; that mere action by one civic body can perhaps lead the way but cannot carry through a broad plan without the help of all of the other civic bodies. If New York City were a tenth of its present size, it would be a simple matter to bring the two or three civic bodies together on a common ground. We who know New York, and the magnitude of its geographical problems, its zoning and residential and business problems, understand that we must deal with the representatives of six or seven million people instead of with the representatives of six or seven hundred thousand people. Nevertheless, the city is notable for the public spirit of its leading business and professional men and women. Furthermore, I am confident that there exist a real sympathy and a great desire to help on the part of those in authority in the city government, and that the officials of the city and the boroughs will be glad to work with the civic organizations toward a common end.

Cast your thoughts back fifty years. The slums of New York were even then a by-word throughout America. Countless books were written describing the horrible conditions of life among the poor in those days. It is a fact that the proportion of residents of this city who in those days lived under slum conditions was extremely large. These fifty years have shown a marvelous change for the better. The proportion of those who are compelled to live under uncivilizing and inhuman conditions has declined steadily, year by year. Nevertheless there are still many focal points, many whole districts scattered throughout the city where men and women and children are still herded together in a way which is not right according to the standard of 1930.

We have a definite goal — the elimination of these conditions altogether — the seeking within our own lifetime of the day when we can say to the world: New York is a city without slums; New

York is a city where every one of its 10,000,000 people can have living conditions which guarantee to them air and light and sanitation; New York is the first American city to get rid of the stigma of the slum.

You who may be interested in the problems of transportation and its sister, trade, are of necessity in a position where you can help to a very great degree in the working out of the plans to bring an approach to this goal — the dwelling places of the inhabitants of our city linked up with the places where our people pursue their daily tasks. There is, indeed, a trinity of problems; the dwelling places, the working places, and transportation, the connecting link between the two. It is for this that I appeal to you to do your very necessary part in this undertaking which is bound in the next few years to demand the attention of the public of the city and of the State.

68 ◖ The Governor Vetoes a Bill Permitting Multiple Occupancy in Tenement Houses. April 4, 1932

Memorandum filed with Senate Bill, Introductory No. 551, Printed No. 1711, entitled:
  "AN ACT to amend the multiple dwelling law, in relation to letting of rooms within apartments in tenement houses."
  NOT APPROVED.

THIS bill is a distinct step backward in proper tenement-house regulation. It proposes to legalize what is now illegal, to wit, the occupancy of a single apartment in a tenement house by more than one family.

Under this bill, any number of families could crowd into a single apartment without alteration of or increase in the number of stairs or public halls or the addition of the necessary sanitary, cooking or other ordinary housekeeping conveniences. Certain minor safeguards are proposed, which as a practical matter would be ineffective and likely to be evaded.

The bill is being urged on the plea that the present law is not being enforced. I do not believe that that argument is a sound one. The practical effect of the bill would be to make permanent and legal what in effect amounts to lodging-house conditions in buildings primarily designed for family occupancy.

69 ❰ The Governor Approves a Bill Limiting Cellar Occupancy in Tenement Houses.
April 4, 1932

Memorandum filed with Senate Bill, Introductory No. 1526, Printed No. 2082, entitled:
"An Act to amend the multiple dwelling law in relation to cellar and basement rooms in tenement houses."
Approved.

This bill permits certain cellar occupancy for janitors only up to April 1, 1933, without the payment of rent.

This is a temporary and final moratorium and I am firmly convinced that when this moratorium is up, this kind of cellar occupancy should be permanently discontinued.

The time for making these basement rooms conform to the new standards is already past. I serve notice on any landlords who have not yet acted in accordance with the purpose of the law that

I will do all in my power to prevent any further extension beyond April 1, 1933. They should act now and not be in the position of law-violators next year.

XI

Prohibition and Repeal of the Eighteenth Amendment

IN ADDITION to the documents printed in this chapter the reader is referred to my campaign speeches during the campaign of 1928 in which I stated my opposition to the enactment of a new State enforcement statute (see, for example, Item 7 of this volume), and to my speeches in the campaign of 1930, in which I definitely advocated the repeal of the Eighteenth Amendment (Items 87 and 89 of this volume). See also Items 81, 131 on page 653, and Item 134 of this volume.

70 ⟨ The Governor Advocates Repeal of the Eighteenth Amendment. September 9, 1930

Dear Bob:

I WANT to tell you how very happy I am that you are slated to be the temporary chairman of the Democratic State Convention, and further to tell you of some of the matters which I think should be stressed at the Convention.

On the matter of the serious unemployment situation, I regret to say that my trips to practically every part of the State this summer confirm the fear that the depression exists not only in a few of the larger cities, but extends to all of the smaller cities and even to the villages and rural districts. You know this situation so thoroughly through your excellent work in the Senate, that I shall not attempt to point out to you the primary causes of this depression, or that it is nationwide as well as statewide. I shall, however, send you data showing the very important practical steps which have been taken by the State Government to improve conditions in our State and also my suggestions for an immediate study of the broad subject of unemployment relief by a contributory system and not dole methods.

I shall also send you a brief outline showing the very important steps which have been taken during the past two years for social welfare, notably the prison and hospital programs, the organization of the parole system, etc., etc.

You are also familiar with the great strides which have been taken this year in relation to the development of State-owned water power and a closer control over public utilities in general, both with the purpose of securing for the consumer more equitable rates.

The very notable achievements in farm relief and in the development of a permanent farm policy are described in my various messages to the Legislature, and I hope that you will read them. The farm population has been relieved of paying approximately thirty million dollars a year of highway tax, real estate tax and school burdens, and we are definitely working out a State program for dirt road improvement.

319

Old age security against want is provided for by the first measure along this line ever adopted by the State. It goes into effect on January first next, and applications are now actually being received.

These are only a few of the high points, and it is worth while to note that all this progress has been made only after determined opposition by the Republican legislative leaders.

Finally, but of very great importance, is the subject of prohibition, which is of great moment in every part of the State. I am convinced that this is true not only in the large cities but also in the smaller communities and in the agricultural districts. It is my belief that in the State of New York an overwhelming public opinion is opposed to the Eighteenth Amendment. The crux of the matter is that the Eighteenth Amendment has not furthered the cause of a greater temperance in our population, but on the contrary (quoting from language used in a resolution adopted by the American Legion) it has "fostered excessive drinking of strong intoxicants" and has "led to corruption and hypocrisy," has brought about "disregard for law and order" and has "flooded the country with untaxed and illicit liquor." I personally share this opinion.

Literally dozens of schemes have been proposed by well-meaning citizens seeking means and methods of improving the existing situation while at the same time leaving the Eighteenth Amendment in full force and effect. The language of the Eighteenth Amendment is so direct and so clear that it seems to me the time has come when these people should no longer try to beat about the bush. It is not merely a matter of the Volstead Act or the Jones Act or any other piece of mere legislation, Federal or State, under the Eighteenth Amendment. It is the Amendment itself.

The force and effect of the Eighteenth Amendment can be eliminated, of course, only by a new constitutional amendment. This would supersede and abrogate the Eighteenth Amendment and substitute therefor a new constitutional provision. That is clear.

The fundamental of a new amendment must be the restoration

of real control over intoxicants to the several States. The sale of intoxicants through State agencies should be made lawful in any State of the Union where the people of that State desire it, and conversely the people of any State should have the right to prohibit the sale of intoxicants, if they so wish, within their own borders. This recognizes the undoubted fact that in a Nation of such wide extent and with such diversity of social conditions public opinion and practical administration in regard to methods of seeking a greater temperance differ very greatly in different parts of the country, and even in different parts of the same State. There is no doubt that in many States the actual sale of intoxicants would continue to be prohibited at least by statute whereas in many other States a reasonable sale of intoxicants through State agencies would in the opinion of the great majority of citizens of these States do much to bring about less intoxication, less corruption and bribery, and more regard and respect for law and order. This latter applies definitely to the State of New York.

It is therefore clear to me that it must remain not only the right but the duty of the Federal Government to protect States which continue to prohibit the sale of intoxicants.

Furthermore, I am positive in saying that there must be some definite assurance that by no possibility at any time or in any place shall the old saloon come back. Therefore, the control of any sale of any intoxicants should be wholly in the hands of the States or of State agencies.

Finally, there should be definite recognition of the extension of home rule to the lower subdivisions of government, in other words, a recognition of the right of cities, villages or towns by popular vote to prohibit the sale of intoxicants within their own borders, even though intoxicants may be sold in other parts of the State through State agencies.

So widespread in this State is the resentment against the results of the Eighteenth Amendment, that the time has come to stop talking and to seek action.

Very sincerely yours,

Hon. Robert F. Wagner
New York City

71 ❨ The Governor Approves a Bill Petitioning the Congress to Take Steps toward Repeal of the Eighteenth Amendment. March 31, 1931

Memorandum filed with Assembly Bill, Int. No. 4, Pr. No. 4, entitled: "AN ACT on the application of the legislature of the State of New York petitioning the Congress of the United States of America to call a national Constitutional Convention to repeal Article Eighteen of the Constitution of the United States." APPROVED.

UP TO the present time five joint resolutions and ten different bills have been introduced in the Legislature, all of them calling for some method of changing the Eighteenth Amendment of the Constitution of the United States. Of these resolutions and bills a number have already been passed, of which this is one. I am informed that several others will without doubt be passed by the Legislature between now and final adjournment. As several members of the Legislature have stated the situation to me, "a majority in both houses will vote aye on any and all legislation which is labeled 'wet' regardless of what the resolution or bill contains." The truth of this remark is fairly well demonstrated by the willingness of the Legislature to support every suggestion that looks to a change in the Eighteenth Amendment.

What is really significant of this frame of mind in the Legislature is not the remedies proposed or the fact that there is no unanimity of opinion as to method, but the demonstration given by the majority in the Legislature that they believe an overwhelming sentiment exists in this State which asks for immediate action to change the Eighteenth Amendment. I believe that this sentiment does exist throughout this State and that the greater part of this sentiment is based on two righteous and sane objectives: first, to eliminate the fundamental source of the greater part of modern organized crime; and, second, to promote a greater temperance. To this policy, as I have repeatedly stated, I subscribe.

In the case of this particular bill it is necessary to call public attention to the fact that the Legislature is asking of Congress an impossibility. It says: "The Legislature . . . applies to the Congress . . . to call a National Constitutional Convention to repeal Article Eighteen . . . and no other article of the Constitution." Anyone familiar with the Constitution of the United States knows that no authority is given to the Congress to call a convention to repeal one article and no other. It is, of course, within the power of a convention when called to confine its recommendations to one article, but it is also clearly within its power to propose such other amendments to or changes in the Constitution as it may see fit.

Article V of the Federal Constitution clearly confers upon the Legislatures the right of applying to the Congress for the calling of a Constitutional Convention. For the Governor to veto this bill would be equivalent to his denying to the Legislature their constitutional right to make such application. I do not feel that I am warranted in denying this right to the Legislature by my veto power, even though the present bill is faulty in its language. I am therefore signing the bill in spite of its defect, in order to cooperate with the Legislature in asserting this right which they have under Article V, and above all in order to transmit to the seat of the Federal Government the prevailing sentiment in my State that something be done at once with the Eighteenth Amendment. The bill will be transmitted in accordance with its directions to the Senate, to the House of Representatives and to the Secretary of State of the United States.

XII

The Welfare of the
Underprivileged, the Crippled,
and the Handicapped

IN ADDITION to the documents printed in this chapter the reader is referred for material on the same general subject to Items 5 and 12 of this volume.

72 ❲ An Address on Rehabilitation of the Mentally and Physically Handicapped. Chautauqua, N. Y. July 13, 1929

A T THE end of a week's trip across the State of New York inspecting State hospitals and schools, it is natural that my thoughts have run to the tremendous strides made by mankind in health and in education during the past generation. Take some comparisons. It is less than fifty years ago in this State, and an even shorter time in some other States, that the care of the insane was definitely recognized as a responsibility of the State itself. Many older people can remember the day when mentally deranged members of families were kept at home in seclusion, or else locked up in some local institution which treated the unfortunate victim as a prisoner and not as a patient.

Today, because of an awakened public responsibility and because of great strides in medical science, mental derangement is treated in modern, well-equipped, State-conducted institutions as an illness from which a growing number of patients may and do recover. It is a fact that the percentage of cures is increasing year by year.

Take then the class of cases which falls under the head of mental deficiency, and not insanity. It is only a few years ago that the backward child, the boy or girl who did not seem "normal," was classed as an imbecile or an idiot and practically laid to one side by the family in the community. Today the State recognizes the obligation of turning the backward child into a useful citizen, able to take his or her part in life, and modern science proves that this end can be accomplished in the great majority of cases.

Take next the boys and girls who are broadly classed as juvenile delinquents. A generation ago these children were given either sharp physical punishment in their own localities and turned adrift, usually to repeat their petty crime and misdemeanors, or else were thrown into a common jail and forced to associate with hardened criminals. Today, Government recog-

327

nizes its responsibility to the juvenile offender, and the fact that in the large majority of cases these boys and girls can be made law-abiding, hard-working citizens. Again the records show that the millions of dollars expended by the State in this great cause are well invested, and that potential criminals are, in large numbers, being turned into law-abiding citizens.

Medical science and a new public conscience are also obtaining magnificent results in the field of physical, as opposed to mental, disabilities. At one of the institutes for the deaf the other day I spoke of the deaf and dumb. The superintendent corrected me immediately, saying:

"There are very few deaf and dumb people in the world. They are deaf and, as a consequence, have not been able to speak, but they are not dumb."

The instruction of these deaf people is working wonders. Girls and boys are being taught to read lips and to make themselves understood sufficiently to make their own way in the world. It is an interesting fact that there is ready employment for all graduates of our deaf schools.

Next we come to the problems of the cripples. A generation ago the crippled had no chance. Today, through the fine strides of modern medical science, the great majority of crippled children are enabled, even though the process may take years, to get about and, in many cases, find complete or practically complete cures. In other words, that large part of humanity which used to be pushed to one side or discarded is now salvaged and enabled to play its own part in the life of the community.

This sketch of the development of a generation brings one naturally to the question, What can be done to take further steps in the generation to come? The answer is a simple one. Further progress must of necessity depend on a deeper understanding on the part of every man and woman in the United States. Knowledge of the splendid results already accomplished is not widespread. You can go into thousands of farming districts in this State and you can go into thousands of closely populated wards in our great cities and find ignorance not only of what has been accomplished but of how to go about utilizing the facilities which we already have. There are literally hundreds of thousands of cases of boys and girls in the United States hidden away on the farm or in the city tenements, boys and girls who are mentally deficient or crippled or deaf or blind. Their parents would give anything in the world to have their mental or physical deficiencies cured, but their parents do not know how to go about it.

In other words, education as to simple facts is of vital importance in every State of the Union, and this education is necessary not only for the dwellers on the remote farms and in the crowded tenements, but it is equally necessary for millions of people who now consider themselves well educated.

I wonder, for example, just how many members of the legislatures in the forty-eight States, just how many members of the Congress of the United States know what is being done by their own State Governments or by the Federal Government in taking care of the mentally or physically crippled. I wonder how many of them have taken steps in their own home districts to bring forward those who need care and are now not getting that care.

I wonder how many so-called leading citizens in any town in the United States know what facilities are offered by State and private institutions, or know what great possibilities for cure exist today with the development of modern medical science.

In other words, the progress which will be made in the coming generation will depend not only on the development and extension of governmental activities and of medical discoveries, but just as important, on the education of the already so-called educated people in this development. Through their efforts thousands of children will receive benefits of modern science which they would otherwise not receive.

This is a problem that demands a crusade. The progress of the past fifty years has been great, but we have marched only a short way. The extension of the work must go on until every child in the United States can be assured of the best that science, Government assistance and private aid can give.

It is a task that appeals to our humanity, but it is a task that appeals also to our future economic success. Every citizen, man, woman or child, who is unable to take his or her part in the normal life of modern civilization is a drag on our economic life. Good humanity and good economics demand that the work must go on.

73 ❬ An Address before the State Charities Aid Association. New York City. January 17, 1930

THE most striking and important difference between the civilization of today and the civilization of yesterday is the universal recognition that the first duty of a State, and by that I mean a Government, is to promote the welfare of the citizens of that State. It is no longer sufficient to protect them from invasion, from lawless and criminal acts, from injustice and persecution, but the State must protect them, so far as lies in its power, from disease, from ignorance, from physical injury, and from old-age want.

It is difficult for us who live in the present day to realize what a tremendous change this is from the time, comparatively recent in the world's history, when the State was the instrument of despots for their own aggrandizement and the great body of its citizens were mere serfs, chattels, or cannon fodder at the service of their overlords.

We speak lightly of this being the era of Democracy without realizing what a tremendous change has been brought about, or how it has revolutionized the everyday existence of every one of us. In this building up of a theory of government "by the people, for the people" our country has been the leader of the civilized nations of the world, and I think I can proudly add that our State has been the leader in our country. Nor do I think it an exaggeration to attribute our progressive position very largely to intelligent, tireless and systematic efforts, for almost sixty years, of the State Charities Aid Association. For while there has been a constantly growing understanding of this real and most important

function of government, legislation, as is always the case, has followed with lagging and hesitant footsteps.

It is easy to say that the State must look after the welfare of its
citizens, but to translate that into terms of law and to create additional agencies of government to make such laws effective is not
an easy matter, and can be expedited only by the rousing of public attention and the wise direction of public interest on the part
of unselfish organizations such as yours.

But while we have made commendable progress toward translating indefinite ideals into definite ideas and again converting
these ideas into actual statutes, we have still a long road to travel.
I want particularly to stress my belief that the time has now arrived to elevate our State Department of Public Welfare to the
position of importance and independence which it deserves in
our State machinery. It has been the Cinderella of our Government household. It has been entrusted, haphazardly, with all sorts
of odds and ends of things — the household tasks, as it were, of our
State establishment — which involve hard work and little glory.
Under our new State Constitution it obtained its first real recognition as a separate and individual function of our Government,
but I believe it should be given far more important duties and
far more support and dignity than have yet been accorded it. And
I want to ask your powerful aid, not only for myself but for those
Governors who will succeed me and who, I feel sure, will be
equally impressed with the importance of its work in eventually,
by carefully considered and not too hasty legislation, raising the
Department of Public Welfare more nearly to a level with its
proud sister, the Department of Education. This must be done
step by step, for as yet we are but laying foundations, and an error
in a foundation will eventually bring about the downfall of however perfect a structure is erected on it.

Let me mention briefly some of these matters in which your
society has been particularly effective in the past and to which the
State must give increasing aid, through our Department of Public
Welfare, in the future.

First of all, take your work in connection with neglected or dependent children. You are holding a twentieth anniversary conference of the County Children's Agents representing County Children's Committees of your society. I wonder if the public realizes that forty counties of our State have profited by their intelligent assistance, and on behalf of the State let me gratefully acknowledge the cooperation they have shown with our County Commissioners of Public Welfare, judges of our Children's Courts, and our Board of Child Welfare administering mothers' allowance. There are only four counties where such committees do not exist, and I hope you will soon be able to show a perfect score. The policy of preventing the breaking up of homes and of keeping children under home influence through State assistance, as opposed to the old way of providing institutions for their care after home life had been destroyed, has done more, and will do more, for the good of the people of this State than I think any of us realize.

To your society I look, as well, for unceasing and loyal assistance in my efforts to secure at least a measure of comfort for those who find old age has overtaken them and who have been unable to lay aside, generally without fault of their own, material provision against that time. As you know, there is a commission working out some practical means of systematically aiding aged and dependent citizens, and I feel sure that their recommendations will be carefully studied by all your members, and, if they are found wise and worthy, will receive your vigorous and wholehearted support.

Then there is another very important matter, and that is our public health. It is becoming increasingly apparent that illness is a thing which can be prevented as well as cured. There is much sound common sense in the traditional Chinese method of paying the doctor for the days you are well instead of for the days that you are sick. Here your society has been and can be particularly helpful because there are limits beyond which, under our theory of home rule, the State cannot go. Much must be done by the counties themselves, and I hope that a centralized system of county health units will become a recognized and necessary part of every county government.

I have left to the last the most pressing and important matter of all — what we now call "mental hygiene." Under that head comes the entire tremendous problem of the insane and the mentally defective, a problem already heavy which, I am sorry to say, is increasing under the stress of our swiftly moving modern civilization. Here, as in the case of our criminals, society too long has been content to concern itself with self-protection. It was not so very long ago that the imprisonment of the criminal and the virtual imprisonment of the insane were considered in much the same light. We have progressed a little more rapidly from that unenlightened viewpoint in the case of the mentally diseased than in the case of the criminal, because here there is obviously no confusing question of moral delinquency involved. We now realize that we must endeavor to cure instead of merely to incarcerate in both instances. But even in the matter of the mentally diseased or defective our facilities for cure are still woefully inadequate. No small part of the large expenditure required by the State this year is made necessary by our past neglect to enlarge these facilities as they must be enlarged from year to year.

The further step, which is something that must be undertaken in each case, is the prevention of both insanity and crime. This has just begun. Money spent for prevention represents many times that amount saved by the State in the future. As a State we have done practically nothing toward the prevention of crime and insanity. It is something I hope we will seriously take up immediately. . . .

74 ❡ Radio Address on a Program of Assistance for the Crippled. February 18, 1931

My Friends:

I BELIEVE it was announced that I was going to talk today on why it pays to do things for crippled children and, I might add to that, other kinds of cripples — grown-up cripples as well. I want to talk, of course, about the big human side of relieving distress and helping people to get on their feet, but at the same time I think there is another phase of the broad question of looking after cripples to which some people have never given much thought — the financial side. For instance, I am told that there are somewhere between three and four hundred thousand cripples in this country today — I mean cripples who are pretty thoroughly put out of business, who cannot get around, who cannot perform any useful task — people, in other words, most of them children, who have to be looked after by other people. Think of it, three or four hundred thousand people out of our total population. This is a tremendous percentage.

Now let us figure for a minute in simple terms. Suppose for the sake of argument that three hundred thousand people are out of useful work when they grow to be older and that each one of them, if he could work, could produce one thousand dollars' worth of new products every year. In other words, if the productive value were one thousand dollars a year apiece, three hundred thousand of them would mean three hundred million dollars added to the annual productive capacity of the United States. That is worth thinking about from the purely money end of things. If we could restore every cripple in this country to some kind of useful occupation it would do much to help the general wealth and well-being of the United States.

People know well that restoring one of us cripples — because as some of you know, I walk around with a cane and with the aid of somebody's arm myself — to useful occupation costs money. Being crippled is not like many other diseases, contagious and otherwise, where the cure can be made in a comparatively short time; not like the medical operation where one goes to the hospital and at the end of a few weeks goes out made over again and ready to resume life. People who are crippled take a long time to be put back on their feet — sometimes years, as we all know. Take it from that angle. Suppose for the sake of argument it costs one thousand dollars a year for a crippled child to be put back on his feet and that it takes five years to do it. The cost to the community — because it has to be community effort in most cases, for most families cannot afford it — is five thousand dollars to put that one individual back on his feet. Remember that most of the cripples can in some shape, manner or form be brought back to useful life. Suppose they are brought back so that at the time they are 20 or 21 they have before them the expectation of a long and useful life, perhaps at least 40 years more. During those 40 years each one of them ought to be able to earn one thousand dollars a year. There is forty thousand dollars added to the country's wealth, at a cost of only five thousand dollars. So the net saving or profit to the State or country as a whole is thirty-five thousand dollars. That shows it pays from the money point of view, if from no other.

At the present time in the United States, they tell me, there are about thirty thousand new cases every year of people who become crippled for one reason or another. The first thing we are trying to do everywhere is to cut down that number of new cases; and I have a letter from my old friend Daddy Allen, whom a great many people all over the United States know as the man who started the International Society for Crippled Children which has branches in every civilized country of the world. He tells me that work is going on in every State in this Union to prevent people from getting crippled, and he hopes that as a result, within a short time, instead of having thirty thousand cases, we shall be able to cut it down to 20,000. It would be a tremendous saving if by preventive measures we can keep ten thousand children every year from becoming crippled.

Of course, modern medical science is trying to prevent diseases and troubles of all kinds just as much as it is trying to make cures. This calls for better understanding on the part of the people, for better education on the part especially of the parents, for better conditions surrounding the birth of children, better care in the home, and, equally important, prevention of many unnecessary accidents of all kinds — automobile accidents, train accidents, and so on. So the first step is to work for the prevention of crippling. This covers the great advances that have been made in preventing industrial accidents — unnecessary injuries that come to people who are at work not only in factories, but also in the field, in nearly every State of the Union. The United States now is working hard and spending much money to prevent these industrial accidents. They are far too common, but much has been accomplished and more will be accomplished in the years to come.

Now for the second step — the work of finding cripples all over the United States. We in the State of New York have had surveys made not only in the cities, but also in the country districts and even out to the remote farms that are not reached by R.F.D. carriers. We have had surveys made and have found literally thousands of children and grown-ups who were crippled and had no medical care of the right kind. There are probably today not only hidden away in the big cities, but also in the agricultural and mountainous parts of the United States, other thousands and thousands of crippled children who have never had any proper care, who have never been to a doctor, who have never been to a hospital or been looked over to see whether they could be brought back to useful life. That second step of finding the cripples is gradually being carried out.

Then the third step — the matter of diagnosing what the trouble is. This step is primarily for the doctors; and yet it is true that our good doctors — even the general practitioners — cannot in many cases consider themselves experienced in what is really orthopedic work. In other words, the average practitioner has to go to a specialist when it comes to treating certain types of patients. All over the United States we are establishing, more and more, clinics run by cities, schools, counties or the State, clinics that are within reasonable travel distance of every home, clinics to which the crippled children can be taken. After they have become crippled or after the people in search of them have found them they are taken to the clinic and the case is diagnosed. Great strides have been made in the past few years in providing facilities for the operations that are essential in some cases. But the medical profession is also realizing that many operations can be avoided through a system of plaster casts, massage exercise and other forms of treatment. The main point is to get the case properly diagnosed by the right kind of doctor in the first instance. Then comes the treatment.

The next medical step, which up to this time has not been developed far in this country, is "after care." After the cause of the trouble is known and the first remedies for it have been applied and the child is able to go home, the treatment must not stop; the parents must be taught what to do. Visiting nurses go in occasionally to see how the child is getting on, and furthermore we are developing new methods by which "after care" is being given in schools for crippled children. We do not want to take the children away from their education, of course, and many schools are putting in special facilities for crippled children where along with their education they can be given the right kind of medical treatment. The point to remember is that the overwhelming majority of children who become crippled can with proper treatment be restored to a useful, active life in the community. It seems to me from somewhat wide experience not only of my own, but of other people, the average cripple in this country has about the finest natural disposition of anyone in the community. There is something that comes to crippled children that gives to them happier, better dispositions. They are seldom cross, they are seldom fretful; we nearly always find them ready to cooperate; we find that they turn out well as scholars and that they are ready to assist in every way in the treatment provided for them. . . .

I want to repeat that we owe to every crippled child in the United States a chance to come back, not merely from the big,

337

broad point of view of humanity. I want to emphasize again that by restoring all of these tens of thousands of children to useful, normal lives, we shall be doing a fine thing, carrying out a great objective for the Nation. I know that we shall have your cooperation. From you who are crippled and you who are absolutely normal we shall have help in furthering this great purpose; we must search out the cripples from every nook and corner of the land; we must do through education everything possible to prevent crippling; we must provide the right medical care; we must spread "after care" to the homes throughout the land.

I am glad to have had this opportunity to say these few words today. We are enlisted in a great cause, one of the greatest causes of humanity that exists in America today.

XIII

Executive Budget Fight—
Separation of Legislative from
Executive Functions

INTRODUCTORY NOTE: THE DISPUTE with the Republican Legislative leaders over the executive budget in New York involved the question as to whether or not the Legislature through its leaders could interfere with the executive function of spending moneys which the Legislature had appropriated for administrative purposes.

The story of the contest in the Legislature and in the courts is told in the documents included in this chapter. They are of additional interest because a similar question arose in 1937, in connection with a Federal appropriation for the New York City World's Fair in which the Congress sought to retain control of the expenditure of the funds appropriated. I vetoed that bill in 1937 for substantially the same principles as controlled the executive budget fight in the State of New York. See also Item 194, Vol. II.

Although the Legislative branch of the Federal or State Governments should have complete discretion as to the amount and purposes of appropriations, subject only to veto power, it should not be permitted to interfere with the functions of the Executive in expending the funds appropriated so long as the purposes of the expenditure are those provided by the Legislative branch, and the disbursements are audited by the Comptroller.

This successful fight in Albany in 1929 was of the highest importance to the maintenance of our forms of government, State and Federal. It will do much to maintain that balance and independence between the two branches — Legislative and Executive — which are so necessary to successful functioning of representative government.

The issue — whether it be in a State capital or in the national capital — is this: The Legislature appropriates under specific laws and the Executive makes the expenditures; shall the Legislature, after the enactment of the law, have any form of control over the expenditure through an agent or agents authorized to make their own interpretations of the law? The answer is obviously no. If the language of the law is not legally clear, it is incumbent on the Executive, through what is known as pre-audit, to pass on the proposed expenditure; and in the event of doubt, to obtain the opinion of the Attorney General who is the principal law officer of the State or Federal Government.

The Legislature of a State or the Congress of the United States is fully entitled to conduct accountings or post-audits just as is done each year by corporations through the hiring of outside accountants.

There is thus a clear line of demarcation — a line which follows the obvious need to keep separate the Legislative and Executive functions of our system of government. The courts definitely recognize this separation. It is a matter of principle, and the principle must be supported by all who believe in our constitutional methods.

75 ❡ The Governor Asserts the Fundamental Principles of an Executive Budget, and Announces His Determination to Defend Them in Court. April 12, 1929

I HAVE given most careful consideration to the steps which, as Governor of the State, I should take to settle the grave doubts which I am advised exist as to the constitutionality of the attempts of the Legislature to supervise and control through two members the spending of appropriations previously made for the support of the State Government. The question at issue is one of far-reaching importance, and involves fundamental principles of our American political institutions which I believe to be vital. It is not a controversy over particular items in an appropriation bill but involves a principle intimately bound up with the new budget system since its inception.

The object of all the agitation, discussion and disinterested service on the part of leading citizens which led up to the reorganization of the State Government and the adoption of the Executive Budget by constitutional amendments cannot be lightly brushed aside. The object clearly was to simplify our administrative machinery, to make the Governor a really responsible executive and to define and fix for all time the separate and distinct functions of the executive and the Legislature. A movement in the same direction has spread all over the country and to the National Government at Washington itself. Since 1910 in every part of the country, in every newspaper, in every political platform, and in the program of every civic organization, there has been growing demand for consolidation of departments under a responsible executive, the establishment of an Executive Budget, and fixed responsibility of administration by the executive head after appropriations are made. Surely the tendency everywhere has been away from the confusing of legislative and executive functions, toward the real separation of powers and the centralization of duty and responsibility in the executive.

This subject was threshed out in the Constitutional Convention of 1915. Administrative consolidation and the Executive Budget were advocated by Elihu Root, its President, who in a memorable speech from the floor insisted that these reforms were vital and the most important of all subjects before the Convention. The program of the Constitutional Convention to create responsible State government was taken up by civic agencies and leaders in the community. After over ten years of discussion, government reorganization was finally written into the Constitution of this State by the people by an impressive majority. The Hughes Commission was appointed to work out the details of consolidation, and they recommended that the Executive Budget be written into the Constitution and stated that government reorganization would be weak and ineffective without it. . . .

The people of the State adopted the Executive Budget amendment in the fall of 1927. The first constitutional Executive Budget was submitted by me on January 28th of this year, and the question now confronting me is whether I shall for the sake of expediency approve a practice now attempted to be introduced and extended which I believe to be fundamentally unsound and which I am advised would be violative of the State Constitution.

Visible, open, responsible budget making was the objective sought by the people in amending the Constitution. The Constitution provides not only that the budget shall originate with the Governor on recommendation of department heads and after hearings and that it shall contain a complete picture of the State's financial condition and proposed expenditures, but also that the budget shall be altered by the Legislature only by striking out or reducing items or by adding items in a separate place distinct from the rest of the budget and each referring to a single object or purpose. The budget was to become law without the Governor's signature, except as to new items which were to be subject to the Governor's veto in whole or in part in the usual way.

The Legislature deliberately violated the spirit and letter of the Constitution. They cut out whole sections of the Executive Budget without indicating by brackets or in any other way what had been deleted. They then added new items here and there throughout the budget, not in a distinct and separate place, and this was done in such a way that no one who did not compare hundreds of pages of each bill could figure out what had been done. They not only cut out and reduced items in this way, but they then restored the same items with different phraseology and conditions so as to produce in effect a totally different result. If this practice is followed to its logical conclusion, all that any subsequent Legislature need do is to cut out all of the Governor's budget the minute it reaches them and start an entirely new one of their own, or by altering the controlling language change completely the intent and purpose of every item in the Governor's budget, and set up a control of every administrative agency by a committee controlled by two of their members as officers.

What is the good of amending the Constitution to consolidate the executive branch of the Government and to fix the duty and responsibility of budget making in the Governor, and what is the use of writing the executive budget into our fundamental law if the very first Legislature can nullify the reforms adopted by the people themselves?

The question before the people of this State in connection with this year's budget appropriations is whether administration is to be in the hands of the Governor elected by all the people to be the head of the executive branch, or whether it is to be shared between the Governor and the Legislature in such a way that all responsibility will be lost. The present legislative leaders take the view that they should have a definite part in administering the Government all the year round and supervising and controlling the expenditure of appropriations. They contend that if furniture is to be bought for the State offices, they shall decide exactly what chairs, desks and coat hangers each department shall have, how they shall be bought and what shall be paid for them. These leaders believe that when a sum of money is appropriated for construction or repair work, other than by contract, they shall decide how many carpenters, mechanics or engineers shall be employed, when they shall be employed and at what salary.

343

Every man and woman in this State with practical experience must know what this means. On this theory, if twenty-five thousand dollars should be appropriated for necessary construction or repair work at a public institution or on a public improvement, if the work is to be done with the forces of the institution or department, as it must be in many cases, and otherwise than by contract, the department head must first have the separate approvals of the Governor and of each of the Legislative Finance Chairmen. This applies to plumbing, sewage, water supply, road work and other construction and repairs. It is impossible to segregate or detail all of these items in advance. It would be improvident in the extreme to attempt to provide in advance exactly what work can be done by contract and what should be done directly by department heads. No one can foretell what the low bid will be in the case of contracts and exactly how much money will be left. It is very difficult at best and impossible in some cases to tell in advance just what forces will be needed to complete the work and when they will be needed. Nothing could be more uneconomical than to force our administrators in all cases to figure out all these things in advance. No sane business man would think of doing it. If two members of the Legislature must be followed around the State and consulted before every bit of construction work can progress, we shall never be able to carry out with reasonable dispatch and economy the great program which we have undertaken nor shall we be able to administer our public improvements when they are completed.

The constitutional amendment reorganizing the State government provided that no new departments should be created. It reduced the number of elective officers, leaving only the Attorney General and Comptroller, besides the Governor and Lieutenant Governor. The Attorney General is a law officer and the Comptroller is really an auditor, and neither are administrative officers. The amendment was intended to do away with the service of legislators on boards and commissions such as the land board. The deliberate purpose of this amendment was to centralize executive responsibility. If two legislators can be set up to share this responsibility with the Governor, the whole intent and purpose of reorganization will be frittered away.

I note that the legislative leaders before acting on the second budget bill sought the advice of the Attorney General who informed them that their procedure was proper and Constitutional.

The executive as well as the legislative branch of the State government has a vital interest in the proper solution of this problem, and I have therefore as Governor sought not only the advice of my official counsel but also the independent advice of eminent counsel. Mr. William D. Guthrie's high reputation as a Constitutional lawyer is national, and he has agreed to present the administrative viewpoint in this matter. The joint opinion of Mr. Guthrie and Mr. Edward G. Griffin, Counsel to the Governor, has been published. I am accepting the second budget except the items objected to by them and with such other disapproval as to new minor items as seem to me to be required.

Mr. Guthrie and my official counsel are prepared to consult with the Attorney General, or with any special counsel who may be designated by the Attorney General or by the Legislature, so as to facilitate a prompt disposition in the courts of any question which may arise as the result of my objections to the second budget bill. I stand firmly upon the principles laid down by them in their opinion. I believe them to be sound and statesmanlike, and I am convinced that the court will sustain their views.

76 ❮ The Governor Discusses the Significance of the Executive Budget Victory. Address before the City Club, New York City.

November 23, 1929

THIS is the first opportunity which has come to me to speak publicly of the very important decision of the Court of Appeals last Tuesday in the so-called State Budget case. I realize fully that the average citizen became confused during the last winter's session, as to the fundamental reason for the controversy between the Legislature and myself. Therefore, it is right to set forth the fundamentals in the simplest kind of language without going into the maneuvers and detailed happenings of last February and March.

First of all, let me make it clear that there was nothing of a personal nature in the controversy. The origin of the famous lawsuit was as follows:

Starting with the Constitutional Convention of 1915 a large body of public opinion in this State, without regard to party, sought a reorganization of the State Government in order greatly to reduce the number of different departments — 118 of them — and in order to create a responsible financial Budget System. As you know, the departments were duly organized and are now eighteen in number. This was followed by the adoption of the amendment to the Constitution, providing for the Executive Budget. The purpose of this budget was to center financial responsibility for making estimates in the Governor, to center administrative duties in the executive departments and to limit the functions of the Legislature to making appropriations and other strictly legislative duties.

During the reorganization period and before the Executive Budget went into effect last January first, a purely stop-gap arrangement was made by compromise between Governor Smith and the Legislature, by which during the reorganization, certain duties of segregating appropriations after they had been made were conferred on the Governor and two of the legislative committee chairmen. It was certainly Governor Smith's thought and that of the public, as well as my own, that when the Executive Budget went into effect the control of executive or administrative functions should vest wholly in the executive or administrative departments. On February first last, I therefore proposed this to the Legislature. The Legislature insisted on coupling the two legislative chairmen with the Governor. I was very certain, after taking careful legal advice, that this was not only contrary to the intention of the people of this State but was also contrary to the general scheme of American Federal and State Governments whereby legislators have constantly been denied the privilege of exercising administrative duties.

Let me make it perfectly clear that this was the crux of my refusal to abide by the desire of the Legislature. At no time did I insist that the Governor himself should have the sole power of segregation, but spoke constantly of the executive or administrative power as a whole, including of course the department heads who are responsible to the Governor. It is an interesting fact that some of the editors of our leading newspapers have been so misinformed that they have, since the Budget decision, said editorially that I had sought powers for the Governor. They fail to catch the difference between the word Executive spelled with a capital E and the same word spelled with a small e.

The decision of the Court of Appeals sustains my contention in every particular. Let that be understood once and for all. That statement is not open to challenge, for the decision definitely upholds my one and only contention, viz.: that members of the Legislature can appropriate moneys but cannot carry on administrative or executive duties in the expenditure of the appropriations. This is a constitutional question, and the decision is so far-reaching that this particular case will be regarded for generations to come as one of the pivots on which the Government of this State and of other States rests.

At the same time some editors have, I hope through lack of information, stated that the Court of Appeals had ruled that neither the Legislators nor the Governor could segregate appropriations in administering them. This is contrary to the clear language of the decision. The decision says that legislators are constitutionally barred from taking part in segregation. The decision further says that in regard to the particular appropriation bill of 1929 the heads of departments and not the Governor shall do the segregating, but the decision clearly allows the Governor the right to segregate if any future Legislature grants that power. In the final analysis it makes little difference whether the Governor or the heads of departments carry out the actual signing of

347

segregation papers, for all the heads of departments are appointees of the Governor and their acts are, therefore, those of the Governor.

The above seems to be a clear statement of a much misunderstood case, and I want to go on record as saying that much of the misunderstanding is due to politicians and their servants who have deliberately sought to becloud and befog the big basic question. The Court of Appeals upholds in its decision the sacred time-honored American principle of the separation of the judicial, legislative and executive departments of Government. Every school child has been taught that this is the fundamental division of our governmental powers. Many attempts have been made in the past to break this clear division down. The highest court of the State of New York sustains this sacred American principle and from now on I trust that instead of constant bickerings and efforts to throw monkey-wrenches into the machinery, we shall have better cooperation and a clearer understanding of the governmental powers in Albany. I am wholly willing to go along with this idea of better understanding and it will not be my fault, if the coming session of the Legislature does not prove to be harmonious and productive of useful legislation and business-like action.

XIV
Public Health

77 (An Address on Public Health and the Development of Saratoga Springs as a Health Center (Excerpts). June 25, 1929

WHEN I was a boy, not far from where we lived there was an unfortunate girl, one who lived seventy summers, who had been a mental defective practically from birth. She was put in the attic, fed and more or less secluded up there for seventy years. Her family and the community regarded it perfectly proper, because she was feebleminded, that she be segregated and kept in the attic and not even allowed to go outdoors. There she was kept all her life and lived to be a little old woman. Not so far away also there was another child, who lived to be an old, old man. He had been a cripple from birth. He, too, had been practically segregated from the community, and no one knew anything about it, except the immediate neighbors. There he was, day after day and year after year, until finally old age took him. That was not so very long ago. You and I could go on enumerating contrasts with the present age. How has this change come about, and to what is it going to lead?

In the first place we have applied common sense. The State has taken care of the mentally deficient, and today in spite of the limited equipment it is carrying out a great work on the whole. A number of years ago the general thought came into the minds of modern civilization that there was a definite duty on the part of the State to do something more, so that the State of New York and almost every State in the Union, not all, have undertaken a general supervision of the health of the communities. Fifty years ago, the matter of health was individual; it was nobody's concern, except that of the family, whether a person was healthy or not, and gradually we have built up a new doctrine — the belief that the State has a positive right, not just an obligation, to see that the health of its individuals is brought up to a higher level. Is it supposed that fifty years from now the citizens of the State will be in the same condition as previously? . . .

The State is going to insist, fifty years from now, on good health, insist on it as a right of what is known as the sovereignty of the people. The old idea of the right of an individual to be sick or of a community to have epidemics no longer exists. That right has been turned around and transferred to the State. I mean by "State" the general governing agencies, and they undoubtedly have the right to insist on good health. If we in this State were a little more awake in our interest in local government, the task would be easy.

As you know I have been doing a great deal of talking during the past four or five months about local government. The larger percentage of the taxpayers' money is spent by the village, township, county or city, and only a very small part of what the people pay goes to the State Government in Albany, and yet, while there is some interest in local matters, there is not half enough. We are much more apt as citizens to look at the fact that the State is spending two hundred and fifty million dollars a year as a governing agency, and overlook entirely the fact that the communities, towns and counties of the State are spending ten times that amount — something like two and a half billion dollars. Most of you are interested in the local end of things, and I recognize the difficulty of your task, and also how hard it is for a Governor to go around the State and get public opinion in favor of a broad public health program. It is easier for us to go to the Legislature and get appropriations for a general, state-wide program. We get the support of the newspapers and civic organizations. In the State Government we are able to work up an active interest in the usual public health program, but what can we spend compared with the local agencies?

In the final analysis, public health must depend upon the locality. Today, in county after county the average amount spent for health improvements is under 50 cents per capita, while those same counties without any hesitation spend four, five or six dollars per capita for improvements to highways. This is just one example. I do not want the highway work to stop, but the proportion is out of line, if we figure it on the population and the future generations. How are we going to increase that rate? By favorable opinion, of course; and that is necessary, if we are going to progress.

I am afraid that local health improvement is not of very vital interest to the supervisors of the average town, the town clerk, the assessors or the road commissioners. There are not many jobs to be given out in the administration of health work. It is not very showy. Health officials cannot get much credit out of improvement to a road that goes to pieces, or for getting some special funds from the board of supervisors of a county. You will not get the good results you think you should out of the average local politician unless you can build a backfire under him. That is your job, a very definite task, and it depends in large part upon the way that you carry out that task that the health work in the average county of the State will progress. I know something about the counties, their local conditions, and the public interest. Some of the widely scattered rural counties are doing better health work than those containing large civic communities. It comes down to the interest aroused among the people themselves, and I am very certain that the work is progressing, although not as fast as it should. We must bring home more and more to the average citizen the fact that health has become a part of Government, that it is no longer a question of charity.

In going through reports, I occasionally find that this or that project will be paid for by private subscription. Why depend upon the rich residents to pay the salary of a local nurse, for instance? This should be a community obligation and privilege, because the success of this work throughout the State is going to depend largely on the citizens who will be living in the State fifty years from now.

Let us consider the question of health census. In spite of the efforts of the State Department of Health and some county organizations, there are still thousands of undisclosed, undiscovered, and untreated cripples in the State of New York. In the far-off Commonwealth of Australia public health goes hand in hand with census, and every year through a continuing census work, in connection with registration for voting as I understand it, a system by which a tabulation is made of the electorate, a report is made on the health of the electorate, and through the electorate a report is made on the health of their families. Perhaps we shall eventually have some such system in this State, through the aid of which every man, woman, and child will have a health record on file with some Government agency. . . .

The State of New York is undertaking an experiment here at Saratoga. When I was a boy I went a number of different summers with my father to some of the German and Austrian health resorts. In those days they were called spas. Before Saratoga became famous for other things I believe it was known as a spa, as we now know the word from the crossword puzzles. The difference between the use of mineral waters, both externally and internally, in this country and on the other side, is that we Americans have treated the subject as part of our vacation.

In the old days, fifty and a hundred years ago, there were a great many springs scattered throughout up-state New York, and people would go there from all over the United States for two reasons: first, to drink the waters without any medical advice and probably their mental attitude while drinking them helped physically; and second, to have a mighty good time and to meet people from this and other States. They came for a vacation period, coupled with which was the idea that they were drinking waters that might benefit them.

I am sorry to say that this is the spirit in which the development of Saratoga Springs has taken place. We have not approached anywhere in this country, except in Hot Springs, Arkansas, the serious use of mineral waters for health in a manner to be compared with the use of these waters in Europe. Some years ago nobody could go to Nauheim to drink the waters and take the baths, unless sent there by a reputable physician. When the people arrived they could not drink or bathe until after complete examination by a physician of long experience, who had served an apprenticeship with an older doctor. If you were accepted by the physician and told that the Nauheim treatment would do you good, you were given a card which would permit you to drink the waters, take the baths and the massages. You were there, however, for cure. Once approved by the doctor, you were given the course of treatment, and if you did not live up to the requirements, "out you would go." That is different from anything in this country. . . .

In order to put the whole thing on a scientific and disciplinary basis we have appointed a commission, and I am very confident, first, that this commission will lay down a definite report that Saratoga can be developed for the good of humanity, and second, that they will submit plans for development in such a way that this particular spot in our State will point the way to all the United States.

In this there are two thoughts: The conviction about the great good that Saratoga can do for many human ills of the people of the State, and the belief that it will point the way so that other States and other mineral springs can be developed along scientific and medical lines. From the Adirondacks to Georgia there are very wonderful springs on both sides of the range, and both in the West and Middle West there are springs going down through the Ozark Mountains and borders of Oklahoma and Texas, and then there are those of the Rockies extending down to Montana and Arizona, and those of the Allegheny Mountains. They are of every known size, form and heat; and I am very hopeful that, while the medical profession of the United States has lagged far behind European doctors with regard to the use of mineral waters, they will recognize the great natural gift we have at our own doors and take advantage of it. I am therefore looking forward to a very splendid development at Saratoga that will help this State and our sister States. . . .

78 ❮ The Governor Transmits to the Legislature a Report of the Special Health Commission. February 19, 1931

To the Legislature:

THE success or failure of any Government in the final analysis must be measured by the well-being of its citizens. Nothing can be more important to a State than its public health; the State's paramount concern should be the health of its people. We in New York can justifiably boast of our accomplishments in public health. The progress which we have made in the last fifteen years is nothing short of phenomenal. For example, in 1913 the death rate in this State from all communicable diseases was 419 per 100,000 population; in 1930 it was only 196; in 1900 the expected span of human life was 47 years; by 1930 it had increased to 57 years. Tuberculosis mortality has declined more than one-half since 1913; typhoid fever, once quite common, is now a rare disease. Diphtheria has declined about two-thirds since 1913; and infant mortality has, in the same period, been reduced by a half.

Much that is enviable in the present status of our health work may be traced, I believe, to the legislation passed in 1913 upon recommendation of a State health commission of which the late Dr. Hermann M. Biggs was chairman. The work of that commission brought about an entire reorganization of the State Department of Health and fundamental changes in its relation to local health authorities. Since 1913 there have been piece-meal amendments to the Public Health Law as new questions arose relative to details of its administration. The rapid strides in medical science, however, and the experience we have gained in public health administration since then, convinced me last year that it was again time to make a comprehensive survey of the entire subject of public health as a governmental function — State and local. For these reasons, on May 1, 1930, I appointed an informal and unofficial commission of fourteen members under the chairmanship of President Farrand of Cornell University, charged with the duty of making such a survey. The membership of that commission is indeed a distinguished one. A mere statement of the names is sufficient to inspire the utmost confidence in and reliance upon their recommendations. Even the preliminary report which the commission has recently sent me, and which I am transmitting herewith to your Honorable Bodies, opens the way for a new health program during the coming years which, if well executed, should bring to New York State far greater advances along every line of health protection than have been achieved during the recent years of which we are justly proud.

The commission makes recommendations for legislation further to improve the public health and administration of the health and sanitation laws of the State. These recommendations are intended to bring the provisions of our Public Health Law up to date and to align our entire attitude on the question of public health more closely with the outstanding achievements and accurate knowledge of modern medical science. The commission in its report points out the important pressing needs to which public health authorities should devote their attention and itemizes its major recommendations along these lines. I desire to call your attention to these recommendations with the earnest request that you proceed at once to translate them into legislation at the earliest possible moment. The expert technical knowledge, the administrative experience in public health and the sound judgment of these commission members, who have so generously given of their wisdom and skill to the public service, should be utilized by us without delay.

An outstanding feature is the recommendation of the Commission that county boards of health should be organized in all counties to provide for our rural areas more effective control of tuberculosis, venereal and other communicable diseases, the protection of maternity and infancy, the safeguarding of public milk and water supplies, more effective public health nursing service and other elements of a modern health program.

Originally local public health duties were imposed on the

cities, towns and villages of the State. As a result there are now in this State as many as 1,099 different local health jurisdictions. This system, originally created to meet the conditions of 1850, cannot possibly be adequate for the needs of 1931. Few, if any, of these small units can afford the services which modern public health demands. The same considerations which prove how obsolete are a great many of our forms of local government likewise prove the present inadequacy of this original arrangement for public health protection. As time has passed new public health duties have become imperative and it has become clear that the small local units could not perform them. Some of them, therefore, such as the maintenance of a county tuberculosis hospital, of a public health laboratory, of a public health nursing service, and others, have been imposed upon county authorities. But it has been on a hit-or-miss plan with no one county authority clearly charged with the duty of developing a balanced and efficient health program. The result has been confusion of responsibility, lack of coordination, waste of effort, and excessive costs for the services rendered. Practically every scientific organization interested in public health has endorsed the idea of establishing boards of health on a county basis with full time personnel. The Commission, therefore, presents as its most vital recommendation, and I urge upon you, the enactment of legislation substituting the county as the unit of local health administration in place of the town and village. It also recommends that cities be made a part of county health districts only when the city requests that it be included, and that villages of more than 5,000 inhabitants be permitted, if they desire, to retain their local boards of health. I call your attention to the itemized list of advantages of a county health unit as compared with the town and village units set forth on pages 16 and 17 of the accompanying preliminary report.

The Commission has not been academic or theoretical in its recommendations. It points out that our statutes have imposed certain health duties upon units which were so small in population and in wealth as to preclude the possibility of efficient performance by them of these duties. It, therefore, recommends that in counties having a population of less than 30,000 people the State Department of Health be empowered, on request of the county board of health, to delegate a member of its staff, without cost, to act as county health commissioner for one or more of such counties.

For like reasons the Commission recommends that the program of tuberculosis hospitalization be rounded out by making hospital provision available to these counties through the establishment by the State of three district State sanatoria of moderate size, the cost of maintenance of which will be charged to the counties from which the patients come; and in admission to which the smaller counties without tuberculosis hospitals of their own would be given special consideration. This seems to be an instance in which further direct participation by the State is the only practicable plan for meeting an important need.

The various other recommendations of the Commission relate to cancer, the venereal diseases, public health nursing, crippled children, maternity, infant and child hygiene, industrial hygiene, public water supplies, stream pollution and public health personnel, all set forth in detail in the accompanying report. I have given them all careful consideration and cannot refrain from congratulating the State upon the serious scientific study which has been given to the whole program by these experts and upon the opportunity which is presented for us to make these strides toward the goal of improved public health.

I need not point out to you how closely bound is the prosperity of the State with its public health. It has been estimated that the average saving from the reduction in tuberculosis alone during the past twenty years, resulting now in 12,000 fewer deaths annually, amounts to a per capita of $5 for every man, woman and child in this State each year, or an amazing total of $60,000,000 per year. Nothing can, of course, have so determining an influence upon the prosperity of the State as the continuous earning power of its citizens, unimpaired by preventable diseases or uninterrupted by premature death. Nor need I point out to you the great humanitarian value of protecting our people from the vast amount of what is so often needless disease and suffering and premature and preventable death.

There can be no reasonable differences of opinion as to the paramount importance of this kind of legislation. I know that you will cooperate with the members of the Commission who have so clearly pointed out the way. These public health experts have sent to me their prescription for their patient, the State of New York. You and I can, and should, join hands in filling this prescription in the form of legislation.

79 ❨ A Recommendation for the Establishment of County Boards of Health in All Counties. April 2, 1931

To the Legislature:

ON THE 19th day of February, 1931, I transmitted to your Honorable Bodies a copy of the report of the special unofficial commission appointed by me to investigate and report remedial measures for the improvement of the public health. I pointed out then, and reiterate now, that nothing can be more important or more worthy of consideration than this subject. Legislation has been introduced to carry out the report of this commission. I am informed that your Honorable Bodies are willing to pass this legislation with the exception of one feature — the establishment of county boards of health in all counties.

The report of the Governor's special health commission, which I transmitted to your Honorable Bodies on February 19th, points out that this is the most important item in the entire health program. The primary responsibility for health protection should be a local one. This responsibility under laws passed more than a half century ago has been imposed on the cities, towns and villages of the State, resulting in the creation of 1,036 local health units, excluding the county and city units. It has been long recognized that these over-numerous and, in many cases, unscientific and untrained local health organizations have been inadequate; and as a result, in recent years, permissive laws have been passed which enable counties to create boards of health and conduct health services which obviously are possible only on a county basis. Unfortunately only four counties so far have availed themselves of this statute.

The report points out that "The present system of town and village boards of health . . . results in a confusion of responsibility, lack of coordination, waste of effort, and excessive costs for the services rendered. The imperative need, therefore, is to seek out the most effective governmental units, and impose upon them the needed powers and full responsibilities. The county is the only available unit for this purpose. . . . The commission feels that this is the most vital matter it has had to consider and urges that legislation be enacted substituting the county as the unit of local health administration in place of the town and village." On pages 16 and 17 of its report the commission points out the advantages of a county health unit, as follows:

1. The unit of population is sufficiently large to permit the employment of trained personnel.
2. One responsible board will be substituted for the many town and village boards of health, the county nursing committee, county milk inspection committee, county clinic committees, and boards of managers of county laboratories.
3. A plan of continuing health service can be developed for the whole county and all of the health personnel can be mobilized to meet emergency conditions in any part of the county.
4. Duplication and overlapping of effort which now exist will be prevented, and better health protection can be furnished for present expenditures.
5. The relative needs for various types of health service in the county can be determined and available public funds allotted in proportion to these needs.
6. School nursing activities now lacking in many rural schools

can be furnished by nurses employed by the county board of health.

7. If school medical inspection is made a function of county boards of health, this important activity can be conducted more effectively on a county-wide basis with trained personnel than under the present system.

8. Through the permissive provision under which tuberculosis control activities may be administered by the county board of health, this activity can be directly coordinated with other health services. This is particularly desirable in the smaller counties.

9. Under the permission granted to cities to join the rest of the county for purposes of health administration, further coordination of health work on a county-wide basis is made possible. Such a union is desirable for cities of less than 50,000 population.

10. New and much-needed health activities can be undertaken which are not now carried out and are not possible under the present system.

11. Vitally important maternity and infant hygiene measures can be organized and efficiently conducted.

12. Treatment facilities for the control of the venereal diseases can be provided.

13. The sanitary quality of milk can be assured through a county-wide inspection service.

14. The sanitary quality of water supplies can be supervised through a county sanitary engineer.

15. Modern epidemiological methods can be applied for control of the communicable diseases in place of the present ineffective system. Toxin-antitoxin, smallpox vaccination and other activities can be conducted by personnel provided for these and other services.

16. Less intimate State supervision and fewer direct services from the Health Department will be required because of the better local organization.

The legislation introduced carries out the recommendations of the commission along these lines and provides that in counties having a population of less than 30,000, the State Department of Health may, on request of the county board of health, delegate a member of its own staff, without cost, to act as county health commissioner for one or more of such counties. It also permits cities and villages of more than 5,000 inhabitants to retain their own local board of health. Under the present provisions of the Public Health Law, the State will share the cost of this local county health program with the county equally. This bill is mandatory in its direction that counties form these health units; but it is merely the substitution of one mandatory unit for many other smaller mandatory units.

No county purpose and no State purpose is more important than this. The people of each county are entitled to the best in the way of health protection that the county and the State together can afford. Selfish local patronage should not be permitted to stand in the way. The opposition of local office holders whose little jobs may be jeopardized should not prevail.

I sincerely urge upon your Honorable Bodies the enactment of this legislation at this session.

80 ⟨ Comment by the Governor on a Report of the Special Health Commission. April 6, 1932

THE report is both an inspiration and an indictment. Other than the indifference of local governments, there is no reason for tuberculosis to be twice as prevalent in some communities as in others; for deaths and illnesses from diphtheria to continue to occur when some municipalities have been able to stamp it out entirely; for twice as many babies to die each year in some counties and cities as in the communities where a modern health program is in force; for certain death rates to be higher in rural communities, with no organized health services, than in urban communities where health service is available; and for those citizens of lower economic rank to suffer a higher death rate from practically *all* causes.

It is apparent from the exhaustive studies made by the Health Commission over a period of nearly two years that our present town and village system of local health administration is as wasteful of lives as of money.

The significance of this report does not lie in its recommendations for needed legislation — important as they are — but in its specific plans for community action covering every phase of public health. It is a report made not only to the Governor, but to the people of the State, and is available for those interested in any aspect of public health. The recommendations of the Commission constitute a broadly conceived, long-range plan for health work in the State which is practical and easy to follow. If well executed it should go far to eliminate our present wastes, inefficiencies and duplications of health effort. It should lighten our heavy economic burden in caring for the unfit and save many lives now needlessly lost.

On April 22 I am calling a conference in Albany with health leaders of the State at which the next steps necessary for carrying out the new health program will be arranged. The expert technical knowledge, the administrative experience in public health and the sound judgment of the members of the Commission, which have found expression in this report, will, I hope, be translated promptly into law and transmitted by practice into the lives of the people.

What I want to make clear to the people of this State is that here is a report which gives us a definite better-health program to work on for a good many years to come. Its effectiveness will be measured by the interest that people take in it in every community. That is why I hope that it will be read and discussed in every county and town in the whole State.

XV

Prisons, Prison Labor, Parole, Probation, and Crime

IN ADDITION to the documents in this chapter, the reader is referred for further material on the same subjects to the following Items in this volume: 11, 17 on page 101, 18 on page 120, 89.

81 ❡ Address before the Conference of Governors, New London, Conn. July 16, 1929

(Suppression of crime — Enforcement of justice — Reform of criminal procedure.)

NO CONSTITUTIONAL sovereign right vested in the forty-eight States which make up our great Nation has been more zealously defended or clearly established than the right of each State to control the police powers and the administration of justice within its borders. What constitutes a crime is a matter which each State determines for itself. What machinery of justice shall be employed to enforce its laws is also a matter for State determination. Only those matters which are violations of such Congressional laws as are based on specific grants of authority by the Constitution to the Federal Government are recognized, not as usurping the State's individual authority, but as necessary measures which the agreement of federation between the different States requires us to acquiesce in, if we are to keep faith one with another.

Our Nation has been a successful experiment in democratic Government, because the individual States have waived in only a few instances their sovereign rights and have permitted the national Government, through its own machinery and its own courts, to enforce within their borders certain particular laws which the States themselves, as represented in Congress assembled, have agreed upon as being proper national legislation.

But there is a tendency, and to my mind a dangerous tendency, on the part of our national Government, to encroach, on one excuse or another, more and more upon State supremacy. The elastic theory of interstate commerce, for instance, has been stretched almost to the breaking point to cover certain regulatory powers desired by Washington. But in many cases this has been due to a failure of the States, themselves, by common agreement, to pass legislation necessary to meet certain conditions.

We are now faced with new and alarming problems in criminal activity. I am very certain that the public is aroused to the neces-

sity of suppressing the outrageous and open lawlessness shown by
the murders committed daily in the public streets of our great
cities, of private feuds between gunmen which flourish with less
punishment than in the darkest days of Sicily. At this constantly
growing disregard of the life and safety of others and crimes
against property, the public has grown alarmed and demands
action. And let me here voice to the Governors of my sister States
my conviction that if our States do not themselves, by cooperation
and earnest, intelligent legislation, remedy the existing condition
of affairs, we shall find the heavy hand of Washington laid on us
by Federal legislation, and the people of our own commonwealths
will raise no voice in protest, because their own State Governments have been inefficient, stupid or negligent.

If we wish to retain our control over the criminal laws and
police powers, we must accept the responsibility for their enforcement; we must clean out the antiquated machinery of justice; we
must meet new kinds of crime with new kinds of laws; and we
must do this, not in this State or that State, but in every State, if
anything is to be really done about this crime problem.

We who have assembled for this conference have no small
moral share in this responsibility. It is the Governor of each State
who has the duty, and the right as well, of calling to the attention
of his State Legislature the need for legislative action, not merely
by a few perfunctory words in an annual message dealing with
many subjects, but persistently, forcibly, and repeatedly, whenever the Legislature fails to take action.

There is no doubt that the citizens of every State will support
their Governor in a demand for proper measures to reduce crime,
and, while the Governor's personal appeal does not always fall
upon sympathetic ears, when it is backed by public opinion, irrespective of political beliefs, it will in the end be heeded by the
most recalcitrant or slow-moving legislative bodies.

I have spoken of the obligation that falls on us, as Governors, to
urge upon our State Legislatures the need of passing proper and
helpful legislation. It may be well asked how may the propriety
or helpfulness of legislation of this character be ascertained? And

here we come at the start to the first great stumbling block in the fight against crime.

Three years ago, when the National Crime Commission, of whose executive committee I happen to be a member, first undertook the investigation as to what practical and immediate steps could be taken to reduce crime, they discovered that, while it is possible to determine with reasonable accuracy how many cases of mumps there had been in the United States during the previous year, no one could tell in even the most inaccurate way how many murders there had been in this same period. We talk about a crime wave. Let me assure you gentlemen, on the word of the National Crime Commission, which has been studying this matter for three years, that no one can today state with any authoritative statistics to back him, whether there is or is not a crime wave in the United States. A certain new and reckless disregard of human life is apparent in some of our large cities, and the records of the courts and State prisons show that a new and most alarming change has taken place in the characters of our criminals, and that the old and hardened "yegg man" has practically disappeared from our police courts and has been replaced by mere lads whose ages range between 16 and 24, who rob and murder with almost a certainty of escape from detection, youngsters who, if detected, are able to defeat justice through clever lawyers with a certainty of safety that is bringing into their ranks new recruits every hour of the day, tempted by the glittering prospect of easy money without real risk. But as to whether or not there is a total increase in the number of crimes committed we have no knowledge whatever. We have no knowledge, in fact, on any subject based on statistics as to criminal acts. Guesses we have from a few cities out of our total population of a hundred odd million people, painstaking research in particular subjects by a few efficient State crime commissions, but of the condition of our country as a whole we may not speak with any certainty, because there are no statistics collected or available.

This was the startling discovery our own commission made three years ago. You will find it emphasized in a letter which I shall read from the chairman of President Hoover's new Federal commission which is just beginning its labors. Until we get more certain knowledge of the amount and character of crime, all our efforts will be mere experiments undertaken in hope, rather than in any confidence based on knowledge.

I want to urge on every Governor present that he take up, as one of the most important matters for the consideration of legislators, the compilation and publication, as a matter of law, of the few vitally necessary criminal statistics to enable us to attack this problem of crime in a businesslike and scientific way.

There are States, and their number I am glad to say is growing, which have already recognized this necessity, my own State being among them, but they are in a pitiful minority as compared with the States where there is no attempt at the collection of statistics of this kind. Let us stop guessing about crime and require a few facts. Do not think that this is a matter which can be turned over to the Government at Washington. Do not think it can be lightly dismissed by saying that it is "something for the census bureau to do." The evasion of State sovereignty has not yet reached the point, thank God, when the Federal Government can issue orders to State officials as to what they shall and shall not do in keeping records, or anything else, and it would be a disgrace on every State that had failed to take this matter up if public opinion should necessitate such meddling with our State machinery as the compiling of crime statistics by orders from Washington would bring about. And unless the Federal Government assumes mandatory authority over our officials, these statistics cannot be collected by Washington. That has been proved by the praiseworthy attempt of the census bureau to collect and publish statistics obtained from our State prisons. They are probably the best national statistics relating to crime in existence, but the director of the census will tell you, as he told our commission, that too often the wardens of our great penitentiaries have replied to his request for information so negligently as to make the figures matters of deep suspicion or, indeed, in some instances, in spite of repeated correspondence, have made no reply at all.

Of all the statistics needed, perhaps the most urgent and the simplest to procure is the record of the numbers and kinds of crimes of violence that have been actually committed, not punished, but committed. Our large cities furnish more or less accurate statistics of arrests and of trials, of convictions, and of imprisonments, but of the crimes committed, where no one is arrested, where no grand jury brings in an indictment, where no court has a record of any kind (we are speaking of the country as a whole), we are profoundly ignorant.

I have spoken at length on this matter of statistics, because as a whole statistics are a dry subject, and it is difficult to interest the public in the necessity of their collection, but I wish to assure this conference that no intelligent body of citizens in these United States, from the President's commission down, has attempted to study and understand this matter of crime and of this new entrance of the young criminal into the problem, but has found itself baffled and disheartened by the lack of obtainable information.

Now as to remedies themselves. There are many causes of crime. Each section of the country, each State within that section, and each city within that State, have peculiar conditions and problems in this connection. Should we, evading our responsibility, cowardly ask the national Government to pass laws which should be enforced throughout the entire country, to provide a system of justice and a criminal code for the entire United States? If the national Government should accept that responsibility, it would find it impossible to draft any national laws which would be equally effective in Maine and California, in Texas and Ohio. Each State must study its own crime conditions, must gather its own statistics and work out its own salvation. By that I do not mean that there should not be the closest possible uniformity in our crime legislation and our criminal codes. All legislation, for instance, against the gun toter has been seriously impaired, because it is not uniform in every State. There are certain fundamental principles, certain uniform treatment of certain crimes, which are absolutely necessary, if we do not want to see our criminals traveling from one State to another in order to take advantage of varying statutes.

I wish this conference would establish a permanent committee on coordination in the enforcing of justice and the reform of criminal procedure which would consider the various suggestions made by our State and national crime commissions, by our various bodies devoted to penal reform and by the bar associations throughout the country, and that such a committee of Governors would recommend for the consideration of all the Governors such proposed legislation as it deem worthy, with the request that it be laid before the Legislatures of the different States. And I wish even more devoutly that it would prove practical to effect some kind of coordination between the chairmen of the respective State legislative committees to whom such legislation would be referred, so that they might know what other States were doing and might agree among themselves as to what was to be reported out, with their favorable recommendation, at the next session of their legislative bodies.

The National Crime Commission has found a spirit of conservatism, speaking in general terms, among many of the bar associations, which should be the first to act. This spirit has been noticed to an even greater extent in the average legislative body. I think I am not exaggerating when I say that, if all the recommendations of properly qualified bodies for legislation simplifying and expediting justice, had been passed by the Legislatures of the different States assembled in session last year, we would have made a tremendous stride toward reducing crime in this country.

It is our duty as Governors, as I have already said, continually to remind our Legislatures of the seriousness of this problem and, if necessary, to ask the people of our commonwealths to support us in our demand for action.

Speaking for my own State, we have found the establishment of a State Crime Commission an invaluable help in meeting this question, and I think the same experience has followed the establishment of such commissions in California and other States. The creation of a proper bureau of identification, such as has been done in Indiana, is another wise step. I have recommended in my own State an investigation as to the possibility of bringing our police methods on a par with those in England, France and Germany, by applying modern science to police protection. In such States as still retain the county jail I hope the system of State-supervised penal institutions will be substituted in the interests of permanent reform of our criminal classes. One of the helpful recommendations of the crime commission in my own State, which has been enacted into law this year, was the establishment in one of our great penitentiaries of a psychiatric clinic to study our prisoners by modern methods, to find out why they became criminals and what course would seem best adapted to bring about their reform.

I do not wish to take up, in opening this discussion, particular things or particular remedies. My own commission has made a number of suggestions, the State commissions of many States have added and improved upon them, and many of those present have doubtless carefully thought out valuable suggestions of their own, but I want again to urge some kind of closer cooperation between the States and the necessity of ceaseless presentation of the matter to our State Legislatures, as being two fundamental things that rest on us as Governors to carry on.

When I started to prepare this opening address I asked the chairman of the President's commission if he had any requests to make of the Governors here assembled for their aid in the tremendous task which they have undertaken. He wrote me in reply a letter so clearly setting out their views that I am going to read it without comment or amplification of any kind of my own in closing. This is what Mr. Wickersham has written.

Letter of George W. Wickersham

Dear Governor Roosevelt:

President Hoover in his inaugural address emphasized the need of an urgent respect for law and the improved treatment of crime and criminals. In his address to the commission on its organization, he said: "A Nation does not fail from its growth and wealth or power, but no Nation can for long survive failure of its citizens to respect and obey the laws which they, themselves, make, nor can it survive decadence of the moral and spiritual contracts that are the basis of respect for law, nor from neglect to organize itself. To defeat crime and the corruption that flows from it, he expressed the hope that his commission shall secure an accurate determination of effect and cause, following them with constructive, courageous, conclusions which will bring public understanding and command public support of its conclusions. In a previous statement to the press the President stated that the purpose of the commission was to examine and critically consider the entire Federal machinery of justice, a reconstruction of its function, simplification of its procedure, the provision of additional special tribunals, and better selection of juries, the moral, effective organization of our agency of investigation and prosecutions. It will also naturally include consideration of the enforcement of the Eighteenth Amendment."

From these statements you will understand what a broad scope we have and what a heavy duty is laid upon us. Every intelligent person must be aware that the general attitude of the American people toward the law has fallen far short of what it should be. It is not only shown in the open disrespect for the Volstead Law, but in the general attitude of "beating the law," so long as one can get by with it.

The first thing our commission did was to endeavor to secure actual, reliable statistics of the existing amount of crime, the increase or decrease of crime during the past decade, the actual delays of the enforcement of justice, and the amount of congestion of the criminal courts. There are no reliable statistics furnishing this information.

The New York Crime Commission, whose admirable reports have been most helpful to us, came upon the same lack, and upon their recommendations the Legislature last year passed an Act to supply this want so far as our State is concerned.

I think if the Governors' Conference would recommend like action by all the States it would be helpful.

Our Commission is studying the subject, and will, I think, recommend a uniform State law on the subject, with a voluntary administration act in the meantime.

Another subject we are inquiring into is the cost of extra-legal protection against crime by the police, armored cars, burglary, robbery, and theft insurance, etc., and a survey of conditions in Boston, nearly completed, indicated that crime in that city actually has diminished during the past decade. The fact that that city has a larger police force in proportion to its population than any other city may have much to do with the favorable condition mentioned, but the challenging fact is in the great number of criminal prosecutions which never come to trial, the number of cases settled by pleas of guilty to a lesser offense than that charged, the great delay in bringing cases to trial, the greater delays in hearing appeals and the abuse of excessive bail on appeal. Justice to be effective should be speedy. It is freely charged that much of the delay is the result of political influence with the police, the prosecutors and even the courts. These are difficult matters to investigate. But if every arrest had to be immediately reported from a central registration office and every step thereafter taken concerning the defendant recorded in the same way, it would be much more difficult for an improper influence to thwart the due administration of justice.

Of course, one of the most serious subjects we must deal with is the enforcement of the Eighteenth Amendment. That measure has written into the Constitution of the United States a prohibition of the importation, manufacture, transportation and sale of intoxicating liquors for beverage purposes. The Amendment confers upon the States concurrent jurisdiction with the national Government for the enforcement of this measure. Thus far the Federal Government alone has borne the brunt of enforcement.

It seems to me that the Governors' Conference might well consider approaching the Federal Government on some feasible proposal to share this burden. If the national Government were to attend to preventing importation, manufacture and shipment in interstate commerce of intoxicants, the State undertaking the internal police regulations to prevent sale, saloons, speakeasies, and so forth, national and State laws might be modified so as to become reasonably enforcible and one great source of demoralizing and pecuniarily profitable crime removed. Every State executive has sworn to support and defend the Constitution of the United States. The Eighteenth Amendment is a part of the Constitution, just as much as any other part of it. Surely, it is pertinent to their Conference to suggest and consider how they may best carry out their solemn undertaking.

My dear Governor, I beg you to excuse this long letter in my own hand. I have no stenographer with me, but I feel that your letter calls for the most helpful reply I can give, and I hope that what I have written may suggest to you something of value in the preparation of your address.

Faithfully yours,

G. W. WICKERSHAM

82 ❨ Address on Prison and Parole Problems. New York City. January 18, 1930

HELL appears to have been the ideal design for a prison in the minds of our forefathers. The narrow cubicles of sweating stone, the little shaft of light that crept between the heavy iron bars, the lack of ventilation, sanitation, of everything which makes life endurable, all to be suffered in sullen silence under the watchful eyes of brutal guards — surely no better form of eternal punishment could be devised to torture lost souls in the hereafter.

In spite of all our remodeling, of all our tinkering and patchwork improving, we have still, in what we boastfully call this "enlightened age," prisons whose physical characteristics have lost little of their ancient horrors so far as their construction goes. Now we are beginning to realize the perfectly obvious fact, to which we have deliberately shut our eyes for so many years, that the men we send to prison with few exceptions will be returned again to live among us, to be, perhaps, our neighbors, to live as we live, and to have the same rights as we have. We at last understand that not philanthropy but mere common sense, and our own self-protection require that these men should be released, chastened and reformed if possible, but at least not rendered more vicious, more degraded, than when they were sentenced.

But while, for some years, we have acknowledged grudgingly the truth of this matter and have made spasmodic and sporadic efforts to better conditions, and while, in so far as treatment and personnel are concerned, we have revolutionized entirely prison government and prison discipline, it has required the recent spectacular uprising of small groups of desperate men to make us finally demand that new prisons, better prisons, and prisons that shall not be places of cruel and unusual punishment must be erected immediately, no matter what they cost.

Our old prisons, such as Auburn, which is the conspicuous example of what a prison should not be, were bad enough when filled only to their normal capacity, but when we attempt, as we are doing at present, to crowd 6500 men into accommodations none too ample for 4500, we obviously are giving the lie to all our vaunted progress in social welfare.

The truth of the matter is that the extraordinary and seemingly callous indifference which has created this condition has resulted from the fact that very few people have thought seriously about the "prison question" at all. Our whole treatment of the criminal has been based not upon any logical theory of crime and punishment, but upon waves of transitory interest created by the events of the day. Having no definite ideas upon the subject, we have swayed first one way and then the other as the result of some outstanding event. First the misery, the discomforts, the inhumanities, the grim hopelessness of prison life will be brought to our attention by some impassioned leader in reform and a wave of sympathy for the convicted will sweep over us. We then demand all manner of hastily considered changes in our whole prison system, based entirely upon our sympathy of the moment for the convicted felon. Immediately, before even this wave of sympathy has had a chance permanently to affect our treatment of the criminal, some series of cold-blooded and inhuman crimes, or, as during the past year, the spectacle of a handful of hardened and hopeless men rising in rebellion against authority, arouses a demand for retaliation and vengeance and we lengthen sentences, increase convictions, and demand stern, unyielding and unsympathetic discipline. This is just as fatal to all real enlightened progress in solving this great problem as that worthy but misdirected sympathy which leads us to consider only the physical comfort of the prisoners, without regard to what is needed to effect a real reformation.

But I think at last we have realized that the time has come to give this matter the same thoughtful study, the same intelligence, the same definite and sustained effort along a carefully planned path toward a clearly understood goal that we have applied to other social problems. We must, in fact, go about this business of prison reform in the same way that we have reformed completely our business methods.

I have pointed out in a special message to the Legislature the five main problems and what we must do by legislation to meet them:

First is the need for new and proper buildings. I have spoken already of the 2000 men sleeping in all kinds of temporary makeshift instead of proper accommodations, and this surplus population is increasing largely because, under our present system of penal treatment, a very great percentage of those whom we release come back again for some new crime. I have outlined a program of building — and building proper prisons is something which may not be done in a few short months — which will give us in 1935 reasonably modern accommodations for 9,000 prisoners. I hope, by other improvements in our whole scheme of treatment of convicted men, by that time we shall have so reduced the number of those who return as to make these accommodations sufficient, with only moderate increases, for years to come. Unless, however, we appropriate the money needed this year and the succeeding four years as well, until the five-year construction program is completed, we shall not be able to reach the goal that we have set. It is not something that may be postponed, if we would end the present intolerable and shameful conditions.

The next thing which is necessary is to work out a plan for the segregation and classification of prisoners. It is obvious that when we place a foolish lad, led into his first crime, in the company of old and hardened offenders, we are making ourselves morally responsible, if he comes out from his comparatively short sentence as hardened and as irredeemable as his associates. It is not pleasant to think of the moral guilt that lies upon us all for this terrible and just accusation, not of making men's bodies uncomfortable, but of destroying their souls.

Now, if we are going to put an end to this — and put an end to it we must — we must know clearly what we intend to do so that we can design our new construction accordingly, for the type of building, the kind of discipline, and even the size and capacity of a prison depend entirely upon the exact use to which we intend to put it.

But granting that these two important things have been worked out, granting that we have proper accommodations and proper classification and segregation, granting that our prisoners have been decently housed and separated so as to avoid making professional criminals out of amateurs, what are we going to give them to do? An idle prisoner becomes a bitter prisoner in an amazingly short time. Work is the only sure preventive of brooding, and this work must be something more than mere routine exercise. It must be interesting, it must be real work that actually achieves something, for it is the feeling of achievement that gives work its power to bring about forgetfulness of the unpleasant.

In no particular have we been more backward than in solving what we know as the "prison labor" problem. It is complex and involves the working out of a plan which shall be acceptable to manufacturers, to our free labor, and to those who are experts as to what will most assist the prisoner to become a useful citizen. If our State Crime Commission in its forthcoming report is not prepared to lay out a definite plan for proper labor for all prisoners, it is my intention immediately to appoint a special commission. This commission will consist of representatives of our manufacturers, our labor organizations and our expert penologists. They are to sit around a table and work out a scheme of prison labor which will be recommended by all three groups. It is also my hope, in consideration of the constantly increasing number of youthful prisoners—boys who have been led into crime from sheer idleness or lack of knowledge of how to earn a living more usefully—that a real trade school education, in as many varied lines as we can find adaptable for this purpose, be given them. I do not know of any one thing which will make these youths useful citizens when they pass out of the prison gates so much as an education in a good trade, under competent supervisors in the use of modern tools and machinery which will make them really skilled workmen and tremendously shorten that most critical period when they must immediately earn a living or return to criminal ways.

The next important thing which we must do, one which is of peculiar importance in view of the necessarily overcrowded conditions which will continue until our building program is completed, is vastly to improve our whole system of parole. We cannot extend the theory of parole under our present plan. It is illogical and wrong to have the work of the Parole Commission undertaken, as at present, by a Board consisting of the wardens of the different prisons and the Commissioner of Correction. It is a man's job in itself, to say nothing of the impropriety of giving the parole power virtually to those in charge of the daily life of the prisoners. We have laid far too many other important duties on these men to expect them to be able to give full attention to working out a scientific extension of the parole theory. I look to the creation of a real Parole Commission consisting of well-paid experts who have, in addition, a real interest in the work. I am asking for the placing of far more authority in such a Commission than the Parole Board now enjoys. Just what changes in our laws are needed for this and just what the functions and duties of this Commission should be are matters to be determined by those who have made a lifelong study of the problem. I shall announce on Monday the appointment of a voluntary committee of six persons, known not only in our State but throughout the country as being peculiarly qualified to speak with authority in this matter, and I have been promised their immediate attention to this question as a public service, to the end that within the next two weeks I may frame a definite working plan based on their years of study which I can submit to the Legislature.

It is my hope to create a body so responsible and so competent as to make it possible to use them as an advisory board in the matter of the hundreds of applications for pardon and commutations of sentence which now lie so heavily on every Governor's shoulders. It is impossible for the Governor to know or for the Governor to investigate all of the many circumstances of which he should be informed in determining these questions of pardon and commutation. It is not legal authority that is needed in this case, but efficient machinery to conduct the preliminary research needed to assure a right determination.

We are at present convicting our criminals under what have come to be known as the "Baumes Laws" which mathematically increase the length of sentence for each new offense until the fourth conviction carries with it a sentence for life. I do not at this time recommend specific changes in these laws. Their effects, their merits, and their faults require expert study from actual observation of conditions since their adoption. But it is my hope, if I can secure the establishment of this real Parole Commission, that after practical experience during the next recess of the Legislature they will be in a position to make recommendations in this matter both to the State Crime Commission and to our Legislature based on actual conditions rather than upon a theory of what would be improvement.

I have tried to explain as briefly as I can our present prison problem and what we propose to do about it. This is certainly one thing in which politics never should be allowed to enter, and on which all parties should reach a common agreement for the common good. I feel confident that although my political party is not the party to which the members of this club belong, I shall receive in this great effort to improve our prisons and our present methods the hearty support of every member.

83 ⟨ Statement on the Appointment of a Committee to Study Prison Labor. March 12, 1930

ANY efficient and effective program for the development of the State's penal institutions along the best modern lines of thought and practice must consist of far more than a mere financial schedule, or a catalogue of structures to be erected or improved in the future. Owing to our failure for many, many years in the past to keep abreast of the times, and to provide each year the comparatively moderate expenditure so to do, we are faced with the necessity of completely remodeling not only our structures but our system in regard to prisons and prisoners.

The first step is, of course, the securing of assurance of sufficient funds to erect certain definite new buildings to meet the growing needs of the State. It is my understanding that the Legislature is in accord with me in this matter and that we may be reasonably assured that this part of the program can be carried through.

Having decided, however, on a prison in the abstract, the next question is: What class of prisoners shall be sent there? It is, I think, universally recognized that the old practice of committing the hardened and practically hopeless offenders to the same institutions as the youth who has committed his first crime results too often in making a professional criminal of the youth upon his release. The character of these prisons, their very integral structure depend, of course, upon the class of prisoners they are designed to accommodate. Thus a five-year program for the gradual proper segregation and distribution of prisoners, to go hand in hand with the new buildings or improvements in old buildings as they are physically completed, is equally essential.

There remains, however, another question which is even more

important and more difficult to answer. Having segregated our prisoners as far as practicable, how are we to keep them occupied during the term of their incarceration? An idle prisoner becomes a brooder and only too often eventually a plotter; yet for various very practical reasons we are more backward in this matter of proper prison labor than in any other part of the work ahead. It is perfectly true that we have had shops of a sort in our prisons, but the finding of employment for every prisoner which will not only keep his mind healthily occupied, but will send him out of the prison better equipped to earn an honest living than he was when he entered, still stares us in the face.

Various solutions have been suggested, but there are three elements which must be considered and reconciled before the prison labor problem is really solved. None of the plans so far has satisfied all of the requirements.

It would be easy to establish industries in our prisons in which every prisoner might be employed, and even to make them profitable to the State, but this can only be done at the expense of those who labor outside the prison walls and, because they have been good citizens, certainly deserve the State's protection from unfair competition from those who have proved themselves bad citizens in relation to law observance. Not only must the right of labor to be protected be considered, but in addition those who manufacture goods which could be easily and more cheaply manufactured in our penal institutions also deserve protection from the competition of goods manufactured within prison walls.

The necessity of providing work which shall be also educational demands industries of some kind in all our prisons for every prisoner. Justice to the manufacturers and the workmen of the State demands that these manufactures do not conflict with similar goods manufactured outside. A possible solution may lie in the establishment of trade schools rather than in factories to turn out finished articles; or it may be necessary to reach a compromise between the three conflicting interests by which mutual concessions are made in the interest of the rehabilitation of the offender which will not fall too heavily on any one group.

In my judgment, the right answer can only be found by a meeting of those understanding the needs of the prisoner, of those representing the State's workers, and of those representing the manufacturing interests of our Commonwealth. I have accordingly determined to appoint a committee consisting of two outstanding experts in prison problems, two representatives of labor, and two representatives of our manufacturing interests to sit around a table together and work this thing out. It cannot be done with the speed with which the admirable report on probation was accomplished. This is a matter of breaking new ground rather than expertly summarizing definite conclusions which have been reached by penal experts after years of study. I intend to ask this committee, whose names will be announced in a few days, to work through the coming summer in the expectation that they may have a definite recommendation for next year's Legislature. . . .

84 (The Governor Reports to the Governors' Conference on Progress in the Suppression of Crime. June 30, 1930

AT THE last session of the Governors' Conference, I was requested to act as an informal committee of one for the purpose of making a report at the next session in regard to progress made by the different State Governments in the war against crime, and particularly as to the necessity of securing by definite legislation fuller and more accurate statistics regarding the character and amount of crime, in order that the whole subject could be considered with more intelligence and with a far better knowledge of actual conditions than are now possessed.

You will hear a special report on the advisability of creating a permanent secretariat for the Conference, which would act as a clearing house of information and generally assist in the coordinating of the activities in our different States along many lines.

The necessity for a universal and central system of reporting of crimes committed, whether in the rural districts or in the great cities, and the publication of statistics in regard thereto, are so obvious as to need no further comment from me. In revising its entire Criminal Code, the State of Louisiana adopted an excellent provision in this respect which requires all sheriffs and peace officers to report not only the crimes on which arrests are made but all crimes which have been committed in their territory.

By making every peace officer, as part of his regular duties, responsible for the report of crimes committed, whether the perpetrator thereof is known or not, and by requiring the proper department of the State machinery to collect, classify and publish at frequent intervals such reports, it will be possible to get a very clear idea of the actual amount of crime in this country without adding any expense for an elaborate statistical bureau.

In case a permanent secretariat is created in accordance with the suggestion made to the Executive Committee, it seems to me to be obvious that a most important function for it to assume would be the duty of preparing a model statute requiring only the most simple statistics, and the forwarding of them to the Governors of the several States in the hope that it will be submitted with a favorable recommendation to the Legislatures.

I have collected considerable material on the subject which I shall turn over to any committee or permanent secretariat which may be created as a result of the action of this session. Should it be decided that such action is not wise, I ask the National Crime Commission, of which I am a member of the Executive Committee, to draw up such a statute and to send it to the Governors during the next few months.

It cannot be said that much progress has been made during the year in attacking crime through legislation. This is largely due to the fact that only nine State Legislatures were in session. Next year the Legislature of practically every State will meet and I hope we shall see a coordinated and real effort made to take legislative action.

I would like to call the attention of all of the Governors to the final report made by the Association sponsored by the American Bar Association which has been working for so many years on the Criminal Code. Many suggestions for the improvement of our criminal codes are embodied in that report. These are worth the serious consideration of every Governor. A previous report covering the same subject, prepared by the late Governor Hadley and made by the National Crime Commission, also contains much valuable material and I shall be glad to forward a copy thereof to any Governor who would like to study it.

There has been an increasing tendency to meet the problem of our overcrowded prisons by seeking to eliminate causes of crime and to reduce the number of prisoners in every way possible. It is generally recognized that unless a prisoner is sentenced for life, he will eventually return to the community, and if our whole theory of prisons and penal treatment is not based so far as possible on the reform of the prisoner while he is in the custody of the State, we shall continue to take in new prisoners at one gate and release hardened criminals through another, and our total criminal population will increase by leaps and bounds in consequence.

There is, of course, a class of offenders from whom society must be protected, men who will always be criminals and who are beyond any efforts at reclamation, but there are many, many cases where a more intelligent treatment of our prisoners will save the State many millions of dollars in providing for their reincarceration at a later date.

There are also many cases of first offenders who undoubtedly can be made useful citizens by placing them on probation and suspended sentence, without herding them with notorious and hardened criminals no matter how short their terms.

There are other cases where a penal sentence is necessary to inflict a sufficiently severe lesson but where scientific observation by trained men will reveal a real willingness to reform and to stay reformed which would make it advisable and wise to release the prisoners on parole at a comparatively early date.

These two great matters, parole and probation, are now receiving consideration in almost every State. I am glad to say that in our own State I think we have made a most noteworthy progress in matters of parole. We have established, on the advice of men who have made the subject a study all their lives, a Parole Commission of three men drawing twelve thousand dollars a year each, who under the law are not allowed to engage in any other business and who have the complete control of the probation system in their hands. This has been made an independent department free from all connection with the heads of the prisons or the Department of Correction. Under this new Parole body a special staff of trained and competent parole officers is created and it is hoped that we can now make a practical demonstration to our sister States of the advantages of competent officials working with complete freedom along modern lines.

I hope next year we shall take the next step and consider seriously the matter of probation which at present is rather left to chance or the individual idiosyncrasies of the different judges.

The tendency of criminals to organize in what might be described as the interstate traffic in crime has increased tremendously during the past two or three years. I feel that we must meet it by a combined effort, working in close cooperation with the Governors and the Legislatures of all the States in order that we may have such uniformity in our criminal procedure and punishments as will leave no place of refuge for the organized gangster in this country.

85 ⟨ Address on Probation and Parole before the National Probation Association. New York City. March 17, 1931

To NO other institutions of learning in the world do so many postgraduates return for advanced instruction as to those "Colleges of crime" which a still unenlightened civilization has erected for a quite different purpose — our penal institutions, State and national. Prison statistics show that from 50 percent to 60 percent of those once sent to jail become habitual offenders and eventually return to jail again. When we consider that this 50 percent represents only those persons who have been caught in the act and have been successfully prosecuted, and that we must add those who have escaped detection or have slipped through the many loopholes in our creaking and antiquated machinery of justice and prosecution, we are forced to admit that, as a protection to society, the whole prison system has been miserably inadequate and ineffective. We are only beginning to realize that the overwhelming majority of our convicted criminals return to society in a short time and become again our neighbors and active members of our community.

We have assumed that the horrors of prison life and the stigma which society brands upon every prisoner, were forcing him through sheer terror into the path of virtue on his release. That is not true. We must always have prisons. There are always those who are criminal by instinct, who must be kept from society and from injuring others because their minds are incapable of reformation, their wills too weak to keep them from lives of crime. These must be rearrested and rearrested and rearrested and rearrested. Our police records are full of criminal biographies of those who have spent, since they reached adolescence, far more time in jail than out of it. For such our prisons must be maintained. But we are finding from practical experience that the permanent reformation of the first-offender is possible in far more instances than we realize. In the State of Massachusetts 80 percent of those who have been placed on probation instead of being sent to jail have made good. In our own State we have placed 250,000 offenders on probation in the last 24 years. We are now placing more than 25,000 yearly, as our courts and our judges have become convinced of the value of the probation system in reducing crime. We have, unfortunately, no figures showing how many of these were permanently reformed, but they have contributed in that time over twenty-three million dollars in fines, restitutions and support of dependents; and I have no doubt that the percentage of permanent reformations closely approximates that of our sister State.

There are three ways of dealing with the first-offender: We can send him to jail and keep him there until the expiration of his sentence; we can parole him before that sentence expires; or we can put him on probation after he is sentenced without his going to jail at all.

For the information of my radio audience let me make clear the difference between probation and parole which are often confused in the public mind. When a convicted prisoner at the time of his sentence is released from custody but kept under the observation of a court officer without going to prison to serve any part of his sentence, he is said to be placed on probation.

If he is actually sent to prison, however, but later found worthy of being released, again under the observation and technically in the custody of a special officer, he is said to be placed on parole.

In both cases his past record is looked into before action is taken and a failure to report to the proper officer, or a new offense against the law, sends him to prison to serve out his sentence with added penalties.

If the criminal's past history gives good reason to believe that he is not of the naturally criminal type, that he is capable of real reform and of becoming a useful citizen, there is no doubt that that probation, viewed from the selfish standpoint of protection to society alone, is the most efficient method that we have. And yet it is the least understood, the least developed, the least appreciated of all our efforts to rid society of the criminal; I am very glad not only to express my appreciation of the work which your association has done in the education of the public, but, in addressing many thousands of people over the radio at the same time, to do what I can to awaken a greater public interest in probation throughout our country generally.

By segregation, by removing the first-offender from the demoralizing society of the habitual criminal, by a study of the criminal himself, treating him as an individual rather than in the mass, we can do much to reduce that staggering percentage of second-offenders. I am proud that this State, largely through the splendid recommendations of our legislative prison commission, has now embarked upon a ten-year program aimed to make our prisons, so far as they can be made, no longer what I have called "Colleges of crime," but true institutions of reform.

By shortening the terms of those who show after their incarceration hopeful symptoms of a real repentence, we can add a still greater number of good citizens to our communities. And here I am again proud to report that our State last year has taken the lead in the development of a powerful, efficient and properly financed Commission of Parole.

By investigation of the past history of first-offenders or of those who, in the opinion of the judge who tries the case, have been the victims, somewhat, of circumstances and who are not hopelessly criminal in their tendencies, and by the placing of such as are found worthy upon probation, I believe we shall empty our prisons still further. While for some years we have had in this State a certain State supervision and support, it is my feeling that this State can go much further than it has. I am recommending to our Legislature this year that this be made a subject of expert study and that next year we inaugurate a real system of State probation as advanced and effective as our new parole system is already showing itself to be.

Economically, probation is to the financial advantage of the State. Statistics show that it costs, roughly, $18 a year to supervise each person released on probation. Under more watchful scrutiny and closer observation it may perhaps eventually cost as much as $25 for each person. Against that set the $350 to $500 a year it costs the State to keep a man in jail. It is my hope that in New York at least, and eventually in all our States, we shall be continually decreasing the number of our prison guards and wardens and increasing the number of our parole and probation officers. Probation officers, however, must be properly trained and competent persons. In this we have been lamentably weak. I am confident if the Legislature agrees to the investigation I have requested, that we shall find a practical way to secure really quali-

fied probation officers, just as we are now insisting on really qualified parole officers. It is the State's affair and this whole matter of
probation should be made the State's business and put under wide
State control.

I urge those interested in this problem of increasing crime,
in this universal crowding of our jails and continual necessity of
building more and more prisons, to support not only in this State,
but in all States, the efforts of those who without attracting anywhere near as much attention as they should, have done so much
to secure the establishment of probation in one form or another
in twenty-one of our forty-eight States.

86 ❡ Address on the Unsolved Problem of Prison Labor. New York City. April 30, 1931

THERE are certain honors which are bestowed, almost automatically, upon the Governor of a State, more in recognition of the
position which he occupies than for any particular merit of his
own. I feel, however, that your Committee, which for more than
twenty years has been striving so intelligently and valiantly to
solve one of the greatest problems in our treatment of convicted
wrongdoers, has not awarded the medal which signifies their
appreciation on account of my position but in recognition of the
fact that I also have been working personally to the same end. I
feel, in consequence, more than usual gratification and appreciation on this occasion because there is nothing so heartening to one
holding public office, as the realization that what he is doing and
trying to do is understood and appreciated and approved by
bodies such as yours.

I have spoken of this problem of prison labor as one of our
great penal questions. I think I might almost refer to it as our
greatest unsolved problem. Along all other roads toward the
proper treatment of the criminal, we have advanced far, and I
think perhaps this State of New York, during the past two years,
has advanced a little further than any other commonwealth. A

prison to us no longer is regarded as an impregnable Bastille into which we can throw, without any consideration, convicted criminals of all grades from the petty thief to the hardened mankiller for certain arbitrary and specified sentences, determined by the judges, without any further sense of responsibility than seeing that they do not escape and are not allowed to return to society until the last hour of their sentence is over.

We have realized for some years past that the criminal is after all a human being and as such is entitled to certain ordinary decencies of civilization — light, air, clean surroundings and a certain amount of exercise and even recreation. We have, however, only fairly recently realized the further great truth, that the average criminal is not only a human being but in nearly all ways very much like ourselves; that up to the time of his conviction he was as much entitled to all the rights of our civilization as we are; and what is more important, that sooner or later, except for those who receive death or life-imprisonment sentences, he will return again to live among us, to become either a useful member of society or a deadly menace to ourselves and our neighbors. With the realization of this fact has come the further understanding that it will be in most cases our blame if he continues in a criminal career and our credit if he quits his evil life.

We are proceeding in consequence along new lines. We are separating the hopeless and hardened criminals from the men who yielded to temptation in a moment of weakness. We are studying each convicted person as an individual. We are trying to make his time of incarceration a period of rehabilitation as well, to find out what is good in him and to develop it, to find what is bad in him and eradicate it so far as is possible. We are trying, too, to remove him from the hardening surroundings of prison life and place him on parole, subject always to return. We are even going a step further and whenever possible we place him on probation after he has been convicted, without imposing on him a prison sentence at all.

By these methods we hope to solve this terrible problem of our overcrowded prisons, so large a proportion of whose population consists of those who having once committed a crime have entered our penal institutions and become so debased that on their release they know no other course, they have no other object but to commit new crimes and to return within the prison walls again, again and again. But all our new methods, based on this new attitude toward convicted men, succeed or fail in proportion to the extent of our ability to make the term of imprisonment a period during which he will not learn new ways of crime from his fellow inmates, but will acquire knowledge and experience and if possible even a definite trade, which will enable him to return to an honest life and to resist the terrible temptations of need and poverty on his release.

Obviously, it will do no good to arrange for a prisoner's parole when he shows evidence of reformation unless we so mold his life in prison as to lead him to desire to reform. There never was a truer adage than that which warns us that "Satan always something finds for idle hands to do." The most demoralizing thing of prison life is, after all, its horrible monotony—the idleness, the lack of anything of interest, the lack of even those small responsibilities which make the busy man almost always a contented man. Only a few have brains so fashioned as to enable them to live in quiet contemplation of nothing in particular. It is self evident that we must have occupation for our prisoners. We do not need to argue that this occupation must be something creative in its nature. To build up a pile of bricks and then tear it down the next day will become after a few days as monotonous as doing nothing at all. This seems obvious and yet it is one of the last things in penal science which we have come to realize.

True, convict labor is not new but convict labor as a means of reformation of the convicts, instead of a mere punishment or an economic machine to turn out manufactured goods at impossible prices wherein the State pays the overhead, is a new idea.

Over one hundred years ago in the first prison establishment in the City of New York and also the first prison of this kind in the State, there was developed a method of prison administration which, you will probably be surprised to know, included proper classification of the prisoners. In addition to this classification there were also established prison industries which were to bring pecuniary returns to the prisoners who received the wages of their industry. The eyes of the whole world were centered on that enterprise and had it succeeded, all that we are trying to do now would have been done many years ago. Perhaps, had we not entered into the machine age, it would have been successful, but with the coming of machines in manufacturing, human greed was allowed to enter, and the exploitation of prisoners for private contractors began. To the horrors of prison life was added slavery as well. The cruelties that ensued, that inevitably must ensue in any plan of using prisoners for the profit of private manufacturers, wrecked the whole scheme. In the end the exploitation of convict-made goods aroused those who are obliged to depend on free labor in the making of their products. There were riots and bloodshed in the streets of New York City in the '30s during the long struggle to end this intolerable practice. Nor was it really abolished until the '80s when private exploitation came to an end as a result of the campaign led by the Workmen's Council. . . . Since then we have had the State use a system whereby the industry of the prisoners is confined to the making of articles used by the State. We have had various experiments but we have been able to provide work only for a portion of our prison population.

It is a difficult problem to keep so many men employed, to keep them employed not only as a prevention of idleness but also as a help in their struggle for existence after their release from prison, to prevent what they make from competing with the labor of the free men who have done no wrong, to prevent their exploitation either to the advantage or disadvantage of private manufacturers. All this is a problem of no small magnitude. In this State I have asked your representatives to meet with representatives of labor and with representatives of the manufacturers, to sit around a common table and arrive at a real solution of the matter. It is a vital part of the effort to coordinate our whole scheme and theory of prisons and punishment. While they are not yet ready to report a final plan, I want to congratulate them for having achieved the hardest part of the work that lay before them. They have brought together, I think, for the first time these four elements, labor, capital, industry, and the science of penology, viewing these questions from four entirely different standpoints; and they are working out the problem in the friendliest spirit with full cooperation.

Other States are watching what we are doing here. If this committee succeeds, even approximately, in solving the first step toward a correct solution of this problem of prison labor, it will have blazed a path which all our sister States will follow, and I shall feel that it far more than myself rightly should deserve the medal of your association.

XVI

The Second Campaign for the Governorship

IN ADDITION to the campaign speeches in 1930, which are printed in this chapter, I made the following other speeches: Address at Democratic State Convention, Syracuse, N. Y. September 30, 1930, *Public Papers* (1930), page 754; Radio Address, Albany, N. Y. October 9, 1930, *Public Papers* (1930), page 762; Radio Address, Albany, N. Y. October 13, 1930, *Public Papers* (1930), page 764; Radio Address, Albany, N. Y. October 16, 1930, *Public Papers* (1930), page 769; Address, Binghamton, N. Y. October 18, 1930, *Public Papers* (1930), page 774; Address, Utica, N. Y. October 23, 1930, *Public Papers* (1930), page 795; Address, Bronx, New York City. October 27, 1930, *Public Papers* (1930), page 806; Address, New York City. October 28, 1930, *Public Papers* (1930), page 811; Address, Yonkers, N. Y. October 28, 1930; Address, Jamaica, L. I. October 29, 1930, *Public Papers* (1930), page 817; Address, Staten Island, New York City. October 30, 1930, *Public Papers* (1930), page 822; Address, Brooklyn, N. Y. October 31, 1930, *Public Papers* (1930), page 826.

My opponent in this campaign was Hon. Charles H. Tuttle, who had been United States Attorney for the Southern District of New York.

The results of the election were Roosevelt 1,770,342, Tuttle 1,045,341.

87 ❨ The Candidate Accepts the Renomination for the Governorship, New York City.

October 3, 1930

(Continuation and maintenance of program of the first term — Social legislation — Water power — Administration of justice — Farm relief — Improvement of local government — Prohibition.)

Two years ago I accepted the nomination for Governor, because I wanted to be a disciple in a great cause — a cause that needed little explaining to the citizens of the State of New York.

I am here once more to accept the nomination for Governor for the simple reason that I still march forward in that cause.

My theme then was that progressive Government, by its very terms, must be a living and a growing thing, that the battle for it is never ending and that if we let up for one single moment or one single year, not merely do we stand still but we fall back in the march of civilization.

During the four administrations of my great predecessor the ground of progress had to be fought for inch by inch, and the same fact holds true of these two years past. Every known kind of wall and boulder has been thrown across our path, sometimes the obstruction of mere inertia, sometimes the opposition of those who for personal, selfish reasons have feared the effect of new things upon their own personal interests. But most often the barrier has been, day in and day out, now in the open, now under cover, the opposition of a Republican leadership which seems to be based primarily on the high-minded, idealistic purpose of discrediting, through me, any and every proposal of the Party which I represent, regardless of merit or reason.

Let me make it perfectly clear that in my judgment this Republican leadership does not represent the great rank and file of the men and women of this State who call themselves Republicans. Let me make it perfectly clear that I am confident that they, in large numbers, will recognize this autumn, as they have recognized before, that Government at Albany must be and shall be progressive, and that they are still as out of step with the leadership of their own Party as they have been in the past.

Now let us look for a moment at the facts. Two years ago in my speech of acceptance I stressed five great objectives:

1. A program of social legislation to make New York the leader among her sister States. This has been adopted and our task now is to see that that leadership shall be maintained in the days to come.

2. I advocated a definite program for the development of the vast water power resources of the State under constant governmental control and possession. The capitulation of the Republican leaders in response to public pressure is still fresh in our minds. One of the great issues this autumn is whether this great policy shall be maintained and carried through or whether the State will revert, either openly or by hidden means, to private ownership.

3. I spoke also of the vital need of a comprehensive study by laymen and lawyers of the whole system of the administration of justice. Here again it took two years before the Republican leaders capitulated, but now at last we are about to take action. Whether the result of this study proves to be more than a mere report of a committee depends on the future drive and leadership in Albany.

4. I spoke also of the great problems that faced our agricultural communities. Once more we have a definite record of definite results, following an agricultural program initiated by me, a program for which I received the splendid cooperation of all of the agricultural interests of the State, regardless of party, a program which the Republican leaders were compelled to adopt when they came to the sudden realization of the fact that for a generation they had been in control of the Legislature and during that whole period had never once gone to the root of the farm problem. Today agriculture in the State of New York is beginning to get on its feet, and the simple question is whether the existing program shall be further extended and amplified during

the next two years or whether we shall go back to the period of inaction and drift.

5. Last of all, I recommended the reorganization of the lower units of county and town government, applying the same principles which had already been so successfully worked out in the reorganization of the State Government. That this should be done under the permissive principle of Home Rule, I have made wholly clear at all times. This great reform has remained pigeon-holed in the desks of the Republican legislative leaders at Albany. It is the one outstanding recommendation of mine which has been thwarted at every turn. The selfish, partisan reasons behind the inaction of these leaders are apparent to everyone; still I am confident that the force of public opinion behind a driving leadership, based on the principles of good government, rather than on the dictates of partisan advantage, will bring inevitable results.

There are, of course, other matters which the voters of the State will scan this autumn. Some of them relate to the individual candidates, now that they have been named by all parties.

For instance, three days ago I asked my distinguished opponent whether or not he would sign a State enforcement act, a question based on a widespread belief that some agreement of this kind was made to secure the support of Assemblyman Jenks and other dry leaders who have fought for this measure for so many years. It required over two days of painful meditation before a reply to this very simple question could be prepared, and it is noteworthy that the answer was not forthcoming until my friend had hastened over to Philadelphia and consulted with the President himself. His answer bears earmarks of the President's policy of being wet and dry at the same time. It is characteristic of the way the question was dodged in the national campaign by calling the Eighteenth Amendment a "noble experiment."

For the benefit of the wet members of his party, my opponent starts out by declaring that he has "no hesitancy" — there is a touch of humor, remembering the forty-eight hours, in that "no hesitancy" phrase — "in declaring that the National Law forms a part of the State Law anyhow and that the urgent thing is to proceed with enforcement rather than to defer to the possible passage of some particular bill." This is a long and lawyer-like way of saying "Yes" and at the same time "No." But the shadow of Assemblyman Jenks falling across his page at this particular point, and remembering his confidential conversations with that gentleman, he hastens to add that the nuisance law already affords a State enforcement possibility and that if "experience demonstrates that this law should be strengthened in order to fulfill its purpose more effectively, I would favor such strengthening." Just what does this mean? Does it mean a State enforcement act in some spots and not in others? It must be clear to everybody what it means. No wonder Mr. Jenks approved of his candidacy. His recent statement only advocates what Mr. Jenks and the drys have tried to do for the past two years, to pass the State enforcement act, and failing that, to pass an enabling act that would give us a Volstead law county by county.

Listen to what he says:

"I believe that legislation extending to counties or other political subdivisions full power within their own borders to use their local courts and police in the enforcement of prohibition should be immediately enacted."

And then he goes on to say:

"I would not approve a state-wide measure following the provisions of the Volstead Act."

I asked him, "Will you, or will you not approve a State enforcement act?" And he said, "I will not approve a state-wide enforcement act."

Who is hedging now? Oh yes, "wet to the wets and dry to the drys." It is the same old story of Republican hypocrisy.

I noticed that my distinguished opponent is troubled and solicitous over what someone has told him. He thinks that there appears to be a discrepancy between my general views as to party planks and the party platform itself. I use the term "what someone has told him" advisedly, because it is evident that he himself cannot possibly have read the platform. The platform says the Democratic Party pledges itself to the repeal of the Eighteenth Amendment and to such measures as will definitely and effectively banish the saloon. I stand definitely on that platform.

I note, too, that he has discovered the existence of the nuisance law — this marvelous weapon which has lain idle and which the drys can feel sure he will strengthen and make effective, if he is elected Governor. In a speech last night, and in articles printed in one of our great papers and to which no denial has been made as yet, a certain Major Campbell flatly claims that his efforts as Prohibition Director to invoke the nuisance law in the City of New York were blocked by Mr. Tuttle whenever called to his attention.

And as long as I am speaking of my distinguished opponent, let me say that I am afraid he has been so long a prosecuting officer, who looks at everything with the viewpoint of securing a conviction in any way possible, that his sense of abstract justice has been somewhat blunted and that he thinks in terms of convictions rather than in terms of judicial determination. This is rather amusingly illustrated by his proclamation that I had given the special Grand Jury a "wooden hatchet" with which to do its work. Permit me to inform him that I did not give the Grand Jury a hatchet of any kind, wooden or otherwise. Their weapons are the scales of justice and the sword of justice, to protect the innocent as well as to punish the guilty.

During the next two weeks, as you know, it will be necessary for me to spend nearly the whole of my time, under the Constitution and the law, in the preparation of the Executive Budget. During this time I can give little thought to the campaign or to myself as your candidate. During these two years I have believed that a personal, first-hand knowledge of the needs and conditions of every part of the State would fit me best for the task of Chief Executive. It is for this reason that I have visited every part of the State and have sought all possible information. I read that my distinguished opponent has announced that he is going to proceed up-State and, as he was quoted in the press, "get down among the people." I know the people will be properly flattered at his condescension, his descent from the high heights he occupies and

I hope, at the same time, he will inform himself on those great matters of State policy about which he has as yet said nothing, those vital questions affecting the welfare and the prosperity of all our fellow citizens, men and women, rich and poor. These are the real issues of this campaign. He will find his visit among the people most illuminating and informative.

We now enter formally into the campaign. Never has a Party gone before the public with a finer record of platform pledges fulfilled. What we have done in the past two years will, I am certain, convince the great majority of our voters that what we promise to do in the next two years, if we are retained in power, is not empty words but solemn pledges which will be fulfilled in the future as our pledges have been fulfilled in the past.

Lack of leadership at Washington has brought our country face to face with serious questions of unemployment and financial depression. Each State must meet this situation as best it can, and I am sure that at this critical period the sober judgment of the electorate of the Empire State will lead them to vote for that Party which for many years past has so wisely guided the policy and so greatly increased the prosperity of this greatest of all Commonwealths of the Union.

88 ❮ Campaign Address (Excerpts), Buffalo, N. Y. October 20, 1930

(Depression and unemployment — "No political party has patent rights on prosperity" — Public works and employment — Rural tax relief — Labor legislation.)

IN DISCUSSING governmental problems, if they are of current interest, it is essential and it is right to give the history of those problems, because the record going back over the past two years has a very direct bearing on the way in which we must approach and seek to solve the problems of the present.

That is why I have been glancing over the files which I had

collected during the 1928 campaign. I find in them a number of quotations made during that campaign which I want at this time to set forth merely for the purpose of the record, and for no other reason. You will recall that I was running for election as Governor of the State of New York against Mr. Albert Ottinger. You will also recall that at that time Mr. Herbert Hoover was running for election as President of the United States. I want to read to you some extracts from speeches during the campaign and from the Republican platform of that year:

"The history of our party demonstrates that . . . through the wisdom of Republican policies, and the capacity of the Republican Administration, the foundations of the high American standard of wage and living have been laid, and the greatness and prosperity of the country firmly established. No better guarantee of prosperity and contentment among our people at home . . . can be given than the pledge to maintain and continue the Coolidge policies. . . ." That is taken from the Republican platform of 1928.

"The people . . . know that the very happiness of their homes, and the comfort of the average man and woman is bound up in the outcome of every Presidential election because prosperity is the key to happiness, and the Republican Party and the Republican protective principles have, more than any other element, created our present-day prosperity, and they will insure that prosperity for the future. . . ." That is an extract from a speech of Albert Ottinger, running for Governor of the State of New York on October 9, 1928.

"We in America today are nearer to the financial triumph over poverty than ever before in the history of any land. The poor man is vanishing from among us. Under these impulses, and the Republican protective system, our industrial output has increased as never before, and our wages have grown steadily in buying power. Our workers, with their average weekly wages, can today buy two and even three times more bread and butter than any wage earner in Europe. At one time we demanded for our workers a full dinner pail. We have now gone far beyond that conception. Today we demand a larger comfort and greater participation in life and leisure. . . ." These are extracts from campaign speeches made by Herbert Hoover in the fall of 1928.

"The way to buttress our prosperity, to give every employer and employee, producer and consumer a feeling of greater security as he looks forward to the next four years with all their uncertainties, to secure the most earnest effort under competent leadership to deal with all the economic difficulties that confront us, is to continue the policies of the Republican Administration under the Presidency of Herbert Hoover. . . ." That is an extract from a speech by Mr. Charles E. Hughes delivered at St. Joseph, Mo., October 23, 1928, in behalf of the election of Herbert Hoover.

Those extracts read strangely tonight.

Then came October, 1929. Again for the record I want to state what I believe to be the simple facts. It has been well said by many national leaders in both parties that during the final period of inflation and stock market plunging not one single step was taken by the responsible officials of the national Administration to put on the brakes, or to suggest even that the situation was economically false and unsound. Thousands of citizens in every part of the United States gained the feeling that the national Government was actually lending encouragement and that all was well with the country. A sound public opinion recognizes today, I am very certain, that if Washington had had the courage to apply the brakes the heights to which the orgy rose would not have been so high, and as a result, even if a slowing up of industry had come, the fall from the heights would not have been so appallingly great.

The other matter of record which today receives censure from many of the most conservative and sound financial and industrial leaders, is the fact that after the crash of last autumn the Republican Administration began and continued to hand out from Washington false information concerning the seriousness of the situation. The President himself very properly called conferences of the leaders of industry from various parts of the country and asked them to do everything possible to maintain production, but he was wrong in saying in December, "I am convinced that through these measures we have reestablished confidence; industrial unemployment and suffering which would otherwise have occurred have been prevented."

The extent of the rapidly growing condition of unemployment was concealed. One optimistic bulletin after another appeared. It was a desperate and futile attempt to restore prosperity by means of proclamations from Washington.

Month after month as conditions became worse, the messages of good cheer became more and more optimistic. As working men were discharged in thousands, they read statements made by the Federal Administration, that "Things were getting better." Although the times called for quick and decisive action by the Federal Government, nothing happened but words. That was the time, if ever, when Government projects should have been accelerated. That was the time, if ever, when public works should have been pushed so as to provide employment. That was the time, if ever, that increased appropriations for Federal aid, roads, river and harbor improvements, veterans' hospitals, military post construction, and public buildings should have been speeded up.

Instead of that, as was pointed out by the Senator from this State, Robert F. Wagner, on September 29, 1930, the total appropriations for the current fiscal year for those purposes were $25,000,000 less than the amount of similar appropriations for the last fiscal year. This same Republican Administration in Washington refused to permit the House of Representatives to enact into law the bills introduced by the Democratic Senator from this State which would have helped the situation and which would have prepared the country against its increase or recurrence.

I need not dwell on the situation today. I need not comment upon the business depression and the cruel condition of unemployment which are upon us.

I have quoted from these various speeches of Republican candidates of two years ago and I have summed up fairly, I think, the two great reasons for blaming the Republican national Administration. But let me make it definite and clear that I do so simply to sum up the record and not for the purpose of obtaining partisan advantage in this campaign.

The one great purpose of setting forth the record as I have is only, and let me stress that word only, to give definite proof of what the Democratic Party has always maintained — that no political party has any monopoly on prosperity. Apparently even the Republican leaders in 1930 have at last come to realize it.

How well do I recall the campaign speeches of two years ago. How well do I recall the repeated appeals for votes on the strength of prosperity at Washington. Speech after speech was devoted to the subject of Republican prosperity and to the necessity of voting under the eagle in order to continue that prosperity. State campaigns have been waged for the last six years by the Republican Party almost exclusively on the question of national prosperity. This year there seems to be a dead silence so far as the Republican Federal Administration is concerned.

Whereas formerly the name of Herbert Hoover or Calvin Coolidge appeared at least five times in the speech of every Republican candidate for office, today we look in vain for mention of the names. Indeed, this attitude of silence, so far as Federal questions of prosperity are concerned, has led some of the Republican candidates even to criticize my party and me for calling it to the public attention. This must seem strange indeed to those of us who remember the campaign speeches of recent years. . . .

And so I have spoken of unemployment and depression in this State and shall continue to do so, not for the purpose of belaboring the Republican national Administration, but for the purpose of proving for all time, that the Democratic Party was right in its claim that no political party has exclusive patent rights on prosperity.

It is my thought, of course, and in this I am perhaps partisan, that the election of Democratic Congressmen from this State this autumn will do much toward helping the Congress of the United

States to build a more sane, a more sound and economic structure for the Nation than has been done in the past.

As to the existing situation in our own State, as Buffalo's greatest citizen, Grover Cleveland, would have said, "that is a condition and not a theory."

We should face this situation honestly and bravely. There is no need for abject pessimism. The strength of this country, the wealth of its natural possessions and resources, the industry, energy and patriotism of its people, are, in the last analysis, the ultimate guarantee of a return to better times.

I have no doubt that capital and labor alike can, and ultimately will, put their shoulder to the wheel to pull our industry out of the deep mud. As a State Government, New York must, of course, and will, of course, do its share and more. It can do it, and has done it, by extending the construction of its public works so as to provide employment for its citizens.

The total amount of money available during this calendar year amounts to $55,000,000. Already, $33,000,000 have been put to work. The balance of $22,000,000 will be put to work as follows: $9,000,000 this month, $7,000,000 next month, and $6,000,000 in December.

In this way we carry on a uniform plan of work — a total amount more than $20,000,000 greater than ever before in the history of the State. When the Legislature meets in January it will give us, I am confident, another large sum to continue the work.

That the record of this State in progress on its public works is ahead of that of any other State is not open to contradiction. . . .

I also wish to point out to you the great savings which have been brought about in your local county and town taxes as a result of the program of rural tax relief which was initiated by me. You will recall that immediately after my election two years ago I appointed an Agricultural Advisory Commission consisting of various professors in agriculture, leaders of various farm and agricultural societies, publishers of farm publications, rural tax experts and practical farmers and dairymen. This commission met and made recommendations to me which I transmitted to the Legislature as soon as I got to Albany. The commission pointed out at the outset that the most crying need of the rural dwellers was relief from their ever-mounting taxes for local purposes.

I want to point out to you that while these taxes have been called rural taxes, they bear down upon dwellers in the cities and in the villages as well. For example, right here in Buffalo, the residents of this city pay a great deal in taxes which go into the County Treasury. In addition to paying city taxes, each and every one of you also pays a county tax. Wherever, therefore, a county is saved expenditures and taxation, that saving helps not only the farmer, but every man, woman and child in the county, including those in the city of Buffalo. . . .

I need not point out to you who initiated and started these reforms. It is true, of course, that both Republicans and Democrats in the Legislature voted for them. But although the Republican Party has been in control of the Legislature absolutely for twenty years, nothing was done to relieve the counties of the State from this staggering burden of taxation until I became Governor, and until I pointed out the way.

This plan of rural tax relief has saved the counties of all the State over $24,000,000 each year. Here in Erie County, the amount which has been saved, $1,400,000, should come off your local tax bills. If it has not, I believe you should make inquiry to ascertain where this tax money is going.

Returning once more to the subject of labor and employment, I am confident that the working men and women of this State have a full realization of the fact that the Democratic Party has been the sponsor of 99 percent of all the progressive labor legislation which is now on our statute books. Labor has come to depend on the Democracy for its progress.

It was in this very city that I received from the President of the American Federation of Labor that hearty commendation for my efforts in behalf of the working classes of the State.

It is with considerable pride that I read from that letter, setting forth the attitude of the American Federation of Labor toward what my Administration has done for labor at Albany. President Green writes to me:

"Your leadership as Governor of the State of New York stands out in a most striking way and the work you are able to do must be classified as a most rare accomplishment. You deserve the support of labor, and of all classes of people who seek to perpetuate our free institutions and who are engaged in preserving our principle of free government through the advancement of the highest and best interests of the masses of the people. I express the earnest hope that all the working people and their friends in the State of New York may give to you their undivided support in your political and social reform policies so that you may be permitted to give to the people the benefit of your service."

I consider that not so much a tribute to what I have been able to do for labor, but rather to the policies of social progress and high-minded legislation which have characterized your party and my party, the Democratic Party of the State of New York, in its continued and untiring efforts to help the physical, mental and moral condition of the average man, woman and child in our State.

In line with this, I regret very much that although, with the help of public opinion, I was able to persuade the Legislature to adopt far-reaching reforms for labor, I was unable to get them to go along with me in my recommendations for further State legislation to regulate private employment agencies.

Too often have the laboring classes of the State been deceived and defrauded by private employment agencies. The State of New York, as well as many cities in the State, is doing what it can to help labor through public employment agencies. I believe that the protection of the strong arm of the State should be afforded to the laboring classes so that fraudulent or dishonest employment agencies will no longer be able to continue their unlawful practices on the honest working people of the State.

I have given you a simple and a true recital of the record. I have spoken of what has occurred in the past. I have given you a background by which you may judge the future.

Now, however, it is time for us to put our shoulders to the wheel and work for that future.

As I have said before, we can all do our share. . . .

It is not a matter of party. It is a matter of good citizenship and good Americanism.

Relief for unemployment, relief for suffering and privation cannot be brought about by Republican remedies alone.

Equally certain is it that it cannot be brought about by Democratic remedies alone. Let us apply united American remedies.

This is not the time to inject party politics or campaign propaganda into the situation in any shape, manner or form. This is not the time for curtailment, for reduction in wages, or for cessation of business activity. On the contrary, this is the time for courage and action.

Let us here and now, regardless of party, pledge ourselves individually and collectively to carry on, to face the future with that high courage and desire for concerted action which have always characterized the American people in every difficult hour.

The path of our duty is clear. You and I know that as good Americans, we will manfully and bravely follow that path.

89 ⁅Campaign Address (Excerpts), Rochester, N. Y. October 21, 1930

(Prisons and parole — Hospitals — Public works by bond issue — "Poor houses" — Old-age assistance — Prohibition.)

WHEN the present history of the State of New York is written a generation hence, the years 1929 and 1930 will be marked with a double star because these two years have seen, in my judgment, a notable change in popular understanding in relation to two great problems of modern humanity.

Most of us know that nearly 100 years ago, an Englishman by the name of Charles Dickens did more than any other individual to revolutionize the whole prison system of England. Through his writings he gave people to understand that for the first time their unfortunate brethren who, for one reason or another, were committed to jail, were still human beings; that jail conditions throughout England were horrible beyond belief; and that these jail conditions had not changed for the better in any material respect since the Dark Ages of a thousand years before.

In the days of Charles Dickens, most of Europe, and we here in the United States also, began to replace the dungeons and filth and starvation and nakedness and immorality of the older prisons with new structures which, in 1830 and 1840, were considered models of their kind. During that period nearly a hundred years ago, the State of New York erected the great prison structures at Sing Sing, Auburn, and Dannemora. And, with the exception of the newer prison at Great Meadow, we have carried on, during this whole time, with these cell blocks of now very ancient vintage.

Is it any wonder that these structures are out of date? It is a fact that for many years, the handful of people who are really interested in prison reform and in bettering the conditions of prisons and prisoners have been demanding new buildings and a new system throughout the State. The difficulty has been, frankly, that the public itself has taken little or no interest, and the result has been that for the past twenty years, we have had only piecemeal reform.

During the past few years, however, startling events all over the United States have brought the whole prison problem to the front. First came the crime wave itself, and with it, a new type of prisoner. Then came a series of riots in the prisons of many different States and in Federal prisons as well. This was followed by a publicity for the whole subject which is at last bearing good fruit.

A year ago last summer I held a conference with the legislative leaders, and we entered into a gentleman's agreement for a building program to cost $30,000,000 — $10,000,000 a year for three years — which program will completely rebuild our antiquated structures, give decent living conditions, good sanitation, plenty of exercise, new forms of labor and instruction, and finally, though by no means the least important, a system of parole which is aimed to give the best possible chance to every individual prisoner to rehabilitate himself as a law-abiding, respected member of the community in which he lives in the shortest possible time. . . .

The second part of this great program relates not to prisons, but to the hospitals of the State. And here it is not because of any particular lack of public interest, but because of an increase in the wards of the State beyond any previous estimate, that we have been facing an emergency during these two years.

Very soon after we took office, Lieutenant-Governor Lehman and I began a systematic inspection of the hospitals of the State. We found the condition of overcrowding to be more than serious. It was disgraceful to our State and a distinct handicap in caring for the patients along modern medical and scientific lines. . . .

In practically every State Hospital and State School the actual sleeping quarters of the patients have been so overcrowded that the beds are literally touching each other, and many of the patients have been forced to sleep out in the corridors. It is impossible to give the individual attention and care to each patient that should be given. . . .

The point I want to drive home tonight is that, both in the hospital and the prison programs, I have laid down a perfectly definite and comprehensive plan pointing to the year 1935. In the case of the prisons, this means the appropriation of $20,000,-000 more, $10,000,000 next year, and $10,000,000 the year after, thus giving us completed prisons by 1935, capable of housing under modern conditions every one of the 9,500 prisoners which the State is estimating to have in that year.

In the case of the hospitals we must provide 6,000 more beds by next year and 6,000 in 1932; and when these buildings are completed by 1935, they will house under proper conditions all of the hospital wards which the State will have on that date, and also relieve the overcrowding in the present institutions.

The total program for hospitals and prisons will cost about $70,000,000 and it will be impossible to pay for this out of current revenues, unless the State raises that amount by new taxation. We are all, I think, opposed to that, and this is the primary reason for the bond issue which will be submitted to the voters of the State on November 4th, this year. This $50,000,000 bond issue is to be used at the rate of not more than $20,000,000 a year toward the program of hospitals and prisons. Here again, partisan politics play absolutely no part. Furthermore, common sense dictates that the cost of the greater part of these splendid new buildings should be spread over a period of years. The buildings themselves are of the most modern permanent fire-proof type of construction; and it is reasonable to assume that they will be useful to the State for at least 100 years to come. To spread this cost over a period of 25 years is in accordance with sound business principles, and at the same time lifts that much burden from the backs of the taxpayers this year and the following two years. It must be clearly understood that if the bond issue does not go through, some next tax will have to be imposed. . . .

We, in this State, have established a new system of parole for prisoners. This system is in charge of a Parole Board of experts recently created at my suggestion by the Legislature. The purpose of the creation of this new Parole Board was not in any sense to make parole more easy or parole supervision more lenient. It was rather to make it more scientific and more effective. It was to give to the case of each prisoner the best that modern thought and modern social science could provide so that his individual case can be studied with a view toward rehabilitating him to good citizenship.

This new Parole Board is now functioning. I believe that under its careful and scientific supervision we shall find that there will be an increase in the proportion of those who, on leaving prison, go straight and become good citizens. Do not forget that out of every 100 men who are sent to prison, 92 of them come out again. Are you not interested in what they are when they return to live as our neighbors?

Let us, by providing accommodations which meet the essentials, at least, of decency, help build for better social conditions in the generations to come.

Along with the dilapidated and antiquated prisons and hospitals which we have inherited from past generations, there is an institution which you and I both want to see eliminated as far as possible. This institution can never be made to conform with our modern social consciousness, no matter how much money we put in it or how much we improve its physical plan.

I mean the "poor house." An alarmingly increasing number of aged persons are becoming dependent on outside help for bare maintenance. No greater tragedy exists in modern civilization than the aged worker, who, after a life of ceaseless effort and useful productivity, must look forward for his declining years to a "poor house."

It is, to my mind, no longer proper to provide for our aged destitute citizens in a "poor house," where that can be avoided. Nothing is so horrible a nightmare to workers of our State as the fear of that gloomy institution. This State, for some time past has abandoned the policy of taking care of orphans in orphan asylums. We have substituted for this archaic system a new one of Child Welfare and Widows' Pensions, whereby the State and locality contribute to the maintenance of children in their own homes, although the breadwinner of the family may have been taken away. Money has been given to the mothers of fatherless children so that they may maintain their children at home instead of sending them to an institution.

Mind you, it is not only a more humane and merciful solution of the problem, but in the long run will be even more economical, since the child can be maintained at home for even less than the cost of decent, modern orphan asylums.

The same arrangement, of course, should be made for our aged poor. They should not be taken away from their homes and placed in hospitals and public institutions. If the State and localities want to aid these people in their declining years, it should not be done in a "poor house," but should be done under conditions where they may maintain in their own homes, their independent lives and hold up their heads as citizens of America. . . .

We, in this State, have at last made a start in our sacred duty of taking care of our dependent aged. It is to my mind, only a start. I hope to see the time come when this relief of old-age assistance will not in any way even resemble a dole system.

I look forward to the time when every young man and young woman entering industrial or agricultural or business activity will begin to insure himself or herself against the privations of old age. The premiums which that young man or young girl will pay should be supplemented by premiums to be paid by the employers of the State, as well as by the State itself. In that way, when the young man or young girl has grown to old and dependent age, he or she will have built up an insurance fund which will maintain them in comfort in their years of reduced activity. In this way, their assistance will be a result of their own efforts and foresightedness. They will be receiving not charity, but the natural profits of their years of labor and insurance. I hope to have the opportunity of continuing my efforts to obtain this kind of old-age insurance which our most progressive thought demands.

Connected with this question of our institutions, and the inmates thereof, is another question of extreme social importance. It is because of my deep interest in modern social problems such as proper housing facilities for the wards of the State and for effective means of combating crime in general that I have considered so earnestly the whole question of temperance. It is bound up, of course, with crime, with insanity, and only too often, with poverty. It is increasingly apparent that intoxication has no place in this new mechanized civilization of ours! In our industry, in our recreation, on our highways, in our very sports, a drunken man is more than an objectionable companion; he is a peril to the rest of us.

The hand that controls the machinery of our factories, that holds the steering wheels of our automobiles, the brain that decides the course of our huge financial organizations, should alike be free from the effects of drugs or alcohol.

To those interested in social progress the question of temperance and the reduction of intoxication has always been a most serious and difficult problem. I believe that the solution which was attempted by the American people after the war, the solution by legislative and constitutional fiat, has been a complete and tragic failure. It has been a failure for two major reasons. In the first place, it has attempted to legislate into being a condition that cannot be attained by legislation but only by the slow and orderly process of education, and, second, because it has attempted to encroach upon fields which should belong exclusively to the respective States of the Union.

I need not point out to you the general encouragement to lawlessness and to a widespread disrespect of law itself which has resulted from this attempt.

I need not point out to you that it has been a prolific source of corruption, hypocrisy, crime, and disorder. The situation has become impossible and intolerable. I, for one, believe that it is time to retrace our steps, for we find that we have wandered far from the firm road toward eventual temperance into a hopeless morass of crime and law defiance.

We must start afresh. And the first step of that start should be as quickly as possible — the repeal of the Eighteenth Amendment.

It is becoming obvious that each sovereign State in the Union should be given the right to determine for itself whether alcoholic beverages should be made, manufactured, sold or transported within its borders.

Following the repeal of the Eighteenth Amendment, New York State must and will take such regulatory measures as will promote temperance definitely and effectively banish the saloon and recognize the principle of home rule in all localities.

I stand flatly upon my party's platform; and I assure you that all of the Democratic candidates are united in this position. There is no diversity or doubt among us. We stand together. We do not attempt, one of us, to appeal to one portion of the State's population, while another appeals to a different portion.

We believe that the people of this State as a whole are interested in temperance, that they want temperance by constitutional and orderly means. While we have the greatest respect for those in our State who still believe that temperance can be best served by the continuance of Federal constitutional and legislative enactment, we disagree with them as to method. We believe that the whole question should be left to the determination of the respective States themselves.

And so we regard this question as a part of that larger program of social reform and progress. We believe indeed that a solution of it will help solve the State's problem with respect to its institutions and with respect to the needs of its citizens. . . .

90 ⟨ Campaign Address (Excerpts), Syracuse, N. Y. October 22, 1930

(Cheap electricity in the home and on the farm.)

I want to talk to you tonight on a subject which I deem of paramount importance to the State, but on which the Republican Party this fall cannot point to its record with great pride. It has been a matter of controversy for many years in this State. It has been discussed at length in practically every gubernatorial election in the last ten years in this State. It has been referred to in this campaign as one of the dominant issues. Apparently, however, so far as possible, the strategy of the Republican campaign seems to be to talk as little as possible about the subject. I refer to the question of the development of the water power resources of the State by a public agency for the public benefit.

I am trying in this campaign to bring this subject as close to the homes of the voters as I can. I am trying to point out to our citizens how the development of electricity by the State will directly affect and benefit them in their daily lives.

While it is true that industry, and particularly manufacturers, have for years enjoyed the benefits and advantages of electricity, it is equally true that the average small consumer in his home is just beginning to realize how important it is for him to obtain not just electricity, but cheap electricity in his home. It was clearly brought out before the Commission on Revision of the Public Service Commission Law why the power companies were willing to sell cheap electricity to big industrial consumers. It was because a large manufacturing corporation could produce its own power very cheaply, and the utility companies were compelled to sell electricity at low rates in order to prevent these large corporations from setting up their own plants and producing their own electric power. In other words, the competitive principle protects the corporations against exorbitant rates, whereas the private home owner is compelled to buy from a monopoly because he could not under any circumstance produce his own electricity.

We all know that the great magic of electricity was originally used for lighting purposes only. It then spread to the factory for industrial uses. Now, however, the time has come when electricity should be carried right into our very homes so as to lighten the drudgery of housekeeping. You and I know that scores of electrically operated household appliances have been invented. Of course, the housewives of the State cannot enjoy these new inventions as long as the rates for current continue to run as high as they now do.

We can observe at close hand the benefits of cheap electricity in the home. Across the St. Lawrence River is the Province of Ontario, Canada. There electricity is developed from water power, by what is known as the Hydro-Electric Commission of Ontario, through a league of municipalities where service is rendered to each class of consumer on a strictly cost of service basis.

It has been estimated by experts that for an average family of four people occupying six rooms, and about 1,000 square feet of space, it would require about 285 kilowatt hours to run a completely electrified household. This means the use of electricity for light, cooking, refrigeration, ironing, toasting, vacuum cleaning, radio operation, washing machine, fans, waffle irons, chafing dish and other kitchen appliances. I need not dwell at length on the reduction in household labor which such electrical appliances could bring about. In Toronto and other large cities of Canada, it would surprise you to know that all of these appliances can be operated for as little as $3.40 per month. I mean that a woman could have all the benefits of these household labor-saving devices for a month, at the rate of $3.40.

I am sure that that is a sharp contrast to what you people in Syracuse, in New York, in any city, or in any country district, would pay for the same thing. As a matter of fact, you in Syracuse would pay almost three times as much; and, at that, you in Syracuse enjoy a rate which is at least cheaper than most other cities of the State. In New York City, for example, the housewife, for the same appliances, would pay almost six times as much per month, or $19.95. Down in Westchester, which pays almost the highest electricity rates of this State — Mt. Vernon or White Plains, for example — the rate would be almost eight times as much, or $25.63. Close by here, in Auburn, and in Rochester, the rate would be $13.40. In other words, whereas a woman in Ontario, Canada, in a city of the size of Syracuse can enjoy a completely electrified household for about $3.40 per month, here in Syracuse you could only get your lights, electric refrigeration and perhaps a toaster. The idea of cooking by electricity at the rates now prevailing in our State is out of the question, except for rich people.

In New York City an amount of $3.40 a month would perhaps buy electric lights and maybe an electric iron and a toaster. In New Rochelle, down in Westchester, you would be lucky to get your lights alone for this amount; and in Geneva, it would all be consumed in paying merely for electric lights.

Now of course there are several reasons why there should be such wide difference in rates between the cities in Ontario and the cities in New York State. A kilowatt of electricity is the same whether it is used in Canada or in New York. It takes the same number of kilowatts to cook a beef stew in Toronto as it does in Syracuse. There are several reasons why there should be the wide difference in cost for these kilowatt hours. Some of these reasons such as our failure in the past to regulate effectively the public utility companies of the State, and more particularly, the electric light and power companies, and the absence in this State of the effective threat of competition by municipalities, I shall discuss in later speeches during this campaign.

It is unquestionably true that the breakdown in regulation has done much to keep our electrical rates high and that we have been far behind other Governments in permitting our municipalities to go into the business of selling their citizens electricity whenever their citizens wish to do so, and whenever they find that they are being charged unreasonable and exorbitant rates by their local utility companies; but I wish to concentrate on what is by far the most important and fundamental reason. In Canada, this League of Municipalities develops electricity from their own water power. They develop it for the benefit of their own citizens. They sell it to their citizens at as near cost as possible. While, for decades, we have been permitting the millions of horsepower lying in the flow of the St. Lawrence River to go idly by on their way to the ocean, the Canadian municipalities have been taking advantage of their natural water power resources so as to convert them into cheap electricity.

Here in New York we have not been so wise. We have given franchises to private corporations to develop electricity from both water power and coal. After the electricity has been developed by these private corporations, they, of course, naturally want to sell it for as great a profit as they possibly can. They naturally are not interested in the consumer. They are interested only in their own profit. In Canada, electricity is more cheaply developed and is sold only with a view toward benefiting the consumer. In New York, we have electricity developed in a more expensive manner, and sold primarily with a view toward benefiting the private corporation. . . .

I had long given the subject much consideration and had come definitely to the conclusion that that policy had been uneconomic and unsound; but as I stood on the banks of the St.

Lawrence and Niagara Rivers and saw this rich possession which should rightfully belong to the people of our State, going into the power houses of private corporations, I formed a firm resolve that so long as I was Governor, and so long as it was at all possible for a State agency to develop these resources, no more would be given or leased to private corporations. . . .

When I first came to Albany we were no nearer a solution than ever before. The Republican leaders were still for private development. They had for years been engaged in an attempt to deceive the people of the State by such phrases as inalienable rights of the people in the fee of their water power resources. They used these high-sounding expressions and at the same time recommended that the development be by means of leases for long terms. . . .

In my speech of acceptance, as the Democratic candidate for Governor, I stated that the time had come for the definite establishment of the principle as a part of our fundamental law, that the physical possession and development of our State-owned water power sites shall not pass from the hands of the people of the State. In my very first annual message to the Legislature, I asked them to take up the question of the development of our water power resources so that the title and constant control of the power generated at the sources shall remain vested in the people and shall not be alienated by long-term leases. I asked the Republican leaders of the Legislature to introduce these bills themselves, so that it could be made a non-partisan measure. They refused to do it. I then asked the Democratic leaders to introduce it, and they not only introduced it, but made motions to discharge the Republican committees from consideration of the bills, so that each individual legislator might have an opportunity to express himself on the matter. The Republican leaders would not even permit the bills to get out of the committee and they were smothered. During the last days of the 1929 session, I again urged the Legislature to pass this legislation, and again they refused.

In the meantime, public opinion had become more and more

aroused. It was becoming more and more felt. Finally, the next year, 1930, after I had again requested the Legislature to take steps toward this development and when they could no longer withstand the force of public opinion, they introduced and passed a bill providing for a commission to be appointed by me to set up a plan whereby the water power resources of the State on the St. Lawrence River could be developed by a State agency for the benefit of the consumers themselves so as to provide the cheapest rates and best service for the people of the State.

That commission has been appointed by me and is now at work formulating a plan by which I hope the people will ultimately obtain the real advantages in cheap electricity which their natural resources contain. . . .

But still the surrender was only a half-hearted one. I was indeed surprised to read this in the 1930 platform of the Republican Party: "We promise a speedy solution of the problem of development of water power resources of the State which shall be based on sound and economic principles rather than on political expediency." Those words have a familiar air. I used to read words like those in the Republican platform which had definitely declared for the policy of private leases. Frankly, I do not like that language. I much prefer, and I am sure the voters of the State will much prefer, the language of the Democratic platform, which says on this subject, "Electric energy should be developed by the State from its water power resources in order to insure low-priced electricity." Now in this campaign, let us face the obvious facts. You and I know who the leaders of the Republican Party are. You and I know that these leaders or at least a great many of them are definitely and publicly aligned with the great electric utility companies of the State. They are officers and they are large stockholders in electric and power companies which, in combination, have almost a monopoly of electricity and power in this State. Do they want the State to develop this water power or would they like to have their own companies do it? Are they interested in providing cheap electricity for you or are they interested in providing large profit for themselves? You and I know that these leaders of the

Republican Party, so closely tied up with the great electric utility companies of the State, are the ones who dictate to the Party, not only their policies, but also, in many cases, their candidates.

You must remember that when this commission which I appointed brings in its report, the work is only half done. I know that that commission will do its full duty. I, myself, personally, went up to the St. Lawrence River with them and personally inspected the sites on which we all hope the State will soon erect its huge power structures.

But when that work is done by the commission, before anything further can be done, the Legislature of the State of New York and the Governor must approve. I cannot believe and I am sure that the voters of the State will not believe that a Republican Legislature and a Republican Governor will look so kindly upon this plan of public development against which they have for so many years and through so many administrations fought and protested. I cannot believe, especially in view of the language of the Republican platform this year, that they will not do all in their power to hamper and prevent and delay any form of public development for the benefit of the people.

It would be only common sense on the part of the people to entrust the development of that plan and the carrying out of those policies to the party which, for so many years, has struggled and fought for its initiation. You can, each one of you, do your share on election day toward the realization of that theory of development which has so long actuated and formed intelligent public opinion in the State.

Some Republican statesmen and party leaders are still renewing the old objection that this plan is putting the State into business. Nothing could be further from the truth. . . .

Once the power is developed, and is ready for sale, then the State is in a position to dictate the price at which it can be delivered to the ultimate consumer. We have no desire to infringe upon the legitimate reasonable profits of any investor in public utility stocks. He is entitled to a fair return on his investment.

That is the whole story, and let us once and for all stop talking about whether the State should be put into business or not.

The important duty of every citizen of the State — lawyers, business men, the press, the agricultural interests, and the average "man in the street" — is from now on to work whole-heartedly for the carrying out of the proposed policy and the plan which, I am confident, will result therefrom. I am confident that the great majority of citizens of the State want to see something done and believe that we must work out a State agency method of development of our great natural electrical resources in such a way that the control of these resources will never pass from the actual possession of the State itself.

91 ⦅ Campaign Address (Excerpts), Albany, N. Y. October 24, 1930

(Regulation of utilities.)

.   .   .   .   .

THERE is another great social reform which the present Democratic Administration in Albany is attempting to accomplish, and which is now in the midst of the same hindering and hamstringing on the part of the Republican legislative leaders. I refer to the proper regulation of public utility companies. These companies, as you know, furnish us electric light, gas light, transportation and telephone service. Their activities must, therefore, necessarily be bound up with the intimate lives of every one of us, the home lives of our families.

Every time we push an electric button which turns on our electric light, every time we lift up the telephone receiver, every time we get on the street car, every time we light our gas stove to boil some water or cook a meal, we are dealing with a public utility company.

Far back in 1907 during the Governorship of Charles E. Hughes, it became apparent that some form of protection must be given to the people who use these various services. This protection was deemed to be necessary in order to protect us from exorbitant rates and to compel the companies to give us decent service, and it was directly in line with principle dating back hundreds of years, that Government has the right and the duty to supervise and regulate these public utility services.

Since that time, however, two important things have been happening which have forcibly brought to the public mind the necessity of reform. The first is that in recent years the Public Service Commission itself has not been performing its original role of a militant protector of public rights. It is contenting itself with acting merely as an occasional judge between the utility companies on the one side and the consumer on the other.

That is not the role that I want to see it fill. It should rather be an ever-watchful protector against exorbitant rates and improper service. It should, more than that, ever be on the lookout so that it, itself, can initiate proceedings to reduce rates if they are too high, or to compel fair service. The reason for this gradual letting down in the functions of the Public Service Commission has been that the Legislature, instead of allowing the Public Service Commission to function as a commission of five men, had so written the law that it was completely under the dominance of whoever happened to be chairman of the commission.

Under the leadership of that chairman, the legitimate functions of the Public Service Commission were completely obscured. It was not until the chairman offered me his resignation because of his inability and unwillingness to go along with my ideas of proper public utility regulation that I was able to obtain for the leadership of that commission a man who, by training and instinct, was sympathetic with the proper functioning of this regulatory body.

You all recall the famous New York Telephone case of last winter. You all recall how after ten years of battle in the courts, and after taking 63,000 pages of testimony, and after examining 4,300 exhibits, the Telephone Company was given permission by the Federal Courts to raise its rates in New York City. You all recall that immediately upon learning of this, I suggested that the Public Service Commission take immediate steps to protect the people's interest in the matter of telephone rates.

You all recall that the chairman of the Public Service Commission at that time resented what he termed my interference in the judicial processes of the Public Service Commission, but still I sent the letter, and still I insisted that the Public Service Commission go through with it.

Shortly thereafter this chairman resigned and I appointed the present chairman, Mr. Maltbie. Already, in the few months since his appointment, there has been an enormous improvement in the activity of the Public Service Commission. Complaints are being immediately investigated and proceedings are being vigorously followed up looking toward cheaper rates for all kinds of public utility services.

Take two practical examples under Chairman Maltbie's leadership: the rates asked by the Telephone Company were drastically reduced this spring, and only yesterday a further reduction was ordered by the Public Service Commission in the long-distance telephone rates.

More and more people of the State are receiving the proper kind of attention from the Public Service Commission. I know that under the present leadership the commission will measure up aggressively to the standards originally expected of it.

But there is a deeper reason for the breakdown in this regulation of public utilities. Ever since the Public Service Commissions were initiated in this State and in other States, there has grown up a body of court-made law. This is not statute law, mind you, which is passed by any Legislature, but law built up by court decisions in the rate cases. The most important of these decisions are centered around the question of value.

This matter is, of course, an extremely technical and complicated one. For that reason I suggested very soon after my arrival at Albany that the Legislature appoint a non-partisan commission to investigate the whole subject, and to revise the Public Service Commission Law so that legislation could be enacted to prevent this court-made law from continuing to force upon our people exorbitant rates for their daily needs. I had hoped that the Legislature would authorize the appointment of a really non-partisan commission, consisting of a small group of experts to work the thing out along scientific and technical lines. That was too much to expect. The Legislature refused. Instead, it followed its usual policy by creating a commission of nine men, of whom they were to appoint six, and I was to name three. Of course, the result was there were six good Republican legislators, and three appointees by me, a Democrat, a Republican and an Independent.

There was the difference in the point of view. The Republican Legislature put on six Republican politicians who knew as much about utilities as my granddaughter does. My point of view was a little different. I declined to take the political faith of my appointees into consideration at all. What I sought and what I got was three experts in public utility and social service problems.

Now this commission brought in a report, a very interesting report, and one which will form the basis for legislation for many years to come, not only in this State, but in other States as well. The report was divided into two parts. One was a majority report signed by the six Republican leaders of the Legislature, and the other was the minority report signed by my three appointees. I need hardly point out that the counsel to the commission was a very good Republican in good Republican standing.

The report of the minority of the Commission, my appointees, went to the very root and essence of the problem. They pointed out that the source of all the difficulty of rate-fixing was this question of value, and they proceeded to point out the remedies to meet the situation.

The Republican, or majority report, while admitting that the basis of the trouble was this question of valuation, was afraid to go to the real root of the difficulty in order to meet the question. Instead, they recommended some very nice innocuous measures, which would have permitted the utility companies, if they wanted to, to submit themselves to various valuation proceedings in order to fix their value. Mind you, they did not say that the utility companies would have to do it, but that they could do it, if they wanted to, for a period of ten years. The minority proposal, however, said that the public utilities of the State would have to submit themselves to a complete revaluation of their property so as to fix the value and that from then on, their values would have to depend upon the real investment by the utility company and not upon any subsequent fictitious value.

It is needless to say that the legislation proposed by the minority received scant attention from the Republican majority, and no consideration at all. Instead, the Republican Party introduced a series of bills carrying out the Republican report. Most of these bills were unimportant and really merited very little attention. I signed them, pointing out that while they did no good, they did no harm.

When it came to the real questions, however, which went to the meat of the matter, the bills passed by the Republican leaders were nothing more than a joke. When they were first introduced, as weak and as ineffective as they were, they immediately aroused the opposition of all the utility companies. They came flocking to Albany. Legislative representatives of gas companies, electric companies, and the telephone companies began swarming through the corridors of the capitol, and into the committee rooms of the Legislature. This would never do. These vast utility combinations, which for years had furnished the sinews of Republican political campaigns in the form of campaign contributions, were going to be subjected to a little regulation, even though it would be absolutely ineffective adequately to protect the rights of the people.

Public hearing after public hearing was held, and I am sure that there were many private hearings held about which the public heard nothing. Pretty soon, amendments began to be introduced, and more amendments and more amendments, and before you knew it, these bills had been so amended that the introducer of two of them refused to vote for them himself on the ground that they had been so often amended that he did not recognize his own bills.

It is an open secret, for example, that the valuation bill and the so-called contract bill had struck a snag in the Senate so severe that although they had been amended and amended to meet the wishes of the utility companies, they still were not going to pass because one utility company in the Western part of the State was opposed to them, and every member of the Assembly from that county had been told to vote against them. It became a source of considerable amusement that Senator Knight, the czar of the Senate, who had backed these bills, could not even get them passed. He could not muster the necessary votes in the Senate and he absolutely refused to let the Senate adjourn unless it would do something about them.

Finally, on the last day, the bills were further emasculated and amended so as to meet the wishes of this utility company, and were rushed through the Legislature in typewritten form so that not one of the Republicans in the Senate who voted for them, except Senator Knight himself, knew what was in the bills. These two bills were passed, not with any intention of their becoming law, because the leaders knew that I could not and would not sign them.

These bills were not passed on any recommendation either from the majority or minority members of the commission. They did nothing to meet the problem. They were absolutely meaningless. They tended to perpetuate a system of regulation which did not regulate; and they were nothing more or less than a cheap and inexcusable fraud on the public.

I do not feel discouraged at the failure of the last Legislature to adopt these measures of regulation. . . .

Of course, your cooperation and assistance are needed. They are needed not only next year; they are needed now. You and I know that the election of a Republican Governor and a Republican Legislature means the end of efforts at regulation of public utilities. We know who the leaders of the Republican Party are. We know their attitude on the public utility question. We know how little they will be interested in fair rates for the consumer, and how much they will be interested in large profits for their utility companies. The Republican campaigners so far have said very little indeed about regulation of utilities. They have tried to keep it in the background as far as possible, but I have an everlasting confidence in the ultimate force of public opinion. I have everlasting confidence that the people of the State can and will see to it that their rights are ultimately protected, and that this great social question of utility regulation will ultimately be solved in the interest of the people themselves.

92 (Campaign Address (Excerpts), New York City. November 1, 1930

(National Republican interference in State campaign — Corruption in New York City.)

For two weeks as candidate for reelection to the Governorship of New York, I have discussed fully, without hate or passion, but with truth and frankness, the issues, the many great issues of this State campaign.

I have told the voters throughout the State the history of the Government of the State during these past two years, a history of which all voters, regardless of party, have a right to be proud.

Further, I have set forth fully the needs of the State for the two years to come, the proposals of my associates and myself for the continuation of orderly and progressive government based on honesty, on efficient administration, on humanity and on law.

Our campaign, as the people of this State know, has not been founded on falsification of the record, and it has not been founded on slander or on promises which cannot be fulfilled.

It has, on the other hand, been based on issues which affect the daily lives of the individual men, women and children in every home of the State, on issues where the State Government comes into direct contact with their work and their play, with their living conditions, with their health and their happiness.

As opposed to this, there stands out a definite and undeniable fact which as the campaign has gone on is being realized more and more by every voter in the State. That fact is that the candidates of the Republican Party have refused to discuss these issues. They have maintained a complete silence on all those many questions which affect all of the people of this State. They have failed even to set forth a constructive program of any kind for the governing of the State during the next two years.

Their campaign, on the other hand, has been based, first, last and all the time, on a falsification of the record and on attacks instigated not by any desire for good government or for progressive legislation or administration, but solely on ambition for office.

To those who believe that candidates should frankly discuss real issues and honestly reveal their views on the fundamental questions of the day, this action of the Republicans has been the most discouraging that we have ever known.

But there was a reason for this so far as Republican leadership was concerned. Before this campaign started, obviously it was necessary for the Republican leaders to find an issue on which to conduct it. Unquestionably they examined carefully the whole range of public subjects to find such an issue.

First, there was water power — the insistent and overwhelming demand that the State should develop the St. Lawrence for the benefit of the consumers at the lowest possible cost. But that was an impossible issue for the Republicans, because year after year they had consistently stood for the virtual gift of this water power to private corporate interests well known to be in close association with the Republican leadership itself.

Then there was labor legislation. They could not use that because year after year they had blocked or weakened every important measure for the protection of the working people of the State, and further because organized labor itself had declared in no uncertain terms in favor of the reelection of the Democratic candidates.

Then there was the necessity for new prisons and new prison

433

methods. They could not use that because the record of the Republican Legislature for fifty years past — a record of neglect and indifference toward prison reform — would make that issue impossible.

Then there was Prohibition. They could not use that because they themselves were split wide apart in the very leadership of their party on that question.

Then there was social welfare. They could not use that for the very obvious reason that it was the Democratic Party and its leaders who for a generation past had initiated every great social reform in this State from workmen's compensation and the forty-eight-hour law down to old-age pensions and the building up of the new parole system, and the securing of new buildings and equipment for the unfortunate wards of the State.

Then there were farm relief and rural tax relief. They could not touch those because all of the great measures for the relief of the agricultural communities, which have become law during these past two years, were first initiated and first pushed by the Governor of the State himself.

Then there were the economic conditions under which the people of the State now find themselves. They could not touch that because that came too close home to the Federal Administration in Washington.

Then there were the parks and parkways — that great program initiated by Governor Smith covering the State like a network. They could not touch that because they had blocked this program on every possible occasion, and furthermore because they remembered that their own leaders on Long Island sought to keep the hundreds of thousands of men, women and children in this city from enjoying the great gifts which nature had bestowed on the shores of Long Island.

There were other issues. But when the Republican leaders examined them and realized their record on those issues they knew that their only hope was to distract the attention of the people of this State from these real issues.

They, therefore, decided to adopt, and have steadfastly adhered to a policy of misrepresenting and distorting a local situation in the City of New York and from the start of the campaign they have refused absolutely to talk about any of the State issues whatsoever. And pursuing misrepresentation, without any sense of justice or propriety, the Republican leaders have made every effort to convince the people of this State and the people of this country that our judiciary is corrupt and judges are unworthy to hold their high offices. No more reprehensible or cowardly act has ever been perpetrated in a campaign in this country than this deliberate attempt to bring dishonor on all — every one — of the members of our judiciary and their families and to break down the confidence of the public in this bulwark of our civilization. I say each and every member of the judiciary from the highest court to the lowest, because the Republican campaign without question has been aimed at making unthinking people believe that all judges should be brought publicly and with a blare of trumpets before a grand jury and subjected to the public task of proving they are honest. The history of the judiciary in this State needs no defense. Men of unquestioned standing, integrity and ability, many of them at a personal financial sacrifice to themselves and their families, have devoted and are devoting their lives to the great cause of justice. I refuse to believe, and further than that I deny, that our judiciary under the leadership and guidance of such men as Chief Judge Cardozo and Presiding Judges Dowling and Lazansky is saturated with corruption.

But, after continuing this campaign of calumny against the judiciary, coupled with utter silence on actual State issues for two whole weeks, the Republican leaders began to realize that the people of the City and the State were beginning to resent this hypocrisy as an insult to their intelligence, and that unless volume and tone could be added to their position they were utterly and hopelessly lost. The whole structure built on a false foundation was bound to crumble unless artificial support for it could be found. So the Republican leaders in their desperation turned to Washington.

What happened? The people of this State have been witnessing a spectacle so novel that its significance has not yet been fully grasped. The Republican national Administration at Washington, suddenly solicitous for our welfare, presumed to send into this State campaign officers of the Cabinet itself to instruct us how to manage our State affairs. These gentlemen have been here and they have instructed us and lectured us on how we should handle our local affairs in this great State.

Who are they? First of all came the Secretary of War himself; then came the Secretary of State, the chief of the President's Cabinet, and tonight you are receiving further instruction from the Treasury Department in the person of its Under Secretary.

I make no personal attack on these three eminent gentlemen. I know them well. They are men of the finest character and I do not dispute their personal fitness to hold the great offices they do, but I do say that they have been misled. I do say that they have shocked the conscience of the fair-minded and thoughtful people of this State by lending the prestige of their great national offices to such a campaign as this and they have even been cajoled into making a personal attack on me.

These same gentlemen and the Republican Administration in Washington sponsoring it and the Republican National Committee financing it, and the New York State leaders and candidates themselves, have persistently cried from the housetops that national issues have no place in this campaign. This is an amazing assertion in view of the fact that for at least the last five State campaigns the Republican candidates for Governor have consistently talked about nothing else but national issues, chiefly the then so-called national prosperity. We in this State in every city and on every farm know the high impropriety of interference by the Federal Government in the purely local affairs of any State and we are fully conscious of the effective manner in which the people of this great State will at the polls show their resentment against such conduct.

Before we look into the soundness of the instructions given to the people of this State by these representatives at Washington we have a right to demand that they show their credentials. Of these

436

three estimable gentlemen, one comes from that great State of Oklahoma which we all respect. He has never lived in New York State; he knows nothing of the problems of New York State; he knows nothing of the situation in New York City; he knows nothing of the requirements and necessities of the twelve million people of this State. Whatever information he has, has been given to him obviously by the members of his own party. It can hardly be said that he has been impartially informed on our affairs. And yet he comes to us presumably only by virtue of his great office. Well may the people of New York State resent this, as would the people of Oklahoma if the tables were turned.

The other two gentlemen of this triumvirate, the Secretary of State and the Under Secretary of the Treasury, are both citizens of this State. The credentials that they present to the people of the State as authorizing them to give instructions are the same in both cases. Both of them have run for Governor in campaigns based largely upon the same kind of tactics as are being employed in this campaign. Both of them were defeated at the polls by the people of this State. The people did not believe in them or in their issues then, and they will not believe in them or in their issues now.

The people of this State who repudiated them are the best judges of whether or not any man is fit to be Governor.

And now having examined the credentials of these gentlemen from Washington who have been telling us how to run our affairs of State, let us examine into the soundness of the instructions which they have given us. The substance of their instructions to us is this: That the only issue in this campaign is judges in New York City, and nothing else counts.

They tell the 12,000,000 people in this State, whether they are so-called "wets" or "drys," who are sincerely interested in the important question of prohibition, and who are seeking a sound solution of the tremendous problem raised by it and who are endeavoring to rid themselves of the crime, violence and corruption bred by it, that that does not count. But I specifically call the attention of the people to the all-important fact that these instructors woefully failed to tell the people of this State where they themselves stand on the prohibition issue. Do they believe in Mr. Hoover's position, or do they stand upon the straddle of the Republican Party in this State? Why is it that they do not dare answer?

They tell the 12,000,000 people of this State interested in the speedy and proper development of its great water power resources to provide cheap electricity for the homes of the State and in keeping them from the hands of private corporations, that that does not count.

They tell the 12,000,000 people of this State who are anxious to protect its aged dependent citizens against the wants and miseries of old age, so that the State may help them to spend their last years in comfort, that that does not count.

They tell the 12,000,000 people of this State interested in its problems of taxation, and desiring that its entire system be revised in order more equitably to distribute its burdens, that that does not count.

They tell the 12,000,000 people of this State who look forward to a scientific study of the prisons of this State to provide a comprehensive plan and policy for prison construction as well as for the proper treatment, punishment, reformation, segregation and labor of prisoners, that that does not count.

They tell the 12,000,000 people of this State who have seen a complete revision of our parole system and the establishment of a modern enlightened system of parole to take care of the 92 percent of the prisoners of our State who return to private life that that does not count.

They tell the 12,000,000 people of this State who are anxious to enlarge and modernize our State hospitals and secure new buildings and equipment for the unfortunate wards of the State that that does not count.

They tell the 12,000,000 people of this State who are anxious to protect its milk and cream supply and to prevent the importation of impure milk and cream from without the State, that that does not count.

They tell the millions of men, women and children of this State who labor for their daily bread that all of the important problems of adequate labor and social legislation, such as the abolition of *ex parte* injunctions in strikes, preference on employment in State and local public works for New York citizens, an eight-hour day and prevailing rate of wage on grade-crossing eliminations, advisory minimum wage boards, elimination of unhealthy living conditions in congested areas, the establishment of the principle that the labor of a human being is not a commodity, adequate appropriations to enforce the labor law and the workmen's compensation law, the increasing of compensation to victims of industrial accidents and their dependents, dispatch in the disposal and payment of compensation claims, the extension of workmen's compensation to include occupational diseases, the adequate regulation by the State of fee-charging employment agencies, the prevention of importation of prison-made goods from other States, that all of these matters affecting the daily lives of every laboring man, woman and child in this State do not count.

They tell the 12,000,000 people of this State who have enjoyed the vast system of parks and parkways inaugurated by Governor Smith and pushed and forwarded in every way by me, who look forward to the completion of the program so that still greater areas through the State from Montauk Point to Niagara may be made available for their health, recreation and enjoyment, that this does not count.

They tell the millions of farmers and other residents of rural communities in this State who are beginning to reap the benefits of that vast program initiated by me of constructive farm and rural tax relief, resulting in better roads, better schools and lower taxes for the rural population of the State and more adequate funds for agricultural surveys and experiment — that those things do not count. And on this question at least, everyone who knows of the complete failure of the Republican Administration in Washington to carry out any form of adequate farm relief, admits they certainly speak with authority.

Having examined the credentials of these Cabinet officers and

439

the nature of their instructions to us, let us see whether they are qualified by success in Washington to instruct the voters in New York. They and their party, this present national Administration; came before this State two years ago soliciting the votes of its people on representations, promises and prophesies. They represented themselves as the creators of the prosperity of the country. They were the originators of sound business; they were its protectors. Under them prosperity had always prevailed and only under them could prosperity continue. Poverty was on its way to be abolished. There is no need for me to demonstrate to you how false were those representations, those promises and those prophecies. There is no need for me to point out to you what has been unfortunately experienced by almost every man, woman and child in the Nation.

I say to these gentlemen: We shall be grateful if you will return to your posts in Washington, and bend your efforts and spend your time solving the problems which the whole Nation is bearing under your Administration. Rest assured that we of the Empire State can and will take care of ourselves and our problems.

And so, with whatever comfort they can find in this Federal support, and persisting in their original intention, the Republican leaders have to this very last day of the campaign refused to talk about the real issues. Instead they have talked only of judges in New York City.

Tonight, therefore, I shall depart from discussing those real issues of the campaign, in order again to repeat to the people of the State my record in this local situation and make that record and my policy clear.

During the last session of the Legislature, Republican leaders having in mind the coming campaign, and realizing that they would have no issue in it, considered the proposition of trying to manufacture publicity by an investigation of New York City. They looked it over and it did not seem to be a very happy thought, so they fell back on one of their most ancient practices of "passing the buck" to the Governor, and trying to put the Governor "in a hole." They went so far as to pass a bill directing me to institute an investigation in New York City; and although I asked them, they refused or were unable to give me any grounds or reasons for such an investigation. I sent the bill right back to them and told them that if they wanted such an investigation in New York City, they were free to go ahead and make one without even submitting the question to me. I pointed out to them that the Legislature not only had full power but was the only one charged with the duty of making any such investigation. They refused to do it. They did not have the courage to do it.

Some months later, my attention was called to evidence which had been presented to a Grand Jury of the County of New York, alleging that a magistrate in the City of New York, had paid a district leader for his appointment. The Grand Jury had failed to indict those who were said to be implicated. Immediately within twenty-four hours I demanded a copy of the minutes. I read them. I deemed that it was appropriate that there should be further investigation. I could have suggested or directed the submission of the matter to another Grand Jury by the District Attorney. I elected, however, for the purpose of removing the matter from all possible criticism, to supersede the District Attorney and place it in the hands of the Republican Attorney General with a Republican judge. I did this within twenty-four hours of receiving the minutes. I foresaw the possibility that in a gubernatorial campaign which was soon to start, a Republican Attorney General who was indeed himself a leading candidate, might use this instrumentality in order to mislead the public. I foresaw that possibility but I did not hesitate to discharge my duty. I never have and I never will, so long as there is any duty to perform. The power of that Grand Jury which I called, is absolutely unlimited to investigate any crime in the County of New York. The Court of Appeals has said so, and these gentlemen from Washington know so. Regardless of all misrepresentations to the contrary, I have never refused to enlarge the powers of the Grand Jury because the Governor of the State has no power either to enlarge those powers or curtail them. But I wish again to point out what Republican candidates and Republican campaign orators and a small portion of the New York press have sought to obscure, that I, a Democratic Governor on the eve of a campaign for reelection, sent into a Democratic county, a Republican Attorney General and a Republican judge with an extraordinary Grand Jury. That investigation was ordered and directed by me.

The next step related to specific abuses in the magistrates courts and in their procedure. I immediately called upon the Appellate Division of the Supreme Court to make a searching investigation of them all. The Appellate Division is the body charged by law with that duty and in accordance with that law I called upon it to perform it. That investigation has been put in the hands of Judge Seabury, a former Judge of the Court of Appeals. I defy anyone even to intimate that that investigation will not be honest, thorough and searching; and I challenge the untruthful assertion made by these gentlemen from Washington that such an investigation is futile. Let them have no doubt that if the Appellate Division discovers corruption in the magistrates courts the Appellate Division will have it punished, no matter where they find it.

Later on, I learned that a Judge had refused to waive immunity before the Ward Grand Jury. In order that I might perform my duty properly I immediately requested that the evidence in this case be sent to me so that the matter could be presented to the Senate of this State if the situation warranted action. Only the Senate of the State could act. I cannot remove a judge or compel him to resign, and the Republican leaders despite their hypocrisy know it. The public knows that the Attorney General advised against my receiving that evidence, and I was denied access to it. Without such evidence I can go no further. Whenever I was in a position to exercise my powers as Governor of this State properly and whenever I believed that those powers should be exercised, I had no hesitation in performing the duties of my office. If there exists evidence before the Ward Grand Jury to warrant my exercising any of the powers of my office, I hear about it only through the newspapers. It has never been presented to me. It may be that there exists such evidence as the special Attorney General informed the press a few days ago, but if it does exist I have no knowledge of it. No word has come to the Governor about it. That latest statement from the Republican Attorney General is only further proof of what the people of this State have long suspected but now know — that the Attorney General is using his office in every way possible in attempting to pervert the function of the Grand Jury itself, solely for the political benefit of Republican candidates.

The Republican candidates and a small section of the local press have sought a definite political object — to make the people of this city believe: (1) That the greater part of the 220 judges in this city are corrupt; (2) that as a result the judiciary as a whole is no longer worthy of the confidence of the people; (3) that neither I nor the Democratic Party in city or State would lift a finger to restore confidence in the courts and punish the guilty.

I, as a citizen of the State and as Governor, resent this campaign, as every person in this State who knows me, and who believes in honest and decent government, resents it.

I, and the members of my Administration, do not yield place to any Republican candidate or editor in abhorrence of a corrupt judiciary. We do not yield place to anyone in indignation against any holder of public office who is recreant to his trust. We do not yield place to anyone in the sincere and honest desire to punish those judges who have or who may prostitute their positions.

If there are corrupt judges still sitting in our courts they shall be removed. They shall be removed by constitutional means, not by inquisition; not by trial in the press, but by trial as provided by law.

If there is corruption in our courts I will use every rightful power of the office of Governor to drive it out, and I will do this regardless of whether it affects or may affect any Democratic or any Republican organization in any one of the five counties of New York City, or in any one of the fifty-seven other counties of the State. That is clear. That is unequivocal. That is simple honesty. That is justice. That is American. That is right.

Now we have come to the close of the campaign. I ask the electorate of the State of New York for their support. I ask this as a rebuke to those Republican national and State leaders who, substituting false charges and deliberate misrepresentation, have had the cowardice to ignore the great problems and issues before the whole State.

I ask this as an expression of confidence in my Administration, as an expression of confidence in the record of these past two years, and of the need, during the next two years, for a continuance of forward-looking, human and honest administration of the affairs of our State.

I ask this of the dwellers in this great metropolis, of the people of the other great cities, of the men and women in the villages and on the farms.

I ask this of the voters of all parties. I ask it in the name of good government.

Cheerfully and confidently I abide the result.

XVII

Unemployment, Unemployment Relief, and Unemployment Insurance

INTRODUCTORY NOTE: AFTER THE crash of 1929, and indeed for some time before that, the State of New York in common with the other States faced the problem of a growing number of unemployed. The Federal Government had adopted the policy of doing very little for the relief of distress among the unemployed either by providing food and shelter, or by furnishing work.

Accordingly, the State was compelled to attempt to do the task with such assistance as it could obtain from local government which was already overburdened by taxes and by debt.

The documents included in this chapter show in detail what was done by the State of New York during my Administration to meet the problem. As early as May, 1930, we began to formulate plans for local relief of distress (*Public Papers,* 1930, page 537) and in November, 1930, we took steps to institute and stimulate public works with a view toward providing employment during the winter of 1930 (*Public Papers,* 1930, page 672).

See also Items 70, 88, 17 on page 103, 18 on page 115.

In 1931 and again in 1932 I recommended to the Legislature that steps be taken to institute a system of unemployment insurance (see Items 96 and 99 of this volume).

As the distress among the unemployed increased, and as the burden on local charity and local government became greater than they could carry, and as the Federal Government continued to refuse to assume any responsibility at all for any relief program, I determined to take the "bull by the horns" and embark

445

upon a State program of relief. I decided to do all I could to carry out what I conceived to be the responsibility of Government: that no one within its jurisdiction, willing but unable to find work, should go without the necessities of life.

Accordingly, during an extraordinary session of the State Legislature, on August 28, 1931 (see Item 97 of this volume), I recommended the creation of a Temporary Emergency Relief Administration and a system of State-financed unemployment relief. The sum of $20,000,000 was appropriated for this purpose. This was the first practical recognition by any State in the United States of a definite responsibility toward the relief of unemployment distress.

The other efforts of my Administration to meet the problem are set forth in the papers in this chapter.

In addition, reference is made to the following, not included for lack of space: Address before welfare workers, October 29, 1931. *Public Papers,* 1931, page 776; Statement on relief, January 1, 1932; Statement on report of Interstate Commission on Unemployment, February 15, 1932 (see Item 99, this volume); Message to Legislature re relief, March 1, 1932; Radio Address, Albany, New York. March 16, 1932; Address, Catholic Charities Luncheon, New York City, April 9, 1932.

During the 1932 campaign for the Presidency, the question was discussed by me in my speeches printed as Items 131, on page 653, 143, and 148 of this volume.

93 ❲ A Statement on Unemployment, and the Appointment of a Committee to Suggest a Plan for Stabilization of Industry. March 29, 1930

I RECENTLY addressed a communication to Chambers of Commerce and labor leaders all over the State with reference to unemployment conditions. Responses have been received from over 200 Chambers of Commerce and over 50 labor bodies. . . . In general the greatest source of hope for the future is reported to be that some kind of public works is either about to be undertaken or now under way. Roads, highways, water works, grade crossing eliminations, school buildings, post office buildings, city buildings, prison and jail buildings, park developments are all mentioned as affording relief from local situations which would otherwise be even more difficult. Many letters urge a larger and speedier program of public works, both local and State. . . .

There is, of course, likely to be some easing of the unemployment situation with the coming of spring — the opening of more public works, the development of agriculture, etc. This will not be sufficient to restore the normal employment so necessary for stable business. Moreover, if we do not make plans now the slump of the autumn and winter of 1930-31 will be more distressing than ever, coming after this year's crisis with its call on savings, reserves, etc. I am convinced that concerted action of all elements in the community can do much to remedy existing unemployment and prevent further depression. Action must be taken with full knowledge of the actual facts, but without hysteria or exaggeration. Political stress must play no part in a program which to be sound must be both scientific and dispassionate.

We appear to have an accumulation of unemployment due to three contributing factors: (1) seasonal fluctuations which have become chronic in some industries; (2) technological unemployment or the displacement of men by labor-saving machinery and methods; this has been greatly accelerated in recent years in New York State and since it is indirectly correlated with cheap mass

447

production we must expect its continuance; (3) the depression due to the business cycle which is an economic phenomenon recurring with some regularity throughout the Nation as well as in this State. . . .

The situation is serious and the time has come for us to face this unpleasant fact as dispassionately and constructively as a scientist faces a test tube of deadly germs, intending first to understand the nature, the cause and the effect, and finally the method of overcoming and the technique of preventing its ravages.

Although serious, local unemployment conditions are spotty, some cities are almost normal, others very bad, still others merely dull.

Unemployment is a problem for the entire community. It is a major social tragedy for the individual who is denied the opportunity to work and earn, but it does not stop there, and if not soon corrected will have a long-time depressive effect on business and trade in the State.

The prosperity of New York State depends upon the prosperity and the spending ability of its own and the Nation's wage earners. As the leading industrial State, it is of first importance to maintain and develop the wage-earner market. A few years ago this would have seemed a wholly impossible task. Today, experiments by industrialists and analysis by economists have established a number of successful methods. Some of these methods are in practice today in industries in New York State, and some are followed in cities as a result of planning by Chambers of Commerce and leading citizens. All of these offer suggestions which can well be studied by others.

Two classes of action are indicated: first, for the relief of the emergency locally; second, for the prevention of future crises.

With respect to the present emergency I strongly urge upon mayors, boards of supervisors and public officials in every community in this State the immediate adoption of the following program:

1. The collection locally by responsible agents of complete

local figures on the number of unemployed in each city and town; the Department of Labor is prepared to suggest forms and methods for such enumeration.

2. The cooperative organization and supervision of public and private philanthropic activities for the giving of such unemployment relief as is locally needed under joint control.

3. The active stimulation of small-job campaigns in every city and town in the State of New York, so that the modicum of unemployment relief can be furnished locally.

4. The establishment of local free employment clearing houses under public auspices in every city and town linked up with the State public employment service, where possible.

5. The starting up of local public works immediately. Road building, sanitation systems, water works, building and building repair are many instances in the control of local officials, and the boards of supervisors should make every effort to begin work on these items promptly.

In addition, the local Chambers of Commerce should appoint committees and plan concretely local means for stimulating trade and industry, at the same time discussing ways and means for the future stabilization of industry in the local communities. Chambers of Commerce must recognize that the prosperity of each town in this State is dependent upon having all of the people in the town at work steadily and thus able with their purchases to keep trade alive.

With regard to efforts to prevent or at least to minimize future unemployment crises, much of the planning must necessarily be done by the industrialists of the State. . . .

I count on the industrialists of this State to strive to overcome recurring unemployment in their industries with the same good will as they have overcome so many other adverse conditions, such as industrial accidents, industrial diseases, child labor, long hours, etc. Effort against unemployment made in the same educational and helpful terms as the campaign against industrial accidents cannot help producing results. In order that such efforts may

449

be organized and sustained until results are produced, I am appointing a special committee of business men and labor representatives, and asking this committee to lay before the employers and the workers of this State every worth-while and significant practice for the stabilization of employment which has come within their range of knowledge and to work out with the business men of the State such practical methods as can be devised for the future control of unemployment.

I wish to stress the fact that in appointing this Committee I am looking forward to a long-time program for industrial stabilization and prevention of unemployment. We do not expect miracles. We do expect to assist the employers of this State in a gradual progress toward stabilization based on authentic American business experience and arising out of and adapted to their own local industrial problem, and on such methods as their good-will and sound business judgment may develop. Surely, both for humanitarian and business reasons, their effort, difficult but urgently necessary, is one in which the Governor of the State may confidently expect the whole-hearted cooperation of the business community.

94 ❪ The Governor Commends the Report of the Committee on Stabilization of Industry.

November 15, 1930

ON THURSDAY evening I received a very important report on the possibilities of stabilizing industry for the purpose of prevention of unemployment. This was made by the committee which I appointed in March of this year. This report is very significant and represents an extremely fine piece of work by an efficient body working under considerable pressure in order to make practical suggestions available to the industrialists of this State at a time when the need for an industrial stabilization program is so pressing.

I am much gratified that this committee, which has worked

hard and earnestly and has carried its own expenses, should have been able to produce something so useful. Its recommendations in this report are definitely those looking toward the long pull for the prevention of future unemployment crises. It was our hope when this committee was appointed that the depression would be short-lived and that we should be spared the emergency of this present winter. Therefore, it was asked to concentrate on the study of preventive measures.

Fortunately, the State of New York is much better organized to meet the emergency situation due to the fact that we began a year ago to stimulate organization and public responsibility to meet the situation. In the course of its conferences with different communities and different industries throughout the State it has acquired a very real knowledge of the unemployment situation in different parts of the State. Among its activities has been the successful promotion of local committees in various communities formed for the purpose of dealing with the problems of relief, emergency employment, and stabilization in those communities.

The Department of Labor has also been definitely promoting such a program for over a year and as a result there is in every large industrial city in the State, with the exception of one, a local emergency committee. In a number of the smaller communities such committees have also been established through the help and recommendation of the stabilization committee.

Because of the success of this activity, and because the present emergency demonstrates the need for a continuing stimulation of local communities to meet their unemployment problem, and also for some central coordinating agency representing the entire State, I am reappointing the stabilization committee, asking it to organize on a more permanent basis and to continue its activities, concentrating for the next few months upon helping communities to devise ways to meet their own problem of unemployment relief and acting as a clearing house and advisory body on all the many plans and schemes which are submitted to State officials having this end in view.

451

At the beginning of the legislative session I shall request the Legislature to make this committee an official commission and to provide for its expenses, which up until this time have been borne by the individual members of the committee. In expanding the duties of this committee I am also asking it immediately to make a plan for the establishment of loan funds on a sound and suitable basis, the loan funds to be under local management and direction and used for the purpose of sustaining those whose incomes are greatly reduced or entirely depleted by the unemployment situation. I am convinced that such loan funds can be very successfully and democratically administered if they are set up on a sound basis with the participation of the banking and business interests.

In effect this committee will act for the State of New York as an EMERGENCY COMMISSION, to act as the coordinating party for the entire State throughout this winter and until the emergency is abated.

The work of the committee will fall under three general heads:

a. To coordinate and encourage the additional employment of men and women out of work;
b. To encourage the establishment of loan funds for the unemployed;
c. To coordinate and prevent duplication in all local public and private housing, clothing and feeding efforts, checking up at the same time in all of the smaller communities of the State so as to initiate relief work for those who need it but who live away from the larger centers of community efforts.

In expanding the duties for this stabilization committee I have acceded to its request for additional membership and especially for membership of persons expert in certain phases of relief work. I am therefore adding to the membership of the committee. . . .

95 ⟨Address on Unemployment Insurance. New York City. March 6, 1931

As MANY of you know I was for years active in the surety branch of the great field of insurance. I am told that suretyship is one of the oldest of all forms of business, for on an ancient tile found in the ruins of Babylon is a record of the pledging of property by the Grand-Vizier of a Babylonian King for the due performance of a royal contract by one of the King's henchmen.

Insurance as a whole is indeed historic—reaching back through hundreds of centuries to meet a very natural human need for protection against all kinds of unforeseen or unknown contingencies.

Life insurance is perhaps one of the younger sisters and yet life insurance today throughout the world has, in its volume of business and in the protection which it affords, become the leader of the whole field.

What impresses me most is that insurance as a whole is a constantly changing and a constantly growing force in our individual lives and in our business lives. As the world becomes more and more civilized and stabilized we are able to give protection against more and more forms of potential dangers or losses. That is why I have at all times been so ready to go along with new forms of insurance to meet new needs. In other words, I have been a consistent opponent of the school which takes the position that because a new form of risk has never been written before it should not be undertaken in the future.

In the various demands which are made by worthy citizens for the protection of business and individuals against new risks, one essential basis for all insurance is often forgotten. I refer to the fundamental principle that insurance must, if it is to survive, be based on human experience. If that fundamental is always kept in mind the stability and the permanence of insurance will be assured and its operations will grow.

I take it that from the very first days of life insurance, for in-

453

stance, the expectation of human life was based on some sort of actuarial tables, no matter how crude these tables may have been in the beginning. As time went on the information concerning human longevity became more accurate and as modern science improved the tables became a true record of the facts.

By the same token underwriting, as you gentlemen call it, has progressed with modern science, recognizing, for instance, as each year goes by that the expectancy of life in this country has appreciably increased. With this recognition has come a lowering of the cost to the individual who seeks to be insured.

It is this reduction of the problem of risk to a business basis which has given the public as a whole the confidence which they now have in properly managed insurance. And this confidence has been further strengthened by the thought that mere private gain is no longer the goal of those who conduct the business.

In line with the thought that the conduct of the insurance business is keeping up with changing conditions, I want to stress one further point. During our own lifetime, we have seen many new forms of insurance, many improvements, many new coverages, and many new methods for the distribution of participating profits and the payment of losses. In our own lifetime we have seen, for instance, the rise of workmen's compensation to an accepted place in the insurance world.

Today we are giving serious thought to still another form of insurable risk — that of providing some form of reserve for individual men and women to be used by them for their maintenance and support in times of involuntary unemployment. Here again, as was the case a quarter of a century ago when workmen's compensation was being considered, there is much unthinking opposition on the principal ground that the proposal is something new. It is not a sound argument to make that a new thing may prove unsound just because it is new.

I take it that in studying what is somewhat loosely referred to as unemployment insurance, the insurance world itself will maintain not only an open mind but will also apply the same fundamental principles of experience and potential risk which it has applied to the existing forms of insurance. It is of the utmost importance that unemployment insurance, like the other forms, be based on sound actuarial tables. This is the fundamental which will prevent a mere dole or gift on the part of either private agencies or Governments themselves.

The other factors entering into unemployment insurance are more methods of administration than matters of fundamentals. Whether we shall have group insurance or general insurance, whether the employer or the employee shall both contribute or only one, what part the State will play in the picture, all of these can, I am very certain, be worked out in the days to come.

I use this example of unemployment insurance for two reasons: First, because I am certain in my own mind that what is now an experiment affecting about one hundred thousand workers in this country will become the universal practice throughout the country during the coming generation; and second, because, I am sure, that the splendid body of men and women who are engaged in this great business of insurance, and who are so successfully solving its problems new and old, will take on this new necessity just as they have taken on other necessities in the past. In so doing you will, I am sure, apply the sound principles of experience and good business which have made life insurance so successful and so necessary to all of us.

96 ❧ A Recommendation for a Commission to Investigate Unemployment Insurance. March 25, 1931

To the Legislature:

IT WOULD be in the public interest if your Honorable Bodies would, before adjournment, enact legislation affecting two important phases of the unemployment problem. The first relates to the present emergency. I sincerely recommend the passage of legislation, which is being introduced in both houses, making an

455

official commission of the unofficial Committee on Stabilization which I appointed in April, 1930. This committee was created for the purpose of making surveys to obtain accurate data relative to unemployment; stabilization of employment; cooperative organization and supervision of public and private philanthropic activities; active stimulation of small-job campaigns in every city and town in the State; establishment of local free employment clearing houses linked up with the State public employment service; and the encouragement of local public works. This committee has been a volunteer unofficial one and I believe that its work should be continued under State auspices in an official manner. It has rendered a fine and useful service.

The second need relates to the broad problem of providing in the future against the results of some new period of economic depression. The serious unemployment situation which has stunned the Nation for the past year and a half has brought to our attention in a most vivid fashion the need for some sort of relief to protect those men and women who are willing to work but who through no fault of their own cannot find employment. This form of relief should not, of course, take the shape of a dole in any respect. The dole method of relief for unemployment is not only repugnant to all sound principles of social economics, but is contrary to every principle of American citizenship and of sound government. American labor seeks no charity, but only a chance to work for its living. The relief which the workers of the State should be able to anticipate, when engulfed in a period of industrial depression, should be one of insurance, to which they themselves have in a large part contributed. Each industry itself should likewise bear a part of the premium for this insurance, and the State, in the interest of its own citizens, and to prevent a recurrence of the widespread hardship of these days, should at the least supervise its operations.

Any Nation worthy of the name should aim in normal industrial periods to offer employment to every able-bodied citizen willing to work. An enlightened Government should look further ahead. It should help its citizens insure themselves during good times against the evil days of hard times to come. The worker, the industry and the State should all assist in making this insurance possible. The successful experience of several large industrial concerns has shown the wisdom and feasibility of some form of unemployment relief.

I strongly recommend that your Honorable Bodies create a commission to investigate this whole subject and report to the Legislature of 1932 a plan for accomplishing some kind of scientific unemployment insurance. As to the nature of the commission, I would suggest that it be a small commission of experts, to be appointed by the Governor, with two or three members to be appointed by and from the Legislature. I mean no disrespect when I state my belief that a large legislative committee is not the proper way to investigate this kind of subject, which will necessarily entail minute technical and expert consideration of various economic, financial and actuarial problems and material. Bills have been introduced creating a commission which I think has the most advisable form, namely, two legislators and four laymen — one to represent labor, one to represent employers, and the others to represent the general public.

I hope that your Honorable Bodies will enact these two recommendations into law.

97 ⟨ New York State Takes the Lead in the Relief of the Unemployed. A Message Recommending Creation of Relief Administration.
August 28, 1931

To the Legislature (in Extraordinary Session):

WHAT is the State? It is the duly constituted representative of an organized society of human beings, created by them for their mutual protection and well-being. "The State" or "The Government" is but the machinery through which such mutual aid and protection are achieved. The cave man fought for existence un- aided or even opposed by his fellow man, but today the humblest citizen of our State stands protected by all the power and strength of his Government. Our Government is not the master but the creature of the people. The duty of the State toward the citizens is the duty of the servant to its master. The people have created it; the people, by common consent, permit its continual existence.

One of these duties of the State is that of caring for those of its citizens who find themselves the victims of such adverse circum- stance as makes them unable to obtain even the necessities for mere existence without the aid of others. That responsibility is recognized by every civilized Nation.

For example, from the earliest days of our own country the consciousness of the proper relationship between the State and the citizen resulted in the establishment of those often crude and unscientific but wholly necessary institutions known as the county poor houses.

In many messages to your Honorable Bodies I have pointed out that this earlier exemplification of the State's responsibility has been sustained and enlarged from year to year as we have grown to a better understanding of government functions. I have mentioned specifically the general agreement of today, that upon the State falls the duty of protecting and sustaining those of its citizens who, through no fault of their own, find them- selves in their old age unable to maintain life.

But the same rule applies to other conditions. In broad terms I assert that modern society, acting through its Government, owes the definite obligation to prevent the starvation or the dire want of any of its fellow men and women who try to maintain them- selves but cannot.

While it is true that we have hitherto principally considered those who through accident or old age were permanently in- capacitated, the same responsibility of the State undoubtedly applies when widespread economic conditions render large num- bers of men and women incapable of supporting either them- selves or their families because of circumstances beyond their control which make it impossible for them to find remunerative labor. To these unfortunate citizens aid must be extended by Government, not as a matter of charity, but as a matter of social duty.

It is true beyond question that aid must be and will be given in large measure through the agencies of private contributions; and in normal times these contributions should be regarded as sufficient to meet normal conditions. However, even here the appeal is not alone on the basis of charity, but is laid on the foundation of the civic duty of all good citizens.

I would not be appearing before you today if these were normal times. When, however, a condition arises which calls for measures of relief over and beyond the ability of private and local assistance to meet — even with the usual aid added by the State — it is time for the State itself to do its additional share.

As my constitutional duty to communicate to your Honorable Bodies the condition of the State, I report to you what is a matter of common knowledge — that the economic depression of the last two years has created social conditions resulting in great physical suffering on the part of many hundreds of thousands of men, women and children. Unless conditions immediately and greatly change, this will, we fear, be aggravated by cold and hunger during the coming winter.

The many reports which I have received from municipal officials, from the Governor's Commission on the Stabilization of Employment, from the State Department of Social Welfare, and from many private organizations for relief and charity, agree that the number of our citizens who, this coming winter, will be in need will, so far as it is possible to estimate, be nearly, if not quite, twice as many as during the winter of 1930-1931.

There are many causes. Many individuals and families, because of prolonged unemployment, have exhausted their savings and their credit. Many who were at work last winter and were enabled to take care of their relatives and friends are now themselves out of work. In the same way, many employers who, up to recently, with fine public spirit have continued to use their resources to prevent the laying-off of workers, are finding that they can no longer do so.

Last winter, distress was to a great extent alleviated along three distinct lines: first, through the recommendations of the Commission on the Stabilization of Employment which pointed out the method of staggering employment in order to provide work for more people, and was largely instrumental in bringing about the coordination of relief work of the various municipalities and private agencies throughout the State; second, by the authorization and construction of large additions to public works on the part of the State and the political subdivisions thereof; third, by a generous response by private individuals in the form of contributions for relief.

We could proceed in accordance with the same program and policy used last winter were it not for two facts which, according to the best information obtainable, seem incontrovertible. The first is that the amount of relief needed will of necessity be vastly greater this coming winter; secondly, the resources hitherto used will not be adequate to meet the additional needs.

There is no escaping the simple conclusion that very large additional funds must be looked for this winter to supplement the lines of assistance given last year.

I am confident that every county, every city and every town will continue its program of public works and add to it wherever possible. Nevertheless, there are many communities in the State which, because they have approached or are approaching their constitutional debt limit or for other equally good reasons, will find themselves unable greatly to add to employment on public works. It is worth while remembering, too, that where these public works are not paid for out of current receipts from taxes, the issuing of notes or bonds by municipalities calls for their subsequent payment out of taxes derived almost wholly from real estate — a form of property which today already bears a heavy load. It is therefore probably correct to estimate that the total of public works giving direct employment to labor will not and cannot be greatly increased during the coming year in the average of the municipalities of the State.

We now come to the source of relief provided by private charity. Even though the generous contributions in previous years of those who appreciate their civic responsibility in this matter should equal the previous sum, it will still fall short of the total needed. Let me make it clear that no individual who can afford it has the right to give one dollar less to private relief work than he has given in the past.

The net result of this survey is that we must recognize these facts; that the local subdivisions of government can in most cases not greatly increase their direct employment of labor and that private charity will prove inadequate to meet the added burden of the next few months.

By a process of elimination, if by nothing else, the responsibility also rests upon the State. It is idle for us to speculate upon actions which may be taken by the Federal Government, just as it is idle for the purpose for which we are here gathered to speculate about the causes of national depression. It is true that times may get better; it is true that the Federal Government may take action to eradicate some of the basic causes of our present troubles; it is true that the Federal Government may come forward with a definite construction program on a truly large scale; it is true that the Federal Government may adopt a well-thought-out concrete policy which will start the wheels of industry moving and give to the farmer at least the cost of making his crop. The State of New York cannot wait for that. I face and you face and thirteen million people face the problem of providing immediate relief.

To supplement and in no way to cut down the existing sources of relief, the State must itself make available at once a large sum of public moneys to provide work for its residents this winter where useful public work can be found; and where such work cannot be found, to provide them with food against starvation and with clothing and shelter against suffering. To wait until the regular session of the next Legislature would mean that half of the winter would be gone before the necessary legislation was passed and the work or organization set up. This answers the suggestion of waiting until it has been definitely established that local endeavor and private charity have failed to meet the needs of the various communities. It is only by using the next two months for the gathering of the necessary facts, the setting up of the machinery, and the collection of the money, that the needs of the winter months can, beyond a doubt, be met. With my deepest sincerity I believe that the State has an immediate duty and that further delay is impossible and wrong.

No Government is infallible; no Government can guarantee that every case of suffering or distress will be taken care of by it or by its agents. All that Government can do is to act with reasonable foresight and so far as its resources allow, to plan for the fullest measure of relief. At best there will be many individual cases of suffering, but the State should take such reasonable steps as lie within its power to make the number of cases of suffering as small as possible.

To carry out with the greatest possible effectiveness the high duty which is the State's, I recommend the following program to care for the relief of distress and the alleviation of unemployment:

1. I suggest that the administration of unemployment and distress relief within the State be placed in the hands of a temporary emergency commission of three persons to be appointed by the Governor to serve without pay. This commission, to be known as the "Temporary Emergency Relief Administration," should be empowered to recommend to the Governor the appointment of local subsidiary commissions of three or more men and women in such cities and counties as it deems advisable. The sum of twenty million dollars, which I am reliably informed is the estimated amount required to meet the needs of the coming year, should be appropriated, and should be apportioned by this commission among the various counties and cities of the State. The distribution should be based in amount on several factors, such as: (1) The number of people and families

462

unemployed in the locality, requiring assistance; and (2) the amount of local effort and initiative as shown by the money raised in the municipality by public and private means, consistent with the financial ability of the municipality and its people.

Based on the theory that the distribution of relief of the poor is essentially a local function, I believe that the State in supplementing the amounts locally raised should seek so far as possible to encourage local initiative by matching local effort; so that the larger the amount raised locally, the larger the contribution by the State.

The actual disbursement of this money should be in the hands of the local welfare officer of the municipality, subject, however, to the approval of the local Temporary Emergency Relief Commission, if one be appointed. The local commission should act in an advisory capacity to the local welfare officer as well as to the State Administration. Such a local commission can do a great deal, not only by coordinating local private relief, but also by inducing people to have as much work done in and about their houses, businesses and farms as is possible in order to provide many additional odd jobs. Much of the strain of the present situation could be relieved if everybody were to engage in an individual, personal, job-furnishing campaign, doing now the work which they might ordinarily postpone for a year or so. The local commission could accomplish much by stimulating this kind of activity. I also contemplate organizing committees throughout the State to encourage this kind of endeavor.

It should be provided by statute that the money be expended as follows: If any form of employment can be found for the public use, prevailing rates of wages should be paid for such work; if, however, it is impossible to locate or provide work of this kind, then the local welfare officer may purchase and give to the unemployed within his jurisdiction necessary food, clothing, fuel and shelter for them and their families. Certain definite restrictions should be embodied within this statute, viz.:

1. That under no circumstances shall any actual money be

paid in the form of a dole or in any other form by the local welfare officer to any unemployed or his family.

2. That this relief should be restricted to persons who have resided in New York State for at least two years prior to the enactment of the statute.

3. That no employment or relief be undertaken except in accordance with rules and regulations laid down by the Temporary Emergency Relief Administration.

The administration should be given the widest latitude and discretion in the apportionment of this money and in its distribution. It should be permitted to retain out of the twenty million dollars a million dollars or more within its discretion to be expended by the State on such work as the State itself may do in the winter months, such as the grading of State lands, construction and maintenance of roads and parkways in such sections of the State as this is possible.

I have so far considered only the proper organization and the prompt distribution of work and supplies where they will be of the greatest assistance. There is another requirement for a scientific and proper system of relief which experience has shown us has not been hitherto properly recognized or organized. Experience has shown that many of the most deserving cases not only refuse to apply for relief until actual starvation has set in, but allow the future health of their children to become permanently undermined by undernourishment rather than seek community help. Any proper relief system must have a thoroughly organized, enthusiastic and tireless department of investigation, constantly seeking out those individuals or families who will not of their own accord come forward. This work must be undertaken by those who are enthusiastic and are sympathetic as well.

I would suggest that this phase of our relief work be laid as a primary duty upon the women of our State; and I shall work in close cooperation with the proposed emergency relief administration to assist in the organization of women as individuals and as groups to carry out this purpose.

2. The necessary money for this unemployment and distress relief should be raised by a tax on personal incomes. It seems logical that those of our residents who are fortunate enough to have taxable incomes should bear the burden of supplementing the local governmental and private philanthropic work of assistance. I believe that this tax should fall proportionately on all incomes, over and above existing exemptions. If each person paying an income tax were required to pay merely half again as much, I am informed by the State Tax Commission, the necessary twenty million dollars will be raised. I have had prepared a computation of what these increases will amount to. You will observe that the burden placed upon the man with a small income is slight indeed; the single man with an income of $3,000, for example, will pay an additional tax of only $2.50; the married man with a family earning $10,000 a year will pay an additional tax of only $26.

The following table shows for typical cases the amount of additional tax for individuals having incomes of certain sizes according to family responsibilities:

Net income	Single persons	Married persons and heads of families (two children or other dependents)
$2,500	$0.00	$0.00
3,000	2.50	0.00
4,000	7.50	0.00
5,000	12.50	1.00
10,000	37.50	26.00
30,000	125.00	102.00
50,000	425.00	402.00
100,000	1,162.50	1,128.00

There were approximately 300,000 personal income tax payers this year. By spreading this burden among those people, few of them will feel it to an appreciable extent and the whole body of our income-making machinery will be sustaining its fair share of the burden. It is clear to me that it is the duty of those who have benefited by our industrial and economic system to come to the front in such a grave emergency and assist in relieving those who under the same industrial and economic order are the losers and sufferers. I believe their contribution should be in proportion to the benefits they receive and the prosperity they enjoy.

There are two alternative ways in which this tax could be levied. First, it could be imposed upon the 1930 incomes. The advantage of this method is that the exact amount of this tax is known because of the fact that the tax returns are now actually on file. The objection to it is that people having already paid their 1930 income tax will feel reluctant to pay a further tax additional thereto. Second, the tax can be levied next April on the 1931 incomes and the money can be provided immediately by the Comptroller through the issuance and sale of short term certificates. This method would obviate the objections of those who have already paid their income tax for 1930, but interposes another fairly important objection that the exact total of the tax is unknown and is therefore speculative. In this connection, I desire to inform you that the present estimate of the Tax Commission, made, however, more than seven months before the receipt of the actual returns next April, is that the amount of the net personal returns for the year 1931 will be about the same as for the year 1930.

3. Legislation should be enacted giving to the various cities and counties of the State authority to borrow money and expend it for the employment of their residents on public works. You will recall that Chapter 284 of the Laws of 1931 extended this authority to the City of New York. I am informed that it has been used in that city with great benefit in the amelioration of the unemployment situation; and I commend it to your consideration for enactment for such other municipalities as may desire to have this power. I believe that municipal obligations to be issued for this purpose should be for no greater period than three years.

4. I recommend that for all future contracts on public works by the State or in a municipality thereof, to be let between October 1, 1931, and June 30, 1932, there be inserted a clause providing for a five-day week for all labor, exclusive of supervisory force, under rules and regulations to be established by the

Department of Labor. In this way the benefits of employment on public works may be spread somewhat more thinly, but certainly more widely.

5. One of the by-products of the economic depression has been the recent application for the State bonus by a great many World War veterans — a bonus to which they were entitled by legislation passed in 1924 after approval by the people. These veterans, not needing the money originally voted to them by the State at that time, failed to make claim therefor. Now the exigencies of the present situation force them to seek assistance where they can find it. This is no new bonus but is the bonus already voted for and approved, but not paid out merely because of failure to make claim therefor. I am informed by the Adjutant-General that these tardy claims will total about $548,000 more than the present fund contains. I therefore suggest that there be allocated out of the twenty million dollar fund hereinabove provided the sum of $548,000 to be turned over to the Adjutant-General for this purpose.

This program is the result of many months of study and reflection on my part. I am convinced that the time for platitudes as to the necessities of the situation has passed. The time for immediate action is at hand and I trust that your Honorable Bodies will act.

Therefore, in compliance with Article IV, Section 4, of the Constitution, I recommend for your consideration the following:

I. The creation of a temporary State agency to carry on the expenditure this winter of State moneys on public State work for the employment of residents of the State.

II. Authorizing such agency to apportion State moneys among the counties and cities of the State to be disbursed by them this winter for employment on local work useful to the public, and for giving necessary food, clothing, shelter and warmth to residents of the State where useful public work cannot be found for them.

III. The appropriation of money out of current revenues to be immediately available for the relief of distress and the amelioration of unemployment, and the laying of a tax on personal incomes to provide the necessary moneys.

IV. Authorizing cities and counties in the State for the period of one year to borrow money for a term not exceeding three years, to be used by them for the employment of local residents on local public works.

V. Legislation providing for a five-day week in all future contracts for labor on State and municipal public work other than supervisory labor.

VI. Providing State money to pay soldiers' bonuses due to World War veterans under the provisions of Chapter 19 of the Laws of 1924 but which have not yet been paid because of delay in filing applications therefor.

98 (A Telegram Urging the Passage of the Federal Emergency Relief Bill. February 10, 1932

I am glad you are working for the unemployment relief bill. It is an important factor in the present emergency. It will equalize the burden throughout the Nation. Although it should not be regarded as a permanent Government policy, nevertheless it is justified as carrying out the definite obligation of Government to prevent starvation and distress in this present crisis. Plans for large public works are possible if the works themselves are carefully planned and economically necessary, but they do not relieve distress at this moment. That is why I hope the Emergency Relief Bill will pass.

Hon. Robert F. Wagner,
United States Senate,
Washington, D. C.

99 ⟨A Message to the Legislature Recommending an Unemployment Insurance Law. February 15, 1932

To the Legislature:

IN JANUARY, 1931, I called a conference of the Governors of the seven industrial States of the Northeast — Ohio, Pennsylvania, New Jersey, Massachusetts, Connecticut, Rhode Island and New York — to discuss and consider various proposals in connection with the current period of unemployment. Among the things accomplished was the appointment of a committee on unemployment insurance to consist of one representative of each of the States. This commission has filed its report with the Governors of the respective States involved and I am forwarding to your Honorable Bodies a copy of this report.

The report offers the following general suggestions for putting an industrial insurance plan into effect:

1. The payment by each employer of a contribution amounting to 2 percent on his payroll; and its reduction to 1 percent when the accumulated reserve per employee shall have exceeded $50.
2. The maximum rate of benefit to be $10 a week, or 50 percent of an employee's wage (whichever is lower); and the maximum period of benefit to be 10 weeks of any 12 months.
3. The payments by each employer to constitute the employment reserve of his firm and not to be added to the common pool.
4. The creation of an Unemployment Administration of three members, representing labor, industry and the public.
5. The State to take prompt steps to extend its public employment service, because no system of unemployment insurance can accomplish its purpose without a properly or-

469

ganized and efficiently operated system of employment exchanges.

6. The Unemployment Commission to encourage cooperative action between firms and industries, because the most effective measures for achieving greater stabilization cannot be accomplished by a single firm.

I recommend the immediate, careful consideration of this report by your Honorable Bodies. I am having prepared legislation to carry out the recommendations made. It is needless for me to point out to you the hardships and misery which have been occasioned to millions of innocent families during the past two years. The plan suggested cannot, of course, in any way prevent a recurrence of all of the conditions through which we have gone. One definite thing that it can do, however, is to alleviate in some small measure the extreme suffering which economic crises always occasion. The plan suggested is not a radical one. It has received the careful and prolonged study of experts. It certainly should be given a trial at the earliest possible moment.

100 ⟪ A Message to the Legislature Urging Continuation of Relief of Unemployment Distress. March 10, 1932

To the Legislature:

ON MARCH 1, 1932, I sent to your Honorable Bodies a message pointing out the urgent necessity for continuing the life and work of the Temporary Emergency Relief Administration in order to continue to alleviate in part the distress caused by current unemployment. Prior to sending that message, and subsequent thereto, I have been in frequent conference with the majority and minority leaders of your Honorable Bodies. I believe that we are all in substantial accord as to the imperative need for continuing this work and providing the necessary funds therefor. It is indeed inconceivable that the State of New York fail to make provision to reduce in so far as possible the suffering of its people from cold and hunger this year and next. The relief furnished last winter should be repeated during the coming winter wherever necessary. It is estimated that the cost would be about $5,000,000 up to November 1, 1932; $15,000,000 additional to February 1, 1933; $15,000,000 additional to January 1, 1934.

I believe that we were all of one mind at our conferences that in normal times the only proper way to provide funds for this purpose would be by a tax of some kind. This form of expenditure clearly comes under the head of current expenses and should be borne from current funds. We cannot, however, blink the fact that the people of our State are already heavily burdened by taxation. The burden is now made even heavier by the present business depression which, of course, reduces ability to pay. It is further expected that additional burdens of taxation will be laid by the Federal Government to make up the huge deficit in the Federal Treasury. Unfortunately, the best economic thought of the country is unable to predict with any certainty any early return to normal conditions which would warrant the hope that by next year the condition of business would make more easy the levy of additional taxes needed for these purposes. In such extraordinary times, I believe that extraordinary measures, otherwise not to be considered, are justified.

It has been suggested in our conferences that the sum of five million dollars be appropriated from current revenues without a new tax, so as to carry the work of the Temporary Emergency Relief Administration up to next election day, and that on election day a referendum be submitted to the people for a bond issue to meet the balance of the requirements up to January 1, 1934. I approve of that suggestion. I am fully aware of the fact that this would be a departure from the pay-as-you-go policy; I am also aware of the fact, however, that conditions which now face us, in their gravity akin to war conditions, warrant this deviation from that principle.

May I point out to you that there are two forms which this bond issue might take?

First, a bond issue might be submitted to take care of the permanent concrete road construction for the next fiscal year. There is, of course, nothing new or startling about this suggestion. Until about twenty years ago it was the policy of the State to build all of its permanent roads by the proceeds of bond issues. To a certain extent this policy was justified by the fact that the ordinary life of that kind of highway is about twenty years and by the theory that the entire burden of the cost thereof should not be borne in any one year. If the necessary funds for the State's construction of concrete highways in 1933-1934 were furnished by a bond issue, this would relieve the current revenues of the State of a sufficient sum of money to pay for unemployment relief out of these current revenues. In that way, without providing any additional tax, relief money could be provided out of current revenues which would be made available by virtue of the fact that the necessary highway money had come from the proceeds of the bond issue. Two facts would be understood by the voters: (1) It would be financially sound to bond highway construction, especially as a temporary method; (2) they would by voting for this bond issue release enough money from existing tax revenues to avoid imposing new taxes for unemployment relief.

The second form would be to submit to the people at the next election a proposal for a bond issue to take care directly of unemployment relief up to January 1, 1934. If the people approve this proposal, the necessary money for the coming winter and part of the succeeding winter would be made available from this issue and the burden of taking care of distress relief would thus be spread over a period of years. While in theory this issuing of highway bonds is preferable because it funds a public improvement which lasts many years, and the funding of unemployment relief does not do this, nevertheless from the practical rather than the theoretical standpoint either method brings a substantially equal amount of cash into the treasury, and on this ground either may be justified. It should be borne in mind that even if the proposition be approved on a referendum, the money need not all be appropriated next year unless the Legislature deems it necessary. Only so much as conditions then make necessary would be spent.

I repeat I am willing to approve either of these methods of funding this expense over a long term, only because of the abnormal and extraordinary situation which faces us. It should not be deemed a precedent for any further deviation from the pay-as-you-go policy. I believe that the legislative and executive branches of the Government are in strict accord on the soundness of the pay-as-you-go principle in State finance for anything other than permanent improvements. It has been the foundation of the credit of our State, which is the strongest in the world, and we should adhere to it under all ordinary conditions. The present crisis, however, cannot be met, except with great hardship, in any way other than as above indicated; and I recommend it to your Honorable Bodies for approval.

101 ⟨The Governor Asks for Public Approval of a Bond Issue to Relieve Unemployment. October 29, 1932

I URGE the voters of the State of New York to give overwhelming approval to Proposition No. 1 on the ballot, authorizing a thirty-million-dollar bond issue to take care of unemployment relief from November 15th on. This will avoid a special session of the Legislature, and new taxes for relief purposes. Most important of all, it will prevent hunger and suffering on the part of hundreds of thousands of our citizens.

XVIII

Land Utilization and
State Planning

THE DOCUMENTS in this chapter show the policy begun during my Administration as Governor, and actively continued by me as President, looking to the proper utilization of the land of the State and Nation. Any comprehensive program for the benefit of that part of our population which lives by agriculture must necessarily include, particularly in its long-range features, provision for the use of each piece of land for the purposes for which nature has made it best fitted.

See also, on this subject, Items 3, 18 on page 119, 21, 22, 131 on page 654 of this volume.

102 ❨ A Proposal for a Survey of Soil and Climatic Conditions. Address at Silver Lake, N. Y. August 15, 1929

IT IS appropriate in the center of one of the important agricultural areas of the State to lay down a part of the agricultural program for the coming year.

People will remember that on the initiation of the Governor's Agricultural Advisory Commission an important program of farm tax relief was put through at the last session of the Legislature. This was in the nature of an emergency program, the result of which could be made of immediate benefit to the farmers of the State. The relief from highway taxes, the reduction in grade crossing elimination contributions by the localities, and the increased State aid for small rural schools will save the agricultural taxpayers many millions of dollars every year from now on.

The same Agricultural Advisory Commission has again been in session, taking up this time one of the important steps for the all-time improvement of agricultural production.

It is a fact not generally realized that the State does not know what its agricultural possibilities are. In other words, no complete survey has been made for the purpose of making definite plans for the more profitable use of each kind of land. There are dozens of different kinds of land in the State, and it is not stretching the point to say that a very large percentage of agricultural lands is now used for the production of the wrong kind of crop.

The commission proposes, therefore, that the first step must be to complete the soil survey of the State. For many years past cooperative work has been going on between the State and the Federal Government but it has resulted in the survey of less than half of the counties of the State. At the present rate of procedure it would require thirty years to finish the soil survey. It is therefore the first step in the program that this soil survey shall be speeded up so as to cover the whole State within the next few years. This will result in knowledge of the kind of soils in every

477

county and every neighborhood and every farm, and will save millions of dollars during the lifetime of the coming generation. For example, it is said that more than half of the orchards of Western New York are planted on the wrong kind of soil. If a knowledge of these soils had been available, millions of dollars would have been saved by the fruit growers of that part of the State.

With increasing specialization in crop growing it is essential to know what soil is best adapted to each crop.

With this soil survey there should go hand in hand a complete survey of the climatic conditions of the State and it is a fact little recognized that one county may have conditions of climate very different from an adjoining county, so different in fact that the effect on the same crop will be marked. This climatic survey applies not only to general crops but especially to orchards and vegetables.

Most people know of the great success of our State in growing fruits of all kinds, but it is less well known that in the last census year the vegetables produced on the farms of New York represented one-fourth of the total value of all farm crops and that the State led all other States.

The third step in the survey is to take an inventory of all of the forest resources of the State. While it is true that the State is consuming far more timber each year than it is growing, it is also true that thousands of owners of wood lots are unable to obtain a dependable market for their forest crops. In other words, we are losing at both ends; we are not growing enough timber, and at the same time not getting what we should for the timber which we have.

There have been much talk and some legislation on reforesting the waste lands of the State, but we have little detailed knowledge of where that land is, what its boundaries are, and what kind of trees should be planted on it for the best returns.

For the above reasons the Governor's Agricultural Advisory Commission feels very strongly that the next important step in the advancement of agriculture in our State is to make a complete survey. This cannot be done in one year, but the work can properly be started at the next session of the Legislature. For the first three years the total cost of the various projects will come to about $110,000 a year. These projects fall into the following classes:

1. Completion of the soil survey, including preparation of detailed maps.
2. Assembling and preparing complete weather data.
3. Classification of land for agriculture, forest, recreation or residential purposes.
4. Survey of the present uses and best adaptations of land, including orchards, vegetables, forests, pastures.
5. Studying the cost of producing milk under the various existing systems of dairying.

I have long been interested in the general subject of city and of regional planning. The present proposed survey of the whole State is merely an intelligent broadening of the planning which heretofore has been localized. It is a study for a statewide plan which will include the use of every acre in the whole State. So far as I know this is the first time in the United States that the city or regional plan idea has been extended to take in a whole State. It will, therefore, be of great interest to everyone who realizes the importance of looking ahead and of using our resources to the best advantage.

I am particularly happy that the Governor's Agricultural Advisory Commission has looked at this big subject in such a broadminded way. The survey which they propose and which I heartily endorse is necessary before we spend millions of dollars which might otherwise be wasted. It is a good businesslike proposition and will in the long run save the agricultural population and also the city dwelling population many millions of dollars through the more economical production of food crops and the increase of our forest resources. I am confident that there will be virtually unanimous support for this excellent program from all parts of the State.

103 ❦ A Message to the Legislature Formulating a Land Policy for the State. January 26, 1931

To the Legislature:

In my Annual Message of January 7, 1931 to your Honorable Bodies, I pointed out that we in this State have in our program of remedial legislation for our farmers and rural dwellers progressed to the point where we should formulate a definite far-reaching land policy for the State. In a literal sense, the adoption of such a land policy affects not merely the rural population of the State, but in an equal degree the entire population of the State. It involves the food supply of all our citizens, their water supply, timber supply, and indeed practically all of their market commodities.

What do we mean by this land policy? Fundamentally, we mean that every acre of rural land in the State should be used only for that purpose for which it is best fitted and out of which the greatest economic return can be derived. New York has about thirty million acres of land, of which twenty-seven million acres are rural and non-industrial. Of these about five million acres are in mountains, forests, swamps, and other lands that have never been cultivated. That leaves about twenty-two million acres which were once in farms. Of this acreage four millions have been abandoned or are no longer used for farm purposes. As a result, about eighteen million acres are now devoted to farming.

I propose that the State proceed to find out as soon as possible for what these eighteen million acres are best suited. It seems almost unnecessary to say that land which is suitable for the raising of crops on a profitable basis should not be left idle or devoted to forest purposes; and that, conversely, land which can be used only for tree planting should not be cultivated year after year in a futile effort to raise profitable crops thereon. And yet, it is unquestionably true, that thousands of farmers, year after year, are spending labor and money in various parts of the State trying to get agricultural products out of land which will never be able to yield a profit in crops, but which should be devoted only to reforestation or recreational purposes.

Our present knowledge of soil conditions enables us to state accurately for what purpose any definite parcel of land is best suited. I believe that the State of New York should be in a position to place at the disposal of its citizens first-hand accurate information as to the actual adaptability of our rural lands for farming in its various phases. To that end, I recommend that the State proceed to make a survey of the rural lands of the State. This survey will probably require about ten years. We should, however, at the earliest possible moment adopt a program of making the survey and start it on its way. As a matter of fact, the first step has been taken. Last year the Legislature on my recommendation appropriated twenty thousand dollars, with a part of which the College of Agriculture at Cornell has made a survey of one whole county—Tompkins County. The survey has been made on the basis of ten-acre squares; and very simple and clear maps have been prepared which can be examined by your Honorable Bodies showing the following data with relation to the plots of land in Tompkins County:

A. The type of soil.
B. The climate.
C. The present use of the land.
D. An analysis of the people who live on the land in relation to the following particulars:
    1. Is the resident a new settler or has his family been on the land a long time?
    2. Are the young people staying on the land or leaving it?
    3. Does the resident make his livelihood out of it or does he occupy it only as a residence?
    4. Does the farm support the farmer in accordance with the American standard of living?
E. The contribution which each farm makes to the food supply of the Nation.

This survey has proved again what is a matter of common

knowledge among agricultural experts, to wit, that a large percentage of the land now in cultivation as farms has no right to remain as farm land. Several generations of farm experience prove that satisfactory living cannot be made from this land by farming. In some of the townships in Tompkins County, as high as 22 percent of the farm land has been proved to be unadaptable to farm purposes.

With time and money, such a survey could be extended to the entire State. It would include, in addition to the data mentioned above, a study of the location of roads, school facilities, resorts, industrial plants, potential water power resources and power, transmission and telephone lines. On the basis of such information approximate boundaries can be laid down of areas in which there appears to be possibility of coordination of economic endeavors. With such maps, agricultural and economic experts can proceed to classify the lands of the State and advise accurately the use for each classification. While, of course, it is not suggested that this classification be in any sense compulsory, continued economic effort will gradually result in using each acre of land for that purpose which will be the most profitable.

The two chief uses of rural land are agriculture and forestry. Land adaptable for one should not be used for the other; and land which cannot be used profitably for either should be declared waste land or wilderness areas in which settlement should be discouraged. Even such land has its usefulness, however, for the natural brush and grass cover which will develop over them will be of some assistance in aiding flood control.

The program can go even further and should be even more far-sighted. It can be used as the basis for planning future State and local developments which depend for their complete efficacy upon accurate knowledge of the proper settling of population. For example, when we proceed to construct or improve roads through the rural areas of the State, whether they be dirt roads or improved roads, we should know whether or not the land through which the roads pass will ultimately support the farm population, or whether the farms will have to be abandoned as unsuitable for agriculture. If we could accurately foresee which areas of lands would ultimately be devoted exclusively to reforestation, we would not of course proceed to construct roads through that area with any idea of using such roads as farm-to-market roads. In the same way, our policy of establishing additional school facilities could be accurately guided toward the end that they be located in spots where they can best serve surrounding population. This conclusion is equally true in connection with electric power and telephone lines. It would, of course, be economically unsound to construct expensive lines into areas where we know that ultimately electricity and telephones will not be introduced on the farms. Such a survey and land policy will therefore help us to attain the highest maximum efficiency in planning farm-to-market roads, rural electrification and telephones, and scientific allocation of school facilities.

Also closely tied up with this survey is the whole question of local land assessment. It is generally conceded that the existing unscientific poor assessment of rural lands is at the root of most local tax difficulties. A great deal of this can be eliminated, of course, by improving the machinery of taxation. This is another subject to which I have invited the attention of your Honorable Bodies on a great many occasions, to wit, a reorganization and modernization of local government. But entirely apart from the disadvantages of an antiquated machinery, local land assessment has rarely, if ever, been scientifically coordinated with the adaptability of the land to various uses, or with the actual or potential income-producing qualities of the land. An accurate scientific survey of each plot of land would necessarily be of inestimable value to a more accurate relative assessment of various parcels of land, called farms.

Hand in hand with this survey there must go a reforestation program on a scale that has never before been attempted by any State. The thousands of abandoned farm areas can be put to their proper use — the growing of trees and the furnishing of recreational opportunities. Fortunately, the State has already definitely embarked upon such a program.

I trust that the reforestation amendment will be again passed by your Honorable Bodies this winter and approved by the people next fall. I hope also that along these lines your Honorable Bodies will pass the various recommendations which I have made in my budget, to wit — $580,000, for the acquisition, maintenance and planting of reforestation areas; ninety-seven thousand dollars for the operation of nurseries and tree planting; one hundred and fifty thousand dollars for the operation of nurseries and tree planting, eight thousand dollars of which has already been made available by Chapter 4 of the Laws of 1931; twenty thousand dollars for the acquisition, maintenance and planting of reforestation areas; twenty-five thousand dollars for the establishment and operation of additional tree nurseries; and twenty-five thousand dollars for the purchase of land for a forest tree nursery.

The adoption of a scientific land policy such as I have outlined, as already begun in Tompkins County, should be extended to all the other counties in the State. The continued maintenance of farms on land which is not adapted to farming will be a drag on the social development of rural life. Such farms cannot support an American standard of living; as Americans we cannot encourage a lower standard of living to continue on them. The social significance of readjusting our rural population gradually but ultimately to the end that only the good farm land be used for farming and the poor land be used for reforesting or other purposes should immediately arouse our attention. It will save the State untold wealth by a more advantageous distribution of highway and school moneys; and in connection with the future development of water power, it will provide a more scientific basis for distribution of electrical energy for any private corporation or municipal agency which ultimately may be engaged in such activity.

I have recommended to your Honorable Bodies an appropriation of ninety-six thousand dollars for land survey and classification by the College of Agriculture at Ithaca and the School of Forestry at Syracuse as a beginning of this State land survey to form the basis of a State land utilization policy. I trust that this recommendation by me will be adopted; and that this State will immediately embark upon this far-sighted program which I know will be of such social and economic moment to both its urban and rural population.

104 ❡ Address before the Conference of Governors on Land Utilization and State Planning. French Lick, Ind. June 2, 1931

Mr. Chairman, Gentlemen of the Conference, Ladies and Gentlemen:

DURING the World War in the Summer of '18, a new Navy destroyer left our shores for the coast of France. About 200 miles off the Irish Channel the commanding officer of this destroyer told one of the young lieutenants who had come into the Navy from civil life to "shoot the sun" at noon; in other words, to determine the position of the ship. The young man "shot the sun," took his figures over the chart board and after about ten minutes the commanding officer noticed he was still scratching his head. He went over and said, "Lieutenant, I will take your figures and work out our position," and the lieutenant moved off.

About five minutes later the commanding officer, after doing a little figuring, summoned the lieutenant to come back, and said, "Young man, take off your hat. This is a solemn moment."

The lieutenant said, "Why, sir?"

The commanding officer said, "My boy, I find from your figures that we are now in the middle of Westminster Abbey."

I take it that we Governors are somewhat concerned with the navigation of a fleet of 48 ships.

At a time when our country, in common with most of the rest of the world, is suffering from a severe dislocation of economic progress, all of the people are naturally and properly asking questions about State and national navigation. It seems strange to them that, with capacities for production developed to the highest degree the world has ever seen, there should come this severe depression, when many who are anxious to work cannot find food for their families while at the same time there is such a surplus of food supplies and other necessities that those who are growing crops or manufacturing can find no markets.

This situation has suggested to many that some new factor is needed in our economic life and this new factor must come from utilizing our experience and our ingenuity to draft and to organize concerted plans for the better use of our resources and the better planning of our social and economic life in general.

It is not enough to talk about being of good cheer. Frankly, I cannot take the Pollyanna attitude as a solution of our problems. It is not enough to apply old remedies. A new economic and social balance calls for positive leadership and definite experiments which have not hitherto been tried.

Our country was of necessity developed in a highly individualistic way. Hardy and determined men went into a new wilderness to carve out homes, to gain a living for their families and to build a future for their race. But the settling of all the land on the continent, the development of a highly organized system of industry and the growth of a huge population have created new and highly complicated problems. In times of booming industry we can overlook defects of organization and danger signals from industry and agriculture, but in times such as the present these symptoms attain a new importance and show us the urgency of the new problems we have to face.

More and more, those who are the victims of dislocations and defects of our social and economic life are beginning to ask respectfully, but insistently, of us who are in positions of public responsibility why Government cannot and should not act to protect its citizens from disaster. I believe the question demands an answer and that the ultimate answer is that Government, both State and national, must accept the responsibility of doing what it can do soundly, with considered forethought, and along definitely constructive, not passive lines.

These lines fall naturally into a number of main heads, such, for instance, as scientific tariff aimed primarily to create a movement of world commodities from one Nation to another; such, for instance, as a better thought-out system of national taxation than we have at the present; such, for instance, as a survey and plan to cut the excessive cost of local government; such, for instance, as the extension of the principle of insurance to cover fields of sickness and of unemployment which are not now reached; such, for instance, as the problem of a dislocation of the proper balance between urban and rural life.

It is this last phase that I am concerned with today and the phrase that best covers all its aspects is "Land Utilization and State Planning."

Land utilization involves more than a mere determination of what each and every acre of land can best be used for, or what crops it can best grow. That is the first step; but having made that determination, we arrive at once at the larger problem of getting men, women and children — in other words, population — to go along with a program and carry it out.

It is not enough to pass resolutions that land must, or should, be used for some specific purpose; Government itself must take steps, with the approval of the governed, to see that plans become realities.

This, it is true, involves such mighty factors as the supply and not the over-supply of agricultural products; it involves making farm life far more attractive both socially and economically than it is today; it involves the possibilities of creating a new classification of our population.

We know from figures a century ago 75 percent of the population lived on farms and 25 percent in cities. Today the figures are exactly reversed. A generation ago there was much talk of a back-to-the-farm movement. It is my thought that this slogan is outworn. Hitherto, we have spoken of two types of living and only two — urban and rural. I believe we can look forward to three rather than two types in the future, for there is a definite place for an intermediate type between the urban and the rural, namely, a rural-industrial group.

On Land Utilization and State Planning

I can best illustrate the beginnings of the working out of the problem by reviewing briefly what has been begun in the State of New York during the past three years toward planning for a better use of our agricultural, industrial and human resources.

The State of New York has definitely undertaken this as a governmental responsibility. Two and a half years ago the State Administration, realizing that the maladjustment of the relationship between rural and city life had reached alarming proportions, undertook a study of the agricultural situation with the immediate purpose of relieving impossible and unfair economic conditions on the farms of the State, but with the broader ultimate purpose of formulating a well-thought-out and scientific plan for developing a permanent agriculture.

The immediate situation was met by the enactment of several types of laws that resulted in the relief of farms from an uneven tax burden and made a net saving to agricultural communities of approximately twenty-four million dollars a year.

First, the State adopted additional State aid for rural education especially in the communities which are so sparsely settled that one-room schools predominate. This State aid gave the smaller rural schools the same advantages already enjoyed by the schools in the large communities.

Second, by a fair equalization of State aid to towns for the maintenance of dirt roads, we put this aid on the basis of mileage rather than assessed valuation, thereby running strictly contrary to the old Biblical formula of "To him who hath shall be given."

Third, through the gasoline tax additional aid is given to the counties for the development of a definite system of farm-to-market roads.

Fourth, the State is embarked on a definite program of securing cheaper electricity for the agricultural communities. We propose to harness the St. Lawrence river as a part of this program, and the electricity developed is by the new law intended primarily for the farmer, the household user, and small industrialist or store-keeper rather than for large industrial plants.

This was a program to relieve immediate needs, but it has

rapidly developed into something which is far deeper and far more important for the future, in other words, State planning. We have felt that if city planning and even county planning are worth while, how much more important is it that the State as a whole should adopt a permanent program both social and economic and statewide in its objectives. In all of this work, it is worth recording that not only the immediate program but also the long-time planning is being worked out in a wholly non-partisan manner. It has, of course, received the benefits of study by the Legislature and legislative commissions. Much of the program has been worked out by the Governor's Agricultural Advisory Commission. This Commission consists of representatives of the great farm organizations such as the Grange, the Farm and Home Bureau, Master Farmers, the Dairymen's League, the G.F.L., members of the Legislature, representatives of State colleges and various Departments of the State Government. It received the hearty cooperation of the Mayors' Conference and of unselfish business men who are willing to give thought to the future of the State and country.

This State program calls for an intensive development of the good land. For the farms that are on a permanent basis, we have definitely embarked on a policy of providing a farm-to-market road that is passable at all times, available electric power, telephone lines, hospital facilities, and a good high school. We believe that as a general State policy, it is better, under present-day conditions, to provide these services and use the good land intensively rather than attempt to use the sub-marginal land.

A good many people, I find, from different parts of the country, visualize the State of New York as consisting primarily of the City of New York, but it is worth while remembering, I think, that nearly 6,000,000 people in the State live outside of that city, and it is worth while remembering, I think, that New York has always ranked high among the States of the Union in the total value of its agricultural products. In recent years we have ranked somewhere between third and seventh in that value among all the

States in the Union, and this in spite of the fact that the State of New York is only twenty-ninth in area.

In spite of this high rank in agriculture, we believe that there is still a large amount of land now being tilled that is better suited for other purposes than for farming.

When we came to the definite acceptance of responsibility for State planning, the first obvious step was to find out what the land area of the State consisted of. I am going somewhat into detail for my colleagues on this for the reason that a great many other States are beginning to embark on the same kind of program, reforestation, drainage, all looking toward the proper use of land, but I hope you will bear in mind that all of this planning for the details dovetails into the larger ultimate picture.

We know, for example, that out of thirty million acres, three million were in cities, villages, residential and industrial areas; five million were in mountains and forests, and by the way, of this five million the State itself has about two million acres of the great Adirondack and Catskill preserves; four million were once farmed but are now abandoned, leaving a total of eighteen million acres for agriculture, divided into one hundred and sixty thousand farms.

The first definite step was to start a survey of the entire State. This involved a study of all the physical factors both above and below the surface of the soil, and a study of economic and social factors, such as market possibilities, what the area is now being used for, for what it is best adapted, and how people live, and so detailed that it gives separate data for each ten-acre square. Already one whole county has been thus surveyed and we expect to cover the entire eighteen million acres involved within the next ten years or less.

Why is this survey being made? We are proceeding on the assumption that good economics require the use of good materials. For example, fifty years ago, the State of New York every year mined thousands of tons of iron ore and turned it into iron and steel. The discovery and development of vast fields of a more economical grade of iron ore in Minnesota and other sections of the country forced the closing of the New York State iron mines. The raw materials did not meet the economic standard. By the same token it may have been profitable when land was first cleared to farm this land, but today, with the tremendous competition of good land in this country and in other parts of the world, it has become uneconomical to use land which does not produce good crops.

Therefore, we propose to find out exactly what every part of the State is capable of producing. From the surveys already made we have come to the belief that a certain percentage of the farm land in the State now under cultivation ought to be abandoned for agricultural purposes. I should not be surprised if that percentage ran as high as somewhere between 20 and 25 percent. We are faced with a situation of hundreds of farmers attempting to farm under conditions where it is impossible to maintain an American standard of living. They are slowly breaking their hearts, their health and their pocketbooks against a stone wall of impossibilities and yet they produce enough farm products to add to the national surplus; furthermore, their products are of such low quality that they injure the reputation and usefulness of the better class of farm products of the State which are produced, packed and shipped along modern economic lines.

If this is true in the State of New York, it is, I am convinced, equally true of practically every other State east of the Mississippi and of at least some of the States west of the Mississippi.

What then are we to do with this sub-marginal land that exists in every State which ought to be withdrawn from agriculture? Here we have a definite program. First, we are finding out what it can best be used for. At the present time it seems clear that the greater part of it should be put into a different type of crop which will take many years to harvest but which, as the years go by, will, without question, be profitable and at the same time economically necessary — the growing of crops of trees.

This we are starting by a new law providing for the purchase and reforesting of these lands in a manner approved by the State, part of the cost being borne by the county and part by the State.

Furthermore, a constitutional amendment will be voted on by the people this autumn providing for appropriations of twenty million dollars over an 11-year period to make possible the purchase and reforestation of over 1,000,000 acres of land, which is better suited for forestry than for agriculture.

We visualized also the very definite fact that the use of this sub-marginal agricultural land for forestry will, in the long run, pay for itself (we shall get that $20,000,000 back many times over) and will from the very start begin to yield dividends in the form of savings from waste. For instance, the farms to be abandoned will eliminate the necessity of maintaining hundreds and even thousands of miles of dirt roads leading to these farms, the maintenance cost of which averages about $100 a mile a year. The reforestation of these farms eliminates the need for providing thousands of miles of electric light and telephone lines reaching out into uneconomical territory. The reforestation of these farms will eliminate the existence and upkeep of many small scattered one-room schools which cost approximately $1,400 each per year to the State Government.

That is why we are confident that over a period of years this State planning will more than pay for itself in a financial saving to the population as a whole.

Modern society moves at such an intense pace that greater recreation periods are needed, and at the same time our efficiency, State and national, in production is such that more time can be used for recreation. That is increasingly evident in this particular year. By reforestation, this land can be turned into a great State resource which will yield dividends at once. The Conservation Commissioner has just issued an order throwing open for hunting and fishing the 25,000 acres recently purchased under this program and all additional reforestation areas when they are purchased.

These reforested areas are largely at the higher elevations at the headwaters of streams. Reforestation will regulate stream flow, aid in preventing floods and provide a more even supply of pure water for villages and cities.

We are asked what will be done for the population now residing on these sub-marginal lands? The answer is two-fold: In the first place, most of the comparatively small number of people on these farms which are to be abandoned will be absorbed into the better farming areas of the State, and, in the second place, we are continuing the idea of the statewide plan by studying the whole future population trend. That is where there is a definite connection between the city dweller and the population engaged in industry, between the rural dweller and the city dweller, between the farmer and the people engaged in industry.

Experiments have already been made in some States looking to a closer relationship between industry and agriculture. These take two forms: first, what may best be called the bringing of rural life to industry; second, the bringing of industry to agriculture by the establishment of small industrial plants in areas which are now wholly given over to farming.

In this particular connection the State of Vermont through a splendid commission seems to be taking the lead in seeking to bring industry to the agricultural regions.

For example, one of the large shoe manufacturing companies was established in a small New York village. Many of the workers live in this village and many others live in the open country within a radius of ten miles or more. Another example is a valley in Vermont where a wood-turning factory for the making of knobs for lids of kettles has already been so successful that the trend of the rural population to the city has been definitely stopped and the population of the valley finds that it can profitably engage in agriculture during the summer with a definite wage-earning capacity in the local factory turning out kettle knobs during the winter months.

As a Nation, we have only begun to scratch the surface along these lines and the possibility of diversifying our industrial life by sending a fair proportion of it into the rural districts is one of the definite possibilities of the future. Cheap electric power, good roads and automobiles make such a rural industrial development possible.

493

In other words, there are without question many industries which can succeed just as well, if not better, by bringing them to rural communities and at the same time these rural communities will be given higher annual income capacity. We are restoring the balance.

It is for these reasons that I have spoken so definitely of a third and new type of American life — the rural-industrial group. It is my thought that many of the problems of transportation, of over-crowded cities, of high cost of living, of better health for the race, of a better balance of population as a whole can be solved by the States themselves during the coming generation.

I have said "by the States themselves" because these experiments should and will be worked out in accordance with conditions which vary greatly in different sections of the country. We should not put all of our eggs into one basket. Some of the State methods of approaching the problem may not be economically sound in the light of future experiences, whereas others may point the way toward a definite national solution of the problem.

I remember many years ago when James Bryce was Ambassador in Washington, I as a young man had the privilege of attending a dinner, and after dinner the discussion came to the permanence of the American form of government. Lord Bryce, I remember, said this: "The American form of government will go on and live long after most of the other forms of government have fallen or been changed, and the reason is this: In other Nations of the world when a new problem comes up it must be tested in a national laboratory, and a solution of the problem must be worked out, and when it is worked out that solution must be applied to the Nation as a whole. Sometimes it may be the correct solution and other times it may be the wrong solution. But you, in the United States, have 48 laboratories and when new problems arise you can work out 48 different solutions to meet the problem. Out of these 48 experimental laboratories, some of the solutions may not prove sound or acceptable, but out of this experimentation history shows you have found at least some

494

remedies which can be made so successful that they will become national in their application."

So, as Lord Bryce says, the American people have 48 laboratories and with all of that competition and cooperation you stand in no danger of falling before the false solution of problems.

In all of this, the States require, of course, the sympathetic cooperation of the National Government as an information-gathering body. The National Government can well act as a clearing house for all of us Governors to work through, and I think that is the correct and most useful function of Washington. Instead of trying to run the whole works and to dictate methods and details to all of the States along some hard and fast program which may or may not apply in the different sections of the country, the National Government can help us in the several States to work out solutions which, in the long run, will get us somewhere.

I am very confident that during the next few years State after State will realize, as we have begun to do in New York, that it is a definite responsibility for Government itself to reach out for new solutions for new problems. In the long run, State and national planning is an essential to the future prosperity, happiness and the very existence of the American people. By those means I think we shall keep out of Westminster Abbey.

105 ⟨ Extemporaneous Address on Regional Planning (Excerpts). New York City. December 11, 1931

I HAVE only been back a few hours from a holiday a thousand miles away from here, down in the State of Georgia where I, too, have been doing some planning as to how to turn the corn fields into cattle pastures and corn fields into forests — planning in the rural sense. And I have come here tonight without any prepared address, but with the thought that I would not make a speech but

495

just talk to you offhand about some of the elements that have developed in regard to planning since the days nearly twenty years ago when Mr. Norton and my uncle, Mr. Delano, first talked to me about regional planning for the city of Chicago. I think that from that very moment I have been interested not in the planning of any one mere city but in planning in its larger aspects. . . .

I have been rather an explorer in the general thought of land utilization. We have heard very often that land is the basis of all wealth. That is true. It has been exemplified by many theories in regard to taxes by Henry George and by many others. But there is an addition to that theme which is actually true. Land is not only the source of all wealth, but it is also the source of all human happiness. Now, that is an important factor in anything ahead. Let me illustrate. How many people are there out of employment today in this country? Well, if you believe the Administration in Washington, four or five millions; if you believe their opponents, nine or ten millions. Take it half way between — a lot of people out of actual employment — and add to those twice that number to represent their dependents. Where do most of those people exist? Where do they live today? Where is the dependent unemployment in this country? I am now speaking in general terms, because there are thousands of exceptions that prove the rule.

Go through the smaller communities of this State, of New Jersey or Connecticut. You will find no starvation, you will find no evictions, you will find few people who do not have an overcoat or a pair of shoes, and in the same way if you go into the farming area, you will not find people starving on the farm. It may be true, there is suffering, there is deprivation but that is not the same kind of thing as being up against it and not knowing where you are going to sleep tonight, or where you are going to get the next meal tonight, in the smaller communities and on the farms, as you will find in the cities of the country. And so I venture the assertion, that at least three-quarters, and probably more, of the dependent unemployed throughout the United States exist today in the cities of the United States. That brings up the question as to whether we have not gone far enough in talking about the mere size of cities, whether we have not gone far enough in, what shall I call it, the old, now out-worn chamber of commerce idea of boosting. . . .

Is it not a false criterion? Are we not beginning now to visualize a different kind of city, with the possibility of a lower cost of living from having a greater percentage of our population a little closer to the source of supply? Some people will object and say that means more people putting out more agricultural products, and thereby increasing the existing surplus. . . .

And yet perhaps in the old days, regional planning could not have been done. We could not have avoided things because we did not have the facilities for fact-finding; we did not know enough about the elements of economics; we did not know enough about the changes in social progress to make any prognostication for the future or to lay down a plan that would be worth the paper it was written on for more than a few years to come. One thing we have learned from this work that has been done by this commission, the Chicago commission and the many bodies that have been organized and are carrying on splendid work all through the United States. We are learning facts, we are learning something about ourselves, many things perfectly obvious, now that they have been pointed out to us, and others perfectly new. I am wondering if out of this regional planning which is extended so widely throughout the country, we are not going to be in a position to take the bull by the horns in the immediate future and adopt some kind of experimental work basis on a distribution of population.

We know, from the point of view of economics, that every skyscraper that goes up in this town puts a dozen older buildings out of business. It is an addition to wealth on the one hand, but a decrease of wealth on the other.

We go glibly and gaily into new projects for more buildings without realizing that there is a limit beyond which we are cutting off more than we are adding on. And that is true not only in the city, but also in the suburbs and in the country.

497

I am convinced that one of the greatest values of this total regional planning is the fact that it dares us to make experiments. This country will remain progressive America just so long as we are willing to make experiments; just so long as we are able to say, "Here is a suggestion that sounds good. We cannot guarantee it. Let's try it out somewhere and see if it works."

Many years ago in Washington James Bryce came back here on a visit. I happened to have the privilege of attending a dinner. After it the men were sitting down in the smoking room talking about the governments of the world. We asked Lord Bryce what he thought of the permanence of government, and he said there would be many changes. This was before the World War broke out, but he said, "I conceive it to be a wise guess, that the American Government will outlive all of the other existing Governments of the world," and we asked, "Why do you say that?"

He said, "For this reason: Modern civilization brings and will bring constantly new social and economic problems, which will have to be met, by some solution of a new character, because the problems are new. In every other country in the world, there is just one laboratory for the testing of the experiment which must make these tests throughout the Nation, make it on a nationwide scale. You in America have a different system. You have one central laboratory, but you have forty-eight other laboratories. And these problems that demand new solutions can be tested out by you in these forty-eight laboratories. Some of the remedies will prove of no use, others devised in these laboratories will prove efficacious, and out of all these forty-eight tests, you will gradually evolve a national remedy to meet these new problems. Therein lies the advantage of America."

And so, I believe that this community, that the State of New York, and our sister States, Connecticut and New Jersey, are greatly to be congratulated upon the work of this Regional Planning Committee. It has opened our eyes to a new vista of the future; it has taken into account the social side, the economic side, the human side, and also the bricks and mortar side — the ports, the playgrounds, the highways, the transportation. Whether the environs of this city remain in the years to come with approximately the same population or whether they continue to grow, this regional plan will mark, I have no doubt, the foundation on which all building in the future will be based. Perhaps there will be changes. But to these men of great vision who have carried this great task to completion, we offer, and we owe, a debt of gratitude which will be repaid not only by us, but by our children and our children's children in all the days to come.

XIX

Subsistence Homesteads and Better Distribution of Population

THE POLICY enunciated in the papers in this chapter with reference to subsistence homesteads and better distribution of population was of course the same as actuated the later efforts of my Administration as President toward the same end. (See Item 100, Vol. II.)

In addition to the documents in this chapter, see also Item 18 on page 116, and Item 135 of this volume.

106 ❧ Address before the American Country Life Conference on the Better Distribution of Population Away from Cities. Ithaca, N. Y. August 19, 1931

IT is not often that I come before an audience with such hearty willingness and even eagerness as I have come here today. I have come not to make a speech, but to offer a proposal and to ask for help, and you have provided the right occasion and have permitted me to present what I have to say to those best qualified to pass upon it.

The experience and the aims of those present here bear in two ways on what I have to present. I am able to speak to those who for more than a generation have been concerned with the attempt to plan in a rational way the conditions of our living in America and at the same time to men and women who have been especially concerned with rural life and rural economic conditions.

Perhaps at times it has seemed to you, Dr. Bailey, and to your associates of President Roosevelt's Country Life Commission, that you have been prophets without due honor in your own country, but I think the time is coming when full honors will be paid to you. You have been pioneers in a work that has never been fully understood by all who should have understood it, but has steadily been working its beneficent effect on the conditions of life in America. To many there may seem something ironical in the fact that the quarter-century in which you have been working for improvement in the status of the country dweller has witnessed a huge transfer of population from farm to city and has seen our civilization transformed from one predominantly rural to one predominantly urban. But the improvement in the standards of living and the extension of comforts and conveniences to American farms and rural homes where at least a quarter of our population lives remove all semblance of irony from it. Education, health safeguards, lightened labor, greater comfort and enlarged social opportunities have come to the rural dweller and they have come largely through the ideas and labor of men of vision rather than by accident.

But I think the improvement in the conditions of rural life has an importance today which transcends the advantages it has brought in the past, great as these are. We have a new situation before us and new need of planning.

We are faced with conditions which cannot be disguised or evaded by optimistic platitudes and which constitute in the belief of sane, well-balanced people a major national crisis. We are about to enter on a third winter of industrial depression and the outlook is one of certain misery among our people on a huge scale. All classes of the population are affected. Prices of all agricultural products are depressed and as to some of the most important — wheat and cotton as major instances — the prices recently have been the lowest for all time, while as to some others markets are almost non-existent.

Wage scales in the cities are normally sustained comparatively well, but this is of no comfort to the huge army of unemployed, which promises to be far greater this winter than at any time in the nation's history, and although the economic difficulties of the farmers are grave, the greatest misery — the distress of lack of food and shelter and warmth — will occur among the industrial population in our cities. It is stating the situation but mildly and conservatively to say that it is viewed with the gravest apprehension and concern by all responsible people.

No one can say with assurance how long this crisis is likely to endure and that very uncertainty makes it all the more our duty not merely to give our support to measures for the immediate relief of unemployed men and women without instituting a dole of money, but to inquire with real energy and courage whether there is not something that can be done — some steps that can be taken either by private initiative or governmental action, or both — if not to prevent such calamities in the future, at least to palliate their effects. I have in mind a course involving private initiative and probably governmental action, which I wish to lay before you today. Let me make it entirely clear, however, that this is not a panacea and in my judgment no single remedy will bring the country as a whole back to normal conditions of employment. Rather must the Federal Government, with the hearty cooperation of State and Municipal Governments, work out a broad and comprehensive plan which will include many important efforts as component parts of the whole. That is why the suggestion I make today is to be considered as only one of many such components. As a prelude to what I wish to offer, let me tell you of an incident in my recent experience.

A few months ago I had a rather extended conversation with a prominent citizen in one of the western cities of our State who has engaged in raising funds for the emergency employment of idle men and for other measures of relief. He quoted figures — staggering and dismaying figures — of the number of heads of families in that one city who were out of work and seeking earnestly for any kind of labor that would bring them a little money to feed their dependents, but had been compelled to list themselves on the rolls of those needing public relief.

"Suppose," I said, "one were to offer these men an opportunity to go on the land, to provide a house and a few acres of land in the country and a little money and tools to put in small food crops — it was then early spring — what proportion of them do you think would accept such a proposition?"

"All of them," he said promptly.

From one point of view the reply merely served to add emphasis to what had been told me of the urgency of the plight in which thousands of families in that city and hundreds of thousands in the country at large found themselves. But I think there may be something more in it and that its implications are worth our very serious consideration.

In times of economic depression we expect to find a concentration of unemployed persons and, as a result, a concentration of distress, in the cities. It is so normal and so usual that it does not seem to merit comment. It is there that the floating industrial population has congregated. There are the headquarters and factories of the luxury industries and the activities that depend upon flush prosperity. There is not only the greatest market for labor, but the center of the forms of employment that have the least economic stability. There the marginal undertakings abound, the hothouse growths that feel the chill winds of depression first. And because there is a large floating labor population and a constantly heavy labor turnover, industry is perhaps a little more ruthless in the urban centers in cutting its payrolls and trimming its budgets to meet conditions of the moment.

It is in the city, and especially in the large city, that unemployment most quickly results in acute need and acute suffering. The urban worker must pay out cash for all he consumes. He is expensively fed, for it requires the labor of many people to supply him. His housing cost is based on high urban land values and heavy taxation. He must have daily transportation that is time-consuming and costly. And he is able to build up little if any reserve against emergency. . . .

Our urban industrial economy is fraught with tremendous perils, as we now see. The faster the wheels of the economic machine turn the greater the disaster when it meets impediments. We now hear the cry of the millions who clamor not primarily for bread but for a chance to work that they may earn their food and their shelter.

Is there no surplus in the production of these necessities of life by which unemployment workers may bridge over from the slack times to the good? If there is, it is not in their hands. We must call upon the generosity of those who have accumulated the means to buy in order to alleviate the distress of those who have not.

But there are surpluses, as we all know. Wheat was lately quoted in the principal markets at the lowest money price ever recorded for this important basic food, and a real price much below that when comparison is made with previous years of low grain prices. There is a great abundance of milk and an exceedingly low price. There are vegetables so abundant that it scarcely pays to take them to market. Our whole agricultural plant is geared to a basis of production more than adequate to feed the whole population abundantly. There are surpluses both of food crops and of the means of growing crops. Why should any hungry person lack food?

A part of the answer, I think, is implied in what I have said heretofore. The difficulty is not solely that purchasing power does not lie in the hands of those who need to buy and must buy to live. There is difficulty also in the fact that those who lack food and shelter are in the very places where it is most inconvenient and expensive for society to help them, for the cost of food in the cities is made up of many charges, the very least of which is the farmer's share in the production of the food supply. City workers must be fed on food transported to the cities and distributed there through an elaborate and highly systematized machine. Food in the country, at the farm, and food in the city are two very different propositions. One represents costs of production, or something much less than that in these times, the lowest price the farmer will take in a "seller's market" rather than permit his crop to rot in the field. Sometimes this is barely enough to pay for his labor in getting it from the field to town. The other represents mainly distribution costs. . . .

It is much easier to point out the anomaly, the economic unsoundness and the tragedy of this situation than it is to suggest any but a visionary remedy. We have had for decades past various "back-to-the-land" movements, but we have seen along with them a steady and continued increase in urban population as compared to rural. There have been good reasons for it in the constantly increasing efficiency of farming as an industry and the growth of agriculture surpluses which have constantly been forcing the less successful farmers to quit the soil and to take their chances in trade and industrial labor for hire. In the present situation of agriculture I do not think anyone could seriously suggest that we need to take men out of industry to put them to farming.

But the question I think we need to examine is whether we cannot plan a better distribution of our population as between the larger city and the smaller country communities without any attempt to increase or any thought of increasing the number of those who are engaged in farming as an industry. Is it not possible that we might devise methods by which the farmer's market may be brought closer to him and the industrial worker be brought closer to his food supply? A farm and a rural home are not necessarily the same thing.

Conditions have changed a great deal since the great rush of workers to the cities began. They have changed materially even since the war period. There have been great changes in means of transportation, changes in the conditions surrounding rural life and changes in industrial methods and facilities, all of which offer enlarged opportunities for rural living. . . .

It is no longer necessary that an industrial worker should live in the shadow of the factory in which he works, and as a matter of fact many of them do not. Especially where factories are situated on the outskirts of cities or in smaller communities the worker should have a wide range of choice for his home in terms of physical distance.

Industry, too, has been freed of a great many old restrictions as to location. It does not need to be located close to a water power, nor does it need to be located in most cases near a fuel supply. High tension transmission of electric current has opened a new era in the transportation of power. The application of electric current to industrial uses has made other advancements. It is not necessary any longer to use power in large quantities or units to use it effectively. The typical factory of a generation ago had huge steam engines driving great line shafts belted to a multitude of machines. Today in the typical installation every machine unit has its own motor and can be placed where it can be used most effectively and conveniently in the process of manufacture. Enlargement of a factory often can be accomplished merely by adding new machine units. In many lines of manufacture small factories have become more feasible economically than before and some large manufacturing institutions have found it advantageous to erect in scattered localities branch plants where a portion of their manufacturing processes is carried on.

Improvements in transportation, too, have had an effect on factory locations. Railroad facilities have been extended and improved to the advantage of lesser centers of population and in New York we have the great resource of the Barge Canal which brings cheap heavy transportation to many communities across the entire State, in effect almost making them seaboard points. The automobile, the bus and the truck have become as important in the transportation of finished products and in some cases of materials as in the movement of workers. Huge vans of manufactured goods travel great distances from factory to market on the public highways.

Communication time between factory and administrative offices and between factory and market has been shortened by telephone improvement and extension, and in this item of administration the automobile and improved highway again play an important part through the means they afford for quick travel from plant to plant and from an administrative center to a plant. Sources of supply of most raw materials, too, have been more widely developed and there is much better organization of facilities for distribution, this in spite of the fact that, in the case of many other products besides those of agriculture, there is still much too great a spread between production costs and consumers' prices due to the product's passing through too many hands from producer to consumer.

All of these circumstances seem to indicate that industry of its own volition is likely to seek decentralization. They seem to point to the probability that we shall see more factories established in small communities and in agricultural regions and fewer comparatively in the largest centers and in old manufacturing communities. Already there has been a trend in that direction. Factories have found it profitable to move from New England to the West and South seeking to divorce themselves from conditions for which their own individual management was partly but not exclusively to blame.

Industry has plainly been feeling its way toward something better in the way of factory location and what has been called for lack of a better term a "labor market," an expression whose implications I detest for the reason that it seems to ignore all human considerations. One of the difficulties of old-established industry today, I am convinced, is due to the fact that it has too often ignored social considerations, has failed to consider that success in industry must in the long run be built on cooperation of human beings on terms which will give all its workers a chance to live decently.

Certainly we want nothing more to do, if we can help it, with the factory town of the old type with its miserable tenements and box-like company houses built in grimy rows on dirty streets —abodes of discouragement and misery—although I could point out examples of the sort in our own State.

There is no doubt that social considerations have had a great part in keeping workers in the cities. City life has had its advantages as well as an attractiveness not based on any actual benefits. Our urban civilization is new enough not to have entirely outworn its lure and its novelty for a population that was once predominantly rural. But the advantages of city life today are less comparatively than they were ten years ago and they will probably continue to grow less, for city conveniences are very rapidly being brought to the country.

We have seen how transportation has reduced distances and made rural living practicable today where it was not a generation or more ago, in the days when the pattern of the factory town of the old style was devised. But there are a hundred other things that contribute to the comfort and practicability of rural living. There are electric lights and electric refrigeration, there are new methods of sanitation for rural homes, there are gas and electric cooking, there is the operation of household power machinery; there is the rural delivery of mail, including the parcel post which puts housewives in close touch with distant shops; there are modern consolidated schools equipped to supply as good primary and high school education as can be had in the city;

there are rural parks which furnish better playgrounds than city people can enjoy; there are the radio and the rural moving picture house showing the same films that the city workers enjoy and there is the opportunity for a freer and more natural community life than can be found in the city streets.

The country has added advantages that the city cannot duplicate in opportunities for healthful and natural living. There is space, freedom and room for free movement. There is contact with earth and with nature and the restful privilege of getting away from pavements and from noise. There is an opportunity for permanency of abode, a chance to establish a real home in the traditional American sense.

But, more than all this, there would be the great advantages for the worker of the opportunity to live far more cheaply and with a greater degree of economic security. The materials for healthful living in the country are cheap and abundant. Established in a country home in an agricultural district the worker, even if he were to grow nothing for himself, could buy a week's supply of healthful food for little more than a day's supply would cost him in the city.

With a considerable movement of workers from city to country there is every reason to believe that the total consumption of agricultural products would be greatly increased. City workers pay 16 cents for a quart of milk for which the farmer receives just now about three. It is well known by health authorities that the city consumption of milk is far less than it should be, that adults and children alike of workers' families would be healthier if they could afford to use more of it. The city price of one quart would buy them at least three in the country. Vegetables whose city price is made up mainly of the costs of many handlings could be obtained with like savings. City workers do not eat enough fresh green vegetables, mainly because they cannot afford them. Many families have them no oftener than twice a week when they should have them twice a day, and could have them that often if they were close to the supply.

The condition of the typical city worker is one of speculative living, with practically no safeguards against the disaster of un-employment that has now fallen on so many of his class. I believe our ingenuity ought to be equal to finding a way by which that condition could be swapped for one of stabilized living in a real home in the country.

Today in fact many city workers have become country dwellers. Both our great and our smaller urban communities are spreading out into the country. It is really surprising to find how many of our country villages are largely inhabited by men and women whose business activity is in some fairly distant city. What is painful about this situation is to see in how many cases families are finding rural homes without finding the real advantages of country living. They are paying more than enough for what they need and desire but are not getting it.

When I see the cheaper city type of houses built on narrow lots of some real estate development far out on the highway, many miles from a city limits, it occurs to me that those who have bought them have been betrayed and that there is urgent need of country life planning for city dwellers. . . .

It seems to me evident that the time has come for public authority to assert jurisdiction over housing conditions in the country and over the character and planning of rural real estate developments. We have precedent for this in the housing and zoning regulations of cities and a beginning of zoning authority in the counties. But I think, with competent advice, we should be able to go much further than this in moving toward an adjustment of the whole problem of distribution of population and the living conditions of workers in the State, which I have been discussing.

With that purpose I propose to appoint a Commission on Rural Homes, to be made up of a group of prominent citizens of the State, all of them having a record of interest in the improvement of social conditions, and to ask the heads of six departments of the State Government to serve with them as ex-officio members so that advice and data on various phases of the problems to be considered may be made available to the commission. Those whom I have asked and who have consented to serve on this commission include men and women with distinguished records of public service who will bring to their new task experience in dealing with housing problems, with conditions of rural life and with industrial affairs on a large scale.

The task I am placing before this commission is, broadly, to determine to what extent and by what means the State and its subdivisions may properly stimulate the movement of city workers to rural homes if such a movement seems desirable; to determine what facilities may be furnished by public authority to assist these workers in getting the right kind of homes in the right locations, and to inquire what encouragement may be offered for the movement of industries from urban centers to rural locations or the establishment of new industries in such locations if such a movement of industry seems desirable.

While the commission will govern the course of its own inquiry I have fixed in my own mind certain definite objectives which will serve to make the undertaking somewhat more concrete. These are:

1. That the commission be prepared to recommend legislation for village, town and county zoning for the whole State, but on a permissive basis, and for village, town and county permanent planning commissions.
2. That the commission explore the possibilities of the enlistment of private capital to aid in the establishment of rural homes within a reasonable distance of industry.
3. That the commission make recommendations as to experiment by the State alone or by the State with the cooperation and assistance of private capital in establishing wholly new rural communities of homes for workers on good agricultural land within reasonable distance of which facilities shall be offered for the establishment of new industries aimed primarily to give cash wages on a cooperative basis during the non-agricultural season.

If we find that the movement of workers to rural homes ought

513

to be encouraged, then it seems to me that we ought to find means of meeting the needs of those who wish to establish themselves in the country. Their requirements suggest themselves to me as follows:

First: Information as to the right type of home to build.

Second: Guidance and assistance in obtaining the most economical use of funds in acquisition and construction.

Third: Advice as to the right area of land to be acquired.

Fourth: Assistance in financing.

The question how best to establish agencies for providing service along this line is within the scope of the commission's task and problem as I have outlined it. I have no doubt that many specific plans for the establishment and organization of rural communities, extending possibly even to suitable types of architecture, layouts of roads and sanitary facilities, planting schemes and methods of community cooperation, will be suggested to the commission. These should furnish valuable data for such temporary or permanent agencies as may be set up as a result of the commission's recommendations.

It will be borne in mind that the objective is to furnish rural homes of an inexpensive sort for unemployed workers and those of small earnings, not to provide for the needs of those who are able to invest ten thousand to fifteen thousand dollars in a country home.

I think I scarcely need to say that this plan does not contemplate any coercive use of State power or any attempt to force either industry or private citizens into a fixed pattern of conduct. On the contrary, it involves merely cooperative planning for the common good. In that cooperative planning it will be essential, naturally, to seek the advice of thoughtful industrial leaders on the trends of industry as to location, character and seasons of employment, and to seek the advice of representatives of labor on other features of the proposal. . . .

While the membership of this commission is representative of the highest type of citizenship and of the sort of expert knowledge that, it seems to me, ought to be brought to bear on the solution of these great questions, I hope sincerely that the problem will not be regarded even for the moment as theirs and mine exclusively. I count upon their being able to call freely on others for advice and aid. I have learned in my own experience that there is a wealth of wisdom and good counsel and willingness to serve the public interest available to any administrator of public affairs who will but ask for it and I expect this commission to be the beneficiaries of that same generous spirit.

107 (Radio Address Advocating Distribution of Population toward the Source of Food Supply. November 13, 1931

I THINK we are all beginning to realize that some new factor is needed in our economic life as a Nation. We are beginning to find that mere drifting is not enough. We are finding that the changing play of economic forces as we know them inevitably leads us to hardships that take the rank of great disasters, which affect all of us and bear most severely on those who have worked faithfully and unquestionably — people who have depended on the leadership of the powerful to find them continuous work.

We are generally agreed today that things are somehow out of balance. It does not need any deep thinking to come to that conclusion. The bald facts are that the natural means for providing plenty of sustenance for all are still abundant. We have the resources of soil and other forms of productivity; we have the knowledge and we have plenty of trained labor. Of most commodities necessary to life and comfortable living we seem even to have a surplus. The producers cannot sell all the goods they would like to make, nor can they buy the goods they want to buy.

What is this lack of balance and how is it caused? The question is one that must occupy every thoughtful mind today. It stands as a challenge to our ability to think.

It is a familiar fact to all of us that this Nation has changed in a relatively few years from one predominantly agricultural to one predominantly industrial. A century ago seventy-five percent of the population lived on farms and twenty-five percent in the cities. Today the figures are almost exactly reversed. There is an explanation, of course. Farm industry has been converted into factory industry. But any suggestion that the pendulum has swung too far brings a prompt rejoinder. It is pointed out that our farmers now produce more crops than they can sell to advantage, that farmers only a few weeks ago were being compelled to let go of their wheat for less than the actual money they had put into its production, and that the situation was the same with respect to all other crops. That is true enough, but it is equally true that the same thing could be said for many forms of manufacturing, and it is also true that the carpenter and the stonemason and the structural iron worker and the machinist—all manufacturers in the broad sense—are frequently unable to sell their labor and their skill, which are their only products, for any price at all.

Let us look one fact in the face. I do not want anyone to think that I am picturing American agriculture as being prosperous—the reverse is true. Nevertheless, when we read statistics that six million or eight million or ten million Americans are out of work do we stop to consider where they are out of work? It is undoubtedly true that the overwhelming majority of these millions of unemployed are living in the cities of the country.

What does unemployment in the city mean? It means that the whole family is not only out of work and out of cash, but is also out of food and is threatened with losing a roof over its heads.

That brings about as serious a picture as we can well imagine —a picture of human misery.

There are unemployed people in the agricultural sections of the country, though they total only a small minority of the whole of the unemployed, and I think it is fair to say that with certain exceptions most of these people in the country are not faced with actual starvation or actual eviction. In other words, while their situation is bad, thoroughly bad, most of them will in some way get through the winter.

I, therefore, come back to the thought that while agriculture is in a thoroughly bad way, actual distress and starvation and lack of fuel and lack of clothing exist primarily in the cities of the Nation. That is where the great bulk of our millions of unemployed is concentrated.

If we accept the theory that in so far as our industries are concerned the present problem is one of distribution — in other words, of distributing to the ultimate consumer the products of industry — then we face the immediate difficulty that population itself is up against the problem of distribution. In other words, the proper distribution of the products of industry cannot be solved until we do something to solve the proper distribution of the population who will use the products.

Let me give you a simple illustration.

A farmer ships milk to a great city two hundred miles away. He gets three cents a quart for his milk. After it has been handled by the milk station and refrigerated and again handled by the railroad and after it gets to the big city and is trucked first to the central distributing point and then delivered either to the home or to the retail store, the cost of handling plus two or three profits on the trip make the mother, the father and three or four children in the city pay fifteen cents a quart for that same milk.

How many quarts of milk can the city family afford to buy at that price? Obviously, very little milk. This inability to buy milk on the part of families who have jobs is aggravated by the total inability to buy on the part of the hundreds of thousands and even millions of families who are wholly out of jobs.

Is it not true that if many of these city families lived a great deal closer to the dairy farmer they could get their milk for half what they are compelled to pay now? Is it not also true that if many of these city families lived nearer the farmer they would consume a great deal more milk, because the same amount of cash would buy more milk?

This situation as to milk applies to nearly all agricultural products. It is a fact that the per capita consumption of farm products in this country has decreased greatly in recent years. The market for what the farmer produces might be very greatly increased if we could find a way to bring more consumers closer to the source of supply. That is something decidedly worth thinking about.

That is why in this very brief talk on the undoubted fact that industry and agriculture are out of balance today I want to propound two simple questions.

The first is this. Is it worthwhile for us to make a definite effort to get people in large numbers to move out of cities where there are thousands and hundreds of thousands of unemployed and bring these people closer to the actual sources of food supply? It seems to me that to that question we must answer an emphatic *yes*.

The second question logically follows the first: What steps can be taken? It seems to me that the answer is this: First we must try to work out a definite plan by which industry itself will seek to move certain forms of industry out of the congested centers where unemployment is greatest into the smaller communities, closer to the primary food supply.

At least it is worthwhile to recognize the fact of the over-population of many of our urban centers, and to try to find some practical means to restore the balance.

XX
Reforestation and Conservation of Natural Resources

108 ❡ Radio Address on the Conservation of Natural Resources as a Function of Government. March 31, 1930

R EAL conservation of our natural resources as a function of State Government is only about twenty years old, although some attempts at it were made sixty years ago. When the country was settled, there appeared to be no need of conserving the forests, the fish, the game or the waters. Within the boundaries of what is now New York State, practically all that was not water was virgin forest — 29,000,000 acres of it. Game was abundant in the forests; and fish, in the streams and rivers. As far as natural resources were concerned, the early settlers really suffered from an embarrassment of riches. Conservation was distinctly not one of their problems. The forests not only were cut to supply the settlers with lumber and wood, but they were burned to clear land for planting and settlement. Fish and game were the common food; "butcher's meat" was a rarity. Two centuries of unrestricted and prodigal use failed to reduce this great natural wealth sufficiently to warn the people that it was not inexhaustible.

One of the first to sound a note of warning was Governor De Witt Clinton. In 1821, when the population of the State was a million and a half and increasing rapidly, he foresaw the need of more intelligent use of the forests, if the economic welfare of the State was to be maintained. In a message to the Legislature he called attention to the fact that we were cutting our forests with no policy of replacement and pointed out the need of such a policy. It took the State sixty years to catch up with Governor Clinton's understanding of the situation and then in 1885 there was established a State Forestry Department. Fifteen years later the State began in a small way a policy of forest replacement by planting 5,000 trees in the forest preserve. From that small beginning we have progressed steadily until there have been planted over 200,000,000 trees from stock raised in the State nurseries, and are now planting more than 25,000,000 each year. I am a firm believer in reforestation as a profitable means of utilizing idle, non-agricultural land and have planted from 8,000 to 10,000 trees a year since 1912 on my farm at Hyde Park.

Sixty years ago the State took its first step in the conservation of wild life by organizing a Fisheries Commission consisting of Horatio Seymour, Seth Green and Robert B. Roosevelt. A few years later a few game protectors were added to this commission and there was built up gradually a Fisheries, Game and Forest Commission. In 1909 the State took over the work of protecting the forests in the Forest Preserve counties from fire and today has a forest fire protective system covering more than 16,000,000 acres and including all the large forested areas in the State.

Conservation grows as the people realize the need of it. Thirty years ago, the Palisades of the Hudson, those rugged cliffs of sheer rock that form one of the most striking scenic features of the lower Hudson, were being converted into trap rock at a rate that insured their speedy destruction. The movement to save the Palisades resulted in the establishment of the Palisades Inter-State Park by New York and New Jersey, with 45,000 acres of mountains, woods and lakes, containing some of the wildest and most rugged scenery to be found in the eastern United States. This great park within less than an hour's ride of New York City, has repaid its cost many times over in the healthful recreation it has afforded the people of New York City during the hot months.

Niagara Falls, America's greatest cataract, Mecca of brides and grooms for nearly a century, was fitted into the State's conservation policy in 1909 when the State Reservation at Niagara was established to preserve the scenic beauties of the Falls.

The State Forest Preserve was established in 1885 and ten years later its integrity for all time was insured when the people wrote into the State Constitution the provisions that it should be "forever kept as wild forest land." The Adirondack and Catskill parks which contain the bulk of the Forest Preserve were established in 1892. Together, they include, roughly, 4,000,000 acres, about half of which are owned by the State. All State-owned land within the Forest Preserve counties belongs to the Forest Preserve whether inside or outside of the parks. The Adirondack Park is the largest State Park in the United States and is larger than any of the National Parks except the Yellowstone. Within the boundaries of these great parks are the State's highest mountains, and the forests on their slopes protect the sources of the State's principal rivers.

It is as a great hunting ground and playground that the Forest Preserve is best known to the public. These great areas with a total acreage larger than some of our neighboring States provide safe and sanitary camping grounds for hundreds of thousands of vacationists every summer who seek the big woods to live close to nature. States all over the eastern half of the country contribute their quotas of campers from late June to early September. This development of forest conservation was started ten years ago as part of the forest fire protective system. Stone fire places were built at attractive places along highways and trails that hunters and campers might have places to build their camp fires without endangering the surrounding forests. The popularity of these public camp sites was immediate and the demand for accommodations at them increased tremendously from year to year. Today many of them will accommodate a population equal to a good-sized village. An abundant supply of pure water, carefully guarded against pollution, is the prime essential at all of these sites, and a forest ranger is in charge of each to see that the camps are kept sanitary and that the regulations regarding fires are obeyed. The Forest Preserve is the home of the State's big game and yields from 7,000 to 10,000 deer each fall with a few hundred bears thrown in for good measure.

In 1911, New York State coordinated its various conservation activities. The Conservation Commission was created and took over the functions of the Forest, Fish and Game Commission and the Water Supply Commission, and since then all conservation work has headed up in this body now known as the Conservation Department. New functions have been added from time to time as conditions required. In 1909 the State took over the remarkable collection of mineral springs whose medicinal waters had made Saratoga Springs famous as a health resort. The springs under private ownership had been pumped for carbonic acid gas to such an extent that many of them had ceased to flow. Under State ownership the pumping for gas was stopped, many of the wells were capped and a scientific study was made to ascertain the amount of water that the wells and springs could be depended to produce without impairment. In 1915 the Saratoga Reservation was placed under the jurisdiction of the Conservation Commission and administered as a division of that body. Water from the restored springs was supplied free to the public at its source and mineral water baths and hydrotherapeutic treatments were given. Patronage of the baths increased from 10,000 in 1915 to 100,000 in 1927. This year a survey of the reservation has been made by a commission to prepare a plan for a broader and more scientific use of the waters with a view to making it a cure center under strict medical direction. This commission was assisted by eminent medical specialists of the United States and Europe and reported a plan under which the drinking of the waters and the taking of the baths will be regulated by competent medical authorities to suit the needs of the individual patient.

Seven years ago the State undertook the development of a unified system of State parks, the purpose of which was to preserve and protect places of scenic and historic interest and also provide adequate recreational areas near large centers of population throughout the State. This movement was initiated in 1923 with the organization of the State Council of Parks and upon the reorganization and consolidation of the State Government in 1926 was made part of the work of the Conservation Department, as the Division of Parks. Today, New York State has a system of State parks extending from the eastern end of Long

Island to Niagara Falls. In the development of a State park program there were taken into consideration the anticipated growth of the State and especially of the larger cities, the need of great parking areas serving the metropolitan districts, the enormous increase in motor cars, and the further conservation needs of the State.

The State is divided into eleven districts, or regions, each under the immediate direction of a park commission. These regions in order are: *(Here followed a detailed description.)*

In the conservation of our natural resources, the intelligent cooperation of the public is of great importance. The laws that are made for the protection of the State's wild life are based upon biological knowledge and if strictly enforced, can be depended upon to prevent the extermination of any species. Knowledge of these laws by the public and cooperation with the duly constituted authorities to prevent violations of these laws tends steadily to raise the standard of wild life conservation.

Everyone can assist in protecting the forests from fire by being careful with fire and smoking materials themselves when in the woods or passing along the highways through the woods, by urging care with fire on the part of others and by promptly reporting fires or violations of fire regulations to the nearest forest ranger.

Not everyone can participate in the tree planting activities of the State, but there are still many thousands who have land not good enough for raising agricultural crops that is suited to growing trees and could be made profitable by reforestation. Forests are valuable not only as a source of timber supply, but they protect the head waters of our rivers and streams. They prevent the too rapid run-off of rain and melting snow and tend to equalize the flow of streams. They return to the land more than they take from it and maintain its fertility. On the watersheds that supply drinking water they are an effective aid against pollution. They are essential to maintaining a supply of wild life — birds, beasts and fish — furnishing homes for the wild birds and beasts and insuring a constant supply of water for the streams.

109 ❪ Radio Address Urging Voters to Support the Reforestation Amendment to the Constitution. October 26, 1931

IN ACCORDANCE with custom I am giving my personal views to the voters of the State on the six amendments to our constitution on which a referendum will be held on Election Day this year. . . .

I come now to an amendment which I regard as of the very greatest importance to the people of this State. This is Amendment Number 3, the reforestation amendment. There has been a great deal of discussion of it and there seems to be some confusion as to just what it means, but after all it is a simple proposition. The amendment puts before the people for their approval a program for the reforestation of idle and unused land in the State — land that is classed by soil experts as useless for agricultural crops because it cannot be cultivated profitably in competion with the good lands of this State and other States.

Surveys have shown that there are close to four million acres of this kind of poor land in the State — land once used for farming but now out of use; and these poor, hilly farms are being abandoned at the rate of a quarter of a million acres a year. But the one way in which this land can be used profitably is in the growing of forest trees. The reforestation program embodied in Amendment Number 3 proposes that the State shall buy a million or more acres of this abandoned land and put it to work.

We are just beginning in this country to wake up to the fact that we need timber and that we need to think of the future. For centuries European countries have been renewing and caring for their forests so as to get the maximum of benefit from them. They treat timber as a crop. We treat our timber resources as if they were a mine, from which the ore can be taken once and once only. The United States is using timber today four times as fast as it is being grown. In New York State, the largest consumer of timber of all the States, we are using it twenty times as fast as we are growing it. We have to haul the bulk of our supply from distant States in the West at a cost of $40,000,000 a year for freight — and even that supply is not going to last forever.

So there is the situation. We have plenty of abandoned farm land on which timber can be grown profitably. We need the timber and will need it more urgently as time passes. Shall we not put this idle land to use to produce it? And incidentally shall we not give employment to many people in the work of planting and caring for these young trees?

New York State, because of its great area of land suited for growing trees and its need of timber, should logically lead other States of our country in this form of intelligent utilization of soil resources. Efforts have been made in this State to encourage reforestation by individuals and communities and counties. The State has been growing in its nurseries young forest trees for planting which have been sold at cost and State aid has been granted for county forests. But the results accomplished have been small in proportion to what needs to be done.

So a commission of eleven, four chosen by the Temporary President of the Senate, four by the Speaker of the Assembly and three by the Governor, of which Senator Hewitt was made chairman, started to study the question in 1928. The commission unanimously worked out what is known as the enlarged reforestation program, which is embodied in Amendment Number 3. This amendment was first passed by the Legislature of 1930 and then by the Legislature of 1931 and I am happy to say that it was considered on a perfectly non-partisan basis, both Republicans and Democrats, leaders and rank and file, giving it their support. Senator Hewitt, who has given his time devotedly for several years to studying and working for reforestation, is here tonight to join me in urging you to vote for this amendment.

Now just what does the amendment propose to do? In the first place it sets up a schedule of appropriations which the Legislature is directed to make over a period of eleven years. The appropriations begin at one million next year and rise gradually

527

each year until they reach two millions. By the way, one million is only one-third of one percent of the State's annual expenditures. The aggregate sum to be appropriated in eleven years is nineteen million dollars. This program, it is estimated, means that not less than a million acres of abandoned farm land and probably considerably more, can be bought and reforested. The small start already made indicates plainly that this result can be achieved.

We are asked why it was thought necessary to include this fixed schedule of appropriations in the amendment. The answer is that it was partly for the sake of obtaining the express approval of the people of the State on the whole program and more definitely for the sake of assured continuity. We must provide nurseries next year for trees to be planted four or five years later. We must obtain land by contract and give time for careful examination of titles before taking possession and planting it. Our whole plan of operations must be suited to the size of the job we have to do. The work cannot be done in hand-to-mouth fashion.

The principle is not new. We have in the last few years morally committed future legislatures to spend specific sums for important social projects. Examples of this are the amendments to the constitution approved by vote of the people, one of them calling on the Legislatures for ten years running to issue bonds and to spend $10,000,000 each year or a total of $100,-000,000, for parks, schools, hospitals and other public improvements; the other was the amendment practically telling the Legislature to spend, from time to time, up to a total of three hundred million dollars ($300,000,000) for the elimination of grade crossings. This year's proposal is a drop in the bucket in comparison with those other two. By the same token when the Friedsam Act for increased State aid to public schools was enacted a few years ago, the Legislature morally bound future legislatures to constantly increasing appropriations, for education, running to a vast sum. Under this Act this State aid to education has risen from $43,000,000 in 1925 to $110,000,000 in 1931. This sum of $110,000,000 means spending each year five and one-half times the total which it is proposed to put into the reforesting of abandoned lands over a period of eleven years. It is true that these constitutional amendments and the Friedsam Act were in form permissive to future legislatures, but I am frank and clear in saying to you that each succeeding Legislature and every member thereof would not dare to go against the expressed will of the people.

Let me clear up once and for all any doubt or fear that the splendid Adirondack or Catskill forest preserves are in any possible danger or are even affected. There is confusion over two wholly different kinds of land.

Please draw a mental picture: sixteen great counties of the State — twelve of them lying between the Mohawk and St. Lawrence and extending from the Vermont line to past Utica, the other four extending from just south of Albany and the Hudson River over to the Pennsylvania line — are known as forest preserve counties. They contain over one-third — nearly one-half — of all the land in the State.

Within these sixteen counties lie two inner areas, one known as the Adirondack Park and the other as the Catskill Park. These inner areas are bounded by what is known as the blue line. Within this blue line not one stick of timber can be cut from State land and not even a twig can be removed, and Amendment Number 3 absolutely reaffirms this State policy in language identical with that used in the constitution at the present time.

What, therefore, does the amendment accomplish? Outside of the Adirondack and Catskill Parks, but still within these sixteen counties, lies one-quarter of all the idle land in the State — not timber land but abandoned farm land.

Under the existing constitution any trees planted on this abandoned farm land would be locked up forever and could not be used for the future benefit of the people of the State. All we seek to do is to put this abandoned farm land to work, including not only the abandoned farm land in the outer margins of the sixteen forest preserve counties but similar land throughout the State.

Heretofore our conservation policy has been merely to preserve as much as possible of the existing forests. Our new policy goes a step further. It will not only preserve the existing forests but create new ones.

I want every man, woman and child in this State to understand this simple point. This amendment does not affect a single acre in the Adirondack or Catskill parks or a single acre now owned by the State in the sixteen bordering counties. Every one of these acres and any future acres to be acquired in the Adirondack or Catskill Parks will be guarded against cutting just as jealously as hitherto. You can take my solemn word for that. What we do seek is to buy abandoned farms outside the Adirondack and Catskill Parks and to make these now useless acres produce a splendid crop of trees for the use of our grandchildren. Remember that these tiny trees will not come to maturity for two generations and in the meantime every year we waste by failing to plant means a greater shortage of timber.

We shall not have to look to the distant future for all the benefits to men, women and children which will flow from this policy. There will be immediate gains. The young forests will clothe what is now barren ugliness with the beauty of new growth. They will serve to prevent soil erosion and floods. They will contribute to purifying water supplies. They will be used also for public hunting areas and for the propagation of game. Already 30,000 acres of the areas planted in the last two years have been thrown open by Conservation Commissioner Morgenthau for this purpose.

There will be still another gain which warrants the prediction that this nineteen millions will be returned to us many times over. These areas of unfit land now call upon the taxpayer for money to support roads and little one-room schools. They draw upon the consumer's purse for the expense of electric light and telephone lines. They default in their tax payments. Remember please that land in proper use is, in the last analysis, still the basis of the prosperity of a State. I want to build up the land as, in part at least, an insurance against future depression.

Thus it seems to me that reforestation as proposed in Amendment Number 3 is a sound business policy and represents besides a moral duty which we owe to ourselves, our State and our children. I ask your support of this amendment.

XXI
Banks and the Protection of Depositors

110 ❡ A Message to the Legislature for the Protection of Thrift Accounts in Commercial Banks. March 24, 1931

To the Legislature:

THERE are now pending before your Honorable Bodies a number of bills which have been introduced at the request of the Superintendent of Banks. Some of these bills relate to the administration of the Banking Department in connection with its supervision over the banking institutions of the State. Other bills seek to increase the powers of the superintendent to protect the depositors of the State from unsafe banking conditions and unsound banking practices.

I know that your Honorable Bodies will appreciate the fact that these bills were proposed by the superintendent in the light of the experiences of the department during the last two years of financial stress. They are based upon conclusions reached by the Banking Department after a close study of conditions affecting the soundness of our banking institutions and bearing upon the protection of the moneys of the depositors of the State. They are the result of earnest study and consideration, and I hope that they will receive further attention from you before the close of this session. The responsibility for strengthening the banking laws rests with you.

But there is another subject covered in the legislation proposed by the Superintendent of Banks, which as a matter of principle directly and immediately affects one and a half million actual depositors out of the thirteen million people of the State: this is the better safeguarding of the thrift accounts owned by these one and a half million people.

I need hardly point out to you that so-called thrift accounts in commercial banks originated from the permission given by the Federal Government to the national banks of the country to engage in this business. Our State, along with other States, followed suit in order not to penalize State banks. It was expected,

535

however, and the original intention of this extension of the powers of our commercial banks was, that only a small percentage of the existing depositors would avail themselves of these facilities, chiefly as a banking convenience to themselves.

Contrary, however, to the original intention, the number of thrift depositors has grown to stupendous figures and the proportion between them and purely commercial depositors has increased beyond all expectation. This increase, of course, has been fostered actively by the commercial banks themselves by advertising and by encouragement of all kinds to the people of the State to open thrift accounts with them.

What, then, is the issue? It is the simple and inescapable fact that in the mind of the average layman, especially the man and woman of limited wealth, there is no nice distinction between thrift accounts and savings accounts. In their minds both are methods for safeguarding and getting a small return on their hard-earned savings. They assume, wrongly perhaps, but none the less naturally, that their thrift deposits are being protected by our State laws in the same way as the deposits of their neighbors who have put their savings in savings banks.

The deposits in thrift accounts can, under existing laws, be placed by the officers of State banks in almost any form of investment. They have a choice as wide and as elastic as for commercial deposits. In savings banks, however, deposits in savings accounts can be placed only in certain types of investments strictly outlined by law. The issue, if thrift accounts are innocently confused with savings accounts by the average depositor, is whether or not the savings bank type of safeguards should be extended to thrift accounts.

I believe that it is nothing more than ordinary good faith to the public that the Legislature at this present session do something to initiate the safeguarding and protection of these thrift accounts. The people of the State not only expect it, but they have a right to demand it. The time to do it is now. Any further delay is inexcusable, and in my opinion is a breach of the trust which the depositors of the State have in their legislative bodies.

The method to be followed is a question for the technical consideration of your banking committees. There is no need for any further investigation of the facts; they have been before the Legislature, in one form or another, for two years, ever since the failure of the City Trust Company in 1929.

It has been obvious for a long time that something should be done; and various plans and suggestions have been advanced to accomplish this end. It is a matter of grave concern to the State that every one of these suggestions advanced has been strenuously opposed by some of the banking interests themselves, though I believe that a majority of our bankers admit that something must be done. So far there has been visible only a campaign of opposition not only to this bill but to the other remedial bills offered this year by the Superintendent of Banks.

At the same time no plan of their own is offered by the banking interests. There is only a continued prayer for delay. To my mind continued delay is not only unwarranted; it is wholly against the public interest. If the banking interests themselves had some substitute plan to correct the evils and dangers which lurk in our banking laws, more reliance might be placed on their wisdom. By merely blocking all reform, as they appear to be doing this year with your Honorable Bodies, they discredit any claim that their efforts are accompanied by any sincere desire to protect the depositors of the State.

I trust that your Honorable Bodies will reconsider the arbitrary action which has been taken so far with reference to all plans which deal with the protection and safeguarding of the depositors' moneys in thrift accounts.

111 ❲ A Message to the Legislature Requesting Additional Facilities for Supervision and Examination of Banks. March 23, 1931

To the Legislature:

I TRANSMIT herewith a copy of a letter received by me today from the Superintendent of Banks. It is in every way the duty of the Legislature and of the Governor to cooperate with the Banking Department in meeting the existing emergency relative to the adequate supervision and examination of all State banking institutions. The recommendations of the Superintendent of Banks, included in this letter, fall under two heads. First, he requests an immediate special appropriation to the Banking Department, to be made available for adding examiners and other employees to his staff. You understand, of course, that all of this money is returned to the State under the Banking Law by the institutions themselves, so that additional examiners and additional employees do not cost the State a single penny. Second, the Superintendent requests an alteration in the methods of appointing and employing the necessary staff.

I shall be glad to cooperate with your Honorable Bodies in regard to the necessary legislation; and I am very confident that the Civil Service Commission will give its hearty cooperation in formulating necessary changes in the rules, regulations and statutes relative to this situation. I know that you will understand the extreme urgency of these matters and the grave responsibility resting upon us to attend to them.

XXII

Annual Radio Reports to the People on the Sessions of the Legislature

THROUGHOUT my Administration as Governor I made very generous use of the radio not only to keep the people of the State informed as to the progress and activities of their State Government, but also, in many instances, to obtain the support of the people for legislation in their interest.

I have selected for this chapter only a few of these radio talks made by me during my Administration. Others, on special subjects, may be found in this volume in the appropriate chapters. Many others were made, for which space was not available in these volumes, including a weekly series of broadcasts after the 1932 session of the Legislature, in which I reported separately in weekly addresses on the workings and the cost of each of the departments of the State Government.

These radio talks are somewhat similar to the radio reports which I have made as President, and which the press has called "Fireside Chats."

112 ❨A Radio Report to the People on the 1929
Session of the Legislature (Excerpts).
April 3, 1929

THIS is in the nature of a preliminary report to the
people of the State on the results of the legislative
session of 1929. As a statewide elected official I feel
I have a distinct duty to keep the people of the State
informed as far as possible as to what goes on in the
State Government, and I am very mindful of the fact that I am
the Governor not just of Democrats, but of Republicans and all
other citizens of the State. That is why this talk and the one
which I hope to make next week will be, just as much as I can
make them, non-partisan in character. I want merely to state
facts and leave the people of the State to draw their own conclusions. . . .

Politically we have two major parties and in State campaigns
each of these parties sets up a so-called platform, giving to the
people of the State a definite statement of what the party proposes
to do in the way of legislation, if it is returned to power.

I want to talk tonight principally about these party platforms
and the promises in them made by both parties to the people of
the State as to what they would do at Albany this winter. Let us
see if these promises have been kept or broken.

It is fair to ask the question at this time, "Has the Republican
party which is in control of the Legislature carried out its promises to the people made last Fall or has it even attempted to do so?"

The same question in regard to the Democratic platform can
properly be put to the Governor as representing the promises
made by the Democratic party.

Unless the responsible party leaders at least make an effort to
carry out the party platform, the platform becomes a meaningless document and might just as well be discarded entirely. To
put it even more strongly a platform which the leaders do not
even attempt to carry out is a fraud and deceit on the voters of
the State of New York.

541

Take up first of all the platform adopted by the Republican Convention at Syracuse on September 29th last year. At that convention the same set of individual leaders wrote the platform and had it adopted as have been responsible for the doings of the Republican majority in the Legislature during the past three months.

Now the most important thing about any promise and particularly about any political promise is whether or not it is made in good faith and in the very first declaration of this solemn pledge to the people made by the Republican party in convention assembled, we find this paragraph:

"We condemn the spirit of waste and extravagance which permeates the present Democratic administration."

Then follow the figures of the State's expenditures last year as compared with 1919, with a closing reference to "the past six years of mounting revenues and profligate spending."

This means that the Republican leaders who drew up this platform wanted the people to think that the State is spending more money than it should and that they intended to cut down these expenses and eliminate what they vaguely term "extravagances." First of all let me make one point clear. The amount of money spent by the State is determined entirely by the Legislature. The action of the Legislature depends on the votes of the party in the majority. The majority party last year fixed the appropriations as recommended by those at the head of the two finance committees. The same gentlemen were among the master minds who drew up this platform. If they really believed that the State had spent too much money, they were condemning themselves and their own party. The Governor has no power to appropriate a single cent of the State's money. He can only veto or reduce what the Legislature decides to be the proper sum. Did these gentlemen really believe that they had been extravagant and had spent more money than was needed for the State? Did they really feel that they could get along with less money this year? Is this paragraph a sort of public confession of incompetence and waste on their part, a sort of figurative sitting in sackcloth amidst the ashes of repentance? Let us judge by what has happened.

The appropriations objected to as too large in 1928 were in round numbers $232,000,000.

This year the same gentlemen have returned to the Governor's desk after weeks of study of the requests of the department heads as the minimum sum required for the next fiscal year appropriations aggregating more than $265,000,000. Is any better proof needed of the insincerity of at least this section in the Republican platform? Now let us see about the rest.

The Republican leaders promised to do something to change what they called our patch-work tax system. That promise was wholly neglected and as a matter of fact in the tax changes which they have proposed they have increased the unsoundness of the present system.

We come next to the Republican platform promise, "To continue this constructive program to meet all our social needs * * * to provide proper care and training for our dependent children, to develop those mentally and physically afflicted to make the most of themselves, to protect women and children in industry and to care for the dependent wards of the State." Let us see what attempt was made to fulfill this pledge. For many years legislation has been sought to secure for women and children in industry a minimum wage or more recently a so-called fair wage. This is in no sense a partisan measure and was advocated by leaders of both parties. It had the support of citizens of all political faiths. Again this year there was introduced a fair wage bill, but the Republican majority in the Legislature, entirely forgetting this pledge, refused even to allow it to be reported out of committee and to receive fair and open discussion in the two houses of the Legislature. Several years ago we placed on the statute books, after a long fight, in which the opponents of the measure were some of the same Republican leaders, a so-called forty-eight-hour law for women in industry. This law was not properly named because it was in effect a forty-nine-and-one-half-hour law. Various attempts have been made to secure a real forty-eight-hour law and this year again a bill for that purpose was introduced. On March 22nd when it became apparent to me that the Republican majority did not intend to let this bill or the fair wage bill or any substitute for them out of committee, I sent a special message to the Legislature hoping to spur the majority leaders to favorable action along these lines. In that message I said that modern social conditions have progressed to the point where such demands as these can no longer be regarded other than as matters of an absolute right. The Republican majority refused to allow the bills even to come to a vote on the floor of the Legislature.

This same section of the Republican platform pledges these legislators who were elected upon it to make adequate provision for the care of the dependent wards of the State and promised a more general distribution of hospital and clinical facilities provided by the State. I pointed out to the Legislature that it would be necessary if we were to care for these dependents properly next year either to issue $50,000,000 in construction bonds, or to impose some new or additional tax in the next year's session of the Legislature. . . .

I am sure that the people do not want increased taxes and I am sure the Republican leaders in the Legislature will be opposed to any such increase next winter. There is no sound reason why hospitals of the type we are now building should not be paid for by the issuance of bonds and the cost thus distributed over part of the life of the buildings.

What happened? My message was read in both houses of the Legislature and bills which were introduced to cover the subject were referred to the finance committees. The Republican leaders refused to give even serious consideration to this need now facing us, and allowed the bills to die in committee.

One of the major problems which is still confronting the State is the development of the valuable State-owned water power resources. This issue has been in the forefront in several State campaigns. There have been differences of opinion as to the course which this development should take, but on one point nearly everyone is agreed, and that is that the ownership of these water power sites should forever remain in the people of the State and that the electricity generated at these sites should be available for the use of all the people and for the development of our State industries at the lowest fair cost. The Republican platform declared for "sound policies in the development of water power which will adequately protect the consumer." Not a single move was made by the writers of this platform to put forward any program, sound or unsound, of water power development, in this session of the Legislature. The Republican majority seem to have lost all interest in this subject. In keeping with my pre-election promises, however, I submitted to the Legislature a program which I believed to be a solution of this problem. The Republican leaders in the Legislature put through a resolution for adjournment without even considering it.

I wish particularly to call to the attention of the people of the State the record of the Republican majority in this session of the Legislature with respect to labor legislation. The Republican platform declares that "The Republican party in this State has done more for Labor than any other party. The labor law and the workmen's compensation law are conceded by labor to be the best in all the States * * * The Republican Legislature has established a commission which has considered and is now considering necessary and beneficent improvements in the Workmen's Compensation Law and all other labor laws and we pledge our party to give full consideration to the recommendations of this commission."

I shall refrain from characterizing this pledge in the light of what happened at Albany this winter. I merely give you the facts and ask you to draw your own conclusions. It is true there has been a legislative commission considering improvement in the Workmen's Compensation Law. That commission submitted its report to the Legislature and made certain recommendations, most of which did not go far enough but which were at least a step forward. The Republican leaders decreed the death of these bills and, then going still further, failed to continue the life of the commission of which they were so proud when they wrote this platform last fall. Not only did they not give full consideration to the recommendations of this commission which they promised, but they were not even willing that the commission should continue its investigations and at the next session submit other and perhaps more suitable bills.

But there were other measures before the Legislature in which labor is vitally interested and which received the same treatment. Most of these other measures were not new, but have been advocated year after year. Neither are they partisan in any sense and they should not be treated as partisan measures by the majority, merely because they have the support of the Democratic minority, particularly in view of the Republican platform pledge. These measures included a bill providing that preliminary injunctions in industrial disputes shall be issued only after a hearing; a bill providing that the labor of a human being shall not be deemed a commodity, and the extension of the Workmen's Compensation Law to all recognized occupational diseases. These measures would extend the necessary protection of the State to those who labor; they are, as I said, matters of absolute right. . . .

I would like to talk a little about the Democratic promises and how we have tried to keep them, but there will not be time to consider this tonight. I must save this subject for the next time that I address the voters of the State. Tonight I wanted to call attention not only to these broken promises of the Republican leaders but to the indefensible way in which most of them have been broken. It would have been bad enough, if having made these promises and secured the votes of at least some of the electorate because of them, they had started out to make their word good by seriously considering and debating measures intended to cover the platform's pledges, and then voting not to do it. But this Legislature cannot by any possible twist of the English language be described as a deliberative body. Measures which would have gone far to make the Republican word good were never allowed to come

546

out of committee for discussion on the floor. This is particularly true of most of the labor legislation. Not only were Democratic bills thus buried, but even proposed Republican legislation. This is un-American and contrary to the whole spirit of our Government. A Legislature is supposed to consider all suggestions of importance, to debate them with an open mind and to pass or reject them according to the arguments for and against which are presented. Under the despotic rule of the chairmen of important committees, bill after bill has been buried in the committee's file, and any attempt to force the committee to report it has been defeated by the lash of the party whip upon the backs of the members of the majority.

For all practical purposes this year's Legislature consisted of the chairmen of a few committees who in most cases have themselves been acting under orders from others, and the majority of the members of the majority party have been merely rubber stamps to register other august wills. I hope the people in this State will realize how completely undeliberative this Legislature has been and that they will insist next year that their representatives sent to Albany, whether they be Democrats or Republicans, will really represent their districts, have minds of their own, and insist on free discussion of important questions and their right to vote as their conscience and their judgment lead them to believe is desired by those who have elected them to the Legislature. I am sure that a clear expression on the part of the voters that this is the sort of legislators they really wish will bring about a complete change in this respect.

If this year's plan of preventing all discussion, of waiting until the last minute before even reporting such measures as the Republican leaders conclude to allow to go through, so that they are hurried through with hundreds of other bills by a mumbled roll call, without any attempt at honest debate, is to be next year's procedure, the fault will lie with the voters of the State who in selecting their candidates take no steps to make it plain that they are to be more than dummies voting "aye" or "no" dutifully when so told to do.

547

113 ❰ A Radio Report to the People on the 1930 Session of the Legislature (Excerpts).
March 26, 1930

THIS is my second radio report to the people on the work of the Legislature this year. I had expected to tell you something more of what has gone on at Albany before this, but I am sorry to say there has been little of consequence to report to you until now. The reason for this may be found in the procedure which our Legislature still follows and which I referred to several times last year as "antiquated." There has been a slight improvement in this regard at the present session, but for the most part, our law-making machine still moves with the speed of an ox-cart in the age of the fast automobile and the airplane.

I have not changed my views with respect to the need for reform in our methods of making laws. In fact, my early experience as a member of the Legislature and my more recent experience with the last Legislature and the present one have convinced me that not only is this reform needed but that sooner or later the people will demand and secure it. . . .

In this connection let me remark that I have felt compelled to veto a large number of local bills which would have increased local government cost for no apparent good reason. Some of my friends of the other party on the "third floor," which is our designation for the Legislature at Albany, have been annoyed by the veto of their pet bills. You may have noticed something about that in the newspapers, but I am sure that the taxpayers who would have had to pay for these salary increases and relatively unnecessary expenses of other sorts are not going to worry so much about these vetoes.

A few of these local bills were designed to cut the cost of local government in certain localities and these bills I signed most readily. One, for instance, relieved Herkimer County from the obligation to furnish and maintain a horse and cow for the sheriff.

However, I am not so much concerned over the fact that the Legislature has to bother with these unimportant local bills, as I am about the system under which the important legislation is considered. Last year I made several appeals for open consideration on the floor of the Legislature of those measures in which the people are really interested. I believe that any bill of state-wide interest which has the support of a considerable number of our citizens is entitled to be reported out of committee and debated on the floor of the two houses. It is our theory of democratic government that minorities shall have a voice in the making of our laws and that every legislator with a meritorious bill shall have the opportunity of trying to convince the majority through a free discussion of its provisions that it should become law. That makes for a deliberative parliament which our Legislature is supposed to be. . . .

I said a moment ago that there has been a slight improvement in the manner of law-making this year. I referred to the debate on the State Budget Bill. It may seem an extraordinary thing to some of my listeners who are not familiar with the method of appropriating money for the support of the State's vast business activities, to learn that never before in this generation has the appropriation bill been debated in detail in the two houses of the Legislature.

Here is what has happened in the past. The chairmen of the Finance Committees of the two houses — in the Assembly it is called the Ways and Means Committee — and latterly the Governor, have prepared a general appropriation bill, which we now call the budget because we are operating under the budget system. The committees would hold no real hearings on the bill, the two chairmen would make their own amendments and then report it out. Well, the budget bill this year had 635 printed pages and never before did the average member of the Legislature, Senator or Assemblyman, even open its covers. There were just two men in the whole State who knew what was in the bill. They were the chairmen of the two committees.

This year we deposed the czars of the budget. I do not mean by that that we took any of their powers away from them, but for the first time there were members in both houses who on the floor asked questions concerning every change made in the budget as submitted by the Executive. Every increase or decrease was scrutinized and the finance chairmen were called upon to explain, out in the open, for public record, why they made the recommendations they did make.

Now, I think this is a very healthy thing. Of course, I do not expect my friends, the two chairmen, to agree with me, for it caused them a few hours of discomfort and inconvenience but it did result in a better understanding of State finances on the part of members of the two houses on both sides of the aisle. . . .

There has been a lot of talk this winter, most of it political, about our prison problem. It has been said the State lacks a prison program. That I emphatically deny. A program we certainly have.

This program is divided into four definite parts:

The first part is the physical one. The State now has four great State Prisons—Sing Sing at Ossining; Great Meadow at Comstock in Washington County; Clinton Prison at Dannemora in Clinton County; and Auburn in Cayuga County. A fifth prison at Attica in Wyoming County is under construction and this present Legislature will authorize surveys and options for a new prison site, to be located somewhere within about 75 miles from New York City.

The plan for the use of these prisons is clear. First of all, it is proposed to use Sing Sing as a sort of a clearing house where prisoners will go after conviction and where they will be sorted out and given the most careful study in order that they may then be sent to other institutions to fit the needs of the individual case. The new prison, the site of which we shall pick this year, will be designed primarily for real first offenders, especially the younger men; it will be conducted more as a school than a penal institution.

The next prison will be Great Meadow to which will be sent

the next grade of prisoners and especially those having comparatively short sentences to serve.

The third prison will be that at Auburn to which will be sent what might be called the middle type of offenders. The other two prisons, Dannemora and Attica, it is planned to use for the more serious type of offenders. This definite physical building program cannot, of course, be carried out in one year but will take three or four years of legislative appropriations to complete. The actual details of construction must, of course, be decided to fit each year's program. For instance, with the proposed use for each of these prisons must come plans for industrial and farm work for the prisoners. The details of this plan will be worked out this summer by a special committee for presentation to the next Legislature.

The second part of the general prison program is the establishment of a permanent and reorganized parole system. The Legislature is about to pass an excellent law for the creation of the new Parole Board which will consist of three full-time commissioners and an adequate staff of parole officers. In this way we hope that this State will take the lead in the reconstruction of those unfortunate people who have committed crimes of various kinds but who must, if it is humanly possible, be restored to useful, honest lives in the community.

The third step in the prison program is the working out of segregation of prisoners by classes. This is an intricate problem never before tried in this State. A special commission will report on this this summer and its program will be made to fit the number and types of actual institutions which the State has. It must be remembered, of course, that the State has an enormous amount of money invested in existing prison buildings and we must utilize them to the best advantage in view of the fact that it is impossible to scrap them all and start everything anew. Furthermore, in this question of segregation, we must remember it is not a rule of thumb matter. For instance, the State must receive a prisoner who is technically a first offender, in that he has never been a prisoner of the State before. Nevertheless he may have a long, criminal history and a proved tendency to commit crime. At the same time the State may receive a boy who has been in several reformatories but who may be of the type that can be made to go straight, if properly educated, trained and looked after by the State. Let us not forget that these are new problems which must be worked out over a period of years, for we have little experience in this matter of segregation of types.

The fourth part of the prison program is the development of proper industries and trades, and occupations for the prisoners. It is not a sufficient answer to set prisoners to work on manufacturing automobile plates or furniture for the State offices, regardless of the individual characteristics of the prisoners. Furthermore, we plan a system by which prisoners will receive more pay than the 1½ cents a day which they now receive for their work in the prison shops. There are three objectives. The first is to give the prisoners healthful occupations; the second is to give them useful occupations; and the third is to make it possible for them either to help support their families or to save up enough money in prison so that when they leave they will have more than the $10 which the State now gives to the men who leave its custody.

One word in regard to the so-called old-age pension bill. I am glad to say that this measure is about to become a law even though I do not think that the commission which drew it up did the very best job of it.

The trouble with the present bill is two-fold: First of all, it allows too much discretion to the local authorities throughout the State, thus failing to provide a uniformity of treatment and allowing individual local factors to creep in to too great an extent. The aged poor, no matter what locality they come from, should have exactly the same kind of consideration and that is why I want a more centralized control by the State Department of Social Welfare in Albany.

My other objection to the bill is that it smacks too much of a mere extension of the present poor laws. A real system of old-age security against want should not have the word "charity" written all over it. Both from the point of view of the old people themselves, and from the point of view of encouraging savings, we should have started this year some system of contribution by the younger men and women in every walk of life so as to build up for their old age not merely a guarantee that they will not be allowed to starve, but also a guarantee that they will be able to live in some kind of comfort in their old age. Progress comes slowly, of course, and I feel that this law is, at least, a step, even though a small one, toward the desired goal.

I am glad to say that there was passed the bill which I consider may in the future be the outstanding accomplishment of this Legislature. This is the bill to take the first step toward the development of the State-owned electric power resources of the St. Lawrence River. When the smoke and dust of partisan speeches clear away, the people of this State will realize a simple fact.

This fact is that the Legislature has after many years of delay, opposition and muddying of the waters, authorized the Governor to appoint five commissioners or trustees who are charged with the primary duty of trying to bring in a definite plan based on a definite policy. The policy is that a direct agency of the State to be known as the Trustees of the St. Lawrence Water Power, shall build a dam, generate the electricity and see that it is sold to the consumer at the lowest possible rate. That is the plain English of the policy and within the next few weeks I shall appoint the five commissioners. I certainly hope and am very confident that their efforts during this summer and autumn will result in a practical plan under this policy so that the people will at least get cheaper electric light and power in their homes.

In closing may I remind you that from now on, our political brethren will be flooding the State with all sorts of wild statements, some with a mere color effect and others made out of whole cloth. You will remember, I know, that this is because we are going to have a State election this fall. It is a pity for the sake of orderly government that we are compelled to have State elections every two years. As you know, I have always advocated elections every four years and that those elections should come in the year half way between Presidential elections. At least this much can be said for the election this fall, that it relates wholly to State officials, and Presidential and Federal policies should not enter into the State campaign in any shape, manner or form.

114 ❧ A Radio Report to the People on the 1931 Session of the Legislature (Excerpts). April 24, 1931

IN ACCORDANCE with what I have made an annual custom during the past two years, I am making this brief report to the people of the State, summarizing the results of the legislative session that has just closed. I take it that the average man and woman in our State have read the highlights of what has taken place in Albany since January first, but I take it also that you will be interested in having me tell you in broad terms of what the Legislature did and what it did not do.

First of all, however, let me make it clear that this is not in any shape, manner or form a partisan plea for though it necessarily represents my own point of view, I shall try to be just as fair as I possibly can in stating the pros and cons of the various problems of public policy with which the Legislature and I have had to deal. . . .

Let me summarize the more important things that the Legislature actually did do — twelve fairly brief résumés of legislation.

1. I place first of all in importance the passage of the bill creating the Power Authority to develop the State-owned water power on the St. Lawrence River. It is my earnest hope that this is the forerunner of cheaper electricity for the homes and farms and small business people of the State.

2. The Legislature took the first steps to carry out the new prison policy of the State, such as authorizing the machinery for classifying and segregating different types of prisoners, appropriating money for the medium security prison and restoring the premium for good behavior in the prisons. I am sorry though that

the Legislature, through a disagreement between the two Houses, did not change the mandatory life term for fourth offenders, without regard to what the offences were.

3. The Legislature recognized the new State policy of utilization of land. This involves continuing the land survey covering the whole State; it involves the program for reforestation of idle lands, and the beginning of the elimination altogether of the poorer land from agriculture.

4. A part, only a part, of the fine health program was adopted and the State will start to build this year the first of the three new regional tuberculosis sanitaria, covering a great many counties in the central and western part of the State.

5. The Legislature took two small steps toward the better regulation of public utilities, for it passed a bill to place bus lines under the control of the Public Service Commission, and another bill to place private water companies also under the control of the Public Service Commission.

6. The Legislature used the first $20,000,000 of the bond issue that was voted last fall, for the State institutions' building program and it added $10,000,000 to this from general revenues. The result is that we are starting this year $20,000,000 more of new hospitals for the insane and $10,000,000 more of new prison facilities. This is carrying out the five-year program which I suggested and proposed two years ago, and we are keeping faith with the people of the State with the purpose and object of having complete facilities for patients and prisoners in actual operation by the year 1935.

7. After five long years of talking and turmoil the Legislature at last has given the necessary authority for the unification of the Rapid Transit system in the five boroughs that make up New York City. Now it will become possible for all of these facilities to be tied together in a practical operating whole, with the hope, of course, that nearly all of us have, that the five-cent fare can be retained for the nearly 7,000,000 people in the greater city.

8. After two years of negotiation with the New Jersey authorities, we have made it possible to consolidate the Hudson Tunnel,

which has been in very successful operation for several years, with the other projects of the Port Authority, thus assuring uniform tolls in this tunnel and in the 38th Street tunnel and on the new Washington bridge across the Hudson River. Incidentally, by refinancing the money which the State put into the Hudson Tunnel during a long course of former years, the treasury of the State has received $24,000,000.

9. In line with this same effort to cooperate with other States, the Legislature authorized the appointment of a Commission to study the question of the pollution of the beaches of Long Island, of the New York and Connecticut shore line and of the New Jersey shore, this commission working with similar commissions set up by our sister States of Connecticut and New Jersey. . . .

10. The Legislature authorized also a new commission to investigate the whole subject of unemployment and this commission will, I am confident, also study and report on the suggestions heretofore made in regard to unemployment insurance. I may add that the Governors of New York and six other States in this neighborhood have cooperated very well and all of the States are making with us a joint study of unemployment insurance. We hope that something practical, safe and sound can be worked out along this line so that in the event, in the days to come, we pass through another period of depression like this one, the real suffering and the real want and the depression itself will not be nearly so serious as in the period we are now going through.

11. A very definite step forward was taken by the Legislature in passing amendments to the law protecting women in industry, something that we have been fighting for in the State for many years, and now we have a statute which comes very close to providing for an enforceable forty-eight-hour week, together with a half holiday every week for working women.

12. Finally, the Legislature has undertaken an investigation of governmental conditions in the City of New York and the two appropriations to carry this out have been approved by me. The total of them is one-half a million dollars. . . .

Now I suppose it is fair to look at the other side of the picture — in other words, the things which this Legislature ought to have done and failed to do. There are a few which I have listed here. I have spoken of 12 of them before and I shall go through them very briefly.

1. The Legislature, outside of the bus and water company bills, did absolutely nothing to strengthen the control of the State over public utilities. Even the very weak recommendations of the majority of the legislative committee which reported a year ago, have not been carried out and there seems to be on the part of the majority a complete disregard in those legislative halls of the real need of strengthening the hands of the Public Service Commission, and of giving to the commission the proper tools with which to meet new problems which have come up during the last few years by mergers, holding companies and other devices on the part of the utility companies. . . .

2. Purely local political considerations prevented the Legislature from even authorizing a commission to study the broad subject of the reorganization of local government. I am convinced — and more and more people every day are convinced — that while the Federal and State Governments are operating on a fairly efficient business basis, the great governmental waste today lies in local government, in city and town and county government. This is where the great bulk of our taxes goes to; that is where tax savings can be most readily made. Let me give you just one example. Under a very old law in our State the supervisors, one in each of the 960 towns of the State, get a rake-off, a 1 percent fee for school building moneys contributed by Albany to the local school districts. All the supervisor has to do is to deposit one check received from Albany and draw another check, and for this important service he gets 1 percent of the amount of the check for himself. He does not even have to do all of that. In many cases, all he has to do is to sign his name on the back of the check and turn it over to somebody else. Some supervisors get several thousand dollars in a year for this small act and they have no further responsibility for the expenditure of the money. A bill to cut off this 1 percent fee failed of passage in the Legislature, but if it had

passed there would have been a saving to the taxpayers of the State amounting to over $130,000 each year. Political influence on the part of local politicians was responsible for the defeat of that bill, but the real blame lay with the members of the Assembly and Senate in listening to this political influence and in failing to have the courage to put through this big saving for the taxpayers and end this rake-off for the supervisors of the towns.

3. Although the splendid commission of doctors, educators and laymen headed by President Farrand of Cornell University recommended the establishment of county health units throughout the State, the majority leaders in the Legislature absolutely declined to pass the bill. . . .

4. In spite of a tremendous demand from millions of people in every part of the State the majority leaders declined to take any steps whatsoever to give further immediate protection to thrift accounts in the State banks. . . . In view of the fact that the Legislature had all the necessary facts and data for studying the subject for two whole years past, it seems almost a dereliction of duty on the part of the legislators that they have deferred this great and important reform for another twelve months.

5. For a long time — five whole years in fact — we have had no legislative reapportionment, even though it is called for by the Constitution. The majority leaders made absolutely no effort even to report out of committee an apportionment bill for senators and assemblymen, even though I begged them to come down and talk it over with me. I knew if they would do that, we would agree on a constitutional bill. There is a grave injustice at the present time toward hundreds of thousands of our citizens. . . .

6. Some congressional districts only have 210,000 inhabitants and others have nearly 350,000. Certainly that is not the intent of the Congress or of the Constitution of our State. For instance, the majority leaders put Suffolk county, at the easterly end of Long Island, into the same congressional district with Staten Island, which is at the westerly end of Long Island, thus leaving a long gap of land and sea between the two parts of this district,

and in that gap are situated a number of other congressional districts.

7. Although the whole State has been shocked by the conduct of some of our judges the Legislature wholly failed to pass two bills which I considered of great importance to the integrity of the judiciary. The first of these was a bill to prevent judges from engaging in private business, and it seems to me that is a perfectly logical and proper measure. The second was a bill to prevent public officers from claiming immunity if called upon to testify in regard to their official conduct, and that seems to me a perfectly proper measure. Both of these bills were approved in principle by the leaders of both political parties, and yet by one of those strange circumstances which cannot always be explained, neither bill got past the Legislature in the closing days.

8. The Legislature wholly failed to provide for the continuation of the Governor's Committee on Stabilization of Industry and Relief of the Emergency of Unemployment. There is nothing I can do about it but I am asking the members of this committee to continue to serve unofficially and without funds for expenses during the coming year, and I hope we can raise the money from private sources to carry on this important work. The committee has done fine work for unemployment relief and the only reason for the failure of the Legislature to give the committee official standing must be the fear of letting me have any credit for the relief of unemployment.

9. The Legislature for an equally unexplained reason failed to do anything to regulate employment agencies through a State agency. Everyone who has studied the subject believes that grave abuses have existed in some employment agencies in the State and there is no reason why they should not come under State regulation.

10. Equally unexplainable was the failure of the Legislature to provide a special bureau in the Department of Labor for the enforcement of the eight-hour day, the enforcement of the prevailing rate of wages law, and the enforcement of the citizens'

preference law, giving preference to New York State citizens in employment.

11. Once again, a Legislature has adjourned without taking any action on the four-year term for Governor proposal with elections held halfway between presidential years. All I have asked it to do for the past three years was to submit this proposition to the voters by referendum, but apparently the legislative leaders are afraid to do even that.

12. Once again, also, the Legislature has declined to enact changes in the election law so as to take certain political and partisan elements out of it. . . .

This then constitutes the summary of legislative action during the past three months. I certainly cannot be truthful in saying that the session was a brilliant success from the point of view of the inhabitants of the State of New York; nor would it be fair of me to say that the Legislature has done nothing. It is my constant hope that as the years go by we shall have, first of all, an improvement in the actual methods of handling proposed legislation — a fairer and freer discussion on important measures, the elimination of a great deal of outworn, time-wasting machinery, and the application of less partisanship in the consideration of bills into which partisanship ought not to enter at all.

I myself hope, after another week of cleaning things up here in Albany, to take a holiday too, but it will only be for a very few weeks, and I shall then be back on the job in Albany around the first of June. At that time I shall have the whole of the summer before me and I expect to do as I have done the two previous summers, to travel through practically every county of the State, visiting State institutions, parks and other projects, going to as many different communities as possible and getting away also as much as possible from the atmosphere of party politics, which I do not believe is a very necessary atmosphere for a Governor to be in except possibly during the months of the legislative session.

Many of you who are listening to my voice I shall hope to have the pleasure of meeting during the course of the coming summer and in the meantime I am very glad to have had this chance of talking to you. I hope to see you very soon.

XXIII
Miscellaneous

115 ❧ A Message to the Legislature Advocating the Initiative and Referendum. March 23, 1929

To the Legislature:

THERE are pending before your Honorable Bodies two proposed constitutional amendments designed to bring closer to the people of the State, control of their State and Federal constitutions. I refer to Bill Senate Print Number 356, Assembly Print Number 415, providing that amendments to our State constitution may be directly initiated by the people themselves, and to Bill Senate Print Number 355, Assembly Print Number 428, providing that any proposed amendment to the constitution of the United States must be submitted to the people before approval by the Legislature of the State.

These measures have for many years been urged by a great number of our citizens, but the leaders of the majority party have refused even to permit them to appear on the floors of your respective bodies for consideration and debate. They must of necessity be submitted to the electorate before they become effective, and I cannot understand the reluctance of the majority party to permit our electorate to express its will on these matters.

I urgently recommend the passage of this progressive legislation granting the people at least a right to say whether they desire a larger share of control over their fundamental law.

116 ❧ Radio Address Urging a Bond Issue for the Construction of State Hospitals and Other Institutions (Excerpts). March 27, 1929

As a result of legislative appropriations at this session it seems clear that at the end of the next fiscal year, that is to say, on June 30, 1930, our State will have a surplus of only about $5,000,000 instead of the surplus of $39,000,000 which we expect to have on June 30th this year.

The chief reason for this is very simple. Out of this coming year's income from taxes of all kinds the State will expend about twenty million dollars for the erection of all kinds of State institutions and buildings such as hospitals, prisons, normal schools, agricultural colleges and so forth and so on.

In other words, the surplus will be greatly reduced, because we shall be drawing on the previous surplus and during the following year we shall not have a big balance upon which to draw.

That means that we shall be at least twenty million dollars short during the following year and it is only fair and right that we should look ahead and discuss ways and means for the following year.

Of course, it would be possible but extremely unwise a year from now to stop building hospitals as I shall explain in a few minutes. If the State could curtail its expenditures, we should be all right. Probably the actual running of the State departments will not go up but under a mandatory law we have to spend next year about eight million dollars more on education than this year and we also have to finish a good many tasks undertaken. The only possible way of saving money next year is by cutting out all appropriations for buildings to house the wards of the State.

I have a very distinct and definite idea that the people of this State are wholly unwilling to fall down in their care of these unfortunate people, mental defectives, for whom the State has always cared. Since 1846 in part and fully since 1889 the State of New York has taken care of these unfortunates.

What is the situation today?

In the State hospitals there are at the present time 10,000 more patients than the hospitals were designed to house. . . .

What does this overcrowding mean? First, in some of the hospitals it means that the space is so limited that beds are actually touching each other side by side, that patients in order to get into bed have to crawl over the foot, that proper standards for air space and floor space must be ignored, that toilet facilities and service of meals in the dining rooms are overtaxed.

It means that in some instances patients must sleep on mattresses placed on the floor for lack of space in which to place beds. It means that this overcrowding increases the chances of accidents and injuries to the patients.

It means that the individual patient cannot have the individual attention and active treatment that he or she is entitled to, and it means that the physicians and nurses cannot produce the best results under such adverse conditions.

Dr. Parsons, the head of the Department of Mental Hygiene, well says: "Unquestionably, overcrowding reacts in the direction of a lowered discharge rate and an increased death rate."

The State is rendering a splendid service to these mentally defective people. Even with the present overcrowding we are curing about twenty percent of them and if we had better conditions for treating them this percentage would increase.

It is an interesting fact that the economic loss to the State — the dollars and cents loss — by reason of mental disorders is four times the cost of caring for one patient. This means that every cure of a patient, every restoration of one of the patients to a normal field for useful activity, pays the cost to the State for taking care of him and three other patients.

The result is that whether we look at this problem from the broad ground of humanity and sympathetic interest or whether we look at it from the dollars and cents point of view of economic value, the result is the same. The State must and will care for those who are properly its wards.

Now, what is the situation, present and future? First of all, we are actually building hospitals which when finished will have a capacity of 7,000 beds. When these hospitals are finished we shall only be 3,000 beds short if we figure on the same number of patients we are caring for today.

But, unfortunately, the total number of patients is increasing at the rate of nearly 2,500 a year. This is due in most part to the simple fact that the population of the State is itself increasing at a fast pace. If somebody could invent a way to limit the population of the State of New York we should not have to put up any new hospitals. That, of course, is an absurd proposition and we must prepare now for the future, because of the very simple fact that we cannot build a hospital in a month or a year.

At the present rate of increase, counting the beds for the necessary nurses, attendants and employees, we shall be nearly 20,000 beds short of the required number by 1936.

The situation was bad enough in this State in 1923 when the last bond issue for hospitals was approved by the people of the State. All of that money has been either expended or is now being expended on actual construction, but the situation will be worse than it was before unless we take immediate steps to prevent an even more serious condition a few years from now.

That is why I have been giving this subject a great deal of study during the past month. I have taken the matter up with the legislative leaders during these past few weeks and the problem resolves itself into two possible solutions.

First of all, it is very clear that if we continue to build these hospitals next year out of current tax receipts, the Legislature will have to pass a law next year putting a new tax on the backs of the people, or else increasing one of the old taxes. That is what is known as the pay-as-you-go plan, which was threshed out and killed a number of years ago by the intelligent opinion of the people of this State.

In other words, it was made perfectly clear to the people that the buildings now being erected for the care of the wards of the State will last as useful structures as hospitals for at least 75 or 100 years. If a private business corporation were putting up these permanent structures that corporation would certainly not try to pay for them out of the current earnings. They would pay for them by issuing bonds running, say for 30 years, a percentage of these bonds being paid for each year. Good business methods prove this to be the right plan.

Why then should the State try to pay for permanent buildings wholly out of its current income? It seems obvious to me that what is good in private business as a principle is also good in State business. There is no reason why the State cannot properly pay for these new hospitals out of a bond issue, the bonds to be paid for over a period of perhaps 30 years.

If we do not issue bonds there will be no escape from a new tax or an addition to an old tax. Personally, I am just as much opposed to raising current taxes as are most of my hearers. Obviously, the State has to balance its budget each year and cannot spend money which it has not. Therefore, next year, if we are to continue with the erection of hospitals out of current tax revenues, we must make those revenues larger and impose additional taxes.

On the other hand, a bond issue will, I think, make the imposition of new taxes next year unnecessary. Even if the people approve on election day the bond issue of fifty million dollars which I am proposing, the bonded indebtedness of the State of New York will be very low compared with that of most of our sister States. The State has a low debt and can well afford to issue fifty million dollars worth of bonds. Incidentally I might add that the credit of the State of New York is of the highest and our bonds sell in the market on a very low yield basis, in many cases less than 4 percent. That means that the bankers and the public have a very high regard for the stability and the credit of the State of New York.

That is why I have asked the Legislature to approve the submission of the question of a fifty-million-dollar bond issue for State institutions to the voters this autumn. I sincerely hope that the Republican leaders will in this particular case, which is certainly not involved in politics and should not be, approve of this recommendation. Unless this Legislature takes action before it adjourns, it will be too late as the question could not be submitted until a year from next autumn. In that event you and I, as citizens of the State, must look forward to an increase in our taxes next year. . . .

The State of New York has a proud record in the care of its wards. We are the model of many other States of the Union. We do not want the present overcrowding to continue nor do we want a repetition in this State of the terrible tragedy which recently occurred in a nearby State when about 200 inmates were burned to death. I am very confident that the people of our State will approve the continuation of our sound financial policy and of the progressive modern care which we give in our hospitals. That is why I want your support for the proposal to submit the question of issuing bonds to the voters at the coming election.

117 ⟨ A Message to the Legislature on Classification of Civil Service Employees. February 10, 1930

To the Legislature:

I HOPE that before the next session of the Legislature a scientific plan may be formulated to improve the present somewhat chaotic condition surrounding the salaries, grades and duties of officers and employees in the civil service of the State. We should recognize the justice of the demands of the many thousands of State civil service employees. A thorough survey of the whole field is needed.

I suggest to your Honorable Bodies the creation of a commission which will not only investigate and study the whole subject of the salaries, grades and duties of the State civil service employees, but will also make possible the remedying of the existing situation in time to be included in the budget which will be prepared by me this year.

Representatives of the employees have called to my attention a resolution introduced in the Legislature, calling for a report by a commission on or before February 15, 1931. I desire to call to your attention in this connection the fact that the budget is made up from the requests of the several department heads submitted before October 15th to the Governor and revised by him during November and December. It is, of course, clear that in this budget the proposed expenditures must be made to balance with the financial condition of the State treasury. Obviously if a committee report is not made until February of next year it cannot be included in the Governor's budget this year, and the relief to the employees cannot go into effect until 1932, the year after next.

It is not fair to the employees to ask them to run the chance of an eleventh-hour available State surplus. The revision of their salaries, grades and duties should become effective as soon as possible.

May I therefore suggest that if any action is taken by your Honorable Bodies, looking to the appointment of the commission, such commission be directed to make a preliminary report, with the necessary figures, to the Governor, on or before September 1, 1930, in order that I may include the figures in the budget totals? In this way the recommendations of the commission can be acted upon this year.

118 ⟨ Radio Address on States' Rights.

March 2, 1930

I HAVE been asked to talk about the respective powers of the National and the State Governments to rule and regulate, where one begins and the other ends. By some curious twist of the public mind, under the terms "Home Rule" or "States' Rights," this problem has been considered by many to apply, primarily, to the prohibition issue.

As a matter of fact and law, the governing rights of the States are all of those which have not been surrendered to the National Government by the Constitution or its amendments. Wisely or unwisely, people know that under the Eighteenth Amendment Congress has been given the right to legislate on this particular subject, but this is not the case in the matter of a great number of other vital problems of government, such as the conduct of public utilities, of banks, of insurance, of business, of agriculture, of education, of social welfare and of a dozen other important features. In these, Washington must not be encouraged to interfere.

The proper relations between the government of the United States and the governments of the separate States thereof depend entirely, in their legal aspects, on what powers have been voluntarily ceded to the central government by the States themselves. What these powers of government are is contained in our Federal Constitution, either by direct language, by judicial interpretation thereof during many years, or by implication so plain as to have been recognized by the people generally.

The United States Constitution has proved itself the most marvelously elastic compilation of rules of government ever written. Drawn up at a time when the population of this country was practically confined to a fringe along our Atlantic coast, combining into one nation for the first time scattered and feeble States, newly released from the autocratic control of the English government, its preparation involved innumerable compromises between the different Commonwealths. Fortunately for the stability of our Nation, it was already apparent that the vastness of our territory presented geographical and climatic differences which gave to the States wide differences in the nature of their industry, their agriculture and their commerce. Already the New England States had turned toward shipping and manufacturing, while the South was devoting itself almost exclusively to the easier agriculture which a milder climate permitted. Thus, it was clear to the framers of our Constitution that the greatest possible liberty of self-government must be given to each State, and that any national administration attempting to make all laws for the whole Nation, such as was wholly practical in Great Britain, would inevitably result at some future time in a dissolution of the Union itself.

The preservation of this "Home Rule" by the States is not a cry of jealous Commonwealths seeking their own aggrandizement at the expense of sister States. It is a fundamental necessity if we are to remain a truly united country. The whole success of our democracy has not been that it is a democracy wherein the will of a bare majority of the total inhabitants is imposed upon the minority, but that it has been a democracy where through a division of government into units called States the rights and interests of the minority have been respected and have always been given a voice in the control of our affairs. This is the principle on which the little State of Rhode Island is given just as large a voice in our national Senate as the great State of New York.

The moment a mere numerical superiority by either States or voters in this country proceeds to ignore the needs and desires of the minority, and, for their own selfish purposes or advancement, hamper or oppress that minority, or debar them in any way from equal privileges and equal rights — that moment will mark the failure of our constitutional system.

For this reason a proper understanding of the fundamental powers of the States is very necessary and important. There are, I am sorry to say, danger signals flying. A lack of study and knowledge of the matter of the sovereign power of the people through State government has led us to drift insensibly toward that dangerous disregard of minority needs which marks the beginning of autocracy. Let us not forget that there can be an autocracy of special classes or commercial interests which is utterly incompatible with a real democracy whose boasted motto is, "of the people, by the people and for the people." Already the more thinly populated agricultural districts of the West are bitterly complaining that rich and powerful industrial interests of the East have shaped the course of government to selfish advantage.

The doctrine of regulation and legislation by "master minds," in whose judgment and will all the people may gladly and quietly acquiesce, has been too glaringly apparent at Washington during these last ten years. Were it possible to find "master minds" so unselfish, so willing to decide unhesitatingly against their own personal interests or private prejudices, men almost god-like in their ability to hold the scales of Justice with an even hand, such a government might be to the interest of the country, but there are none such on our political horizon, and we cannot expect a complete reversal of all the teachings of history.

Now, to bring about government by oligarchy masquerading as democracy, it is fundamentally essential that practically all authority and control be centralized in our National Government. The individual sovereignty of our States must first be destroyed, except in mere minor matters of legislation. We are safe from the danger of any such departure from the principles on which this country was founded just so long as the individual home rule of the States is scrupulously preserved and fought for whenever it seems in danger.

Thus it will be seen that this "Home Rule" is a most important thing, a most vital thing, if we are to continue along the course on which we have so far progressed with such unprecedented success.

Let us see, then, what are the rights of the different States, as distinguished from the rights of the National Government. The Constitution says that "the powers not delegated to the United States by the Constitution, nor prohibited by it to the States, are reserved to the States, respectively, or to the people," and Article IX, which precedes this, reads: "The enumeration in the Constitution of certain rights shall not be construed to deny or disparage others retained by the people."

Now, what are the powers delegated to the United States by the Constitution? First of all, the National Government is entrusted with the duty of protecting any or all States from the danger of invasion or conquest by foreign powers by sea or land, and in return the States surrender the right to engage in any private wars of their own. This involves, of course, the creation of the army and navy and the right to enroll citizens of any State in time of need. Next is given the treaty-making power and the sole right of all intercourse with foreign States, the issuing of money and its protection from counterfeiting. The regulation of weights and measures so as to be uniform, the entire control and regulation of commerce with foreign nations and among the several States, the protection of patents and copyrights, the erection of minor Federal tribunals throughout the country, and the establishment of postoffices are specifically enumerated. The power to collect taxes, duties and imposts, to pay the debts for the common defense and general welfare of the country is also given to the United States Congress, as the law-making body of the Nation.

It is interesting to note that under the power to create post-offices the Constitution specifically provides for the building of post roads as a Federal enterprise, thus early recognizing that good roads were of benefit to intercommunication between the several States, and that districts too poor to afford to construct them at their own expense were entitled to some measure of Federal assistance. It is on this same principle that New York and other States are aiding rural counties, or constructing entirely at State expense improved through-thoroughfares suited to modern traffic. The Constitution also contains guarantees of religious freedom, of equality before the law of all citizens, of protection from confiscation of property and from other possible acts of injustice to the individual citizen; and Congress is empowered to pass laws enforcing these guarantees of the Constitution, which is declared to be the supreme law of the land.

On such a small foundation have we erected the whole enormous fabric of Federal Government which costs us now $3,500,-000,000 every year, and if we do not halt this steady process of building commissions and regulatory bodies and special legislation like huge inverted pyramids over everyone of the simple Constitutional provisions, we shall soon be spending many billions of dollars more.

A few additional powers have been granted to the Federal Government by subsequent amendments. Slavery has been prohibited. All citizens, including women, have been given the franchise; the right to levy taxes on income, as well as the famous Eighteenth Amendment regarding intoxicating liquors, practically complete these later changes.

So much for what may be called the "legal side of national versus State sovereignty." But what are the underlying principles on which this Government is founded? There is, first and foremost, the new thought that every citizen is entitled to live his own life in his own way so long as his conduct does not injure any of his fellowmen. This was to be a new "Land of Promise" where a man could worship God in the way he saw fit, where he could rise by industry, thrift and intelligence to the highest places in the Commonwealth, where he could be secure from tyranny and injustice — a free agent, the maker or the destroyer of his own destiny.

But the minute a man or any collection of men sought to achieve power or wealth by crowding others off the path of progress, by using their strength, individually or collectively, to force the weak to the wall — that moment the whole power of Government, backed, as is every edict of the Government, by the entire army and navy of the United States, was pledged to make progress through tyranny or oppression impossible.

On this sure foundation of the protection of the weak against the strong, stone by stone, our entire edifice of Government has been erected. As the individual is protected from possible oppression by his neighbors, so the smallest political unit, the town, is, in theory at least, allowed to manage its own affairs, secure from undue interference by the larger unit of the county which, in turn, is protected from mischievous meddling by the State.

This is what we call the doctrine of "Home Rule," and the whole spirit and intent of the Constitution is to carry this great principle into the relations between the National Government and the Governments of the States.

Let us remember that from the very beginning differences in climate, soil, conditions, habits and modes of living in States separated by thousands of miles rendered it necessary to give the fullest individual latitude to the individual States. Let us further remember that the mining States of the Rockies, the fertile savannas of the South, the prairies of the West, and the rocky soil of the New England States created many problems and introduced many factors in each locality, which have no existence in others. It must be obvious that almost every new or old problem of government must be solved, if it is to be solved to the satisfaction of the people of the whole country, by each State in its own way.

There are many glaring examples where exclusive Federal

control is manifestly against the scheme and intent of our Constitution.

It is, to me, unfortunate that under a clause in our Constitution, itself primarily intended for an entirely different purpose, our Federal Courts have been made a refuge by those who seek to evade the mandates of the State Judiciary.

I think if we understand what I have tried to make clear tonight as to the fundamental principles on which our Government is built, and what the underlying idea of the relations between individuals and States and States and the National Government should be, we can all of us reason for ourselves what should be the proper course in regard to Federal legislation on any of the questions of the day.

119 ⟪ Radio Address on the Advantages of Outdoor Life. June 24, 1931

BECAUSE this is the month of June and because the thoughts of more people in our Nation than ever before are turning to the out of doors, I want to say a few words tonight about camping and some of the reasons why many more people should try out this wonderful way of spending a part of the summer. As a matter of fact living in the outdoors is an historical attribute of the American people. From the earliest days of the settlements along the Atlantic Seaboard in every generation for two hundred and fifty years up to the completion of the pioneer settling of the great West, a very large proportion of our population was at all times engaged in camping out in one form or another. George Washington spent the greater part of his early years before the outbreak of the Revolution in camps, first with the troops of Braddock and then as a surveyor of a very wide stretch of territory. Lincoln himself spent many of his earlier years in camping when his family was moving on from place to place in search of new land and in the creation of new homesteads.

It was only during the past eighty years or so that so many

575

American families lost the habit of living more or less out of doors. The tendency to concentrate in cities, the growth of industry and the greater comforts that came into modern homes led many families to forget the opportunities for health and enjoyment that lay in country life or in returning to more simple ways of life even for short periods during the year. It is only within the past few years that we have remembered our heritage and rediscovered the old joys of getting closer to nature. With this have come a better understanding of health conditions and a realization that the stress and strain of modern civilization require a complete change from city conditions if the race is to maintain itself.

A few years ago a great French doctor made some interesting and intensive studies in various large cities of Europe and he came to the conclusion that the average family will die out in the course of three or four generations if it lives continuously in the city and has no addition of country bred stock through intermarriage with people of country ancestry. I do not know whether modern medical science supports this theory that the race will die out if it is confined to cities over a long period of time but I do know that every doctor encourages outdoor life and fresh air in as large quantities as possible to every city dweller.

Much has certainly been accomplished to spread the gospel of fresh air during the past few years. I remember as a boy going into New York City by train and passing along the elevated structure that passes through the northern part of the city. In those days when one came into the city on a train late at night every one of the windows in the tenement houses on both sides was firmly and tightly shut. It was the almost universal rule for people to sleep in hermetically sealed rooms. Today if you enter New York late at night on the same railroad and look out you will see practically every window in those same tenement houses wide open to let in the fresh air. That health lesson has been pretty thoroughly learned.

We have been helped in the opportunities for outdoor life

more than anything else by the advent of the automobile and especially the cheap automobile. They have made it possible for whole families to get out into the real country districts at less cost and greater speed than formerly. When the automobile first came into fairly general use, large numbers of families wanted to take up camping but they could go for miles along country roads or through woods and find only private property from which they were barred by "no trespass" signs. But the demand for camping places was soon met. Hundreds and thousands of farmers and other property owners found that they could earn an honest penny by providing camping places and even more important, the Federal Government and most of the State Governments were prompt to recognize their own obligation by opening up State and Federal owned land for camping purposes. For instance, today the Nation has a hundred and sixty-seven million acres of National Forest preserve to visit and camp in and the States and counties have another eleven million acres which are open to the public. Those of you who know what the State of New York has done will appreciate the marvelous opportunities for campers in the Adirondacks, in the Catskills and in the splendid park areas that have been developed by the Regional Commission on Long Island, in the Palisades of the Hudson, in the Taconic area, in the Central New York Region, among the Finger Lakes and in the great Allegany State Park in the southwest corner of the State. The State itself has put up the cost of paying for and developing these splendid areas for campers and the State expects no reimbursement for the sums which have been thus expended. All it asks is that the campers and other visitors will keep fires from starting and remember that orderly conduct and the preventing of litter are really a public duty on the part of each group of campers toward those who follow them. The State furnishes the camp sites, the water supply and the sanitary facilities and only in some areas does the State receive a very small fee in return in order to pay a part of the upkeep.

Every year that passes sees some new group organize for the encouragement of camping. We all know of the hundreds of thousands of boys and girls who have been taught to understand and love camping through the effort of the Boy Scouts, the Girl Scouts, the Camp Fire Girls, the Young Men's and Young Women's Associations and the thousands of school and health and religious and educational associations which are maintaining camps. That the whole movement is growing is shown by the simple fact that since the State of New York started its camp facilities in the Adirondack Preserve a number of years ago the actual attendance at these camp sites has practically doubled with each year that has gone by. That includes 1930, when in spite of the economic depression twice as many people used the Adirondack camps as had done so the year before.

That reminds me that people are beginning to realize that camping out is just as much meant for the poor family as for the rich family. It is easy to figure out that provided a family can afford the initial cost of some kind of transportation and some kind of camping outfit of the simplest sort, the actual cost of living in camp is lower than it is in almost any hotel, and it is actually lower, under the conditions that most people live, than in the city itself.

I am told that the national agencies alone, such as the Boy Scouts, the Girl Scouts, and the Health Camps of various kinds probably have two million people in camp during the summer. And the campers in commercial and family and tourist and park camps probably run to many times that figure.

I do not need to enlarge on the health values of camping out for old and young but I do want to say a few words about the social and educational values. We Americans need to get to know all of the phases of American life. To stay within our own little, narrow circle in our own communities, whether it be a big one or a little one, narrows our perspective and keeps us from a better understanding of the problems and needs of the country as a whole. We need a fresh point of view, a mental stimulus that will fit us better for the coming winter's tasks, whether they be the tasks of business or the tasks of home life.

Furthermore, in camping out I think that we learn to adjust

578

ourselves to other personalities, to meet and rub elbows with lots of other people whom otherwise we should never see. Camping is not only a leveling influence in that it brings in all sorts of new influences but it is also leveling in that we get a new insight into the characteristics of other people. Furthermore, we get new chances to develop leadership, to meet and solve new problems, to devise new and interesting experiments and to show what we can do in all kinds of delightful emergencies that we will talk about for months to come after we get home.

Finally, I like to think of the camper as one who is standing off at a little distance and looking at his normal and usual life. He is free to have the time for a little thinking, free to survey the conditions in which crowded humanity lives, free to ask himself questions as to whether improvement along various lines cannot be made in our much vaunted civilization. It is a time for stock-taking, a time for a calm survey, not only of one's own personal problems, but also of community problems and even national problems. I am convinced that in this way we can build up a saner, more intelligent citizenship which will do much to provide sane yet new solutions for the many difficulties that confront us at the present time.

My one regret is that there are still millions of individuals and even millions of families throughout the land whose circumstances are such that they cannot possibly even consider taking a camping trip of some kind. That is one of the problems which has not yet been solved. Nevertheless, to every man and woman and every boy and girl who can in some way manage to get off into camp for even a few days, let me say that it is well worth-while. I hope, if you have not done it before, that you will try it out this summer and if you can arrange to do so let me wish you a happy and delightful outing.

120 ❨ The Governor Hails the Appointment of Judge Benjamin N. Cardozo to the United States Supreme Court. February 18, 1932

I CONGRATULATE the President and the people of the United States on the selection of Judge Benjamin N. Cardozo as a Justice of the Supreme Court. I know of no jurist in the law more liberal in its interpretation, more insistent that simple justice must keep step with the progress of civilization and the bettering of the law of the average individuals who make up mankind. This State gives to the Nation a man who has made our highest court noteworthy among all the tribunals of America.

121 ❨ A Memorandum on the Removal of Sheriff Thomas A. Farley of the County of New York. February 24, 1932

THIS is a proceeding brought by Samuel Seabury, Esq., for the removal of Thomas M. Farley, Sheriff of the County of New York. After the filing of the charges and the answer of the sheriff thereto, I directed a public hearing to be held before me on February 16, 1932, in the Executive Chamber. The sheriff attended with his counsel and was there given an opportunity to be heard in his defense.

The complainant brings his charges in a private capacity as a citizen, but on testimony evoked by him as the official counsel of a joint legislative investigating committee.

The fact should be recorded that in regard to the charges filed, the complainant, as counsel, did not call any witnesses for the respondent before the committee, nor was respondent given opportunity to call witnesses for himself or to be heard with his own counsel. Complainant now asks the Governor to remove the sheriff on the evidence brought before the investigating committee by the complainant himself. It would be unjust to remove a public officer as a result solely of this testimony without giving him his own full day in court. Public clamor cannot make the Executive shut his eyes to these plain requirements of justice.

All of the alleged facts in connection with the charges of professional gambling and structural changes in the Farley clubhouse received publicity at the time of the raids in 1926. This was all more than three years prior to the election of the sheriff; and the electorate at the time of voting subsequently for Thomas M. Farley for the office of sheriff will be presumed by me to have known of these allegations and to have elected him with such knowledge. These charges alone would, therefore, be insufficient on which to remove the sheriff. The only relevance which they might have in this proceeding would be in connection with the charge made that the sheriff under oath before the Joint Legislative Committee denied the truth of the facts and therefore committed perjury. It would, of course, be impossible for the Governor to determine whether or not perjury was committed merely by the existence of a conflict in the evidence; and certainly a great deal more would have to be shown to sustain a charge of definite perjury. In view, however, of my decision on other charges, it seems unnecessary to pass upon the quality or bearing of the evidence relating to this charge.

Complainant asks for the removal of the sheriff on the further ground that in violation of law he wilfully refused to testify in secret and private examination before a sub-committee of one member of the joint legislative committee. I dismiss this charge. At the time Sheriff Farley declined to testify in secret before a sub-committee of one, he did so not only on advice of counsel, but also with knowledge that the legality of a private, secret examination by a legislative committee had not been passed upon by any court, even a court of first instance. Even to this day, the legality of secret legislative investigations has not been definitely upheld. The question of examination by a sub-committee of one has been upheld by a lower court; but the power to compel the investigation to be held in secret instead of in public presents grave questions of public policy and of the rights of individuals, which should at the least be passed upon clearly and definitely by the Court of Appeals of this State. It is at least open to question whether an accused public official is not entitled to the choice of being examined in public or in private. Sheriff Farley made it clear that he was ready and willing to testify in public and to sign any required waiver of immunity. In the absence of a ruling by the Court of Appeals I hold that he was justified in his action.

The charge relative to employees and subordinates does not impress me as being in itself sufficient to warrant removal.

I do not find from the testimony and evidence submitted that the sheriff was, on all the evidence, so unfamiliar with his duties and so incompetent and unqualified as to justify removal on this charge.

The charge that Sheriff Farley appropriated interest on funds of judgment creditors collected and held by him in his official capacity rests to a degree on the determination by the courts as to who had title to this interest. Putting aside the legality of the acceptance of this interest, it is sufficient to say that, though long continued, this has been a highly improper practice in New York County, and that legislation should be adopted making this practice impossible in the future.

Nevertheless, I express regret that Sheriff Farley did not, when the question of interest was first raised, make immediate tender of the full amount he had placed in his personal account and demand definitely and as a matter of right that the courts determine forthwith whether the interest belonged to him or to the litigants.

In regard to the charge that Sheriff Farley is unable to explain the sources of large sums of money deposited by him in his bank accounts, in addition to his official income, I have already at the hearing held by me laid down the following rule:

"As a matter of general sound public policy, I am very certain that there is a requirement that where a public official is under inquiry or investigation, especially an elected public official, and it appears that his scale of living, or the total of his bank deposits far exceeds the public salary which he is known to receive, he, the elected public official, owes a positive public duty to the community to give a reasonable or credible explanation of the sources of the deposits, or the source which enables him to maintain a scale of living beyond the amount of his salary.

"While this rule may seem to be an enlargement of any previous ruling by a Governor of this State, it is time, I believe, that the standard of the conduct of public officer be put on a plane of personal as well as official honesty and that, therefore, there is a positive duty on the part of the public official to explain matters which arise on an inquiry which involves the expenditure or the depositing of large sums of money."

Passive acquiescence by unthinking people in the actions of those who shrewdly turn to personal advantage the opportunities offered by public office is out of step with modern ideals of Government and with political morality. Such personal gain is not to be excused because it is accompanied by the respondent's popularity of person and great public generosity. Public office should inspire private financial integrity.

The stewardship of public officers is a serious and sacred trust. They are so close to the means for private gain that in a sense not at all true of private citizens their personal possessions are invested with a public importance in the event that their stewardship is questioned. One of their deep obligations is to recognize this, not reluctantly or with resistance, but freely. It is in the true spirit of a public trust to give, when personally called upon, public proof of the nature, source and extent of their financial affairs.

It is true that this is not always pleasant. Public service makes many exacting demands. It does not offer large material compensation; often it takes more than it gives. But the truly worthy steward of the public is not affected by this. His ultimate satisfaction always must be a personal sense of a service well done, and done in a spirit of unselfishness. Standards of public service must be measured in this way. The State must expect compliance with these standards because if popular Government is to continue to exist it must in such matters hold its stewards to a stern and uncompromising rectitude. It must be a just but a jealous master.

Public office means serving the public and nobody else.

Since the hearing before me, I have carefully examined the evidence given by Sheriff Farley, the argument of his counsel, together with further analyses of Sheriff Farley's bank accounts submitted to me subsequent to the date of hearing. I am compelled to hold that the charge relates to transactions arising before and continuing during the Sheriff's term of office. I am not satisfied with the explanation of the sources of a large portion of the sums of money involved; and I hold that Sheriff Farley has not complied with the spirit or the letter of the rule which should guide public officers.

An order will issue removing Thomas M. Farley as Sheriff of the County of New York.

122 ❨ Address before the Boy Scout Foundation. New York City. April 8, 1932

It is a rare treat, this opportunity to meet again with my associates of the Boy Scout Foundation.

I was startled with Mr. Collier's reminder that we have rounded out our first ten-year period. I feel that I am particularly indebted to him and his associates on the Board and the members of the Advisory Council for what has been accomplished. And it appears to me that this Tenth Annual Meeting of the Boy Scout Foundation can well be transformed into a report of stewardship to the people of this great city.

The progress which has been made in service to the youth of New York City and the Nation is due entirely to that vast army of more than 100,000 volunteers, who in one role or another, sacrifice time and effort to the cause for boys. To them the Nation owes a debt of gratitude.

It is somewhat difficult to visualize volunteer service on such a scale. Few fully realize the extent to which the burdens of public service — and I use that term in a very strict way — are assumed by volunteers. Few realize how helpless the regular agencies of Government would be without this service. Hundreds of thousands of men and women are now engaged in emergency employment relief. Other hundreds of thousands of volunteers are regularly supplementing the work of the Government from week to week through the agencies with which they are identified. And so it is the volunteer, typical of the spirit of service, who is the backbone of social progress.

While my primary concern at the moment is that of the Boy Scouts, and the thousands of volunteers serving it, I want to project a plea in behalf of all character building and social service agencies during this difficult period. These agencies reflect an important phase of our recent progress; they are an integral part of our life of today; they express the hope of the future. Never perhaps in our history was the social service agency so urgently needed as now. My plea is that this great service to America be protected from interruption or curtailment at this time.

The Boy Scout Foundation came into being ten years ago because it was felt that there was a bigger opportunity in Greater New York for service to boys, which it was our responsibility to fill. There were then 16,000 Scouts. Today there are in excess of 32,000. We feel that progress toward one of our objectives has been made. But we recognize that there is a greater opportunity ahead. For in New York City 60,000 Scouts would not be considered adequate.

We realized then that the outdoor features of our program were paramount, but that our camping facilities were inadequate. Accordingly, we acquired and developed a wonderful 10,000-acre tract of land — a place the boys now call their own on which they are building not merely for their own use but for the joy of helping other boys in years to come.

The magnitude of that camping project is indicated by the substantial summer enrollment; 3,500 boys can be accommodated daily.

That, too, was an achievement. But the full utilization of that tract, drawing thousands and thousands of New York City boys for citizenship and outdoor training each year, is but partially accomplished.

The outdoors is of special significance to the city boy living under crowded conditions. Life in the large city has lost its out-of-door opportunities. Artificial interests have been substituted. Normal, natural growth is threatened. Thus, the organized camp has a special mission. And it was in that sense that we projected plans for this big summer camp, supplemented by nearby camps where boys go for week-ends and short periods. It was visualized as something that would supplement in a fundamental way the effort of the public school and the church to build the boys physically, mentally and spiritually. I wish that each of you within the hearing of my voice could visit the new camp which serves Greater New York.

It is gratifying to note that in the development of this great camp several friends have erected memorials.

I know of no more fitting tribute than to make it possible for some boy, or boys in generations to come, to have the benefit of this great outdoor university of character.

This is one direction in which we must provide for the permanency of the Boy Scout Movement. I am happy to know that announcement of intention to make special gifts, or bequests, to the Endowment Fund, or specifically for the permanency of this camp, have been made.

Scouting, however, is not just camping. It is a leisure time program intended to give the boy something that challenges his interest and encourages self-improvement by diverting and directing his interest into worth-while channels. Its unique methods of operation are of interest to educators and psychologists. To you and me, as citizens, the interest is primarily in results.

This is what Scouting achieves:

It inculcates in the boy a definite sense of civic responsibility.

It develops respect for the rights of others.

It places the emphasis on honor and decency.

It is constructive prevention.

But is not prevention rather than correction the solution of the crime problem? It is our positive duty to make the boy resourceful and trustworthy and he will not seek a gun at the point of which to make his livelihood. The racketeer and the gangster go out the window when Scouting comes in the door!

Thousands and thousands of New York City boys are eager to become Scouts. The outstanding opportunity offered to us is to make this program available to them. Our record of accomplishment so far should serve merely as a challenge to expand the Boy Scout enrolment of this great City. That should be our objective! And I hope, in keeping with the proposals already made, the Boy Scout Foundation and its associated councils will undertake a most aggressive campaign to help more boys.

123 ❦ A Tribute to George Washington. Address before the Conference of Governors, Richmond, Va. April 27, 1932

Governor Pollard, my fellow Executives, and you, my friends of Virginia:

IN THE olden days the welcome of the fathers and mothers of Virginia drew hither guests from all the colonies and from all the Nations of Europe: you, Governor Pollard, and you, the people of the Commonwealth of today, are giving to us a welcome of equal sincerity, a welcome which we and our families appreciate to the full and will always cherish. Ask us again, and we will come again.

At this hour when the purposes of civilization are challenged; when unrest is apparent; when new problems and new valuations call for a new leadership, it is well for America to view again the honor, the purity and the unselfish devotion of him who became the keystone in the making of the Nation, and who rightly won the imperishable title of Father of his Country.

A Tribute to George Washington

In many ways this great gathering in the Capitol of Virginia constitutes the perfect tribute to the memory of George Washington. To this Commonwealth of his birth have come the Chief Executives of the Sovereignties of the Nation he founded to join with Governor Pollard, and, with you, his fellow-Virginians, in recreating in our hearts a deeper understanding of one who, by the grace of God, continues to shed his influence upon mankind.

You my fellow Governors, representing not the thirteen original States alone, but States which include vast territories that were unknown and unexplored in the days of the founding of the American Republic — you have equal right in our common heritage; and I am certain that the gallantry of Virginia will permit to the State of New York a natural pride in the thought that during the War of the Revolution, and later at the founding of constitutional government, General and President Washington's service to his country lay so greatly in my State.

I call tonight's great gathering a perfect tribute because I am confident that Washington himself would have desired a national tribute. His every prayer, his every thought, his every action, which related to his fellow men — all were founded upon a breadth of view and a breadth of vision that allowed no part to obscure the whole.

I like to believe that at this very hour his spirit is dwelling among us, helping us to turn away from sordid desires, and summoning us to a renewal of the ancient faiths.

It is generally agreed that more has been said and written about George Washington than about any other American. His biographers constitute a varied multitude, from the dry-as-dust scholastic who spends a life upon minutiae, to the "humanizer" who in brisk patois seeks to clothe the eighteenth-century gentleman in the latest garb of the modern, and not, it seems to me, to the end that we shall understand him any the better.

Far more interesting and, I believe, infinitely more profitable, is what Washington wrote and said and did himself. He made no pretense to oratory or to authorship, and yet in perfect detail and with painstaking industry Washington himself has set forth for us the wisdom of his life. Examination easily puts to rest an all too prevalent impression that Washington was an emblem merely, and that Hamilton and others constituted the real directing genius of that great era. His own letters indicate the extent to which the policies of these brilliant minds were in the last analysis given initial shape and direction by Washington himself. If one will but read he will see the extent to which Washington, in his painstaking way and enlightened by a vast experience, actually directed the making of a Nation. Out of his letters emerges the man himself. One is struck by that habit of forceful but homely expression in which, while still a mere boy, he tells us of assuming great responsibilities, of his deep interest in developing the western lands, of his seeking after every kind of knowledge.

This diversity of knowledge, which, after all, is the foundation stone of his superbly realistic statesmanship, came from the fact that he was probably the most travelled man in the colonies.

My mind has perhaps unconsciously given first emphasis to Washington, the traveller, because we Governors in the space of three days have been given the privilege of seeing more of the Old Dominion's territory and landmarks than he could have covered in three weeks. It was perhaps fortunate for our life and limb and comfort that we have substituted a motorized caravan on splendid concrete roads for the chaise, the coach and the saddle on red clay roads. . . .

No other President has brought to his office a more complete knowledge of the country — and most of it acquired on horseback at that! Yet, notwithstanding his unique equipment President Washington decided that it was one of "the duties of (his) station to visit every part of the United States in the course of (his) administration of government." He wanted "to acquire knowledge of the face of the Country, the growth and agriculture thereof, and the temper and disposition of the inhabitants themselves."

His many journeys carried him north to Crown Point in New York; south to Savannah in Georgia; west to Gallipolis in Ohio;

east to Boston and to Kittery in Maine. A student of his travels has recently plotted, after months of careful research, the routes followed. That map shows that Washington covered vast distances, if we keep in mind the means of transportation of those days.

This first President of ours was enormously in touch with his United States—the States that he, perhaps more than any individual, made United in fact.

Extraordinarily for an individual, he animated his country, motivated it, inspired it. In the eyes of universal adulation he became its symbol. The special point is that he did all of this at first hand: he did nothing vicariously; he delegated next to nothing in his Americanization.

He knew at this same first-hand every geographical section of the Colonies he made into a Nation. Even in these days of Pullmans, motor-cars and airplanes such itineraries would be a remarkable achievement on the part of a public man half as busy as he was. . . .

While he loved best the serene life of a master farmer at Mount Vernon, it was not given him to enjoy such peace for any considerable time. His life was a succession of long, arduous periods of public service. For six years, military duties relating to the conflict with the French and Indians exacted his energies and at times seriously endangered his health. For the next sixteen years his life at Mount Vernon was more and more disturbed by that growing spirit of revolt against the Mother country which stirred the colonies. Then followed the eight years of Revolution with interludes of despair and disaster. When peace with England came, the affairs of the young Nation were still critical and nearly six years were given to the making of the new Nation. Finally, there were eight years of the Presidency—perhaps the most arduous of all. It is difficult to find any parallel in history for this career, made up of a hard succession of tasks, each, it would seem, harder than its predecessor. It was a lifetime of stern and seemingly endless difficulties. Other lives in other Nations and other times have been similarly filled with action and with tasks. America has no Caesar, America has no Charlemagne, America has no Henry the Eighth, America has no Napoleon, America has no Lenin: America prefers and always will prefer her Washington.

When he laid down the care of office in 1797, he had completed practically forty-five years of service for his Country and his countrymen—a period covering a succession of infinitely critical times of stress. In spite of a constant burden of treachery, of injustice, of slander and criticism and often of the stupidity of his associates, he maintained—with a few exceptions, when he displayed delightfully human fits of temper—a calm and patient devotion to fundamental issues.

We who have suffered ourselves the pains of public criticism can realize what he meant when he said toward the end of his long career, that he had been "assailed in such exaggerated and indecent terms as could scarcely be applied to a Nero, a notorious defaulter or even to a common pick-pocket."

He met his problems by patient and informed planning, enlightened by a lively imagination but restrained by practical prudence. This practical and prudent manner of working has made him seem to many historians ultra-conservative, but careful examination of his policies shows that they were far-reaching and liberal for the time and circumstances under which he was working.

Speculation, for example, was prevalent during his career. Some of this, of course, was unavoidable in a period of rapid expansion in a virgin and immature country, but its effect on the industry and habits of the people and on normal economic affairs he deeply deplored. In writing to Jefferson in 1788, he said, "I perfectly agree with you that an extensive speculation, a spirit of gambling, or the introduction of anything which will divert our attention from agriculture must be extremely prejudicial, if not ruinous to us." Some of my fellow Governors have given voice to this same thought during these past three days.

With respect to the rise of manufacturing, he did not commit himself to a governmental policy of encouraging only manufac-

591

turing, constantly pointing out that manufacturing should be considered as an aid to what he conceived to be the dominant economy of the country — agriculture. In a letter to Lafayette, he stated in substance, that he would regret to see manufacturing draw vast numbers of workers from the land, and that he felt that such a result was not necessary.

Washington repeatedly emphasized the responsibility of Government for the encouragement of agriculture. This real Father of his Country spoke repeatedly of the wisdom of developing agricultural aid and in 1796, his message said, "It will not be doubted, that, with reference either to individual or national welfare, agriculture is of primary importance. In proportion as Nations advance in population and other circumstances of maturity, this truth becomes more apparent, and renders the cultivation of the soil more and more an object of public patronage." What a pity that recent national leadership and, therefore, recent national thought have so little heeded that precept!

Because he saw that agriculture was a thing that was not susceptible to the principles of competition, it followed for him that it was intimately related to and dependent on governmental policy. Consequently, in his magnificent matter-of-fact manner, he reasoned directly from what he saw to what he thought ought to be done by the Government, not disturbing his mind by mere efforts to reconcile conflicting schools of economic theory. It is some such matter-of-fact attitude that modern statesmen might apply in greater measure to public problems. To concern ourselves less with theory and more with a realism based on the hard lessons of experience, is to serve well the memory of Washington and also the fundamental interests of popular government.

Of the nationalism that dominated Washington's policies, another Virginian President said, speaking at the darkest moment of the Great War, July 4, 1918, at Washington's tomb in Mount Vernon: "It is significant — significant of their own character and purpose and of the influences they were setting afoot — that

Washington and his associates, like the barons at Runnymede, spoke and acted not for a class, but for a people . . . They entertained no private purpose, desired no advantage." So spoke your President and mine — Woodrow Wilson.

This absence of sectionalism, together with his interest in the means of knitting the scattered people of the new Nation together, was the imperishable contribution of Washington. And it was born, as we know, of a firm and accurate knowledge. He saw that nothing could be gained by preaching a mere theory of unity. He first grasped the units and then sought the means of union. He identified the sections and interests, sought with a sympathetic and penetrating mind their special problems and needs and stated them with fairness and courage. Then he sought whether by roads or waterways or by the less material instrumentality of education, the means of national unity. First identify, then unify. "The separate interests," he said, "as far as it is practicable, must be consolidated; and local views must be attended to, as far as the nature of the case will admit . . . If the union of the whole is a desirable object, the component parts must yield a little in order to accomplish it."

It is of interest to note at this Conference of Governors the essential part of a circular letter addressed by him to the Governors of the States at the close of the War of the Revolution. He said: "With this conviction of the importance of the present crisis, silence in me would be a crime. I will therefore speak to your Excellencies the language of freedom and of sincerity without disguise . . . There are four things which I humbly conceive are essential to the well being, I may even venture to say, to the existence, of the United States, as an independent power: —

"First. An indissoluble union of the States under one federal head.

"Second. A regard to public justice.

"Third. The adoption of a proper peace establishment; and,

"Fourth. The prevalence of that pacific and friendly disposition among the people of the United States, which will induce them to forget their local prejudices and policies; to make those mutual concessions which are requisite to the general prosperity; and in some instances to sacrifice their individual advantages to the interest of the community."

Nearly a century and a half later we, as Governors, can accept that calm advice from our First President. We can accept from him those fine fundamentals, and learn from him that theory without practical action moves a Nation but a short distance along the path of progress. . . .

Our styles may change, our means of unity are ever transformed by mechanical invention and by increasing knowledge. To the roads and waterways of his age and generation are now added railroads, air transportation, the telegraph and telephone, the radio and that portentious and enormously valuable national interest, giant electrical power. To surround new means of national usefulness with proper safeguards and legitimate assistance is the way of a statesmanship that depends upon knowledge and facts rather than theory and prejudice. We need education, justice, foreign relations, all cut to the pattern of modern necessity, but above all, unity in the spirit and form of Washington's common sense — a unity based upon a deep and sympathetic knowledge of differences; for knowledge puts away fear, and fear is the father of disunion.

May his spirit watching over us here in his native State and his native land breathe upon us his courage, his sympathy, his knowledge, to the end that we his children may safeguard and foster through all the years the great trust he has given into our keeping.

Join me therefore in these his words:

"That your union and brotherly affection may be perpetual; that the free constitution which is the work of your hands may be sacredly maintained; that its administration may be stamped with wisdom and virtue; that, in fine, the happiness of the people of these States under the auspices of liberty may be made complete — this is my unceasing prayer to Heaven."

124 ❧ A Thanksgiving Day Proclamation. November 18, 1932

I, FRANKLIN D. ROOSEVELT, Governor of the State of New York, do proclaim Thursday, the twenty-fourth day of November, in this year of our Lord one thousand nine hundred and thirty-two, as Thanksgiving Day.

I ask the people of the State to come together in families, in communities and in churches for the giving of thanks to God.

May the many of our people fortunate in their temporal well-being, and the many who are bearing the stress of poverty, unite in the common purpose of seeking divine guidance toward the greater extending of unselfish charity and help in behalf of their fellow men.

It is fitting that men and women of all creeds should join in the words of the prayer:

"O God, almighty and merciful, who healest those that are broken in heart, and turnest the sadness of the sorrowful to joy; let thy fatherly goodness be upon all that thou hast made.

"Remember in pity such as are this day destitute, homeless or forgotten of their fellow men. Bless the congregation of thy poor. Uplift those who are cast down. Mightily befriend innocent sufferers, and sanctify to them the endurance of their wrongs.

"Cheer with hope all discouraged and unhappy people, and by thy heavenly grace preserve from falling those whose penury tempteth them to sin; though they be troubled on every side, suffer them not to be distressed; though they be perplexed, save them from despair."

125 ❧ Radio Greeting to the Christmas Ship for Puerto Rico. December 21, 1932

AT THIS hour a unique ceremony is taking place on board the S. S. *Coamo* at her pier in the East River, New York City. Members of the Puerto Rico Child Feeding Committee, representatives of our churches and Governor Beverley with a group of friends from Puerto Rico, are assembled on this ship to bless its cargo and to bid the ship "God Speed" on her errand of mercy.

This is the Christmas Ship for Puerto Rico. It will not carry toys and games or Christmas trees; its cargo consists of food for the desperately needy children of our own American Island, which in these recent years has been visited time and again with disasters so severe that a less courageous people might have given up in despair.

On this occasion, our Nation again witnesses a practical demonstration of the true spirit of Christmas. When we know of the hunger of thousands of children, our hearts are touched and we are moved to do something to share a little that these boys and girls, who are not unlike those of our own firesides, may have something to eat.

I am deeply impressed with the work of the Puerto Rico Child Feeding Committee. It is good to know that there is no additional cost to this Committee for the preparation and distribution of the food. Not only has the Island Government wholeheartedly cooperated, but the people of Puerto Rico themselves have been very generous, especially the local Parent-Teacher Associations, which have contributed so much in time and money. I admire the splendid courage of these loyal American citizens.

For the past two years over 40,000 boys and girls have been receiving one meal a day in 900 emergency feeding stations on the Island. Not less than 65,000 different children have received help through the work of this Committee.

As Chairman of the New York State Puerto Rico Child Feeding Committee, I am glad to know that so much has been accomplished. There could be no more substantial testimony of the sincere interest and friendship which our people here on the mainland have for their fellow-citizens in Puerto Rico, than is shown in our willingness, even in these difficult times, to sacrifice and share something with the people of Puerto Rico, who have suffered so much.

The Christmas Ship for Puerto Rico

The poverty in Puerto Rico, caused in part by the hurricane of 1928 and aggravated by the financial depression of the past three years, has been made extremely serious by another very recent great storm, which swept across the island. Forty-four complete municipalities, comprising a population of over 800,000 people, lay in the path of this terrific hurricane. Losses suffered by agriculture are estimated at over $20,000,000. Total property destruction is fixed at at least $40,000,000. Naturally the children are the first and greatest sufferers at a time like this. They should be the first to receive our help. I am told that at least 125,000 boys and girls in this ravaged area alone are in urgent need of food.

We must look to a constructive vigorous program for the welfare and rehabilitation of the entire island. I am familiar with its many problems and am confident that any philanthropic investment made in Puerto Rico will bring good and lasting returns.

The heart of America has been repeatedly touched by the suffering of those far removed from us, but let us remember that Puerto Rico is in no sense foreign. The port to which this Christmas Food Ship will sail is within the boundaries of our own Nation. It is true that at this hour we are compelled to meet more obligations of one kind and another than have been known for generations, and we must meet them with greatly curtailed resources. At a time like this, however, we cannot fail to realize more fully the deep significance of the Biblical admonition: "Bear ye one another's burdens."

This is the spirit in which the Christmas Ship sails. May I send with it my own sincere Christmas greetings and the good wishes of all our people.

126 ❧ A Memorandum on the Hearing of Charges Preferred against James J. Walker, Filed after His Resignation as Mayor of the City of New York (Excerpts). December 29, 1932

FORMAL charges against Honorable James J. Walker, Mayor of the City of New York, having been submitted to the Governor, the latter, as required by law, gave the Mayor a copy of the charges and an opportunity of being heard in his defense. Mayor Walker, accompanied by counsel, attended before the Governor. The hearing began on August 11, 1932, and was terminated on September 2, 1932, following notification of the Mayor's resignation.

The purpose of this memorandum is to record for convenient reference the proceedings incidental to the hearing, including the controversies that arose during its progress relative to the Governor's power of removal and to his conduct of the inquiry.

The charges against Mayor Walker grew out of testimony given before a Joint Committee of the Legislature. . . .

On June 8, 1932, Hon. Samuel Seabury, who had been appointed counsel by the Joint Legislative Committee and had examined the witnesses at the public hearings, transmitted to the Governor the stenographic transcript of the testimony taken before the Committee in so far as it related to the conduct of the Honorable James J. Walker, Mayor of the City of New York, with a communication containing certain charges, designated as conclusions, respecting the conduct of the Mayor and an analysis of the evidence.

The letter from Judge Seabury to the Governor concluded, as follows:

"From the record submitted, and after a hearing, you can determine whether the public interest and the maintenance of decent standards among public officials require that the Hon.

James J. Walker should be removed from the office of Mayor of the City, and can take such action as may be just to Mayor Walker and the people of the City of New York."

The charges preferred by Judge Seabury and the others against the Mayor of New York invoked the exercise of the responsibility resting upon the Governor to demand accountability to the State for the conduct of the officer under attack.

The hearing began on August 11, 1932. The Mayor appeared personally and with counsel.

The Governor indicated the procedure that would be followed. After opening statements by counsel for the Mayor and counsel preferring the charges, Mayor Walker was informed by the Governor that he would be questioned on the charges and was then sworn and examined regarding each of the Seabury charges in turn.

At the conclusion of the Mayor's testimony a motion to dismiss each of the Seabury charges was made by the Mayor's counsel. The motion was argued at length, the discussion occupying the whole of one day and part of another. After denial of the motion, counsel for the Mayor examined a number of witnesses in the Mayor's defense, some of whom attended in response to subpoenas issued by the Governor at the instance of the Mayor.

The examination of witnesses had not been concluded when the hearing closed. The testimony to the termination related exclusively to the Seabury charges.

The termination of a removal proceeding by the resignation of the officer sought to be removed, as in this instance, would in most circumstances render unnecessary any form of report, but, in this case, certain claims were advanced relating to the jurisdiction of the Governor to remove the Mayor of the City of New York and to the procedure adopted by the Governor, which are of sufficient importance to justify review in permanent form.

The entire procedure was, of course, in virtue of the power of removal from office with which the Governor is invested.

This power of removal is the power to require and enforce

accountability to the State for the official conduct of public officers. In a recent opinion, the Appellate Division, Fourth Department, observed with reference to this power, that "Its object was not to punish the offender, but to improve the public service." (*Matter of Newman v. Strobel,* 236 App. Div., 371, 373.)

Originally when the power of removal was a mere incident to the power of appointment, which applied to local as well as State officers, the dominant consideration in exercising the power of removal was to substitute for those removed others more acceptable to the appointing power.

The method of selecting local officers by non-local agencies was changed by the Constitution of 1821, which, as Governor Tilden explained in his Municipal Reform Message to the Legislature of May 11, 1875, "substituted election by the people of the localities or appointment by local authorities, with respect to a large share of the local offices."

Though the method of selection was changed, the interest of the State in the conduct of officers whose selection had been thus transferred to the localities continued, and that object was thenceforth attained by vesting a power of removal for cause, under constitutional and statutory provisions, in the Governor or in other officers or tribunals.

It was logical and reasonable to vest such power in the Governor because the executive power is, under the Constitution (Art. IV. Sec. 1), vested in the Governor and the Governor "shall take care that the laws are faithfully executed." (Art. V, Sec. 4). This duty to see that the laws are faithfully executed was imposed on the Governor by the Constitution of 1777 and by every succeeding Constitution down to the present. It is made particularly effective by the power of removal when that power is vested in the Governor. (Lincoln, Constitutional History of New York, Vol. 4, p. 471.)

"Indeed," says Governor Tilden, "it is a characteristic peculiarly of the present Constitution to distinguish between the power of electing or appointing an officer and the power of holding him to account. In the words of my annual message, 'It is while dispersing the one to the localities to reserve the other to the State, acting by its general representation and as a unit; to retain in the collective state a supervisory power of removal in addition to whatever other accountability may result to the voters or authorities of the locality from the power to change the officer at the expiration of his term or from special proceeding of law. The two ideas are not incompatible; on the contrary, one is the complement of the other. Such dispersion of the appointing power has become possible only because these devices have been invented to preserve accountability to the State.'" (Tilden's *Public Writings and Speeches*, Vol. II, p. 126)

It is to maintain the principle of accountability to the State, on appeal by a minority or by individuals against wrongdoing by Government officials, that the Governor is invested with the power of removal, and when exercising that power the Governor does so in the interest of the people of the State of New York and not as a judge or an arbitrator between individuals with conflicting interests. The inquiry conducted by him and before him is for the purpose of informing him whether the officer under charges should be removed from his office. There are no parties, in the sense of litigants, to such a proceeding. The Governor is discharging an executive power in the interests of the State. When the Governor has complied with the constitutional requirement of "giving to such officer a copy of the charges against him, and an opportunity of being heard in his defense," the power to decide whether the officer should be removed and the responsibility for a right decision rest solely upon the Governor.

In order that there may be no misapprehension on this point, it seems advisable that attention be directed to the pertinent decisions of the Court of Appeals, which is our court of last resort.

In the *Matter of Guden*, 171 N. Y. 529, Governor Odell removed Charles Guden, Sheriff of Kings County. An action was thereafter brought by the removed sheriff seeking from his successor the delivery of books and papers of office. The case went to the Court of Appeals and that court denied all power in the courts to review the action of the Governor, which was held conclusively to be an executive act. The following from the opinion of the court by Chief Judge Parker disposes of the controversial possibilities of this subject:

"These powers the people of this State have by a written Constitution separated, and distributed among the three departments of government created by it — the executive, legislative and judicial — carefully enumerating the powers and defining their limits. And the Constitution must be so construed as to preserve rather than to destroy the powers of the coordinate branches of the government, thus securing the full exercise of all the powers conferred by the people."

"In this country the power of removal is an executive power, and in this State it has been vested in the Governor by the people." (Constitution, Art. IV, Sec. 1.)

"It does not require argument to persuade the mind that the power thus conferred is executive, not judicial, and that it was intended to be vested exclusively in the Governor."

"The suggestion that, if the courts do not interfere, some chief executive may proceed in disregard of those principles which courts of impeachment have established, should not be given weight, for the ability to act quickly in the removal of administrative officers and clerks is as important in the conduct of government as in the management of a gigantic corporation or large individual enterprise."

"Therefore, we do not examine into the merits for they do not concern the courts, inasmuch as both the power to decide whether Guden should be removed from the office of sheriff, and the responsibility for a right decision, rest solely upon the Governor of the State."

·   ·   ·   ·   ·

At the outset of the hearing of the charges against Mayor Walker, the power of the Governor to remove a Mayor of New York City was challenged, and other claims were advanced looking to the imposition of certain limitations upon the exercise of the removal power. Briefly stated, these latter claims were that the Governor was precluded from consideration of charges relating to conduct in a prior term of office, and was not within his prerogative in making use of the testimony taken before the Joint Legislative Committee.

The basis of the objection that the Governor has no power

to remove the Mayor of the City of New York was the claim that Section 122 of the Charter of Greater New York is unconstitutional. In disposing of the objection, the Governor, at the very beginning of the hearing, ruled as follows:

"The Legislature provided in the New York City Charter, Section 122, that the Mayor may be removed from office by the Governor in the same manner as Sheriffs, except that the Governor may direct the inquiry provided by law to be conducted by the Attorney General; that after the charges have been received by the Governor and pending the investigation, he may suspend the Mayor for a period of not exceeding thirty days.

"The manner of removing Sheriffs from office is provided for in the State Constitution, Section 1, Article 10, the last sentence of which is the one in point, viz.

" 'The Governor may remove any officer in this section mentioned, within the term for which he shall have been elected; giving to such officer a copy of the charges against him, and an opportunity of being heard in his defense.'

"Section 122 of the present Charter of the City of New York, providing for the removal of the Mayor by the Governor, has been in the Charters of the City of New York continuously for a great many years — I think over sixty years. The Court of Appeals of this State has sustained it as a valid constitutional enactment.

"The power of removal so vested in the Governor has not been transferred by the Home Rule Amendments to the Constitution, to any other officer or body. The power remains with the Governor, in whom it has resided for a long time, and the exercise of that power is one of the duties of his office which the Governor is obliged to discharge whenever the public interest requires that he shall do so."

This was not the first time that the claim had been made that the Governor has no jurisdiction to entertain removal charges against officers of the City of New York.

A similar contention that Section 122 of the New York City Charter was unconstitutional was advanced at the opening of the proceeding before Governor Hughes, in 1907, to remove John F. Ahearn as President of the Borough of Manhattan. Before filing an answer to the charges against Ahearn, his counsel, on a special appearance, moved to vacate the notice issued by Governor Hughes requiring Borough President Ahearn to appear and answer the charges, and to dismiss the proceeding on the ground that the Governor had no jurisdiction to remove Ahearn from his office as President of the Borough of Manhattan, for the reason that the Charter provision for the removal of the president of a borough of the City of New York was unconstitutional and void because inconsistent with and repugnant to the home rule provisions of the State constitution.

The Charter provision for the removal of a borough president (Sec. 382, Charter of the City of New York) reads:

"The president of a borough may be removed in the same manner as the Mayor, as provided in other sections of this Act."

The contention, therefore, that the section authorizing the removal of a borough president is unconstitutional involved necessarily the constitutionality of Section 122 of the Charter of the City of New York, under which the removal of the Mayor is authorized.

Governor Hughes denied the motion to dismiss the proceeding. His opinion contains a careful consideration of the sections of the New York City Charter, including Section 122, which were under discussion in the case before him, the provisions of the State constitution, the rulings of prior Governors, and extensive quotations from "the very able message of Governor Tilden under date of May 11, 1875," (New York State, Public Papers of Governor Hughes, 1907, pp. 268-274).

The constitutionality of the Charter provision authorizing the removal of the Mayor of New York City does not, however, rest for authoritative support solely upon decisions of the Executive Department. The Court of Appeals has upheld the constitutionality of those provisions in no uncertain language as appears from the opinion of that Court on the attempt to restore Ahearn to the office from which he was ousted: . . .

"Section 382 of the Charter of New York (Ch. 466 of the Laws of 1901) by its own terms and by reference to other constitutional and statutory provisions relating to removal of county officers, provided for the removal of the defendant by the Governor on charges after an opportunity to be heard in his defense, and no claim is made that all provisions for the trial and protection of the defendant were not observed in the proceedings which resulted in his removal. It is, however, somewhat argued that the provisions purporting to confer upon the Governor the power of removal of defendant conflict with what are commonly known as the Home Rule provisions of the Constitution, and are, therefore, invalid. We are so agreed that this argument is not well founded, that the provisions under which the Governor proceeded are constitutional and valid, and that they do not violate either the letter or the spirit of those provisions which secure and guarantee the principles of local self-government, that it does not seem necessary to discuss them." (*People v. Ahearn,* 196 N. Y., 221, 225.)

Chief Judge Cullen dissented from the opinion of the majority of the Court that Ahearn was not eligible for re-election, but, in so doing, expressed concurrence with the determination as to the constitutionality of the Charter provision conferring upon the Governor the power of removal. He said:

"I have no doubt that the statute under which the Governor removed the defendant from office is valid and constitutional. By the Greater New York Charter (Sec. 382) it is enacted that the president of a borough may be removed in the same manner as the Mayor, as provided in other sections of the act. By Section 122 it is provided that the Mayor may be removed from his office by the Governor in the same manner as sheriffs, and by Section 1 of Article 10 of the Constitution a sheriff may be removed by the Governor, giving such officer a copy of the charges against him and an opportunity to be heard in his defense. A provision authorizing the removal of the Mayor by the Governor will be found in the charters of the City of New York ever since the office was made elective, with the exception of a brief period." (*Ibid.,* p. 245)

It is deserving of notice that the brief period referred to by Chief Judge Cullen is that between 1870 and 1873. In 1870, under the pretense of local self-government the Governor's power of removal was taken away.

"The existing law, which had stood for many years, by which the mayor, comptroller, and street commissioner had been removable by the governor, as in the case of sheriffs, was repealed." (Tilden's *Public Writings and Speeches,* vol. II, p. 131)

Then, in 1871, came the discovery of the Tweed Ring's frauds, and there was a demand in that year for return of the power of removal, which was restored in 1873.

Despite the fact that in 1909, the Court of Appeals had upheld the constitutionality of the Governor's power of removal, two proceedings were initiated in the Supreme Court, Albany County, during the hearing on the Walker charges, to prohibit the Governor from discharging the duty imposed upon him by the provisions of the Charter of the City of New York, on the ground that Section 122 of the Charter is unconstitutional. The very same contentions, which had been passed upon twenty-three years before, were again advanced with several additional references to more recent home rule legislation.

One of these proceedings was brought by a taxpayer. The other, to quote its title, was an application by James J. Walker for an order of prohibition against Honorable Franklin D. Roosevelt as the trier of facts, acting in pursuance of Section 122 of the Greater New York Charter of the City of New York, and Section 1 of Article 10 of the Constitution of the State of New York.

On Mayor Walker's application to prohibit the Governor from proceeding with the hearing on the charges, the familiar contention, made at the opening of the hearing, was repeated, and once more it was insisted that Section 122 of the Greater New York Charter was unconstitutional and void.

The learned Justice, who heard the argument, wrote an opinion (*Matter of Donnelly v. Roosevelt* [*In re Walker*], 144 Misc. 523), in which, after referring to the decision of the Court of Appeals in *People v. Ahearn*, he observed:

"The conclusion is obvious that the authority conferred upon the Governor under Section 122 of the Greater New York Charter is a valid enactment and that such enactment exists in full force and effect and gives the Governor jurisdiction of the subject matter."

The Court, in addition to confirming the constitutional power of the Governor to entertain the charges, found that the essentials to invest the Governor with power to proceed were present in the hearing under consideration.

In this respect Justice Staley wrote as follows:

"With jurisdiction free from constitutional restraint, the power of the executive to act is made complete by compliance with the direction of Section 1 of Article 10 of the Constitution by giving to the accused officer a copy of the charges against him and an opportunity of being heard in his defense. Such compliance with the essentials to invest the Governor with power to proceed with the hearing has been made in the proceedings now before him."

The Justice directed that orders

"be entered denying the application of the petitioners and dismissing the proceedings without cost."

Thus was again rejected the venerable objection of unconstitutionality of a provision of law that has been in New York City charters for at least sixty years.

The further contention was raised in the answer of Mayor Walker and repeated at the beginning of the hearing, that the Governor might not entertain charges relating to conduct in a prior term of office, because whatever misconduct the officer had been guilty of during a prior term would be so far condoned by his reelection as to be eliminated as a possible ground for his removal, upon the assumption that the electorate had tacitly pardoned the offending officer for previous misconduct and incontestably reestablished his eligibility to hold the same office.

It must be clear that this contention is not only wrong in principle but is based upon assumptions too violent to afford it any support. It is unthinkable, for instance, that a community may be compelled to accept the consequences of the reelection of an officer who had been guilty of gross acts of malfeasance in a prior term, where the electorate did not have full and detailed knowledge of the acts of malfeasance at the time of reelection. The power of removal can not be made ineffectual by any such affront to what is right and decent in Government.

Nor is it the fact that derelictions of duty are or can always be known to the voters when asked to pass upon the merits of a candidate for reelection. There might be many violations of duty which, occurring before election, even after nomination, would not come to the attention of the electorate until revealed by investigation after the voters had again registered their preference for the unworthy incumbent.

As Governor Dix said in the Gresser removal proceeding:

"There is no ground of belief that when the voters elected him in November, 1909 they were aware of the wrongdoing in the departments under Mr. Gresser and which were fully set out in the commissioner's report; hence he is not entitled to claim immunity as from a vote of confidence."

(State of New York, Public Papers of Governor Dix, 1911, p. 481.)

Furthermore, it will immediately suggest itself that derelictions might occur between the day of election and the end of the term that the reelected officer was then serving under a prior election. Could it be said that such offenses were condoned by an election that took place prior to the commission of the offenses?

The single circumstance of a reelection cannot suffice to prevent inquiry into acts committed during a prior term. Even the power of selection by a majority is not absolute, but is subject to the power to remove, and the purpose of that power "is to purge the public service of an unfit officer. Such unfitness may arise from conduct in an office held continuously, although during the term of an earlier election." (*Attorney-General v. Tufts,* 239 Mass. 459.)

Accordingly, at the very beginning of the hearing, the Governor overruled the objection in the Mayor's answer that a public officer might not be removed for acts of omissions occurring prior to a present term of office, and pointed out that such a contention was raised on the trial of the charges against Governor Sulzer, and that the majority of the Court for the Trial of Impeachments had rejected it. This had been the ruling also in the trial of Justice George G. Barnard, a Justice of the Supreme Court who had been impeached for misconduct during a prior term of office. The question was argued extensively and with great learning and abundance of authority by those who participated in the Barnard and Sulzer trials.

In the Sulzer trial, Chief Judge Cullen of the Court of Appeals, who sat as President of the Court of Impeachments, referring to the ruling in the Barnard impeachment proceedings, said:

"Some of the offenses charged had been committed in a previous term. The contention of the respondent in that case, that he was not liable to impeachment during one term for acts done in the previous one, was overruled and probably the weight of precedent throughout the country is in accord with that decision."

(State of New York, Court for the Trial of Impeachments, *The People of the State of New York v. William Sulzer,* 1913, Vol. II, p. 1623.)

Chief Judge Cullen's insistence was that:

"liability for offenses during a previous term and liability for offenses when not in office were entirely distinct propositions."

(*Ibid.,* p. 1624)

The opinion of the Appellate Division in *Matter of Newman v. Strobel,* 236 App. Div. 371, is the most recent pronouncement on the question whether a public officer can be removed during one term of office for misconduct in a previous term. It was rendered on September 28, 1932, about four weeks after the Walker hearing closed. The authorities are reviewed at length and the following paragraph will suffice to indicate the conclusion at which the Court unanimously arrived:

"The whole purpose of the Legislature in enacting this statute (Section 36 of the Public Officers Law) could easily be lost sight of, and the intent of the law-making body be thwarted, if an unworthy official could not be removed during one term for misconduct in a previous one. A public officer is none the less unfit to hold office, and the interests of the public are none the less injuriously affected because the misdeeds which portray his unfitness occurred on the last day of one term rather than on the first of the next succeeding term." (236 App. Div. at p. 373)

The remaining contention advanced by counsel for the Mayor was that the testimony taken in public and under oath before the Legislative Committee should not be received by the Governor. This was urged at the beginning of the hearing. In over-ruling it, the Governor informed the Mayor's counsel that if the defense required that any person, who was available as a witness, whether he had or had not testified before the Legislative Committee, should be called before the Governor for examination, the Governor, upon receipt of the name or names of such witness or witnesses, with a statement showing the purpose for which such testimony was desired, would, upon due consideration, require the attendance of such witnesses.

This ruling was made even more liberal upon the second day of hearing, when the Governor stated that those portions of the evidence referred to in Judge Seabury's analysis were before the Governor for consideration: that if the Mayor desired to put in any other portions of the testimony, they would be received, and that if the Mayor's counsel desired to cross-examine any material witness whose testimony was contained in those portions of the Legislative Committee's records which Judge Seabury had specified, "the Governor would require the attendance of such witness to enable the Mayor or his counsel to cross-examine."

The Mayor's counsel at the session of August 17 requested that subpoenas be issued for cross-examination to all the witnesses who had appeared before the Legislative Committee and whose testimony was contained in the volumes submitted by Judge Seabury. The Governor signed such subpoenas that same evening and on the following day tendered them to counsel for the Mayor, who declined to take them. The Governor then directed his Counsel to keep the subpoenas, so that they might be available to the Mayor's Counsel at any time.

The Governor himself exercised the power of subpoenaing witnesses for the purpose of obtaining testimony on matters relating to the charges. In this manner the attendance of the witness Walter R. Herrick was compelled and others were under subpoenas to attend issued by the Governor *sua sponte* at the time that the hearing terminated.

The objection that the testimony of the witnesses before the Joint Legislative Committee might not be received by the Governor was nothing more than a mere repetition of an objection raised in the Ahearn case with reference to the testimony taken by the Commissioners of Accounts.

In that case, the petitioners for the Borough President's removal offered the report of the Commissioners of Accounts and the official record of the testimony taken before such Commissioners. Objection was made by counsel for Ahearn upon the ground that the report was the *ex parte* opinion of the Commissioners of Accounts, that the report of the evidence taken before the Commissioners of Accounts constituted only hearsay statements of a number of witnesses in a proceeding in which the respondent was denied the right of counsel, and that such witnesses were not cross-examined and did not confront the officer against whom their testimony was received. These are the very grounds which were urged by counsel for Mayor Walker on objection to the receipt of the testimony of witnesses before the Legislative Committee.

Governor Hughes overruled the objection and, in so doing, said:

"This is an official report of an examination made into the conduct of the office of the Borough President in accordance with the provisions of the Greater New York Charter and, as I understand it, at the instance of the Borough President himself. I see no reason why the evidence that has been taken before the Commissioners of Accounts should be retaken here. This hearing is not bound by technical rules and as I must in the last event be personally satisfied with regard to every matter upon which I am called to pass, I think the public interests and the interests of Justice require that I should not insist upon all this testimony being taken *de novo*. I shall of course have in mind the absence of cross-examination and when the conclusion of the matter is reached and Mr. Ahearn has been heard, you may be assured that the case will be dealt with in accordance with substantial principles of equity.

"As far as the technical ground, that the witnesses have not been cross-examined, is concerned, I think the public interest in having this matter disposed of without a long-drawn-out hearing for the retaking of this testimony and spreading it upon the records, is paramount.

"I of course understand the importance of cross-examination and when we get to the close of the entire case that matter may be one of importance.

I do not think, however, that it is sufficient ground for refusing to take the official record. I shall, therefore, receive it."

(S. M. of hearing in the matter of the Charges against John F. Ahearn, President of the Borough of Manhattan, pp. 129-133)

At a later stage of the Ahearn hearing, counsel for the Borough President made the following motion:

"I move that the prosecution be required to produce the witnesses whose testimony has been read into this record for purposes of cross-examination; and in the alternative, that the evidence be stricken from the record on the ground that it is unfair to the respondent to try him on that kind of evidence.

"THE GOVERNOR: If at any time I find that cross-examination of any of these witnesses is necessary to the reaching of a definite conclusion, I shall order it or have the portion of the testimony removed from consideration, but I shall not make such a ruling at this moment." (*Ibid.*, p. 185)

Still later:

"THE GOVERNOR: You are not going to be prejudiced by any evidence because of the fact that there was no cross-examination. That is a subject of proper scrutiny, but you are here to answer for the administration of your department and I propose to learn the facts of the case, and you might as well get down to that." (*Ibid.*, pp. 255-6)

A condition did develop later which required the attendance of witnesses who had testified before the Commissioners of Accounts and, to remove any possible conflict of testimony, Governor Hughes directed they should be produced "for such examination as may be proper within a reasonable limit upon the basis of their testimony." (*Ibid.*, p. 351)

Thereafter such witnesses were produced and duly cross-examined by counsel for the Borough President.

The foregoing discussion in the Ahearn case took place with reference to the first charge. When the second charge was taken up, the following is indicated by the minutes:

"THE GOVERNOR: All this evidence before the Commissioners of Accounts is in and the portions as to particular charge have been identified, and in taking up the first charge the witnesses were cross-examined and that examination led to the consideration of specifications and so that charge has been introduced. Now this sheet of particulars as to the testimony relied upon contains references to witnesses connected with the charges in relation to the specifications. Those portions may be read now or later and if there is dispute as to any questions of facts involved I shall want the witnesses presented here for cross-examination if desired. So I will leave it to you to proceed in the way you think most expedient." (*Ibid.*, pp. 900, 901)

Manifestly this decision was directly relevant to the hearing on the charges against Mayor Walker. When Governor Hughes said that "the public interests and the interests of justice" required he should not insist upon having the testimony before the Commissioners of Accounts taken *de novo*, and that the public interest, as he put it, "in having this matter disposed of without a long-drawn-out hearing for the retaking of this testimony and spreading it upon the records, is paramount," he was stating reasons for his action which were at least equally fatal to the demand for the retaking of the testimony given before the Joint Legislative Committee. That testimony had been taken in public, under oath, before a committee appointed by the representatives of the people of this State. To have required that the witnesses who had given the testimony should be re-examined *in extenso* would have resulted in an unjustifiable protraction of the proceeding. Of course, if it became evident that the obligation resting upon the Governor to ascertain the truth could not be discharged without the further appearance of any of such witnesses, indication to the Governor to that effect would lead to the issuing of a subpoena for the witness concerned. Thus there was reserve in the precedent set by Governor Hughes of the right to cross-examination if the need for its exercise arose, and in the Walker case the position of the Mayor was protected by the readiness of the Governor to require witnesses to attend when there was a conflict between the testimony given at the hearing and that taken before the Joint Legislative Committee.

Such a conflict did arise between the testimony of Mayor Walker before the Governor and the testimony of Commissioner Herrick before the Committee and the latter was accordingly re-

613

quired by subpoena issued by the Governor to attend for examination. Another instance of such conflict was when Mr. Paul Block testified before the Governor respecting checks that he asserted had been shown him at private hearings held by counsel for the Legislative Committee. In contradiction of this testimony, one of Judge Seabury's associates was examined before the Governor.

Nor is it beside the point now being considered to note that the Mayor himself had been examined as a witness before the Joint Legislative Committee (Minutes of testimony before the Joint Legislative Committee, pp. 8672-8741; 8750-8779; 8780-8796; 8798; 8811-8816; 8818; 8823; 8824-8830; 8838-8883; 8891-8943), that the charges were in part based upon the testimony which he had given, and that, as to other witnesses, with the exception of those whose testimony was purely formal, consisting of the identification of bank accounts and corporate records, such witnesses, in the main, had been associated with Mayor Walker in the transactions which were under investigation, and some of them were his intimates.

In view of the nature of the transactions to which the testimony of these witnesses was directed, it would certainly have been productive of nothing except an utterly unjustifiable waste of time to have required that the direct testimony, which filled six typewritten volumes and had occupied a great many days, should be again taken and the hearings prolonged while such repetition was in progress.

The weight to be given testimony not taken before him was, of course, for the Governor to determine. The Governor, conducting a hearing on charges, as Governor Hughes said, in the Ahearn case, is not bound by technical rules. His attitude toward all available sources of information bearing on such charges has been explained as follows:

". . . it is with the Governor, who is to act in the matter, to determine, himself, whether the cause of removal exists, from the best lights he can get, and no mode of inquiry being prescribed for him to pursue, it rests with him to adopt that method of inquiry and ascertainment as to the charge involved which his judgment may suggest as the proper one, acting under his official responsibility, and it is not for the courts to dictate to him in what manner he shall proceed in the performance of his duty, his action not being subject to their revision." *Wilcox, et al. v. The People, ex rel. Lipe, et al.,* 90 Ill. 186, 205. See also: *In re Application for Removal of William N. Nash,* 147 Minn. 383, 386-7.

Summarizing the foregoing discussion, which covers the principal objections urged in the Walker case, it is apparent that each is the repetition of an attempt that had been made in other instances to challenge the Governor's power and the method of its exercise.

The claim that Section 122 of the Charter of the City of New York was unconstitutional had, in the Ahearn case, been urged before Governor Hughes, and in all of the courts of this State up to the Court of Appeals; the objection that conduct in a previous term of office could not constitute a ground for removal had been urged and overruled in impeachment proceedings brought against Supreme Court Justice George G. Barnard and against Governor Sulzer; and the insistence upon the production for cross-examination of witnesses who had testified in another place and before other officers had been urged in the Ahearn case and disposed of by Governor Hughes as hereinbefore indicated.

This concludes the examination of those features of the case, which, because of their general importance, seem to justify, for the information of those who will hereafter occupy this office, a review of the rulings that were made. A report of the case would not be complete, however, if it left unnoticed certain statements contained in the opinion of the learned justice who passed upon the applications for orders to prohibit the Governor from proceeding with the hearing.

If the learned justice, having reached the conclusions expressed in those parts of his opinion quoted above and on which he directed that the petitions for orders of prohibition should be denied, had contented himself with the direction that he gave for dismissal of the proceedings, thereby exhausting his judicial power and function, there would be no occasion to make further reference to these abortive attempts to prevent the Governor from proceeding with the hearing of the charges, but for some unaccountable reason Justice Staley, having thus disposed of the matter pending before him, and thereby fully discharged his judicial duty, indulged in observations that can only be described as ill-advised.

In the course of his opinion the learned Justice wrote:

"The respondent, as Executive of the State, through his special appearance herein, has declined to submit himself or the subject matter of this proceeding to the jurisdiction of the court. He stands upon his prerogative as Executive and asserts his freedom from judicial process.

"Under such circumstances, the power and responsibility for the acceptance or rejection of the application of these precedents in the conduct of the proceeding pending before the Governor rests solely with him. It is not within the power of the court to impose or coerce compliance therewith upon the Executive. With jurisdiction of the proceedings, wherein the Governor is required to perform an executive act, the judicial branch of the government is powerless to command him how to act or that he refrain from action." (*Matter of Donnelly v. Roosevelt, (In re Walker)* 144 Misc. 525 at pp. 531-2)

In so far as this language implies that the Governor could have transferred the removal proceedings to the courts, it indicates an amazingly erroneous conception of judicial as well as executive functions and assumes a relation between the executive and judicial branches of the Government which is violative of basic principles of constitutional law.

Since the Governor's power of removal is a distinctly executive function, not only would it create confusion if the judicial branch of the Government attempted to direct its exercise, but the invasion of the executive domain would be fundamentally objectionable even if temporarily expedient. On this point we have the lucid statement of Judge Vann, speaking for the Court of Appeals in *People ex rel. Burby v. Howland*, 155 N.Y., 270 at p. 282:

"The object of a written constitution is to regulate, define and limit the powers of government by assigning to the executive, legislative and judicial branches distinct and independent powers. The safety of free government rests upon the independence of each branch and the even balance of power between the three. Unite any two of them and they will absorb the third with absolute power as a result. Weaken any one of them by making it unduly dependent upon another and a tendency toward the same evil follows. It is not merely for convenience in the transaction of business that they are kept separate by the constitution, but for the preservation of liberty itself, which is ended by the union of the three functions in one man or in one body of men. It is a fundamental principle of the organic law that each department should be free from interference in the discharge of its peculiar duties by either of the others."

The constitutional scheme of assignment and regulation of powers is so elemental that it is difficult to realize that a Justice of the Supreme Court could assume that the Governor could do otherwise than decline "to submit himself," whatever that may mean in these circumstances, "or the subject matter" of a removal proceeding before him to a jurisdiction which could not acquire authority to act by any such method. It need only be stated to be accepted that the abdication by the Governor of his prerogative as executive could not accomplish a transfer of that prerogative to the judicial branch of the Government.

The expressions regarding the method of conducting the proceedings to which the learned Justice refers in the last quotations from his opinion related to matters which were altogether exterior to the Court's appropriate business. As was to be expected, they were given wide publicity at the time and though it was then generally recognized, and has since been judicially declared that they were mere dicta (*Matter of Newman v. Strobel,* 236 App. Div. 371, at p. 377),* the very fact that they were uttered by a Justice of the Supreme Court of this State and are now perpetuated in the law reports (144 Misc. 525) requires that they should not pass unnoticed in this memorandum.

What the learned Justice said can only be construed as, and undoubtedly was meant to be, gratuitous advice or instruction

---

* "In some cases what is said is simply *obiter dictum.*" Opinion by Edgcomb, J., referring to the Staley decision.

on the manner in which the executive function should be discharged, with particular reference to the contentions hereinbefore discussed, which had been urged by counsel for the Mayor in the hearing on the charges. Opinion was indicated on the question whether executive action could relate to matters antedating the present term of an officer against whom charges are preferred, and also as to the method that should be adopted by the Governor in relation to the presentation of testimony bearing upon official fitness.

Had the learned Justice understood, as he should have, that the Governor was sensible of his obligation to his own conscience, the control provided against abuse in the historical development of the removal power, he would have realized the offensive implication of his advice and of the unwarranted intimation of restrictions to be placed upon the Governor's freedom to make certain of the circumstances by which his action might be justified to his conscience. In no aspect of his own duty or decent regard for discharge of the Governor's duty could intervention by the learned Justice be permissible.

On the matters in issue before him the Governor was at pains to be guided by reason and by precedent. The Court for the trial of Impeachments is the supreme tribunal created by our constitution for the exercise of the power of removal by the method of Impeachment. It consists of the members of the Court of Appeals and of the Senate. The Governor followed the rulings of that Court, whereas in utter disagreement with those rulings, the learned Justice expressed the opinion that the Governor was precluded from considering "charges dealing with official acts or omissions occurring prior to the present term of the officer" whose conduct was under consideration by the Governor in the pending hearing.

It seems strange that the learned Justice should be unfamiliar with the rulings of the Court of Impeachments, but even more strange is his failure to realize that in expressing any opinion in a judicial pronouncement on the conduct of the hearing, he was, in his own words, guilty of "judicial encroachment" upon the performance of executive duties.

The only questions which the learned Justice was called upon to decide were whether the Governor had authority to entertain the charges for the removal of the Mayor of the City of New York under Section 122 of the City Charter, and whether the essentials to invest the Governor with power to proceed were present. When, having decided those questions, he attempted to indicate what the Governor's procedure should be, his expressions passed out of the realm even of dicta, and his irrelevant observations deserved the censure which has generally been pronounced upon them.

It was unfortunate that the learned Justice should have regarded the adventitious circumstance that the Walker case came before him as an opportunity to express his personal views on the conduct of the hearing, especially since the language of his opinion was not subject to judicial or other authoritative review. His utterances could have no effect except the possible one of influencing public opinion adversely to the Executive in the discharge of the latter's duty and so bring implication of blame upon a coordinate branch of the Government. It is incumbent upon public officers, under our system, to respect the constitutional division of authority and to remain within the limits prescribed for their own action. Failure to do so, if repeated, would create suspicion of intentional misuse of power.

There is a singular appositeness to this concluding reflection, if the appropriate substitution be made, in the closing sentence of Grover Cleveland's "The Independence of the Executive," wherein referring to his own accomplishment in freeing the President from another claim of tutelage, he describes the Executive as

"the independent agent of the people, representing a coordinate branch of their government, charged with responsibilities which under his oath he ought not to avoid or divide with others, and vested with powers not to be surrendered, but used in the guidance of patriotic intention and an unclouded conscience."

Where this memorandum indicates or implies uncompromising opposition to any kind of attempt to require the Governor to surrender his powers or avoid responsibility for the discharge of his duties by dividing that responsibility with any other branch of the Government, the justification for the position taken by the present Governor was actuated by the same considerations which served as guides for his illustrious predecessors, Governors Tilden, Cleveland and Hughes.

XXIV

The First Campaign for the Presidency, 1932

PART I. Before the Nomination at Chicago, July 1, 1932
PART II. After the Nomination at Chicago, July 1, 1932

INTRODUCTORY NOTE: DURING my first campaign for the Presidency, several campaign trips were made: a Western trip to the Pacific Coast, September 12 to October 3, 1932; a Midwestern and Southern trip, October 18 to October 25; and a New England trip, October 29 to October 31.

I have included in this chapter only a small number of the speeches made by me. In addition to those included I also made campaign speeches at the following places: Bellefontaine, Ohio, September 12; Indianapolis, Indiana, September 13; Jefferson City, Missouri, September 13; Goodland, Kansas, September 15; Limon, Colorado, September 15; Denver, Colorado, September 15; Brown Palace Hotel, Denver, Colorado, September 15; Cheyenne, Wyoming, September 16; Laramie, Wyoming, September 16; Hanna, Wyoming, September 16; Ogden, Utah, September 18; Brigham, Utah, September 18; Cache Junction, Utah, September 18; Pocatello, Idaho, September 18; Butte, Montana, September 19; Deer Lodge, Montana, September 19; Everett, Washington, September 20; Portland, Oregon, September 21; Dunsmuir, California, September 22; Davis, California, September 22; Sacramento, California, September 22; Civic Auditorium, San Francisco, California, September 23; Santa Barbara, California, September 24; Glendale, California, September 24; Hollywood Bowl, September 24; Capitol, Phoenix, Arizona, September 25; Wickenburg, Arizona, September 25; Prescott, Arizona, September 25; Ash Fork, Arizona, September 25; Lamy, New Mexico, September 27; Las Vegas, New Mexico, September 27; Ratoon,

Colorado, September 27; La Junta, Colorado, September 27; Pueblo, Colorado, September 27; Broadmoor Hotel, Colorado Springs, Colorado, September 27; Benkelman, Nebraska, September 28; Holdrege, Nebraska, September 28; McCook, Nebraska, September 28; Sumack Farm, near Omaha, Nebraska, September 29; South Omaha, Nebraska, September 29; Council Bluffs, Iowa, September 29; Freeport, Illinois, September 30; Milwaukee, Wisconsin, September 30; Radio Address, Detroit, Michigan, October 2; Democratic State Convention, Albany, N. Y., October 4; Syracuse, N. Y. (Back Platform), October 18; Rochester, N. Y., October 18; Buffalo, N. Y., October 18; Wheeling, West Virginia, October 19; Indianapolis, Indiana, October 20; Terre Haute, Indiana, October 20; Mattoon, Illinois, October 20; Louisville, Kentucky, October 22; Lebanon, Kentucky, October 22; Corbin, Kentucky, October 22; Knoxville, Tennessee, October 22; Etonah, Tennessee, October 22; Atlanta, Georgia, October 23; Georgia Warm Springs Foundation, October 23; Atlanta, Georgia, October 24; Alexandria, Virginia, October 25; Southern Pines, North Carolina, October 25; Raleigh, North Carolina, October 25; Ayer, Massachusetts, October 29; Portland, Maine, October 31; Brooklyn Academy of Music, Brooklyn, New York, November 4; Poughkeepsie, New York, November 7.

The results of this election were as follows: Roosevelt 22,821,-857; Hoover 15,761,841; Roosevelt electoral vote 472 (42 States); Hoover electoral vote 59 (6 States).

PART ONE

127 ❨ The Governor Enters the First Primary Campaign for the Presidential Nomination. January 22, 1932

My dear Mr. McLean:

I F IT is the desire of our party leaders in your State that my name be presented at your coming primaries as a candidate for the Democratic nomination for the Presidency, I willingly give my consent, with full appreciation of the honor that has been done me.

It is the simple duty of any American to serve in public position if called upon. One who believes in new standards of Government for meeting new problems, in the translation of forward-looking thought into practical action, must welcome a chance to do his share toward that end.

As Governor of a State containing nearly thirteen million people, I am, especially at this time, obligated to a still higher duty. These people when they reelected me in 1930 gave to me a great confidence that I would continue the task of helping to solve the serious problems which confront us. Our Legislature is now in session. If I am to be faithful to this trust I must devote myself to the obtaining of progressive laws, and the immediate administering of executive duties in the interest of the people of this State.

Were I now to divert my efforts in any degree by personal efforts in furtherance of my own political future, I would not only be untrue to my own convictions, but I would also stamp myself as one unworthy to be my party's choice as leader.

I know that you will understand the good faith in which I tell you this; and also my hope that our party will place before the Nation candidates who stand for progressive ideals of Government, who represent no mere section, no narrow partisanship and no special class.

I am grateful that my friends of North Dakota wish to present my name in the primary elections for the approval of the people of North Dakota, and I accede to that request.

Faithfully yours,

Hon. F. W. McLean,
Secretary, State Central Democratic Committee,
Grand Forks, North Dakota

128 ❡ The "Forgotten Man" Speech. Radio Address, Albany, N. Y. April 7, 1932

ALTHOUGH I understand that I am talking under the auspices of the Democratic National Committee, I do not want to limit myself to politics. I do not want to feel that I am addressing an audience of Democrats or that I speak merely as a Democrat myself. The present condition of our national affairs is too serious to be viewed through partisan eyes for partisan purposes.

Fifteen years ago my public duty called me to an active part in a great national emergency, the World War. Success then was due to a leadership whose vision carried beyond the timorous and futile gesture of sending a tiny army of 150,000 trained soldiers and the regular navy to the aid of our allies. The generalship of that moment conceived of a whole Nation mobilized for war, economic, industrial, social and military resources gathered into a vast unit capable of and actually in the process of throwing into the scales ten million men equipped with physical needs and sustained by the realization that behind them were the united efforts of 110,000,000 human beings. It was a great plan because it was built from bottom to top and not from top to bottom.

In my calm judgment, the Nation faces today a more grave emergency than in 1917.

It is said that Napoleon lost the battle of Waterloo because he forgot his infantry — he staked too much upon the more spectacular but less substantial cavalry. The present administration in Washington provides a close parallel. It has either forgotten or it does not want to remember the infantry of our economic army.

These unhappy times call for the building of plans that rest upon the forgotten, the unorganized but the indispensable units of economic power, for plans like those of 1917 that build from the bottom up and not from the top down, that put their faith once more in the forgotten man at the bottom of the economic pyramid.

Obviously, these few minutes tonight permit no opportunity to lay down the ten or a dozen closely related objectives of a plan to meet our present emergency, but I can draw a few essentials, a beginning in fact, of a planned program.

It is the habit of the unthinking to turn in times like this to the illusions of economic magic. People suggest that a huge expenditure of public funds by the Federal Government and by State and local governments will completely solve the unemployment problem. But it is clear that even if we could raise many billions of dollars and find definitely useful public works to spend these billions on, even all that money would not give employment to the seven million or ten million people who are out of work. Let us admit frankly that it would be only a stopgap. A real economic cure must go to the killing of the bacteria in the system rather than to the treatment of external symptoms.

How much do the shallow thinkers realize, for example, that approximately one-half of our whole population, fifty or sixty million people, earn their living by farming or in small towns whose existence immediately depends on farms. They have today lost their purchasing power. Why? They are receiving for farm products less than the cost to them of growing these farm products. The result of this loss of purchasing power is that many other millions of people engaged in industry in the cities cannot sell industrial products to the farming half of the Nation. This brings home to every city worker that his own employment is directly tied up with the farmer's dollar. No Nation can long endure half bankrupt. Main Street, Broadway, the mills, the mines will close if half the buyers are broke.

I cannot escape the conclusion that one of the essential parts of a national program of restoration must be to restore purchasing power to the farming half of the country. Without this the wheels of railroads and of factories will not turn.

Closely associated with this first objective is the problem of keeping the home-owner and the farm-owner where he is, without being dispossessed through the foreclosure of his mortgage. His relationship to the great banks of Chicago and New York is pretty remote. The two billion dollar fund which President Hoover and the Congress have put at the disposal of the big banks, the railroads and the corporations of the Nation is not for him.

His is a relationship to his little local bank or local loan company. It is a sad fact that even though the local lender in many cases does not want to evict the farmer or home-owner by foreclosure proceedings, he is forced to do so in order to keep his bank or company solvent. Here should be an objective of Government itself, to provide at least as much assistance to the little fellow as it is now giving to the large banks and corporations. That is another example of building from the bottom up.

One other objective closely related to the problem of selling American products is to provide a tariff policy based upon economic common sense rather than upon politics, hot-air, and pull. This country during the past few years, culminating with the Hawley-Smoot Tariff in 1929, has compelled the world to build tariff fences so high that world trade is decreasing to the vanishing point. The value of goods internationally exchanged is today less than half of what it was three or four years ago.

Every man and woman who gives any thought to the subject knows that if our factories run even 80 percent of capacity, they will turn out more products than we as a Nation can possibly use ourselves. The answer is that if they run on 80 percent of capacity, we must sell some goods abroad. How can we do that if the outside Nations cannot pay us in cash? And we know by sad experience that they cannot do that. The only way they can pay us is in their own goods or raw materials, but this foolish tariff of ours makes that impossible.

What we must do is this: revise our tariff on the basis of a reciprocal exchange of goods, allowing other Nations to buy and to pay for our goods by sending us such of their goods as will not seriously throw any of our industries out of balance, and incidentally making impossible in this country the continuance of pure monopolies which cause us to pay excessive prices for many of the necessities of life.

Such objectives as these three, restoring farmers' buying power, relief to the small banks and home-owners and a reconstructed tariff policy, are only a part of ten or a dozen vital factors. But they seem to be beyond the concern of a national administration which can think in terms only of the top of the social and economic structure. It has sought temporary relief from the top down rather than permanent relief from the bottom up. It has totally failed to plan ahead in a comprehensive way. It has waited until something has cracked and then at the last moment has sought to prevent total collapse.

It is high time to get back to fundamentals. It is high time to admit with courage that we are in the midst of an emergency at least equal to that of war. Let us mobilize to meet it.

129 ℭ "A Concert of Action, Based on a Fair and Just Concert of Interests." Address at Jefferson Day Dinner, St. Paul, Minn. April 18, 1932

W HAT is the real reason that Jefferson Day Dinners are being given throughout the length and breadth of the land, a century and a quarter after Thomas Jefferson was at the height of his career? No doubt it is in part because Democrats use the opportunity of the anniversary to assemble in furtherance of party plans and for the advancement of candidacies. But in a larger sense they are held to give renewed allegiance to the foundation principles of which Jefferson was the chief builder and on which still rests the social and political structure of the Republic.

It is not necessary for us in any way to discredit the great financial genius of Alexander Hamilton or the school of thought of the early Federalists to point out that they were frank in their belief that certain sections of the Nation and certain individuals within those sections were more fitted than others to conduct Government.

Federalism, as Woodrow Wilson so wisely put it, was a group "possessed of unity and informed by a conscious solidarity of interest." It was the purpose of Jefferson to teach the country that the solidarity of Federalism was only a partial one, that it represented only a minority of the people, that to build a great Nation the interests of all groups in every part must be considered, and that only in a large, national unity could real security be found. The whole life and all of the methods of Jefferson were an exemplification of this fundamental. He has been called a politician because he devoted years to the building of a political party. But this labor was in itself a definite and practical act aimed at the unification of all parts of the country in support of common principles. When people carelessly or snobbishly deride political parties, they overlook the fact that the party system of Government is one of the greatest methods of unification and of teaching people to think in common terms of our civilization.

We have had in our own history three men who chiefly stand out for the universality of their interest and of their knowledge — Benjamin Franklin, Thomas Jefferson and Theodore Roosevelt. All three knew at first hand every cross-current of national and international life. All three were possessed of a profound culture in the best sense of the word, and yet all three understood the yearnings and the lack of opportunity, the hopes and fears of millions of their fellow beings. All true culture finally comes down to an appreciation of just that.

And of the three Jefferson was in many ways the deepest student — the one with the most inquiring and diversified intellect and, above all, the one who at all times looked the farthest into the future, examining the ultimate effects on humanity of the actions of the present.

Jefferson's methods were wholly illustrative of this purpose of Government based on a universality of interest. I can picture the weeks on horseback when he was traveling into the different States of the Union, slowly and laboriously accumulating an understanding of the people of his country. He had done the same thing throughout the Provinces of France in the critical days before the Revolution, and he was not only drinking in the needs of the people in every walk of life, but he was also giving to them an understanding of the essential principles of self-government. He was one of the first to recognize the community of interest between the shipowner in New York and the boatman on the upper reaches of the Ohio. He was one of the first to try to reconcile the problems of the South with those of the North. He was one of the first to preach the interdependence of town and country and he was one of the first to bring to the crusty conservatism of leaders of the Eastern seaboard the hopes and aspirations of the pioneer. He was willing to stake his fortunes on the stroke of a pen which purchased an imperial domain which trebled the size of the Nation over night. He was no local American! He was no little American!

Jefferson was so big in mind and in spirit that he knew the average man would understand when he said "I shall often go wrong through defective judgment. And when right, I shall often be thought wrong by those whose positions will not command a view of the whole ground. I ask your support against the errors of others who may condemn what they would not, if seen in all its parts." His, after all, was the essential point of view that has been held by our truly great leaders in every generation.

Andrew Jackson had it. I like his blunt statement that "the spirit of equity requires that the great interests of agriculture, commerce, and manufactures should be equally favored."

Abraham Lincoln had it. We could say today, as he said in 1861, "physically speaking we cannot separate. We cannot remove our respective sections from each other nor build an impassible wall between them. A husband and wife may be divorced, and go out of the presence and beyond the reach of each other, but the different parts of our country cannot do this. They cannot but remain face to face, and intercourse must continue between them."

Theodore Roosevelt brought home to us once more the fundamental point of view when he said:

"The kind of business prosperity that blunts the standard of honor, that puts an inordinate value on mere wealth, that makes a man ruthless and conscienceless in trade, and weak and cowardly in citizenship, is not a good thing at all, but a very bad thing for the Nation. This Government stands for manhood first and for business only as an adjunct of manhood.

"In the past the most direful among the influences which have brought about the downfall of republics has ever been the growth of the class spirit, the growth of the spirit which tends to make a man subordinate the welfare of the public as a whole to the welfare of the particular class to which he belongs, the substitution of loyalty to a class for loyalty to the Nation. This inevitably brings about a tendency to treat each man not on his merits as an individual, but on his position as belonging to a certain class in the community.

"It is the man's moral quality, his attitude toward the great questions which concern all humanity, his cleanliness of life, his power to do his duty toward himself and toward others, which really count; and if we substitute for the standard of personal judgment which treats each man according to his merits, another standard in accordance with which all men of one class are favored and all men of another class discriminated against, we shall do irreparable damage to the body politic. This Government is not and never shall be government by a plutocracy. This Government is not and never shall be government by a mob."

It is to this national community of interest that we should dedicate ourselves tonight.

The great size of the country, enlarged by Jefferson's Louisiana Purchase, offers vast advantages for those who live in it.

But it imposes grave problems upon those who are vested with its direction and control. In normal times it is likely to live in the isolation of sectionalism. It becomes a loose association of communities, with little common thought and little realization of mutual interdependence.

This reminds me of what Chesterton keenly remarked concerning the members of the British Empire. They are, he says, like the passengers in an omnibus. They get to know each other only in case of an accident.

It is only in a crisis that we look back to our common concerns.

The stress of a vast emergency rudely wakes us all from our local concerns and turns us to wider concerns. Then for the first time we look to a larger measure of cooperation, a more exact measuring of our resources, and what is most important, a more imaginative and purposeful planning.

Two weeks ago I said that we were facing an emergency today more grave than that of war. This I repeat tonight.

That a great fear has swept the country few can doubt. Normal times lull us into complacency. We become lazy and contented. Then with the coming of economic stress we feel the disturbing hand of fear. This fear spreads to the entire country and with more or less unity we turn to our common Government at Washington.

In meeting this appeal, what has the present Republican administration done and what is the policy and spirit that has guided it?

Let us see first what this policy has been. Mr. Eugene Meyer, Governor of the Federal Reserve Board, in speaking for the creation of a Reconstruction Finance Corporation in December said: "I believe the main result . . . would be through the removal of fear. The present situation is peculiar, in that, instead of the weak being afraid of the strong, the strong are afraid of the weak and the main object aimed at is the removal of that fear from the strong institutions, so that they may go ahead and conduct business in a normal way."

This, I submit, is spoken in the true Hamiltonian tradition—

631

that while manifestly no one can claim a monopoly of fear, the allaying of it must proceed from the strong to the weak.

And what has the Administration provided to meet the situation?

First, an appeal to charity. Second, the moratorium declared after a hesitation and delay of months and without calling the Congress into session. Third, the creation of the Emergency Finance Corporation, the spirit of which, I submit, is well embodied in Governor Meyer's words just quoted. Finally, unscientific, belated — almost frantic — economy in Government.

Compare this panic-stricken policy of delay and improvisation with that devised to meet the emergency of war fifteen years ago.

We met specific situations with considered, relevant measures of constructive value. There were the War Industries Board, the Food and Fuel Administration, the War Trade Board, the Shipping Board and many others.

I am not speaking of an economic life completely planned and regimented. I am speaking of the necessity, however, in those imperative interferences with the economic life of the Nation that there be a real community of interest, not only among the sections of this great country, but among its economic units and the various groups in these units; that there be common participation in the work of remedial figures, planned on the basis of a shared common life, the low as well as the high. In much of our present plans there is too much disposition to mistake the part for the whole, the head for the body, the captain for the company, the general for the army. I plead not for a class control but for a true concert of interests.

The plans we may make for this emergency, if we plan wisely and rest our structure upon a base sufficiently broad, may show the way to a more permanent safeguarding of our social and economic life to the end that we may in a large number avoid the terrible cycle of prosperity crumbling into depression. In this sense I favor economic planning, not for this period alone but for our needs for a long time to come.

Let me cite a practical example of the control of the use of Government as an agency for the oppression of the general average of the population by any individual or small group of individuals — the historic and fundamental control over certain industries which, by their very nature, are monopolistic. Many generations before our American independence it was a fundamental of the British constitution that such services as toll roads and ferries should be regulated by the Government for the good of the public. This was recognized throughout the thirteen colonies; and later this control was extended to other similar services, such as canals and railroads and gas and electricity and telephones. It is not stretching the imagination to declare that this principle of regulation has been for centuries a component part of the common law; and that concentrated in its simplest terms this control has involved two very simple mandates: First, that the service itself should be adequate to the needs of the public; and, second, that the price charged should be reasonable to the extent that it provides a reasonable return for the labor expended and for the actual cash which has been wisely and necessarily invested in the property.

I have stated the principle and the purpose of the principle which underlie Government regulation of public utilities. Every court has recognized the principle and it is only in the application of the principle that we have gone astray. The great problem today is how we shall return to a simple clearcut carrying out of the purpose of the common law.

Let me illustrate by telling you simply and briefly the story of the long fight which I have had in the State of New York for making available for the use of the public of the State a million and one-quarter horsepower provided by nature and capable of development at an exceedingly low price on the St. Lawrence River.

There is no doubt that because the people of the State have always owned the bed of the St. Lawrence River out to the international boundary, the people of the State and not private corporations have the definite right to build the necessary dam or dams to develop the power. Twenty-five years ago, when the people of the State were little aware of their great heritage, a Legislature attempted to alienate this great possession to the Aluminum Company of America. This was happily frustrated and then began a twenty-year struggle to prevent a new alienation of this great possession under the guise of a lease running for fifty years or more. In this contest, my distinguished predecessor, Governor Smith, was happily able to prevent the control from passing out of the hands of the State.

When I took office, I undertook at once a definite plan for the development of this great power and I laid down a very definite application of the principle to which I have alluded. In order to be absolutely certain that the actual possession of the power itself should never be alienated from the people, I insisted that the actual dam or dams and the actual power houses should be constructed by a public authority and always remain in the physical possession of that public authority.

Then came the question of how and under what terms this power should be distributed to the actual consuming public. I laid down the principle that this task of transmission and of distribution should be offered in the first instance to private capital and private management, but under very definite terms. These terms were intended to carry out the purpose of getting the electricity into the homes of the people at the lowest reasonable price. This price would be made up of the following items: First, a payment to the State at the power house of an amount necessary to pay the interest and amortization on the cost of the plant; second, an item representing the actual cost of transmission and a reasonable return on the actual money wisely and necessarily invested in transmission lines; and third, the cost of distribution plus a reasonable return on the amount wisely and necessarily invested in the properties engaged in distribution.

The sum of these three items would represent the actual cost of electricity to the home owner, and we have believed that this cost would be far below the average price now charged to the home owners in the State. The very definite plan has been to invite private capital to contract with the State to do this transmitting and distribution on these entirely proper and reasonable terms. But at that point it became necessary to provide an alternative in the event that private capital was unwilling to undertake transmission and distribution on terms involving only a reasonable profit to that private capital.

I said in my message to the Legislature at that time: "Are the business men of this State willing to transmit and distribute this latent water power on a fair return on their investment? If they are satisfied, here is their opportunity. If not, then the State may have to go into the transmission business itself." That is the obvious development of any sound Government control over private utilities — that Government itself should not engage in the utility business if it can find private initiative and private capital willing to undertake the business for a reasonable and fair return on the capital which it is necessary and wise to invest in the project, and on the other hand, that if Government is not able to find private individuals or corporations willing to do this, then Government must step in and do it itself.

If, during this past generation, these fundamentals had been observed by our courts, by all of our public service commissions, by our legislatures, there would be no problem of the control of utilities today. It is an unfortunate fact, which is not denied by the leading bankers or the leading utility men themselves, that largely through the building up of a series of great mergers and a series of great holding companies, the capital structure, especially in the case of the electric utilities, has been allowed to expand to an extent far beyond the actual wise and necessary cash investment. It is a simple fact that in thousands of cases throughout the United States electric utility companies have sought, and in many instances have succeeded in obtaining permission to charge rates which will bring a fair return, not on this cash investment, but on a definite inflation of capital.

I am putting this case very calmly and conservatively. It could be put much more forcibly and it would be easy to make accusations against many of the great utility companies now operating in this country. Recrimination, however, is not particularly useful. It is more useful to state the principles that go back for centuries in such a way that the people of this country will understand them and will understand how, in losing sight of them, we have made ourselves the victims. The net result of our blindness, of our failure to regulate, and of our failure to say that if private capital will not operate for a reasonable profit, Government will have to operate itself, is that in most places in the United States the householders and the farmer and the small business man are paying vastly more for that very necessary part of our modern life — electricity — than they should be paying. It is neither radical, nor a violation of any principle of sound business, for me to state in definite terms that public servants with a proper regard for the interests of the people themselves must exert every effort to restore the fundamentals of public control. And this applies not only in every State capitol, but also in the control by the national Government over those great sources of power which fall under its jurisdiction.

One final point goes with this. A very deep study over many years makes it clearer to me with every passing day that where a public service like the transmission of electricity passes beyond State lines and becomes interstate in its actual operation, in such a case the control cannot effectively be maintained by States alone, or through agreements between neighboring States. That problem is national in its scope and can be solved only by the firm establishment of national control.

It is a great unifying interest doing more to make us a united Nation than any other material factor. To control it for the common good requires national thinking by a national party.

The same broad national view must direct our dealing with the tariff. The Republican Administration has greatly intensified the depression by its tariff policy. The Hawley-Smoot tariff law of 1930 was a drastic revision of the tariff upward. The existing tariff levels were already high enough to protect American industries which needed protection. The increases which the Hawley-Smoot bill made were not based on any scientific analysis of tariffs. The increases were political favors — in large measure to contributors to the Republican campaign fund. The consequences of the Hawley-Smoot bill have been tremendous, both directly and indirectly. Directly, American foreign trade has been steadily dwindling. Indirectly, the high schedules of the Hawley-Smoot bill caused European Nations to raise their own tariff walls, and those walls were raised not only against us but against each other. The result has been that the value of goods exchanged internationally in the last year or so has been less than fifty percent of what it was three or four years ago. When the Hawley-Smoot bill was passed, European States were endeavoring to negotiate reciprocal arrangements which might have caused the lowering of European tariff walls. Our action prevented such an arrangement, and since 1930 when Congress acted and the President signed the law, European tariff barriers have gone higher and higher. This means a lower standard of living in many quarters because prosperity exists only when goods are exchanged internationally.

Just before the Hawley-Smoot bill was presented to President Hoover for his signature, a thousand American economists told President Hoover that he should not sign the law. I am told that never before in history have so many economists been able to agree upon anything. But the faults of this bill were so open and palpable that they found easy agreement. With really prophetic insight they warned him in detail of what would happen, and the detail that they gave him is the detail of what has happened: no benefit to the farmers; injury to American export trade; weakening of the security of American investments abroad; increase of unemployment; and encouragement of a world-wide tariff war. President Hoover ignored this warning. Would he have ignored a warning by a thousand engineers that a bridge which the national Government was building was unsafe?

To my mind a proper tariff policy must be a complete reversal of the methods of the present administration. The scientific determination of economic facts and the scientific determination of probable results of proposed changes are all for the good and should, of course, be used. But this action in itself does nothing to bring about the actual reciprocal exchange of goods so necessary to us and to all Nations. That is the only realistic method of making goods move. The task of statesmanship is to determine what these products are, to bring about bi-lateral or group international agreements to effectuate their exchange. The world is looking for that type of statesmanship and for such a plan that goes far beyond mere scale reductions, that fills in the gaps in the mere advocating of "export" tariff boards and, above all, that provides a real beginning of that international resumption of business that everyone favors and expects.

If Jefferson would return to the councils of the party, he would find that while economic changes of a century have changed the necessary methods of government action, the principles of that action are still wholly his own. As the great Virginian sat at Monticello in the twilight of his life he saw the rise of manufacturing and the growth of the cities and he still held fast to the first principles that a truly national economy is many sided. A great disciple of Jefferson said: "Jefferson's principles are sources of light because they are not made up of pure reason, but spring out of aspiration, impulse, vision, sympathy. They burn with the fervor of the heart; they wear the light of the interpretation he sought, the authentic terms of honest, human ambition. And the law, in his mind, was the guardian of all legitimate ambition. It was the great umpire standing by to see that the game was honorably and fairly played in the spirit of generous rivalry and to open the field free to every sportsman-like contestant."

That was spoken in 1912 by Woodrow Wilson. It was the voice that the people of the country recognized as the authentic and clear spokesman of the Jeffersonian heritage.

There will be many in this Nation during the coming months who will implore you not to swap horses crossing a stream; there will be others who will laughingly tell you that the appeal should have been worded, "Do not swap toboggans while you are sliding downhill." But it seems to me that the more truthful, the more accurate plea to the people of the Nation should be this: "If the old car in spite of frequent emergency repairs has been bumping along downhill on only two cylinders for three long years, it is time to get another car that will start uphill on all four."

Jefferson labored for a widespread concert of thought, capable of concert of action, based on a fair and just concert of interests. Jefferson labored to bring the scattered farmers, the workers, the business men into a participation in national affairs. This was his purpose and this is the principle upon which the party he founded was based. It should now present itself as an agency of national unity.

I say with Lincoln, "Having thus chosen our course, without guile and with pure purpose, let us renew our trust in God and go forward without fear and with manly hearts."

130 ⟪ "The Country Needs, the Country Demands Bold, Persistent Experimentation." Address at Oglethorpe University. May 22, 1932

President Jacobs, members and friends of Oglethorpe University, and especially you, my fellow members of the Class of 1932:

FOR ME, as for you, this is a day of honorable attainment. For the honor conferred upon me I am deeply grateful, and I felicitate you upon yours, even though I cannot share with you that greater satisfaction which comes from a laurel worked for and won. For many of you, doubtless, this mark of distinction which you have received today has meant greater sacrifice by your parents or by yourselves, than you anticipated when you matriculated almost four years ago. The year 1928 does not seem far in the past, but since that time, as all of us are aware, the world about us has experienced significant changes. Four years ago, if you heard and believed the tidings of the time, you could expect to take your place in a society well supplied with material things and could look forward to the not too distant time when you would be living in your own homes, each (if you believed the politicians) with a two-car garage; and, without great effort, would be providing yourselves and your families with all the necessities and amenities of life, and perhaps in addition, assure by your savings their security and your own in the future. Indeed, if you were observant, you would have seen that many of your elders had discovered a still easier road to material success. They had found that once they had accumulated a few dollars they needed only to put them in the proper place and then sit back and read in comfort the hieroglyphics called stock quotations which proclaimed that their wealth was mounting miraculously without any work or effort on their part. Many who were called and who are still pleased to call themselves the leaders of finance celebrated and assured us of an eternal future for this easy-chair mode of living. And to the stimulation of belief in this dazzling chimera were lent not only the voices of some of our public men in high office, but their influence and the material aid of the very instruments of Government which they controlled.

How sadly different is the picture which we see around us today! If only the mirage had vanished, we should not complain, for we should all be better off. But with it have vanished, not only the easy gains of speculation, but much of the savings of thrifty and prudent men and women, put by for their old age and for the education of their children. With these savings has gone, among millions of our fellow citizens, that sense of security to which they have rightly felt they are entitled in a land abundantly endowed with natural resources and with productive facilities to convert them into the necessities of life for all of our population. More calamitous still, there has vanished with the expectation of future security the certainty of today's bread and clothing and shelter.

Some of you — I hope not many — are wondering today how and where you will be able to earn your living a few weeks or a few months hence. Much has been written about the hope of youth. I prefer to emphasize another quality. I hope that you who have spent four years in an institution whose fundamental purpose, I take it, is to train us to pursue truths relentlessly and to look at them courageously, will face the unfortunate state of the world about you with greater clarity of vision than many of your elders.

As you have viewed this world of which you are about to become a more active part, I have no doubt that you have been impressed by its chaos, its lack of plan. Perhaps some of you have used stronger language. And stronger language is justified. Even had you been graduating, instead of matriculating, in these rose-colored days of 1928, you would, I believe, have perceived this condition. For beneath all the happy optimism of those days there existed lack of plan and a great waste.

This failure to measure true values and to look ahead extended to almost every industry, every profession, every walk of life. Take, for example, the vocation of higher education itself.

If you had been intending to enter the profession of teaching, you would have found that the universities, the colleges, the normal schools of our country were turning out annually far more trained teachers than the schools of the country could possibly use or absorb. You and I know that the number of teachers needed in the Nation is a relatively stable figure, little affected by the depression and capable of fairly accurate estimate in advance with due consideration for our increase in population. And yet, we have continued to add teaching courses, to accept every young man or young woman in those courses without any thought or regard for the law of supply and demand. In the State of New York alone, for example, there are at least seven thousand qualified teachers who are out of work, unable to earn a livelihood in their chosen profession just because nobody had the wit or the forethought to tell them in their younger days that the profession of teaching was gravely oversupplied.

Take, again, the profession of the law. Our common sense tells us that we have too many lawyers and that thousands of them, thoroughly trained, are either eking out a bare existence or being compelled to work with their hands, or are turning to some other business in order to keep themselves from becoming objects of charity. The universities, the bar, the courts themselves have done little to bring this situation to the knowledge of young men who are considering entering any one of our multitude of law schools. Here again foresight and planning have been notable for their complete absence.

In the same way we cannot review carefully the history of our industrial advance without being struck with its haphazardness, the gigantic waste with which it has been accomplished, the superfluous duplication of productive facilities, the continual scrapping of still useful equipment, the tremendous mortality in industrial and commercial undertakings, the thousands of dead-end trails into which enterprise has been lured, the profligate waste of natural resources. Much of this waste is the inevitable by-product of progress in a society which values individual endeavor and which is susceptible to the changing tastes and customs of the people of which it is composed. But much of it, I believe, could have been prevented by greater foresight and by a larger measure of social planning. Such controlling and directive forces as have been developed in recent years reside to a dangerous degree in groups having special interests in our economic order, interests which do not coincide with the interests of the Nation as a whole. I believe that the recent course of our history has demonstrated that, while we may utilize their expert knowledge of certain problems and the special facilities with which they are familiar, we cannot allow our economic life to be controlled by that small group of men whose chief outlook upon the social welfare is tinctured by the fact that they can make huge profits from the lending of money and the marketing of securities — an outlook which deserves the adjectives "selfish" and "opportunist."

You have been struck, I know, by the tragic irony of our economic situation today. We have not been brought to our present state by any natural calamity — by drought or floods or earthquakes or by the destruction of our productive machine or our man power. Indeed, we have a superabundance of raw materials, a more than ample supply of equipment for manufacturing these materials into the goods which we need, and transportation and commercial facilities for making them available to all who need them. But raw materials stand unused, factories stand idle, railroad traffic continues to dwindle, merchants sell less and less, while millions of able-bodied men and women, in dire need, are clamoring for the opportunity to work. This is the awful paradox with which we are confronted, a stinging rebuke that challenges our power to operate the economic machine which we have created.

We are presented with a multitude of views as to how we may again set into motion that economic machine. Some hold to the theory that the periodic slowing down of our economic machine is one of its inherent peculiarities — a peculiarity which we must grin, if we can, and bear because if we attempt to tamper with it we shall cause even worse ailments. According to this theory, as I see it, if we grin and bear long enough, the economic machine will eventually begin to pick up speed and in the course of an indefinite number of years will again attain that maximum number of revolutions which signifies what we have been wont to miscall prosperity, but which, alas, is but a last ostentatious twirl of the economic machine before it again succumbs to that mysterious impulse to slow down again. This attitude toward our economic machine requires not only greater stoicism, but greater faith in immutable economic law and less faith in the ability of man to control what he has created than I, for one, have. Whatever elements of truth lie in it, it is an invitation to sit back and do nothing; and all of us are suffering today, I believe, because this comfortable theory was too thoroughly implanted in the minds of some of our leaders, both in finance and in public affairs.

Other students of economics trace our present difficulties to the ravages of the World War and its bequest of unsolved political and economic and financial problems. Still others trace our difficulties to defects in the world's monetary systems. Whether it be an original cause, an accentuating cause, or an effect, the drastic change in the value of our monetary unit in terms of the commodities is a problem which we must meet straightforwardly. It is self-evident that we must either restore commodities to a level approximating their dollar value of several years ago or else that we must continue the destructive process of reducing, through defaults or through deliberate writing down, obligations assumed at a higher price level.

Possibly because of the urgency and complexity of this phase of our problem some of our economic thinkers have been occupied with it to the exclusion of other phases of as great importance.

Of these other phases, that which seems most important to me in the long run is the problem of controlling by adequate planning the creation and distribution of those products which our vast economic machine is capable of yielding. It is true that capital, whether public or private, is needed in the creation of new enterprise and that such capital gives employment.

But think carefully of the vast sums of capital or credit which in the past decade have been devoted to unjustified enterprises — to the development of unessentials and to the multiplying of many products far beyond the capacity of the Nation to absorb. It is the same story as the thoughtless turning out of too many school teachers and too many lawyers.

Here again, in the field of industry and business many of those whose primary solicitude is confined to the welfare of what they call capital have failed to read the lessons of the past few years and have been moved less by calm analysis of the needs of the Nation as a whole than by a blind determination to preserve their own special stakes in the economic order. I do not mean to intimate that we have come to the end of this period of expansion. We shall continue to need capital for the production of newly-invented devices, for the replacement of equipment worn out or rendered obsolete by our technical progress; we need better housing in many of our cities and we still need in many parts of the country more good roads, canals, parks and other improvements.

But it seems to me probable that our physical economic plant will not expand in the future at the same rate at which it has expanded in the past. We may build more factories, but the fact remains that we have enough now to supply all of our domestic needs, and more, if they are used. With these factories we can now make more shoes, more textiles, more steel, more radios, more automobiles, more of almost everything than we can use.

No, our basic trouble was not an insufficiency of capital. It was an insufficient distribution of buying power coupled with an oversufficient speculation in production. While wages rose in many of our industries, they did not as a whole rise proportionately to the reward to capital, and at the same time the purchasing power of other great groups of our population was permitted to shrink. We accumulated such a superabundance of capital that our great bankers were vying with each other, some of them employing questionable methods, in their efforts to lend this capital at home and abroad.

I believe that we are at the threshold of a fundamental change in our popular economic thought, that in the future we are going to think less about the producer and more about the consumer. Do what we may have to do to inject life into our ailing economic order, we cannot make it endure for long unless we can bring about a wiser, more equitable distribution of the national income.

It is well within the inventive capacity of man, who has built up this great social and economic machine capable of satisfying the wants of all, to insure that all who are willing and able to work receive from it at least the necessities of life. In such a system, the reward for a day's work will have to be greater, on the average, than it has been, and the reward to capital, especially capital which is speculative, will have to be less. But I believe that after the experience of the last three years, the average citizen would rather receive a smaller return upon his savings in return for greater security for the principal, than experience for a moment the thrill or the prospect of being a millionaire only to find the next moment that his fortune, actual or expected, has withered in his hand because the economic machine has again broken down.

It is toward that objective that we must move if we are to profit by our recent experiences. Probably few will disagree that the goal is desirable. Yet many, of faint heart, fearful of change, sitting tightly on the roof-tops in the flood, will sternly resist striking out for it, lest they fail to attain it. Even among those who are ready to attempt the journey there will be violent differences of opinion as to how it should be made. So complex, so widely distributed over our whole society are the problems which confront us that men and women of common aim do not agree upon the method of attacking them. Such disagreement leads to doing nothing, to drifting. Agreement may come too late.

Let us not confuse objectives with methods. Too many so-called leaders of the Nation fail to see the forest because of the trees. Too many of them fail to recognize the vital necessity of planning for definite objectives. True leadership calls for the setting forth of the objectives and the rallying of public opinion in support of these objectives.

Do not confuse objectives with methods. When the Nation becomes substantially united in favor of planning the broad objectives of civilization, then true leadership must unite thought behind definite methods.

The country needs and, unless I mistake its temper, the country demands bold, persistent experimentation. It is common sense to take a method and try it: If it fails, admit it frankly and try another. But above all, try something. The millions who are in want will not stand by silently forever while the things to satisfy their needs are within easy reach.

We need enthusiasm, imagination and the ability to face facts, even unpleasant ones, bravely. We need to correct, by drastic means if necessary, the faults in our economic system from which we now suffer. We need the courage of the young. Yours is not the task of making your way in the world, but the task of re-making the world which you will find before you. May every one of us be granted the courage, the faith and the vision to give the best that is in us to that remaking!

PART TWO

131 ❦ "I Pledge You—I Pledge Myself to a New Deal for the American People." The Governor Accepts the Nomination for the Presidency, Chicago, Ill. July 2, 1932

(Breaking of foolish precedents and traditions—Interdependence of economic groups—Economies in government—Repeal of Prohibition Amendment—Truth in sales of securities—Public works for unem-ployed—Shorter work day and work week—Proper land use—Re-forestation work for unemployed—Farm relief—Agricultural sur-pluses—Farm and home mortgage interest reduction—Reciprocal trade agreements—Federal responsibility for relief of unemployment distress.)

Chairman Walsh, my friends of the Democratic National Con-vention of 1932:

I APPRECIATE your willingness after these six arduous days to remain here, for I know well the sleepless hours which you and I have had. I regret that I am late, but I have no control over the winds of Heaven and could only be thankful for my Navy training.

The appearance before a National Convention of its nominee for President, to be formally notified of his selection, is un-precedented and unusual, but these are unprecedented and un-usual times. I have started out on the tasks that lie ahead by breaking the absurd traditions that the candidate should remain

647

in professed ignorance of what has happened for weeks until he is formally notified of that event many weeks later.

My friends, may this be the symbol of my intention to be honest and to avoid all hypocrisy or sham, to avoid all silly shutting of the eyes to the truth in this campaign. You have nominated me and I know it, and I am here to thank you for the honor.

Let it also be symbolic that in so doing I broke traditions. Let it be from now on the task of our Party to break foolish traditions. We will break foolish traditions and leave it to the Republican leadership, far more skilled in that art, to break promises.

Let us now and here highly resolve to resume the country's interrupted march along the path of real progress, of real justice, of real equality for all of our citizens, great and small. Our indomitable leader in that interrupted march is no longer with us, but there still survives today his spirit. Many of his captains, thank God, are still with us, to give us wise counsel. Let us feel that in everything we do there still lives with us, if not the body, the great indomitable, unquenchable, progressive soul of our Commander-in-Chief, Woodrow Wilson.

I have many things on which I want to make my position clear at the earliest possible moment in this campaign. That admirable document, the platform which you have adopted, is clear. I accept it 100 percent.

And you can accept my pledge that I will leave no doubt or ambiguity on where I stand on any question of moment in this campaign.

As we enter this new battle, let us keep always present with us some of the ideals of the Party: The fact that the Democratic Party by tradition and by the continuing logic of history, past and present, is the bearer of liberalism and of progress and at the same time of safety to our institutions. And if this appeal fails, remember well, my friends, that a resentment against the failure of Republican leadership — and note well that in this campaign I shall not use the words "Republican Party," but I shall use, day in and day out, the words, "Republican leadership" — the failure of Republican leaders to solve our troubles may degenerate into unreasoning radicalism.

The great social phenomenon of this depression, unlike others before it, is that it has produced but a few of the disorderly manifestations that too often attend upon such times.

Wild radicalism has made few converts, and the greatest tribute that I can pay to my countrymen is that in these days of crushing want there persists an orderly and hopeful spirit on the part of the millions of our people who have suffered so much. To fail to offer them a new chance is not only to betray their hopes but to misunderstand their patience.

To meet by reaction that danger of radicalism is to invite disaster. Reaction is no barrier to the radical. It is a challenge, a provocation. The way to meet that danger is to offer a workable program of reconstruction, and the party to offer it is the party with clean hands.

This, and this only, is a proper protection against blind reaction on the one hand and an improvised, hit-or-miss, irresponsible opportunism on the other.

There are two ways of viewing the Government's duty in matters affecting economic and social life. The first sees to it that a favored few are helped and hopes that some of their prosperity will leak through, sift through, to labor, to the farmer, to the small business man. That theory belongs to the party of Toryism, and I had hoped that most of the Tories left this country in 1776.

But it is not and never will be the theory of the Democratic Party. This is no time for fear, for reaction or for timidity. Here and now I invite those nominal Republicans who find that their conscience cannot be squared with the groping and the failure of their party leaders to join hands with us; here and now, in equal measure, I warn those nominal Democrats who squint at the future with their faces turned toward the past, and who feel no responsibility to the demands of the new time, that they are out of step with their Party.

Yes, the people of this country want a genuine choice this year, not a choice between two names for the same reactionary doctrine. Ours must be a party of liberal thought, of planned action, of enlightened international outlook, and of the greatest good to the greatest number of our citizens.

Now it is inevitable — and the choice is that of the times — it is inevitable that the main issue of this campaign should revolve about the clear fact of our economic condition, a depression so deep that it is without precedent in modern history. It will not do merely to state, as do Republican leaders to explain their broken promises of continued inaction, that the depression is worldwide. That was not their explanation of the apparent prosperity of 1928. The people will not forget the claim made by them then that prosperity was only a domestic product manufactured by a Republican President and a Republican Congress. If they claim paternity for the one they cannot deny paternity for the other.

I cannot take up all the problems today. I want to touch on a few that are vital. Let us look a little at the recent history and the simple economics, the kind of economics that you and I and the average man and woman talk.

In the years before 1929 we know that this country had completed a vast cycle of building and inflation; for ten years we expanded on the theory of repairing the wastes of the War, but actually expanding far beyond that, and also beyond our natural and normal growth. Now it is worth remembering, and the cold figures of finance prove it, that during that time there was little or no drop in the prices that the consumer had to pay, although those same figures proved that the cost of production fell very greatly; corporate profit resulting from this period was enormous; at the same time little of that profit was devoted to the reduction of prices. The consumer was forgotten. Very little of it went into increased wages; the worker was forgotten, and by no means an adequate proportion was even paid out in dividends — the stockholder was forgotten.

And, incidentally, very little of it was taken by taxation to the beneficent Government of those years.

What was the result? Enormous corporate surpluses piled up — the most stupendous in history. Where, under the spell of delirious speculation, did those surpluses go? Let us talk economics that the figures prove and that we can understand. Why, they went chiefly in two directions: first, into new and unnecessary plants which now stand stark and idle; and second, into the call-money market of Wall Street, either directly by the corporations, or indirectly through the banks. Those are the facts. Why blink at them?

Then came the crash. You know the story. Surpluses invested in unnecessary plants became idle. Men lost their jobs; purchasing power dried up; banks became frightened and started calling loans. Those who had money were afraid to part with it. Credit contracted. Industry stopped. Commerce declined, and unemployment mounted.

And there we are today.

Translate that into human terms. See how the events of the past three years have come home to specific groups of people: first, the group dependent on industry; second, the group dependent on agriculture; third, and made up in large part of members of the first two groups, the people who are called "small investors and depositors." In fact, the strongest possible tie between the first two groups, agriculture and industry, is the fact that the savings and to a degree the security of both are tied together in that third group — the credit structure of the Nation.

Never in history have the interests of all the people been so united in a single economic problem. Picture to yourself, for instance, the great groups of property owned by millions of our citizens, represented by credits issued in the form of bonds and mortgages — Government bonds of all kinds, Federal, State, county, municipal; bonds of industrial companies, of utility companies; mortgages on real estate in farms and cities, and finally the vast investments of the Nation in the railroads. What is the measure of the security of each of those groups? We know well that in our complicated, interrelated credit structure if any one of these credit groups collapses they may all collapse. Danger to one is danger to all.

How, I ask, has the present Administration in Washington treated the interrelationship of these credit groups? The answer is clear: It has not recognized that interrelationship existed at all. Why, the Nation asks, has Washington failed to understand that all of these groups, each and every one, the top of the pyramid and the bottom of the pyramid, must be considered together, that each and every one of them is dependent on every other; each and every one of them affecting the whole financial fabric?

Statesmanship and vision, my friends, require relief to all at the same time.

Just one word or two on taxes, the taxes that all of us pay toward the cost of Government of all kinds.

I know something of taxes. For three long years I have been going up and down this country preaching that Government — Federal and State and local — costs too much. I shall not stop that preaching. As an immediate program of action we must abolish useless offices. We must eliminate unnecessary functions of Government — functions, in fact, that are not definitely essential to the continuance of Government. We must merge, we must consolidate subdivisions of Government, and, like the private citizen, give up luxuries which we can no longer afford.

By our example at Washington itself, we shall have the opportunity of pointing the way of economy to local government, for let us remember well that out of every tax dollar in the average State in this Nation, 40 cents enter the treasury in Washington, D. C., 10 or 12 cents only go to the State capitals, and 48 cents are consumed by the costs of local government in counties and cities and towns.

I propose to you, my friends, and through you, that Government of all kinds, big and little, be made solvent and that the example be set by the President of the United States and his Cabinet.

And talking about setting a definite example, I congratulate this convention for having had the courage fearlessly to write into its declaration of principles what an overwhelming majority here assembled really thinks about the 18th Amendment. This convention wants repeal. Your candidate wants repeal. And I am confident that the United States of America wants repeal.

Two years ago the platform on which I ran for Governor the second time contained substantially the same provision. The overwhelming sentiment of the people of my State, as shown by the vote of that year, extends, I know, to the people of many of the other States. I say to you now that from this date on the 18th Amendment is doomed. When that happens, we as Democrats must and will, rightly and morally, enable the States to protect themselves against the importation of intoxicating liquor where such importation may violate their State laws. We must rightly and morally prevent the return of the saloon.

To go back to this dry subject of finance, because it all ties in together — the 18th Amendment has something to do with finance, too — in a comprehensive planning for the reconstruction of the great credit groups, including Government credit, I list an important place for that prize statement of principle in the platform here adopted calling for the letting in of the light of day on issues of securities, foreign and domestic, which are offered for sale to the investing public.

My friends, you and I as common-sense citizens know that it would help to protect the savings of the country from the dishonesty of crooks and from the lack of honor of some men in high financial places. Publicity is the enemy of crookedness.

And now one word about unemployment, and incidentally about agriculture. I have favored the use of certain types of public works as a further emergency means of stimulating employment and the issuance of bonds to pay for such public works, but I have pointed out that no economic end is served if we merely build without building for a necessary purpose. Such works, of course, should insofar as possible be self-sustaining if they are to be financed by the issuing of bonds. So as to spread

653

the points of all kinds as widely as possible, we must take definite steps to shorten the working day and the working week.

Let us use common sense and business sense. Just as one example, we know that a very hopeful and immediate means of relief, both for the unemployed and for agriculture, will come from a wide plan of the converting of many millions of acres of marginal and unused land into timberland through reforestation. There are tens of millions of acres east of the Mississippi River alone in abandoned farms, in cut-over land, now growing up in worthless brush. Why, every European Nation has a definite land policy, and has had one for generations. We have none. Having none, we face a future of soil erosion and timber famine. It is clear that economic foresight and immediate employment march hand in hand in the call for the reforestation of these vast areas.

In so doing, employment can be given to a million men. That is the kind of public work that is self-sustaining, and therefore capable of being financed by the issuance of bonds which are made secure by the fact that the growth of tremendous crops will provide adequate security for the investment.

Yes, I have a very definite program for providing employment by that means. I have done it, and I am doing it today in the State of New York. I know that the Democratic Party can do it successfully in the Nation. That will put men to work, and that is an example of the action that we are going to have.

Now as a further aid to agriculture, we know perfectly well — but have we come out and said so clearly and distinctly? — we should repeal immediately those provisions of law that compel the Federal Government to go into the market to purchase, to sell, to speculate in farm products in a futile attempt to reduce farm surpluses. And they are the people who are talking of keeping Government out of business. The practical way to help the farmer is by an arrangement that will, in addition to lightening some of the impoverishing burdens from his back, do something toward the reduction of the surpluses of staple commodities that hang on the market. It should be our aim to add to the

654

world prices of staple products the amount of a reasonable tariff protection, to give agriculture the same protection that industry has today.

And in exchange for this immediately increased return I am sure that the farmers of this Nation would agree ultimately to such planning of their production as would reduce the surpluses and make it unnecessary in later years to depend on dumping those surpluses abroad in order to support domestic prices. That result has been accomplished in other Nations; why not in America, too?

Farm leaders and farm economists, generally, agree that a plan based on that principle is a desirable first step in the reconstruction of agriculture. It does not in itself furnish a complete program, but it will serve in great measure in the long run to remove the pall of a surplus without the continued perpetual threat of world dumping. Final voluntary reduction of surplus is a part of our objective, but the long continuance and the present burden of existing surpluses make it necessary to repair great damage of the present by immediate emergency measures.

Such a plan as that, my friends, does not cost the Government any money, nor does it keep the Government in business or in speculation.

As to the actual wording of a bill, I believe that the Democratic Party stands ready to be guided by whatever the responsible farm groups themselves agree on. That is a principle that is sound; and again I ask for action.

One more word about the farmer, and I know that every delegate in this hall who lives in the city knows why I lay emphasis on the farmer. It is because one-half of our population, over 50,000,000 people, are dependent on agriculture; and, my friends, if those 50,000,000 people have no money, no cash, to buy what is produced in the city, the city suffers to an equal or greater extent.

That is why we are going to make the voters understand this year that this Nation is not merely a Nation of independence, but it is, if we are to survive, bound to be a Nation of interdependence — town and city, and North and South, East and West. That is our goal, and that goal will be understood by the people of this country no matter where they live.

Yes, the purchasing power of that half of our population dependent on agriculture is gone. Farm mortgages reach nearly ten billions of dollars today and interest charges on that alone are $560,000,000 a year. But that is not all. The tax burden caused by extravagant and inefficient local government is an additional factor. Our most immediate concern should be to reduce the interest burden on these mortgages.

Rediscounting of farm mortgages under salutary restrictions must be expanded and should, in the future, be conditioned on the reduction of interest rates. Amortization payments, maturities should likewise in this crisis be extended before rediscount is permitted where the mortgagor is sorely pressed. That, my friends, is another example of practical, immediate relief: Action.

I aim to do the same thing, and it can be done, for the small home-owner in our cities and villages. We can lighten his burden and develop his purchasing power. Take away, my friends, that spectre of too high an interest rate. Take away that spectre of the due date just a short time away. Save homes; save homes for thousands of self-respecting families, and drive out that spectre of insecurity from our midst.

Out of all the tons of printed paper, out of all the hours of oratory, the recriminations, the defenses, the happy-thought plans in Washington and in every State, there emerges one great, simple, crystal-pure fact that during the past ten years a Nation of 120,000,000 people has been led by the Republican leaders to erect an impregnable barbed wire entanglement around its borders through the instrumentality of tariffs which have isolated us from all the other human beings in all the rest of the round world. I accept that admirable tariff statement in the platform of this convention. It would protect American business and American labor. By our acts of the past we have invited and received the retaliation of other Nations. I propose an invitation to them to forget the past, to sit at the table with us, as friends, and to plan with us for the restoration of the trade of the world.

Go into the home of the business man. He knows what the tariff has done for him. Go into the home of the factory worker. He knows why goods do not move. Go into the home of the farmer. He knows how the tariff has helped to ruin him.

At last our eyes are open. At last the American people are ready to acknowledge that Republican leadership was wrong and that the Democracy is right.

My program, of which I can only touch on these points, is based upon this simple moral principle: the welfare and the soundness of a Nation depend first upon what the great mass of the people wish and need; and second, whether or not they are getting it.

What do the people of America want more than anything else? To my mind, they want two things: work, with all the moral and spiritual values that go with it; and with work, a reasonable measure of security—security for themselves and for their wives and children. Work and security—these are more than words. They are more than facts. They are the spiritual values, the true goal toward which our efforts of reconstruction should lead. These are the values that this program is intended to gain; these are the values we have failed to achieve by the leadership we now have.

Our Republican leaders tell us economic laws—sacred, inviolable, unchangeable—cause panics which no one could prevent. But while they prate of economic laws, men and women are starving. We must lay hold of the fact that economic laws are not made by nature. They are made by human beings.

Yes, when—not if—when we get the chance, the Federal Government will assume bold leadership in distress relief. For years Washington has alternated between putting its head in the sand and saying there is no large number of destitute people in our midst who need food and clothing, and then saying the States should take care of them, if there are. Instead of planning two and a half years ago to do what they are now trying to do, they kept putting it off from day to day, week to week, and month to month, until the conscience of America demanded action.

I say that while primary responsibility for relief rests with localities now, as ever, yet the Federal Government has always had and still has a continuing responsibility for the broader public welfare. It will soon fulfill that responsibility.

And now, just a few words about our plans for the next four months. By coming here instead of waiting for a formal notification, I have made it clear that I believe we should eliminate expensive ceremonies and that we should set in motion at once, tonight, my friends, the necessary machinery for an adequate presentation of the issues to the electorate of the Nation.

I myself have important duties as Governor of a great State, duties which in these times are more arduous and more grave than at any previous period. Yet I feel confident that I shall be able to make a number of short visits to several parts of the Nation. My trips will have as their first objective the study at first hand, from the lips of men and women of all parties and all occupations, of the actual conditions and needs of every part of an interdependent country.

One word more: Out of every crisis, every tribulation, every disaster, mankind rises with some share of greater knowledge, of higher decency, of purer purpose. Today we shall have come through a period of loose thinking, descending morals, an era of selfishness, among individual men and women and among Nations. Blame not Governments alone for this. Blame ourselves in equal share. Let us be frank in acknowledgment of the truth that many amongst us have made obeisance to Mammon, that the profits of speculation, the easy road without toil, have lured us from the old barricades. To return to higher standards we must abandon the false prophets and seek new leaders of our own choosing.

Never before in modern history have the essential differences between the two major American parties stood out in such striking contrast as they do today. Republican leaders not only have failed in material things, they have failed in national vision, because in disaster they have held out no hope, they have pointed out no path for the people below to climb back to places of security and of safety in our American life.

Throughout the Nation, men and women, forgotten in the political philosophy of the Government of the last years look to us here for guidance and for more equitable opportunity to share in the distribution of national wealth.

On the farms, in the large metropolitan areas, in the smaller cities and in the villages, millions of our citizens cherish the hope that their old standards of living and of thought have not gone forever. Those millions cannot and shall not hope in vain.

I pledge you, I pledge myself, to a new deal for the American people. Let us all here assembled constitute ourselves prophets of a new order of competence and of courage. This is more than a political campaign; it is a call to arms. Give me your help, not to win votes alone, but to win in this crusade to restore America to its own people.

132 ⁋ The Candidate Discusses the National Democratic Platform. Radio Address, Albany, N. Y. July 30, 1932

I HOPE during this campaign to use the radio frequently to speak to you about important things that concern us all.

In the olden days, campaigns were conducted amid surroundings of brass bands and red lights. Oratory was an appeal primarily to the emotions and sometimes to the passions. It always has been my feeling that with the spread of education, with the wider reading of newspapers and especially with the advent of the radio, mere oratory and mere emotion are having less to do with the determination of public questions under our representative system of Government. Today, common sense plays the greater part and final opinions are arrived at in the quiet of the home.

In this quiet of common sense and friendliness, I want you to hear me tonight as I sit here in my own home, away from the excitement of the campaign. I am weighing all the things which I have learned in all my years in public service — first in Albany, twenty-one years ago, then during eight busy years in Washington, interspersed with visits into all the States of the Union and, during and after the War, to the Nations of Europe; then, in these latter years, in my tasks as Governor of New York.

In order that the way may be clear for the more detailed discussion and debate which will come as the campaign proceeds, I propose tonight to state the broad policies of my party and to sketch the first outline of the final picture.

Where do we look for this? In the platform, of course. A platform is a proposal and at the same time a promise binding on the party and its candidates.

Now even the partisan opposition press has found it hard to criticize the Democratic platform this year. It is brief, only one-fifth of the length of the Republican platform, and easily understood. Eighty percent of it is constructive; only twenty percent critical. Moreover, it is forthright and genuine — honest to the core.

The entire platform needs to be read in the light of its short preamble. This indicates that our present economic condition — how it came, what it is, and how it can be remedied — is the main issue of this campaign. I can do no better than to read it exactly as it stands.

"In this time of unprecedented economic and social distress, the Democratic Party declares its conviction that the chief causes of this condition were the disastrous policies, pursued by our Government since the World War, of economic isolation fostering the merger of competitive businesses into monopolies and encouraging the indefensible expansion and contraction of credits for private profit at the expense of the public.

"Those who were responsible for these policies have abandoned the ideals on which the War was won and thrown away the fruits of victory, thus rejecting the greatest opportunity in history to bring peace, prosperity and happiness to our people

660

and to the world. They have ruined our foreign trade, destroyed the values of our commodities and products, crippled our banking system, robbed millions of our people of their life savings and thrown millions more out of work, produced widespread poverty and brought the Government to a state of financial distress unprecedented in times of peace.

"The only hope for improving present conditions, restoring employment, affording permanent relief to the people and bringing the Nation back to its former proud position of domestic happiness and of financial, industrial, agricultural and commercial leadership in the world lies in a drastic change in economic and governmental policies.

"Believing that a party platform is a covenant with the people to be kept by the party when entrusted with power, and that the people are entitled to know in plain words the terms of the contract to which they are asked to subscribe, we hereby declare this to be the platform of the Democratic Party.

"The Democratic Party solemnly promises by appropriate action to put into effect the principles, policies and reforms herein advocated and to eradicate the policies, methods and practices herein condemned."

Immediately after this statement of principle, there follow three important declarations:

"An immediate and drastic reduction of governmental expenditures by abolishing useless commissions and offices, consolidating departments and bureaus and eliminating extravagance, to accomplish a saving of not less than 25 percent in the cost of Federal Government, and we call upon the Democratic Party in the States to make a zealous effort to achieve a proportionate result.

"Maintenance of the national credit by a Federal budget annually balanced on the basis of accurate Executive estimates within revenues, raised by a system of taxation levied on the principle of ability to pay.

"A sound currency to be preserved at all hazards, and an international monetary conference called, on the invitation of

661

our Government, to consider the rehabilitation of silver and related questions."

With these declarations—for a balanced budget and for a sound currency—the Democratic Party sets its face against the time-serving and disastrous fiscal policy of recent years.

What did that policy do?

1. In highly prosperous times, when taxes were easy to obtain, it repealed taxes on abnormal profits and incomes, with the result that the war debt was not drastically reduced.
2. When the depression began, the Administration, instead of reducing annual expenses to meet decreasing revenues, became sponsor for deficits which at the end of this fiscal year will have added $5,000,000,000 to the national debt.
3. To meet this staggering deficit, the Administration has resorted to the type of inflation which has weakened public confidence in our Government credit both at home and abroad.

High-sounding, newly invented phrases cannot sugar-coat the pill.

Let us have the courage to stop borrowing to meet continuing deficits. Stop the deficits. Let us have equal courage to reverse the policy of the Republican leaders and insist on a sound currency.

Our party says clearly that not only must Government income meet prospective expenditures, but this income must be secured on the principle of ability to pay. This is a declaration in favor of graduated income, inheritance and profits taxes, and against taxes on food and clothing, whose burden is actually shifted to the consumers of these necessities of life on a per capita basis rather than on the basis of the relative size of personal incomes.

Something more is needed than a domestic balanced budget and a just revenue system. Muddled Government finance creates a general uncertainty concerning the value of national currencies; this uncertainty has a way of spreading from country to country. The world is tormented with it now. The United States could well afford to take the lead in asking for a general conference to establish less changeable fiscal relationships and to determine what can be done to restore the purchasing power of that half of the world's inhabitants who are on a silver basis, and to exchange views regarding governmental finance.

It is obvious that sound money is an international necessity, not a domestic consideration for one Nation alone. Nothing is more needed than such an exchange of opinion; nothing could do more to create stable conditions in which trade could once more be resumed.

We face a condition which, at first, seems to involve either an unbalanced budget and an unsound currency or else failure of the Government to assume its just duties — the relief of distress and protection against loss of savings built up through many years by numberless small investors. This concerns you, my friends, who managed to lay aside a few dollars for a rainy day.

This dilemma can be met by saving in one place what we would spend in others, or by acquiring the necessary revenue through taxation. Revenues must cover expenditures by one means or another. Any Government, like any family, can for a year spend a little more than it earns. But you and I know that a continuation of that habit means the poorhouse.

At best, the Federal Government will necessarily bear a heavy burden. It has been the theory of Republican leaders that relief is a local responsibility, a theory stated repeatedly and modified only with the greatest reluctance. The Democratic platform was framed with an eye to actual human needs. What could be finer than that bold and humanitarian statement pledging "continuous responsibility of the Government (meaning the Federal Government) for human welfare, especially for the protection of children."

In view of this statement, the plank concerning relief for the unemployed becomes significant:

"We advocate extension of Federal credit to the States to provide unemployment relief wherever the diminishing resources of the States make it impossible for them to provide for the needy; expansion of the Federal program of necessary and useful construction affected with a public interest, such as flood control and waterways, including the Great Lakes-St. Lawrence deep waterways; the spread of employment by a substantial reduction in the hours of labor, the encouragement of the shorter week by applying that principle in Government service; advance planning of public works."

Following this there is the party declaration concerning agriculture.

"We advocate for the restoration of agriculture, the Nation's basic industry, better financing of farm mortgages through reorganized farm bank agencies at low rates of interest, on an amortization plan, giving preference to credits for the redemption of farms and homes sold under foreclosure; extension and development of the farm cooperative movement and effective control of crop surpluses so that our farmers may have the full benefit of the domestic market.

"Enactment of every constitutional measure that will aid the farmer to receive for basic farm commodities prices in excess of cost of production.

"We condemn the extravagance of the Farm Board, its disastrous action which made the Government a speculator in farm products and the unsound policy of restricting agricultural production to the demands of domestic markets."

The platform contains admirable statements about a group of subjects which logically go together — the tariff and foreign policy. The tariff plank reads as follows:

"We advocate:

"A competitive tariff for revenue, with a fact-finding tariff commission free from Executive interference, reciprocal tariff agreements with other Nations and an international economic conference designed to restore international trade and facilitate exchange.

"We condemn:

"The Hawley-Smoot tariff law, the prohibitive rates of which have resulted in retaliatory action by more than forty countries, created international economic hostilities, destroyed international trade, driven our factories into foreign countries, robbed the American farmer of his foreign markets and increased his cost of production."

A tariff is a tax laid on certain goods passing from the producer to the consumer. It is laid on these goods rather than other similar ones because they originate abroad. This is obviously protection for the producers of competing goods at home. Peasants who live at lower levels than our farmers, workers who are sweated to reduce costs, ought not to determine prices for American-made goods. There are standards which we desire to set for ourselves. Tariffs should be high enough to maintain living standards which we set for ourselves. But if they are higher, they become a particularly vicious kind of direct tax which is laid doubly on the consumer. Not only are the prices of foreign goods raised, but those of domestic goods also.

It is a difficult and highly technical matter to determine standards and costs of production abroad and at home. A commission of experts can be trusted to find such facts, but not to dictate policies. The facts should be left to speak for themselves, free from presidential interference.

One of the great needs of the world is to set international trade flowing again. The proper procedure is to ascertain all the pertinent facts, to publish them widely and then to negotiate with each country affected. Trade barriers of all kinds ought to be lowered, not by rule of thumb, but with due regard to safety and justice — lowered, nevertheless, as quickly and definitely as possible. Policy needs to be dominated by the realities we discover and by the national purposes we seek.

This tariff policy, however, cannot be separated from our other relations with foreign countries; the whole thing ties in together. The platform is explicit here also:

"We advocate:

"A firm foreign policy, including peace with all the world and the settlement of international disputes by arbitration; no interference in the internal affairs of other Nations; the sanctity of treaties and the maintenance of good faith and of good-will in financial obligations; adherence to the World Court with the pending reservations; the Pact of Paris, abolishing war as an instrument of national policy, to be made effective by provisions for consultation and conference in case of threatened violation of treaties; international agreement for reduction of armaments; and cooperation with Nations of the Western Hemisphere to maintain the spirit of the Monroe Doctrine. We oppose cancellation of due debts owing to the United States by foreign Nations."

This problem of the debts is complex. Its solution has, however, been brought measurably nearer by the recent results at Lausanne. Great Britain, France and Germany have at last agreed among themselves concerning reparations. The danger now is that they may turn a united front against us. This comes, I am convinced, not so much from the debts they owe us, as from our barriers against their trade, which make the problem so difficult.

The debts will not be a problem — we shall not have to cancel them — if we are realistic about providing ways in which payment is possible through the profits arising from the rehabilitation of trade. The Republican platform said nothing at all about this; but their position has been the absurd one of demanding payment and at the same time making payment impossible. This policy finally forced a moratorium as it was bound to do. Our policy declares for payment, but at the same time for lowered tariffs and resumption of trade which open the way for payment.

Up to this point, you and I have been considering both the immediate relief for the present emergency and also the immediate initiating of plans to bring us back to a more normal economic condition. At the same time it is equally our duty to guard against repetition of the evils and errors which have cost us so much. It is not enough to say that when prosperity is restored we shall then consider how to avoid repeating all the old errors. Today we recognize these errors. Today they should be outlawed for all time to come. It must be made more difficult for a depression to happen in the future; it must be made impossible for its indefensible features to show themselves again. Concerning the necessary revision of some of our institutions for this purpose, I shall have more to say later. At present I read you the party's stand:

It advocates:

"Strict and impartial enforcement of anti-trust laws to prevent monopoly and unfair trade practices, and revision thereof for the better protection of labor and the small producer and distributor; conservation, development and use of the Nation's water power in the public interest.

"Protection of the investing public by requiring to be filed with the Government and carried in advertisements of all offerings of foreign and domestic stocks and bonds true information as to bonuses, commissions, principal invested and interests of sellers. Regulation to the full extent of Federal power of:

"Holding companies which sell securities in interstate commerce;

"Rates of utility companies operating across State lines;

"Exchanges trading in securities and commodities.

"Quicker methods of realizing on assets for the relief of depositors of suspended banks, and a more rigid supervision of national banks for the protection of depositors and the prevention of the use of their moneys in speculation to the detriment of local credits.

"The severance of affiliated securities companies and the divorce of underwriting schemes from commercial banks; and further restriction of Federal Reserve Banks in permitting the use of Federal Reserve facilities for speculative purposes."

It condemns:

"Action and utterances of high public officials designed to influence stock exchange prices.

"The usurpation of power by the State Department in assuming to pass upon foreign securities offered by international bankers, as a result of which billions of dollars in questionable bonds have been sold to the public upon the implied approval of the Federal Government."

Now we come to the famous repeal plank. It is simple and it has meaning:

"We favor the repeal of the Eighteenth Amendment.

"To effect such repeal we demand that the Congress immediately propose a constitutional amendment to truly representative conventions in the States called to act solely on that proposal.

"We urge the enactment of such measures by the several States as will actually promote temperance, effectively prevent the return of the saloon and bring the liquor traffic into the open under complete supervision and control by the States.

"We demand that the Federal Government effectively exercise its power to enable the States to protect themselves against importation of intoxicating liquors in violation of their laws.

"Pending repeal, we favor immediate modification of the Volstead Act to legalize the manufacture and sale of beer and other beverages of such alcoholic content as is permissible under the Constitution and to provide therefrom a proper and needed revenue."

Nothing need be added to that, except that if the present Congress takes no action, I shall urge the new Congress to carry out these provisions.

There are a number of other plans of importance, but less in need of elaboration, which, because my time is so short, I shall only read to you.

They are as follows:

"We advocate a navy and an army adequate for national defense, based on a survey of all facts affecting the existing establishments, that the people in time of peace may not be burdened by an expenditure fast approaching one billion dollars annually.

"The full measure of justice and generosity for all war veterans who have suffered disability or disease caused by or resulting from actual service in time of war and for their dependents.

"Unemployment and old-age insurance, under State laws.

"Independence for the Philippines; ultimate statehood for Puerto Rico; the employment of American citizens in the operation of the Panama Canal.

"Simplification of legal procedure and reorganization of the judicial system to make the attainment of justice speedy, certain and at less cost.

"Continuous publicity of political contributions and expenditures, strengthening of the corrupt practices act and severe penalties for misappropriation of campaign funds.

"We condemn:

"The improper and excessive use of money in political activities.

"Paid lobbies of special interests to influence members of Congress and other public servants by personal contacts.

"The open and covert resistance of administrative officials to every effort made by Congressional committees to curtail the extravagant expenditures of the Government, and to revoke improvident subsidies granted to favored interests."

And now, my friends, I close my talk with you tonight with this concluding declaration:

"To accomplish these purposes and to recover economic liberty we pledge the nominees of this convention, and the best effort of a great party whose founder announced the doctrine which guides us now: in the hour of our country's need, equal rights to all, special privilege to none."

133 ❨ The Failures of the Preceding Administration. Campaign Address at Columbus, Ohio. August 20, 1932

(Encouragement of overspeculation and overproduction — Foreign trade — Tariff barriers — Loans to backward and crippled countries — "Alice-in-Wonderland" economics — Optimistic misleading statements after crash of 1929 — Concentration of economic power — Supervision of security sales and exchanges, bank deposits, and holding companies — Separation of investment banking from commercial banking.)

WHEN I opened my campaign in Chicago seven weeks ago I spoke briefly and plainly of the issues of this campaign. Following that address I outlined to the people of the country the platform of my party. In the order of logic I should devote this address to the Republican platform and the speech of acceptance of my opponent. I find it necessary, therefore, not only to discuss these statements, but to consider them in the light of Republican policies and promises of the past few years. To do so without severe criticism is impossible.

I regret that necessity, for destructive criticism is never justified for its own sake. And yet, to build we must first clear the ground. We must find out why the Republican leadership — and mind you, all the way through this campaign I am not talking about the millions of fine men and women who make up the Republican Party, I am addressing my remarks to the Republican leadership — why that Republican leadership built so unwisely. We must determine the causes that made the whole structure collapse.

We must take borings to determine the necessary character of the foundation. To justify our right to build we must show not only a sound plan, but why, in contrast, this plan leads to hope of better things.

Both platforms and the speeches of acceptance of both candidates at least have agreed upon one thing: that the major issue in this campaign is the economic situation. The people are now asked to judge whether the present Administration has been wise in its economic policies, as revealed in the President's statements and actions. Only in this sense is this criticism directed at an individual.

I propose to show that this leadership misunderstood the forces which were involved in the economic life of the country, that it encouraged a vast speculative boom, and that when the reckoning came the Administration was not frank, not honest, with the people, and by blundering statements and actions postponed necessary readjustments.

Much of our trouble came from what the President described as "a new basis in Government relation with business; in fact, a new relationship of Government with its citizens."

The fact that he believes this policy definitely affects business he has asserted many times. For example, in taking credit for the expansion of export trade, he said, "It is not chance. . . . Things like this don't happen."

Here is the case summed up in the President's own words. At St. Louis in 1928 he said, "Without the wise policies which the Republican Party has made effective through the past seven and a half years, the great prosperity we now enjoy would not have been possible."

Remember this, my friends, in the face of present assertions that Government cannot affect business conditions. He even claims he must take the responsibility of what the army does and where it goes.

This mobilization of business as the President practices it by promotion and advertising methods will always be defective. His power to influence public opinion is great, but this driving will, as it has been well put, always be back-seat driving—ineffective and dangerous.

Apart from the futility and danger of such interference the President's thought is a wide departure from the Republican tradition as voiced by President Harding's slogan of less government in business. Republicans everywhere should understand and see this in this year, 1932. It is completely alien to the traditions of their party. The coincidence of the two policies is as dangerous a mixture as fire and powder. This is the tragic folly of the past four years.

Even before the election of Mr. Hoover a terrible race began between the rising tide of bubble fortunes in the stock market and the rising tide of unemployment. Mr. Hoover's own records in the Department of Commerce showed that there were 2,000,-000 fewer men at work in the four principal fields of employment in 1925 than there had been six years previously, although the population and production had vastly increased and many new industries had appeared.

Despite huge profits in a handful of large corporations, the fact remained that more than half the corporations of the country were reporting no net income. Nevertheless, we were, said Mr. Hoover in that campaign, on the verge of the "greatest commercial expansion in history."

High wages would create new consuming power, accelerated mass and machine production would lower costs. Buy more! Owe more! Spend more! This was the program. This caused the deluge of high-pressure selling, lavish extravagance, head-on plunges into debt and yet more debt, and all this, coupled with the President's idea of Government sponsorship of the whole headlong plunge, was the dangerous doctrine called "the new economics."

It was the heyday of promoters, sloganeers, mushroom millionaires, opportunists, adventurers of all kinds. In this mad whirl was launched Mr. Hoover's campaign. Perhaps foreseeing it, a shrewd man from New England, while in the cool detachment of the Dakota hills, on a narrow slip of paper wrote the historic words, "I do not choose to run."

It was already obvious even to the Administration that the forced production of our industry was far too great for our domestic markets. The President had to meet this fact and he did meet it by an audacious and fateful suggestion. We were to sell what he called "the constantly increasing surplus." We were to sell it abroad.

But how could this be done in the collapsed state of world finance? He answered, "It is an essential part of the further expansion of our foreign trade that we should interest ourselves in the development of backward or crippled countries by means of loans."

Obedient to this suggestion, the United States, which had already loaned fourteen billions abroad, was lending overseas at a rate of two billion dollars per year. Thus was produced, my friends, the crop of foreign bonds which American investors know to their cost today. The old economics had gone out of business. To the suggestion that mass and machine production ultimately destroys employment, the President simply observed, and again I quote his words, "This is the re-echo of a century ago."

And the new economics went merrily on. The agitation had already begun for the raising of protective tariffs, according to good Republican principles. There were protests, of course, that you could not increase protective tariffs, preventing foreigners from selling, and at the same time expect a greater expansion of our foreign trade.

Said the President: "This theory was sound enough in the old days of direct barter." And after discussing polyangular trade, he concluded in these words: "This, I believe, finally extinguishes the already depleted importance of the theory that our tariff seriously damages the buying power of foreign countries."

I think the President himself knew better; but behind him was the insistent Mr. Grundy. They had let the President have his foreign loans — not unnaturally, in view of the huge banking commissions which were being made out of these loans.

But Mr. Grundy and the Republican leaders, looking for something more substantial than the fanciful promises from abroad that were being sold to American investors, asked for a copper-riveted American market, sealed by the highest tariff in the history of the world.

The President hesitated, because he must have seen at that time the awful nature of the choice. But his courage failed. Grundyism had its way; and American industry, accelerated to a pace never before known, suddenly found the brakes locked on a slippery road. The law of gravity did the rest.

Back in 1928, when the Republican candidate told us that our prosperity was permanent and safe, red flags of warning were already flying unheeded.

For some years the collapse of farm prices had prostrated agriculture, with nothing done to help. In industry, the number of corporations reporting net income was steadily diminishing.

In banking, Paul Warburg, a great financial authority and a great man who had given years of his life to the original building up of the Federal Reserve System, issued early in 1929 a public warning that speculation had gone wild and that the country would have to pay for it.

Notwithstanding the appearance of prosperity, unemployment was steadily increasing. Months before, the American Federation of Labor had sounded an alarm with regard to the rapid decrease in the number of jobs.

And the Federal Reserve Board saw the clouds, too, but did little to help.

The Administration lined up with the stock market, and the warnings went unheeded. The President apparently forgot that in 1922 he himself had written as follows: "Thirty years ago our business community considered the cyclic financial panic inevitable. We know now that we have cured it through the Federal Reserve Board." And yet in 1929 he took the opposite course, nullifying the Board's effort.

It has been suggested that the American public was apparently elected to the role of our old friend, Alice in Wonderland. I agree that Alice was peering into a wonderful looking-glass of the wonderful economics. White Knights had great schemes of unlimited sales in foreign markets and discounted the future ten years ahead.

The poorhouse was to vanish like the Cheshire cat. A mad hatter invited everyone to "have some more profits." There were no profits, except on paper. A cynical Father William in the lower district of Manhattan balanced the sinuous evil of a pool-ridden stock market on the end of his nose. A puzzled, somewhat skeptical Alice asked the Republican leadership some simple questions:

"Will not the printing and selling of more stocks and bonds, the building of new plants and the increase of efficiency produce more goods than we can buy?"

"No," shouted Humpty Dumpty. "The more we produce the more we can buy."

"What if we produce a surplus?"

"Oh, we can sell it to foreign consumers."

"How can the foreigners pay for it?"

"Why, we will lend them the money."

"I see," said little Alice, "they will buy our surplus with our

674

money. Of course, these foreigners will pay us back by selling us their goods?"

"Oh, not at all," said Humpty Dumpty. "We set up a high wall called the tariff."

"And," said Alice at last, "how will the foreigners pay off these loans?"

"That is easy," said Humpty Dumpty, "did you ever hear of a moratorium?"

And so, at last, my friends, we have reached the heart of the magic formula of 1928. Strange as it may seem, the road to abolition of poverty was a constantly increasing maze of machine production. The absorption of the surplus was to be through what I quoted before, the "development of backward and crippled countries by means of loans."

The "lift-yourself-up-by-your-own-boot-straps" theory was believed. Yes, it appeared to work. People voted the exponent of the new economics into office and rushed into the markets to buy. Under the spell of this fable they sacrificed on the altar of the stock market the frugal savings of a lifetime.

Business men sincerely believed that they had heard expert advice and risked their solvency by a new burst of expansion. Common sense was hushed before the spell of an economic necromancy sponsored by Washington itself.

Between that day when the abolition of poverty was proclaimed, in August, 1928, and the end of that year, the market balloon rose. It did not stop. It went on, up and up, and up for many fantastic months. These were as the figures of a dream. The balloon had reached the economic stratosphere, above the air, where mere man may not survive.

Then came the crash. The paper profits vanished overnight; the savings pushed into the markets at the peak dwindled to nothing. Only the cold reality remained for the debts were real; only the magnificently engraved certificates not worth the cost of the artistic scroll work upon them!

And now came what I believe to be the real crime of the Republican Administration. It had a sea of statistics at hand, but the Administration did not tell the truth. On October 25, 1929 — the day after the big break — the President observed: "The fundamental business of the country, that is, production and distribution of commodities, is on a sound and prosperous basis."

And further he insisted, and these are his words: "There is no reason why business could not be carried on as usual."

On December 3, 1929, the President sent a message to Congress as follows: "The sudden threat of unemployment and the recollection of the economic consequences of previous depressions under a much less secure financial system created unwarranted pessimism and fear. We have re-established confidence."

And again, with what seems now like ghastly humor, the speech continued: "I wish to emphasize that during the past year (1929) the Nation has continued to grow in strength. Our people have advanced in comfort."

Meanwhile, common citizens in their family affairs, and industrial and commercial agencies, began to trim their sails, but the President disapproved of this prudence.

"I have," said he, "instituted systematic and voluntary measures of cooperation with the business institutions and with the State and municipal authorities to make certain that the fundamental business of the country shall continue as usual."

On March 7, 1930, came the classic remark of the whole depression. Said the President to the press: "All evidence indicates that the worst effects of the crash and unemployment will have passed during the next sixty days."

On May 1, 1930, the White House once more insisted, "We have now passed the worst." In October, 1930, after the false start and the disastrous aftercrash of that fateful summer, proclaimed the White House: "The depression is but a temporary halt in the prosperity of a great people. The income of a large part of our people has not been reduced."

On December 2, 1930, it was announced that "we have already weathered the worst of the storm." And then, my friends, as the depression steadily continued, all was silence.

That was the measure of Republican leadership.

Finally, when facts could no longer be ignored and excuses had to be found, Washington discovered that the depression came from abroad. In October of last year, the official policy came to us as follows: "The depression has been deepened by events from abroad which are beyond the control either of our citizens or our Government" — an excuse, note well, my friends, which the President still maintained in his acceptance speech last week.

Not for partisan purposes, but in order to set forth history aright, that excuse ought to be quietly considered. The records of the civilized Nations of the world prove two facts: first, that the economic structure of other Nations was affected by our own tide of speculation, and the curtailment of our lending helped to bring on their distress; second, that the bubble burst first in the land of its origin — the United States.

The major collapse in other countries followed. It was not simultaneous with ours. Moreover, further curtailment of our loans, plus the continual stagnation in trade caused by the Grundy tariff, has continued the depression throughout international affairs.

So I sum up the history of the present Administration in four sentences:

First, it encouraged speculation and overproduction, through its false economic policies.

Second, it attempted to minimize the crash and misled the people as to its gravity.

Third, it erroneously charged the cause to other Nations of the world.

And finally, it refused to recognize and correct the evils at home which had brought it forth; it delayed relief; it forgot reform.

So much for a dispassionate review of the facts of history. I have placed the blame. But to place the blame is not enough.

The logical question before us now is this: What steps have been taken to recognize the errors of the past? What concrete remedies have been proposed to prevent them from happening in the future?

The real point at issue is this. Has the Republican Party, under a captaincy distinguished during the past four years for errors of leadership and unwillingness to face facts, whose whole theory of curing the country's ills has been to call his leading sufferers together in conference to tell him how they may be helped, has this party, I ask, under this leader, suddenly become the Heaven-sent healer of the country who will now make well all that has been ill?

In other words, has the Republican elephant, spotted with the mire through which it has wandered blindly during these past four years, suddenly by miracle overnight become a sacred white elephant of spotless purity, to be worshiped and followed by the people, or has it merely been scrubbed and whitewashed by cunning showmen in the hope that they can deceive a credulous electorate for four years more?

Let's look at the records. The Republican platform provides the familiar explanation that the length and depth of the depression came from abroad. But there is no recognition of the part played by unsound investing policies under a lax and indifferent leadership. That caused, as we know, a very considerable part of the losses sustained by the people of this country.

The only constructive suggestion regarding investments is an evasion. It says that serious problems have arisen from uniting investment to commercial banking; but it does not have the courage to suggest a separation of the two. It provides no remedy.

The acceptance speech of the distinguished gentleman who is running against me is equally empty of hope on this subject. There is an eloquent description of the storm through which we are passing; there are glimpses through the clouds, of troubled officers pacing the deck wondering what to do.

He speaks with feeling of a soil poisoned by speculation in which grew ugly weeds of waste, exploitation and the abuse of financial power, but he speaks not of the beneficent rays of the sun of administrative approval under which these weeds sprouted and flourished.

The only approach to the protection of the investing public

beyond temporary and immediate loans is a vague reference to a stronger banking system which will not, he says, "permit the credit of the country to be made available without adequate check for wholesale speculation in securities."

He adds that "for seven years I have repeatedly warned against credit loans abroad for non-productive purposes," whatever that may be.

I have set forth thus in the words of Republican leaders the rise, the decline and the fall of the Administration. We now come to the philosophy which, the President maintains, is behind all this. Here we have a strange contrast. We have in many utterances, ending with the acceptance speech, an exposition of the doctrine of American individualism. Set over against that theory is an actual policy that is directly in conflict with it.

Appraising the situation in the bitter dawn of a cold morning after, what do we find?

We find two-thirds of American industry concentrated in a few hundred corporations, and actually managed by not more than five human individuals.

We find more than half of the savings of the country invested in corporate stocks and bonds, and made the sport of the American stock market.

We find fewer than three dozen private banking houses, and stock-selling adjuncts of commercial banks, directing the flow of American capital.

In other words, we find concentrated economic power in a few hands, the precise opposite of the individualism of which the President speaks.

We find a great part of our working population with no chance of earning a living except by grace of this concentrated industrial machine; and we find that millions and millions of Americans are out of work, throwing upon the already burdened Government the necessity of relief.

We find a tariff that has cut off any chance of a foreign market for our products, that has had the effect of cutting the earnings of the farmer to the extent of threatening him with foreclosure and want.

We find the Republican leaders proposing no solution except more debts, more conferences under the same bewildered leadership, more Government money in business but no Government attempt to wrestle with basic problems. And we have a stirring appeal to the intrepid soul of the American people.

Now I believe in the intrepid soul of the American people; but I believe also in its horse sense. I am going on now to outline my own economic creed, and a substantial part of the constructive program that I hope to initiate.

I, too, believe in individualism; but I mean it in everything that the word implies.

I believe that our industrial and economic system is made for individual men and women, and not individual men and women for the benefit of the system.

I believe that the individual should have full liberty of action to make the most of himself; but I do not believe that in the name of that sacred word a few powerful interests should be permitted to make industrial cannon fodder of the lives of half of the population of the United States.

I believe in the sacredness of private property, which means that I do not believe that it should be subjected to the ruthless manipulation of professional gamblers in the stock markets and in the corporate system.

I share the President's complaint against regimentation; but unlike him, I dislike it not only when it is carried on by an informal group, an unofficial group, amounting to an economic Government of the United States, but also when it is done by the Government of the United States itself.

I believe that the Government, without becoming a prying bureaucracy, can act as a check or counterbalance to this oligarchy so as to secure the chance to work and the safety of savings to men and women, rather than safety of exploitation to the exploiter, safety of manipulation to the financial manipulators, safety of unlicensed power to those who would speculate to the bitter end with the welfare and property of other people.

Yes, the word "individualism" is a bitter word in the mouths of Republican leaders, who have fostered regimentation without stint or limit. Opposition to financial exploitation is a ghastly sham in men who have created, encouraged and brought into being the very power of exploitation. We must go back to first principles; we must make American individualism what it was intended to be—equality of opportunity for all, the right of exploitation for none.

Some of the Democratic policies I have already set forth.

Today I lay before you another, and I do so in direct and plain English.

Let me ask you a practical question: If by manipulation or as the result of economic law a definite, even though partial, improvement in industrial production and commodity values were to begin in the near future, would the people of this country be satisfied to have a continuance of the same governmental policies toward speculation that were definitely practiced before the crash?

Would the people of this country welcome a return of practices in banking, in the sale of foreign securities, in the flotation of mergers or in concealed and unsound practices of corporate finance to which the Nation was treated in the years prior to 1929?

For every sane man and woman in this country I answer no. I now ask one further question, a question to which current history also answers no. Does the Republican platform or do the Republican nominees and leaders promise concrete and immediate remedies to prevent a return of what has so largely been instrumental in bringing us where we are today? A thousand times no.

In contrast to a complete silence on their part, and in contrast to the theories of the year 1928, which I have shown that the Republican leaders still hold, I propose an orderly, explicit and practical group of fundamental remedies. These will protect not the few but the great mass of average American men and women

681

who, I am not ashamed to repeat, have been forgotten by those in power.

These measures, like my whole theory of the conduct of Government, are based on what? Based on telling the truth.

Government cannot prevent some individuals from making errors of judgment. But Government can prevent to a very great degree the fooling of sensible people through misstatements and through the withholding of information on the part of private organizations, great and small, which seek to sell investments to the people of the Nation.

First — Toward that end and to inspire truth telling, I propose that every effort be made to prevent the issue of manufactured and unnecessary securities of all kinds which are brought out merely for the purpose of enriching those who handle their sale to the public; and I further propose that with respect to legitimate securities the sellers shall tell the uses to which the money is to be put. This truth telling requires that definite and accurate statements be made to the buyers in respect to the bonuses and commissions the sellers are to receive; and, furthermore, true information as to the investment of principal, as to the true earnings, true liabilities and true assets of the corporation itself.

Second — We are well aware of the difficulty and often the impossibility under which State Governments have labored in the regulation of holding companies that sell securities in interstate commerce. It is logical, it is necessary and it is right that Federal power be applied to such regulation.

Third — For the very simple reason that the many exchanges in the business of buying and selling securities and commodities can by the practical expedient of moving elsewhere avoid regulation by any given State, I propose the use of Federal authority in the regulation of these exchanges.

Fourth — The events of the past three years prove that the supervision of national banks for the protection of the public has been ineffective. I propose vastly more rigid supervision.

Fifth — We have witnessed not only the unrestrained use of bank deposits in speculation to the detriment of local credit, but we are also aware that this speculation was encouraged by the Government itself. I propose that such speculation be discouraged and prevented.

Sixth — Investment banking is a legitimate business. Commercial banking is another wholly separate and distinct business. Their consolidation and mingling are contrary to public policy. I propose their separation.

Seventh — Prior to the panic of 1929 the funds of the Federal Reserve System were used practically without check for many speculative enterprises. I propose the restriction of Federal Reserve Banks in accordance with the original plans and earlier practices of the Federal Reserve System under Woodrow Wilson.

Finally, my friends, I propose two new policies for which legislation is not required. They are policies of fair and open dealing on the part of the officials of the American Government with the American investing public.

In the first place, I promise you that it will no longer be possible for international bankers or others to sell foreign securities to the investing public of America on the implied understanding that these securities have been passed on or approved by the State Department or any other agency of the Federal Government.

In the second place, I assure you that high public officials in the next Administration will neither by word nor by deed seek to influence the prices of stocks and bonds. The Government has access to vast information concerning the economic life of the country, but the present Administration has all too often issued statements that have had no relation to the scientific information which it possessed. That has shaken public confidence and it is going to stop.

My friends, these assurances which I am here giving you are to my mind greatly important in the long list of remedies that we propose. Restored confidence in the actions and statements of Executive authority is indispensable. This Administration during these four years has risked the lives and property and welfare of the people of the country through a policy of disastrous governmental speculation.

It is no wonder that stagnation has resulted — a stagnation born of fear. But this is a distrust not of ourselves, not in our fundamental soundness, not in our innate ability to work out our future. It is a distrust in our leaders, in the things they say and the things they do.

Therefore, the confidence that the Administration has asked us as individual citizens to have in ourselves is not enough. The kind of confidence we most need is confidence in the integrity, the soundness, the liberalism, the vision, and the old-fashioned horse sense of our national leadership.

Without that kind of confidence we are forever insecure. With that kind of confidence in the leadership of America, represented by the Government in Washington, the future is ours to conquer and to hold.

134 ⟨ Campaign Address on Prohibition, Sea Girt, N. J. August 27, 1932

(Prohibition — Repeal of the Eighteenth Amendment.)

My friends:

ONCE upon a time an orator who was describing the scenery of his State remarked that in the North it was "mountaineous" and that in the South it was "moisterious."

That classic description reminds me of the Republican national ticket this year — "high and dry" at one end and at the other end "increasing moisture."

But before I come to further elucidation on that point let me make another clear.

However we may differ as to method, we all agree that temperance is one of the cardinal virtues. In dealing with the great social problems in my own State, such as the care of the wards of the States, and in combating crime, I have had to consider most earnestly this question of temperance. It is bound up with crime, with insanity and, only too often, with poverty. It is increasingly apparent that the intemperate use of intoxicants has no place in this new mechanized civilization of ours. In our industry, in our recreation, on our highways, a drunken man is more than an objectionable companion, he is a peril to the rest of us. The hand that controls the machinery of our factories, that holds the steering wheel of our automobiles, and the brains that guide the course of finance and industry, should alike be free from the effects of over-indulgence in alcohol.

But the methods adopted since the World War with the purpose of achieving a greater temperance by the forcing of Prohibition have been accompanied in most parts of the country by complete and tragic failure. I need not point out to you that general encouragement of lawlessness has resulted; that corruption, hypocrisy, crime and disorder have emerged, and that instead of restricting, we have extended the spread of intemperance. This failure has come for this very good reason: we have depended too largely upon the power of governmental action instead of recognizing that the authority of the home and that of the churches in these matters is the fundamental force on which we must build. The recent recognition of this fact by the present Administration is an amazing piece of hindsight. There are others who have had foresight. A friend showed me recently an unpublished letter of Henry Clay, written a hundred years ago. In this letter Clay said that the movement for temperance "has done great good and will continue to do more" but "it will destroy itself whenever it resorts to coercion or mixes in the politics of the country."

Another statesman, given to the Nation by this State of New Jersey, pointed out this necessary course when Federal Prohibition first became a great issue. President Wilson foresaw the economic and social results of such an attempt. It was not necessary for him to live through the disastrous experience in order to come to the conclusion now confessed by our present President.

In statesmanship an ounce of foresight is better than a pound of hindsight.

The experience of nearly one hundred and fifty years under the Constitution has shown us that the proper means of regulation is through the States, with control by the Federal Government limited to that which is necessary to protect the States in the exercise of their legitimate powers. This I submit is the principle embodied in our Democratic platform; and I state further that it is not the principle stated in the Republican platform or in the speeches of acceptance of the two candidates of the Republican Party.

This time of depression has caused us to see even more plainly than before not only the political and moral consequences of our action but its economic results as well.

We threw on the table as spoils to be gambled for by the enemies of society the revenue that our Government had theretofore received, and the underworld acquired unparalleled resources thereby. The multiplication of enforcement agencies created resentment and a cynical and complacent attitude toward lax enforcement resulting from connivance between such agencies and the law breakers. The general disregard for and defiance of such law of nationwide application bred disrespect for other law. The attempt to impose the practice of virtue by mandate of the fundamental law produced an attitude of intolerance to other forms of restraint and a denial even of the basis of authority. The violation of fundamental principles set in motion a chain of consequences that no one not politically blind could fail to see; and all the time a steady flow of profits, resulting from the exactions of a newly created industry, was running into the pockets of racketeers. The only business of the country that was not helping to support the Government was in a real sense being supported by the Government. This was the business that was the direct product of the 18th Amendment and the Volstead Law—a business which is lucrative, vicious and corrupting in its influence on the enforcement agencies of Government.

Unquestionably our tax burden would not be so heavy nor the

forms that it takes so objectionable if some reasonable proportion of the uncounted millions now paid to those whose business has been reared upon this stupendous blunder could be made available for the expenses of Government.

On this subject the two parties offer the voters a genuine choice this year. On the one hand a definite method of relief in the true American tradition, with the States authorized to carry out their part of the responsibility, and the Nation doing what it is practically and constitutionally able to do; on the other side, evasion and indirection.

I should be something less than candid — in fact I should be dishonest — if I did not in this campaign continue to speak very plainly of these evasions, insincerities and deceptions. As I have repeatedly pointed out. Republican leaders are attempting to fight this battle with words. And in fighting with words we may use them either as a flaming sword, frankly, honestly and with courage, to press home the cause of truth, or we may use them as shields, to turn aside, evade and obstruct the attack of an adversary. It is in this latter sense that the Republicans have been fighting a battle of words. Now a shield is a bigger thing than a sword and so when they would use words as a defense, they must use more of them. Witness the Republican platform — long, indirect, ambiguous, insincere, false, compared with the concise sincerity of our own platform. And this is especially true of what they say about Prohibition. We first have a long, rambling party pronouncement in the Republican platform. And then we have long, rambling explanations of its meaning. Words upon words. Evasions upon evasions. Insincerity upon insincerity. A dense cloud of words. We rush into the cloud to find whether there is meaning and substance at the bottom of it all, and we find nothing. When we emerge from the cloud, we see another in the distance and we rush over to that. And again we find nothing. And so we rush from cloud to cloud and find at the bottom of each, nothing but dust, meaningless, worthless dust, at the bottom of a cloud of words.

One of the stories that we learned in our youth was that of the famous Oracle of Delphi. In ancient Greece, it is told, there was a place where volcanic gas came forth from a crevice in the earth. Over this crevice the pagans built a temple, and directly above the fumes arising from the earth, they set the throne of the Oracle. When the Oracle was partially stupefied by the poisons in the gas, she uttered strange and incoherent words. The high priests of the temple were supposed to tell the people the meaning of these incoherent words. The people never suspected that the priests were not possessed of a real understanding of these words and that they interpreted them to suit their own convenience. But great issues were decided by this method. Pagan kings came to the Oracle and on its incoherent mumblings the fate of Nations was sometimes staked.

In June, the Republican Oracle sat in Chicago. There was a fume of heated oratory; clouds of Prohibition proposals were emitted; the Resolutions Committee and the Convention itself succumbed to the stupefying influence. It uttered words in the party platform — words and more words, till meaning was lost and reason slumbered. And then when the Convention ended and the people asked the high priests of the party what it all meant, the answers were so diverse that one was tempted to suspect the worst — that it meant nothing at all. The Secretary of State explained in the choicest phrases of Republican diplomacy; Senator Borah spoke out in his forthright fashion and said it sounded wet to him; President Butler said the words were dry.

I suspect that those who wrote that plank thought that it would sound dry to the drys and wet to the wets. But to the consternation of the high priests it sounded dry to the wets and wet to the drys. This was very serious indeed. Something had to be done about it.

Well, something was done about it. The Democratic Party fairly and squarely met the issue. It adopted, by an overwhelming vote, a plank so plain and clear and honest that no one could doubt its meaning and the candidates accepted this statement one hundred percent.

And then public opinion, moved by a true American admiration for brave and honest statement, expressed itself in no uncertain terms. It liked the Democratic platform. It liked people who spoke their minds. It liked courage and candor. This must have been disturbing to the high priests of the Republican Party, but, as always, they hesitated and temporized. And then in the six weeks following the Democratic Convention, a vast air of expectancy surrounded the White House. Rumors came forth that the high priests were to speak. People were to be told at last the meaning of what the June Oracle had said.

There were difficulties in the way, because the high priests had often spoken of this subject before. In 1928 the Republican candidate for the Presidency said: "I do not favor the repeal of the Eighteenth Amendment," and, amplifying his meaning at that time, he added that it was "a great social and economic experiment noble in motive and far-reaching in purpose."

He brought about the creation of the Commission on Law Enforcement and Obedience composed of "an able group of distinguished citizens of character and independence of thought, representative of different sections of the country." When, after eighteen months of sincere and painstaking work, this Commission reported its findings to him, he submitted the report to the Congress commending all of the minor findings of the Commission but not approving of the Commission's proposed revision of the Eighteenth Amendment.

He condemned the report with faint praise, thus: "It should stimulate the clarification of the public mind and the advancement of public thought." It did stimulate and clarify the public mind to the extent that it showed it what it had long suspected was true, that national Prohibition had not been and could not be enforced. But it apparently did not stimulate and clarify the Presidential mind because the White House, so far as Prohibition was concerned, fell into a deep silence. As the Republican Convention approached, according to the newspapers of the time, appeal after appeal was made to him and innumerable drafts of a Prohibition plank were submitted to him. Out of it all came the incoherent utterance of the Chicago Oracle to which I have alluded.

At last, on the eleventh day of August, the President spoke to the people. To anyone who will read the Prohibition plank in the Republican platform and the remarks of the President on this question in his acceptance speech, the difficulty under which the President labors will become obvious and the reason for his use of meaningless words will become clear. It is the difficulty that always attends sacrificing principles for votes, and attempting to conceal that fact by the use of pussy-cat words. That statement can be no better substantiated than by the President's own statement that "I have always sympathized with the high purpose of the Eighteenth Amendment." Does that spell out a prohibitionist attempting to retain the support of the drys?

But the President has at last learned what the facts have shown these many years — that laws opposed by majority sentiments "create resentment which undermines enforcement and in the end produces degeneration and crime."

This seems to mean State Home Rule. But apparently the President does not really believe in State Home Rule, if by the use of force there can be effective Federal control. He is willing to believe in the principle of State control only when the Federal Government cannot get away with the destruction of State control.

His statement proceeds deliberately to misrepresent the position of the Democratic Party. He says: "Our opponents pledge the members of their party to destroy every vestige of constitutional and effective Federal control of the traffic."

I have the right to assume that the President read the Democratic platform and on that assumption I charge that this statement was made to mislead the people of this country and I assert that a mere reading of the plain, unequivocal provisions of the Democratic platform will sustain that charge. So that there can be no possible misunderstanding, let me read the provisions of the Democratic platform on this point. It begins:

"We advocate the repeal of the Eighteenth Amendment. To

effect such repeal we demand that the Congress immediately propose a Constitutional Amendment to truly representative conventions in the States called to act solely on that proposal."

So much for repeal. Now what does it tell the States to do:

"We urge the enactment of such measures by the several States as will actually promote temperance, effectively prevent the return of the saloon and bring the liquor traffic into the open under complete supervision and control by the States."

It then clearly states what the President either accidentally overlooked or deliberately misrepresented:

"We demand that the Federal Government effectively exercise its power to enable the States to protect themselves against importation of intoxicating liquors in violation of their laws." It then goes on to speak of the Volstead Law:

"Pending repeal, we favor immediate modification of the Volstead Act to legalize the manufacture and sale of beer and other beverages of such alcoholic content as is permissible under the Constitution and to provide therefrom a proper and needed revenue."

Thus the Democratic platform expressly and unequivocally opposes the return of the saloon and with equal emphasis it demands that there be Federal control of the liquor traffic to protect dry States. Only on the theory of seeking to return to power by the mere use of words can such statements of the President of these United States be explained.

But, meanwhile, another high priest has been heard from. In the period following August eleventh, the anti-repealists of the Republican Party raised their voices in lamentation, like Jeremiah of old.

The Republican candidate for Vice-President heard this wailing. He hastened to avow his devotion to the Republican platform, but he found in the words of the Oracle full justification for the belief that the Eighteenth Amendment should not be repealed. And so, in the true spirit of those who in ancient times controlled the Oracle for their own ends, provision is made for all possible contingencies.

691

It is said that an ancient King when he consulted the Oracle as to the probability of his success in a war that he was about to undertake, was told that if he went to war a great army would be destroyed. But he did not realize that the Oracle had not made it clear that it might be his own army that would be destroyed. My friends, the high priests have failed to inquire of the Oracle the answer to the question that the King of old forgot. A great army is to be destroyed. But they do not realize which army it is to be.

In New York State in 1930 there was a party which tried to ride two horses at the same time. The Republican Party had one foot, its candidate for Governor, on the wet horse, and the other foot, its candidate for Lieutenant Governor, on the dry horse. The voters of New York State saw that it was a circus stunt. Honest wets and honest drys — Democratic, Republican and Independent — were disgusted. They threw the ticket into the discard.

This year the Republican national leaders have tried the same circus stunt. The answer of the voters throughout the Nation will be precisely the same.

In the last analysis, my friends, the Prohibition issue comes down to a question of faith and confidence in leadership and in the words of leaders.

However people may differ as to the principle of Prohibition, national or State, they all will agree that a temporizing and insincere policy is disastrous not only to the cause of Prohibition, but to that of temperance as well. The present leadership stands convicted of attempting to evade and confuse this issue. The honest dry will, I know, honor more the honest wet than the shifty dry; and the anti-prohibitionist prefers, I know, the four-square dry to the uncertain wet. All will join in condemning a fearful and timid practice of evasion.

Here, as before, I emphasize that the deep question in this campaign is one of confidence in leadership — in leaders. The measure of the truth of what they say is what they have said; the measure of what they will do is what they have done.

135 ❨ "A Restored and Rehabilitated Agriculture." Campaign Address on the Farm Problem at Topeka, Kans. September 14, 1932

(Farm relief — Land use — Population distribution — Reciprocal foreign tariff adjustments — Essentials of an effective plan for relief of agriculture — Republican neglect of the farmer — Federal Farm Board.)

Governor Woodring, my friends:

I HAVE come here not alone to talk to you about farms and farming. I have come just as much and even more to listen and to learn. On this whole trip I am seeking, as on many previous occasions, first-hand contacts with that section of the Nation which is responsible for the major part of the food supply of the Nation.

In my contacts here and in the discussions that I have, I want to hear from men and women of all parties and of all views on the question of farm relief. I am going to follow one simple principle in this discussion and that is complete and absolute frankness. This question is too serious to be trifled with by empty political platitudes or by specious and ingenious tricks of language or of thought. In dealing with the subject I want to avoid on the one hand political sky-writing, and on the other hand political wise-cracking.

In keeping faith with this principle of getting down to business, let me say what I think we all recognize — that there is no single remedy that will by itself bring immediate prosperity to the agricultural population of all parts of the United States. You know that, and I know that, and it is a good point from which to start.

I know this personally for four reasons. First, I have lived on a farm in the State of New York for fifty years. Second, I have run a farm in the State of Georgia for eight years, and run it without profit. Third, ever since I went into public life, I have made it a point to travel over this country and in so doing I have maintained what I think modesty would permit me to say is a genuine and practical interest in the farm problems of the various parts of this country at first hand. And, finally, as Governor of the State of New York, the farm products of which rank fifth or sixth among all the forty-eight States of the Union, I have in four years devoted myself to building a farm program of which the people of my State, regardless of party, have some reason to be proud.

Four years ago, in the campaign for the governorship in 1928 the fact was properly stressed that even though New York is often thought of as a State primarily urban, yet its own farm problem was of immediate and critical importance. Some of the distress that you and the Middle West as a whole have felt was present in parts of New York and in the East in the same acute form. Without indulging in excessive promises, I assured the farmers of New York that their problems would be met by practical and definite action.

In the creation of a State plan I recognized the principle of bringing more than one mind to bear on the problem and of putting more than one shoulder to the wheel. Not alone through the process of appointing commissions and calling conferences, but by the actual enactment of practical legislation, we built our policies. In the years that have followed we have attempted a number of substantial things. They are set forth in the public record. Existing tax obligations of local communities were lightened to the extent of twenty-four millions a year. State aid for roads was redistributed on a mileage basis instead of on an assessment basis, so that the poorer communities could enjoy exactly the same assistance per mile in the improvement of dirt roads as that given to the richer suburban communities.

The same principles of aid were applied to rural schools in order to guarantee a modern education for the children of farmers even in the most sparsely settled communities. The State assumed the entire cost of constructing and reconstructing roads and bridges in the state highway system, thus lifting another heavy tax burden from farm property. The State paid all except a very small fraction of the cost of grade-crossing elimination so

694

that safety might be afforded to the less as well as the more fortunate districts of the State. Appropriations for the safeguarding of rural health were increased. A provision for funds for a soil survey of the State was made and this is already paying a substantial dividend in more profitable farming, in its aid to our State reforestation program and in enabling farmers to get necessary road improvements, telephone lines and electric power lines. In addition to that, the cooperative corporation law and the laws regulating traffic in farm produce were revised and strengthened in the interest of the farmer. Very recently, legislation was enacted to create a new system of rural credit organizations to meet the emergency created by the collapse of rural banks.

Why do I tell you all this? I cite these examples to illustrate the many angles that attended the building up of this program. The great lesson of it all — a lesson for every State in the Union — is that there is no single cure-all, but that progress comes from a comprehension of many factors and a sincere attempt to move forward on many lines at the same time.

I see no necessity for discussing in detail the acute distress in which the farmers of America find themselves. You all know that better than anyone can tell you. You have felt it in your own lives and experiences. And you have seen it reflected in limiting the opportunities that you have wanted to give to your families. This experience of yours is far more moving than any phrases of mine or of anyone else. This distress has grown for more than eleven years over a radius of hundreds of miles from where I stand, in as productive and fertile a country as the world has ever seen. We have poverty, we have want in the midst of abundance. With incomparable natural wealth within the reach of these progressive farmers they struggle with poverty and unbelievably hard times. They try to hold their farms under conditions produced by corn, hogs, cotton, wool, cattle and wheat selling on the farm at prices as low as or lower than at any time in the history of the United States. There has been some slight rise from these low levels, but in spite of that, there remain in millions of farm homes continuing uncertainty and continuing apprehension.

695

This means that the farmer misses not only the things that make life tolerable but those that make decent living possible. It means — and this is most important — that the farmer's children must suffer the denial of those chances for education that justice and fairness should assure to them. We all of us hoped that our children would have a "better break" than we had. But the economic turn has almost blasted that hope for the farm parent. This means nothing less, my friends, than the shadow of peasantry.

There are six and one-half million families to whom this deepening shadow is a grim reality. These six and one-half million families represent 22 percent of the total population of the United States. They are the men, women and children actually living on farms. It is fair to ask what percentage of the national income comes each year to this 22 percent of the population. Let us remember these figures: Twelve years ago, in 1920, this 22 percent of the population got 15 percent of the national income; in 1925 it received 11 percent. By 1928 agriculture's share had dropped to only just above 9 percent, and the most recent estimate, based on the figures of the United States Department of Agriculture itself, shows that farm income has today dropped to about 7 percent. Remember well that during the past four years when he has been the Chief Executive of the Nation, and also as a member of the Cabinet during the previous six years, the dominant factor in our governmental economic policies has been the distinguished gentleman who is running against me.

But let us not stop at our six and one-half million farm families. Let us remember that fifty million men, women and children within our borders are directly and immediately concerned with the present and the future of agriculture.

Again, let us not stop there. Another fifty or sixty million people who are engaged in business or in industry in our large and small city communities are at last coming to understand the simple fact that their lives and futures are profoundly concerned with the prosperity of agriculture. They realize more and more that there will be no outlet for their products unless their fifty million fellow Americans who are directly concerned with agriculture are given the buying power to buy city products.

Our economic life today is a seamless web. Whatever our vocation, we are forced to recognize that while we have enough factories and enough machines in the United States to supply all our needs, those factories will be closed part of the time and these machines will lie idle part of the time if the buying power of fifty million people on the farms remains restricted or dead as it is today.

Two months ago I pointed out in my speech of acceptance the interdependence of the people of the United States — the fact that we cannot have independence in its true sense unless we take full account of our interdependence in order to provide a balanced economic well-being for every citizen of the country.

Industrial prosperity can reach only artificial and temporary heights as it did in 1929 if at the same time there is no agricultural prosperity. This Nation cannot endure if it is half "boom" and half "broke."

That word "interdependence" applies not only to the city on the one hand and the farm on the other, but it applies also to the relationship between the different parts of our country. If in the South a cotton-raising population goes into bankruptcy because the price of cotton is so low that it does not pay for the cost of production, you in the wheat belt or in the corn belt are directly affected by a tragedy a thousand miles away. If you who raise wheat or corn lose your homes through foreclosure, every other farmer in the East, or in the South, or out on the Pacific Coast, and every factory worker in every part of the country, is directly affected by your distress.

Interdependence within the field of agriculture itself is a vital fact. Every kind of farming is related to every other kind, and a disturbance anywhere within the structure causes repercussions everywhere.

If we would get to the root of the difficulty, we shall find it in the present lack of equality for agriculture. Farming has not had an even break in our economic system. The things that our

697

farmers buy today cost 9 percent more than they did before the World War in 1914. The things they sell bring them 43 percent less than then. These figures, as of August first, authenticated by the Department of Agriculture, mean that the farm dollar is worth less than half of what it represented before the war. Remember this, my friends: The things that farmers buy, protected by Mr. Grundy's tariff, are 9 percent above pre-war; the things that farmers sell — and remember world prices fix domestic prices — are 43 percent below pre-war prices. The correction of that condition must in some way bring the purchasing power of the farmer within reach of the things that Mr. Grundy has protected. It means finding a cure for the condition that compels the farmer to trade in 1932 two wagon-loads for the things for which in 1914 he traded one wagon-load. And that is as short a way as I know of stating the farm problem.

There are two undeniable historic facts of the past twelve years:

First, the present Administration, and the two previous Administrations, in all of which the President was an important member, failed utterly to understand the farm problem as a national whole, or to plan for its relief; and second, they destroyed the foreign markets for our exportable farm surplus beginning with the Fordney-McCumber Tariff and ending with the Grundy Tariff, thus violating the simplest principle of international trade, and forcing the inevitable retaliation of foreign countries.

I cannot forbear at this point expressing my amazement that in the face of this retaliation — inevitable from the day the Grundy Tariff became law and predicted by every competent observer at home and abroad — not one effective step to deal with it or to alleviate its consequences has been taken or proposed by the national Administration. In that attitude the Republican leadership, from the President down, shows an incredible disregard of plain facts, combined with what I shall politely term a stubborn indifference to the consequence of its own folly.

Of some steps which should have been taken and which should now be taken to meet this situation I have already spoken and

698

I shall have more to say. But at this moment I want to speak of other phases of the problem of permanent farm relief. Let us pause for a moment and take a look at the problem in the longer perspective. We must have, I assert with all possible emphasis, national planning in agriculture. We must not have, as now, the scattering of our efforts through the heterogeneous and disassociated activities of our governmental agencies dealing with the problem. On the other hand, we must avoid the present tendency to jump from one temporary expedient to another. We need unity of planning, coherence in our Administration and emphasis upon cures rather than upon drugs.

On my part, I suggest the following permanent measures:

First, I would reorganize the United States Department of Agriculture, looking toward the administrative machinery needed to build a program of national planning. I should be the last person in the world to become a harsh and thoughtless critic of a department that has done many good things. But I know enough of government and of the ways of government to know that the growth of a department is often irregular, illogical and haphazard. It is always easy to add to a department; additions mean more jobs. But to cut away unnecessary functions, eliminate useless jobs or redirect routine activities toward more fruitful purposes is a task that must be and shall be undertaken.

Second, I favor a definite policy looking to the planned use of the land. We already have more than enough tilled land to meet our needs for many years to come, since our population has ceased to expand so rapidly and agriculture is becoming each year more efficient. But we have in the thirteen original States of the East, and a few others, great areas of relatively poor land hardly worth cultivation, which provide either actual or potential competition with better land. This lowers the quality of farm products, depresses the prices of better farm products, creates great added expense because of the faulty distribution of the population and consumes public and private resources in attempting the development of means of living and communication that ought not to be needed. The sum total result of all this is waste and hardship. To provide the necessary guidance for the correction of this faulty distribution of farms and of farming energy there is need for an economic soil survey, especially in the Eastern States, to be carried on jointly by the Nation and the States through the initiative of the Federal Government. This soil survey should have a much broader scope than present surveys, and should be directed toward the problems of proper utilization of the land and future distribution of population along sound economic lines. It should lead to mapping and classification of land of all kinds, to determine which lands are best suited for agricultural production, which lands are marginal and which lands are suited only to growing tree crops.

Let me give you this simple example of something I have actually done. Remember, at the same time, that this does not apply to the wheat belt; it applies only in small measure to the corn belt, but it does apply fully to most of the Eastern States. We in the State of New York have approved, by vote of the people, the expenditure of ten millions of dollars toward the elimination of marginal lands from actual farming. This year in a short time we have bought, as I said, over two hundred thousand acres of unprofitable marginal farm lands and we have turned these acres into the growing of trees for lumber and pulp. I do not have to point out to you the fact that this Eastern program is not only good for the East but is also of value in that it removes the competition of marginal hill farms from your own crops in the West.

Planning of that kind, designed primarily to gain a better and less wasteful distribution of agricultural productive effort, inevitably will point the way to readjustments in the distribution of the population in general. The pendulum is swinging back from the intense concentration of population in cities. We know the possibilities for the greater ease and comfort of modern rural and small town living. This does not mean a "back-to-the-land" movement in the ordinary sense of a return to agriculture, but it does mean definite efforts to decentralize industry.

It will effect cheaper and more wholesome living for many

millions of our population. To the farmer it will mean bringing a considerable part of his market closer to his own dooryard.

A third process of permanent relief for agriculture can come through national leadership in the reduction and more equitable distribution of taxes. We all agree on that. With respect to this I propose to exert through the Presidency, as I have done through the Governorship, such influence as I can, in favor of a national movement to reorganize local government in the direction of eliminating some of the tax burden which now bears so heavily on farms of the Nation. There are too many taxing districts, too many local units of government, too many unnecessary offices and functions. The governmental underbrush which has sprouted for years should be cleared away. In addition, we need a clearer separation of fields of taxation as between the Nation, the States and the localities. By so doing, we can lift some of the tax burden resting on land, and I mean to stress that objective by every means at my command. These three objectives are of the sort that will require slow-moving development. They constitute a necessary building for the future. In meeting the immediate problem of distress, however, it is necessary to adopt quick-acting remedies.

In the first place, there is the necessity, as we all know, for the refinancing of farm mortgages in order to relieve the burden of excessive interest charges and the grim threat of foreclosure. Much was done in the last session of Congress to extend and liquefy and pass on to the Federal Government — the Nation — the burden of debt of railroads, banks, utilities and industry in general. Something in the nature of a gesture was made in the direction of financing urban homes. But practically nothing was done toward removing the destructive menace of debt from farm homes. It is my purpose, if elected, to direct all the energy of which I am capable to the formulation of definite projects to relieve this distress. Specifically, I am prepared to insist that Federal credit be extended to banks, insurance or loan companies, or other corporations or individuals holding farm mortgages among their assets, but that these credits must be made on the condition that every reasonable assistance be given to the mortgagors where the loans are sound, with the purpose of preventing foreclosure. These conditions must be enforced. Lower interest rates and an extension of principal payments will save thousands of farms to their owners. And hand in hand with this we must adopt the definite policy of giving those who have lost the title to their farms, now held by institutions seeking credit from governmental agencies, the preferential opportunity of getting their property back.

The second immediate necessity is to provide a means of bringing about, through governmental effort, a substantial reduction in the difference between the prices of things the farmer sells and the things he buys. One way of attacking this disparity is by restoring international trade through tariff readjustments.

The Democratic tariff policy consists, in large measure, of negotiating agreements with individual countries permitting them to sell goods to us in return for which they will let us sell to them goods and crops which we produce. An effective application of this principle will restore the flow of international trade; and the first result of that flow will be to assist substantially the American farmer in disposing of his surplus. It is recognized, however, that to take up the slack until international trade is sufficiently restored, we must devise means to provide for the farmer a benefit which will give him in the shortest possible time the equivalent of what the protected manufacturer gets from the tariff. You farmers put this well in a single phrase: "We must make the tariff effective."

In the last few years many plans have been advanced for achieving this object. None has been given a trial. The circumstances are so complex that no man can say with definite assurance that one particular plan is applicable to all crops or even that one plan is better than another in relation to a particular crop.

One fact I want to make clear, with all possible emphasis. There is no reason to despair merely because defects have been found in all of these plans; or because some of them have been discarded by responsible leaders in favor of new plans. The fact that so much earnest study and investigation of this problem has been made, from so many angles, and by so many men is, in my opinion, ground for assurance rather than despair. Such a wealth of information has been accumulated, so many possibilities explored, so many able minds enlisted, and, more important still, so much education on the subject provided for and by the farmers themselves, that the time has come when able and thoughtful leaders who have followed this development from the beginning are now focusing on the basic elements of the problem and the practical nature of its solution.

Within the past year many of our principal industrialists also have come to the conclusion that — since the great decline of our export trade — the chief hope for industrial rehabilitation lies in some workable and immediate method of dealing with farm surpluses.

Support for the trial of some plan to put the tariff into effect seems to be found everywhere except in the Administration at Washington. This official lack of sympathy has probably done more to prevent the development of concrete, generally acceptable plans than any other single force. To me it appears that the Administration takes an attitude that is wholly unfair. It says, in substance, that since a perfect plan has not been developed nothing can be done; and at the same time it takes a position wholly inimical to every effort made during the past eleven years to provide workable means of relief. This negative position taken by the Administration is more than a mere failure to assume leadership. It is an absolute repudiation of responsibility. This negative, even hostile position, has included, as we know, a disposition on the part of the Administration to set proponents of one plan off against the proponents of another, the apparent object being to create a situation in which it is possible for Administration leadership to say, "How can we do anything for agriculture when it is not agreed within itself as to what it wants to do?"

It will be my purpose, my friends, to compose the conflicting elements of these various plans, to gather the benefit of the long study and consideration of them, to coordinate efforts to the end that agreement may be reached upon the details of a distinct policy, aimed at producing the result to which all these efforts and plans are directed — the restoration of agriculture to economic equality with other industries within the United States. I seek to give to that portion of the crop consumed in the United States a benefit equivalent to a tariff sufficient to give you farmers an adequate price.

I want now to state what seem to me the specifications upon which most of the reasonable leaders of agriculture have agreed, and to express here and now my whole-hearted accord with these specifications.

First: The plan must provide for the producer of staple surplus commodities, such as wheat, cotton, corn in the form of hogs, and tobacco, a tariff benefit over world prices which is equivalent to the benefit given by the tariff to industrial products. This differential benefit must be so applied that the increase in farm income, purchasing and debt-paying power will not stimulate further production.

Second: The plan must finance itself. Agriculture has at no time sought and does not now seek any such access to the public treasury as was provided by the futile and costly attempts at price stabilization by the Federal farm board. It seeks only equality of opportunity with tariff-protected industry.

Third: It must not make use of any mechanism which would cause our European customers to retaliate on the ground of dumping. It must be based upon making the tariff effective and direct in its operation.

Fourth: It must make use of existing agencies and so far as possible be decentralized in its Administration so that the chief responsibility for its operation will rest with the locality rather than with newly created bureaucratic machinery in Washington.

Fifth: It must operate as nearly as possible on a cooperative basis and its effect must be to enhance and strengthen the co-operative movement. It should, moreover, be constituted so that it can be withdrawn whenever the emergency has passed and normal foreign markets have been reestablished.

Sixth: The plan must be, in so far as possible, voluntary. I like

704

the idea that the plan should not be put into operation unless it has the support of a reasonable majority of the producers of the exportable commodity to which it is to apply. It must be so organized that the benefits will go to the man who participates.

These, it seems to me, are the essential specifications of a workable plan. In determining the details necessary to the solution of so vast a problem it goes without saying that many minds must meet and many persons must work together. Such cooperation must of necessity come from those who have had the widest experience with the problem and who enjoy to the greatest degree the confidence of the farmers in this country. Without in any sense seeking to avoid responsibility, I shall avail myself of the widest possible range of such assistance. My willingness to do this is fully attested to by the extent to which the development of our agricultural program in New York has been brought about through the assistance given to me, on a non-partisan, non-paid basis, by the leaders of agriculture in the State of New York. This cooperation and advice which I received in New York came not only from those directly interested in agriculture but from the leaders in the Legislature as well. There were there, as there are in the Congress of the United States, farsighted and patriotic public servants, Republicans and Democrats, who are willing to put the welfare of agriculture and of the country as a whole ahead of party advantage. To such leaders in all parties I shall look for guidance, good-will and support.

After all, the farmer's hope for the future must rest upon the policy and the spirit in which his case is considered. His problem is one of difficulty. It is for him to decide whether he wants the solution of this problem to be committed to leaders who are determined to relieve the inequities which have caused his distress, or to leaders whose record clearly shows that they are determined to preserve a staggering subsidy for industry, but to give agriculture only a measure of words and more words. The essence of this question comes down to a matter of keeping faith with American agriculture. On my part, I can stand on my own record and on the policies I have just set forth.

On the opposite side, you have the long record of the present Administration.

In setting forth that record you know better than I that the farmers' hope has had to rest upon the policy and spirit in which his case was considered by the Government. We can fully test the policy and spirit of the present Administration. It runs back a long time, because those leaders have held public office before. In those offices they have had ample opportunity to demonstrate their attitude toward agriculture.

When the depression in agriculture began in 1921, Republican leaders first sought to belittle the plight of agriculture. They claimed that the old familiar tariff remedy would suffice; and they offered the Fordney-McCumber tariff act, passed, God save the mark, under the ironic label of farm relief. The Republican leaders in positions of national responsibility at that time — and this, of course, includes the then Secretary of Commerce — either did not or would not realize the change in international conditions due to international debts. They closed their eyes to the outstanding economic fact. Prior to the war we had paid our interest on our debts to Europe by means of agricultural exports. After the war, because we had changed to a creditor, and Europe was in debt to us, it was necessary that we demand either goods or gold in return. The Fordney-McCumber tariff barrier shut off the normal tide of trade. Europe could not pay, so she could not buy. Specifically, she began to stop buying our surplus farm products.

To offset the harmful effect of this tariff situation, intelligent and responsible farm leaders worked out, in 1922, what they called a program for equality for Agriculture. Plans to achieve this equality for agriculture were brought before members of the President's Cabinet at that time. They moved in the direction of a Republican agricultural conference to consider it. The conference met. It took the amazing position that production should be reduced to the demands of the domestic market by the cheerful means, it appeared, of "starving out" the farmers who had formerly exported to Europe. It is matter of common knowledge that the President, then the Secretary of Commerce, was not without influence in the determination of this result.

In fact, the conclusions of that grim agricultural conference were strikingly similar to those voiced subsequently by the Secretary of Commerce himself. In 1925, for example, he said "continuance of overproduction means surplus, and that can only be corrected by prices low enough to make production unprofitable for some of the acreage of use." In plain English this meant "lower the price; starve out one-third of the farms; then see what happens." Throughout the whole agricultural agony of the ensuing three years the Secretary of Commerce set himself like adamant against all relief proposals. Farm leaders suggested segregation of export surplus from the domestic market. With marked acerbity he stated in a letter that such a step would "subsidize the British Empire."

The McNary-Haugen legislation called forth violent and abusive veto messages. There was, to put it mildly, no protest from the then Secretary of Commerce. The Secretary of the Treasury, in 1926, well phrased the attitude of the Administration. He insisted that any attempt to raise domestic prices was a "subsidy" and he stated that "if given to five agricultural commodities the Government could not logically refuse to give the same treatment to the textile, boot and shoe, coal and other industries" — sublimely disregarding the plain fact that the tariff was already giving those industries, in effect, the highest subsidy in history.

Now to put forth, as the Secretary of Commerce did, the idea of limiting farm production to the domestic market was simply to threaten agriculture with a terrific penalty. Apparently, either he did not see, or did not care, that this meant allowing wheat land in Kansas to remain idle, forcing foreclosure of farm mortgages, wrecking farm families, while our withdrawal from the world's markets principally benefited foreign producers. He did not ask the manufacturers to reduce their exports. As Secretary of Commerce, he made no fight for American agriculture's share of world's trade, though he could find time to assist foreign sales of every non-agricultural product. In his campaign speeches of 1928 he offered merely a program of cooperative marketing and self-help. This was to be developed through a farm board as a means of handling the surplus, although he should have known, as responsible farm leaders knew, that the cooperatives obviously could not undertake the burden of controlling the great surplus cut adrift by tariff barriers. He could and should have seen that they handled only a relatively small volume, and that it would be impossible for the members to shoulder the load and the cost. The idea of "stabilizing" through speculative operations was conceived and was written into the platform of 1928 and was vigorously supported by the candidate for the Presidency. You now know to your cost what stabilizing meant in practice.

Meanwhile, the familiar old song of the benefits to be derived from the tariff was heard. In 1928, in his acceptance speech, Mr. Hoover said: "An adequate tariff is the foundation of farm relief." He and his supporters insisted in 1928 that we were importing $3,300,000,000 of farm products and that an adequate tariff laid on these would be sufficient for the relief of agriculture. It was a ghastly fraud. The principal items of "agricultural" imports were rubber, silk, coffee, tea and the like — a long list of exotic and tropical goods, including such American farm products as elephants' tusks, skins of the Russian ermine and wallaby, and elk hides. The fact was that imports which competed with products grown in America amounted only to $460,-000,000; and sugar represented over half of this figure. The truth was that our farmers do not produce the items proposed to be protected by a tariff. They consume them. The "remedy" handed the farmer was not to raise his selling price, but to raise his cost of living.

I take it that the process of education through hard knocks has gone far enough to make it unnecessary for me to comment further. The claim that the Republican discriminatory tariff methods are a benefit to the farmer is a cynical and pitiless fraud.

Shortly after his inauguration in 1929, the President assembled a special session of Congress. He went through the form of fulfilling his campaign promises by the passing of his agricultural marketing act and the Hawley-Smoot Tariff. The decline of prices increased, a slump was apparent. The cooperatives could not meet the situation. The Farm Board began its stabilizing operations. This resulted in a tremendous undigested surplus overhanging the market; it put a millstone around the neck of the cooperatives. The effort resulted in squandering hundreds of millions of the taxpayers' money. Farm Board speculative operations must and shall come to an end.

When the futility of maintaining prices of wheat and cotton, through so-called stabilization, became apparent, the President's Farm Board, of which his Secretary of Agriculture was a member, invented the cruel joke of advising farmers to allow twenty percent of their wheat lands to lie idle, to plow up every third row of cotton and to shoot every tenth dairy cow. Surely they knew that this advice would not — indeed, could not — be taken. It was probably offered as the foundation of an alibi. They wanted to be able to say to the farmers: "You did not do as we told you to do. Now, go blame yourselves."

Now, after the harm has been done, the President's acceptance speech of 1932 fully recognizes the futility of the stabilizing experiment and merely apologizes for the results. In order to avoid responsibility he claims that the Farm Board departed "from its original purpose by making loans to farmers, cooperatives to preserve prices from panic." It was his Farm Board. Why did he permit such a departure?

The President's acceptance speech, with its artful excuses and its empty promise, will bear careful reading by the farmers of this country in the light of the promises of 1928. I wish that the Republican campaign organization would provide every farmer with a copy of the President's acceptance speech. I can imagine a farmer sitting on his door-step meditating on the questions that have caused him so much concern, while he reads that speech.

The farmer asks the question: "How may we expect that our exports will be restored and some way provided by which our customers may pay for our surplus produce with goods which we farmers can use?" He reads the answer in the acceptance speech: "I am squarely for a protective tariff."

"Does this," asks the farmer, "mean the Grundy Tariff Bill that you signed?" The acceptance speech is silent on that point.

Again the farmer asks, "Maybe the tariff can be made effective on farm produce consumed at home? Time after time the organized farmers of the United States and the friends of agriculture have sought to do just that." The answer of the President in his acceptance speech is an attempt to close the door of hope on this subject: "No power on earth can restore prices except by restoration of general recovery and markets. Every measure we have taken looking to general recovery is of benefit to the farmer."

And that, if you please, is the record. That is what we have to expect from the present Republican leadership: more Republican tariffs, implacable opposition to any plan to raise the price of farm products, a program of "starving out" a third of the present farm population. A splendid prospect, this! Reduced to lowest terms, the present administration asks farmers to put their interests into the hands of their bitterest opponents—men who will go to any and all lengths to safeguard and strengthen a protected few, but who will coldly say to American farmers: "One-third of you are not needed. Run a race with bankruptcy to see which will survive." It is no new theory of Government. It has been reactionary policy since time immemorial. Help the few; perhaps those few will be kind enough to help the many.

This is unsound; it is unfair; it is unjust; it is not American! Industry can never prosper unless the agricultural market is restored and farm buying power returns. Without tariff readjustment the President's program is hopeless; without active assistance, the Grundy schedules can break the farmer long before the farmer can find a market for his goods. It suggests that if industry revives, the farmer will be taken care of; though you all know that the boom of 1929 brought nothing but lower prices and more debts to the farm.

The situation challenges every responsible statesman in America to seek in agricultural circles an active remedial plan. The

President has indicated his attitude in advance. His laconic "I shall oppose them" closes the last door of hope in him.

I cannot share his view. I will not believe that in the face of a problem like this we must merely throw up our hands. I have unbounded faith in a restored and rehabilitated agriculture. In this profession of faith I invite you to join. May those of us who intend a solution and decline the defeatist attitude join tirelessly in the work of advancing to a better-ordered economic life. The time has come. The hour has struck.

136 ❨ "The Railroad Mesh Is the Warp on Which Our Economic Web Is Largely Fashioned." Campaign Address on Railroads at Salt Lake City, Utah. September 17, 1932

My friends:

I AM having, as I have repeated many times these past few days, a glorious time — a delightful time. Never have I met people more cordial, more interested, more enthusiastic in their hospitality. To my mind it is no mere personal tribute to me. I think this enthusiasm, this interest, are an expression of the hope that people have that a new deal will mean better and happier days for all of us. This, it seems to me, is what I have learned as I have passed over the westward trail of the pioneer.

My visit here in Salt Lake City is, I assure you, one of the brightest spots of a happy trip. As I have viewed the scene in this valley, it is easy to see how a distinguished citizen of your State, arriving in this place eighty-five years ago, exclaimed: This is the place! And every time I come back to it I want to pay a new tribute to those splendid American pioneers who made it possible in the early days.

Pessimists tell me that for some of the great problems of American life, such as the prices the farmer gets for his products and the prices the miner gets for his toil, nothing can be done because these things are locked in the jaws of an unchangeable economic law. But when I see, as I have seen here, what human beings have done in the work of reclamation and in other attempts to change, through the efforts of man and for the benefit of man, the face of nature itself, the complaint of these pessimists seems just a bit absurd. It is clear to me that if we can change the conditions of nature that made a place a desert, we ought to have faith in the possibility of changing the economic conditions sufficiently to bring the producer and the consumer more closely together for the benefit of each.

The tasks that we face in the reordering of economic life are great. They call for courage, for determination and what you have abundantly out here, the hardihood of the pioneer. We still have before us, as had those who settled this great West, battles with hunger, battles with human selfishness and, what is more important, the battle with our own spirits, seeking, in the face of discouragement, the means of restoration and relief.

As the life of the pioneer came to be more widely extended with the coming of the railroads and the development of commerce, things that were local came to be national, and things that were national came to be international. Interdependence is the watchword of this age. For example, when due to unwise tariff schedules of our national Government in Washington, some far-away Nation is driven to retaliation, we know now that the farmers in Iowa, in Kansas, in Colorado, and in Utah suffer. I need not tell you of the importance of these far-flung relationships. For example, the independence of the Philippines, five thousand miles away, which, by the way, our Party in its platform heartily advocates, is not without significance to you in your daily lives and in your future happiness.

And one of the greatest of these questions of international relationship, let us say it frankly, is that of money, of gold and of silver! I am glad to take official notice of the fact that the administration in Washington apparently has at last come to recognize the existence of silver. To move in the direction of consideration of that question is in thorough accord with the Democratic platform, which says: "We favor a sound currency to be preserved at all hazards and an international monetary conference called on the invitation of our Government to consider the rehabilitation of silver and related questions."

The elements of this question, of course, have changed profoundly in the past generation. The economists of the world have come to recognize that the problem of money is largely one of international concern. I propose to speak of this in more detail very shortly, outlining the difference between the platforms and policies of the two major parties.

I have spoken tonight of the building of the West. In that great development the railroad, of course, was the dominant factor. For ninety years railroads have been the means of tying us all together in national unity. I need not tell you that in this development we have seen great heroism, great faith and, unfortunately, also great injustice. When the railroads first stretched out across the plains and into these mountains and valleys, they were regarded as a miracle, challenging the imagination of the people. Later there came an age when the railroads, controlled by men who unfortunately did not recognize the large public interest at stake, were regarded by these same people as an octopus, crushing out their life and sapping their substance. But that day has passed. The railroad is becoming more and more a servant of the people, largely owned by the people themselves. It is this new relationship of the railroad that should and must guide our consideration of its problems. The railroad that was first a miracle, and then a sinister threat, has now become a part of our national economic life. We are concerned with the preservation of the railroad of the Nation.

My friends, the problem of the railroads is the problem of each and every one of us. No single economic activity enters into the life of every individual as much as do these great carriers. It is well to pause a moment and examine the extent of this interest. As I have done before in other matters, I want to think the issue through in terms of individual men and women. Directly a "railroad" affects three great groups. Indirectly it affects everyone within its vast territory.

First, take its owners. These are not, as too many suppose, great railway magnates sitting in luxurious offices and clubs. They are the people throughout the country who have a savings bank account, or an insurance policy, or, in some measure, an ordinary checking account. Figures, though they may be dull, nevertheless do talk. There are more than eleven billions of railroads bonds outstanding — about half as great an amount as there are United States Government obligations outstanding. Of these eleven billions nearly five billions are owned by savings banks and insurance companies; that means that they are owned, not just by the banks and insurance companies, but by the millions of policy holders and savings bank depositors. When you put money in the bank or pay that insurance premium, you are buying an interest in the railroads. Some two billions more are held by churches, hospitals, charitable institutions, colleges and other institutions of endowment. The remaining bonds are scattered far and wide among a host of people whose life savings have been invested in what has come to be a standard American industry. Even railroad stocks are held in small units of a few shares here and there, by school teachers, doctors, salesmen, thrifty workmen in every State. Experts in railroad finance know that perhaps thirty million people out of our population have a stake, a direct stake, in these great American enterprises.

Next are the people who work in the railway systems, either directly on the lines, or in the industries which furnish railroad supplies. There are over 1,700,000 railroad employees required to handle normal traffic; and to these must be added, in direct interest, hundreds of thousands of other men and women who supply coal, forge rails, cut ties, manufacture rolling stock and contribute labor to maintain the systems.

And then, most numerous of all, are the people who travel or ship goods over our steel highways. And that includes just about all of us.

Now there is no reason to disguise the fact that the railroads as

a whole in this Nation are in serious difficulty. They are not making both ends meet. I do not share the opinion which has been
aired recently that the railroads have served their purpose and
are about to disappear. Capable students of American transportation do not support that view. As Professor Ripley of Harvard
pointed out, if you tried to carry all railroad freight by motor
truck you would have to have a fleet of trucks which would make
a solid line, bumper to bumper, all the way from New York to
San Francisco; or, to put it differently, you would have a ten-ton
truck moving every thirty seconds over every mile of improved
highway in the United States. That brings it home!

Let me put it another way. In a normal year, our railroads are
called upon to transport over thirty million people one thousand
miles each, and to transport 440 million tons of freight one thousand miles. No other machine in existence today is available to
carry that load. And that is why I say that the day of the railroads
is not over yet.

No, there is no danger of the railroads going out of business.
They have a great economic place in the scheme of things for a
good long time to come.

Why, then, the difficulty? In the first place — let us be frank with
ourselves — we did unbalance the system of things, as we have had
a habit of doing, badly. We built — properly — hundreds of thousands of miles of first-class, hard-surfaced highways directly paral-
lelling the railway tracks. These we paid for out of our taxes, or,
in some cases out of bond issues. Today many thousands of buses
and trucks engaged in interstate commerce use these rights-of-way,
built by the people — use them and pay nothing for the investment. You and I, in our annual tax bills, of course, pay for most
of the maintenance of the highways and interest charges on their
construction. The motor vehicles pay only a small part. Naturally, that being so, they can often haul passengers and freight at
a lower rate than the railroads. They can operate with a relatively
smaller overhead and capital, lower taxes and lower maintenance
costs for their right-of-way. Also we, the National Government,
allow them to operate free from many restrictions that would

715

insure a greater safety to the public and fairer working conditions for labor. We must not give to these buses and trucks any unfair competitive advantages over the railroads themselves.

We do not desire to put motor vehicle transportation out of its legitimate field of business, because it is a necessary and important part of our transportation system; but motor transportation ought to be placed very definitely under the same Federal supervision as railroad transportation itself.

Second, while thus forcing the railroads to meet unfair competition we have not only permitted but frequently required them to compete unreasonably with each other. In regulating the railroads, we preserved the policy that at all times, between principal points, there must be competing railroad systems. There is a great deal to be said for that policy, so long as — let us make this clear — so long as there is traffic enough to support the competing lines. As long as you have that traffic, the competition helps to insure efficiency. But as the railroads have been allowed to increase their capacity far beyond traffic needs, the wastes of competition have become more and more insupportable. Now we have to face the issues: Shall we permit them — in fact, force them — to bankrupt each other? Or shall we permit them to consolidate and so to economize through reducing unprofitable services? In other words, shall we permit them to divide traffic and so eliminate some of the present wastes? No solution is wholly attractive, because we have the problem of an overbuilt plant, of partially unemployed capital, a problem similar in its difficulty to that of unemployed labor. But a definite sound public policy actually carried out will hasten improvement. We cannot, my friends, as the present Republican leadership has done, rest upon a feather-bed of false hopes.

Third, we can cut out some expensive deadwood in the shape of unnecessary or duplicated facilities. The public generally does not realize that thirty percent of railroad mileage in this Nation carries only two percent of the freight and passenger traffic. This does not mean that all that mileage can be or ought to be immediately scrapped. But it does suggest that a considerable amount of — what shall I say — judicious pruning gradually can be done in this unpaying mileage without public detriment.

Finally, there has been entirely too much maneuvering for position among the railroads themselves in the past ten years. We have had an epidemic of railroad holding companies whose financial operations were, to say the least, not generally beneficial to the orderly development of transportation. They were financial comets, free to rove through the system, spending other people's money in financial gambles and in acquiring side enterprises outside of the direct sphere of railroading itself. A great deal of money throughout the Nation has been lost, and a good deal of damage has been done, by these companies. This policy, I can assure you, will have no sympathy from the National Administration that takes charge in Washington next March.

All that I have said should indicate that one chief cause of the great present railroad problem has been that typical cause of many of our problems — the entire absence of any national planning for the continuance and operation of this absolutely vital national utility. The individual railroads should be regarded as parts of a national transportation system. That does not mean all should be under one management. Indeed, the principal doubt of the efficiency of consolidations has been caused by the repeated demonstration in our history that a great railroad is made by good executives; and experience has shown that the mileage over which one manager can be effective is limited to a small fraction of our national mileage as a whole. In other words, as in most things, the human equation enters.

But it is necessary that a single railroad should have a recognized field of operation and a definite part to play in the entire national scheme of transportation. It is necessary that each rail service should fit into and be coordinated with other rail services and with other forms of transportation. Let it be noted, for instance, that our postal service uses every variety of transport: rail, automobile, steamship, and airplane; but it controls few of these vehicles. We might well approach the railroad problems from a similar point of view, survey all of our national transportation needs, determine the most efficient, the most economical means of distribution and substitute a national policy for national lack of planning, and encourage that growth and expansion which are most healthful to the general welfare. In common counsel and in common purposes we shall find the corrective of the present unhappy tendency to look for dictators. The wisdom of many men will save us from the errors of supposed supermen.

I do not share the view that Government regulation per se is responsible for any great amount of the present difficulties. Had this been true, we should have known it long before the depression came. In the words of one of our own railway presidents, "there is no question whatever that the regulation of the railroads of the Nation has been in the public interest." Regulation, in fact, has protected investors as well as patrons, and I think no enlightened railroad man would care to go back to the old days when unregulated railroad operation landed one-third of the railroad mileage in receivership.

When the depression came with its great loss of tonnage, the combined effect of uneconomic competition, unproductive and overextended mileage, imprudent financial adventures, and frequently ill-advised management resulted in a situation where many railroads literally were unable, are still unable, to earn their interest charges on their own debt. The Government then undertook to tide over the emergency by lending money freely to the railroads, with a view to keeping them afloat. I am glad to approve this policy as an emergency measure, though I do not go along with many of the details of the methods. As far as it goes, this policy — and I speak in the broader sense of the word policy — is good. We had far too great a stake in the situation to allow a general smash-up. If elected, of course I shall continue the policy of trying to prevent receiverships. But I do not believe that it is more than a stop-gap just to lend money and more money. Lending money is all right if — but only if — you put your borrower into a position so that he can pay you back.

Let us face the facts squarely. We may as well realize first, rather than last, the fundamental issues.

Railroad securities in general must not be allowed to drift into default. The damage done to savings banks, insurance companies and fiduciary institutions generally would be too great.

But, let me make it clear that the extension of Government credit will be largely wasted unless with it there are adopted the constructive measures required to clean house. In individual railroads these turn on the financial conditions peculiar to each case. In certain situations, where fixed charges impose an unsound overstrain on the road, they must be reduced. In general, corrective measures must be adopted making for a sounder financial structure along the lines I now propose to set out. Unless the underlying conditions are recognized, you and I are wasting our time and our money.

Concretely — and I have to be fairly concrete in this campaign — I advocate:

First: that the Government announce its intention to stand back of the railroads for a specified period, help of the Government being definitely conditioned upon acceptance by the railroads of such requirements as may in individual cases be found necessary to readjust top-heavy financial structures that are strangled half to death today, through appropriate scaling down of fixed charges. I propose the preliminary development of a national transportation policy with the aid of legislative and administrative officials and representatives of all interests most deeply concerned with the welfare and with the service of the railroads, including investors, labor, shippers and passengers. I propose that in the application of this policy to the railroads the Reconstruction Finance Corporation, working, of course, with the Interstate Commerce Commission, shall share the work of planning the reorganization or readjustment, for the protection of public investments and those of innocent security holders.

And I also propose that when such plans have been worked out, the same agencies shall indicate a specified period of support to see the railroads through, in the carrying out of these plans.

Second: To aid in the rehabilitation of roads which are unable to meet the present unprecedented strain or which may succumb to past or future mismanagement, I propose a thorough overhauling of the Federal laws respecting railroad receiverships and indeed of all kinds of public utility receiverships. As the usual procedure in bankruptcy now stands, it suggests Mr. Dooley's famous dictum that it is arranged so that every member of the Bar may get his fair share of the assets. Yes, and I speak as a lawyer myself. There is urgent need to eliminate a multiplicity of court actions, a maze of judicial steps, a long period of business chaos and a staggering expense account allowed to lawyers, receivers, committees, bankers and so forth—world without end. Included in that revised procedure there should also be a provision by which the interests of security holders and creditors shall be more thoroughly protected at all points against irresponsible or self-interested reorganization managers.

Third: I advocate the regulation by the Interstate Commerce Commission of competing motor carriers. Where rail service should be supplemented with motor service to protect the public interest, the railroads should be permitted in this manner to extend their transportation facilities; and indeed, they should be encouraged to modernize and adapt their plant to the new needs of a changing world.

Fourth: I believe the policy of enforced competition between railroads can be carried to unnecessary lengths. For example, the Interstate Commerce Commission may well be relieved of requiring competition where the traffic within the competitive area is insufficient to support competing lines, recognizing, of course, the clear and absolute responsibility for protecting the public against any abuses of monopolistic power.

Fifth: After many long years of getting nowhere, the proposed consolidations of railroads, which are lawful and in the public interest, should be pressed to a conclusion. At the same time the provisions of the law should be revised in line with the policies here proposed and with repeated suggestions of the Interstate Commerce Commission and of representatives of the shippers, the carriers and their employees, to insure further protection of public and private interests involved.

All the appropriate agencies of the Federal and State Governments should have a part in a national effort to improve the health of these great arteries of commerce.

Sixth: So-called "railroad holding companies" must be definitely put under the regulation and control of the Interstate Commerce Commission in like manner as railroads themselves, because we cannot let our fundamental policies be blocked by screens of what we call corporate complexities.

Last of all, we must realize that Government encouragement and cooperation, more than mere restriction and repression, will produce lasting improvement in transportation conditions. The economy and efficiency of railroad operations will depend upon the capacity of railroad management and its freedom from undue burdens and restraints when this is balanced by acceptance of public responsibilities. It will depend also in large measure upon the competence and morale of railroad employees, constituting perhaps the largest body of skilled workers functioning as a unit in all of our industrial life. Transportation is not a mechanized service. It is a service of human beings whose lives are worthy of even more intelligent care than that necessary to preserve the physical mechanisms which they operate. And it is very clear to me that all the men and women who are employed on our great transportation systems are entitled to the highest possible wages that the industry can afford to pay.

You and I know in the last analysis that every great economic interest in the Nation requires the continuous, efficient operation of the railroads. The products of our farms, our mines and our forests flow into the markets. The fabricated products of our manufactures flow back to these primary producers along the highways of steel. We must pay the fair cost of this transportation, which is in truth a tiny fraction of the selling price of commodities themselves. But we cannot burden our producers or restrict their markets by excessive costs of transportation. So the constant improvement in the economy and efficiency of transportation is a matter of ever-present national concern. Under stimulus of good times and under pressure of hard times also, much has been done in the way of this improvement. More can be done still, and I assure you it is going to be done.

The net situation today is that most of our railroads throughout the Nation, railroads owned by us, are failing month by month to earn the fixed charges on their existing debts. Continuance of this failure spells only one thing — bankruptcy.

Here is the difference in a few words between the policies of the President of the United States and policies which I propose.

The President suggests only this as one of his nine points relating to the economics of the Nation — the extension of further credits to the railroads, thus obviously increasing their debt and increasing their fixed charges. That policy, my friends, may put off the evil day for a short period but, standing alone and by itself, it makes the day of reckoning more tragic for the Nation when it comes.

My policy goes to the root of the difficulty. While I would do everything possible to avert receiverships which now threaten us, I seek to bring the operating balance sheets of the railroads out of the red and put them into the black. In other words, I want the railroads to stand on their own feet, ultimately to reduce their debts instead of increasing them and thereby save not only a great national investment, but also the safety of employment of nearly two million American railway workers. I make the point clear that the maintenance of their standard of living is a vital concern, not only to us, their fellow citizens, but to the national Government itself.

In this great task of reordering the dislocated American economics, we must constantly strive for three ends: efficiency of service, safety of financial structure, and permanence of employment. The railroad mesh is the warp on which our economic web is largely fashioned. It has made a continent into a Nation. It has saved us from splitting, like Europe, into small, clashing, warring units. It has made possible the rise of the West. It is our service of supply. These are not matters of private concern; they have no place in the excesses of speculation, nor can they be allowed to become springboards of financial ambition. Such readjustments as must be made, should be so made that they will not have to be done again; and the system must become, as it should be, secure, serviceable, national in the best sense of that word.

That, my friends, is the transportation policy of the Democratic Party.

The problem today may be new in form, but it is old, very old in principle; and principles have not changed.

Avoid financial excesses; adjust plant to traffic; protect the workers; coordinate all carrier service in a great national transport policy, and, above all, serve the public, serve them reasonably, serve them swiftly, serve them well.

That is the road to economic safety, and I ask you to choose that road.

137 ❰ Campaign Address on Reciprocal Tariff Negotiations (Excerpts). Seattle, Wash. September 20, 1932

Governor Hill, Mr. Mayor, my friends of the State of Washington:

I AM glad to visit Seattle once more, this beautiful city and great seaport, on the one hand facing the Orient, with its great future significance in the life of the world, and on the other hand, Alaska, our own Alaska, with its needs and its possibilities.

I have often visited this city, and always with pleasure. While I was in the Navy Department, the line of my duty often led me here.

I am glad to renew old associations under the pleasant auspices that have brought me here today, and, in addition to that, I am glad to make these new associations as well.

I regret that I have such little opportunity to see more of the beauties of Seattle, its neighboring city, Tacoma, and this part of the country. I have seen enough, however, and heard enough today, to know how heavily the hand of the great depression has fallen upon this Western country. To see what has happened in this great seaport brings back with keen irony some of the things that Republican leaders used to tell us about stimulating foreign trade. As I pointed out in my speech at Columbus, one of the ways that they were going to stimulate foreign trade in 1928 was to lend money to backward nations, to crippled countries, so as to enable them to buy goods from us with our money. Well, that is one way to carry on business transactions. Another way would be just to give things away! I am not sure that this latter way of giving things away is not better than the first, because at least when we give things away we save the cost of keeping books. And, moreover, when we give things away we at least have no disappointment in failing to receive payment from our debtors.

Another method that the present Republican leaders conjured up to provide for our prosperity was the Hawley-Smoot, otherwise known as the Grundy, Tariff. . . .

President Hoover probably should have known that this tariff would raise havoc with any plans that he might have had to stimulate foreign markets. But he did not, I am afraid, sufficiently understand how insistent are the demands of certain types of Republicans for special high tariff protection. When that tariff bill was passed, with its outrageous rates, the President yielded to the demand of those leaders and started us down the road to the place where we now find ourselves. It is the road to ruin, if we keep on it!

That tariff, as you in the State of Washington well know, had the inevitable result of bringing about retaliations by the other nations of the world. Forty of them set up, just as you and I would have done, their own tariff defenses against us.

For example, our next-door neighbor, Canada, imposed retaliatory tariffs on your peaches, so that their tariff is now higher than the freight rates to Canada. And there is a retaliatory tariff on asparagus, and on other vegetables and other fruits, so high that practically none of your agricultural product can be sold to your logical customers, your neighbors across the border. The

724

market for your surplus is destroyed and thereby fair prices for your whole crop are made impossible.

Embargoes by France, embargoes by other European nations on apples and other products of the Pacific Coast, make it impossible to ship your surplus apples abroad through the Panama Canal.

Retaliatory tariffs on condensed milk have closed milk condensaries on the Northern Pacific Coast. Companies have sold their cows. Let us see the effect of that. As you and I know, that cuts off the market for the hay crops raised by the farmers. That is a good example of the fact, the undeniable, undisputed fact of the interdependence of industry and agriculture. I am told that one great company has gone to Holland, Germany and other European nations, and built condensers there. And I am told that the people of Washington are at this time appealing to the Secretary of State to use his good offices with Germany to prevent the placing of canned salmon on a quota basis. In short, because we have built unjust tariff walls ourselves, other countries are now using our own poison against us.

To remedy this I have advocated and continue to advocate a tariff policy based on reason, on the same good old-fashioned horse sense that you and I would use in dealing in our own business with our own neighbor. It is a tariff policy based in large part upon the simple principle of profitable exchange, arrived at through negotiated tariff, with benefit to each Nation.

If I am any judge of conditions in this country today and of thought in this country today, that policy will be initiated on March 4, 1933.

This principle of tariff by negotiation means to deal with each country concerned, on a basis of fair barter; if it has something we need, and we have something it needs, a tariff agreement can and should be made that is satisfactory to both countries. That, of course, avoids a violent and a general shake-up in business. It is a just method of dealing with our foreign customers. It keeps the general structure of international trade, stable and sound. And it makes for world peace. It is practical, it is American! Let us lead the way!

Out here on the Pacific Coast, another factor has had a destructive effect upon our foreign trade. Trade with the Orient has suffered to a great extent on account of tariffs; but it has also suffered because of the abnormal depreciation of the buying powers of the countries of the far east.

It is widely recognized by enlightened financial leaders, conservative and liberal alike, that to remedy this we shall have to look to international action. And in line with the plan suggested by the Democratic platform I shall advocate immediate action by our Government in cooperation with other Governments of the world.

There are many ways of producing the results desired without disturbing the currency of the United States.

In this whole matter of restoration of export trade with all countries, east and west, through the methods that I have outlined and shall continue to speak of, I am absolutely determined that our Nation shall take the initiative and the leadership.

That constitutes again the application of the rules of common sense. It constitutes what I conceive to be a new deal in the restoration of foreign trade; and with it goes a partial restoration of prosperity in our own country. It is the way to economic peace and stability; it is the way to a reasonable and sound prosperity.

My friends, it is the way of fairness and justice too — fairness to our customers abroad, justice to our own citizens who have suffered so bitterly because of the loss of this export trade. This measure of justice can come only through a revival of industry and employment — not charity, but a chance for us to earn our own living. That is the hope, that is the demand of the man and the woman forgotten in the policies of the present Republican leadership.

138 ❡ "A National Yardstick to Prevent Extortion against the Public and to Encourage the Wider Use of That Servant of the People — Electric Power." Campaign Address on Public Utilities and Development of Hydro-Electric Power, Portland, Ore. September 21, 1932

MY FRIENDS, I have journeyed many times to this beautiful Pacific Coast, but I want to assure you that I have never comprehended, as I have this time, the warmth of your hospitality, the greatness of your resources and opportunities and, I want to add with all earnestness, the great importance of the problem that I am discussing tonight.

I have come, not primarily to speak but, rather, to hear; not to teach, but to learn. I want to hear of your problems, to understand them and to consider them as they bear on the larger scene of national interest.

I have strengthened the belief that I have had for a long time and that I have constantly set forth in my speeches and papers in my work as Governor of the State of New York, that the question of power, of electrical development and distribution, is primarily a national problem.

Speaking in the language of the Navy, with which I was associated for many eventful years, I want at the outset of this discussion to take my bearings, to know my destination, to chart my course. In discussing electrical power, the speaker, like a ship sailing in dangerous waters, must avoid not only unseen shoals and rocky reefs, he must also be on his guard against false lights on the shore. His only protection against all of these dangers is to set squarely and fairly before him the course that he must steer. Let me do that in a few sentences.

As I see it, the object of Government is the welfare of the people. The liberty of people to carry on their business should not

727

be abridged unless the larger interests of the many are concerned. When the interests of the many are concerned, the interests of the few must yield. It is the purpose of the Government to see not only that the legitimate interests of the few are protected but that the welfare and rights of the many are conserved. These are the principles which we must remember in any consideration of this question. This, I take it, is sound Government — not politics. Those are the essential basic conditions under which Government can be of service.

It is scarcely necessary to tell you this out here on the Pacific Coast. In no other section of the country have there been a greater interest in Government and a more intelligent application of the principles of sound Government in its legislation in the action of the administrative authorities, and nowhere, may I add, are the people less bound by mere political factionalism than here.

When questions like these are under consideration, we are not Democrats, we are not Republicans; we are a people united in a common patriotism. This is the spirit of my entire campaign. If the spirit and the method that I am applying to public questions are in line with that of progressive citizens of parties other than my own, I invite them to join me now, as I have invited them many times before. In the face of present national emergencies we must distinguish between parties and their leaders.

When the great possessions that belong to all of us — that belong to the Nation — are at stake, we are not partisans, we are Americans.

It is, therefore, fitting that I should choose this great State of the Coast to set forth my ideas respecting the question of electrical power and to discuss it not only with you here in Portland and in Oregon, but with all of the people in all of the States to whom this subject is a concern affecting their individual lives.

This subject has been discussed so much in complex language, in terms which only a lawyer can understand, or in figures which only accountants can understand, that there is need for bringing it back into the realm of simple, honest terms understood by millions of our citizens.

This is particularly true because there has not only been lack of information — and information difficult to understand — but there has been in the past few years, as the Federal Trade Commission has shown, a systematic, subtle, deliberate and unprincipled campaign of misinformation, of propaganda, and, if I may use the words, of lies and falsehoods. The spreading of this information has been bought and paid for by certain great private utility corporations. It has permeated the schools, the editorial columns of newspapers, the activities of political parties, the universities and the printed literature in our book stores. A false public policy has been spread throughout the land, through the use of every means, from the innocent school teacher down to a certainly less innocent former chairman of the Republican National Committee itself.

Let us go back to the beginning of this subject. What is a public utility? Let me take you back three hundred years to old King James of England. The reign of this king is remembered for many great events — two of them in particular. He gave us a great translation of the Bible, and, through his Lord Chancellor, a great statement of public policy. It was in the days when Shakespeare was writing Hamlet and when the English were settling Jamestown, that a public outcry rose in England from travelers who sought to cross the deeper streams and rivers by means of ferry-boats. Obviously these ferries, which were needed to connect the highway on one side with the highway on the other, were limited to specific points. They were, therefore, as you and I can understand, monopolistic in their nature. The ferry-boat operators, because of the privileged position which they held, had the chance to charge whatever the traffic would bear, and bad service and high rates had the effect of forcing much trade and travel into long detours or to the dangers of attempting to ford the streams.

The greed and avarice of some of these ferry-boat owners were made known by an outraged people to the King himself, and he invited his great judge, Lord Hale, to advise him.

The old law Lord replied that the ferrymen's business was quite different from other businesses, that the ferry business was, in fact, vested with a public character, that to charge excessive rates was to set up obstacles to public use, and that the rendering of good service was a necessary and public responsibility. "Every ferry," said Lord Hale, "ought to be under a public regulation, to-wit: that it give attendance at due time, keep a boat in due order, and take but reasonable toll."

In those simple words, my friends, Lord Hale laid down a standard which, in theory at least, has been the definition of common law with respect to the authority of Government over public utilities from that day down to this.

With the advance of civilization, many other necessities of a monopolistic character have been added to the list of public utilities, such as railroads, street railways, pipelines and, more lately, the distribution of gas and electricity.

The principle was accepted, firmly established, and became a basic part of our theory of Government long before the Declaration of Independence itself. The next problem was how to be sure that the services of this kind should be satisfactory and cheap enough while at the same time making possible the safe investment of private capital.

For more than two centuries, the protection of the public was vested in legislative action, but with the growth of the use of public utilities of all kinds in these later days, a more convenient, direct and scientific method had to be adopted — a method which you and I now know as control and regulation by public service or public utility commissions.

Let me make it clear that I have no objection to the method of control through a public service commission. It is, in fact, a proper way for the people themselves to protect their interests. In practice, however, it has in many instances departed from its proper sphere of action, and, I may add, has departed from its theory of responsibility. It is an undoubted and undeniable fact that in our modern American practice the public service commissions of many States have often failed to live up to the very high purpose for which they were created. In many instances their selection has been obtained by the public utility corporations themselves. These corporations, to the prejudice of the public, have often influenced the actions of public service commissions. Moreover, some of the commissions have, either through deliberate intent or through sheer inertia, adopted a theory, a conception of their duties wholly at variance with the original object for which they were created.

Let me illustrate: When I became Governor, I found that the Public Service Commission of the State of New York had adopted the unwarranted and unsound view that its sole function was to act as an arbitrator or a court of some kind between the public on the one side and the utility corporations on the other. I thereupon laid down a principle which created horror and havoc among the Insulls and other magnates of that type.

I declared that the Public Service Commission is not a mere judicial body to act solely as umpire between complaining consumer or the complaining investor on the one hand, and the great public utility system on the other hand. I declared that, as the agent of the Legislature, the Public Service Commission had, and has, a definitely delegated authority and duty to act as the agent of the public themselves; that it is not a mere arbitrator as between the people and the public utilities, but was created for the purpose of seeing that the public utilities do two things: first, give adequate service; second, charge reasonable rates; that, in performing this function, it must act as agent of the public, upon its own initiative as well as upon petition, to investigate the acts of public utilities relative to service and rates, and to enforce adequate service and reasonable rates.

The regulating commission, my friends, must be a Tribune of the people, putting its engineering, its accounting and its legal resources into the breach for the purpose of getting the facts and doing justice to both the consumers and investors in public utilities.

731

This means, when that duty is properly exercised, positive and active protection of the people against private greed!

So much for the simple, clear and definite theory of regulation —a theory which today is observed more in the breach than in the observance.

Now, I come to another principle which, in spite of having been befogged and bedeviled by many utility companies—and, I am sorry to say, by many of our courts as well—is nevertheless clear and simple when you get down to the roots of it.

The ferryman of old, under King James, through regulation and control of the Government, was compelled to give fair service for a fair return on his labor and a fair return on his property. It is only in recent days that the direct descendants of the old English ferryman have in hundreds of cases found ways of paying to themselves inordinate and unreasonable profits and overcapitalizing their equipment, three, five—yes, even ten times the money which they themselves have put into it.

I am not going to confuse the issue by setting forth a lot of figures, but I do ask you to remember a few simple facts which are so tremendously important in our economic life.

Our good friend, Senator Norris, of Nebraska, using the figures of the Federal Trade Commission, summarized this in a great speech in the Senate of the United States only two months ago. He pointed out the overcapitalization of many companies by name, in definite figures, and summed up the discussion by setting forth in round numbers that these main companies had been found to be overcapitalized to the extent of $520,000,000!

This means, my friends, that the people of the United States were called upon to supply profits upon this amount of watered stock. It means that someone was deriving profits from the capitalization into which he had put no substantial capital himself. It means that the people had to pay these unjust profits through higher rates.

As Senator Norris eloquently pointed it out, on the floor of the Senate, in these words: "Just try to comprehend what that means. With the investigation only partially finished, the Federal

Trade Commission has disclosed 'write-ups' (and this means water) in round numbers to the amount of five hundred and twenty million dollars upon which the poor people, the common people, must pay a profit for all times — not for a day, not for a year, but unless some change is made in public authority, it must be paid forever." And Senator Norris added this: "As I showed yesterday in the beginning, all this investigation would have been stopped (meaning the investigation by the Federal Trade Commission) if President Hoover had his way. He is opposed to it all."

These were the deliberate spoken words of Senator Norris on the floor of the United States Senate July 14, 1932, a permanent record for the benefit of the American people — uncontroverted and uncontrovertible!

Let us consider for a moment the vast importance of the American utilities in our economic life; and in this, I am not including the railroads and other transportation companies, which I have already discussed. The utility industry in 1931 collected over four billion dollars in one year from the users of electricity, gas, telephone and telegraph. That means an average of $133 from each and every family in the United States.

According to the figures of the industry itself, the American public has invested nearly twenty-three billions in public utilities, again excluding the railroads which account for about eleven billions more.

You will readily see that this "lusty younger child" of the United States needs to be kept very closely under the watchful eye of its parent, the people of the United States.

But these cold figures do not measure the human importance of the electric power in our present social order. Electricity is no longer a luxury. It is a definite necessity. It lights our homes, our places of work and our streets. It turns the wheels of most of our transportation and our factories. In our homes it serves not only for light, but it can become the willing servant of the family in countless ways. It can relieve the drudgery of the

733

housewife and lift the great burden off the shoulders of the hard-working farmer.

I say "can become" because we are most certainly backward in the use of electricity in our American homes and on our farms. In Canada the average home uses twice as much electric power per family as we do in the United States.

What prevents our American people from taking full advantage of this great economic and human agency? The answer is simple. It is not because we lack undeveloped water power or unclaimed supplies of coal and oil.

The reason is that we cannot take advantage of our own possibilities. The reason is frankly and definitely that many selfish interests in control of light and power industries have not been sufficiently far-sighted to establish rates low enough to encourage widespread public use. I wish that every community in the United States could have rates as low as you have them here in Portland. The price you pay for your utility service is a determining factor in the amount you use of it.

Low prices to domestic consumers will result in their using far more electrical appliances than they do today. Again let me speak plainly. Through lack of vigilance in State capitals and in the national Government, we have allowed many utility companies to get around the common law, to capitalize themselves without regard to actual investment made in property, to pyramid capital through holding companies and, without restraint of law, to sell billions of dollars of securities which the public have been falsely led into believing were properly supervised by the Government itself.

And now for a personal word. I am speaking to you as the Governor of the State of New York, who for four years has been attacked by the propaganda of certain utility companies as a dangerous man. I have been attacked for pointing out the same plain economic facts that I state here tonight.

My answer has been, as it is tonight, to point out these plain principles that seek to protect the welfare of the people against

734

selfish greed. If that be treason, my friends, then make the most of it!

But, I have found new converts to my treason.

The President's Federal Trade Commission has just come out with a report which, if I am not mistaken, is a last-minute effort to fall in line with the plain implication of the present understanding—the present temper—of the public of this country. Some of its conclusions bear careful reading, in the light of what the President has said on many occasions in the past.

Back in 1925, the then Secretary of Commerce, now the President, said: "Nothing could be more hideous extension of centralization in Federal Government than to undermine State utility commissions and State responsibility." Somewhat later he said: "The argument is sometimes used that the power situation is parallel with the railroads where Federal regulation has been found absolutely necessary. This is an illusion. It differs in several profound respects. Power has no such interstate implication as transportation. Furthermore, there has been outrageous exaggeration of the probable extent of interstate power. For economic reasons these power districts will, in but few cases, reach across State lines."

Thus spoke the present President of the United States in opposition to Federal regulation and control of any power public utilities. His statement of facts then is now contradicted by his own Federal Power Commission.

That Commission states what I have long been saying, that power has grown into interstate business of vast proportions and requires the strict regulation and control of the Federal Government. The Commission says: "Analysis of information furnished by ninety-one holding companies shows that forty-eight major projects under public utilities are subject to control by ten top companies and these ten groups serve 12,478 communities with a population of more than forty-two million people."

Let me give you an illustration, not only to show the vast extent of operations of some of these great companies, but the unsound conditions created by the policies of the Federal noninterference which the President of the United States still so valiantly maintains.

The crash of the Insull empire has given excellent point to the truth of what I have been arguing for four long years.

The great "Insull monstrosity," made up of a group of holding and investing companies, and exercising control over hundreds of thousands of operating companies, had distributed securities among hundreds of thousands of investors, and had taken their money to an amount running over one and a half billions of dollars — not millions, but billions!

That "Insull monstrosity" grew during the years of prosperity until it reached a position where it was an important factor in the lives of millions of our people. The name was magic. The investing public did not realize then, as it does now, that the methods used in building up these holding companies were wholly contrary to every sound public policy.

They did not realize that there had been arbitrary write-ups of assets and inflation of vast capital accounts. They did not realize that excessive prices had been paid for property acquired. They did not realize that the expense of financing had been capitalized. They did not realize that payments of dividends had been made out of capital. They did not realize that sound subsidiaries had been milked and milked to keep alive the weaker sisters in the great chain. They did not realize that there had been borrowings and lendings, an interchange of assets, of liabilities and of capital between the component parts of the whole. They did not realize that all these conditions necessitated terrific overcharges for services by these corporations.

The Insull failure has done more to open the eyes of the American public to the truth than anything that has happened. It shows us that the development of these financial monstrosities was such as to compel inevitable and ultimate ruin; that practices had been indulged in that suggest the old days of railroad wild-catting; that private manipulation had outsmarted the slow-moving power of Government.

As always, the public paid and paid dearly. As always, the

public is beginning to understand the need for reform after the same public has been fleeced out of millions of dollars.

I have spoken on several occasions of a "new deal" for the American people. I believe that the "new deal," as you and I know it, can be applied to a whole lot of things. It can be applied very definitely to the relationship between the electric utilities on the one side, and the consumer and the investor on the other.

True regulation is for the equal benefit of the consumer and the investor. The only man who will suffer from true regulation is the speculator, or the unscrupulous promoter who levies tribute equally from the man who buys the service and from the man who invests his savings in this great industry.

I seek to protect both the consumer and the investor. To that end I now propose and advocate, as I have proposed and advocated heretofore, the following remedies on the part of the Government for the regulation and control of public utilities engaged in the power business, and companies and corporations relating thereto:

First: Full publicity as to all capital issues of stocks, bonds and other securities; liabilities and indebtedness; capital investment; and frequent information as to gross and net earnings. In other words, let us "turn on the light!"

Second: Publicity on stock ownership of stocks and bonds and other securities, including the stock and other interest of every officer and every director in every company.

Third: Publicity with respect to all intercompany contracts and services and interchange of power. Again, "let in the light!"

Fourth: Regulation and control of holding companies by Federal Power Commission, and the same publicity with regard to such holding companies as provided for the operating companies.

Fifth: Cooperation of Federal Power Commission with Public Utilities Commissions of the several States, obtaining information and data pertaining to the regulation and control of such public utilities. I speak with experience as to this, as Governor of a State!

Sixth: Regulation and control of the issue of stocks and bonds and other securities on the principle of prudent investment only.

Seventh: This is a technical matter, but it goes to the root of the subject. Abolishing by law the so-called reproduction cost theory for rate-making, and establishing in place of it the actual money prudent-investment principle as the basis for rate-making.

Eighth: Legislation making it a crime to publish or circulate false or deceptive matter relating to public utilities, or public utility commissions anywhere, and at any time.

I come now to the other great problem of the relationship of the Government to the development through Government itself of power resources and power manufacture.

I do not hold with those who advocate Government ownership or Government operation of all utilities. I state to you categorically that as a broad general rule the development of utilities should remain, with certain exceptions, a function for private initiative and private capital.

But the exceptions are of vital importance, local, State and national, and I believe that the overwhelming majority of the people in this country agree with me.

Again we must go back to first principles: A utility is in most cases a monopoly, and it is by no means possible, in every case, for Government to insure at all times by mere inspection, supervision and regulation that the public get a fair deal — in other words, to insure adequate service and reasonable rates.

I therefore lay down the following principle: That where a community — a city or county or a district — is not satisfied with the service rendered or the rates charged by the private utility, it has the undeniable basic right, as one of its functions of Government, one of its functions of home rule, to set up, after a fair referendum to its voters has been had, its own governmentally owned and operated service.

That right has been recognized in a good many of the States of the Union. Its general recognition by every State will hasten the day of better service and lower rates. It is perfectly clear to me, and to every thinking citizen, that no community which is sure that it is now being served well, and at reasonable rates by a private utility company, will seek to build or operate its own plant. But on the other hand the very fact that a community can, by vote of the electorate, create a yardstick of its own, will, in most cases, guarantee good service and low rates to its population. I might call the right of the people to own and operate their own utility something like this: a "birch rod" in the cupboard to be taken out and used only when the "child" gets beyond the point where a mere scolding does no good.

That is the principle which applies to communities and districts, and I would apply the same principles to the Federal and State Governments.

State owned or Federal owned power sites can and should and must properly be developed by Government itself. That has been my policy in the State of New York for four years. When so developed by Government, private capital should, I believe, be given the first opportunity to transmit and distribute the power on the basis of the best service and the lowest rates to give a reasonable profit only. The right of the Federal Government and State Governments to go further and to transmit and distribute where reasonable and good service is refused by private capital, gives to Government — in other words, the people — that very same essential "birch rod" in the cupboard.

This Nation, through its Federal Government, has sovereignty over vast water-power resources in many parts of the United States. A very few of these are in process of development. A few more are in the blueprint stage, and many others have not even been surveyed.

We have undertaken the development of the Boulder Dam on the Colorado River. The power will be sold by the United States Government at a cost that will return the Government investment with 4 percent interest in fifty years.

Long before that, we undertook the development at Muscle

Shoals, and all that we have got out of it has been a series of Presidential vetoes. We have spent millions on this project.

In contrast, let me repeat the position which I took when I was first inaugurated Governor of New York in January, 1929, and which I have maintained ever since. I said then, and I say now: "The water power of the State should belong to all the people. The title to this power must rest forever in the people. No commission — not the Legislature itself — has any right to give, for any consideration whatever, a single potential kilowatt in virtual perpetuity to any person or corporation whatever. It is the duty of our representative bodies to see that this power is transferred into usable electrical energy and distributed at the lowest possible cost. It is our power — and no inordinate profits must be allowed to those who act as the people's agent in bringing this power to their homes and workshops."

We have, as all of you in this section of the country know, the vast possibilities of power development on the Columbia River. And I state, in definite and certain terms, that the next great hydro-electric development to be undertaken by the Federal Government must be that on the Columbia River.

This vast water power can be of incalculable value to this whole section of the country. It means cheap manufacturing production, economy and comfort on the farm and in the household. Your problem with regard to this great power is similar to our problem in the State of New York with regard to the power development of the St. Lawrence River.

Here you have the clear picture of four great Government power developments in the United States — the St. Lawrence River in the Northeast, Muscle Shoals in the Southeast, the Boulder Dam project in the Southwest, and finally, but by no means the least of them, the Columbia River in the Northwest. Each one of these, in each of the four quarters of the United States, will be forever a national yardstick to prevent extortion against the public and to encourage the wider use of that servant of the people — electric power.

Although the President, in his acceptance speech, recommends the Federal regulation of interstate power, he has in the past, and as Secretary of Commerce in the Harding and Coolidge Cabinets, opposed Federal regulation of interstate holding and transmission companies. He has been silent on the non-enforcement of the Federal Water Power Act. He has been evasive on valuation methods and high rates and is apparently satisfied with the present type of forty-eight different varieties of State regulation.

Since 1928 the distinguished gentleman who is running against me has done nothing to enforce the regulatory sections of the Federal Water Power Act. He has done nothing to block the financial operations incident to the great post-war power development as planned by its promoters. The history of the Federal Power Commission, prior to the creation of a full-time commission under the Couzens bill after a Congressional investigation, the character of the appointments made when this Commission took office, the Muscle Shoals veto, and the closing of the White House doors to the public interest in the St. Lawrence project — all demonstrate that the policy of the present Republican leadership is dominated by private rather than public interest.

In 1925 Secretary Hoover said that while there was a considerable amount of speculation going on, especially in the stocks of holding companies, he wished to make it clear that with an intelligent State regulation neither watered capital nor speculation could affect the rates paid by consumers and that there was no need for Federal control.

While President Hoover now urges Federal control, no administration bill has been introduced in Congress in the past four years.

My distinguished opponent is against giving the Federal Government in any case the right to operate its own power business. I favor giving the people this right where and when it is essential to protect them against inefficient service or exorbitant charges.

As an important part of this policy the natural hydro-electric power resources belonging to the people of the United States, or the several States, shall remain forever in their possession.

To the people of this country I have but one answer on this subject. Judge me by the enemies I have made. Judge me by the selfish purposes of these utility leaders who have talked of radicalism while they were selling watered stock to the people and using our schools to deceive the coming generation.

My friends, my policy is as radical as American liberty. My policy is as radical as the Constitution of the United States.

I promise you this: Never shall the Federal Government part with its sovereignty or with its control over its power resources, while I am President of the United States.

139 ❡ "New Conditions Impose New Requirements upon Government and Those Who Conduct Government." Campaign Address on Progressive Government at the Commonwealth Club. San Francisco, Calif. September 23, 1932

My friends:

I COUNT it a privilege to be invited to address the Commonwealth Club. It has stood in the life of this city and State, and it is perhaps accurate to add, the Nation, as a group of citizen leaders interested in fundamental problems of Government, and chiefly concerned with achievement of progress in Government through non-partisan means. The privilege of addressing you, therefore, in the heat of a political campaign, is great. I want to respond to your courtesy in terms consistent with your policy.

I want to speak not of politics but of Government. I want to speak not of parties, but of universal principles. They are not political, except in that larger sense in which a great American once expressed a definition of politics, that nothing in all of human life is foreign to the science of politics.

I do want to give you, however, a recollection of a long life spent for a large part in public office. Some of my conclusions and observations have been deeply accentuated in these past few weeks. I have traveled far — from Albany to the Golden Gate. I have seen many people, and heard many things, and today, when in a sense my journey has reached the half-way mark, I am glad of the opportunity to discuss with you what it all means to me.

Sometimes, my friends, particularly in years such as these, the hand of discouragement falls upon us. It seems that things are in a rut, fixed, settled, that the world has grown old and tired and very much out of joint. This is the mood of depression, of dire and weary depression.

But then we look around us in America, and everything tells us that we are wrong. America is new. It is in the process of change and development. It has the great potentialities of youth, and particularly is this true of the great West, and of this coast, and of California.

I would not have you feel that I regard this as in any sense a new community. I have traveled in many parts of the world, but never have I felt the arresting thought of the change and development more than here, where the old, mystic East would seem to be near to us, where the currents of life and thought and commerce of the whole world meet us. This factor alone is sufficient to cause man to stop and think of the deeper meaning of things, when he stands in this community.

But more than that, I appreciate that the membership of this club consists of men who are thinking in terms beyond the immediate present, beyond their own immediate tasks, beyond their own individual interests. I want to invite you, therefore, to consider with me in the large, some of the relationships of Government and economic life that go deeply into our daily lives, our happiness, our future and our security.

The issue of Government has always been whether individual men and women will have to serve some system of Government or economics, or whether a system of Government and economics exists to serve individual men and women. This question has persistently dominated the discussion of Government for many

743

generations. On questions relating to these things men have differed, and for time immemorial it is probable that honest men will continue to differ.

The final word belongs to no man; yet we can still believe in change and in progress. Democracy, as a dear old friend of mine in Indiana, Meredith Nicholson, has called it, is a quest, a never-ending seeking for better things, and in the seeking for these things and the striving for them, there are many roads to follow. But, if we map the course of these roads, we find that there are only two general directions.

When we look about us, we are likely to forget how hard people have worked to win the privilege of Government. The growth of the national Governments of Europe was a struggle for the development of a centralized force in the Nation, strong enough to impose peace upon ruling barons. In many instances the victory of the central Government, the creation of a strong central Government, was a haven of refuge to the individual. The people preferred the master far away to the exploitation and cruelty of the smaller master near at hand.

But the creators of national Government were perforce ruthless men. They were often cruel in their methods, but they did strive steadily toward something that society needed and very much wanted, a strong central State able to keep the peace, to stamp out civil war, to put the unruly nobleman in his place, and to permit the bulk of individuals to live safely. The man of ruthless force had his place in developing a pioneer country, just as he did in fixing the power of the central Government in the development of Nations. Society paid him well for his services and its development. When the development among the Nations of Europe, however, had been completed, ambition and ruthlessness, having served their term, tended to overstep their mark.

There came a growing feeling that Government was conducted for the benefit of a few who thrived unduly at the expense of all. The people sought a balancing—a limiting force. There came gradually, through town councils, trade guilds, national parlia-

744

ments, by constitution and by popular participation and control, limitations on arbitrary power.

Another factor that tended to limit the power of those who ruled, was the rise of the ethical conception that a ruler bore a responsibility for the welfare of his subjects.

The American colonies were born in this struggle. The American Revolution was a turning point in it. After the Revolution the struggle continued and shaped itself in the public life of the country. There were those who because they had seen the confusion which attended the years of war for American independence surrendered to the belief that popular Government was essentially dangerous and essentially unworkable. They were honest people, my friends, and we cannot deny that their experience had warranted some measure of fear. The most brilliant, honest and able exponent of this point of view was Hamilton. He was too impatient of slow-moving methods. Fundamentally he believed that the safety of the republic lay in the autocratic strength of its Government, that the destiny of individuals was to serve that Government, and that fundamentally a great and strong group of central institutions, guided by a small group of able and public spirited citizens, could best direct all Government.

But Mr. Jefferson, in the summer of 1776, after drafting the Declaration of Independence turned his mind to the same problem and took a different view. He did not deceive himself with outward forms. Government to him was a means to an end, not an end in itself; it might be either a refuge and a help or a threat and a danger, depending on the circumstances. We find him carefully analyzing the society for which he was to organize a Government. "We have no paupers. The great mass of our population is of laborers, our rich who cannot live without labor, either manual or professional, being few and of moderate wealth. Most of the laboring class possess property, cultivate their own lands, have families and from the demand for their labor, are enabled to exact from the rich and the competent such prices as enable them to feed abundantly, clothe above mere decency, to labor moderately and raise their families."

These people, he considered, had two sets of rights, those of "personal competency" and those involved in acquiring and possessing property. By "personal competency" he meant the right of free thinking, freedom of forming and expressing opinions, and freedom of personal living, each man according to his own lights. To insure the first set of rights, a Government must so order its functions as not to interfere with the individual. But even Jefferson realized that the exercise of the property rights might so interfere with the rights of the individual that the Government, without whose assistance the property rights could not exist, must intervene, not to destroy individualism, but to protect it.

You are familiar with the great political duel which followed; and how Hamilton, and his friends, building toward a dominant centralized power were at length defeated in the great election of 1800, by Mr. Jefferson's party. Out of that duel came the two parties, Republican and Democratic, as we know them today.

So began, in American political life, the new day, the day of the individual against the system, the day in which individualism was made the great watchword of American life. The happiest of economic conditions made that day long and splendid. On the Western frontier, land was substantially free. No one, who did not shirk the task of earning a living, was entirely without opportunity to do so. Depressions could, and did, come and go; but they could not alter the fundamental fact that most of the people lived partly by selling their labor and partly by extracting their livelihood from the soil, so that starvation and dislocation were practically impossible. At the very worst there was always the possibility of climbing into a covered wagon and moving west where the untilled prairies afforded a haven for men to whom the East did not provide a place. So great were our natural resources that we could offer this relief not only to our own people, but to the distressed of all the world; we could invite immigration from Europe, and welcome it with open arms. Traditionally, when a depression came a new section of land was opened in the

West; and even our temporary misfortune served our manifest destiny.

It was in the middle of the nineteenth century that a new force was released and a new dream created. The force was what is called the industrial revolution, the advance of steam and machinery and the rise of the forerunners of the modern industrial plant. The dream was the dream of an economic machine, able to raise the standard of living for everyone; to bring luxury within the reach of the humblest; to annihilate distance by steam power and later by electricity, and to release everyone from the drudgery of the heaviest manual toil. It was to be expected that this would necessarily affect Government. Heretofore, Government had merely been called upon to produce conditions within which people could live happily, labor peacefully, and rest secure. Now it was called upon to aid in the consummation of this new dream. There was, however, a shadow over the dream. To be made real, it required use of the talents of men of tremendous will and tremendous ambition, since by no other force could the problems of financing and engineering and new developments be brought to a consummation.

So manifest were the advantages of the machine age, however, that the United States fearlessly, cheerfully, and, I think, rightly, accepted the bitter with the sweet. It was thought that no price was too high to pay for the advantages which we could draw from a finished industrial system. The history of the last half century is accordingly in large measure a history of a group of financial Titans, whose methods were not scrutinized with too much care, and who were honored in proportion as they produced the results, irrespective of the means they used. The financiers who pushed the railroads to the Pacific were always ruthless, often wasteful, and frequently corrupt; but they did build railroads, and we have them today. It has been estimated that the American investor paid for the American railway system more than three times over in the process; but despite this fact the net advantage was to the United States. As long as we had free land; as long as population was growing by leaps and bounds; as long as our industrial plants were insufficient to supply our own needs, society chose to give the ambitious man free play and unlimited reward provided only that he produced the economic plant so much desired.

During this period of expansion, there was equal opportunity for all and the business of Government was not to interfere but to assist in the development of industry. This was done at the request of business men themselves. The tariff was originally imposed for the purpose of "fostering our infant industry," a phrase I think the older among you will remember as a political issue not so long ago. The railroads were subsidized, sometimes by grants of money, oftener by grants of land; some of the most valuable oil lands in the United States were granted to assist the financing of the railroad which pushed through the Southwest. A nascent merchant marine was assisted by grants of money, or by mail subsidies, so that our steam shipping might ply the seven seas. Some of my friends tell me that they do not want the Government in business. With this I agree; but I wonder whether they realize the implications of the past. For while it has been American doctrine that the Government must not go into business in competition with private enterprises, still it has been traditional, particularly in Republican administrations, for business urgently to ask the Government to put at private disposal all kinds of Government assistance. The same man who tells you that he does not want to see the Government interfere in business — and he means it, and has plenty of good reasons for saying so — is the first to go to Washington and ask the Government for a prohibitory tariff on his product. When things get just bad enough, as they did two years ago, he will go with equal speed to the United States Government and ask for a loan; and the Reconstruction Finance Corporation is the outcome of it. Each group has sought protection from the Government for its own special interests, without realizing that the function of Government must be to favor no small group at the expense of its duty to protect the rights of personal freedom and of private property of all its citizens.

In retrospect we can now see that the turn of the tide came with the turn of the century. We were reaching our last frontier; there was no more free land and our industrial combinations had become great uncontrolled and irresponsible units of power within the State. Clear-sighted men saw with fear the danger that opportunity would no longer be equal; that the growing corporation, like the feudal baron of old, might threaten the economic freedom of individuals to earn a living. In that hour, our anti-trust laws were born. The cry was raised against the great corporations. Theodore Roosevelt, the first great Republican Progressive, fought a Presidential campaign on the issue of "trust busting" and talked freely about malefactors of great wealth. If the Government had a policy it was rather to turn the clock back, to destroy the large combinations and to return to the time when every man owned his individual small business.

This was impossible; Theodore Roosevelt, abandoning the idea of "trust busting," was forced to work out a difference between "good" trusts and "bad" trusts. The Supreme Court set forth the famous "rule of reason" by which it seems to have meant that a concentration of industrial power was permissible if the method by which it got its power, and the use it made of that power, were reasonable.

Woodrow Wilson, elected in 1912, saw the situation more clearly. Where Jefferson had feared the encroachment of political power on the lives of individuals, Wilson knew that the new power was financial. He saw, in the highly centralized economic system, the despot of the twentieth century, on whom great masses of individuals relied for their safety and their livelihood, and whose irresponsibility and greed (if they were not controlled) would reduce them to starvation and penury. The concentration of financial power had not proceeded so far in 1912 as it has today; but it had grown far enough for Mr. Wilson to realize fully its implications. It is interesting, now, to read his speeches. What is called "radical" today (and I have reason to know whereof I speak) is mild compared to the campaign of Mr. Wilson. "No man can deny," he said, "that the lines of endeavor have

749

more and more narrowed and stiffened; no man who knows anything about the development of industry in this country can have failed to observe that the larger kinds of credit are more and more difficult to obtain unless you obtain them upon terms of uniting your efforts with those who already control the industry of the country, and nobody can fail to observe that every man who tries to set himself up in competition with any process of manufacture which has taken place under the control of large combinations of capital will presently find himself either squeezed out or obliged to sell and allow himself to be absorbed." Had there been no World War — had Mr. Wilson been able to devote eight years to domestic instead of to international affairs — we might have had a wholly different situation at the present time. However, the then distant roar of European cannon, growing ever louder, forced him to abandon the study of this issue. The problem he saw so clearly is left with us as a legacy; and no one of us on either side of the political controversy can deny that it is a matter of grave concern to the Government.

A glance at the situation today only too clearly indicates that equality of opportunity as we have known it no longer exists. Our industrial plant is built; the problem just now is whether under existing conditions it is not overbuilt. Our last frontier has long since been reached, and there is practically no more free land. More than half of our people do not live on the farms or on lands and cannot derive a living by cultivating their own property. There is no safety valve in the form of a Western prairie to which those thrown out of work by the Eastern economic machines can go for a new start. We are not able to invite the immigration from Europe to share our endless plenty. We are now providing a drab living for our own people.

Our system of constantly rising tariffs has at last reacted against us to the point of closing our Canadian frontier on the north, our European markets on the east, many of our Latin-American markets to the south, and a goodly proportion of our Pacific markets on the west, through the retaliatory tariffs of those countries. It has forced many of our great industrial institutions which exported their surplus production to such countries, to establish plants in such countries, within the tariff walls. This has resulted in the reduction of the operation of their American plants, and opportunity for employment.

Just as freedom to farm has ceased, so also the opportunity in business has narrowed. It still is true that men can start small enterprises, trusting to native shrewdness and ability to keep abreast of competitors; but area after area has been preempted altogether by the great corporations, and even in the fields which still have no great concerns, the small man starts under a handicap. The unfeeling statistics of the past three decades show that the independent business man is running a losing race. Perhaps he is forced to the wall; perhaps he cannot command credit; perhaps he is "squeezed out," in Mr. Wilson's words, by highly organized corporate competitors, as your corner grocery man can tell you. Recently a careful study was made of the concentration of business in the United States. It showed that our economic life was dominated by some six hundred odd corporations who controlled two-thirds of American industry. Ten million small business men divided the other third. More striking still, it appeared that if the process of concentration goes on at the same rate, at the end of another century we shall have all American industry controlled by a dozen corporations, and run by perhaps a hundred men. Put plainly, we are steering a steady course toward economic oligarchy, if we are not there already.

Clearly, all this calls for a re-appraisal of values. A mere builder of more industrial plants, a creator of more railroad systems, an organizer of more corporations, is as likely to be a danger as a help. The day of the great promoter or the financial Titan, to whom we granted anything if only he would build, or develop, is over. Our task now is not discovery or exploitation of natural resources, or necessarily producing more goods. It is the soberer, less dramatic business of administering resources and plants already in hand, of seeking to reestablish foreign markets for our surplus production, of meeting the problem of underconsumption, of adjusting production to consumption, of distributing wealth and products more equitably, of adapting existing economic organizations to the service of the people. The day of enlightened administration has come.

Just as in older times the central Government was first a haven of refuge, and then a threat, so now in a closer economic system the central and ambitious financial unit is no longer a servant of national desire, but a danger. I would draw the parallel one step farther. We did not think because national Government had become a threat in the 18th century that therefore we should abandon the principle of national Government. Nor today should we abandon the principle of strong economic units called corporations, merely because their power is susceptible of easy abuse. In other times we dealt with the problem of an unduly ambitious central Government by modifying it gradually into a constitutional democratic Government. So today we are modifying and controlling our economic units.

As I see it, the task of Government in its relation to business is to assist the development of an economic declaration of rights, an economic constitutional order. This is the common task of statesman and business man. It is the minimum requirement of a more permanently safe order of things.

Happily, the times indicate that to create such an order not only is the proper policy of Government, but it is the only line of safety for our economic structures as well. We know, now, that these economic units cannot exist unless prosperity is uniform, that is, unless purchasing power is well distributed throughout every group in the Nation. That is why even the most selfish of corporations for its own interest would be glad to see wages restored and unemployment ended and to bring the Western farmer back to his accustomed level of prosperity and to assure a permanent safety to both groups. That is why some enlightened industries themselves endeavor to limit the freedom of action of each man and business group within the industry in the common interest of all; why business men everywhere are asking a form of organization which will bring the scheme of things into balance, even though it may in some measure qualify the freedom of action of individual units within the business.

The exposition need not further be elaborated. It is brief and incomplete, but you will be able to expand it in terms of your own business or occupation without difficulty. I think everyone who has actually entered the economic struggle—which means everyone who was not born to safe wealth—knows in his own experience and his own life that we have now to apply the earlier concepts of American Government to the conditions of today.

The Declaration of Independence discusses the problem of Government in terms of a contract. Government is a relation of give and take, a contract, perforce, if we would follow the thinking out of which it grew. Under such a contract rulers were accorded power, and the people consented to that power on consideration that they be accorded certain rights. The task of statesmanship has always been the re-definition of these rights in terms of a changing and growing social order. New conditions impose new requirements upon Government and those who conduct Government.

I held, for example, in proceedings before me as Governor, the purpose of which was the removal of the Sheriff of New York, that under modern conditions it was not enough for a public official merely to evade the legal terms of official wrongdoing. He owed a positive duty as well. I said in substance that if he had acquired large sums of money, he was when accused required to explain the sources of such wealth. To that extent this wealth was colored with a public interest. I said that in financial matters, public servants should, even beyond private citizens, be held to a stern and uncompromising rectitude.

I feel that we are coming to a view through the drift of our legislation and our public thinking in the past quarter century that private economic power is, to enlarge an old phrase, a public trust as well. I hold that continued enjoyment of that power by any individual or group must depend upon the fulfillment of that trust. The men who have reached the summit of American business life know this best; happily, many of these urge the binding quality of this greater social contract.

The terms of that contract are as old as the Republic, and as new as the new economic order.

Every man has a right to life; and this means that he has also a right to make a comfortable living. He may by sloth or crime decline to exercise that right; but it may not be denied him. We have no actual famine or dearth; our industrial and agricultural mechanism can produce enough and to spare. Our Government formal and informal, political and economic, owes to everyone an avenue to possess himself of a portion of that plenty sufficient for his needs, through his own work.

Every man has a right to his own property; which means a right to be assured, to the fullest extent attainable, in the safety of his savings. By no other means can men carry the burdens of those parts of life which, in the nature of things, afford no chance of labor; childhood, sickness, old age. In all thought of property, this right is paramount; all other property rights must yield to it. If, in accord with this principle, we must restrict the operations of the speculator, the manipulator, even the financier, I believe we must accept the restriction as needful, not to hamper individualism but to protect it.

These two requirements must be satisfied, in the main, by the individuals who claim and hold control of the great industrial and financial combinations which dominate so large a part of our industrial life. They have undertaken to be, not business men, but princes of property. I am not prepared to say that the system which produces them is wrong. I am very clear that they must fearlessly and competently assume the responsibility which goes with the power. So many enlightened business men know this that the statement would be little more than a platitude, were it not for an added implication.

This implication is, briefly, that the responsible heads of finance and industry instead of acting each for himself, must work together to achieve the common end. They must, where necessary, sacrifice this or that private advantage; and in reciprocal self-denial must seek a general advantage. It is here that formal Government—political Government, if you chose—comes in. Whenever in the pursuit of this objective the lone wolf, the unethical competitor, the reckless promoter, the Ishmael or Insull whose hand is against every man's, declines to join in achieving an end recognized as being for the public welfare, and threatens to drag the industry back to a state of anarchy, the Government may properly be asked to apply restraint. Likewise, should the group ever use its collective power contrary to the public welfare, the Government must be swift to enter and protect the public interest.

The Government should assume the function of economic regulation only as a last resort, to be tried only when private initiative, inspired by high responsibility, with such assistance and balance as Government can give, has finally failed. As yet there has been no final failure, because there has been no attempt; and I decline to assume that this Nation is unable to meet the situation.

The final term of the high contract was for liberty and the pursuit of happiness. We have learned a great deal of both in the past century. We know that individual liberty and individual happiness mean nothing unless both are ordered in the sense that one man's meat is not another man's poison. We know that the old "rights of personal competency," the right to read, to think, to speak, to choose and live a mode of life, must be respected at all hazards. We know that liberty to do anything which deprives others of those elemental rights is outside the protection of any compact; and that Government in this regard is the maintenance of a balance, within which every individual may have a place if he will take it; in which every individual may find safety if he wishes it; in which every individual may attain such power as his ability permits, consistent with his assuming the accompanying responsibility.

All this is a long, slow talk. Nothing is more striking than the simple innocence of the men who insist, whenever an objective is present, on the prompt production of a patent scheme guaranteed to produce a result. Human endeavor is not so simple as that. Government includes the art of formulating a policy, and using the political technique to attain so much of that policy as will receive general support; persuading, leading, sacrificing, teaching always, because the greatest duty of a statesman is to educate. But in the matters of which I have spoken, we are learning rapidly, in a severe school. The lessons so learned must not be forgotten, even in the mental lethargy of a speculative upturn. We must build toward the time when a major depression cannot occur again; and if this means sacrificing the easy profits of inflationist booms, then let them go; and good riddance.

Faith in America, faith in our tradition of personal responsibility, faith in our institutions, faith in ourselves demand that we recognize the new terms of the old social contract. We shall fulfill them, as we fulfilled the obligation of the apparent Utopia which Jefferson imagined for us in 1776, and which Jefferson, Roosevelt and Wilson sought to bring to realization. We must do so, lest a rising tide of misery, engendered by our common failure, engulf us all. But failure is not an American habit; and in the strength of great hope we must all shoulder our common load.

140 ⟨ Campaign Address on Agriculture and Tariffs at Sioux City, Iowa. September 29, 1932

MR. CHAIRMAN, my friends in Sioux City, my friends in this great State, and, indeed, all of you through the country who are listening on the radio tonight, let me tell you first of all that I appreciate this remarkable welcome that you have given me, and I appreciate, too, the performance put on by the mounted patrol of my fellow Shriners.

Two weeks ago, when I was heading toward the Coast, I presented before an audience in the City of Topeka, what I conceived to be the problem of agriculture in these United States, with particular reference to the Middle West and West, and what the Government of the Nation can do to meet that problem of ours.

I have been highly gratified to receive from all parts of the country and particularly from farm leaders themselves, assurances of their hearty support and promises of cooperation, in the efforts that I proposed to improve the deplorable condition into which agriculture has fallen. The meeting of this farm problem of ours is going to be successful only if two factors are present.

The first is a sympathetic Administration in Washington, and the second is the hearty support and patient cooperation of agriculture itself and its leaders.

I cannot avoid a word concerning this plight of agriculture — what it means to all. It means that the product of your labor brings just half of what it brought before the war. It means that no matter how hard you work and how long and how carefully you save, and how much efficiency you apply to your business, you face a steadily diminishing return. As a farm leader said to me, you have been caught like a man in a deep pit, helpless in the grip of forces that are beyond your control. Still, my friends, it has meant that in spite of the maxims that we have learned when we were in school, that we ought to work and save, to be prudent and be temperate, in spite of all of the rest of the homely virtues, the return on these virtues has belied the hopes and the promises on which you and I were raised.

That is one of the tragic consequences of this depression. The things that we were taught have not come true. We were taught to work and we have been denied the opportunity to work. We were taught to increase the products of our labor and we have found that while the products increased the return has decreased. We were taught to bring forth the fruits of the earth, and we have found that the fruits of the earth have found no market.

The results of our labor, my friends, have been lost in the

smash of an economic system that was unable to fulfill its purposes.

It is a moral as well as an economic question that we face — moral because we want to reestablish the standards that in times past were our goal. We want the opportunity to live in comfort, reasonable comfort, out of which we may build spiritual values. The consequences of poverty bring a loss of spiritual and moral values. And even more important is the loss of the opportunity that we had hoped to give to the younger generation. We want our children to have a chance for an education, for the sound development of American standards to be applied in their daily lives at play and work. Those opportunities can come only if the condition of agriculture is made more prosperous.

Now, the farmer — and when I speak of the farmer I mean not only you who live in the corn belt, but also those in the East or the Northwest who are in the dairy business, those in the South who are raising cotton, and those on the plains who are raising cattle and sheep, and those in the many sections of the country who are raising cattle, all kinds of things, small fruits and big fruits — in other words, the farmer in the broad sense, has been attacked during this past decade simultaneously from two sides. On the one side the farmer's expenses, chiefly in the form of increased taxes, have been going up rather steadily during the past generation, and on the other side, he has been attacked by a constantly depreciating farm dollar during the past twelve years, and it seems to be nothing less than old-fashioned horse sense to seek means to circumvent both of these attacks at the same time. That means, first, for us to seek relief for him from the burden of his expense account and, second, to try to restore the purchasing power of his dollar by getting for him higher prices for the products of the soil.

Now, those two great purposes are, quite frankly, the basis of my farm policy, and I have definitely connected both of them with the broadest aspects of a new national economy, something that I like to label in simpler words, "A New Deal," covering every part of the Nation, and covering industry and business as well as farming, because I recognize, first of all, that from the soil itself springs our ability to restore our trade with the other Nations of the world.

First of all, I want to discuss with you one of the angles of the mounting expenses of agriculture in practically every community and in every State — the problem of the taxes which we have to pay.

Let us examine the proportion of our expenditures that goes to the various divisions of Government. Half of what you and I pay for the support of Government — in other words, on the average in this country fifty cents out of every dollar — goes to local government, that is, cities, townships, counties and lots of other small units; and the other half, the other fifty cents, goes to the State and Nation.

This fifty cents that goes to local government, therefore, points to the necessity for attention to local government. As a broad proposition you and I know we are not using our present agencies of local government with real economy and efficiency. That means we must require our public servants to give a fuller measure of service for what they are paid. It means we must eliminate useless office holders. It means every public official, every employee of local government must determine that he owes it to the country to cooperate in the great purpose of saving the taxpayers' money.

But it means more than that, my friends. I am going to speak very frankly to you. There are offices in most States that are provided for in the Constitution and laws of some of the States, offices that have an honorable history but are no longer necessary for the conduct of Government. We have too many tax layers, and it seems to me relief can come only through resolute, courageous cutting.

Some of you will ask why I, a candidate for the office of President of the United States, am talking to you about changes in local government. Now, it is perfectly clear that the President has no legal or constitutional control over the local government under which you people live. The President has, nevertheless,

759

my friends, the right and even the duty of taking a moral leadership in this national task because it is a national problem, because in its scope it covers every State, and any problem that is national in this broader sense creates a national moral responsibility in the President of the United States himself.

And I propose to use this position of high responsibility to discuss up and down the country, in all seasons and at all times, the duty of reducing taxes, of increasing the efficiency of Government, of cutting out the underbrush around our governmental structure, of getting the most public service for every dollar paid in taxation. That I pledge you, and nothing I have said in the campaign transcends in importance this covenant with the taxpayers of the United States.

Now, of the other half dollar of your taxes, it is true that part goes to the support of State Governments. I am not going to discuss that end. In this field also I believe that substantial reductions can be made. While the President rightly has no authority over State budgets, he has the same moral responsibility of national leadership for generally lowered expenses, and therefore for generally lowered taxes.

It is in the field of the Federal Government that the office of President can, of course, make itself most directly and definitely felt. Over 30 percent of your tax dollar goes to Washington, and in this field also, immediate reforms can be accomplished. There are, of course, items such as the interest on the public debt which must be paid each year, and which can be reduced only through a reduction in the debt itself, by the creation of a surplus in the place of the present deficit in the national treasury, and it is perhaps worth while that I should tell you that I spent nearly eight years in Washington during the Administration of Woodrow Wilson, and that during those eight years I had a fair understanding of the problem of the national expenses, and that I knew at first hand many of the details of actual administration of the different departments. Later in this campaign I propose to analyze the enormous increase in the growth of what you and I call bureaucracy. We are not getting an adequate return for the money we are spending in Washington, or to put it another way, we are spending altogether too much money for Government services that are neither practical nor necessary. And then, in addition to that, we are attempting too many functions. We need to simplify what the Federal Government is giving to the people.

I accuse the present Administration of being the greatest spending Administration in peace times in all our history. It is an Administration that has piled bureau on bureau, commission on commission, and has failed to anticipate the dire needs and the reduced earning power of the people. Bureaus and bureaucrats, commissions and commissioners have been retained at the expense of the taxpayer.

Now, I read in the past few days in the newspapers that the President is at work on a plan to consolidate and simplify the Federal bureaucracy. My friends, four long years ago, in the campaign of 1928, he, as a candidate, proposed to do this same thing. And today, once more a candidate, he is still proposing, and I leave you to draw your own inferences.

And on my part I ask you very simply to assign to me the task of reducing the annual operating expenses of your national Government.

Now I come to the other half of the farmer's problem, the increase of the purchasing power of the farm dollar. I have already gone at length into the emergency proposals relating to our major crops, and now I want to discuss in more detail a very important factor, a thing known as the tariff, and our economic relationship to the rest of this big round world.

From the beginning of our Government, one of the most difficult questions in our economic life has been the tariff. But it is a fact that it is now so interwoven with our whole economic structure, and that structure is such an intricate and delicate pattern of causes and effects, that tariff revision must be undertaken, without question, with scrupulous care and only on the basis of established facts.

I have to go back in history a little way. In the course of his 1928 campaign, the present Republican candidate for President with great boldness laid down the propositions that high tariffs interfere only slightly, if at all, with our export or our import trade, that they are necessary to the success of agriculture and afford essential farm relief; that they do not interfere with the payments of debts by other Nations to us, and that they are absolutely necessary to the economic formula which he proposed at that time as the road to the abolition of poverty. And I must pause here for a moment to observe that the experience of the past four years has unhappily demonstrated the error, the gross, fundamental, basic error of every single one of those propositions — but four years ago! — that every one of them has been one of the effective causes of the present depression; and finally that no substantial progress toward recovery from this depression, either here or abroad, can be had without a forthright recognition of those errors.

And so I am asking effective action to reverse the disastrous policies which were based on them. As I have elsewhere remarked, the 1928 Republican leadership prosperity promise was based on the assertion that although our agriculture was producing a surplus far in excess of our power to consume, and that, due to the mass and automatic machine production of today, our industrial production had also passed far beyond the point of domestic consumption, nevertheless, we should press forward to increase industrial production as the only means of maintaining prosperity and employment. And the candidate of that year insisted that, although we could not consume all those things at home, there was some kind of unlimited market for our rapidly increasing surplus in export trade, and he boldly asserted that on this theory we were on the verge of the greatest commercial expansion in history. I do not have to tell you the later history of that.

And then, in the spring of 1929, ostensibly for the purpose of enacting legislation for the relief of agriculture, a special session of Congress was called, and the disastrous fruit of that session was the notorious and indefensible Grundy-Smoot-Hawley tariff.

As to the much-heralded purpose of that special session for the relief of agriculture, the result, my friends, was a ghastly jest. The principal cash crops of our farms are produced much in excess of our domestic requirements. And we know that no tariff on a surplus crop, no matter how high the wall — 1,000 percent, if you like — has the slightest effect on raising the domestic price of that crop. Why, the producers of all those crops are as effectively thrust outside the protection of our tariff walls as if there were no tariff at all. But we still know that the tariff *does* protect the price of industrial products and raises them above world prices, as the farmer with increasing bitterness has come to realize. He sells on a free trade basis; he buys in a protected market. The higher industrial tariffs go, my friends, the greater is the burden of the farmer.

Now, the first effect of the Grundy tariff was to increase or sustain the cost of all that agriculture buys, but the harm to our whole farm population did not stop there.

The destructive effect of the Grundy tariff on export markets has not been confined to agriculture. It has ruined our export trade in industrial products as well. Industry, with its foreign trade cut off, naturally began to look to the home market — a market supplied for the greater part by the purchasing power of farm families — but for reasons that you and I know, when industry turned its eye to the American market, it found that the Grundy tariff had reduced the buying power of the farmer.

So what happened? Deprived of any American market, the other industrial Nations in order to support their own industries, and take care of their own employment problem, had to find new outlets. In that quest they took to trade agreements with other countries than ourselves and also to the preservation of their own domestic markets against importations by trade restrictions of all kinds. An almost frantic movement toward self-contained nationalism began among other Nations of the world, and of course the direct result was a series of retaliatory and defensive measures on their part, in the shape of tariffs and embargoes and import quotas and international arrangements. Almost immediately international commerce began to languish. The export markets for our industrial and agricultural surpluses began to disappear altogether.

In the year 1929, a year before the enactment of the Grundy tariff, we exported 54.8 percent of all the cotton produced in the United States — more than one-half. That means, Mr. Cotton Grower, that in 1929 every other row of your cotton was sold abroad. And you, the growers of wheat, exported 17 percent of your wheat, but your great foreign market has been largely sacrificed; and so, with the grower of rye, who was able to dispose of 20 percent of his crop to foreign markets. The grower of leaf-tobacco had a stake of 41 percent of his income overseas, and one-third of the lard production, 33 percent, was exported in the year 1929. Where does that come in? Well, it concerns the corn grower because some of us, even from the East, know that corn is exported in the shape of lard.

How were your interests taken care of? Oh, they gave you a tariff on corn — chicken feed — literally and figuratively, but those figures show how vitally you are interested in the preservation, perhaps I had better say the return, of our export trade.

Now, the ink on the Hawley-Smoot-Grundy tariff bill was hardly dry before foreign Nations commenced their program of retaliation. Brick for brick they built their walls against us. They learned the lesson from us. The villainy we taught them they practiced on us.

And the Administration in Washington had reason to know that would happen. It was warned. While the bill was before Congress, our State Department received 160 protests from 33 other Nations, many of whom after the passage of the bill erected their own tariff walls to the detriment or destruction of much of our export trade.

Well, what is the result? In two years, from 1930 to May, 1932, to escape the penalty on the introduction of American-made goods, American manufacturers have established in foreign countries 258 separate factories; 48 of them in Europe; 12 in Latin America; 28 in the Far East, and 71 across the border in Canada.

The Prime Minister of Canada said in a recent speech that a factory is moving every day of the year from the United States into Canada, and he assured those at the recent conferences at Ottawa that the arrangements made there with Great Britain and other colonies would take $250,000,000 of Canadian trade that would otherwise go to the United States. So you see, my friends, what that tariff bill did there to put more men on the street here, and to put more people to work outside our borders.

Now, there was a secondary and perhaps even more disastrous effect of Grundyism. Billions of dollars of debts are due to this country from abroad. If the debtor Nations cannot export goods, they must try to pay in gold. But we started such a drain on the gold reserves of the other Nations as to force practically all of them off the gold standard. What happened? The value of the money of each of these countries relative to the value of our dollar declined alarmingly and steadily. It took more Argentine pesos to buy an American plow. It took more English shillings to buy an American bushel of wheat, or an American bale of cotton.

Why, they just could not buy our goods with their money. These goods then were thrown back upon our markets and prices fell still more.

And so, summing up, this Grundy tariff has largely extinguished the export markets for our industrial and our farm surplus; it has prevented the payment of public and private debts to us and the interest thereon, increasing taxation to meet the expense of our Government, and finally it has driven our factories abroad.

The process still goes on, my friends. Indeed, it may be only in its beginning. The Grundy tariff still retains its grip on the throat of international commerce.

There is no relief in sight, and certainly there can be no relief if the men in Washington responsible for this disaster continue in power. And I say to you, in all earnestness and sincerity, that unless and until this process is reversed throughout the world, there is no hope for full economic recovery, or for true prosperity in this beloved country of ours.

The essential trouble is that the Republican leaders thought they had a good patent on the doctrine of unscalable tariff walls and that no other Nation could use the same idea. Well, either that patent has expired or else never was any good anyway; or else, one other alternative, all the other Nations have infringed on our patent and there is no court to which we can take our case. It was a stupid, blundering idea, and we know it today and we know it has brought disaster.

Do not expect our adroit Republican friends to admit this. They do not. On the contrary, they have adopted the boldest alibi in the history of politics. Having brought this trouble on the world, they now seek to avoid all responsibility by blaming the foreign victims for their own economic blundering. They say that all of our troubles come from abroad and that the Administration is not in the least to be held to answer. This excuse is a classic of impertinence. If ever a condition was more clearly traceable to two specific American-made causes, it is the depression of this country and the world. Those two causes are interrelated. The second one, in point of time, is the Grundy tariff. The first one is the fact that by improvident loans to "backward and crippled countries," the policy of which was specifically recommended by the President, we financed practically our entire export trade and the payment of interest and principal to us by our debtors, and even in part, the payment of German reparations.

When we began to diminish that financing in 1929 the economic structure of the world began to totter.

If it be fair to ask, What does the Democratic Party propose to do in the premises?

The platform declares in favor of a competitive tariff which means one which will put the American producers on a market equality with their foreign competitors, one that equalizes the difference in the cost of production, not a prohibitory tariff back of which domestic producers may combine to practice extortion on the American public.

I appreciate that the doctrine thus announced is not widely different from that preached by Republican statesmen and politicians, but I do know this, that the theory professed by them is that the tariff should equalize the difference in the cost of production as between this country and competitive countries, and I know that in practice that theory is utterly disregarded. The rates that are imposed are far in excess of any such difference, looking to the total exclusion of imports — in other words, prohibitory rates.

Of course the outrageously excessive rates in that bill as it became law, must come down. But we should not lower them beyond a reasonable point, a point indicated by common sense and facts. Such revision of the tariff will injure no legitimate interest. Labor need have no apprehensions concerning such a course, for labor knows by long and bitter experience that the highly protected industries pay not one penny higher wages than the non-protected industries, such as the automobile industry, for example.

But, my friends, how is reduction to be accomplished? In view of present world conditions, international negotiation is the first, the most practical, the most common-sense, and the most desirable method. We must consent to the reduction to some extent of some of our duties in order to secure a lowering of foreign tariff walls over which a larger measure of our surplus may be sent.

I have not the fear that possesses some timorous minds that we should get the worst of it in such reciprocal arrangements. I ask if you have no faith in our Yankee tradition of good old-fashioned trading? Do you believe that our early instincts for successful barter have degenerated or atrophied? I do not think so. I have confidence that the spirit of the stalwart traders still permeates our people, that the red blood of the men who sailed our Yankee clipper ships around the Horn and Cape of Good Hope in the China trade still courses in our veins. I cannot picture Uncle Sam as a supine, white-livered, flabby-muscled old man, cooling his heels in the shade of our tariff walls. We may not have the astuteness in some forms of international diplomacy that our more experienced European friends have, but when it comes to good old-fashioned barter and trade — whether it be goods or tariff — my money is on the American. My friends, there cannot and shall not be any foreign dictation of our tariff policies, but I am willing and ready to sit down around the table with them.

And next, my friends, the Democrats propose to accomplish the necessary reduction through the agency of the Tariff Commission.

I need not say to you that one of the most deplorable features of tariff legislation is the log-rolling process by which it has been effected in Republican and Democratic Congresses. Indefensible rates are introduced through an understanding, usually implied rather than expressed among members, each of whom is interested in one or more individual items. Yes, it is a case of you scratch my back and I will scratch yours. Now, to avoid that as well as other evils in tariff making, a Democratic Congress in 1916 passed, and a Democratic President approved, a bill creating the bipartisan Tariff Commission, charged with the duty of supplying the Congress with accurate and full information upon which to base tariff rates. That Commission functioned as a scientific body until 1922, when by the incorporation of the so-called flexible provisions of the Act it was transformed into a political body. Under those flexible provisions — reenacted in the Grundy tariff of 1930 — the Commission reports not to a Congress but to the President, who is then empowered on its recommendation to raise or lower the tariff rates by as much as 50 percent. At the last session of Congress — this brings us down to date — by the practically unanimous action of the Democrats of both houses, aided by liberal-minded Republicans led by Senator Norris, of Nebraska, a bill was passed by the Congress, but vetoed by the President, which, for the purpose of preventing log-rolling, provided that if a report were made by the Tariff Commission on a particular item, with a recommendation as to the rates of duty, a bill to make effective that rate would not be subject to amendment in the Congress so as to include any other item not directly affected by the change proposed in the bill. And in that way each particular tariff rate proposed would be judged on its merits alone. If that bill had been signed by the President of the United States, log-rolling would have come to an end.

I am confident in the belief that under such a system rates adopted would generally be so reasonable that there would be very little opportunity for criticism or even caviling as to them. I am sure that it is not that any duties are imposed that complaint is made, for despite the effort, repeated in every campaign, to stigmatize the Democratic Party as a free trade party, there never has been a tariff act passed since the Government came into existence, in which the duties were not levied with a view to giving the American producer an advantage over his foreign competitor. I think you will agree with me that the difference in our day between the two major parties in respect to their leadership on the subject of the tariff is that the Republican leaders, whatever may be their profession, would put the duties so high as to make them practically prohibitive — and on the other hand that the Democratic leaders would put them as low as the preservation of the prosperity of American industry and American agriculture will permit.

Another feature of the bill to which reference has been made, a feature designed to obviate tariff log-rolling, contemplated the appointment of a public counsel who should be heard on all applications for changes in rates whether for increases sought by producers, sometimes greedy producers, or for decreases asked by importers, equally often actuated by purely selfish motives. And I hope some such change may speedily be enacted. It will have my cordial approval because, my friends, it means that the average citizen would have some representation.

Now, just a few words in closing. I want to speak to you of one other factor which enters into the dangerous emergency in which you farmers find yourselves at this moment. For more than a year I have spoken in my State and in other States of the actual calamity that impends on account of farm mortgages. Ever since my nomination on the first day of July, I have advocated immediate attention and immediate action looking to the preservation of the American home to the American farmer. But I recognize that I am not at the head of the national Administration nor shall I be until March 4th next. Today I read in the papers that for the first time, so far as I know, the Administration of President Hoover has discovered the fact that there is such a thing as a farm mortgage or a home mortgage.

I do not have to tell you that, with the knowledge of conditions in my State which ranks fifth or sixth among the agricultural States of the Union and with the knowledge I have gleaned on this trip from coast to coast, I realize to the full the seriousness of the farm mortgage situation. And at least we can take a crumb of hope from his proposal for just another conference, a conference of some kind at least to discuss the situation. Seriously, my friends, all that I can tell you is that with you I deplore, I regret the inexcusable, the reprehensible delay of Washington, not for months alone, but for years. I have already been specific on this subject, upon mortgages, in my Topeka speech. All that I can promise you between now and the fourth of March is that I will continue to preach the plight of the farmer who is losing his home. All I can do is to promise you that when the authority of administration and recommendation to Congress is placed in my hands I will do everything in my power to bring the relief that is so long overdue. I shall not wait until the end of a campaign, I shall not wait until I have spent four years in the White House.

141 ⟨ "The Philosophy of Social Justice through Social Action." Campaign Address at Detroit, Mich. October 2, 1932

My old friend Mayor Murphy, my old friend Governor Comstock, and you — many of you — my old friends of Detroit and of Michigan:

You know today is Sunday, and I am afraid that some of you people today in Detroit have been talking politics. Well, I am not going to. I want to talk to you about Government. That is a very different thing. And I am not going to refer to parties at all.

I am going to refer to some of the fundamentals that antedate parties, and antedate republics and empires, fundamentals that are as old as mankind itself. They are fundamentals that have been expressed in philosophies, for I don't know how many thousands of years, in every part of the world. Today, in our boasted modern civilization, we are facing just exactly the same problem, just exactly the same conflict between two schools of philosophy that they faced in the earliest days of America, and indeed of the world. One of them — one of these old philosophies — is the philosophy of those who would "let things alone." The other is the philosophy that strives for something new — something that the human race has never attained yet, but something which I believe the human race can and will attain — social justice, through social action.

From the days of the cave man to the days of the automobile, the philosophy of "letting things alone" has resulted in the jungle law of the survival of the so-called fittest. The philosophy of social action results in the protection of humanity and the fitting of as many human beings as possible into the scheme of surviving. I am sorry to say that among the followers of that first philosophy of "letting things alone" are a lot of people in my community back home, which is a little village, and in the farming districts of the Nation and in the great cities, such as yours. We can place in that philosophy a great many splendid people who keep saying, not only to themselves and to their friends, but to the community as a whole, "Why shouldn't we 'let things alone'? In the first place they are not as bad as they are painted, and in the second place they will cure themselves. Time is a great healer." An easy philosophy! The kind of philosophy, my friends, that was expressed the other day by a Cabinet officer of the United States of America, when he is reported to have said, "Our children are apt to profit rather than suffer from what is going on."

While he was saying that, another branch of our Government, the United States Public Health Service, which believes in my kind of philosophy, I think, said this: "Over six millions of our public school children do not have enough to eat. Many of them are fainting at their desks. They are a prey to disease. Their future health is menaced."

In which school do you believe?

In the same way, there are two theories of prosperity and of well-being: The first theory is that if we make the rich richer, somehow they will let a part of their prosperity trickle down to the rest of us. The second theory—and I suppose this goes back to the days of Noah—I won't say Adam and Eve, because they had a less complicated situation—but, at least, back in the days of the flood, there was the theory that if we make the average of mankind comfortable and secure, their prosperity will rise upward, just as yeast rises up, through the ranks.

Now, my friends, the philosophy of social justice that I am going to talk about this Sabbath day, the philosophy of social justice through social action, calls definitely, plainly, for the reduction of poverty. And what do we mean when we talk about the reduction of poverty? We mean the reduction of the causes of poverty. When we have an epidemic of disease in these modern days, what do we do? We turn in the first instance to find out the sources from which the disease has come; and when we have found those sources, those causes, we turn the energy of our attack upon them.

We have got beyond the point in modern civilization of merely trying to fight an epidemic of disease by taking care of the victims after they are stricken. We do that; but we do more. We seek to prevent it; and the attack on poverty is not very unlike the attack on disease. We are seeking the causes and when we have found them, we must turn our attack upon them. What are the causes that destroy human beings, driving millions of them to destruction? Well, there are a good many of them, and there are a good many of us who are alive today who have seen tremendous steps taken toward the eradication of those causes.

Take, for instance, ill health: You and I know what has been accomplished by community effort, State effort, and the efforts and association of individual men and women toward the bettering of the health of humanity.

We have spent vast sums upon research. We have established a wholly new science, the science of public health; and we are carrying what we call today "instruction in health" into the most remote corners of our cities and our country districts. Apart from the humanitarian aspect, the result has been an economic saving. It has been money which has been returned to the community a thousand times over. You and I know that a sick person — a man, woman or child, who has to be taken care of — not only takes the individual who is sick out of active participation and useful citizenship, but takes somebody else, too. And so, from the purely dollars and cents point of view that we Americans are so fond of thinking about, public health has paid for itself.

And what have we done along other lines for the prevention of some of the causes of poverty?

I go back twenty-two years to a time when, in my State of New York, we tried to pass in the Legislature what we called a Workmen's Compensation Act, knowing, as we did, that there were thousands of men and women who every year were seriously injured in industrial accidents of one kind or another, who became a burden on their community, who were unable to work, unable to get adequate medical care. A lot of us youngsters in the Legislature in those days were called radicals. We were called Socialists. They did not know the word Bolshevik

773

in those days, but if they had known that, we would have been called that, too. We put through a Workmen's Compensation Act. The courts, thinking in terms of the Seventeenth Century, as some courts do, declared it to be unconstitutional. So we had to go about amending the Constitution, and the following year we got a Workmen's Compensation Act.

What has it done? We were not the first State to have it. One of the earliest States, by the way, was New Jersey, which, the year before the action in the State of New York, passed a Workmen's Compensation Act at the bidding of that great humanitarian Governor, Woodrow Wilson. The result has been that almost every State of the Union has eliminated that cause of poverty among the masses of the people.

Take another form of poverty in the old days. Not so long ago, there were in every part of the Nation — in country districts and in city districts — hundreds and thousands of crippled children who could get no adequate care, who were lost to the community and who were a burden on the community. We have, in these past twenty or thirty years, gradually provided means for restoring crippled children to useful citizenship; and it has all been a factor in going after and solving one of the causes of poverty and disease.

And then in these later years, we have been wondering about old people; and we have come to the conclusion in this modern civilization that the old-fashioned theory of carting old people off to the county poorhouse is not the best thing after all.

I shall tell you what sold me on old age insurance — old age pensions. Not so long ago — about ten years — I received a great shock. I had been away from my home town of Hyde Park during the winter time and when I came back I found that a tragedy had occurred. I had had an old farm neighbor, who had been a splendid old fellow — Supervisor of his town, Highway Commissioner of his town, one of the best of our citizens. Before I had left, around Christmas time, I had seen the old man, who was eighty-nine, his old brother, who was eighty-seven, his other brother, who was eighty-five, and his "kid" sister, who was eighty-three.

They were living on a farm; I knew it was mortgaged to the hilt; but I assumed that everything was all right, for they still had a couple of cows and a few chickens. But when I came back in the spring, I found that in the severe winter that followed there had been a heavy fall of snow, and one of the old brothers had fallen down on his way out to the barn to milk the cow, and had perished in the snow drift. The town authorities had come along and had taken the two old men and had put them into the county poorhouse, and they had taken the old lady and had sent her down, for want of a better place, to the insane asylum, although she was not insane but just old.

That sold me on the idea of trying to keep homes intact for old people.

In another respect modern science has been good to us. It is not so very long ago that a young person, or an old person, who had any trouble with his mentality, was put into what was called an asylum and not long before that they used to call it a "madhouse." Even when I was a boy, the States of the Nation used to provide asylums. And when anybody was not entirely right mentally — when anyone was a mental defective as we would say today — he used to be carted off to the asylum to stay there until he came out to go to the graveyard.

Today that is no longer true. Medical science is now doing two things: first, for the young people who are not mentally deficient but who require special mental training we are applying special treatment and special education so that, instead of becoming a burden when they grow up, they are going to be useful citizens.

And then, on the other side of it, there is the special treatment for the older people, who do have to go to hospitals for mental troubles. The other day, just before I left Albany, I got a report from my State Department of Mental Hygiene showing that instead of the old-fashioned system in which the rule was observed of "once in, always in," this past year in the State of New York we had sent back to their families 23 percent of all those who were in our hospitals for mental cases — cured.

Now, those are some of the causes that have destroyed in past ages countless thousands of our fellow human beings. They are the causes that we must attack if we are to make the future safer for humanity. We can go on taking care of the handicapped and the crippled and the sick and the feeble-minded and the unemployed; but common sense and humanity call on us to turn our back definitely on these destroyers. Poverty resulting from these destroyers is largely preventable, but, my friends, if poverty is to be prevented, we require a broad program of social justice.

We cannot go back to the old prisons, for example, to the old systems of mere punishment under which a man out of prison was not fitted to live in our community alongside of us. We cannot go back to the old system of asylums. We cannot go back to the old lack of hospitals, the lack of public health. We cannot go back to the sweatshops of America. We cannot go back to children working in factories. Those days are gone.

There are a lot of new steps to take. It is not a question of just not going back. It is a question also of not standing still.

For instance, the problem of unemployment in the long run — and I am not talking about the emergency of this year — can be and shall be solved by the human race. Some leaders have wisely declared for a system of unemployment insurance throughout this broad land of ours; and we are going to come to it.

But I do not believe the Secretary of the Interior would be for it. He would say that great good is coming to this country because of the present situation. Yes, the followers of the philosophy of "let alone" have been decrying all of these measures of social welfare. What do they call them? They call them "paternalistic." All right, if they are paternalistic, I am a father.

They maintain that these laws interfere with individualism, forgetful of the fact that the causes of poverty in the main are beyond the control of any one individual or any czar, either a czar of politics or a czar of industry. The followers of the philosophy of "social action for the prevention of poverty" maintain that if we set up a system of justice we shall have small need for the exercise of mere philanthropy. Justice, after all, is the first goal we seek. We believe that when justice has been done individualism will have a greater security to devote the best that individualism itself can give. In other words, my friends, our long-range objective is not a dole, but a job.

At the same time, we have throughout this Nation — and I know you have in Detroit, because Frank Murphy has talked to me of it many times in the past year or two — widespread suffering which all of us in the city and country alike have to do everything we can to tide over. All agree that the first responsibility for the alleviation of poverty and distress and for the care of the victims of the depression rests upon the locality — its individuals, organizations and Government. It rests, first of all, perhaps, upon the private agencies of philanthropy, secondly, other social organizations, and last, but not least, the Church. Yet all agree that to leave to the locality the entire responsibility would result in placing the heaviest burden in most cases upon those who are the least able to bear it. In other words, the communities that have the most difficult problem, like Detroit, would be the communities that would have to bear the heaviest of the burdens.

And so the State should step in to equalize the burden by providing for a large portion of the care of the victims of poverty and by providing assistance and guidance for local communities.

Above and beyond that duty of the States the national Government has a responsibility.

I would like to enlarge on that a lot, but that would be politics, and I cannot. My friends, the ideal of social justice of which I have spoken — an ideal that years ago might have been thought over-advanced — is now accepted by the moral leadership of all of the great religious groups of the country. Radical? Yes, and I shall show you how radical it is. I am going to cite three examples of what the churches say, the radical churches of America — Protestant, Catholic and Jewish.

And first I will read to you from the Sunday Sermon, the Labor Sermon sent out this year by the Federal Council of Churches of Christ in America, representing a very large proportion of the Protestants in our country.

Hear how radical they are: They say:

"The thing that matters in any industrial system is what it does actually to human beings. . . .

"It is not denied that many persons of wealth are rendering great service to society. It is only suggested that the wealthy are overpaid in sharp contrast with the underpaid masses of the people. The concentration of wealth carries with it a dangerous concentration of power. It leads to conflict and violence. To suppress the symptoms of this inherent conflict while leaving the fundamental causes of it untouched is neither sound statesmanship nor Christian good-will.

"It is becoming more and more clear that the principles of our religion and the findings of social sciences point in the same direction. Economists now call attention to the fact that the present distribution of wealth and income, which is so unbrotherly in the light of Christian ethics, is also unscientific in that it does not furnish purchasing power to the masses to balance consumption and production in our machine age."

And now I am going to read you another great declaration and I wonder how many people will call it radical. It is just as radical as I am. It is a declaration from one of the greatest forces of conservatism in the world, the Catholic Church. I quote, my friends, from the scholarly encyclical issued last year by the Pope, one of the greatest documents of modern times:

"It is patent in our days that not alone is wealth accumulated, but immense power and despotic economic domination are concentrated in the hands of a few, and that those few are frequently not the owners but only the trustees and directors of invested funds which they administer at their good pleasure. . . .

"This accumulation of power, the characteristic note of the modern economic order, is a natural result of limitless free competition, which permits the survival of those only who are the strongest, which often means those who fight most relentlessly, who pay least heed to the dictates of conscience.

"This concentration of power has led to a three-fold struggle for domination: First, there is the struggle for dictatorship in the economic sphere itself; then the fierce battle to acquire control of the Government, so that its resources and authority may be abused in the economic struggle, and, finally, the clash between the Governments themselves."

And finally, I would read to you from another great statement, a statement from Rabbi Edward L. Israel, Chairman of the Social Justice Commission of the Central Conference of American Rabbis. Here is what he says:

"We talk of the stabilization of business. What we need is the stabilization of human justice and happiness and the permanent employment of economic policies which will enable us to preserve the essential human values of life amid all the changing aspects of the economic order. We must have a revamping of the entire method of approach to these problems of the economic order. We need a new type of social conscience that will give us courage to act. . . .

"We so easily forget. Once the cry of so-called prosperity is heard in the land, we all become so stampeded by the spirit of the god Mammon, that we cannot serve the dictates of social conscience. . . . We are here to serve notice that the economic order is the invention of man; and that it cannot dominate certain eternal principles of justice and of God."

And so, my friends, I feel a little as if I had been preaching a sermon. I feel a little as if I had been talking too much of some of the fundamentals, and yet those fundamentals enter into your life and my life every day. More, perhaps, than we can realize. If we realized that far more, it would result throughout this country in a greater activity, a greater interest on the part of the individual men and women who make up our Nation, in some of the problems which cannot be solved in the long run without the help of everybody.

We need leadership, of course. We need leadership of people who are honest in their thinking and honest in their doing. We need leadership if it is straight thinking and unselfish; but in the last analysis we must have the help of the men and women all the way from the top to the bottom, especially of the

779

men and women who believe in the school of philosophy which is not content to leave things as they are.

And so, in these days of difficulty, we Americans everywhere must and shall choose the path of social justice — the only path that will lead us to a permanent bettering of our civilization, the path that our children must tread and their children must tread, the path of faith, the path of hope and the path of love toward our fellow man.

142 ❧ Radio Address to the Business and Professional Men's League Throughout the Nation. October 6, 1932

(Interdependence of business interests with those of agriculture and labor — Reciprocal tariffs.)

I AM glad to have this opportunity of speaking to luncheons in many parts of the United States of the Roosevelt Business and Professional Men's League. I have heartily welcomed the support of your organizations. You represent a very large group of the thoughtful business and professional men throughout the Nation. You represent a liberal and understanding point of view toward the relationship of business and Government, and you include in your membership all political parties.

It sometimes has been said that it takes a great national crisis to rouse the interest of business men in the affairs of Government but I do not believe that this is any more true of business men than it is of any other occupation or profession in the country. It is, however, undoubtedly true that for many years Republican leaders have been able by assiduous advertising to persuade a large percentage of business men that their best interests lay in the success of the Republican Party.

It is needless for me to point out that the events of the past three years have proved to very many of these same business men that the Republican leadership is by no means proof against unsound economics resulting in disastrous speculation and subsequent ruin. Furthermore, this same leadership has been unable to do more than put temporary patches on a leaking roof without any attempt to put a new roof on our economic structure. And you all know that a roof that has to be mended in some new place after every rain will not last long, but must be rebuilt as quickly as possible.

Business men in every part of the country have learned this other lesson from the depression: that an artificial, over-stimulated business boom is an unsound menace, especially if it affects only one portion of the population, while other portions of our population are getting poorer and poorer. That is why I have so greatly stressed the necessity of restoring prosperity to our agricultural interests, to our cattle interests, to our mining interests, as an essential adjunct to restoring general business prosperity.

This doctrine I have been preaching ever since the day I was nominated, and I am happy that the President, in his speech on Tuesday, finally has come to agree with me on this point when he says, "Every thinking citizen knows that the farmer, the worker and the business man are in the same boat and must all come to shore together."

I am glad also that he thereby admits that the farmer, the worker and the business man are now all of them very much at sea!

I have just returned from a visit to a score of the States of the Nation. I made this trip primarily to learn at first hand the problems and the conditions in the various sections of the country. I took occasion to explain various aspects of the program which I propose as a chart to guide my Administration if I am elected President.

Back in April, in discussing certain questions, I used the term "a concert of interests" to describe my policy. It is not a new term, but one which had historic standing. I have conceived it to be a necessity in the present state of affairs to keep this constantly in mind.

To do otherwise is to go from group to group in the country, promising temporary and oftentimes inexpedient things. It is to go to the farmers and promise them something and then to the business men and promise them another thing. In fact, we have had an excellent example recently of belated promises addressed specifically to a group in the hope that with some new temporary expedient, suggested a month before election, the minds of farmers may be turned away from the grim fact of a consistently unfriendly attitude on the part of the Administration over many years.

This type of campaigning, which might be called a "pork-barrel" campaign, is not my notion of what the country needs in a time like this. It is my profound conviction that the Democratic candidates are to be entrusted with the administration of Government at the coming election. There will be high responsibility and I am not going to enter upon that responsibility without charting a course sufficiently broad and deep to make certain a successful voyage.

I am not going to confuse the long view by small items of temporary expediency. Hence, I have described the entire compass of my policy as a "concert of interests" — North and South, East and West, agriculture, industry, mining, commerce and finance.

With this broad purpose in mind, I have further described the spirit of my program as a "new deal," which is plain English for a changed concept of the duty and responsibility of Government toward economic life. Into this general plan and actuated by this spirit, I have been setting the details of the program intended to right specific troubles of specific groups without, at the same time, inflicting hardships upon other groups. Above all, my program has looked to the long view, intending to see that the factors that brought about our present condition may not occur again.

The central fact of our economic life is its failure to see beyond the barriers of immediate concerns. Perhaps it is too strong a word to call this ignorance but it certainly means that we do not know enough about ways to produce and we do not know enough about ways of keeping on producing. With the most efficient system of industry ever devised, our country has been brought to the point of reducing its output by one-half, while most of us sit around and look at each other in bewilderment and indecision. We need to know how to keep on working. If we can learn this, and I believe we can, all our other problems can be solved with ease.

The theory upon which we have been proceeding for ten years is a shocking impossibility; it is that goods can be produced which cannot be bought.

There were two unusual features that characterized business during our late decade of prosperity. First, great strides toward productive efficiency were made. Second, the goods produced by this efficiency were in large part being purchased on credit. Credit is, of course, a necessity to business. But today we know that our recent use of credit was ungoverned and unmeasured. To reduce it to homely terms, people incurred more debts than they could safely carry and the incurrence of this debt, encouraged as it was by reckless statements from Washington, had much to do with the crash that we have experienced.

To prevent such a recurrence of unmeasured expansion of credit is the task of statesmanship in the next few years. That is not to say that I favor complete Government control over the use of credit, but that I do propose the use of governmental assistance in bringing to the attention of producer and consumer alike such enlightened information as will enable the people to protect themselves against unwarranted and headlong plunges into excessive debt.

It is up to the Government to maintain its most sacred trust to guard the welfare of its citizens. This trust requires the achievement of such balance among productive processes as will tend to a stabilization of the structure of business. That such a balance ought to be maintained by cooperation within business itself goes without saying. It is my hope that interference of Government to bring about such a stabilization can be kept at a minimum, limiting itself perhaps to wise dissemination of information.

The other factor is that whenever income in any great group in the population becomes so disproportionate as to dry up purchasing power within any other group, the balance of economic life is thrown out of order. It is a proper concern of the Government to use wise measures of regulation which will bring this purchasing power back to normal. This emergency exists among the farmers in the Nation today, and I have not hesitated to say that the Government owes a duty with respect to the restoration of their purchasing power.

Industries have problems which in many essentials are similar to those of agriculture, and they ought to be met in similar ways. Most of the industries are more highly integrated, however, and their planning policies are frequently further advanced.

I spoke of two categories of those who are suffering the worst of contemporary distresses. Besides the farmers, there are the workers in industries. We need for them a greater assurance of security. Old-age, sickness and unemployment insurance are minimum requirements in these days. But they are not enough. Whether we are thinking of the heart-breaking problem of present distress and of the possibility of preventing its recurrence in the future, or whether we are merely thinking about the prosperity and continuity of industry itself, we know that some measures of regularization and planning for balance among industries and for envisaging production as a national activity must be devised.

We must set up some new objectives; we must have new kinds of management. Business must think less of its own profit and more of the national function it performs. Each unit of it must think of itself as a part of a greater whole; one piece in a large design.

I believe with all my heart that business and professional men have a high sense of their responsibilities as American citizens and a high regard for the public welfare. Therefore I am confident that they will go along with me in working wholeheartedly toward the national good in the broadest sense of that term.

One more word to you, my friends. It is true that many business men have been taught the glittering generality that high tariffs are the salvation of American business. You and I today know the final absurdity of a tariff so high that it has prevented all outside Nations from purchasing American-made goods for the very simple reason that because of our exclusive tariff they could not pay us in goods, and did not have the alternative of paying us in gold.

I remind you that for romantic adventurings in foreign markets we expect and hope to substitute realistic study and actual exchange of goods. We shall try to discover with each country in turn the things which can be exchanged with mutual benefit and shall seek to further this exchange to the best of our ability. This economic interchange is the most important item in any country's foreign policy. Out of economic disputes arise the irritations which lead to competitive armament and are fruitful causes of war.

More realistic mutual arrangements for trade, substituted for the present system in which each Nation attempts to exploit the markets of every other, giving nothing in return, will do more for the peace of the world and will contribute more to supplement the eventual reduction of armament burdens, than any other policy which could be devised. At the same time it will make possible the approach to a national economic policy at home which will have as its central feature the fitting of production programs to the actual probabilities of consumption.

At least, the issue will no longer be confused by the impossible hopes of selling in foreign markets which cannot now pay for our products. There will no longer be that excuse for the overbuilding of American industries. And they can begin the process, too long delayed, of accommodation to markets on which they can count.

The relations between Government and business will necessarily be in process of definition during the coming years. I said in a speech which redefined individualism in modern terms, that business leaders are now expected to assume the responsibilities which accompany their power. It must be the policy of the Government to see that they do it. A good deal can be done in this way, especially if we mobilize public opinion. It is a way we must honestly try. The time has come when industrial leadership must serve the public interest. I am sure that you will not fail to improve.

I have discovered in my journeying that, as I suspected, the American people are thoroughly disillusioned concerning our economic policies at home and abroad. There is arising an insistent demand for a new deal. I have been telling you some of the ways in which I conceive those insistent demands ought to be met. I should like to say again that there is neither magic nor cure-all in any of this. Hard necessity drives us now. The mandate is clear and peremptory. These are the things we must do.

We are engaged in a national enterprise. There are no sacred highly privileged special interests which we are pledging ourselves to protect. There is no panacea for our economic ills. There are, however, methods to be tried for attaining a genuine concert of interests. I desire to pledge myself to this service. It will be long and arduous; with the help of all of you we shall reach the goal.

143 ❧ Radio Address on Unemployment and Social Welfare. Albany, N. Y. October 13, 1932

(Responsibility of local, State, and Federal Governments for relief of unemployment distress — Public works to lessen unemployment — Better housing — Unemployment insurance — Children — Public health and welfare.)

I AM speaking to you from my desk in the Executive Mansion in Albany of a subject which is not in the narrower sense of the word political, but which, because it is connected with Government, vitally affects the life of almost every man, woman and child in the United States.

I cannot, of course, answer the hundreds of questions which come to me in every mail, but a letter signed by ten of the leading social welfare workers permits me to use their questions as a text for the expression of certain great basic principles which are vital to us in this time of stress.

The first question asks my position in relation to the duty of the Federal and State and local Governments to provide funds and aid for the relief of those who are out of work.

The problem therein outlined is one which is very real in every section of the country, as I have good reason to know. This was accentuated by what I saw and heard on my recent trip to the Pacific Coast.

Let me answer it by laying down what I believe to be certain cardinal principles.

In the first place, even in an ideal community where no one is out of work, there would always be the need of welfare work conducted through the churches, through private charity and by local government—the need for clinics and hospitals and vocational training, the need for the care of the aged, for care of mental cases and for care of the crippled.

Such communities where there is no unemployment are almost utopian, for even in times of prosperity there are always some unemployed—people who want to work but can find no work.

The first principle I would lay down is that the primary duty rests on the community, through local government and private agencies, to take care of the relief of unemployment. But we then come to a situation where there are so many people out of work that local funds are insufficient.

It seems clear to me that the organized society known as the State comes into the picture at this point. In other words, the obligation of Government is extended to the next higher unit.

I practice what I preach. In 1930 the State of New York greatly increased its employment service and kept in close touch with the ability of localities to take care of their own unemployed. But by the summer of 1931 it became apparent to me that actual State funds and a State-supervised system were imperative.

I called a special session of the Legislature and they appropriated a fund of $20,000,000 for unemployment relief, this fund to be reimbursed to the State through the doubling of our income taxes. Thus the State of New York became the first among all the States to accept the definite obligation of supplementing local funds where these local funds were insufficient.

The administration of this great work has become a model for the rest of the country. Without setting up any complex machinery or any large overhead, the State of New York is working successfully through local agencies, and in spite of the fact that over a million people are out of work and in need of aid in this one State alone, we have so far met at least the bare necessities of the case.

This past spring the Legislature appropriated another $5,-000,000 and on November 8 the voters will pass on a $30,000,000 bond issue to tide us over this winter and at least up to next summer.

Finally, let me come to the last step in the statement of the principle. I am very certain that the obligation extends beyond the States and to the Federal Government itself if and when it becomes apparent that States and communities are unable to take care of the necessary relief work.

It may interest you to have me read a short quotation from my message to the Legislature in 1931:

"What is the State? It is the duly constituted representative of an organized society of human beings, created by them for their mutual protection and well being. One of the duties of the State is that of caring for those of its citizens who find themselves the victims of such adverse circumstances as make them unable to obtain even the necessities of mere existence without the aid of others.

"In broad terms, I assert that modern society, acting through its Government, owes the definite obligation to prevent the starvation or the dire want of any of its fellow men and women who try to maintain themselves but cannot. To these unfortunate citizens aid must be extended by the Government — not as a matter of charity, but as a matter of social duty."

That principle which I laid down in 1931, I reaffirm. I not only reaffirm it, I go a step further and say that where the State itself is unable successfully to fulfill this obligation which lies upon it, it then becomes the positive duty of the Federal Government to step in to help.

In the words of our Democratic national platform, the Federal Government has a "continuous responsibility for human welfare, especially for the protection of children." That duty and responsibility the Federal Government should carry out promptly, fearlessly and generously.

It took the present Republican Administration in Washington almost three years to recognize this principle. I have recounted to you in other speeches, and it is a matter of general information, that for at least two years after the crash, the only efforts made by the national Administration to cope with the distress of unemployment, were to deny its existence.

When finally this year, after attempts at concealment and minimizing had failed, it was at last forced to recognize the fact of suffering among millions of unemployed, appropriations of Federal funds for assistance to States were finally made.

I think it is fair to point out that a complete program of unemployment relief was on my recommendation actually under way in the State of New York over a year ago, and that in Washington relief funds in any large volume were not provided until this Summer and at that they were pushed through at the demand of Congress rather than through the leadership of the President of the United States.

At the same time, I have constantly reiterated my conviction that the expenditures of cities, States and the Federal Government must be reduced in the interest of the Nation as a whole. I believe that there are many ways in which such reduction of expenditures can take place, but I am utterly unwilling that economy should be practiced at the expense of starving people.

We must economize in other ways, but it shall never be said that the American people have refused to provide the necessities of life for those who, through no fault of their own, are unable to feed, clothe and house themselves. The first obligation of

Government is the protection of the welfare and well-being, indeed the very existence of its citizens.

So much for that.

The next question asks my attitude toward appropriations for public works as an aid to unemployment. I am perfectly clear as to the principles involved in this case also.

From the long-range point of view it would be advisable for Governments of all kinds to set up in times of prosperity what might be called a nest egg to be used for public works in times of depression. That is a policy which we should initiate when we get back to good times.

But there is the immediate possibility of helping the emergency through appropriations for public works. One question, however, must be answered first, because of the simple fact that these public works cost money.

We all know that Government treasuries, whether local or State or Federal, are hard put to it to keep their budgets balanced, and in the case of the Federal Treasury thoroughly unsound financial policies have made its situation not exactly desperate, but at least threatening to future stability, if the policies of the present Administration are continued.

All public works, including Federal, must be considered from the point of view of the ability of the Government treasury to pay for them. There are two ways of paying for public works.

One is by the sale of bonds. In principle such bonds should be issued only to pay for self-sustaining projects or for structures which will without question have a useful life over a long period of years.

The other method of payment is from current revenues, which in these days means in most cases added taxes. We all know that there is a very definite limit to the increase of taxes above the present level.

From this point, therefore, I can go on and say that if funds can be properly provided by the Federal Government for increased appropriations for public works, we must examine the character of these public works. I have already spoken of that type which is self-sustaining. These should be greatly encouraged.

The other type is that of public works which are honestly essential to the community. Each case must rest on its own merits. It is impossible, for example, to say that all parks or all playgrounds are essential. One may be and another may not be.

If a school, for instance, has no playground, it is obvious that the furnishing of a playground is a necessity to the community. But if the school already has a playground and some people seek merely to enlarge it, there may be a very definite question as to how necessary that enlargement is.

Let me cite another example. I am much interested in providing better housing accommodations for the poor in our great cities. If a slum area can be torn down and new modern buildings put up, I should call that almost a human necessity, but on the other hand, the mere erection of new buildings in some other part of the city while allowing the slums to remain raises at once a question of necessity. I am confident that the Federal Government working in cooperation with States and cities can do much to carry on increased public works and along lines which are sound from the economic and financial point of view.

Now I come to another question. I am asked whether I favor a system of unemployment insurance reserves made compulsory by the States, supplemented by a system of federally coordinated State employment offices to facilitate the reemployment of jobless workers.

The first part of the question is directly answered by the Democratic platform, which advocates unemployment insurance under State laws.

This is no new policy for me. I have advocated unemployment insurance in my own State for some time, and indeed last year six Eastern Governors were my guests at a conference which resulted in the drawing up of what might be called an ideal plan of unemployment insurance.

This type of insurance is not a cure-all, but it provides at least a cushion to mitigate unemployment in times of depression. It is

791

sound if, after starting it, we stick to the principle of sound insurance financing. It is only where Governments, as in some European countries, have failed to live up to these sound principles that unemployment insurance has been an economic failure.

As to the coordinated employment offices, I can only tell you that I was for the bills sponsored by Senator Wagner of my own State and passed by the Congress. They created a nationally coordinated system of employment offices operated by the individual States with the advisory cooperation of joint boards of employers and employees.

To my very great regret this measure was vetoed by the President of the United States. I am certain that the Federal Government can, by furnishing leadership, stimulate the various States to set up and coordinate practical, useful systems.

These first three questions which I have discussed related to the relief of those who are unemployed, and it is perhaps logical that the next two questions should relate to children, because we know that unemployment works a great hardship on the young people of the coming generation.

I certainly favor the continuance of the fine work which has been done by the Children's Bureau in Washington, but at the same time we must not forget that the Federal Government through several other agencies is constantly working for the welfare of children.

Attempts have been made to cut the appropriations for child welfare work. It seems to me that this is the last place in which we should seek to economize. I cannot agree with the member of President Hoover's Cabinet who suggests that this depression is not altogether a bad thing for our children.

You and I know the appalling fact that malnutrition is one of the saddest by-products of unemployment. The health of these children is being affected not only now but for all the rest of their lives.

Furthermore, a depression takes thousands of children away from schools and puts them to work to help the family income. They are underpaid and only too often work under conditions

792

which, physically and morally, are often dangerous. It is well to remember, too, that the use of these untrained children in industry keeps many adults out of employment and has the effect of cutting down wages below a decent living standard.

These are only a few of the many reasons why the Federal Government must continue to act as an agency to disseminate information about child welfare and to encourage State and local governments to raise their standards to the highest possible levels.

The last question relates to keeping children in school to the age of sixteen. I am in favor of that. Furthermore, I go along with the thought that we must increase vocational education for those children who otherwise would not receive adequate training. That kind of vocational training will raise the standards of worthwhile employment, not only now but also in normal times.

My own observation leads me to believe that in many parts of the country we have tended to an educational system devised too greatly for academic training and professional careers.

We know that already many of the professions are oversupplied, and it is a fair guess that during the coming generation we shall devote more attention to educating our boys and girls for vocational pursuits which are·just as honorable, just as respectable and in many instances just as remunerative as are the professions themselves.

The Federal Government, without in any way taking away the right and the duty of the several States to manage their own educational affairs, can act as a clearing house of information and as an incentive to higher standards.

But the Federal Government has had no continuing policy for dealing with problems of public health and social welfare. In this as in other activities a multiplicity of unrelated agencies has been developed hit-or-miss to deal with aspects of the same problem. The result has been waste of men and money and a more costly and less efficient service than we should have.

The Administration has done nothing to reorganize this or other branches of the Federal Government, in spite of campaign promises at the last three Presidential elections. I propose to inaugurate a definite long-range plan for dealing with all phases of public health and welfare, which are a proper concern of the Federal Government.

May I add that in the State of New York during the past four years we have accomplished definite and practical results by coordinating and planning the work of the State?

I cite as a simple example the public health program, which is a part of my Administration. It has been referred to in other States as the most important contribution to practical public health work during this generation. And all of this we have taken out of politics.

The same principles can and should be applied to the health and welfare work of the Federal Government.

In closing, will you let me make an appeal to the entire country — an appeal with all my heart, with all my mind and with all my soul — to let nothing interfere with the duty and obligation of coming forward as individuals and as groups to the support of the unemployed and their dependents during the coming winter.

By proclamation I can make official appeal to the State of which I am Governor, but I think that I have the right, as a Presidential candidate, to make an unofficial appeal to my fellow Americans in every other State.

I wish that every man, woman and child above the age of reason in the whole country would make the coming Thanksgiving Day and the coming Christmas Day occasions to contribute with money or food or clothing, or all three, to the direct relief of local needs.

Let us remember that in addition to whatever it may be possible for the Federal Government or State Government or municipalities to do in relieving the tremendous and increasing burden of relief work, misery and distress will still be great unless individuals, societies and churches practice actual charity — actual love of their neighbor — to an extent even greater than at any time in the past.

Let us who have jobs or money or shelter for ourselves and our own families share with the less fortunate. Thanksgiving Day and Christmas Day of 1932 will take on an added significance — the significance of a higher American ideal of social justice.

144 ⟪ Campaign Address on the Federal Budget at Pittsburgh, Pa. October 19, 1932

My friends of Pennsylvania:

IT IS fitting that I should choose Pittsburgh to sound a solemn note of warning, addressed not only to the Republican leaders, but also to the rank and file of American voters of all parties. There are some prices too high for the country to pay for the propaganda spread abroad in a Presidential election.

That, my friends, is proved when, as now, the Republican campaign management and people like Henry Ford and General Atterbury of the Pennsylvania Railroad are guilty of spreading the gospel of fear.

That is true when in a desperate, futile, last-minute effort to dam the tide of popular disapproval that is steadily growing against the Administration, they become alarmists and panic breeders.

This policy of seeking to win by fear of ruin is selfish in its motive, brutal in its method and false in its promise. It is a policy that will be resented as such by men and women of all parties in every section of the country on November eighth.

It is an insult to the intelligence of the American voters to think that they can be fooled by shifting the boast of the full dinner pail made in 1928, to the threat of the continued empty dinner pail in 1932.

I assure the badly advised and fear-stricken leaders of the Republican Party that not only Democrats but also the rank and file of their own party, who are properly dissatisfied with that leadership, are still American patriots and that they still cherish in their hearts, as I do, the safety of the country, the welfare of its people and the continuance of its institutions.

What is the normal and sensible thing to do when your neighbor gets all excited and starts calling you and your family bad names over the back fence? I take it that nothing is gained by your calling your neighbor worse names or by losing your own temper. As a matter of fact, the peace of the community is best served by sitting down and quietly discussing the problems without raising one's voice. That is why I decline to answer vituperation merely by more vituperation.

Sometime, somewhere in this campaign, I have to talk about dollars and cents. It is a terrible thing to ask you people to listen for forty-five minutes to the story of the Federal budget, but I am going to ask you to do it; and I am going to talk to you about "dollars and cents" in terms that I think not only public accountants, but everybody else can understand.

One of these great problems — and a very vital one to my family and your family and to the whole community — is the financial problem of making both ends meet. I want to discuss this problem with you tonight. To do so sincerely I must tell the facts as they are and conceal nothing from you. It is not a pretty picture, but if we know that picture and face it we have nothing to fear. This country is the richest and most resourceful Nation in the world. It can and will meet successfully every problem which it faces; but it can do so only through intelligent leadership working unselfishly for the good of all people. That it has not had such leadership in its financial affairs will become obvious from the facts I am going to relate to you tonight.

We all know that our own family credit depends in large part on the stability of the credit of the United States. And here, at least, is one field in which all business — big business and little business and family business and the individual's business — is at the mercy of our big Government down at Washington, D. C.

What I should like to do is to reduce, in so far as possible, the problem of our national finances to the terms of a family budget.

The credit of the family depends chiefly on whether that

family is living within its income. And that is equally true of the Nation. If the Nation is living within its income, its credit is good. If, in some crises, it lives beyond its income for a year or two, it can usually borrow temporarily at reasonable rates. But if, like a spendthrift, it throws discretion to the winds, and is willing to make no sacrifice at all in spending; if it extends its taxing to the limit of the people's power to pay and continues to pile up deficits, then it is on the road to bankruptcy.

For over two years our Federal Government has experienced unprecedented deficits, in spite of increased taxes. We must not forget that there are three separate governmental spending and taxing agencies in the United States — the national Government in Washington, the State Government and the local government. Perhaps because the apparent national income seemed to have spiraled upward from about 35 billions a year in 1913, the year before the outbreak of the World War, to about 90 billions in 1928, four years ago, all three of our governmental units became reckless; and, consequently, the total spending in all three classes, national, State and local, rose in the same period from about three billions to nearly thirteen billions, or from 8½ percent of income to 14½ percent of income.

"Come-easy-go-easy" was the rule. It was all very merry while it lasted. We did not greatly worry. We thought we were getting rich. But when the crash came, we were shocked to find that while income melted away like snow in the spring, governmental expense did not drop at all. It is estimated that in 1932 our total national income will not much exceed 45 billions, or half of what it used to be, while our total cost of Government will likely be considerably in excess of 15 billions. This simply means that the 14 percent that Government cost has risen to has now become 33 1/3 percent of our national income. Take it in terms of human beings: It means that we are paying for the cost of our three kinds of Government $125 a year for every man, woman and child in the United States, or $625 a year for the average family of five people. Can we stand that? I do not believe it.

797

That is a perfectly impossible economic condition. Quite apart from every man's own tax assessment, that burden is a brake on any return to normal business activity. Taxes are paid in the sweat of every man who labors because they are a burden on production and are paid through production. If those taxes are excessive, they are reflected in idle factories, in tax-sold farms, and in hordes of hungry people, tramping the streets and seeking jobs in vain. Our workers may never see a tax bill, but they pay. They pay in deductions from wages, in increased cost of what they buy, or — as now — in broad unemployment throughout the land. There is not an unemployed man, there is not a struggling farmer, whose interest in this subject is not direct and vital. It comes home to every one of us!

Let me make it perfectly clear, however, that if men or women or children are starving in the United States — anywhere — I regard it as a positive duty of the Government — of the national Government if local and State Governments have not the cash — to raise by taxes whatever sums may be necessary to keep them from starvation.

What I am talking about are the taxes which go to the ordinary costs of conducting Government year in and year out. That is where the question of extravagance comes in. There can be no extravagance when starvation is in question; but extravagance does apply to the mounting budget of the Federal Government in Washington during these past four years.

The most obvious effect of extravagant Government spending is its burden on farm and industrial activity, and, for that nearly every Government unit in the United States is to blame. But when we come to consider prodigality and extravagance in the Federal Government, as distinguished from State or local government, we are talking about something even more dangerous. For upon the financial stability of the United States Government depends the stability of trade and employment, and of the entire banking, savings and insurance system of the Nation.

To make things clear, to explain the exact nature of the present condition of the Federal pocketbook, I must go back to 1929.

Many people throughout the land—rich and poor—have believed the fairy story which has been painstakingly circulated by this Administration, that the routine spending of our Federal Government has been kept on a fairly even keel during these past five years. It was perhaps easy to give this impression because the total outlay each year up to the emergency appropriations of this year did not increase alarmingly. But the joker in this is that the total outlay includes interest and sinking fund on the public debt; and those charges were going down steadily, right up to this year.

On the plain question of frugality of management, if we want to compare routine Government outlay for 1927 with that for 1931 for example—four years later—we must subtract this so-called "debt service charge" from the total budget in each year. If we do this, we find that the expenditure for the business of Government in 1927 was $2,187,000,000, and in 1931, $3,168,-000,000.

That represents an increase of actual administrative spending in those four years of approximately one billion dollars, or roughly, 50 percent; and that, I may add, is the most reckless and extravagant past that I have been able to discover in the statistical record of any peacetime Government anywhere, any time.

It is an ultimate fact proved by the record which is the exact reverse of the thing announced as fact by Republican leaders.

Let me repeat those figures so that the whole country can get them clearly in mind. Leaving out "debt service charges" in both instances, the cost of carrying on the usual business of the United States was $2,187,000,000 in 1927, $3,168,000,000 in 1931—an increase in four years of one billion dollars!

That, my friends, is the story on the spending side of the ledger. But you and I know that there are always two sides—or ought to be—to a ledger that is supposed to balance. It is bad enough—that story of the spending side, and a billion dollar increase, that 50 percent increase in four years! But it is less than half of the whole appalling story. And I am telling the Nation that on the income side of our ledger, the record is worse.

799

Unlike other taxing agencies, the Federal Government does not levy a direct tax on property. Therefore, you do not have to be an expert to know that when anything happens that violently contracts sales and incomes and the prices of securities and commodities, there is sure to be a similar violent contraction of Federal income and that a Government charged with maintaining the financial stability not only of the United States itself, but of the whole American Nation under all conditions, is under a very solemn duty, in such an event, to take immediate steps to avoid a deficit.

Although six weeks had elapsed since the worst economic crash in history, the panic of 1929, the Federal budget that was submitted by the President in December, 1929, did not even refer to it. It estimated receipts for the year ending June 30, 1931, at 4.2 billions, actually more than they had been in the preceding year of economic fantasy, a figure which obviously could not possibly be attained without an immediate return to the exaggerated speculations of 1929. The Administration advised no economy. On the contrary, it proposed a reduction of taxes and it blandly and cheerfully remarked — here are its own words: "Our finances are in sound condition. . . . Our estimated expenditures . . . are well within our expected receipts." That was six weeks after the panic had broken!

Against those estimated receipts, placed at 4.2 billions by the Secretary of the Treasury, the sad fact is that the actual revenue turned out to be 3.3 billions, or nearly a billion short of the estimate.

I recite that 1929 Federal incident to clarify what happened at Washington in the next two years, in 1930 and 1931. In December of 1930 a new budget appeared. Vast declines in every form of business activity were at that time deadly certain. In fact, the national income was in a nosedive, or perhaps it was in a tailspin. It was therefore certain that Federal income was on the verge of a catastrophe. Yet, that new budget of December, 1930, recommended neither increased taxes nor decreased expenditures, although upon its recommendations depended the credit standing of the United States.

The Budget Message of the President asserted that the deficit for 1931 would be only $180,000,000; and it contained the statements :"Nor do I look with great concern upon this moderate deficit," and, again, "Our Government finances are in a sound condition." He actually estimated a surplus for the year 1932.

At this time the President and his Secretary of the Treasury had had plenty of experience with falling tax receipts — just as you and I had had with falling income.

The astonishing and inescapable fact is that no such results as those estimated could have been achieved without an immediate and complete business recovery from the practical paralysis then existing. That 1930 budget cannot fairly be called an estimate at all. It was an extreme hazard on the hope of an economic miracle, a gamble, if you please, a gamble with your money and mine — and a hidden one at that.

There is something much more than mere error in that kind of thing. Our people and the world are entitled to reasonable accuracy and reasonable prudence; and above all they are entitled to complete frankness. They have a right and a duty to place in retirement those who conceal realities, those who abuse confidence.

I am going to talk about more figures — but figures talk.

We remember these simple facts: On December 3, 1930, the President estimated that the following summer there would be a deficit of $180,000,000, but that in the summer of 1932 there would be a profit of $30,000,000, or a total estimated deficit for the two years of $150,000,000.

Now, I am going to give you good people a real shock. Instead of the Government running into the red for those two years to the tune of $150,000,000, the deficit on June 30, 1932, was, for the two fiscal years, three and three-quarters billion dollars.

No, I fear we cannot call this budget an estimate — or even a fair gamble. I do not know what to call that kind of representation or that kind of fact, but the name for it certainly is not candor.

Nineteen hundred and thirty-one proved to be the worst year experienced in the depression up to that time. For my distinguished opponent, 1931 was the year in which all his distinctive 1928 economic heresies seemed to come home to roost, all at the same time.

Let us call the roll of those economic heresies:

1. Those famous loans to "backward and crippled countries," which he said would provide uninterrupted employment and uninterrupted industrial activity by expanding our export trade, no longer could be made.

2. Retaliation against his monstrous Grundy tariff — and you people in Pennsylvania ought to know something about that — against which the best economic and industrial thought in the country had stood in almost unanimous protest, and against which it once more protested within the past week, and which was to cure our agriculture and maintain our industry, had already begun to strangle the world trade of all Nations, including our own.

3. Debtor Nations, no longer sustained by our improvident loans and no longer able to export goods, were drained of gold for debts and, one by one, were forced to abandon specie payments.

4. Finally, as a direct result of all these influences, our export markets dried up, our commodity prices slumped and our own domestic business itself declined at a more rapid rate than business in some of the backward and crippled countries.

Unemployment began to rise here in even greater proportions than in Europe. To top this ruin of all these seductive 1928 theories — which were to bring the millennium of abolished poverty and the chicken, or maybe it was two of them, in every pot —

came the complete collapse of the 1929 and 1930 Administration fiscal policy.

The truth about the shattering effect of all these homing heresies began to leak out as the summer of 1931 advanced; and it is my opinion that in the conduct of national finances, as in the conduct of corporation finances or family budgets, if things are not going as well as one had hoped, it is far better to face the truth than to try to hide it. That is why, when history comes to be written, it will be shown that it was far more harmful to the Nation last autumn—in 1931—and all through this year of 1932, to have the facts leak out, than it would have been to have had them boldly and frankly disclosed to us when they were actually taking place.

The result of such a combination of disquieting revelations was inevitable. The very basis of confidence in our economic and financial structure both here and abroad was impaired. A fresh wave of liquidation ensued. Foreigners took $1,000,000,000 of their gold back in that black year of 1931.

I emphasize this history because our opponents have now become almost frantic in their insistence that this entire sequence of events originated abroad. I do not know where; they have never located "abroad," but I think it is somewhere near Abyssinia. They insist that no American policy was in the least to blame, and that to say otherwise is what they call "hideous misrepresentation." The "foreign cause" alibi is just like ascribing measles on our little boy to the spots on his chest, instead of to the contagious germ that he has picked up somewhere.

No, we need not look abroad for scapegoats. We had ventured into the economic stratosphere — which is a long way up — on the wings of President Hoover's novel, radical and unorthodox economic theories of 1928, the complete collapse of which brought the real crash in 1931. The Grundy tariff accelerated the drop. As hard reality rushed up to meet our fall, this Administration did not see fit to adapt its fiscal policies to this inevitable consequence. It is a responsibility which no campaign alibi can avert, and less than three weeks off, the day of reckoning will come.

The Administration's recent strategy in this campaign is a direct appeal to public sympathy for its agony of spirit in the dark hours of last year and this year, when retribution for our chasing after strange economic gods overtook us. It protests against any assessment of just blame. But it protests in vain.

I want to say, with all sincerity, that I recite this record with reluctance. No man with a spark of decency or humanity can fail to sympathize with our responsible leaders in hours of crisis. Politics or no politics, I pay my tribute to the devotion of the President of the United States. It is not true to say that he has not been unremitting in his efforts, and I for one have never heard it said.

But I do indict his Administration for wrong action, for delayed action, for lack of frankness and for lack of courage. Before the Administration partisans complain of this arraignment, they must remember that the American people are now about to exercise their democratic right of self-determination of their own fate and their own future. They must make a choice. That appeal for sympathy is not based on any frank acknowledgment of the failure of the policies so clearly portrayed by these tragic events. On the contrary, it is a denial that these principles have failed. It persists in the same course and even presumes to ask admiration for the stubborn ruggedness of that persistence.

Under those circumstances I should fail utterly in my duty to the American people, if I did not fearlessly portray these errors and link them directly to the havoc which they have brought and which they threaten to continue.

The autumn of 1931 witnessed the complete wreckage of the Administration program to that date, the collapse of its entire economic philosophy. The convening of the 72nd Congress last December started the last phase. The President appeared with his December, 1931 Budget Message. It was a fateful moment. That was the time — last December — for an honest demonstration to the world that might have set the whole world trend of economic events in an upward direction or at least checked the decline. All that it was necessary to do was finally to end once and for all the

804

two years of vacillation and secretiveness, to tell the truth to the Congress of the United States, and to rely on that Congress to balance the budget and establish American credit in the eyes of all the world.

In a way the Administration did acknowledge the necessity for that. It started off by saying that it was going to balance the budget. Fine! Then it said it was balancing the budget. Fine! And finally, it said it had balanced the budget. Better yet! And now, months later, it insists that because it has balanced the budget, it has saved the Gibraltar of world stability and prevented the overthrow of our form of Government.

If all that is true, the Administration has done well. If it is not true, then the Administration stands convicted of a new and fatal trifling with the welfare of our people and the credit of our country.

Let me not waste words. I now quote from the daily Treasury statement, made three weeks ago, on the result of the first three months of operation under the new budget this year, the statement covering the months of July, August and September, the first quarter of the fiscal year. Here is what it says:

"Excess of expenditures over receipts, $402,043,002." There you are!

For the corresponding quarter of last year the deficit was only $380,495,584, but at the end of the year it was $2,885,000,000. There is, therefore, strong indication that we are in for another staggering deficit. If the present rate on that budget continues, the true deficit as of June 30th next year will be over $1,600,-000,000 — a deficit so great that it makes us catch our breath.

I regret to say that the appeal of this Administration for applause for its soundness and courage last winter is simply not based on facts. The budget is not balanced and the whole job must be done over again in the next session of Congress.

I have shown how unreliable these constant assurances are. It is not seemly to conjecture motives, but I think it is fair to say the whole record of Administration policy in the last four years reveals that it has been afraid to trust the people of the United

States with the true facts about their affairs. That is a fundamental error which shows unfamiliarity with the true basis of American character.

While the President claims that he did finally recommend new taxes, I fear this courage came two years too late and in far too scanty measure. Perhaps it explains the underlying thought of the phrase "prosperity is just around the corner." Perhaps it explains two complete concealments of deficits and the insufficiency of the action taken last winter. It is an error of weakness and an error which I assure you I will not make.

Our Federal extravagance and improvidence bear a double evil; first, our people and our business cannot carry these excessive burdens of taxation; second, our credit structure is impaired by the unorthodox Federal financing made necessary by the unprecedented magnitude of these deficits.

Instead of financing the billion-dollar deficit of 1931 in the regular way, the Government simply absorbed that much of the lending capacity of the banks and by so much impaired the credit available for business. In that year the amount of Government obligations held by our banks increased by a little more than one billion dollars.

You and I know that this Administration's claims that it has provided credit for industry and agriculture by pouring credit into banks are not wholly frank. Commercial credit has continuously contracted and is contracting now. The truth is that our banks are financing these great deficits and that the burden is absorbing their resources. All this is highly undesirable and wholly unnecessary. It arises from one cause only, and that is the unbalanced budget and the continued failure of this Administration to take effective steps to balance it. If that budget had been fully and honestly balanced in 1930, some of the 1931 troubles would have been avoided. Even if it had been balanced in 1931, much of the extreme dip in 1932 would have been obviated. Every financial man in the country knows why this is true. He knows the unnecessary muddle that has accumulated and is still accumulating in Washington.

Now, how can we continue to countenance such a condition? That is a practical question. In all conscience, can an Administration which has so frequently failed in a matter so directly touching its own responsibilities ask for your support and trifle with your common sense by these campaign alibis about mysterious foreign forces and by this specious talk about sound fiscal policies? Would it not be infinitely better to clear this whole subject of obscurity, to present the facts squarely to the Congress and the people of the United States, and to secure the one sound foundation of permanent economic recovery—a complete and honest balancing of the Federal budget? In all earnestness I leave the answer to your common sense and judgment.

The other bad effect of this fiscal mismanagement is not the least bit technical. It is the burden of high cost on the backs of all our people. I can state the condition best by quoting one paragraph from a document published a week ago and signed by both Calvin Coolidge and Alfred E. Smith. They say:

"All the costs of local, State and national Government must be reduced without fear and without favor. Unless the people, through unified action, arise and take charge of their Government, they will find that their Government has taken charge of them."

Every word of that warning is true; and the first and most important and necessitous step in balancing our Federal budget is to reduce expense.

The air is now surcharged with Republican death-bed repentance on the subject of economy, but it is too late. We must look deeper than these eleventh-hour pronouncements. You cannot go very far with any real Federal economy, without a complete change of concept of what are the proper functions and limits of the Federal Government itself.

Perhaps we can get some glimpse of the President's underlying philosophy about the Federal Government by going back and opening the volume of his 1928 speeches. He proposed, you remember, as he said, "a new thing in Government." He says that he "reorganized the Department of Commerce on a greater scale than has ever been attempted or achieved by any Government in the world." In his book, called *The New Day*, he says this: "A Nation which is spending ninety billions a year can well afford a few hundred million for a workable program."

I could go on quoting for a good many minutes, but perhaps the point could be made clearer by recalling that the Department of Commerce went through even the heavy war strain, back in the days of the World War, on about 13 millions a year. When Secretary Hoover left it, it was spending 39 millions a year; and this year it is estimated that it will be spending 43 millions a year. And the Department of Commerce is now housed in that great marble building which is facetiously called in Washington the "Temple of Fact Finding," which cost the people considerably more than the Capitol of the United States.

That little example, my friends, may explain the 50 percent increase in Government overhead in four years, 1927-1931, and I am sure that the whole group of quotations reveal why you can never expect any important economy from this Administration. It is committed to the idea that we ought to center control of everything in Washington as rapidly as possible — Federal control. That was the idea that increased the cost of Government by a billion dollars in four years. Ever since the days of Thomas Jefferson, that has been the exact reverse of the democratic concept, which is to permit Washington to take from the States nothing more than is necessary to keep abreast of the march of our changing economic situation.

In the latter philosophy, and not in the philosophy of Mr. Hoover — which I think is responsible for so much of our trouble — I shall approach the problem of carrying out the plain precept of our Party, which is to reduce the cost of current Federal Government operations by 25 percent.

Of course that means a complete realignment of the unprecedented bureaucracy that has assembled in Washington in the past four years. I am no stranger to Washington. I knew it at firsthand during the administrations of President Roosevelt and President Taft. I served in Washington for seven and a half years under President Wilson. I have some familiarity with the national Government. In addition to that, for more than four years I have been conducting the Administration and the policies of a State that has thirteen million inhabitants.

Now, I am going to disclose to you a definite personal conclusion which I reached the day after I was nominated in Chicago. Here it is: Before any man enters my Cabinet he must give me a two-fold pledge:

1. Absolute loyalty to the Democratic platform and especially to its economy plank.
2. Complete cooperation with me, looking to economy and reorganization in his Department.

I regard reduction in Federal spending as one of the most important issues of this campaign. In my opinion it is the most direct and effective contribution that Government can make to business.

In accordance with this fundamental policy it is equally necessary to eliminate from Federal budget-making during this emergency all new items except such as relate to direct relief of unemployment.

As a part of that phase of the budget problem, I take note that former President Coolidge is reported as having said in a speech in New York City:

"An early and timely word from the Democratic candidate for President that he would reject the proposal to increase the national debt by $2,300,000,000 to pay a bonus would have been a great encouragement to business, reduced unemployment, and guaranteed the integrity of the national credit. While he remained silent economic recovery was measurably impeded."

That charge is baseless and absurd for the very good reason that last April my views on the subject were widely published and have been subsequently frequently quoted. I said this:

"I do not see how, as a matter of practical sense, a Government running behind two billion dollars annually can consider the anticipation of bonus payment until it has a balanced budget, not only on paper, but with a surplus of cash in the treasury."

No one, for political purposes or otherwise, has the right in the absence of explicit statement from me to assume that my views have changed. They have not. So much for another effort by Republican leaders to preach an unwarranted gospel of fear and panic to the American electorate.

I have sought to make two things clear: First, that we can make savings by reorganization of existing departments, by eliminating functions, by abolishing many of those innumerable boards and those commissions which, over a long period of years, have grown up as a fungus growth on American Government. These savings can properly be made to total many hundreds and thousands of dollars a year.

Second, I hope that it will not be necessary to increase the present scale of taxes, and I call definite attention to the fact that just as soon as the Democratic platform pledge is enacted into legislation modifying the Volstead Act, a source of new revenue amounting to several hundred millions of dollars a year will be made available toward the balancing of the budget. I refer specifically to a Federal tax on beer, which would be raised through the sale of beer in those States and those States only which by State law allow the sale of beer. At the same time I reiterate the simple language of the Democratic platform which in good faith opposes the return of the old-time saloon:

"We urge the enactment of such measures by the several States as will actually promote temperance, effectively prevent the return of the saloon and bring the liquor traffic into the open under complete supervision and control by the State."

The above two categorical statements are aimed at a definite balancing of the budget. At the same time, let me repeat from now to election day so that every man, woman and child in the United States will know what I mean: If starvation and dire need on the part of any of our citizens make necessary the appropriation of additional funds which would keep the budget out of balance, I shall not hesitate to tell the American people the full truth and ask them to authorize the expenditure of that additional amount.

These have been unhealthy years for prophets, and I hasten to disclaim such a role. But one thing I know: A powerful cause contributing to economic disaster has been this inexcusable fiscal policy and the obscurity and uncertainty that have attended and grown out of it. There it remains for all to see — a veritable cancer in the body politic and economic. Is it prophecy to assure you that if we remove that destructive growth we shall move on to better health and better life?

To my mind, that is so plain and persuasive as scarcely to be open to argument. As I said in the beginning, this is the one field in which business is wholly in the grip of Government. It is a field where Government can make a great contribution to recovery.

To that contribution I here pledge the utmost of my faith and my ability. I am as certain as mortal man can be certain of anything in the future, that from the moment that you and I set our hands openly and frankly and courageously to that problem, we shall have reached the end of our long, hard, downward road. We shall have started on the upward trail. We shall have built for economic recovery a firm footing, on a path that is broad, true and straight. Join me, and "let's go!"

NOTE: The Democratic platform of 1932, called for "an immediate and drastic reduction of governmental expenditures by abolishing useless commissions and offices, consolidating departments and bureaus, and eliminating extravagance, to accomplish a saving of not less than 25 percent in the cost of Federal Government." The foregoing speech reiterated the promise of reduced expenditures.

But the platform also advocated "the extension of Federal credit to the States to provide unemployment relief wherever the diminishing resources of the States make it impossible for them to provide for the needy; expansion of the Federal program of necessary and useful construction affected with a public interest . . . [and the] continuous responsibility of Government for human welfare. . . ."

In this speech I also pointed out that: "If starvation and dire need on the part of any of our citizens make necessary the appropriation of additional funds which would keep the budget out of balance, I shall not hesitate to tell the American people the full truth and ask them to authorize the expenditure of that additional amount."

Immediately upon assuming office, I recommended and effected drastic economies in the regular expenditures of Government. (See Vol. II, Items 12, 28.) I vetoed subsequent Congressional action in restoring some of the cuts made by me in Government costs (see Vol. III, Item 55); but the bill was passed over my veto.

The great increase in the expenditures of Government came from the new extraordinary agencies of Government created to meet the emergency and from the necessities of meeting the widespread needs of the unemployed. Neither the platform nor the speech intended, in letter or in spirit, to permit the emergency and the distress of the unemployed to go on without assistance from the Government's treasury.

And the simple historical fact remains that the regular expenses of the departments of the Government as they existed in the summer of 1932, were reduced drastically by the Congress and the Executive in the spring of 1933.

145 ⟨ Campaign Address on Farm Mortgages at Springfield, Ill. October 21, 1932

It is good to be here with you in Springfield, Illinois, in the political and geographic center of this great State. Three weeks ago I visited Chicago, representative of the industrial area of Illinois. Down here the problem of agriculture looms, but as I have often said, these two great interests are by no means strangers, nor are they really separated in interest at all. Each is dependent on the other to a degree often overlooked in American politics.

I want to call to your attention one of the aspects of the great American agricultural problem. More than a month ago at Topeka, Kansas, I set forth a comprehensive national program for agriculture.

Today it is my purpose again to take up this subject and to enlarge upon it. This program is conceived to meet a condition which cannot longer be endured in a Nation endowed with so much natural wealth. I indulge in no magic formula. I do not attempt the task of misleading you into hoping I have arrived at a single panacea for the manifold problems of agriculture. I propose, therefore, fundamental cures, and I do so in the spirit of honest frankness, with the belief that such a method is the sure way to win your cooperation in this great task that will face the new Administration.

May I also add that I would be the last person to claim sole credit for the program which I enunciated at Topeka or indeed for the enlargement of it which I propose to give you here today? It is a program worked out in cooperation with the wisest leaders of agriculture itself, and I pledge to you a continuance of that policy of cooperation in order that the program may be enacted into workable law, a law set into operation at the earliest possible moment. No attempt by the present Administration to belittle this first, honest effort to meet the problem of the American farmer can hide the essential fact that my three-point program goes to the root of the problem.

The three great steps which we must take are: First, the Federal Government owes it to agriculture to see that it gets a fair price for its products. That means that the prices of farm products must be raised above the present ruinously low levels to which they have fallen. A properly adjusted tariff can do much in this direction, but the present tariff policies of the Republican Administration have done precisely the opposite. Pending the relief that will be afforded by properly adjusted tariff policy, measures must be taken to give the farmer immediate tariff benefit. This means in substance a practicable plan agreed to by agricultural leaders which will provide for the farmer a higher return for certain of his crops. I set forth these principles which such a plan must embody, in my Topeka speech, and these principles have been widely accepted as a basic plan of action in formulating the necessary legislative relief.

Second, there must be lifted from the backs of every farmer the heavy load of taxation which today weighs upon him. This load is made up of three parts, the local, State and national units. At Pittsburgh I outlined the position of the Democratic Party, and my position on the question of the honest balancing of the Federal budget and the imperative need of immediate economy in national expenditures. I also reiterate now my promise to exert

813

all available influence in the position as the President of the United States toward the reduction of all State and local taxes.

Third, we come to the vastly important principle concerning the burden which farm mortgages now bear on every agricultural community. I want to take this occasion at this time to amplify that part of my program. Let me first repeat what I said about farm mortgages at Topeka:

"It is my purpose, if elected, to direct all the energy of which I am capable to the formulation of definite projects to relieve this distress. Specifically, I am prepared to insist that Federal credit be extended to banks, insurance or loan companies, or other corporations or individuals holding farm mortgages among their assets, but that these credits must be made on the condition that every reasonable assistance be given to the mortgagors where the loans are sound, with the purpose of preventing foreclosure. Those conditions must be enforced."

I further said that "lower interest rates and an extension of principal payments will save thousands of farms to their owners. And hand in hand with this we must adopt the definite policy of giving those who have lost the title to their farms, now held by institutions seeking credit from governmental agencies, the preferential opportunity of getting their property back."

To that may I add that the Government should make it a definite condition when advancing Federal credit, that wherever possible interest rates must be lowered for renewed or extended mortgages? Whenever the Government of the United States exercises any control over the situation it is the duty of that Government to demand every practicable and possible assistance to the farmer seeking credit to finance his crops, and his farm, to obtain for him the very lowest reasonable rate of interest. The magnitude of the problem may be seen when we realize that the total farm mortgage debt in the United States, according to the figures of the Department of Agriculture, was, at the end of 1930, $9,241,-390,000 or nearly three times that of 1910, and you farmers here in Illinois alone owed $631,266,000. On this debt I believe today that the farmer is called upon to pay too heavy an interest charge, especially when we realize that to this burden are added taxes which today are two and a half times as great as they were in 1914.

In order to enable him to pay these fixed charges the farmer must depend upon the prices for which his products may be sold, and yet we must face the fact that with this heavy mortgage indebtedness grown three-fold in twenty years, and with his taxes increased more than two-fold, the prices which he receives for his products have shrunk in half. In concrete figures the farmer's income in 1919 of 16 billion dollars shrank in the year 1931 to 7 billion dollars. These appalling figures point all too clearly to the devastating economic catastrophe that has overtaken agriculture in the past few years.

Those who live in the industrial areas know now to their sorrow the importance of that 9 billion dollars, which, being taken from the farmer's income, have likewise contributed to a reduction in buying power which has contributed directly to an enormous degree to the catastrophe that has more recently overtaken industry and labor.

The solution of this problem is our first concern in national rehabilitation. We cannot have national prosperity without farmer prosperity. The farm mortgage which has caused thousands of farmers to lose their homes remains a constant threat to business and the success of agriculture. My program is opposed to, and aims to stop, the ruthless foreclosure of farm mortgages. It is economically unsound to sell out an honest, hard-working efficient farmer, but more than that such a procedure constitutes in most cases a social, moral and a human wrong. And moreover the position of the institution, the bank or the insurance company, holding the mortgage is not bettered by thus becoming a large land owner. The natural result of tax sales and mortgage foreclosures is the lowering of most farm land values to a point below what should be their true worth.

In 1916 a Democratic Congress under the leadership of President Wilson enacted the Federal Farm Loan Act. This Act provided means for the Federal Government to deal with this problem and effectively to furnish relief for the borrowers in the

Federal Loan System and to lead the way for other mortgage institutions not directly supervised by the Federal Government itself to give like relief to their borrowers. By the end of 1931 these Federal Land Banks became very important units in our financial life. Their loans at the end of that year amounted to approximately $1,168,000,000 while those of the Joint Stock Land Banks approximated $532,000,000.

Some of these Joint Stock Land Banks have pursued a policy of destructive selfishness contrary to the spirit and purpose of the Farm Loan Act, an Act framed to improve the farm mortgage condition of the Nation. Some of them have foreclosed upon the farm debtors with callous disregard of the interest of these debtors and of the public interest generally. They have sold these farms at distressingly low values and in some instances have retired the corresponding farm bonds purchased in the open market at even lower prices. Thus there has been shown a net profit to those banks on these sordid transactions. Actually there has been a heavy loss to the general community.

Apparently after belated recognition of these disastrous and unfair practices President Hoover in his speech at Des Moines on October 4th took occasion to disclaim responsibility for the policies of these Joint Stock Land Banks but he overlooked the provisions of Section 17 of the Federal Farm Loan Act which defines the powers of the Federal Farm Board and which provides that Federal Farm Board with the power "to exercise generally supervisory authority over the Federal Land Banks, the National Farm Associations, and the Joint Stock Land Banks." For the failure to enforce this duty and the law the President and his Administration are to blame.

This is just another example of this Administration's failing to use or misusing agencies already created, and which if properly used would have saved this country much of its suffering.

I propose that these powers of the Federal Farm Board shall be fully exercised to the end that this distressing situation shall be immediately remedied and to the end that the enlightened purposes of the Democratic-created Farm Loan Act shall be fully carried out.

The present Administration has been derelict in another particular. The last Congress recognized the necessity for stopping the wholesale ouster of farm owners. In an Act approved by the President February 2, 1932, Congress provided that the United States Treasurer should subscribe for $125,000,000 of stock in the Federal Land Banks. Of this amount $25,000,000 was provided in order that the banks might extend the time for the payment of past due mortgage instalments. The Act specifically provided that this sum should be used exclusively to supply any bank with funds to use in place of the amount of which such banks might be deprived by reason of the granting of extensions of mortgage payments.

A great many banks have given extensions and have been reimbursed out of this fund, but they violated the obvious intention of the law and of the Congress which passed it, and destroyed the usefulness of the purposes of this Act when they frequently required borrowers to give crop loans and other miscellaneous securities for such extensions. They thus made it difficult and often impossible for farmers who were delinquent in their payments, to use their credit for normal farm production purposes and indeed for family maintenance. These banks pursued this narrow and indefensible policy. The blame for not enforcing the intention of the law must be borne by the Hoover Administration and is typical of the unsympathetic attitude of that Administration toward the farmer and his problems. As President I shall propose to Congress a definite plan for the refinancing of farm mortgages in line with the principles which I stated in my Topeka speech, and which I repeated here today. I shall recommend legislation to the Congress for the scaling down of amortization installments of Federal Land Bank borrowers when in the judgment of bank directors conditions justify such action, with provision for deferring such unpaid amounts to the end of such amortization periods. And I shall enforce such legislation.

This partial and temporary extension will help the farmers to save their farms until they can secure a better net income through the working out of the plans which I have discussed for the solution of the general farm program. As for those farm mortgage institutions, not under the control of the Federal Government, I renew the statement made in my address at Topeka declaring for loans by Federal financial agencies to such concerns to enable them to carry defaulted mortgages of deserving borrowers. It must never be forgotten that the funds so loaned the banks are primarily for the benefit of the farmer and must be so employed. Finally I propose consideration by Congress of the necessity for a complete reorganization of the means provided to operate in the field of agricultural finance.

At the present time we have at least seven agencies concerned with farm mortgages. Some of these are direct agencies of the Federal Government. Some of them are corporations operating with funds provided by the Federal Government, others are still more removed from the Government but are under partial governmental authority. Within my broad agricultural program I advocate the coordination of such agencies to the end that the Federal agricultural policy in regard to farm mortgages may be guided by a single purpose and be so concentrated in its operation that it may really become an effective aid to the farmer.

I ask your study of this general agricultural policy for the agricultural people of this country in the same practical and sympathetic spirit in which it is made, and I invite your comparison of this program with the piece-meal and grudging concessions made by the present Administration. As a definite example, may I call to your attention the cautious commitment made by the President in his Des Moines speech when he stated as follows:

"But further and more definitely than this I shall propose to the Congress at the next session that we further reorganize the Federal land banks and give to them the resources and liberty of action necessary to enable them definitely and positively to expand in the refinancing of the farm-mortgage situation where it is necessary to give men who want to fight for it a chance to hold their homes."

After a long-continued period of complete silence and negative action this is his answer to the strong challenge of the Democratic program on this subject. I would point out to you that the farm mortgage situation has existed for many years, that it has been critically bad during the past three years, and yet this is the only approach to positive action which the President is willing to make when impelled to promise to do so in the midst of a political campaign. It is but a grudging and hastily improvised attempt to hang on to the coat-tails of the policy enunciated by the Democratic party this year. The ultimate effectiveness of such vague promises I leave to you to judge in the light of the past acts of this Administration.

The rising tide of agricultural protest is being shown by independent thinking and a resolute determination to bring about a new deal. I have offered a policy and a program, national in scope, providing for a community of effort on the part of the citizens of this country who seek so earnestly for nothing more or less than a fair chance to live as American citizens. The assurance of support and approval of this definite and concrete program which has come to me since that day when I first enunciated it at Topeka, marks, I feel sure, the first signs of dawn after the long night for agriculture.

I extend my grateful appreciation to those who have indicated not only their sympathy but their cooperation in my efforts. November 8th is near at hand, beyond that March 4th, beyond that to agriculture, again I say, a new deal.

146 ❡ Campaign Address on the Eight Great Credit Groups of the Nation. St. Louis, Mo. October 21, 1932

FAITH is a delicate though powerful factor in our economic life, and a party that sounds a note of alarm from high places is performing no decent service to the American Nation.

One of the most artful and plausible of Administration whip-crackers started this campaign of fear on the eve of the Maine election. At that moment our people were in low spirits. Millions of men who had tramped the streets for months feeling hopeless, friendless and alone were listening to his words and he told them that if they did not vote for the Republican candidate in the Maine election it would be practically impossible for the administration remaining in power from election to March to save them from dire disaster. The good people of Maine were not disturbed by these false-faces of disaster. They saw that this horrible menace was only a painted mask, that the artificially created eclipse of the sun was nothing but a low lying smoke screen, so light as to be blown aside by the first breath of fresh air.

They knew that the fire so artfully whipped into life was nothing but a campaign sky-rocket, and that the rumblings of disaster that were intended to sound so near and so menacing were simply the old-fashioned melodramatic campaign stage properties patented by Mark Hanna and Matt Quay, and for these long years lying dust-covered in the attic of American politics. The people of Maine saw through this, and I well remember that on the night when we started on our Western trip, the night before I greeted the citizens of St. Louis here in September, the news came that the electorate of Maine had registered their disapproval of this sort of silly entertainment in no uncertain terms.

All of the good, old spectres are snatched from the grave, but the mantles of the giant actors of the past now hang in a shabby and ill-fitting manner on the diminutive forms of these new apostles of disaster. The workers and the farmers of today have heard from their fathers of the old terroristic threats that were put into their pay envelope just before election. They have heard of the warnings originating from the Republican National Committee in past campaigns, and pasted on the walls of their factories just before election. And they are not being scared by these things any more.

American labor has educated itself too well. American agriculture has learned too much in the bitter school of experience to be frightened by any new variations of the old terrorism of the past. We are living in another age. These stage properties are out of date.

As a last resort, the President and the Ex-President advance and attempt to throw political and economic tear bombs among the people of the country. Now, my friends, you all know what tear gas is. It is one of the new inventions by which a few people can control a lot of people. A few do it by blinding the eyes of the many, by causing tears to flow; and in the midst of the confusion that thus results a determined minority seeks to accomplish its selfish purposes.

You and I know that this tear gas has no permanent effect; it is the temporary and very painful effect that counts. The tears, I can assure you, are not tears of sympathy, but the purpose of the users of tear gas is not to create sympathy but to blind you for the occasion. No, my friends, the purpose of the panic-creating tear gas which the Republican leaders are now hurling is not to open your hearts but to blind your eyes.

Let me tell you from the bottom of my heart that I, for one, favor having you keep your eyes wide open, and I, for one, favor keeping my own heart wide open.

I want to take this occasion to say that in my opinion such efforts cast a deep reflection upon the principles for which this country has stood. The American working men and the American farmers are free men, citizens of a great Republic. The life blood of this Republic is the integrity and independence of the electorate. You American farmers and American workmen are entitled, by all of the fundamental rights that you have acquired in generations of fighting, to a free and untrammeled choice on election day. The politician or employer who tries to deny to you these rights and to use a gospel of fear to blind you to the true facts presented in this campaign is an enemy not only of fairness and sportsmanship in politics, but of the very principles upon which this country has been established. To protect these rights men have suffered and died. The principles they have won in such a bitter fight are chiseled for all the centuries to come on the granite walls of our American system of Government. The man who tries, for political or economic advantage, to chip away these rights is an untrustworthy leader in business and politics.

And now to the business of conducting a campaign in the proper spirit, a spirit of good reason, good sense and good humor.

I have spoken of human rights and of social justice and tonight in the confident spirit that the present temper of the country affords me I am going to talk with you about a form of property rights which has a direct bearing on our present and future enjoyment of life. You and I know that many millions of Americans have some kind of an interest in some form of property. From the point of view of the average citizen this interest in property takes the form of bank deposits, of trust funds, of insurance policies, or of land or security ownership.

In addition to individuals, thousands upon thousands of institutions created for the public good have similar interests — the Churches, the hospitals, the relief funds, the schools and colleges and other non-profit-making organizations of many kinds.

Most of the property of these individuals and of these institutions is invested in some form of long-term security. Let me illustrate: Our national economic life is in large part tied up in underlying bonds that represent in fact mortgages on American railroads, on American industry, on American land and on three forms of American Government — the national, State and local Governments of the United States.

These securities are bought and sold; and it is a fact that the prices at which they sell are important to everyone of us, even though we individually and immediately may own none of them.

It may be said that they are the medium by which the savings of Americans are put to work. For example, your savings in the savings bank do not go into the vaults of the savings bank, but are put out by the bank at interest for your benefit. In the same way, the premium that you pay to a building and loan association goes in each case into investments. All of them represent some interest in the stable institutions of America.

Many months ago in attempting to see the economic situation

of this country as a whole in simple terms and in terms so full of meaning that I could at a glance encompass the need of the entire country, I set down a list of the eight great credit groups of this country. I conceive this list to represent the credit interest of the Nation, north and south, east and west, employer and employee, industry, commerce and agriculture. I conceive these eight groups as representing the foundation stones upon which the permanent credit of this country rests.

I said then, and I say now, that the stability of the country rests not on any one, but on all of these, and that when we want to know whether anything is disturbing the stability of the country we look to see whether any of these foundation stones are crumbling away, or whether the ground underlying these stones is weakened by any cause.

This is the way to comprehend the stability of the country as a whole, and in my opinion it is the only way. It was with this in mind that I conceived the plan of my campaign. It was with this in mind that I ordered the presentation of the various subjects that I have discussed with the people of this country. I made my plan in accordance with this comprehensive picture of national needs. I attempted to discuss these in an orderly fashion, carefully, simply, with system and with a deep regard for the facts.

I have not been shaken from this plan. I have refused to be intimidated by my opponents. I have kept the faith with this plan as I have kept the faith with the platform of my party, because I believe in the sound sense of the American people. I knew they would hear me, and I knew they would hear me to the end, in spite of all the fear and all the terrorism that the leaders of the Republican Party have been seeking to instill.

And now, at the end of October, I come to a resume of this subject of credit. I want to set forth these points, these eight credit groups, and to talk briefly about the condition of each. At the end of my discussion, which in the last analysis is a summary of what I have been talking about for many weeks, you will see what the condition of the country is with reference to credit, what these groups need and what the Democratic Party proposes to do about them.

First: Federal Obligations:

At the very top of the credit structure of the country, surpassing all other groups in moral and material importance, stand the obligations of the Federal Government. These are paramount, because Government is essential to all ordered economic life. When they go, everything goes. Happily these obligations are secure. They suffer only to the extent that Government is permitted to be extravagant, wasteful, or ill-managed. They suffer if the Federal budget is not balanced, and particularly where the deficit of one year is not cleared up in the succeeding year.

I spoke two nights ago in Pittsburgh about balancing the Federal budget—and I meant it. I pointed two obvious ways. The first is to cut down expenses. That is something that all of us can understand. The second is to raise more money but not, if we can possibly avoid it, by increasing any of the present taxes; but rather by carrying out the mandates of the Democratic Platform by restoring to the several States their own rights to handle the liquor question through the repeal of the Eighteenth Amendment, and by placing a tax on beer which in the meantime will increase our Federal revenues by several hundred million dollars a year.

I called attention in my address at Pittsburgh on Wednesday night to the great importance of Federal budget making as the foundation of the national credit. I pointed out that the Hoover Administration had been responsible for deficit after deficit; that as one disastrous year succeeded another no attempt was made to arrange the finances of the country so that at least the mounting loss of revenue might not be turned into a deficit for the next year. It is my pledge and promise that this dangerous kind of financing shall be stopped and that rigid governmental economy shall be enforced by a stern and unremitting Administration policy of living within our income.

Second: State Obligations:

State obligations constitute one of the most sound and safe groups of the entire credit structure. A State is generally required by dire necessity, if for no other reason, to live within its income. If it runs a deficit in one period, it must make provision for that deficit in the budget of the following period.

In fact, in New York when we run a deficit the Constitution of the State requires us to provide in the budget for the following year not merely for current needs, but also for revenue with which to pay the deficit of the past year. I have strictly lived up to this requirement. This is the best guarantee of credit stability known, and it accounts for the fact that the credit of the State of New York makes its bonds almost the highest grade of investment known to the country.

Third: Municipal Bond Issues:

The next great credit group includes the obligations of cities, counties, towns, villages and other local units. This is a very large group; a fair estimate is over 17 billions of these local bonds. They are largely held by individuals and by institutions, and are properly a matter of deep public concern. The soundness of these bonds is directly bound up with the honesty and capability with which American cities are run.

I have as the Governor of New York State concerned myself very definitely with the finance of its cities. I have exercised what influence I could to keep the credit of these cities sound and secure. I have set my face sternly not only against municipal dishonesty, but likewise against municipal mismanagement. I want to record, here and now, the belief that every public official, from the President of the United States down, owes it to himself to use every scrap of influence he can to prevent the frittering away of the revenues exacted from the sorely pressed taxpayers of every city in the United States, so that, if necessary, they must be compelled to walk in the way of municipal honesty and efficiency.

I want to reaffirm what I have said many times, that while the legal power of the President in this respect is limited, his power to lead public opinion in the way of improvement in local government can be a very definite and useful force for cheaper and better government in American cities. This is what I propose to do toward the credit represented by the 17 billions of municipal bonds.

Fourth: Foreign Obligations:

The next group of obligations comprises what are known as foreign bonds. This is an unsavory chapter in American finance. These bonds in large part are directly the fruits of a disastrous policy pursued by the present Administration in Washington — none other, if you please, than the policy of lending to backward and crippled Nations.

Flagrant instances of the abuse of American investors occurring under this system are well known. When, after my address at Columbus last August, the Secretary of State chose to come to the defense of the Administration, his apology was smothered by irrefutable and devastating statements of fact by Senator Glass, Senator Barkley and many others. The Administration has not since attempted to defend the indefensible fallacy of the Department of State with regard to these investments. If we were depending upon these bonds as an integral part of American finance we should be fearful indeed. But fortunately, or unfortunately, as you choose to look at it, the returns on the foreign bond list have already come in. Many are in default. Others have lost the major part of their original face value. The best that can be said is that that danger is in great part behind us, and not ahead of us.

I have already announced the policy of my own administration in this regard. My job will be to prevent a recurrence of this incident, to prevent the hard-earned dollars of American investors from being frittered away in foreign fields, with the encouragement of the Federal Government of the United States, and with profit only for certain international financiers whose greed exceeds their patriotism.

Fifth: Domestic Industrial Bonds:

These obligations do not represent major difficulties. They are not widely held by banks, insurance companies, savings banks, or the credit institutions of the country. They are largely in the hands of private investors. The amount is relatively small in quantity, for the industrial companies during the past few years were engaged, not in creating debts, but in paying them. On the great chessboard of American finance, the industrial obligations do not constitute a danger.

The problem of industry is not, strictly speaking, a problem of finance. It is a problem which I dealt with in my speech at San Francisco. So far as possible, industry should be organized so that it will give every workman the right to earn a living through his own effort. Such influence as the Federal Government may exert should be directed to this end.

Sixth: Public Utility Obligations:

In connection with public utility obligations, I am not speaking now of the financial excrescences on the public utility system represented by pyramided holding companies, some of which are already in bankruptcy and others of which have already been discounted by the public markets. I speak rather of those companies that are engaged not in stock jobbing, but in the sound and important business of distributing light, power, heat and public service. They have obligations outstanding which do not at this time constitute a problem in American finance. As a group they are currently earning their interest charges. I have already set forth in my Portland speech my attitude toward the problems of these companies.

The outlines of my public utility policy are definitely in the direction of protecting the investor, as well as the consumer. Certainly the integrity of the financial obligations included in this group will be conserved to a greater degree than ever before through an adoption of my policy toward public utilities. There has not been, so far as I have been able to determine, a single responsible criticism of the program there set forth.

827

I ask the simple question, "What leadership has the President exerted toward the elimination of the type of abuse which resulted in the Insull failure?"

The indifference of the present Administration has permitted the savings of thousands of our citizens to be swallowed up and lost for all time.

Seventh: Railroads:

Railroad obligations, mostly bonds, amount to 11 billion dollars. They bear interest charges of nearly half a billion dollars a year. Such bonds are held in savings banks, insurance companies, commercial banks, and similar institutions.

In the year 1931, admittedly a bad year, the railroad system as a whole earned slightly more than its interest charges on this entire group of bonds. The year 1932 has not been so happy, although railroad earnings are beginning to show slight increases.

I have discussed the Democratic plan of meeting this problem, not only in the interest of maintaining railroads at a fair degree of efficiency, but what is more important, in the interest of protecting the savings of millions of persons in this country, invested in the securities of these railroads. I made it a cardinal point in my railroad address that the railroads should be freed from certain destructive competition and that the Government should undertake for a specified period to see the railroads through, provided they put their own houses in order. Note the difference between this and the program of the Administration. Without plan and apparently without thought, the best that it could do was to advance a dole to the railroads month by month as emergencies might arise, leaving both the railroad and the bondholder uncertain as to whether each dole would not be the last.

This is not meeting problems. It is merely sticking financial mustard plasters on the railroads.

There is only one way to do this job, and that is to do it. Where adjustments are to be made, let us find out what they are. Let us arrange for handling them in a swift and orderly method. Let us make a definite commitment that once the railroad's house is in order the Government can stand firmly behind it. Our Democratic plan has been before the country now for some weeks. Experts on the situation, representing railroad managements, railroad unions, employers, workers and investors have joined in almost universal approval of the soundness of this plan.

Eighth: Real Estate Obligations:

We come now to real estate obligations: There is, first, a great body of mortgages on city and suburban homes. These represent money borrowed by you and me, and our friends, with which to buy homes. Most of these are mortgages on small homes. They are paid by the little man — "the forgotten man" if you like, of whom no one thinks because he does not beg for help. Yet these men are not only the backbone of the American financial system, they are in the aggregate about the safest credit risks we have.

This group does not constitute a financial danger to the country, but it does call for wise financial handling. We propose to do whatever we can to free these homes of the burden of excessive taxation. This will definitely help these home owners to protect their homes. I have said that these home owners were "forgotten men." But they are no longer forgotten, because in the midst of the campaign, the Federal Administration has finally begun to consider their difficulties. We agree to the necessity of home loan banks, but, in the administration of these banks, we shall insist that they shall not be subject to the unwise and improper administration that has characterized the Federal and Joint Stock Land Bank Systems under which the bank makes money while the mortgagor goes unaided. To the extent that the home loan banks effect this, I shall be glad to approve the policy; and I shall be glad to make whatever modifications are needed to insure that the relief reaches the spot it is intended to reach.

And finally I come to farm mortgages. I have discussed this question twice in my campaign. Only today in Springfield I set forth in some detail my proposals with respect to this. What I said there, was an amplification of my pledge in my Topeka speech of a month ago.

I seek definite action by the Federal Government — and I stress the word "action" — to prevent farmers from losing their homes, to provide lower interest rates for them where, as in many cases, such rates are excessive, and to extend and defer the capital payments due under the original mortgage terms.

We have seen too many farmers driven from their homes and from their lands. It is time to reverse that process.

Those are the eight great credit groups of the country. And that is, in brief, what the Democratic Party proposes to do with regard to each. I submit to your fairness, your intelligence, and your insight, the case of the Democratic Party with regard to what it means to do about our credit system.

I have taken you over the great field of permanent American finance. I have tried to summarize for you in a few minutes the result of many months of public discussion of the various problems connected with these credit groups.

I know that the tasks before me are heavy. Some are very difficult; but all are possible. The question is not whether the situation could be worse; the question is, how can we make it better?

The financial fabric of America is, as I have said before, a seamless web held together by the infinitely complex loyalties of men. We must protect it against men who would tear it to pieces rather than face defeat. There is every reason to face the future with confidence. Let us bend our minds and our wills to performing this plain duty, because the unmistakable temper of the American people is going to place this responsibility upon the Democratic Party. That is the lesson of the past few weeks. It is the answer of the American people.

147 ❧ "I Am Waging a War in This Campaign against the 'Four Horsemen' of the Present Republican Leadership—Destruction, Delay, Deceit, Despair." Campaign Address at Baltimore, Md. October 25, 1932

Governor Ritchie, and my friends:

TODAY, for me, is a double anniversary. It was some years ago in this great Armory that I had some small part in the convention that resulted in the nomination of our great leader, Woodrow Wilson. The other anniversary is one in advance, for it is two weeks from tonight that the American people are going to speak.

I cannot tell you how deeply I feel and appreciate this great reception which you have given me in a State whose people from the beginning have led in the fundamental principles of Democracy, whose people from the first settlement of Maryland have preached and practiced the doctrine of the liberty of mind and the liberty of soul.

And may I say here, and over the radio to my friends in the District of Columbia, that it was only because of this meeting in Maryland that I could not stop there today to greet them at the station, and that I shall have to defer that honor and privilege until the 4th of March.

It is well that the people of our Nation should keep in mind that it was this colony of Maryland which first proclaimed freedom of religious belief, freedom of practice according to the dictates of one's own conscience and soul.

As you and I know, that principle was greeted by the skeptics of the time as an idea visionary, fantastic and unworkable.

A worthy spokesman for this principle, a gallant defender of it year in and year out, a brave and tried general in the war to preserve human rights and human liberty, is your great Governor, Albert C. Ritchie.

We are approaching the end of this campaign — I am all here, except a small fraction of my voice — and I am determined now, as I have been from the beginning, that the people of this country keep before them the fundamental issues of this campaign. To that end I have refused to be diverted or confused by the misrepresentations of my opponents, the fears of the weak, the madness of the unreasoning. No amount of hysteria on the part of a bankrupt Republican leadership will divert the American people at the eleventh hour from the decision they have already reached.

I am waging a war in this campaign — a frontal attack — an onset — against the "Four Horsemen" of the present Republican leadership: The Horsemen of Destruction, Delay, Deceit, Despair. And the time has come for us to marshal this "Black Horse Cavalry"!

First of all, the "Horseman of Destruction": The embodiment of governmental policies so unsound, so inimical to true progress that it has left behind in its trail everywhere economic paralysis, industrial chaos, poverty and suffering. You have heard that Horseman clattering down your streets.

Echoing down the trail of this first "Horseman" we might imagine the voice of the Book of Revelations saying, "A measure of wheat for a penny, three measures of barley for a penny; and see thou hurt not the oil and the wine."

Next comes the "Horseman of Delay": Emblazoned on his banner also are words of the Revelation, "And it was said unto them, that they should rest yet for a little season."

I suppose this is what the Republican leaders mean when they say, "Don't change horses while crossing the stream." What they really mean is, "Don't run the risk of crossing the stream at all."

The delay that they have practiced is the delay that they want you to adopt when they say, "Give us another term, and maybe we can do better," or, perhaps, that inspiring battle cry, "Give us another term and we will not do worse."

There is no time for delay when we have been led by these people into quicksand. There is no time for delay when nearly half of our people cannot buy the bare necessities of life. There is no time for delay when eleven millions of honest, industrious and willing men and women are tramping the streets and roads of our Nation looking for work. There is no time to wait when the prosperity and happiness of this country are at stake.

And we of the Democratic Party will not wait!

Next in line is the third Horseman — the "Horseman of Deceit." It is his purpose to cover the trail of the Horsemen of Destruction and Delay. He tells you things that are not true. He wears a mask. He attempts by misrepresentation and the distortion of facts to blind your eyes, to destroy your sense of direction, and to paralyze your power of action.

He carries a great shield to hide from you the ugly ruin and terror which his comrades have left in their wake.

Bringing up the rear, is the fourth Horseman — the "Horseman of Despair." He tells you that our Government has no control over conditions that are handled from overseas. He tells you that economic conditions must work themselves out. He tries to close the door of hope in your face.

Take them up one by one: The first Horseman of Destruction suddenly appeared on the scene of this country, the most powerful in the world, with the greatest potentiality in wealth, in natural resources, intelligence and the efficiency of its people; where starvation and serious unemployment did not exist. Abroad in this land, however, was an unsound spirit of speculation which had been encouraged by the false doctrine of "borrow and buy."

The Horseman of Destruction in the Republican Administration gleefully gave encouragement to this speculation. The Presidential candidate of that Party in 1928 said unwisely that there would never be another panic in this country; that we were on the eve of the greatest prosperity that we had ever known. That is when we heard about the "chicken in every pot."

The White House and the Treasury Department issued statements that definitely encouraged and stimulated that speculative boom. They led the people on to certain and disastrous destruction.

There is the record. No partisan words will ever wipe it out. That record stands, and the lost savings of millions bid us remember it all our days.

The Horseman of Destruction came likewise from the false policy of lending money to backward and crippled countries. The Administration encouraged the policy that sought to open markets in foreign lands through the lending of American money to these countries. This was definitely sponsored by the Republican candidate for President in 1928, and for a time it became a cardinal factor in the policy of his Administration. It was utterly and entirely unsound, as I have demonstrated many times. It brought upon us a terrible retribution, and the record shows that this charge which I have made repeatedly in this campaign has never been answered. The State Department presented a laborious alibi which was immediately answered in such a devastating fashion by Senator Glass of Virginia and other members of the Congress that the State Department has gone fishing ever since.

You will search the President's speeches in vain for any attempt to explain this policy of destruction.

The Horseman of Destruction rode into every town and every county when the Grundy Tariff Bill was passed and signed, for this Horseman was insatiable.

He struck at the crumbling prosperity of the country.

A special session of Congress was called by the President for the declared purpose of "farm relief and limited changes in the tariff." The farmers were denied adequate relief while the President and his Administration raised practically unscalable tariff walls against international trade. This foolish act was done notwithstanding that our tariff already carried unreasonably high rates, in spite of the protests of thirty foreign Governments and threats of retaliation. Our doors were closed to our principal European purchasers. Retaliatory walls were erected against us by forty foreign Governments. The President is making no answer to this plain fact when he says, as he did in Des Moines, that there had been retaliatory tariffs before the Hawley-Smoot Tariff Act was passed. Of course there were such acts passed before the Hawley-Smoot Act. No one said there were not; but remember, my friends, that eight years before the Hawley-Smoot Act the Republican Congress had passed the Fordney-McCumber Act which was itself the cause of retaliation by foreign Governments.

After the Hawley-Smoot Act foreign trade throughout the world fell into a condition of stagnation.

Our exports between the passage of the Act in June, 1930, up to the present time fell off more than sixty percent. Two hundred and fifty-eight of our American factories were moved to foreign countries. And our factories are still moving daily — moving abroad. Demand for labor has dropped. Our surplus productions, excluded from their normal foreign markets, were thrown back on the domestic markets to the destruction of commodity prices. The purchasing power of over half of our people was destroyed and demand for products in the domestic market fell, resulting in bankruptcy, foreclosures and unemployment. Every city and every farm knows these facts. Every city and every farm is waiting for Tuesday, November 8th, to arrive.

My distinguished opponent is declaring in his speeches that I have proposed to injure or destroy the farmers' markets by reducing the tariff on products of the farm. That is silly. Of course I have made no such proposal, nor can any speech or statement I have made be so construed. I said in my Sioux City speech, in discussing the Hawley-Smoot Tariff Act of 1930:

"Of course outrageously excessive rates in that bill as it became law, must come down. But we should not lower them beyond a reasonable point indicated by common sense and facts."

The point indicated was that no tariff duty should be lowered to a point where our natural industries would be injured. Again in my Sioux City speech I made the Democratic position plain, where I said that negotiated treaties would be accomplished "by consenting to reduce, to some extent, some of our duties in order to secure a lowering of foreign tariff walls that a larger measure of our surplus may be sold abroad."

Of course, it is absurd to talk of lowering tariff duties on farm products. I declared that all prosperity in the broader sense springs from the soil. I promised to endeavor to restore the purchasing power of the farm dollars by making the tariff effective for agriculture, and raising the price of the farmers' products. I know of no effective excessively high tariff duties on farm products. I do not intend that such duties shall be lowered. To do so would be inconsistent with my entire farm program, and every farmer in the United States knows it and will not be deceived.

Next in line I want to talk to you about the Horseman of Delay, who followed closely on the heels of the Horseman of Destruction. To take action — strong, vigorous action — to repair and rebuild destruction, is to admit that there has been destruction.

The Republican leaders would never be willing to admit that. And so they delayed. When they should have taken vigorous action to relieve the Federal budget of its crushing burden in December, 1929, they failed to do so. Their delay to take action to reduce expenditures continued from year to year, 1929, 1930, 1931.

With regard to unemployment relief their action was the same. Far-sighted people told them long ago that here was a human emergency that demanded action. But they were at all times hoping — guessing — that things somehow would get better and that they would not be brought to a stern reckoning for the consequences of their acts. So they kept on delaying providing relief. On this tombstone of the present Republican leadership will be written for all time the words "Too late."

My friends, this is one of the most inexcusable actions of the present Administration. I want to say with all of the emphasis that I can command, that this Administration did nothing and their leaders are, I am told, still doing nothing. Their leaders are still ridiculing my proposal for action. They still maintain the policy of delay. They ask for the right to continue it for four years more.

And now we come to the Horseman of Deceit:

The Horseman of Deceit rides by night. He rode when the Administration told the public that the crash of 1929 was not serious. He rode when it said prosperity was just around the corner. He rode when people were told to buy and invest and to continue business as usual. He is riding now, when spokesmen of the Administration misrepresent what I say and what my Party says and what my associates say. Let me illustrate.

The President contends that the danger to our credit structure was due primarily to the failure of the Government to balance its budget. Right now, let us see who is responsible for that failure. After March 4, 1929, the Republican Party was in complete control of all branches of the Federal Government — the Executive, the Senate, the House of Representatives and, I might add for good measure, the Supreme Court as well.

The crash came in October, 1929. The President had at his disposal all the instrumentalities of Government. From that day to December 31st of that year, he did absolutely nothing to remedy the situation. Not only did he do nothing, but he took the position that Congress could do nothing. The deficit in the Treasury continued to increase, but never once did he urge that the budget be balanced, until December, 1931 — two long years later — after the leaders of the new Democratic House of Representatives had announced their determination to balance the budget. Then, my friends, the President urged that this same thing be done. He was right — dead right — but as usual, he was right at the wrong time — two years too late.

The passage of the revenue bill was delayed because the President and the Secretary of the Treasury constantly changed their estimates as to the amount of revenue necessary to balance the budget. It will be recalled that on December 3, 1930, the President estimated that on June 30, 1932 — this year — the Treasury would have a deficit of only $150,000,000. But the people of America now know that on that date the deficit amounted to three and three-quarter billion dollars. I care not whether this misleading statement was due to deliberate misrepresentation, or to inefficiency; in either event it must convince the thoughtful

837

people of this Nation that the conduct of our fiscal affairs should be placed in the hands of men upon whose financial statements some reliance can be placed. I propose that the Treasury, in issuing statements as to the condition of our finances, shall substitute efficiency for inefficiency, and candor for deception.

I know that it cannot be successfully contradicted that after the budget estimate was submitted to the last Congress by the President, the Democrats of the House and Senate voted to reduce appropriations for the departments. I know that the President publicly announced his approval of a policy of economy. But the members of his Cabinet appeared before the committees of Congress and opposed the efforts of the Congress to reduce appropriations of the departments.

Under the provisions of the old Budget Act of 1921, the President has specific authority to recommend the elimination and consolidation of bureaus — not only bureaus, but boards and commissions. If he has recommended the consolidation of any of these bureaus it has certainly escaped my attention, and that of the people of the country as well. Then, on top of that, the economy bill of 1932 gave to him the absolute power to consolidate Government activities. That act was approved June 30, and to this day there has been no consolidation of such activities; and therefore there is no justification for our entertaining the hope of any reorganization of the departments of the Government under the leadership of President Hoover.

I think the President's idea of economy is illustrated pretty well by the only section of the relief bill which is of Republican origin, namely, the appropriation of $15,000,000 for the construction of theaters, gymnasiums, service clubs, recreation halls and riding academies at army posts throughout the Nation; construction projects, by the way, which the Congress itself had failed to provide for in the regular appropriation bills; problems that were unessential and placed an unjust and unfair burden upon the American taxpayers. The President's idea of economy is further illustrated by his approval of an appropriation of $500,000 for the creation of something that you have all heard about — the Wickersham Commission, one of the outstanding achievements of the present Administration.

The Horseman of Deceit rode when the Republican Convention wrote its plank on prohibition. While nothing could be more clear than the declaration of the Democratic Platform and nothing can be more clear than my acceptance of that Platform, the Republican Convention, as you know, adopted a Prohibition statement that was intended to sound wet to the wets, and dry to the drys. The trouble was that it ended by deceiving no one. It sounded dry to the wets, and wet to the drys.

And so, after a month and a half of keeping his ear to the ground, the Presidential candidate attempted to correct it. He added new elements of confusion. In his speech of acceptance, he promised to work for the repeal of the Eighteenth Amendment with some very important reservations. Everything went well for several days, but suddenly the Vice President was heard from. He attempted to make provision for a dry interpretation of what the President meant as an appeal to the wets. Thus it looked as if the ticket was facing both ways. But on close examination it was found that the Vice Presidential candidate was without a doubt wholly dry, and the Presidential candidate was only half dry. The result of this curious attempt to move both ways on a one-way street was not only to get traffic all tangled up from the point of view of Republican votes, but also to resolve the Republican Ticket in a sort of whirling motion — round and round — that meant to the voter honestly attempting to make a choice, only a dizzy exhibition of uncertainty. So that is where the issue stands, my friends. No honest wet and no honest dry can approve of such political tactics. It seems to me that it is the most palpable attempt to defraud the American people that we have seen in our day's generation.

Now a word as to beer. I favor the modification of the Volstead Act to permit States to authorize the manufacture and sale of beer just as fast as the law will let us. This is a way to divert three hundred million dollars or more by way of taxes from the pockets of the racketeers to the Treasury of the United States.

The Horseman of Deceit was certainly riding high when the Republican leaders were trying to make up their minds about the Eighteenth Amendment.

Finally there now rides abroad in a stricken country, among a people impoverished, confused, sore and weary, the fourth Horseman. He is the Horseman of Despair.

This Administration has resorted finally to the most plaintive diagnosis of a doctor in despair that any country has ever heard from responsible statesmen. The most devastating example of this kind of preaching is contained in the President's acceptance speech when he addressed himself to the farmers of the Nation. He told them that he sympathized with their stricken condition; that he wished he could do something to help them; that his attempt to help them through stabilization had been a disastrous failure; that he had considered various remedies and had finally come to the conclusion that nothing but the general revival of business could restore the American farmer. That was bitter medicine for the agricultural population of the United States. Its fallacy was apparent, for we all know that only by restoring this vast potential market, involving the needs of fifty million people, can American industry in the cities also be restored. How, it may be asked, can industry, which depends for its restoration upon the farming population, recover and thus contribute to the recovery of agriculture? That this economic doctrine is absurd is attested by the fact that industrialists have come to the conclusion that the future of industry depends upon establishing a market for American-made goods among American farmers.

Another example of the doctrine of despair has been uttered recently by the President of the United States. In his speech at Detroit he quarrels with the statement which I made to the effect that it was the responsibility of Government to see to it that workers should be kept on their jobs wherever possible and that when they were out of jobs they should be restored. I have no apology for that statement. It means precisely what it says. But the President's interpretation of it, however, is based on what he apparently has come to believe, that ten million people of the United States must remain unemployed unless the Government provides employment for all of them. The exact meaning of his statement is, if I understand English correctly, that there is no hope for a restoration of normal employment for these ten million people.

Despair is written all over this statement of the President. It is a despairing cry which says to the ten million or more American unemployed that normal employment is not for them and is not in sight. That is pure unadulterated despair. He apparently is opposed to any optimism in the face of present conditions. He apparently feels that the way to restore the spirit of the American people is to tell the ten million unemployed — the vast, weary army of unemployed — that they are going to remain unemployed. That is pure and unadulterated pessimism. It is, I submit, hair-shirt hypocrisy with a vengeance.

If my opponents feel that I am to be diverted by puerile criticism, I answer them by returning to the attack.

My statements are a matter of public record. They are correct. They are clear. They are directly and clearly addressed to the needs of the country.

Do not be deceived in these, the last moments of the campaign, by false lights on the shore, by smoke screens, by theatrics, by magic, by juggling, by the calling of names, by misrepresentation.

The Four Horsemen about which I have told you tonight have passed on their way.

Destruction has done its worst. But there still remains a country of vast resources, filled with people of spirit and strength.

Delay has made destruction ten times the worse. But it is not too late to build a policy of reconstruction.

They have sought to deceive. They have sought to confuse. But the American people have learned how to know deceit because they met it. They will take care of that, too, on Tuesday, November 8th. We, the people of this country, have lived too long and suffered too deeply to be frightened, to be intimidated by selfish and unAmerican employers, and other mongers of fear.

841

We Americans will rise from destruction; we Americans will conquer despair; we Americans are facing new things. With confidence we accept the promise of a "New Deal."

148 ⟪ "We Are Through with 'Delay'; We Are Through with 'Despair'; We Are Ready, and Waiting for Better Things." Campaign Address on a Program for Unemployment and Long-Range Planning. Boston, Mass. October 31, 1932

Governor Ely, Mayor Curley, my friends of Massachusetts:

I AM GLAD that a moment ago I had the privilege of standing under the flag of the Commonwealth of Massachusetts. There is a reason why I am particularly proud and happy of that. It is because, my friends, exactly one-half of me — my mother's half — comes from Massachusetts.

This trip to New England, I assure you, has brought back many happy memories. I have had a wonderful day from the early morning when I left the old school which I once attended and, where, I am told, I received some kind of culture, all the way up through Lawrence and Haverhill, and then on through New Hampshire and to Portland, Maine; and then this afternoon, coming back through the cities of Maine, New Hampshire and back into Massachusetts. I am more than ever convinced that those three States that I have visited today are going to be found in the Democratic column on November 8th.

I have met a multitude of old friends, with whom I have been associated in public life for more years than I care to tell you. If I were to start referring to each of them by name, I should have to call the roll of Massachusetts Democracy, and a good many of the Republicans as well. I appreciate the fact that today, a week before election, we have a united party — a party which, in securing a great victory on November 8th, will be supported

not only by Democrats but by free-spirited Republican and independent voters. My only regret is that I could not have been
here last Thursday night when Governor Smith was here. Anyway, the very day that he was here I had a good long talk with
him, and I heard about the splendid and deserved welcome you
gave him here in Boston.

Other memories, too, have come from far back beyond my
earliest political experience. As a boy, I came to this State for
education. To that education I look back with open and sincere pride and gratitude.

Then I came and lived not very far from here at a great institution for the freeing of the human mind from ignorance, from
bigotry of the mind and the spirit. Knowledge — that is, education in its true sense — is our best protection against unreasoning prejudice and panic-making fear, whether engendered by
special interests, illiberal minorities, or panic-stricken leaders
who seek to perpetuate the power which they have misused.

I hope I have learned the lesson that reason and tolerance
have their place in all things; and I want to say frankly that
they are never so appropriate as when they prevail in a political
campaign.

I say this with some feeling because I express widespread
opinion when I note that the dignity of the office of President
of the United States has suffered during the past week. The President began this campaign with the same attitude with which he
has approached so many of the serious problems of the past three
years. He sought to create the impression that there was no
campaign going on at all, just as he had sought to create the
impression that all was well with the United States, and that
there was no depression.

But, my friends, the people of this country spoiled these plans.
They demanded that the administration which they placed in
power four years ago, and which has cost them so much, give
an accounting. They demanded this accounting in no uncertain
terms.

This demand of the people has continued until it has become

an overwhelming, irresistible drift of public opinion. It is more than a drift. It is a tempest.

As that storm of approval for the Democratic policies has grown, several moods have come over the utterances of the Republican leader.

First, they were plaintively apologetic. Then the next move was indignation at the Congress of the United States. Finally, they have in desperation resorted to the breeding of panic and fear.

At first the President refused to recognize that he was in a contest. But as the people with each succeeding week have responded to our program with enthusiasm, he recognized that we were both candidates. And then, dignity died.

At Indianapolis he spoke of my arguments, misquoting them. But at Indianapolis he went further. He abandoned argument for personalities.

In the presence of a situation like this, I am tempted to reply in kind. But I shall not yield to the temptation to which the President yielded. On the contrary, I reiterate my respect for his person and for his office. But I shall not be deterred even by the President of the United States from the discussion of grave national issues and from submitting to the voters the truth about their national affairs, however unpleasant that truth may be.

The ballot is the indispensable instrument of a free people. It should be the true expression of their will; and it is intolerable that the ballot should be coerced — whatever the form of coercion, political or economic.

The autocratic will of no man — be he President, or general, or captain of industry — shall ever destroy the sacred right of the people themselves to determine for themselves who shall govern them.

An hour ago, before I came to the Arena, I listened in for a few minutes to the first part of the speech of the President in New York tonight. Once more he warned the people against changing — against a new deal — stating that it would mean changing the fundamental principles of America, what he called the sound principles that have been so long believed in in this country. My friends, my New Deal does not aim to change those principles. It does aim to bring those principles into effect.

Secure in their undying belief in their great tradition and in the sanctity of a free ballot, the people of this country—the employed, the partially employed and the unemployed, those who are fortunate enough to retain some of the means of economic well-being, and those from whom these cruel conditions have taken everything—have stood with patience and fortitude in the face of adversity.

There they stand. And they stand peacefully, even when they stand in the breadline. Their complaints are not mingled with threats. They are willing to listen to reason at all times. Throughout this great crisis the stricken army of the unemployed has been patient, law-abiding, orderly, because it is hopeful.

But, the party that claims as its guiding tradition the patient and generous spirit of the immortal Abraham Lincoln, when confronted by an opposition which has given to this Nation an orderly and constructive campaign for the past four months, has descended to an outpouring of misstatements, threats and intimidation.

The Administration attempts to undermine reason through fear by telling us that the world will come to an end on November 8th if it is not returned to power for four years more. Once more it is a leadership that is bankrupt, not only in ideals but in ideas. It sadly misconceives the good sense and the self-reliance of our people.

These leaders tell us further that, in the event of change, the present Administration will be unable to hold in check the economic forces that threaten us in the period between election day and inauguration day. They threaten American business and American workers with dire destruction from November to March.

They crack the "whip of fear" over the backs of American voters, not only here but across the seas as well.

845

Ambassador Mellon, the representative of the United States at the Court of St. James's, an Ambassador who should represent the whole American people there — every faith, the whole Nation, Democrats, Republicans and Independents alike — appeals to an English audience, on English soil, for the support of a party candidate 3000 miles away, and invokes the same sinister threat and seeks to spread that threat to the rest of the civilized world.

I read somewhere in a history book about a Roman Senator who threw himself into a chasm to save his country. These gentlemen who represent us are of a new breed. They are willing to throw their country into a chasm to save themselves.

There is another means of spreading fear — through certain Republican industrial leaders. I have said, without being controverted, that 5,000 men in effect control American industry. These men, possessed of such great power, carry likewise a great responsibility. It is their duty to use every precaution to see that this power is never used to destroy or to limit the sound public policy of the free and untrammeled exercise of the power of the ballot.

In violation of that duty, some of these 5000 men who control industry are today invading the sacred political rights of those over whom they have economic power. They are joining in the chorus of fear initiated by the President, by the Ambassador, by the Secretary of the Treasury, and by the Republican National Committee.

They are telling their employees that if they fail to support the Administration of President Hoover, such jobs as these employees have will be in danger. Such conduct is unAmerican and worthy of censure at the ballot box. I wonder how some of those industrial leaders would feel if somebody else's "baby had the measles." In other words, would they agree that it would be equally reprehensible if any political leader were to seek reprisal against them — against any coercing employer who used such means against political leaders? Let us fight our political battles with political arguments, and not prey upon men's economic necessities.

846

After all, their threats are empty gestures. You and I know that their industries have been sliding downhill. You know, and I know, that the whole program of the present Administration has been directed only to prevent a further slipping downhill. You know, and I know, that therein lies the difference between the leaderships of the two parties.

You know, and I know, that the Democratic Party is not satisfied merely with arresting the present decline. Of course we will do that to the best of our ability; but we are equally interested in seeking to build up and improve, and to put these industries in a position where their wheels will turn once more, and where opportunity will be given to them to reemploy the millions of workers that they have laid off under the Administration of President Hoover.

It is not enough merely to stabilize, to lend money! It is essential to increase purchasing power in order that goods may be sold. There must be people capable of buying goods in order that goods may be manufactured and sold. When that time comes, under our new leadership, these same gentlemen who now make their threats will be found doing business at the old stand as usual.

The American voter, the American working-man and working woman, the mill-worker of New England, the miner of the West, the railroad worker, the farmer, and the white-collar man will answer these silly, spiteful threats with their ballots on November eighth.

As I have pointed out before in this campaign, in a good many States and during many weeks, the fruits of depression, like the fruits of war, are going to be gathered in future generations. It is not the pinch of suffering, the agony of uncertainty that the grown-up people are now feeling that count the most; it is the heritage that our children must anticipate that touches a more vital spot. It is not today alone that counts. Under-nourishment, poor standards of living and inadequate medical care of today will make themselves felt among our children for fifty years to come.

I stood in Topeka, Kansas, two months ago, and said to the farmers that the tragic effects of 40¢ wheat and 9¢ corn and 6¢ cotton are not so much what the farmer himself must feel when he sees the labor of his hands wasted on a product that does not yield him a living, that the bitterness of it all is what it means for his children and for their children.

It is the same for you — workers in industry and in business. There are none of us who do not hope that our children can get a better break than we have had, that the chance for an education, for a reasonable start in life, may be passed on to our children, an opportunity for them built out of the hard work of our own hands. We want them to have opportunity for profitable character building — decent, wholesome living — good work, and good play. We want to know somehow that, while perfection does not come in this world, we do try to make things better from one generation to another.

That is why I emphasize that this depression, with its vast unemployment, has swept away much of the material gains that we had hoped to use. Grim poverty stalks throughout our land. I know it well for I have seen it, all the way to the coast and back again, as I have traveled up the length and breadth of 36 States of the Union. It embitters the present and darkens the future.

Against this enemy every ounce of effort and every necessary penny of wealth must be raised as a defense. It is not that we lack the knowledge of what to do. The tragedy of the past years has been the failure of those who were responsible to translate high-sounding plans into practical action. There's the rub.

The present leadership in Washington stands convicted, not because it did not have the means to plan, but fundamentally because it did not have the will to do. That is why the American people on November eighth will register their firm conviction that this Administration has utterly and entirely failed to meet the great emergency.

The American people are a heart-sick people for "hope deferred maketh the heart sick."

Let me offer you an example. In 1921 and 1922 there was a

depression — very mild, compared with the present one, but nevertheless, a depression. There was, as you will remember, a large amount of unemployment. The President of the United States, President Harding, in September, 1921, called what was known as the "President's Conference on Unemployment," the first, my friends, of a long and distinguished series of President's conferences. This Conference employed a number of experts who prepared a highly competent report. It happens that this report did not appear until after that depression was ended — which was another characteristic of those conferences. The report was published in 1923, six years before the present depression began.

It said many sound things. It proposed the control of credit expansion by the banks; it proposed the prevention of over-expansion of industry; it proposed the control of public and private construction in boom periods, and it proposed security against the suffering that might come from unemployment.

It was a good report, my friends. Sound and intelligent people worked on it, and contributed to it.

The Chairman of that Unemployment Conference in 1921 was the then Secretary of Commerce of the United States, Secretary Herbert Hoover.

The President complains, President Herbert Hoover, because I have charged that he did nothing for a long time after the depression began. I repeat that charge. It is true. I can further add to that charge by saying that from the time this report by Secretary of Commerce Hoover was published in 1923, for the six years that preceded the crash in 1929, he did nothing to put into effect the provisions advocated in 1923 against the possibility of a future depression.

Instead of doing something during these six years, and especially the last year or two, he participated in encouraging speculation, when the sound business brains of the country were saying that speculation should be discouraged, and in spite of the fact that his own report in 1923 said that depressions are in large part due to over-speculation. He failed to prepare by positive action against the recurrence of a depression. On the contrary — the exact contrary—he intensified the forces that made for depressions by encouraging that speculation.

He did not do what in his 1923 report he said ought to be done. Instead of that, and on top of that, he did what he said ought not to be done.

Now, my friends, we are considering unemployment tonight, and I am going to start by setting forth the positive policy which the President's Commission under the leadership of the Secretary of Commerce urged should be done. There is a lot of it which is still good.

It was a 5-point program. And as a program it was good.

First, it urged that Government should reduce expenditures for public works during periods of prosperity, and that, during those periods, Government should build up reserves with which to increase expenditures during periods of unemployment and industrial depression. But was that done? Not one penny's worth. No reserves were built up for the rainy day.

Second, the report said that the Federal Government should work with the railroads in the preparation of a long-time constructive program. Was that done? No. The Republican Administration did not give effect to this proposal. Instead of working with the railroads, to consolidate their lines and put them on a sound, economical basis, the Administration waited until the depression had laid them low, and then had nothing for them except to loan them more money, when they were already heavily in debt.

Third, the report proposed the setting up of safeguards against too rapid inflation, and consequently too rapid deflation of bank credit. As I have shown, the President and his Secretary of the Treasury went to the other extreme and encouraged speculation.

Fourth, the report recommended an adequate system of unemployment insurance. No one in the Administration in Washington has assumed any leadership in order to bring about positive action by the States to make this unemployment insurance a reality. Some day, in our leadership, we are going to get it.

Fifth, it suggested an adequate system of public employment

850

offices. But when Senator Wagner introduced a bill to establish Federal employment offices, President Hoover vetoed the measure that Secretary Herbert Hoover had sponsored. It seems to me, speaking in this great section of the country where there are so many business men, that business men who believe in sound planning and action, must feel that there is danger to the country in the continuance of a leadership that has shown such incapacity, such ineptitude, such heedlessness of common sense and of sound business principles. What we need in Washington is less fact finding and more thinking.

Immediate relief of the unemployed is the immediate need of the hour. No mere emergency measures of relief are adequate. We must do all we can. We have emergency measures but we know that our goal, our unremitting objective, must be to secure not temporary employment but the permanence of employment to the workers of America. Without long-range stability of employment for our workers, without a balanced economy between agriculture and industry, there can be no healthy national life.

We have two problems: first, to meet the immediate distress; second, to build up on a basis of permanent employment.

As to "immediate relief," the first principle is that this Nation, this national Government, if you like, owes a positive duty that no citizen shall be permitted to starve. That means that while the immediate responsibility for relief rests, of course, with local, public and private charity, in so far as these are inadequate the States must carry on the burden, and whenever the States themselves are unable adequately to do so the Federal Government owes the positive duty of stepping into the breach.

It is worth while noting that from that disastrous time of 1929 on the present Republican Administration took a definite position against the recognition of that principle. It was only because of the insistence of the Congress of the United States and the unmistakable voice of the people of the United States that the President yielded and approved the National Relief Bill this summer.

In addition to providing emergency relief, the Federal Government should and must provide temporary work wherever that is possible. You and I know that in the national forests, on flood prevention, and on the development of waterway projects that have already been authorized and planned but not yet executed, tens of thousands, and even hundreds of thousands of our unemployed citizens can be given at least temporary employment.

Third, the Federal Government should expedite the actual construction of public works already authorized. The country would be horrified if it knew how little construction work authorized by the last Congress and approved by the President has actually been undertaken on this date, the 31st of October. And I state to you the simple fact that much of the work for which Congress has given authority will not be under way and giving employment to people until sometime next summer.

Finally, in that larger field that looks further ahead, we call for a coordinated system of employment exchanges, the advance planning of public works, and unemployment reserves. Who, then, is to carry on these measures and see them through? The first, employment exchanges, is clearly and inescapably a task of the Federal Government, although it will require the loyal and intelligent cooperation of State and local agencies throughout the land. To that Federal action I pledge my administration. The second, the advance planning of public works, again calls for a strong lead on the part of the Government at Washington. I pledge my administration to the adoption of that principle, both as to enterprises of the Federal Government itself and as to construction within the several States which is made possible by Federal aid; and I shall urge upon State and local authorities throughout the Nation that they follow this example in Washington. The third, unemployment reserves, must under our system of Government be primarily the responsibility of the several States. That, the Democratic platform, on which I stand, makes entirely clear.

In addition to all this, there has been long overdue a reduction of the hours of work and a reduction of the number of working days per week. After all, the greatest justification of modern industry is the lessening of the toil of men and women. These fruits will be dead fruits unless men earn enough so that they can buy the things that are produced, so that they can have the leisure for the cultivation of body, mind and spirit, which the great inventions are supposed to make possible. That means that Government itself must set an example in the case of its own employees. It means also that Government must exert its persuasive leadership to induce industry to do likewise.

Here then is a program of long-range planning which requires prompt and definite action and the cooperation of Federal and State and local Governments, as well as of forward-looking citizens of both parties throughout the land. The proposals are specific, they are far-reaching. To advocate a less drastic program would be to misread the lessons of the depression and to express indifference to the country's future welfare.

There is one final objective of my policy which is more vital and more basic than all else. I seek to restore the purchasing power of the American people. The return of that purchasing power, and only that, will put America back to work.

We need to restore our trade with the world. Under Republican leadership we have lost it, and the President of the United States seems to be indifferent about finding it again.

And now I am going to talk to a city audience about farming. I do not make one kind of speech to a farm audience and another kind of speech to a city audience. We need to give to fifty million people, who live directly or indirectly on agriculture, a price for their products in excess of the cost of production. You know how and why that affects you in the cities. To give them an adequate price for their products means to give them the buying power necessary to start your mills and mines to work to supply their needs. Fifty million people cannot buy your goods, because they cannot get a fair price for their products. You are poor because they are poor.

I favor—and do not let the false statements of my opponents deceive you—continued protection for American agriculture as well as American industry. I favor more than that. I advocate,

853

and will continue to advocate, measures to give the farmer an added benefit, called a tariff benefit, to make the tariff effective on his products. What good does a 42-cent tariff on wheat mean to the farmer when he is getting 30 cents a bushel on his farm? That is a joke. The most enlightened of modern American business men likewise favor such a tariff benefit for agriculture. An excellent example is your own fellow Bostonian, Mr. Harriman, President of the Chamber of Commerce of the United States, who has recently proclaimed a plan for the restoration of agriculture not unlike my own.

The President of the United States does not favor a program of that kind, or, so far as I can make out, of any practical kind. He has closed the door of hope to American agriculture, and when he did that, he closed the door of hope to you also.

He says proudly that he has effectively restricted immigration in order to protect American labor. I favor that; but I might add that in the enforcement of the immigration laws too many abuses against individual families have been revealed time and time again.

But when the President speaks to you, he does not tell you that by permitting agriculture to fall into ruin millions of workers from the farms have crowded into our cities. These men have added to unemployment. They are here because agriculture is prostrate. A restored agriculture will check this migration from the farm. It will keep these farmers happily, successfully, at home; and it will leave more jobs for you. It will provide a market for your products, and that is the key to national economic restoration.

One word more. I have spoken of getting things done. The way we get things done under our form of Government is through joint action by the President and the Congress. The two branches of Government must cooperate if we are to move forward. That is necessary under our Constitution, and I believe in our constitutional form of Government.

But the President of the United States cannot get action from the Congress. He seems unable to cooperate. He quarreled with a Republican Congress and he quarreled with a half Republican Congress. He will quarrel with any kind of Congress, and he cannot get things done.

That is something that the voters have considered and are considering and are going to remember one week from tomorrow. You and I know, and it is certainly a fact, that the next Congress will be Democratic. I look forward to cooperating with it. I am confident that I can get things done through cooperation because for four years I have had to work with a Republican Legislature in New York.

I have been able to get things done in Albany by treating the Republican members of the Legislature like human beings and as my associates in Government. I have said that I look forward to the most pleasant relations with the next Democratic Congress, but in addition to that let me make it clear that on that great majority of national problems which ought not to be handled in any partisan manner, I confidently expect to have pleasant relations with Republicans in the Senate and the House of Representatives as well as with Democrats.

After the fourth of March, we — meaning thereby the President and the members of both parties in the Halls of Congress — will, I am confident, work together effectively for the restoration of American economic life.

I decline to accept present conditions as inevitable or beyond control. I decline to stop at saying, "It might have been worse." I shall do all that I can to prevent it from being worse but — and here is the clear difference between the President and myself — I go on to pledge action to make things better.

The United States of America has the capacity to make things better. The Nation wants to make things better. The Nation prays for the leadership of action that will make things better. That will be shown in every State in the Union — all 48 of them — a week from tomorrow. We are through with "Delay"; we are through with "Despair"; we are ready, and waiting for better things.

149 ❲ Campaign Address before the Republican-for-Roosevelt League on Cooperation between Executive and Legislative Branches in Government (Excerpts), New York City.

November 3, 1932

Mr. Childs, Mr. Young, my fellow Americans:

I AM HERE tonight at the invitation of a group of public-minded citizens who have placed principle above party. These citizens, whose party affiliation has been Republican, have publicly declared that they consider that a change in the administration of this Government is necessary, that it is, in fact, indispensable to a restoration to normal conditions. And so, on such an occasion it is fitting for me to speak as a citizen rather than as a partisan. . . .

And now I want to talk to you very simply from my own personal experience in regard to the actual conduct of Government itself — what a business man would call the executive and operating task of the corporation.

It is necessary, first of all, for us to recognize the simple fact that, apart from the occasional judicial interpretations relating to Government, we have in Washington, as in all the States, two constant factors which are working year in and year out, side by side and in constant contact with each other — in the case of States the Governor and the Legislature, and in Washington the President and the Congress.

Many unthinking people have inveighed against the Congress in every generation of our Republic, little realizing that they are striking at the very fabric of our Constitution. If they would but think for a moment, they would realize that if we were to eliminate the Congress of the United States, we would automatically cease to be a Republic.

The real purpose of the Constitution was based on the rightful assumption that the President and the Congress would be sufficiently right-minded, sufficiently practical and sufficiently patriotic to make every effort to cooperate the one with the other. It is not an overstatement either of the fact, or of the opinion of the American public, to say that the present Chief Executive of our Nation has shown a singular lack of ability to cooperate with the Congress. I am not speaking only of the past eleven months since the House of Representatives became Democratic by the margin of a handful of votes. I am speaking also of the previous two and one-half years, during which time the Congress in both of its branches was controlled by the same party to which the President himself belongs. From the earliest days of the special session which he summoned in the spring of 1929, the relations between the Capitol and the White House have, to say the least, lacked cordiality, understanding and common national purpose.

Let me make it clear that I do not assert that a President and the Congress must on all points agree with each other at all times. Many times in history there has been complete disagreement between the two branches of the Government, and in these disagreements sometimes the Congress has won and sometimes the President has won. But during the Administration of the present President we have had neither agreement nor a clear-cut battle. Either would have cleared the atmosphere and would have been far preferable to the smouldering ill-feeling that has prevailed during the past three and one-half years in Washington.

I believe that I have the right to point out my own conception of the relationship between an executive and a legislative body. I have served as a legislator and as a Chief Executive. I believe that from the point of view of a Governor or a President, his relations with the legislative body can be based on cooperation. The fact is that with the great majority of problems mere partisanship should, in so far as possible, be kept in the background. In meeting this great majority of problems, they can and should be treated primarily from the point of view of national good rather than of party good. Let me add that in the case of most

857

reconstruction legislation, there ought to be no great difference in the policy of the two great political parties.

We are all influenced by our personal experiences. For four long years, as Governor of New York, I have been faced by a Legislature Republican in both of its branches. From the beginning I have worked on the assumption that the members of this Legislature were human beings, that they were patriotic, and that most of our State problems could best be solved by cooperation between them and myself. We have differed on certain matters of fundamental policy. In those cases, I have given them battle. Sometimes they have won, sometimes, and I think in the majority of cases, I have won; but in all these cases we have had good, clean, open fights. And the people have known the full story of each case.

But, when the problem has been one affecting human welfare, the Legislature and I have always ended by sitting around a table and getting something practical done. That was the history of the labor legislation in this State during the past four years — of the legislation for the improvement of our hospitals and our prison system, of the legislation that enacted that old-age security law, of the legislation that made this State the leader among all the States in providing unemployment relief. In the latter case, I called a special session. I proposed a bill, the Republican leaders proposed another bill, and we had a good old-fashioned "knock-down and drag-out" fight. Finally, we sat around a table; I met them 20 percent of the way, they met me 80 percent of the way; they passed the bill, I signed the bill; the relief work was started — all in less than a month. Contrast that with the fact that it took the Congress six months to get the President to see that such measures were necessary in the Nation as well.

I want to drive home the point that I have practiced what I preach — that there can be cooperation between an Executive and a legislative body in the interest of getting things done.

And while I draw from my personal experience one part of my record in Albany well illustrates my point. Up to the time I was inaugurated as Governor, the record for vetoes in this State belonged to former Governor Grover Cleveland. But in each of the last four years I have vetoed more legislative acts than did Cleveland himself, and the percentage of laws passed which received my executive disapproval has run from 25 percent to as high as 31 percent of all bills passed. That is not all. During those four years, not one single bill which received my disapproval has been passed by the Legislature over my veto. It is likewise with my record of appointments. As in the Federal Government, nearly all important administrative or judicial appointments require confirmation by the Senate. During my four years as Governor, not a single one of my appointments has been rejected by the Senate of the State of New York.

One final point on this subject of cooperation. It seems, of course, fairly obvious that the next Congress of the United States will have a majority of Democrats in both its branches. Any child can understand that it will be easier for a Democratic President to cooperate with the next Congress than it would be if the present Chief Executive were reelected. But, let me at the same time add this in all seriousness and from my heart. I honestly believe that even if the Congress of the United States were to be Republican in one or both of its branches I could get along with it better than the gentleman who is running for President on the Republican ticket.

The great issue this year is national, comprehensive and humane. I have painted it with broad lines because it is a program for a great Nation. That is why, from the beginning, insisting upon the principle of a new deal, I have invited to join our cause Republicans who believe that this country needs the tonic of a new alignment of party loyalties, a new and enlightened support of our national faith. This country needs the tonic effect of such a reiteration of American principles. It calls to its service with particular emphasis the independent and courageous spirits who are willing to leave the household of a betrayed faith, who are asking for substance, not shadows, who are seeking for truth, not names for truth.

In speaking for the common purposes of all of these forward-

859

looking men and women I have, I believe, avoided the delusion that this is a campaign of persons or of personalities. To indulge in such a fantastic idea of my own individual importance would be to betray the common hope and the common cause that has brought us all together this year. A great man left a watchword that we can well repeat: "There is no indispensable man."

But there are indispensable principles without which Government cannot serve its purpose. These are the principles of fair and open dealing with the public, of using the great powers of the Government to serve no mean party advantage, of keeping promises made to agriculture and labor, of friendly relations between the Executive and the Legislature, of economic peace with foreign Nations, of protection for those who must entrust their savings to others, of social justice for all, and relief for those who are in need.

Reducing it to all the essentials of my speech of acceptance, we want to get for the American people two great human values —work and security. To achieve this end I invite you all. It is no mere party slogan. It is a definition of national need. It is a philosophy of life. I repeat it with a courage lent by the knowledge that I speak a philosophy of Government as well—the ideals which have made us and kept us a Nation.

150 ⟨ "I Believe that the Best Interests of the Country Require a Change in Administration." Campaign Address at Madison Square Garden. New York City. November 5, 1932

TONIGHT we close the campaign. Our case has been stated and made. In every home, to every individual, in every part of our wide land, full opportunity has been given to hear that case, and to render honest judgment on Tuesday next.

From the time that my airplane touched ground at Chicago up to the present, I have consistently set forth the doctrine of the present-day democracy. It is the program of a party dedicated to the conviction that every one of our people is entitled to the opportunity to earn a living, and to develop himself to the fullest measure consistent with the rights of his fellow men.

You are familiar with that program. You are aware that it has found favor in the sight of the American electorate. The movement comes not from the leaders of any group, of any faction, or even of any party. It is the spontaneous expression of the aspirations of millions of individual men and women. These hopes, these ambitions, have struggled for realization in different ways, on the farms, in the cities, in the factories, among business men and in the homes. These have found at length a common meeting ground in the Democratic program.

Tonight we set the seal upon that program. After Tuesday, we go forward to the great task of its accomplishment and, we trust, to its fulfillment.

There can be only one great principle to guide our course in the coming years. We have learned the lesson that extravagant advantage for the few ultimately depresses the many. To our cost we have seen how, as the foundations of the false structure are undermined, all come down together. We must put behind us the idea that an uncontrolled, unbalanced economy, creating paper profits for a relatively small group, means or ever can mean prosperity.

Exactly four years ago, on a similar occasion, the Democratic Party, in closing its campaign, stigmatized the condition, then called "Prosperity," in truly prophetic language with the label "False Prosperity." You know now, and America knows, the justice of that label. The reasoning then was as simple as is the analysis now. While the families upon our farms are in want, there can be no safety for the families of the workers in our cities.

There is an interdependence in economics, just as there is a brotherhood in humanity. Loss to any is loss to all.

Today we struggle against the inevitable result of wandering after false gods. Confident in the sinew and fiber of American life, we know that our losses are not beyond repair. We know that we can apply to the great structure we have built, our power of organization, our fertility of mind and the intelligence and the foresight needed to make that structure more serviceable. We refuse to be oppressed by baseless fears that our firesides are to become cold or that our civilization will disappear. We know that by the united effort of us all, our fear can be dissipated, our firesides protected, our economic fabric reconstituted and our individual lives brought to more perfect fulfillment.

In that united effort, I make bold to include not only you, the members of my own party; not only the great independent masses who seek relief from an Administration which has served them ill; not only the liberal-minded elements in all parts of the country who have joined in creating the program we are proud to offer; but also the men and women in the ranks of the Republican Party, whose interests must also be ours.

The next Administration must represent not a fraction of the United States, but all of the United States. No resource of mind or heart or organization can be excluded in the fight against what is, after all, our real enemy. Our real enemies are hunger, want, insecurity, poverty and fear. Against these there is no glory in a victory only partisan.

The genius of America is stronger than any candidate or any party. This campaign, hard as it has been, has not shattered my sense of humor or my sense of proportion. I still know that the fate of America cannot depend on any one man. The greatness of America is grounded in principles and not on any single personality. I, for one, shall remember that, even as President. Unless by victory we can accomplish a greater unity toward liberal effort, we shall have done little indeed.

Let us turn from consideration of leadership and think of the loyal voters who constitute the great army that has brought us to the gates of victory. Let us give thought to the men and women in the ranks. There are many millions of them. What have they in mind? Why have they enlisted?

There is among you the man who is not bound by party lines. You vote according to your common sense and your calm judgment after hearing each party set forth its program. To you I say that the strength of this independent thought is the great contribution of the American political system. You, and millions like you, have appraised the Democratic program, and have rallied to its standard. Your thought makes wider our vision in handling our national policies.

There is among you the woman who knows that women's traditional interests — welfare, children and the home — rest on the broader basis of an economic system which assures her or her husband of a job. The old expression that "a woman's place is in the home" has a wider meaning today. Your interests may be in your home, but you now know that they are no longer disassociated from the interests of the State. Into your home, for instance, comes electricity. What you pay for it is largely determined by the attitude of your Government. Your family budget must provide for a tax bill as well as for your baby's clothes. And you know now that your baby's clothes are apt to depend upon the amount of taxes your family pays. You who have had the clarity of vision to trace many of your private problems back to their roots in Government policy, best appreciate the program we lay before you.

There is among you the man in business or in trade who has heard the cry that change was a fearful thing but who, unafraid, has decided to change. You know now that when things are going wrong, only partisan prejudice and stupidity can countenance a continuance. You know now that the logical remedy for mistaken policy is a change in policy. You have decided to make this change. You have decided to put the conduct of affairs into other hands.

All of you, consciously or not, have helped shape the policies of the Democratic Party in this, its war on human suffering. Your own experiences and your own fears and your own problems — all have written themselves into our program. There is something of you in all of us.

There is among you the man who has been brought up in the good American tradition to work hard and to save for a rainy day. You have worked hard. You have stinted yourself to save. You now find your savings gone. You now find your job gone. Your resentment comes not from discontent alone but from a feeling of deep injustice. You have joined us not because of discontent, but because in our program you find the hope that this cannot come again. We have not enticed you with offers of magic, or lured you with vain promises. We have given you the hope of a better ordered system of national economy. We have pledged you our word and our will to do.

There is among you the man who has been brought up to believe that a livelihood could always be wrung from the soil by willing labor. You have broken your back in your efforts to make the soil produce. And when you have gathered your harvest you have found that harvest worthless. In bewilderment, you have learned that when you had something to buy the cost was great; but when you had something to sell, the price was low or the price was nil. For years you have endured this until at length the mounting tide of debt has threatened your very home. You have entered our ranks. No promised cure-all led you there. You came because by careful analysis you were convinced where your difficulty lay.

You knew that your difficulties were beyond your individual control to prevent or cure. Our plan offered to you a mobilization of the resources of Government to bring to you the fruits which your labor deserved.

There is among you the man who has been able to save something from this wreck. You have joined our ranks because you, too, have come to realize the falsity of the 1928 economics and to look for your safety in a new and stronger philosophy of constitutional Government.

All of you, in all places, in all walks of life, have joined in proving that only by a true conception of the interdependence of the American economic system, can there be hope of safety and security for all.

Today there appears once more the truth taught two thousand

years ago that "no man lives to himself, and no man dies to himself; but living or dying, we are the Lord's and each other's."

It may be said, when the history of the past few months comes to be written, that this was a bitter campaign. I prefer to remember it only as a hard-fought campaign. There can be no bitterness where the sole thought is the welfare of America.

It is with this spirit and in this spirit that I close the campaign. I believe that the best interests of the country require a change in administration. Every sign points to that change. But I would have you realize that the strength of the country is the strength of union. Let us restore that strength.

It was said at the close of the World War that "America had come of age." After that War, we had a unique opportunity to build permanently for America. That opportunity we did not grasp.

But even in our mistakes we have learned how strength can best be used to the common benefit of us all. The millions of unchronicled heroes who by self-denial and patience have carried this Nation through this economic crisis must give us new hope. We can and will bring to the problem of the individual the maturity of the united effort of a Nation come of age. America, mature in its power, united in its purpose, high in its faith, can come and will come to better days.

XXV

Between Election and Inauguration—November, 1932, to March 4, 1933

INTRODUCTORY NOTE: On NOVEMBER 17, 1932, I telephoned President Hoover in response to his letter to me of November 12, 1932 (see Item 151, this volume), that I would visit him at the White House on November 22, 1932, for the purposes mentioned in his letter. This conference took place on that date.

The President repeated to me in greater detail what he had already written, and explained the status of the proposed International Economic Conference which was to be held at some date, not yet chosen, during the course of the year 1933. Little discussion took place, as the principal objective of this meeting at the White House was to put me in touch with the current international economic situation, partly in relation to foreign Government debts owed to the United States Government, but principally in relation to the international monetary problem. Domestic matters were not discussed, and on the subject of foreign debts no tangible suggestion was forthcoming. It will be remembered that the Congress had already declined to authorize Executive negotiation of debt settlements and that the Congress elected in 1930 was still in office.

I left Washington on November 23, 1932, for Warm Springs, Ga., and remained in Warm Springs until December 6, 1932, when I returned to Albany because of the special session of the Legislature which had been called on the subject of the financial situation of New York City.

Between December 17th and December 21st, there was the

correspondence between President Hoover and myself, which is printed as Item 152 of this volume.

It will be seen from my letter of December 19th that I wholly agreed with President Hoover's policy toward disarmament; that I wholly approved preliminary conversations by the Chief Executive to determine facts and explore possibilities relating to debts; and that in respect to the Economic Conference I felt that because the Conference would not be held until long after I came into office, my hands should not be tied by preliminary limitations. Again, it will be noted that domestic matters form no part of the interchange of letters in December. I made it clear that I would welcome any steps which President Hoover might take in foreign matters in the way of exploratory work and preliminary survey.

On January 20, 1933, I again visited the White House to confer with President Hoover. At this meeting the foreign debt situation was again discussed. It seemed to be the thought of President Hoover and Secretary of the Treasury Mills that a solution of the debt question would act as a principal cure for our domestic ills, that it was a necessary complement to the distant Economic Conference and that the debtor Nations were at that time in a position to make a substantial and immediate settlement. At no time did I discourage the President from making the necessary surveys and obtaining practical proposals from other Nations. I felt, however, that the world economic situation at that time would prevent any proposal to the United States which could possibly receive the approval of the Congress, and that a wholly different line of action should be initiated — the emphasis being placed on practical steps on a wide front at home, supplementing a broad domestic program with protection for the American dollar in international exchange. When the whole machinery needed overhauling, I felt it to be insufficient to repair one or two minor parts.

After this conference on January 20, 1932, the following statement was given out at the White House: "The conference between the President and the President-elect this morning was attended by Secretaries Stimson and Mills and Messrs. Norman Davis and Moley. The discussions were devoted mainly to a canvass of the foreign situation and the following statement covering the procedure to be followed was agreed upon:

" 'The British Government has asked for a discussion of the debts. The incoming Administration will be glad to receive their representative early in March for this purpose. It is, of course, necessary to discuss at the same time the world economic problems in which the United States and Great Britain are mutually interested, and therefore, that representatives should also be sent to discuss ways and means for improving the world situation.

" 'It is settled that these arrangements will be taken up by the Secretary of State with the British Government.' "

Thereafter I left for Warm Springs and Muscle Shoals. During the course of this trip I made various speeches printed as Items 154 and 155 in this book, and also additional speeches at Birmingham, Ala., January 21; Decatur, Ala., January 21; and Florence, Ala., January 21, which are not included in these volumes.

On February 4, 1933, I went on a vacation fishing trip, returning to Miami, Florida, on February 15, 1933. I there made the short informal talk which is printed as Item 156 of this volume. This preceded the attempted assassination, which resulted in the fatal wounding of Mayor Anton Cermak of Chicago.

On February 17th I returned to New York City and went to Hyde Park. I left from New York City on March 2, 1933, for the Inauguration in Washington.

On February 21st, Mr. William H. Woodin accepted the post of Secretary of the Treasury in my Cabinet. Shortly thereafter he got in touch with Secretary of the Treasury Ogden L. Mills and was in daily contact with the Treasury and, through the Treasury, with the White House, every day thereafter until we both arrived in Washington on March 2nd. Mr. Woodin telephoned to me several times each day, and we both concluded that the banking situation throughout the Nation was becoming so acute that only immediate and drastic measures could save the banks from having to close their own doors. Increasing lines of depositors were withdrawing their funds in gold or gold certificates. A proposal was made to give authority to the Treasury to deposit Government funds directly in any bank—but the Treasury did not have sufficient funds to deposit.

On my arrival in Washington on the evening of March 2nd, Mr. Woodin told me of a suggestion that the President and I should join in a statement reiterating confidence in the fundamental soundness of American banks, and appealing to depositors to stop withdrawing funds. Many similar appeals and statements —all to the effect that nothing was wrong with the country—had been made during preceding years. Again, I felt that strong, positive, definite action should take the place of appeals.

The following day, March 3rd, I visited the White House with my family to pay official respects to the President. For generations it had been the custom of the President-elect to visit the President on March 3rd and for the President to return the call immediately on the President-elect at the house or hotel of the latter. After tea at the White House on March 3, 1933, a short conference was held by me with President Hoover. Messages had been coming in all day, reporting that some banks had closed their doors, that some Governors were declaring moratoria, and that more gold was being withdrawn. Later in the evening, by telephone, I told the President that while I was wholly agreeable to his closing all the banks by Proclamation, I could not, as a private citizen, join him in such a Proclamation.

I told the President, however, that I believed that he had such authority under the Trading with the Enemy Act. I understood it to be the belief of the President that while some of his advisers had told him that he could do this, others had told him that it would not be legal. I had already asked Senator Thomas J. Walsh, who was to have become my Attorney General, to give me a report on such Presidential authority. As Senator Walsh had died suddenly, however, on March 2d, I had asked Mr.

Homer S. Cummings to become Attorney General and had requested him for an opinion. On the evening of March 4th, I received the verbal opinion of the new Attorney General on which I based the Presidential Proclamation signed during the night of March 5th-6th, closing all banks.

During the whole of the day and evening of March 3d, Mr. Woodin was in conference with Secretary of the Treasury Mills and was in complete touch with the situation as it developed in every part of the country.

It is well to remember that during the trying days of January, February and the first three days of March, prior to my Inauguration, I was a private citizen wholly without authority, express or implied. The Congress of the United States was Democratic by a narrow margin in both Houses. For me to have taken part in the daily relations between the Executive and the Congress would have been not only improper, but wholly useless. On only one occasion was my opinion asked by Congressional leaders. It had been suggested that a general sales tax be imposed to meet the great and growing deficit in the Treasury. For many years I had expressed my opposition to a general sales tax, on the ground that such a tax bore inevitably far more heavily on the poor than on the rich. This I told to the Democratic Congressional leaders. The proposed tax was not pressed.

Furthermore, it was abundantly clear to me then and has become abundantly clear to the country since that time that appeals for confidence and minor legislative changes could not during that period stop the downward spiral and turn its course upward. For the President-elect to dabble with superficial remedies would have been to impair or destroy the efficacy of the drastic, far-reaching actions which were put into effect in the "One Hundred Days" immediately following March 4th. To attack one symptom by weak methods would have impaired the broad attack on a score of fronts which came later. No participation by me as a private citizen would have prevented the crisis; such participation in details would have hampered thoroughgoing action under my own responsibility as President.

871

151 ❮ An Exchange of Letters between President Hoover and President-Elect Roosevelt. November 12, 1932, and November 14, 1932

Governor Franklin D. Roosevelt,
Albany, N. Y.

THE SECRETARY of State has informed me that the British Ambassador, on behalf of his Government, has handed him a note stating that "they believe that the régime of intergovernmental financial obligations as now existing must be reviewed; that they are profoundly impressed with the importance of acting quickly and that they earnestly hope that the United States Government will see its way clear to enter into an exchange of views at the earliest possible moment."

The British Ambassador further asks for a suspension of the payments due by the British Government to our Government for the period of the discussion suggested or for any other period that may be agreed upon. This last suggestion clearly relates to the payment of $95,000,000 which will fall due on December 15, 1932. I have requested the Secretary of State to transmit to you a full copy of that note.

The Secretary of State has also just been informed that similar requests are to be made by other debtor Governments, which likewise are obligated to make payments to the United States on December 15 next. One debtor Nation has defaulted on a payment due November 10 and another debtor Nation has served notice on our Government of its incapacity to make a payment due in December. Thus our Government is now confronted with a world problem of major importance to this Nation.

The moratorium which I proposed a year ago in June — that is, the year's postponement of intergovernmental debts and the spread of the deferred payment over ten years — was approved by the Congress. It served a great purpose in staying destruction in every direction and giving to Europe a year in which to realize and so modify their attitude on solely European questions as to support their credit structure from a great deal of further destruction. They have made very substantial progress during that year in financial adjustments among themselves and toward armament reduction.

Practically all of our World War debt settlements were made not by the Executive, but by the commission created by act of Congress, and all were approved in the form of legislation enacted by both houses. A year ago in recommending to the Congress the ratification of the moratorium I presented a statement of my views as to the whole of the relationship of ourselves to our debtor countries, and pointed out that debts to us bore no relationship to debts between other Nations which grew out of the War.

At the same time I recommended to the Congress that a new debt commission be created to deal with situations that might arise owing to the temporary incapacity of any individual debtor to meet its obligations to our country during the period of world depression. Congress declined to accede to this latter recommendation; it passed a joint resolution, reading in part as follows:

"It is hereby expressly declared to be against the policy of the Congress that any of the indebtedness of foreign countries to the United States should be in any manner canceled or reduced; and nothing in this joint resolution shall be construed as indicating a contrary policy or as implying that favorable consideration will be given at any time to a change in the policy hereby declared."

The limitation to purely temporary and individual action as to those incapable of payment during the depression expressed in the "communiqué" referred to in the British note, and in my recommendation to the Congress, was evident in these documents. The refusal of the Congress to authorize even the examination of this limited question, together with the above resolution, gave notice to all debtor Governments of the attitude of this Government toward either cancellation or reduction of existing obligations. Therefore, any commitments which European Governments may have made between themselves could not be based upon any assurances of the United States.

Moreover, the tenor of negotiations asked for by the debtor Government goes beyond terms of the Congressional resolution referred to.

I have publicly stated my position as to these questions, including that I do not favor cancellation in any form, but that we should be receptive to proposals from our debtors of tangible compensation in other forms than direct payment in expansion of markets for the products of our labor and our farms. And I have stated further that substantial reduction of world armament which will relieve our own and world burdens and dangers has a bearing upon this question. If negotiations are to be undertaken as requested by these Governments, protracted and detailed discussions would be necessary which could not be concluded during my Administration.

Any negotiation of this question on the basis of the requests of these Governments is limited by the resolution of the Congress, and if there is to be any change in the attitude of the Congress it will be greatly affected by the views of those members who recognize you as their leader and who will properly desire your counsel and advice.

This outlines where the question stands at the present moment.

I am prepared to deal with the subject as far as it lies in the power of the Executive, but it must be our common wish to deal with this question in a constructive fashion for the common good of the country. I am loath to proceed with recommendations to the Congress until I can have an opportunity to confer with you personally at some convenient date in the near future.

There are also other important questions as to which I think an interchange of views will be in the public interest. The building up of world economic stability is, of course, of the greatest importance in the building up of our recovery. As you know, a world economic conference will be held during the course of the coming Winter. Already two American experts have met with the technical experts of other Governments to prepare tentative agenda. While this conference may be begun during my Administration, it is certain that it will not complete its labors until after you have assumed office.

Parallel with this, of course, is the disarmament conference in which the United States has taken a leading part. This also has a great economic purpose, as well as the advancement of world peace.

Time is of great importance in all these questions, and I understand that you are planning to come through Washington some time during the latter part of next week, and I hope you will find it convenient to stop off long enough for me to advise with you.

I should, of course, be only too glad to have you bring into this conference any of the Democratic Congressional leaders or other advisers you may wish.

HERBERT HOOVER

November 12, 1932

The President,
Pratt, Kansas.

I APPRECIATE your cordial telegram. On the subjects to which you refer, as in all matters relating to the welfare of the country, I am glad to cooperate in every appropriate way, subject, of course, to the requirements of my present duties as Governor of this State.

I shall be delighted to confer with you in Washington, but I have been confined to the house with a slight cold and I am, therefore, not able to suggest a definite date. I shall call you on the telephone as soon as the time of my departure for the South has been determined.

May I take the liberty of suggesting that we make this meeting wholly informal and personal. You and I can go over the entire situation.

I had already arranged to meet a number of the Democratic leaders of the present Congress late this month at Warm Springs.

It will be helpful for me to have your views and all pertinent information when I meet with them.

I hope that you also will see them at the earliest opportunity, because, in the last analysis, the immediate question raised by the British, French and other notes creates a responsibility which rests upon those now vested with executive and legislative authority.

My kindest regards,

FRANKLIN D. ROOSEVELT

152 ❪ A Second Exchange of Letters between President Hoover and President-Elect Roosevelt. December 17, 1932, to December 21, 1932

Governor Franklin D. Roosevelt,
Hyde Park, N. Y.

December 17, 1932

My Dear Governor:

As you have seen from the press, the position of the debtor Governments in respect to the December 15th payments is now largely determined. In accord with both your expressions and my own statements, it is the duty of the United States to survey and exchange views on these questions individually with some of the debtor Governments. It is necessary to consider the character of machinery to be erected for this purpose.

These problems cannot be disassociated from the problems which will come before the World Economic Conference and to some degree those before the Conference on World Disarmament. As the economic situation in foreign countries is one of the dominant depressants of prices and employment in the United States, it is urgent that the World Economic Conference should assemble at as early a date as possible. The United States should be represented by a strong and effective delegation. This delegation should be chosen at an early moment in order that it may

877

give necessary consideration and familiarize itself with the problems, and secure that such investigation and study is made as will be necessary for its use at the conference.

Beyond this such problems as the exchange of views in respect to debts cannot be accomplished in satisfactory manner through the ordinary routine of diplomatic contacts. Satisfactory conclusions can only be reached by free and direct round-table discussion with each Government separately where agreement may be had upon fact and where conclusions can be reached. It has been an almost universal practice in our Government where unusual and vital questions are involved to appoint special delegations to undertake such discussions. The routine machinery of diplomacy neither affords the type of men required nor can they give the time from other duties which such discussions require.

While we must not change our established policy of dealing with each debtor separately — and, indeed, no other course could be entertained in view of the widely divergent conditions which exist in the different countries and the very different situations in which they find themselves — and while the decision heretofore reached not to consider the debt question at the coming World Economic Conference is a wise one, it seems clear that the successful outcome of the World Economic Conference will be greatly furthered if the debt problems can be satisfactorily advanced before that conference, although final agreement in some cases may be contingent upon the satisfactory solution of certain economic questions in which our country has a direct interest and the final determination of which may well form a part of the matters coming before the Economic Conference.

It is desirable that such delegation should include members of the Congress in order that such intricate facts and circumstances can be effectively presented to the Congress. It is no derogation of Executive authority to choose members from that quarter. It might be well to consider whether this delegation should also embrace in its membership some of the old or new members of the delegation to the arms conference in order that these three important questions should be given coordinate consideration.

If it were not for the urgency of the situation both at home and abroad and the possible great helpfulness to employment and agricultural prices and general restoration of confidence which could be brought about by successful issue of all these questions and the corresponding great dangers of inaction, it would be normal to allow the whole matter to rest until after the change of administration, but in the emergency such as exists at the moment I would be neglectful of my duty if I did not facilitate in every way the earliest possible dealing with these questions.

It is obvious that no conclusions would be reached from such discussion prior to March 4th, but a great deal of time could be saved if the machinery could be created at once by the appointment of the delegates as I have mentioned.

I shall be informing the Congress of the economic situation and of the desirability of the above proposed machinery for dealing with these conferences. I should be glad to know if you could join with me in the selection of such delegation at the present time or if you feel that the whole matter should be deferred until after March 4th. I believe there would be no difficulty in agreeing upon an adequate representation for the purpose. In such selection the first concern would be the selection of a chairman for the delegation.

HERBERT HOOVER

The President,
The White House.

December 19, 1932

Dear Mr. President:

I HAVE GIVEN earnest consideration to your courteous telegram of December 17th and I want to assure you that I seek in every proper way to be of help. It is my view that the questions of disarmament, intergovernmental debts and permanent economic arrangements will be found to require selective treatment even though this be with full recognition of the possibility that in the ultimate outcome a relationship of any two or of all three may become clear.

1. As to disarmament: Your policy is clear and satisfactory. Some time, however, is required to bring it to fruition. Success in a practical program limiting armaments, abolishing certain instruments of warfare and decreasing the offensive or attack power of all Nations will, in my judgment, have a very positive and salutary influence on debt and economic discussions.

2. As to the debts: If any debtor Nation desires to approach us, such Nation should be given the earliest opportunity so to do. Certainly in the preliminary conversations the Chief Executive has full authority either through the existing machinery of the diplomatic service or by supplementing it with specially appointed agents of the President himself, to conduct such preliminary investigations or inquiries without in any way seeking formal Congressional action. I am impelled to suggest, however, that these surveys should be limited to determining facts and exploring possibilities rather than fixing policies binding on the incoming Administration. I wholly approve and would in no way hinder such surveys.

3. As to the economic conference: I am clear that a permanent economic program for the world should not be submerged in conversations relating to disarmament or debts. I recognize, of course, a relationship, but not an identity. Therefore, I cannot go along with the thought that the personnel conducting the conversations should be identical.

By reason of the fact that under the Constitution I am unable to assume authority in the matter of the agenda of the economic conference until after March 4th next, and by reason of the fact that there appears to be a divergence of opinion between us in respect to the scope of the conference, and further by reason of the fact that time is required to conduct conversations relating to debts and disarmament, I must respectfully suggest that the appointment of the permanent delegates and the final determination of the program of the economic conference be held in abeyance until after March 4th.

In the meantime I can see no objection to further informal conferences with the agenda committee, or to the carrying on of
preliminary economic studies which would serve an undoubtedly
useful purpose.

I feel that it would be both improper for me and inadvisable
for you, however much I appreciate the courtesy of your suggestion, for me to take part in naming representatives. From the
necessity of the case, they could be responsible only and properly
to you as President for the effective performance of their assign-
ments, particularly in matters calling for almost daily touch with
and directions of the Executive. I would be in no position prior
to March 4th to have this constant contact.

I think you will recognize that it would be unwise for me to
accept an apparent joint responsibility with you when, as a matter of constitutional fact, I would be wholly lacking in any
attendant authority.

FRANKLIN D. ROOSEVELT

Governor Franklin D. Roosevelt,
Albany, N. Y.

December 20, 1932

My Dear Governor:

I HAVE your telegram expressing the difficulties which you find
in cooperation at the present time. In the face of foreign conditions which are continually degenerating agriculture prices, increasing unemployment and creating economic difficulties for
our people, I am unwilling to admit that cooperation cannot be
established between the outgoing and incoming Administrations
which will give earlier solution and recovery from these difficulties.

If you will review my previous communications and conversations I think you will agree that while outlining the nature of the
problems my proposals to you have been directed to the setting
up not of solutions but of the machinery through which by pre-
paredness the ultimate solution of these questions can be ex-

pedited and coordinated, to the end that many months of delay and increasing losses to our people may be avoided.

I fully recognize that your solution of these questions of debt, the world economic problems and disarmament might vary from my own. These conclusions obviously cannot be attained in my Administration and will lie entirely within your Administration. I wish especially to avoid any embarrassment to your work and thus have no intention of committing the incoming Administration to any particular policy prior to March 4th. Even the exploratory work you suggest should be participated in by men in whom you have confidence, and I wish to facilitate it. What I deem of the utmost importance is that when you assume responsibility on March 4th machinery of your approval will be here, fully informed and ready to function according to the policies you may determine.

My frequent statements indicate agreement with you that debts, world economic problems and disarmament require selective treatment, but you will agree with me that they also require coordination and preparation, either in the individual hands of the then President or in the hands of men selected to deal with them and advise him. There is thus no thought of submerging the World Economic Conference with other questions, but rather to remove the barriers from successful issue of that conference.

With view to again making an effort to secure cooperation and that solidarity of national action which the situation needs, I would be glad if you could designate Mr. Owen D. Young, Colonel House, or any other men of your party possessed of your views and your confidence and at the same time familiar with these problems, to sit with the principal officers of this Administration in an endeavor to see what steps can be taken to avoid delays of precious time and inevitable losses that will ensue from such delays.

HERBERT HOOVER

The President,
The White House.

December 21, 1932

Dear Mr. President:

I THINK perhaps the difficulties to which you refer are not in finding the means or the willingness for cooperation, but rather in defining clearly those things concerning which cooperation between us is possible.

We are agreed that commitments to any particular policy prior to March 4th are for many reasons inadvisable and indeed impossible. There remains, therefore, before that date only the possibility of exploratory work and preliminary surveys.

Please let me reiterate not only that I am glad to avoid the loss of precious time through delay in starting these preliminaries but also that I shall gladly receive such information and expression of opinion concerning all of those international questions which because of existing economic and other conditions must and will be among the first concerns of my Administration.

However, for me to accept any joint responsibility in the work of exploration might well be construed by the debtor or other Nations, collectively or individually, as a commitment, moral even though not legal, as to policies and courses of action.

The designation of a man or men of such eminence as your telegram suggests would not imply mere fact-findings; it would suggest the presumption that such representatives were empowered to exchange views on matters of large and binding policy.

Current press dispatches from abroad already indicate that the joint action which you propose would most certainly be interpreted there as much more of a policy commitment than either you or I actually contemplate.

May I respectfully suggest that you proceed with the selection of your representatives to conduct the preliminary exploration necessary with individual debtor Nations and representatives to discuss the agenda of the World Economic Conference, making it clear that none of these representatives is authorized to bind this Government as to any ultimate policy.

If this be done, let me repeat that I shall be happy to receive their information and their expressions of opinion.

To that I add the thought that between now and March 4th I shall be very glad if you will keep me advised as to the progress of the preliminary discussions, and I also shall be happy to consult with you freely during this period.

FRANKLIN D. ROOSEVELT

153 ❬ Address at the First Inauguration of Governor Herbert H. Lehman of New York.

January 2, 1933

IN TAKING leave of you, my friends, my neighbors and my associates, after four years in Albany, I could not fail to have many regrets at the parting. They have been happy years — made more so by the loyalty and common purpose of the many men and women who have so unselfishly aided me in the conduct of the administrative Government of the State. To all of you who have been my colleagues, from the members of my Cabinet on through all of the ranks of the departments and the Civil Service, I extend my personal appreciation.

I have seen much of Government of many kinds, and in many places, and I do not hesitate to say to the people of this State that their public servants in the Executive branch of the State Government take high rank for faithful service and high integrity.

Four years ago it fell to me to succeed a Governor who had set a standard founded on unselfish effort and a keen understanding of the needs of the people of the State. To maintain a Government of definite action founded on liberal thought has been my aim. It is, therefore, of special moment both to Governor Smith and to myself that we see today the responsibility that was ours, passing into the hands of Governor Lehman.

Any Executive who has been able to put into practical effect a philosophy of Government, a measure of accomplishment that transcends mere theory or the mere duties of routine administration, must rejoice that the thirteen million human beings within the borders of our State are to be led for at least two years to come by one who understands human needs and has the purpose to meet them.

A clear view must include all functions of governing. The Governor of this State, while giving full recognition to the desirability of home-rule in local affairs, must, at the same time, encourage every sensible effort to improve the efficiency of local government. Though we have been negligent in the past, the very times in which we live have focused attention on the comparative inefficiency in almost all of our lesser units.

The sovereignty of the State — in other words, the people themselves — are, in my judgment rightly, asking both structural changes and the elimination of unessential personnel and of unnecessary functions. Therein lies a definite relationship between the State Governments and the localities themselves.

Less well-defined but of great importance nevertheless, is another relationship — that between the Government of the State and the Government of the Federal Union. The crisis has brought new problems and, at the same time, new possibilities, whereby Washington and the several State capitals may become more mutually helpful, especially in the matters which with increasing frequency involve overlapping functions. It is time to define more clearly where the Federal machinery of Government ends, and where the State machinery of Government begins. It is time likewise for closer contacts between the President and the Governors.

That is another reason why I rejoice today in the privilege of taking part in the inauguration of my long-time friend and colleague, Governor Lehman. I shall have a friend in Albany and he will have a friend in Washington. In the years to come, may the people of our State give to him the same fine loyalty which they have been good enough to give to me.

154 ❮ Informal Extemporaneous Remarks at Sheffield, Ala., on Muscle Shoals Inspection Trip. January 21, 1933

Governor Miller, my friends:

I THINK I can almost say, "My neighbors," because, from my little cottage at Warm Springs, from Pine Mountain which lies back of it, I can look into Alabama.

I am here for two reasons: The first is to fulfil a promise made to myself, because, during the campaign, I said that I wanted to see Muscle Shoals. The other is that I do not believe that any person in the world can act or make a recommendation in regard to any great project unless he has seen the project himself.

Today I am looking forward with the greatest interest to seeing this particular part of the Tennessee Valley. I am very confident that the distinguished gentlemen who are with me from the Congress of the United States will be able to work with me and get something practical done.

Every single part of the United States is represented here today. Senator Norris is the author of Muscle Shoals. Senator Dill, who has taken such a great interest in the power question as a whole, comes from the Pacific Northwest. Mr. Scattergood is a gentleman who has done so much to build up the use of electricity in the Southwest. And, finally, another section of the country is well represented by the gentleman who has been for some years the chairman of my own Power Authority in the State of New York; he represents the great St. Lawrence Development. So you might say that all four corners of the United States are here today.

We are here because the Muscle Shoals Development and the Tennessee River Development as a whole are national in their aspect and are going to be treated from a national point of view.

And so, my friends, I am looking forward with the greatest of pleasure to my day here. It is going to give me a great advantage in putting Muscle Shoals back on the map.

155 ❦ Informal Extemporaneous Remarks at Montgomery, Ala., on Muscle Shoals Inspection Trip. January 21, 1933

Governor Miller, my friends and neighbors of Alabama:

THIS MEETING tonight is a fitting climax to one of the most interesting days that I have ever spent. It is a great privilege to me to stand in this sacred spot where a great American took oath of office as the President of the Confederacy.

I have been thinking, as I came here through the State, of how little the younger generation in the South and in the North knows today of the failings and the effects that were brought out by the war between the States. I am not so very old — just half a century, that is all — and yet even I, in my boyhood, can remember the troubles and the difficulties within a family, that were caused by that war.

As some of you may know, one of the Roosevelts married into a Georgia family and I can remember, as a small boy, that two very distinguished gentlemen, intimately connected with the Navy of the Confederacy — mind you, this was in the 80's — came to New York to visit the Roosevelt family. Because those two brave and distinguished officers had fought in the Navy of the Confederacy, there were some Roosevelts who still regarded them as "Pirates."

Now, that is hard to understand by the younger generation in all parts of this country; yet it was less than half a century ago that that happened. I know, and I am glad to know, that my own daughter who is with me today and all the rest of my children and all of the younger generation just laugh heartily at hearing brave officers of the Confederate Navy referred to as pirates.

The war between the States is not only over, but I believe that I can say, here in the birthplace of the Confederacy, and be rightly understood in the North, South, East and West, that in many ways that war between the States has done more than anything else to bind the Nation into a unified whole.

I am particularly happy, as one who is about to occupy another White House, to have had the privilege of seeing the first White House of the Confederacy as I turned the corner to come here to the Capitol.

This morning, early, I saw with my own eyes what I have been waiting to see ever since the days when I served in Washington as a Lieutenant of that great Democrat and great American President, Woodrow Wilson. I was not only impressed with the size of the great operation at Muscle Shoals, but I can tell you frankly that it was at least twice as big as I ever had any conception of its being. It was distressing to me, and I think it was distressing to almost every other member of the party—we had with us distinguished members of the Senate and of the House of Representatives, together with engineers and others from every part of the United States—to see that so much of that great plant has been lying in idleness all these years.

My friends, I am determined on two things as a result of what I have seen today. The first is to put Muscle Shoals to work. The second is to make of Muscle Shoals a part of an even greater development that will take in all of that magnificent Tennessee River from the mountains of Virginia down to the Ohio and the Gulf.

Muscle Shoals is more today than a mere opportunity for the Federal Government to do a kind turn for the people in one small section of a couple of States. Muscle Shoals gives us the opportunity to accomplish a great purpose for the people of many States and, indeed, for the whole Union. Because there we have an opportunity of setting an example of planning, not just for ourselves but for the generations to come, tying in industry and agriculture and forestry and flood prevention, tying them all into a unified whole over a distance of a thousand miles so that we can afford better opportunities and better places for living for millions of yet unborn in the days to come.

So, my friends, I believe that the Governor was right in at least one sense when he spoke of this being a red-letter day, because I am convinced that what was seen by the members of the national Senate and by the national House of Representatives and by your President-elect means that just as soon as we possibly can, we are going to start something up in Washington practical, useful and necessary.

My one regret in coming here is that it is dark and I shall not have the opportunity tonight of seeing this wonderful old city. I hope it will be my privilege to come back here some day from Warm Springs, when the sun is shining.

And I shall always regard this as a red-letter day for another reason. I have had the opportunity to come here and stand where Jefferson Davis once stood.

156 ⟨ Informal Extemporaneous Remarks at Miami, Fla., Immediately Preceding Attempted Assassination of the President-Elect.

February 15, 1933

Mr. Mayor, my friends of Miami:

I AM NOT a stranger here because for a good many years I used to come down here. I have not been here for seven years, but I am coming back, for I have firmly resolved not to make this the last time.

I have had a very wonderful twelve days' fishing in these Florida and Bahama waters. It has been a splendid rest and we have caught a great many fish, but I am not going to attempt to tell you any fishing stories. The only fly in the ointment on my trip has been that I have put on about ten pounds so that means that among the other duties that I shall have to perform when I get North is taking those ten pounds off.

I hope very much to be able to come down here next winter, and to see all of you, and to have another enjoyable ten days or two weeks in Florida waters.

Many thanks.

Index

Index

Index

Index

Index

Index

Index by Miss K. C. Blackburn